FINDING
and
BUYING
YOUR PLACE
in the
COUNTRY

FINDING
and
BUYING
YOUR PLACE
in the
COUNTRY

Les Scher
Attorney at Law

Carol Scher
Consumer Advocate

Artwork by

Roger Bayless and Pearl Hurd

COLLIER BOOKS
Macmillan Publishing Company
New York

COLLIER MACMILLAN PUBLISHERS
London

The purpose of this book is to give guidance and general information to the public in the purchase of real estate. It is not intended to give legal advice regarding any specific legal problem. Because this book is a guide for the purchase of real estate throughout the United States and Canada, and laws are complex and constantly changing, anyone with a specific legal problem should consult an attorney locally.

Copyright © 1988 by Les Scher and Carol Scher

Artwork by Roger Bayless and Pearl Hurd

Collier Books
Macmillan Publishing Company
866 Third Avenue, New York, NY 10022
Collier Macmillan Canada, Inc.

Library of Congress Cataloging-in-Publication Data
Scher, Les.
   Finding and buying your place in the country.

   Includes index.
      1. Country homes—United States—Purchasing.
2. Country homes—Canada—Purchasing.   3. Vacation
homes—United States—Purchasing.   4. Vacation homes—
Canada—Purchasing.   I. Scher, Carol.   II. Title.
HD256.S27   1987   643′.2   87-24246

   ISBN 0-02-008400-5

Macmillan books are available at special discounts for bulk purchases for sales promotions, premiums, fund-raising, or educational use. For details, contact:

Special Sales Director
Macmillan Publishing Company
866 Third Avenue
New York, NY 10022

10 9 8 7 6 5 4 3 2 1

Printed in the United States of America

To our children,
Paula Heather and Sarah Jenée,
who fortunately know
the joys of
growing up in the country

CONTENTS

Part I

Looking for Land

Part II

Checking Out the Land

Part III

The Land and the Law

Part IV

Deciding on a Fair Price

Part V

Financing Your Purchase

Part VI

The Contract of Sale

Part VII

Going through Escrow

Part VIII

Alaska, Hawaii, and Canada

Part IX

Using a Lawyer

Part X

Protecting Your Property after Your Purchase

Part XI

Property Evaluation Checklist

Appendix

ILLUSTRATIONS

MODEL FORMS

ACKNOWLEDGMENTS

Over the years since our first book was published in 1974, we have received many letters from readers offering their own stories and new ideas. This book brings together fifteen years of new information and is completely updated as to every aspect of buying property. Assembling this massive amount of new information and resource material depended on the help of many people, but special thanks go to our senior researcher and information specialist, Gerald H. Scher, who spent a year, including a fact-finding trip to Washington, D.C., gathering all the new Useful Resources listed throughout the book; and to our office manager, typist, and loyal co-worker, Rebecca Campbell, who worked many fifteen-hour days and gave up weekends helping us get this book ready for you.

We are indebted to Thomas G. Willcock, of the H. M. Dignam Corporation Ltd., Canada, for traveling from Toronto to our home in northern California to bring us information and advice for our greatly expanded section on buying land in Canada. Thanks also to Michael McGee, L.S., for proofreading and editing our chapter on surveying.

A new perspective on the law as it relates to society has been provided to us by Harry Philo, another attorney who believes in sharing his knowledge and making information available to help people.

We are grateful to our editor, David Wolff, for his efforts in helping us publish this new book for a new generation of land buyers.

We continue to enjoy the encouragement and moral support of our parents, Meyer and Hannah Scher, and Howard and Evelyn Wilcox, and we greatly appreciate the work done by Brian and Cindy Wilcox to make our country home energy-self-sufficient.

Our life continues to be enhanced by the inspired music of American jazz musicians, who continue to create timeless works of art for the enjoyment of all of us.

Finally, we thank our friends, neighbors, and clients, who have made our first twenty years of life in the country so pleasurable.

—*Carol Scher*
Les Scher

INTRODUCTION

My father told me when I was very young the first thing a man must do is to own a piece of land. When you go into a store and you buy something it's chattel, but when you own a piece of land, that's real. And that's where the words "real estate" originated.

—Chuck Berry

We have now been living in the country for nearly twenty years, having purchased our place in the rural-land movement of the late sixties. Our land was undeveloped except for an open-framed horse barn. I can remember when we handed our down payment money to the real estate agent wondering if we were making the biggest mistake of our lives. Fortunately, it was the best decision we ever could have made.

We soon learned about carpentry, cement, plumbing, and electric wiring; about springs, pumps, and holding tanks; about tree-planting, gardening, and dirt-road maintenance; and about alternative energy systems. We now supply our own power using solar cells, a water turbine, and storage batteries with a gas generator as a backup. Our house is built, as are a shop, laundry room, and game room. We have fresh fruit and vegetables and a business in town that supports us.

My commute to my office in the small rural town of Garberville in the redwood tree country of northern California is only a thirty-minute drive through the hills, along the river, and under the redwoods. We can still drink pure water from a spring and breathe clean air. And I know that thousands of other people across the United States and Canada have had similar good fortune in their moves to the country, and many more seek to leave the congestion of the major cities and suburbs.

xvii

A recent Gallup poll commissioned by the National League of Cities found that one-third of those residing in municipalities of fifty thousand or more would migrate to the country if they had the chance. Beginning in the mid-seventies for the first time in 150 years, the flow of the population in the United States switched direction away from the cities and their immediate surroundings.

This pattern remains the same today. The population seems to be responding naturally to overcrowding, congestion, pollution, depersonalization, and a decline in the quality of life in urban areas, as well as to the increasing high cost of living in a metropolitan area.

The last twenty years have seen new kinds of cars and trucks especially suited to the rural lifestyle, rugged and economical with fuel. Rural roads and accessibility of rural areas to the city are being improved at an accelerated rate. It is easier now than at any other time in history to live in a rural area and reasonably commute to the heart of a major city, if that is what you choose to do.

Folks in retirement continue to seek a peaceful rural community to live in, and they bring their hard-earned life savings with them, making more opportunities for people who work and have businesses in the area. Retirees see the value in selling their urban or suburban property at a high price and buying a comparable property in the country for one-third the price, putting the rest of the money in savings, kicking back, and enjoying life.

The younger pioneers are willing to accept the lower income in rural areas for the joys of country living. However, the net disposable income is increased because the cost of living is lower. For example, in California in 1986 the average price statewide for a single family home was $131,530, but in the rural areas the average price was in the range of $70,000—significantly cheaper. New construction continues to occur throughout the rural areas of the country. In 1986, 11 percent of all new homes were built outside metropolitan areas, in places with populations of ten thousand or less and rural in character.

The second-home or vacation-home market is also healthy. Originally there was some fear that the Tax Reform Act of 1986 would have a detrimental effect by removing certain breaks, but this did not occur. Any owner of a vacation retreat, as long as it is used by the owner for more than fourteen days a year or more than 10 percent of the number of days the property is rented out, may qualify for all tax breaks accorded a primary residence such as deductibility of interest and tax payments.

Therefore, I do not expect to see a decline in the desire to own a second home as a retreat. In fact, many owners of vacant rural lots will likely start developing them to take advantage of the tax breaks.

The U.S. Department of Housing and Urban Development recently pointed out that in 1976 one American family in twelve owned either a second home or a vacant recreational lot and that by 1985 that figure had doubled.

Although prices were high and interest rates ridiculous in the late seventies and early eighties, things have now returned to normal. It now appears that the years of the late eighties and well into the nineties will be the best years to purchase rural real estate in the last quarter of the twentieth century, not necessarily as a get-rich investment, but as an investment in a better life-style for you and your family.

HOW TO USE THIS BOOK

This book is meant to be a tool that you should carry with you as you go through the processes of finding and buying your place in the country. You will have to read parts of it more than once in order to absorb all of the information. Many of the things I discuss will become much clearer when you actually get out and start dealing with real estate agents, looking at land, and delving into the public records at the local city hall. If you have the time and inclination to follow the course of investigation I outline, you will be protected with the minimal need for a lawyer. Even when you retain counsel for some aspect of the purchase, such as inspecting the final draft of your contract of sale or title documents, it will be very helpful for you to have this background information available to you. After your purchase, you will continue to find this book useful for such contingencies as fighting an increase in property taxes, confronting the building inspector, appropriating water from a stream, and protecting yourself if you have trouble making your mortgage payments.

The chapters in this book are divided into eight

parts with an appendix at the end. Part I, "Looking for Land," should be used in conjunction with the Appendix. This first section gives basic information on how to find out about land for sale, and it teaches you how to protect yourself when dealing with real estate agents by explaining the role they play and the sales tactics they use. Part II, "Checking Out the Land," outlines in detail the factors you should consider when choosing the general location of the land and evaluating the various aspects of a specific parcel, especially the soil, the water, and the condition of the structures. Part III, "The Land and the Law," explains in an easy-to-follow manner the legal protections you need and how to investigate them. Part IV, "Deciding on a Fair Price," will help you evaluate the fair market value of the land and bargain skillfully with the seller to get his asking price down to a figure you consider reasonable. Part V, "Financing Your Purchase," explores the types of financing, the sources of loans, and available government programs. Because the financial world has a language all its own, a glossary of terms and a checklist for evaluating a loan are also included. Part VI, "The Contract of Sale," presents a model form that you can copy from the book and modify for your own transaction; this helps to insure that you will be adequately protected in your purchase. This is the heart of the book and the most important section. *You must get everything in writing when you are dealing with real estate.* Nothing you are told verbally is legally binding, unless you can prove what was said, and that is often impossible to do. Part VII, "Going through Escrow," demystifies the escrow process and explains title searches, abstracts of title, and title insurance. The various forms of co-ownership are outlined and a Model Owners Agreement is included. Different types of deeds are then described. Part VIII, "Alaska, Hawaii, and Canada," contains resource information for evaluating property purchases in these three unique areas. Part IX, "Using a Lawyer," discusses how to select and use a lawyer. Part X, "Protecting Your Property after Your Purchase," gives you vital information on how to protect your property interest after you purchase your land and includes the pertinent information from the 1986 Income Tax Reform Act. Part XI, "Property Evaluation Checklist," sums up the entire book in a simple-format checklist that you should take with you every time you go property hunting. It contains a complete and basic summary of all points raised throughout the book and will remind you of every question you need to ask and every piece of information you will need to be a safe and wise buyer.

The Useful Resources at the end of the chapters and the appendixes at the end of the book contain hundreds of addresses and sources of information for everything from real estate catalogues to solar energy systems and prefab log houses. When writing for any of the pamphlets, also ask for a recent catalogue or list of their publications to get the most recent information and prices. You may find publications that you are particularly interested in that we haven't included.

The Useful Resources also include the material available from government and private agencies and books, magazines, and other data not readily available in local libraries or bookstores. Even if you send for only the free resources you will have a valuable personal library of information that will aid you before and after you purchase your place in the country.

I

LOOKING FOR LAND

CHAPTER 1

How to Start Your Search

Purchasing land should be done as carefully as selecting the person you will share it with. The more land you see, the more you will learn about differences in value and about your expectations. Try to keep an open mind when land hunting. Many people find that, after seeing many kinds of places, they choose a different type of environment than they had originally sought. Take your time and approach your search with a relaxed but probing attitude. Even if you are not ready actually to buy land at the present time you should begin looking, since it takes time to find the right place and you

want to find out as much information as you can about country property before you buy.

Take your outdoor camping equipment, or your trailer if you have one, when you go land hunting. Some real estate agents and sellers will allow you to stay on the land for a day or two so that you can get a sense of what it is like. (The aspects of the land that you can explore while camping or visiting there are discussed in Part II, "Checking Out the Land.") You can't begin to get an idea of whether the property will be right for you unless you spend some time on it. You should stay at least a day on the land. You will probably be able to do this only if it is vacant land.

You want to see the property at its best and at its worst. Most land is sold in the spring and early summer, from April through July. This is usually the most beautiful time of year. The weather is getting warm, the wildflowers are in bloom, the grass is green, and water is plentiful. People are beginning to think of getting a place to spend the approaching summer and those to follow. Sales usually drop a little during the driest summer months but increase again in the early fall, from September through October. Land prices are highest during these seasons because the demand is greater. (The effect of the number of interested buyers on the price of a piece of property is discussed in chapter 20, ''Bargaining to Get the Seller's Asking Price Down.'') The best time to buy is in the late fall and winter when the number of buyers diminishes and prices are at an annual low level. Few people will venture forth to look at land in the dead of winter when many country roads are impassable. If you see some land you like in the spring, try to wait until December or January to buy it. Not only will you probably get it for a much better price at that time, but you will also be able to see it under both good and bad conditions. If you still like it when the roads are muddy and rutted and the skies are overcast, you know you will be happy with your purchase. However, if you see some land for the first time in the middle of winter when it is covered with snow, do not buy it until you see it after the snow melts. A beautiful covering of snow can disguise a poor piece of land.

If possible, try to live in the area in which you want to buy before actually making your purchase. You may find that you do not like the area as well as you imagined you would. It is usually easy to find a house or cabin to rent for a few weeks or a month. If you ask around you might be able to find a job as caretaker on someone's property. This is an economical way to live in the country while looking for your own piece of land. If you are a resident, you will probably hear about places for sale that an outsider would not find out about. Many people do not sell their land through real estate agents in order to avoid paying an agent's commission. Some do not even advertise in the local paper or post signs, but simply rely on friends passing the word. There are several common ways to find out about property for sale without living in the area, however.

Most real estate agencies print up listings of available properties which they will send to you on request. Go to the main branch of your local library or telephone company and ask to see the yellow pages of the directory for the area in which you are interested in purchasing land. You can then send letters to all the real estate agents there asking for their listings and telling them what you want. They will send you the current listings and let you know when something comes into their offices that might interest you.

Large real estate agencies publish land catalogues listing various pieces of property they have for sale. In the appendix at the end of the book, I list the catalogues now available free from major real estate companies that have local franchises throughout the rural areas of the United States. (One of the most famous companies is United National Real Estate.) The different catalogues are fun to look at, and they will give you an idea of prices in various areas of the country, but their major purpose is to lure you into the local offices so that the agents can show you whatever properties they have available—not necessarily the ones they advertise. Because of the lag time in printing up the catalogues, often properties listed are already sold before the catalogue comes out. Other deals that sound fantastic in the catalogue may be difficult to recognize because of the subjective nature of describing and advertising a piece of property.

When reading any real estate advertisement, notice what is excluded as well as what is included. Any piece of land can be written up to sound good or can look beautiful in a tiny photograph. An ad will always refer to a parcel's good qualities. For example, if no mention is made of water availability, there is a good chance that water supply will be a problem.

Another common advertising technique used by many real estate agencies is illustrated by the following quote from a real estate promotion:

From this brochure select the property or section that suits you best and see it now! Delay might mean that someone else might beat you to the bargain you have chosen. The brochure will be in the hands of thousands of other people in every corner of the United States, and the first person on the ground with the necessary deposit is the one who gets the place of his choice!

Don't let such ads scare you into thinking that you must buy land immediately because nothing will be left if you don't. Lots of land is still available, and more becomes available every day as large land holdings, ranches, and farms split up. Although land prices continue to fluctuate, good deals are constantly coming up, and if you know what you are doing, you will be able to get a good piece of land at a reasonable price for many years in the future.

Another common way to locate land for sale is to look in the local papers in the area and in the classified ads of major newspapers of a nearby city. The Sunday editions of large newspapers carry the most real estate advertisements, and many rural brokers advertise in the urban areas because that is where the market is. Often there is a separate classification for country property.

When you go to an area you should prepare index cards containing a description of the type of land you want and hang them on the local bulletin boards with an address at which you can be reached. You can also place an ad in the local paper for a small fee.

It is possible to purchase land other than from a private party. The federal and state governments sell and lease land to the general public. Although homesteading is no longer possible, even in Alaska, mining claims have been used to obtain land on a short-term basis. A program exists whereby summer homes can be leased in the national forests. Information on how to obtain all the available literature on the above subjects is given in the appendix. Also included therein is resource information on land in Alaska and Canada for the heartier land buyers and the addresses of land agencies in each state that sell state-owned land.

Land can also be purchased at tax sales held when property taxes have not been paid by the owner. This land seems to be a bargain, but many technical aspects are involved, and I do not recommend that you buy such land without consulting an attorney. In most cases, you must pay cash for the land and after you buy it the owner still has a legally specified period of time to pay the back taxes and redeem the land. If this happens, you will get your money back with interest, but you will lose the land. Tax sales are discussed in chapter 17, ''Property Taxes and Assessments.'' You can get all the facts on the local laws in your area from the county tax collector.

A variation on buying land at a tax sale is to look in the tax collector's public file in the county tax collector's office to find parcels that have back taxes due on them. You can then contact the owners and ask them if they would like to sell. You might find an owner who is desperate and willing to sell his place at a bargain price.

Buying land at a foreclosure or trustee sale also involves technical legal problems and should not be attempted without hiring an attorney to explain the intricacies of these sales and how to protect yourself.

You will not have any problems finding land for sale. Your main concerns will be the quality of the land and improvements, the price you will pay for it, the inclusion in your contract of sale of all the necessary legal protections, and the method of financing your purchase. The remainder of the book is devoted to these things.

CHAPTER 2

Real Estate Agents, Realtors, and Salespeople

BROKERS SERVE A USEFUL AND NECESSARY FUNCTION

Over the years I have grown to appreciate the useful function served by real estate agents in the world of country property. Unlike urban realtors, country agents spend time ferrying buyers over hill and dale to show them property. They can't just send a buyer out to an address to look at a house. Personal tour-

ing must be done, and this is very time-consuming. A broker might have to drive an hour or more on numerous occasions before a property is sold. Of course, a broker can show a property many times and never make a sale. Although it might seem that they make an unfair amount of money (5 to 10 percent of the sales price) on a deal, many times they never make a sale. They have high advertising costs running newspaper ads and mailing out brochures. This is part of their overhead and is not a separate cost to the seller. Because most sellers of rural property are not available to show the property, a nonresident owner would have a difficult time selling his or her property without the help of a good real estate agent.

Brokers also lead the way in fighting to keep country property available for sale. They often fight restrictive laws against subdividing and developing land, thus protecting their livelihood and helping you move to the country at the same time. They counteract the tendency of the rural residents to close the door to newcomers, thus helping all of us realize our dream of finding and buying a place in the country.

CAVEAT EMPTOR—LET THE BUYER BEWARE!

In the last fifteen years land buyers have become considerably more sophisticated, and because of that, the more unscrupulous real estate agents have fared badly. Also, federal and state agencies have been more vigorous in regulating subdivisions and prosecuting the crooks. However, some brokers have just become more subtle, and others are just not well informed. So whether you are dealing with honest or dishonest, informed or misinformed real estate people, remember the cardinal rule: Caveat emptor, ''Let the buyer beware!'' You will now have the knowledge and ability to double-check anything a real estate person tells you and demand to get all important statements in writing. *Never* let a real estate salesperson intimidate you into refraining from asking questions or from cross-checking anything he or she tells you. In order to play the game of real estate you must know who the players are.

Remember, the real estate agent works for the seller, not the buyer! The real estate agent makes money only if a sale is made!

THE DIFFERENCES BETWEEN THE REAL ESTATE AGENT, THE REALTOR, AND THE SALESPERSON

A person who is licensed by the state to sell land will be either a real estate *agent* or *broker*, a *realtor*, or a real estate *salesperson*. The terms *agent* and *broker* are used interchangeably.

The Real Estate Agent or Broker

States generally require that a person aspiring to become a real estate agent serve as an apprentice to an already licensed agent for a specified period of time, that he take a few college courses, and that he pass an examination on basic real estate law. However, brokerage laws are not very detailed, and licenses are easy to obtain. The real estate agent acts as a middleman throughout the negotiations between you and the owner who is selling his land. For example, if you want to make an offer to buy some land, you will give your offer to the broker to deliver to the seller. The seller then gives his response to the agent, who delivers it to you. The agent cannot legally refuse to inform the seller of any facts involving a possible sale, even if the amount of money or terms you offer seem outrageous. Usually an agent can accept a deposit from you on behalf of the owner, although he rarely has the power to actually accept your offer and sign a final contract of sale on the seller's behalf. Some states permit real estate agents to write certain documents, such as deposit receipts and contracts of sale, although many areas consider contract drafting to be an illegal practicing of law. (See chapter 28, ''The Model Contract of Sale.'')

The Realtor

In an attempt to create an aura of professionalism for the land-selling industry, the National Association of Realtors, consisting of over 700,000 members, established a code of ethics by which its members swear to abide. A realtor is any real estate agent who has been accepted as a member into one of the local real estate boards. In my experience, realtors generally seem more anxious than the average real estate agent to comply with state and local real estate laws. Because of the extra status they enjoy, they are usually cautious to avoid doing anything that would cause them to lose their membership in NAREB, the National Association of Real Estate Boards. An agent or salesman working under a realtor is kept under close supervision by that realtor. Although you will encounter few realtors in small towns, you can always identify an agent who is a realtor by a sign in his window displaying the round emblem and big *R*.

Subsidiary groups within the National Association of Realtors include the Realtors Land Institute and the Accredited Farm and Land Member (AFLM) designation. The realtor with the AFLM logo designation specializes in farms and recreation land.

7

Because of the specialized nature of these realtors there are only 350 in the country. See Useful Resources for obtaining the names of these specialists.

The Real Estate Salesperson

To become a real estate salesperson one is usually required only to pass a very simple examination. No apprenticeship is required and no experience is necessary. For this reason, most people you will meet selling land will be salespeople. Salespeople must work under a licensed real estate agent and can show land only under the agent's authority. A salesperson usually cannot sign any documents or receive any money in his own name, but he can do so in the agent's name. The average salesperson knows very little about land, real estate laws, or the property he is showing. His knowledge about the parcels he is instructed to show comes solely from his employer, the real estate agent and/or the seller.

The following story is a typical example of how a purchaser can get in trouble. I know the principals involved in this case and saw how the buyer was taken. A salesperson convinced a buyer to purchase some land by assuring him that a beautiful creek ran across the property. The buyer, without double-checking anything the salesperson told him, signed a contract, paid the purchase price, and closed the deal. Then he decided to get a survey done before beginning to build his house to be sure that it would be on the property. He should have demanded that a survey be conducted before he bought the land. The survey showed, to the buyer's surprise, that the creek was not on his property. Since the land was worthless without water from the creek, he went to the former owner to try to get his money back, but was unsuccessful. The former owner had never promised him that the creek was on the property and, in fact, had never even met him. The buyer then tried to locate the salesperson, but he had since left the agent's employment. The agent claimed he had never told his salesperson that the creek was on the property. But he did admit that when the salesperson asked if the creek was on the property, he said that he thought it might be but that he could not be sure without a survey. Getting nowhere, the buyer filed a complaint with the district attorney against the salesperson and real estate agent for fraud. The district attorney found the salesperson and brought him in for questioning, at which time he stated that the agent did tell him the creek was on the land and that he knew nothing about the property other than what he had been told by the agent. The district attorney refused to get involved and referred the victim to a private attorney. But the buyer had nothing in writing to prove he had been told the creek came with the land. The buyer, after consulting several lawyers about suing the parties involved, decided that the costs and fees were too high. He decided to spend the money on a well instead. The buyer did not get what he paid for and will have to pay still more for the well. This could have been avoided by demanding a survey before the close of the sale.

When a salesperson misinforms a buyer, by the time the buyer realizes something is wrong, the salesperson may be long gone. There is a huge turnover in salespeople because the requirements are so easily met and because many people become salespeople in order to make some quick money or find a good deal on a piece of land themselves and then drop out of selling. Few salespeople are paid a regular salary. Usually they get a fraction of the agent's commission for a sale they work on, so there is little incentive to work regularly, and they come and go as they please. Unless a salesperson intends to apply for a license to become a real estate agent, there is no pressure on him to be well informed or particularly honest. Though a buyer who has been defrauded can always sue the seller, the agent, and the salesperson, going to court is easier said than done.

Even if you are positive that you have the law on your side and that you will have no problem proving your case, you still have to hire an attorney, pay court costs, and follow through with a lengthy and costly litigation. And if the defendant agrees to settle the matter out of court, you will still have legal fees to pay. In many areas, the courts are jammed with cases, and a year or two or more may pass before you can even get into court. If you do not have evidence in writing you will have a difficult time proving your case.

Never depend on your ability to bring a successful case against someone should he defraud you. Your goal is to investigate the property so thoroughly before you buy that you will not have any reason to bring a court action later. As a safety factor, make sure your contract of sale specifies all the terms and conditions of the deal so that you will have a good case if those terms are not met.

THE REAL ESTATE AGENT WORKS FOR THE SELLER

A basic fact to remember when dealing with the real estate agent is that he is working for the seller.* Although he is a middleman, he is not an independent person who simply tries to find a buyer for a piece of property. Usually the seller has signed a form of listing contract, making the agent an employee, and when the agent finds an acceptable buyer the seller will pay him a commission. Thus the agent is directly responsible, and owes complete loyalty, to the seller. Since the agent's commission is based on a percentage of the selling price, it is in his interest to get the highest price possible for the land. Commissions usually start at 6 percent of the selling price and often go as high as 10 percent. The agent's role in setting the asking price for the property is explained in chapter 20, "Bargaining to Get the Seller's Asking Price Down."

Since a broker showing you property legally represents the seller, he or she is obligated to seek the highest possible price for the seller and thus may not be able to advise you what approximate lower price the seller may be willing to accept.

If you tell a broker the true top price you are willing to pay for the property, such information might be passed on to the seller without your knowledge or approval. That could result in the seller's asking for that higher price and your paying more than you otherwise might have paid. As a buyer you will not want to disclose confidential information to a broker who does not represent you.

A seller usually gives his property to an agent under one of the following common types of listing contracts. The most desirable contract for an agent is an *exclusive right to sell* the property, which means that he is the only person allowed to sell the land during the period the contract is in force; if the property is sold by anyone else, including the owner, the broker gets all or part of the commission. No other agent can show the land, and if the seller finds a buyer on his own, a commission must still be paid to the agent under contract.

*Throughout the remainder of this book, I will refer to the owner of land as the seller and the person who sells his land for him as the broker or real estate agent. It is implied that the "agent" could be a realtor or salesperson.

Often a broker will allow other brokers to show the property under a *multiple listing* arrangement, and if another broker finds a buyer for the property both brokers will share the commission. If the seller himself finds a buyer the broker can demand all of his commission, but will often agree to reduce his commission under those circumstances.

A variation on that form of listing is one sometimes called an *exclusive agency* contract, which is the same as an exclusive right to sell except that the seller reserves the right to sell the land himself without being obligated to pay any commission to the agent.

The third type of contract is the *open listing,* in which the seller is free to list his land with several different brokers. The first one to find a satisfactory buyer gets the commission. The seller can also sell the land himself and not pay anyone a commission. Most brokers dislike this type of listing because they are competing with everyone else in town and will show open-listed land only after showing their exclusive listings.

If you see land that is listed by several brokers under an open listing, you can choose the broker you like best and buy directly from him.

Since most sellers figure the price of the commission into their asking price in order to pass the expense on to the buyer, if the seller is not selling through an agent you can use that fact when bargaining to get the price reduced.

Frequently a seller will list his land as a *net listing*. This means he tells the broker he wants to net a fixed sum of money, and the broker can keep any money received over the fixed sum, regardless of the amount.

Land seekers are occasionally successful in locating property owners and purchasing directly from them in cases where their property is not even being advertised for sale. Many owners of rural land, particularly if it is underdeveloped or used only as a second home, will not live in the area. But you can identify the parcel on a map and go to the tax assessor's office to obtain the owner's name and address. (This is explained in chapter 17, "Property Taxes and Assessments.")

Get It in Writing!

An agent makes money only if he sells some property, and competition for listings in rural areas is extremely tough. Some real estate agents will take

any listing they can get, regardless of the condition of the property. It might be lacking in adequate water, legal access rights, well-drained soil, or other features of good land, but that won't stop some agents from taking the listing. Eventually someone may buy it.

Most agents are not going to mention the bad points of a piece of property. Only by asking the right questions and demanding specific answers do you stand any chance of learning the true facts. Don't be satisfied with equivocal statements, such as "I think so," "I don't think there's been a problem in the past," or "Nobody can make a guarantee about that in this area." This type of statement is meaningless. The ancient rule of caveat emptor, "Let the buyer beware," applies: it is up to you to clarify all the facts of the situation. By giving an equivocal answer to a question, the agent is not committing himself to anything. Even if he makes a definite statement, unless you get it in writing, it is worthless. You must receive more than equivocal, worthless statements when preparing to lay down thousands of dollars.

Work Out Everything before the Deal Is Closed

Never buy land on the agent's promise or assurance that a problem can be worked out after the deal is closed. For example, if you are supposed to share a well with adjoining landowners but no agreement has been drawn up as to what the arrangement will be, the agent might tell you that your neighbors are great people and that you will have no problem working out an arrangement after you buy the land. This is a common and dangerous sales hustling technique. Once you pay your money and take title, the agent is out of the picture. If your neighbors

don't turn out to be so nice, you can be in real trouble. Don't assume the agent is going to help you with problems once he gets his commission. If he can't arrange all the details in writing before you buy the land, he certainly won't do so afterwards.

These Lines Are Always Good for a Laugh

"I'll let you in on a secret about the seller."

"I'm going to show you something nobody else has seen."

"The land is really worth more than the seller is asking."

"So far, nobody else has seen this property."

"If I had the money, I'd buy this piece myself."

"Look, a lot of people are interested in this property, so you had better make up your mind quickly."

"If your creek or spring dries up, you can always drill a well."

"I am sure the seller will not negotiate."

"You have a prescriptive right-of-way; you don't need a deeded easement."

THE BROKER'S PSYCHOLOGY

After dealing with countless real estate agents, I have found two standard psychological approaches used in selling country property. The first I call the "Welcome to the country, smile, and don't worry about a thing" approach, and the second is the "Why are you trying to complicate the deal by asking all those questions?" approach.

10

1. How to Read a Real Estate Ad

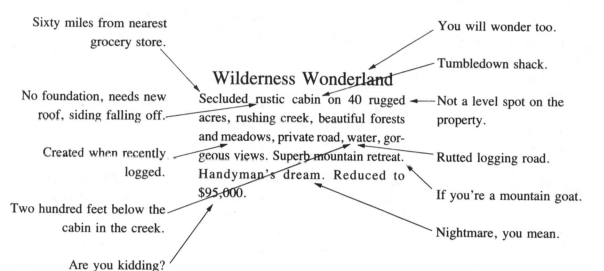

Sixty miles from nearest grocery store.

No foundation, needs new roof, siding falling off.

Created when recently logged.

Two hundred feet below the cabin in the creek.

Are you kidding?

Wilderness Wonderland

Secluded rustic cabin on 40 rugged acres, rushing creek, beautiful forests and meadows, private road, water, gorgeous views. Superb mountain retreat. Handyman's dream. Reduced to $95,000.

You will wonder too.

Tumbledown shack.

Not a level spot on the property.

Rutted logging road.

If you're a mountain goat.

Nightmare, you mean.

"Welcome to the Country, Smile, and Don't Worry about a Thing"

The rural land dealer often exudes this attitude. The first thing you notice is the informal, unbusinesslike appearance. But don't let the absence of a necktie mislead you into thinking he is necessarily more down-home and honest than slick, high-pressure city agents. Coming from the city, you will be easily soothed by the country ambiance. The agent will try to make you feel completely at ease and will assure you he can help you find a nice piece of land. If he can convince you that he has nothing but your interests in mind, he hopes that you won't question anything he tells you.

In the last fifteen years there has been a great increase in the number of women involved in selling rural property. They are very successful salespersons and should be treated the same as a male broker. The same caution should be exercised by you in dealing with both sexes.

Extreme caution should be used when dealing with developers who fly customers to their subdivisions for the weekend, provide free meals and drinks, let them ride horses and go swimming, and then make a big sales pitch. These sales gimmicks place extreme pressure on the captive buyer, and sales contracts should never be signed until you have returned home for a few days to cool off and think about what you are getting yourself into.

Several brokers have given their personal tips for selling property in the country. The most interesting one is to make sure the owner-seller has bread baking or coffee brewing when the prospective purchaser is shown the house. These are two favorite smells for most people and lend a subconscious edge to a sales pitch. One broker makes sure the house is warm and a big fire is going in the fireplace, with drinks available and fresh flowers on the table. Sometimes prearranged telephone calls will come in from "prospective buyers" while an interested party is being shown the house.

"Why Are You Trying to Complicate the Deal by Asking All Those Questions?"

This approach is extremely effective, particularly when used with buyers who know little about what they are doing. Nobody wants to sound stupid. Thus when a buyer asks too many questions, the real estate agent gives him a look that implies, "What's the matter, are you stupid or something?" Most agents dislike anyone who asks a lot of questions, especially lawyers who "complicate things with all kinds of trivial conditions." The broker would have you believe that buying land is simply a process of finding a parcel that looks good to you and paying your money. The rest is just "paperwork." This is exemplified by the common statement made by brokers that the deposit receipt is just a receipt for some money and only one of many forms the buyer will get. Little does the buyer know that once the deposit receipt is signed by both parties, it becomes the binding contract for the land purchase. (See chapter 28, "The Model Contract of Sale.")

An experienced agent knows very quickly whether a buyer is going to be an "easy sale." He bases his judgment on how much knowledge you appear to have about real estate, how much money you intend to spend, and whether you have "buyer's fever." Thus, when a buyer starts asking questions about extremely important legal matters, such as title insurance, easements, water rights, building permits, and financing, some brokers pass them off as if they are merely secondary to the deal. They are secondary to the broker. His goal is to sell the land. He cannot get a commission, regardless of how large or small, unless he sells the property. Anything that delays the sale he will try to avoid. For example, if you ask to have the land surveyed or to be shown the wording of easements that are to be contained in your deed, he will give you the impression that you are imposing on his valuable

time and getting on his nerves—because you will be. Or he will try to scare you into thinking you will blow the deal by making demands on the seller.

Once you have read this book, you will have many questions to ask the agent selling the property about every aspect of your purchase, and you will probably sound like a lawyer to him. Never let a broker's comments that you are paranoid, uptight, or concerned with minor points embarrass or impede you when investigating your prospective purchase. A broker has nothing to lose when he takes your money. You are the only one who can lose anything.

MANY AGENTS WILL CUT INTO THEIR COMMISSIONS TO MAKE A SALE

A real estate agent must sell a piece of property before he can make a commission. Depending on the circumstances, a broker might personally pay to clear up a problem which a seller won't pay for in order to make a sale. For example, a client of mine wanted to buy some land that had not been surveyed, and one of our conditions was that a legal survey be completed with all boundary lines marked on the ground. (Every buyer should have the basic protection of knowing what he is buying.) The seller absolutely refused to spend the $800 for a survey, and I would not let my client go ahead with the deal until she was certain where the boundary lines were. Everything else was satisfactory and we made it clear to the broker that the only thing holding up the sale was the seller's refusal to conduct a survey.

The broker stood to make about a $4,000 commission on the sale. His listing contract was about to terminate, and he was afraid that if he did not sell the property by the final date, the seller would go to a different broker and he would lose the right to sell the land. Therefore, he decided to personally hire and pay for a licensed surveyor to conduct the survey, after which my client purchased the property. The broker thus cut his commission by $800, but the $3,200 he still made on the deal was better than nothing.

If a seller is intransigent on a condition of your purchase, such as getting a survey, a test drilling for water, an easement or water right, or structural and pest inspection, ask the broker to pay for it. If he is desperate for a sale or is worried about the seller taking the property to someone else, he might be willing to give you what you want and pay for it himself. This is done more frequently than you might imagine.

BROKERS ALSO NEGOTIATE LOANS

A broker might tell you that he can get you the loan you need. Brokers often have very close ties with local banks and savings and loan associations. But you have to be careful of two things. The first is that a broker will probably charge you for this service. Second, the loan he will get for you might have a higher interest rate, origination fee, and other costs than you can get elsewhere. In most states, brokers must have special licenses to negotiate loans. In any event, you should always compare the broker's loan terms with those of other available lending institutions. (See chapter 25, "Borrowing from Third Party Lenders.")

A REAL ESTATE AGENT AND HIS OR HER REPUTATION

A real estate agent develops a reputation—good or bad—very quickly in a small town. Spend some time around town, in the restaurants, at the gas station, in the hardware store, and in the retail shops. Talk to folks about your interest in moving to the area. Ask for recommendations about a broker. Pay attention to what you hear. When I first came into my area looking for land, every time I asked the locals who not to deal with in town I was given the same two names. Those two brokers are no longer in business, and for good reason.

The fact that a broker shows you a piece of land does not commit you to continue to patronize him. If you hear that a particular broker has lost his license or is being investigated by the district attorney or local real estate board, find out if this is true before buying land from him. Write to your state department of real estate and ask what the current status of the broker is and whether he has been charged with fraudulent sales practices. It is illegal for a person to claim he is a broker if he is not, and most states require a person to be licensed to sell property belonging to someone else.

PREPARING TO DEAL WITH AN AGENT

Many real estate agents prefer that you write or call to make an appointment to view land rather than just drop in. Go to the phone company or to the public library to get a copy of the phone book for the area you want to investigate. Look under *real estate* in the yellow pages, write down the addresses of all the brokers in town, and send duplicate letters to every agency telling them when you will be in the area and requesting an appointment to view their property. Most brokers will send you pamphlets describing what they have for sale. If some of the described properties are already sold, the honest broker will have marked them with a Sold stamp.

The broker will want to know what kind of place you are looking for and how much money you have to spend. If you are restricting your search to land with electricity that is not more than fifteen minutes from the nearest town and has a year-round creek running through it, the broker will know immediately if he has anything that will interest you. You should always try to get him to show you everything he has that meets your requirements. Never tell the broker the actual amount of money you have to spend so you will be in a better position to bargain to get the purchase price down later. (See chapter 20, "Bargaining to Get the Seller's Asking Price Down.") Simply tell him the price range of property you can afford. But always act like a serious customer or the broker might not show you the best of what he has, particularly if it is far from his office.

If you do not like any of the property a broker shows you, you can leave your name with him and tell him to write you a card if something comes up that meets the description of what you want. This does not mean that he is working for you, and he should not charge you for his service. It is possible to hire a broker to find property for you, but I don't think the expense is worth it, and this is rarely done. The conscientious broker who believes you are serious will notify you when something comes on the market. But you should keep the contact open by communicating regularly with the agents in town.

WARNING—NEVER TRY TO CHEAT A BROKER OUT OF A COMMISSION

Unfortunately, some buyers try to cheat brokers out of a commission. I have successfully sued both buyer and seller for doing so. A buyer will be shown a parcel of land by a broker, and then the buyer makes contact directly with the seller and negotiates a selling price. The buyer and seller close the deal without informing the broker, hoping that the broker never finds out. This is illegal. The buyer is liable for damages for interfering with the contractual relationship between the seller and bro-

ker and for conspiring with the seller to deprive the broker of his lawful commission. The seller is liable for breach of contract with the broker. They both will lose in court should the broker sue for his commission.

USEFUL RESOURCES

The following pamphlet is free from:
  Federal Trade Commission
  Office of Consumer and Business Education
  Bureau of Consumer Protection
  Washington, DC 20580

Real Estate Brokers

For a roster of Accredited Farm and Land Members (AFLM) of the Realtors Land Institute, write to:

  Farm and Land Institute
  430 N. Michigan Ave.
  Chicago, IL 60611

II

CHECKING OUT THE LAND

CHAPTER 3

Climate

DO YOU KNOW WHAT TO EXPECT?

The first thing a person who moves from the city to the country notices is the weather. As a resident or worker in the city you probably spend most of the day indoors under artificial lighting, insulated from the climate by permanently sealed and tinted windows and air-conditioning. You imagine that when you move to the wide open spaces you will delight in the smell of the earth after a light rain and the warmth of the early morning sun shining on fields and trees. But getting in and out of an isolated area on a slippery, rutted dirt road in the snow and rain; trying to start your car in subfreez-

ing weather; using a cold, damp outhouse; having your water pipes freeze; and keeping yourself and your animals warm are also part of country life.

Urban expatriates often make the mistake of moving to an area of the country where the weather is completely different from what they are used to, and then often find they are unable to adjust to the new climate conditions. I strongly recommend that you spend part of each of the four seasons, and preferably a whole year, in an unfamiliar area where you intend to buy land in order to assure yourself that you are willing and able to keep yourself happily alive in that area's climate.

CLIMATE REGIONS MAP

The basic elements of climate that you should consider and research when land hunting are temperature, humidity, rain and snow, drought, floods, winds, frost, sunshine, fog, cloudiness, hurricanes, cyclones, tornadoes, and dust storms. The U.S. Department of Agriculture Climate Regions Map divides the country into thirty-two separate climate regions. It is reprinted here as illustration 2, followed by a description of each region.

REGION 1 comprises the Pacific Coast west of the Coast Range from Santa Cruz Bay to the Canadian line. Its characteristics are cool, dry summers with frequent fogs and heavy winter rainfall with lowest temperatures 8 to 10 degrees below freezing in the north to about freezing in the south.

REGION 2 includes the Willamette Valley in Oregon and the region of similar climate north of it in Washington, including the shores of Puget Sound. The summers are warmer and drier than in Region 1, and the average lowest temperatures are from 10 to 20° F.

REGION 3 includes the Sacramento and San Joaquin valleys in California. This region has hot, dry summers and mild winters with 10 to 20 inches of rainfall. The temperature drops to 8 to 10 degrees below freezing on the valley floor, with slightly higher temperatures on the hillsides.

REGION 4 includes the Sierra Nevada and Cascade mountain ranges. This region has hot, dry summers except for occasional scattered showers in the mountains. Most of the winter precipitation, from 20 to over 50 inches, falls on the western slopes, where winters are moderate to cold. East of the mountains, wide variations in temperatures occur frequently. The Sierra Nevadas have snow annually as low as 2,000 feet. Throughout this entire area, conditions vary considerably according to elevation.

REGION 5 comprises the coast west of the Coast Range from Santa Cruz to Santa Barbara, thence to San Diego, Redlands, and Riverside, including what is popularly known as southern California. The summers are dry, cool on the coast, and warm inland; the winters are moderately rainy, from 30 inches in the mountains to 10 inches in the valleys, being nearly free from frost on the coast and in the foothills.

REGION 6 is the Columbia River Valley in eastern Washington. The summers are warm; the winters have ordinary temperatures of 10 to 15° F, with extremes occasionally of zero. The annual rainfall varies from 7 to 20 inches, mostly in winter and spring.

REGION 7 includes the plateau of the eastern part

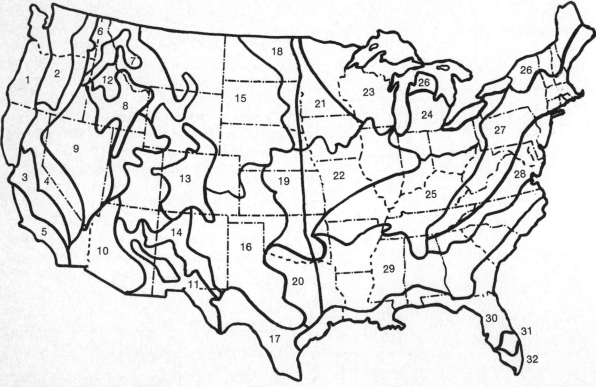

2. Climate Regions Map

of the state of Washington and the valleys of northern Idaho and western Montana. The summers are warm, and the lowest winter temperatures range from 0 to 15° F, with an annual rainfall of 10 to 20 inches.

REGION 8 is the Snake River Plains and the Utah Valley. It is semiarid country with water available for irrigation. The summers are hot, and the winters often have minimum temperatures of 0 to −10° F with a rainfall of 9 to 15 inches, mostly in winter.

REGION 9 is the northern part of the great arid interior plateau included in the states of Oregon, Nevada, and Utah. Its characteristics are hot days and occasional frosty nights in summer with cold winters and about 10 inches of rainfall annually.

REGION 10 includes all the southwestern desert, including portions of California, Arizona, and a corner of Nevada. The climate is hot to scorching, with a rainfall of 3 to 10 inches.

REGION 11 comprises the southern part of the great arid interior plateau included in New Mexico and Arizona. Its characteristics are the same as the plateau farther north (Region 9), except that the temperatures are higher.

REGION 12 is that part of the Rocky Mountains included in Idaho, Montana, Wyoming, Washington, and Oregon. The temperature and rainfall vary greatly, depending on elevation and exposure.

REGION 13 includes the Rocky Mountains of Utah and Colorado. It is similar to the region farther north, except that the temperatures for the same elevation are about 7 degrees warmer.

REGION 14 includes the Rocky Mountains of Arizona and New Mexico. It is similar to the region farther north, except that temperatures for the same elevation average about 6 degrees warmer than Region 13 and 13 degrees warmer than Region 12.

REGION 15 is the northern Great Plains area south to Kansas and Colorado, extending from the 5,500-foot contour on the west to the black soils on the east. It is extremely cold in winter in the northeastern portions, usually dropping to −30° or −40° F, while close to the mountains it is 20 degrees warmer. The summers are moderately warm. It is generally recognized as the northern part of the dry-farming area, with a rainfall of about 15 inches.

REGION 16 is the central portion of the Great Plains including the plains portions of Kansas, Oklahoma, and New Mexico as well as portions of the plains in Colorado and Texas. It extends eastward from about the 6,500-foot contour on the west to the black soils on the east. The rainfall varies from 12 to 22 inches. The climate is warmer and has greater evaporation than Region 15. It is the southern portion of the dry-farming area.

REGION 17 is the dry, hot portion of southwestern Texas, with 12 to 22 inches of rainfall, but with excessive evaporation.

REGION 18 is the subhumid black-soils country lying east of the dry-farming area of the northern Great Plains and is intermediate as to moisture between Region 15 and the more humid area to the east of it. The winters are very cold and dry.

REGION 19 is the subhumid black-soils area of Kansas, southern Nebraska, and much of Oklahoma. There is more moisture than in the dry-farming country to the west of it and less than in the area farther east. It is a locality of sudden variation in winter temperatures and of hot winds in summer.

REGION 20 is the subhumid or transition region of central Texas with black and chocolate-colored soils. In moisture conditions it is intermediate between the dry-farming regions farther west and the humid climate of eastern Texas.

REGION 21 is the northern part of the prairie country with frequent droughts of more than thirty days in the western portion and cold winters with drying winds. The rainfall is 20 to 30 inches, occurring mostly in the summer season.

REGION 22 is that portion of the prairie country having higher temperatures than Region 21, but subject to similar cold, drying winds in winter. The rainfall is 30 to 40 inches.

REGION 23 is the western part of the Great Lakes forest area. The eastern portion is slightly warmer and more humid than the western portion, the latter much resembling Region 21.

REGION 24 is largely that part of the country influenced by the Great Lakes, lying east of Lake Michigan, exending south into Ohio and eastward to Lake Ontario. There is considerable moisture in the atmosphere in addition to a rainfall of 30 to 40 inches rather well distributed through the year. The winter temperatures are more moderate than in Region 23.

REGION 25 includes the Ohio and lower Tennessee River valleys and the Ozark Mountain region. The winter temperatures are rather moderate with much alternate freezing and thawing, while the summer is warm with a thirty-day drought often occurring near its close. The rainfall is 40 to 50 inches.

REGION 26 includes the colder sections of the eastern United States, comprising much of Maine, New Hampshire, and Vermont, the mountainous portions of New York, and a portion of northern Michigan. It is characterized by cold winters with heavy snowfall and short summers of long days and cool nights.

REGION 27 is the Appalachian Mountain country, including much of New England and New York, most of Pennsylvania, and the mountainous portion of the states southward. The rainfall is abundant, usually from 35 to 50 inches, and is well distributed through the season. In the colder parts the snowfall is abundant.

REGION 28 lies just east of Region 27 and includes the Piedmont and some adjoining sections with similar growing conditions. It extends from northern Alabama northeastward across the Carolinas and Virginia to New Jersey and the coast of Massachusetts. It is warmer than Region 27, with abundant rainfall except in late summer, when thirty-day droughts often occur. The winters are open, with much freezing and thawing, and there is but little snow protection to be relied upon.

REGION 29 includes most of the cotton country, extending from what is known as east Texas eastward and northward to the Atlantic Ocean in North Carolina and Virginia. It lies between the Piedmont region and the swampy lower coastal plain that borders the Gulf of Mexico and the Atlantic Ocean. The rainfall is abundant, being from 45 to 60 inches, and is well distributed, except toward the last of the rather warm summer, when a long drought frequently occurs, particularly in the western portion.

REGION 30 is the swampy coastal plain from Wilmington, North Carolina, southward along the Atlantic Ocean, and westward along the Gulf of Mexico. It has moderate summer temperatures with hot sunshine, short winters, an abundance of rainfall (50 to 60 inches), except in the Texas portion, and is almost subtropical.

REGION 31 is southern Florida, with the exception of the subtropical fringe. It is subject to annual frosts, often becoming sufficiently cold to kill the tops of tender plants without killing their roots, and has rather warm summers and a rainfall of about 50 inches.

REGION 32 is the tropical coast of southern Florida. It has slight range of temperature with no killing frosts and a rainfall of 50 to 60 inches.

GEOGRAPHICAL DIFFERENCES BETWEEN EAST AND WEST

The East is less mountainous than the West, and geographical changes are relatively gradual from one section to another. (See illustration 3.) Likewise temperatures generally increase slowly as you go from north to south. The West, on the other hand, contains large rugged mountain ranges with great differences in elevation over short distances. For example, Mount Whitney, one of the highest peaks in the United States (14,495 feet), and Death Valley, a desert wasteland containing the lowest point in the United States (276 feet below sea level), are less than eighty-five miles apart. These extremes of topography cause the climate to be much more diverse throughout the West than in the East. Temperature differences tend to be based on elevation and can vary greatly within a small area. When looking for land, especially in the West, don't assume that the climate of your prospective homestead is the same as the climate of the nearest town twenty miles away. For instance, the areas all around us often get fog in the mornings and afternoons whereas our valley, protected from the ocean on one side and the river valley on the other by two mountain ranges, gets almost no fog throughout the year.

RAIN AND SNOW—THE HUMID EAST AND ARID WEST

An average of thirty inches of water fall as rain or snow in the United States each year, but this precipitation is not divided evenly over the country. Illustration 4 indicates the dividing line between the humid East and the arid West.

Although the heaviest mean annual rainfall is over 100 inches near the north Pacific Coast, and several other locations in the West have a mean annual precipitation in excess of 40 inches, most of the West, from Texas north to Montana and the

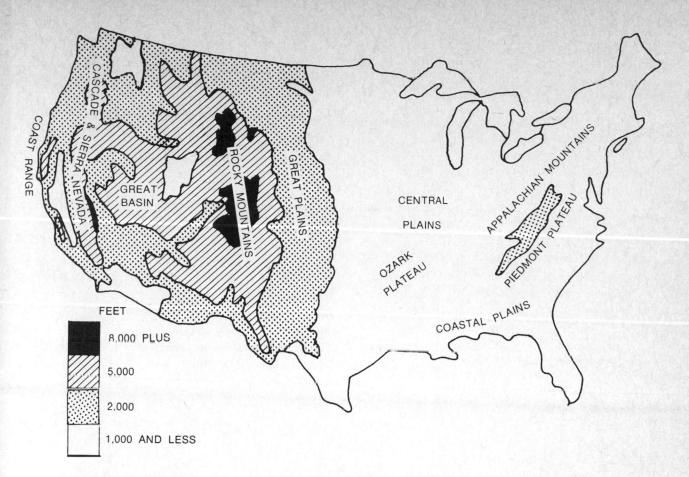

COAST RANGE

CASCADE & SIERRA NEVADA

GREAT BASIN

ROCKY MOUNTAINS

GREAT PLAINS

CENTRAL PLAINS

OZARK PLATEAU

APPALACHIAN MOUNTAINS

PIEDMONT PLATEAU

COASTAL PLAINS

FEET

8,000 PLUS

5,000

2,000

1,000 AND LESS

3. Prominent Physical Features of the United States

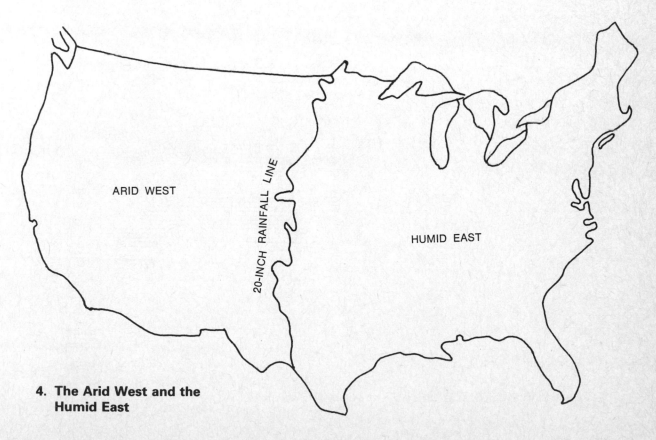

ARID WEST

20-INCH RAINFALL LINE

HUMID EAST

4. The Arid West and the Humid East

Dakotas through the Great Plains area, averages less than 20 inches of rainfall annually, and much of the Southwest averages less than 10 inches a year.

The East gets considerably more rain because of the mixing of Arctic air with the semitropical air masses from the South. The warm southern air flow curves across the Gulf of Mexico, up the Mississippi, and then turns east over the Appalachians to the Atlantic. The Artic air mass from the north pushes the warm air upward, which lowers the temperature, resulting in heavy rains in both summer and winter. Illustration 5, the "Average Annual Precipitation," and illustration 6, the "Average Summer Precipitation," show the great difference in precipitation between the humid East and the arid West. The eastern half of the United States, which contains about 40 percent of the country's total land area, gets 75 percent of the rain and

snow. It is because of this excessive water that most of the floods occur in that part of the country.

FLOODS

In whichever part of the country you are looking, if the land is next to a river or stream you should seriously consider the possibility of a flood. (See illustration 7 to find the season in which floods generally occur in your area.) In our area, a devastating flood wiped out several towns along our main river in 1964. I have met a few people who bought land since then along that river. They all know about the 1964 flood but none have actually studied the history of flood damage or the likelihood of future floods occurring. They know only that their homesteads might be wiped out some

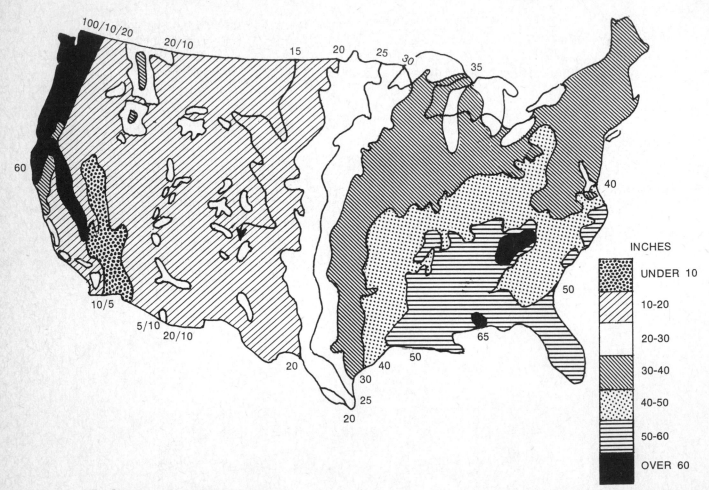

5. Average Annual Precipitation

INCHES
UNDER 10
10-20
20-30
30-40
40-50
50-60
OVER 60

22

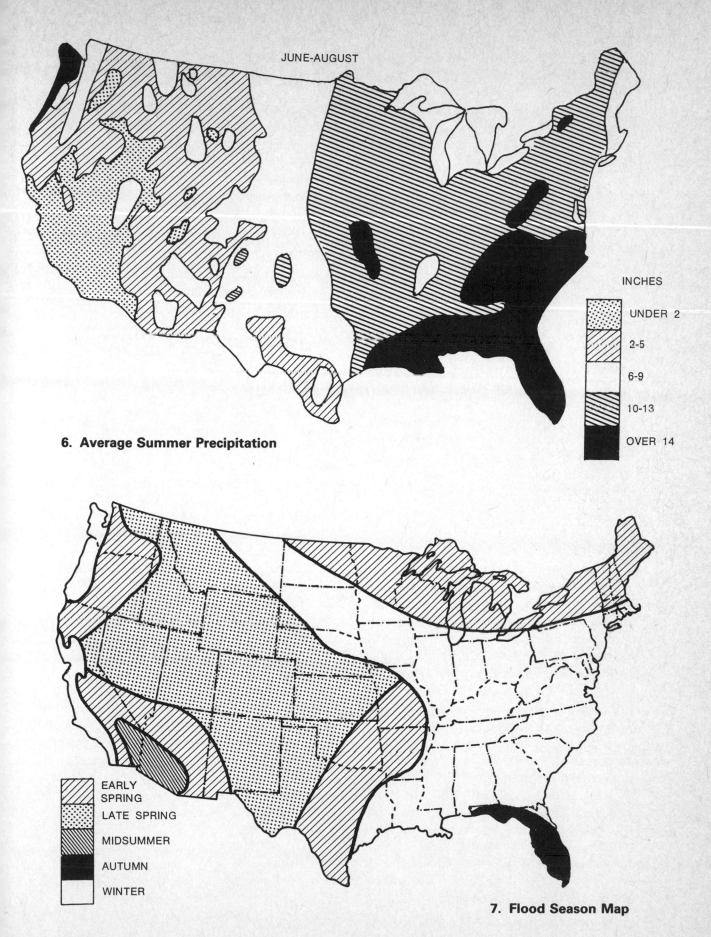

JUNE-AUGUST

6. Average Summer Precipitation

INCHES

UNDER 2

2-5

6-9

10-13

OVER 14

EARLY
SPRING

LATE SPRING

MIDSUMMER

AUTUMN

WINTER

7. Flood Season Map

23

winter and have accepted perennial anxiety.

Most county libraries maintain a local history section that contains a large collection of information on past floods including photos, newspaper and magazine articles, and maps indicating where the worst damage occurred. They also have information on flood-control measures subsequently taken by the county.

Unfortunately some of the finest land is located in vulnerable flood-plain areas along large rivers, but most rural areas are developing flood-control projects, which lessen potential hazards. You should examine the progress of local flood-control plans if you are looking for land along a watercourse. Be especially cautious when buying land along a river that has had a forest fire or extensive logging operations conducted on its banks. Removing the trees increases the amount of surface water runoff and greatly increases the potential for floods where none have occurred in the past. Heavy grazing and farming also help to cause floods by destroying the natural ground cover.

The size of a stream does not indicate its propensity to flood. Even the smallest streams have sent several feet of water into living rooms during heavy storms. Carefully balance your desire to live in a flood area with the potential dangers to your homestead.

Flash Floods

In many parts of the United States flash floods are a chance threat. These are local floods of great volume and short duration, generally resulting from heavy rainfall, and are often the most damaging floods because they occur on short notice and are highly unpredictable. During a recent flash flood in the James River basin in Virginia, twenty-seven inches of rain fell in about eight hours, drowning 153 people and destroying everything in the area. Some of the states most seriously affected by flash floods are Maine, New Jersey, North and South Carolina, Ohio, Virginia, and West Virginia. However, flash floods are not limited to the East. In May 1972, the Guadalupe River in Texas overflowed in a flash flood when twelve inches of rain fell in one day, raising the river nine feet above flood level. The National Weather Service is setting up automatic alarm systems in flash-flood areas throughout the East. If an alarm system has been installed in your area, the price of the land may

increase slightly, but the added cost will be worthwhile.

Storms of flash-flood proportion occur in the Great Plains states when moist tropical air moves in and collides with dry polar air, causing heavy rains, thunder, and lightning. In these storms, one-third of the average annual precipitation can fall in twenty-four hours; occasionally one-fifth of the annual supply falls in one hour, and then four months pass without any rain at all.

DROUGHT

Too little rain and snow can be as bad as too much. Drought is a serious threat to many areas of the country. The usual problems in the arid West have already been mentioned earlier and will be described in great detail in chapter 4, "Is There Enough Water on the Land?" Recurring droughts are a normal feature of the climate in southern parts of the Great Plains area, which has had four major droughts since 1880. The most severe occurred during the 1930s throughout the Dust Bowl and caused many farmers to lose their land. The latest drought in that area lasted for four years in the 1950s.

Major water supply crises also occur in other parts of the country. Between 1961 and 1966 most of the fourteen northeastern states suffered a serious lack of water. The areas most affected extended from eastern Massachusetts to eastern Pennsylvania. Many rural inhabitants found their wells completely dry during most of the year, and trees, grass, flowers, and crops showed the serious effects of the long water shortage. In addition, wells along the Atlantic Coast were contaminated by seawater seeping into the ground as large amounts of fresh water were withdrawn during dry periods. Other parts of the humid East suffered major droughts in the 1930s and 1949, as well as through the sixties.

In 1986 the South suffered the worst drought in over one hundred years, and the devastating effects of the summer of 1986 will be felt for many years to come. A depleted water table can take years to revive itself.

A thorough study of the drought history of an area, and the community's ability to meet future crises, will give you the best indication of what might be in store for you if you buy property there.

Legend for map 8:
- JUNE
- MAY 10-30
- APRIL 10-MAY 10
- MAR. 20-APR. 20
- FEB. 28-MAR. 10
- FEB. 0-28
- JAN. 30-FEB. 8

8. Average Dates of the Last Killing Frost in the Spring

FROST AND SUNSHINE—THE LENGTH OF THE GROWING SEASON

If you are interested in growing your own food you will want to know the number of frost-free days the area has, since many fruits and vegetables cannot tolerate freezing weather. Illustrations 8, 9, and 10 together indicate the average frost-free periods throughout the country. These maps are very general but can aid you in determining where the best areas are for what you intend to grow. You should check local conditions, visit farms and nurseries in the area, and talk to longtime residents about the weather, the length of the growing season, and the crops that are grown there.

Legend for map 9:
- BEFORE AUG. 30
- AUG. 30-SEPT. 30
- SEPT. 30-OCT. 30
- OCT. 30-NOV. 30
- NOV. 30-DEC. 10
- AFTER DEC. 10

9. Average Dates of the First Killing Frost in the Fall

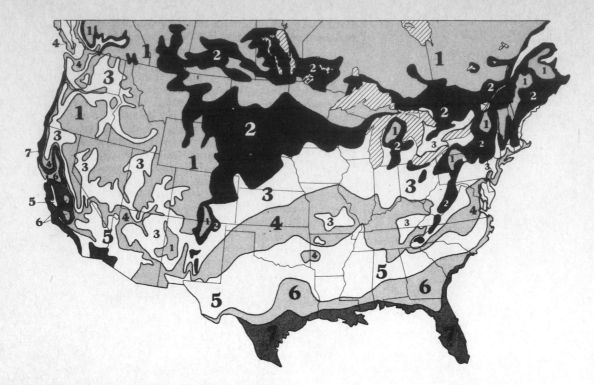

10. Number of Frost-Free Days per Year

1 30–120 days
2 120–150 days
3 150–180 days
4 180–210 days
5 210–240 days
6 240–270 days
7 270–365 days

ACID RAIN

Acid rain refers to any precipitation having a pH less than that of rainwater. Rainwater is naturally slightly acidic, with a pH of around 5.6, but this may vary considerably. It is a weak acid because carbon dioxide from the atmosphere combines with rainwater to form a mild carbonic acid.

Acid rain, on the other hand, is much more acidic because sulfur and nitrogen oxides combine with rainwater to form sulfuric and nitric acids. Acid rain can have a pH of around 2.0, up to 5.6. Because the pH scale is logarithmic, a pH of 3 is ten times more acidic than a pH of 4 and one hundred times more acidic than a pH of 5.

Sulfur and nitrogen oxides are released into the atmosphere by natural phenomena, such as volcanoes, forest fires, ocean spray, lightning, and decomposition of organic matter, as well as by related human activities. However, in heavily industrialized and urbanized areas of eastern North America, human activities cause more than ten times the amount of emissions of sulfur and nitrogen oxides into the atmosphere than do natural sources.

About two-thirds of the United States currently receives acid rain precipitation. Acid rain occurs mostly east of the Mississippi River because the prevailing winds and frequent routes of storm centers are from west to east carrying airborne pollutants from some midwestern states. The pH of average annual rainfall in most states east of the Mississippi River is presently less than 4.5, which is at least ten times more acidic than normal rain.

Fish are particularly sensitive to acid rain. Waters with pH levels of 4 or 5 can kill fish indirectly because females fail to reproduce. In waters of a pH of 3 or lower fish suffocate from the formation of excess mucus in their gills. Also, some heavy metals, such as aluminum and lead, are more easily dissolved in water with a lower pH and are leached from the soil into the runoff and groundwater and then into lakes and rivers. Eventually, fish may die from accumulation of these heavy metals. Even a short pulse of acid rain, such as from melting snow in the springtime, may lower the pH of a large body of water enough to prevent spawning during that critical period.

Acid rain affects other wildlife also, although it is not so well documented. Acid rain is an increasingly important consideration when buying country property, especially in the eastern portion of North America, particularly if you are considering raising fish or crops that are sensitive to acidity.

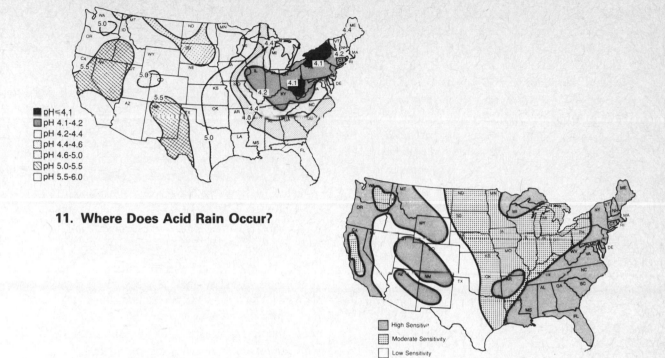

11. Where Does Acid Rain Occur?

12. What Areas in the United States Are Susceptible to Acid Rain?

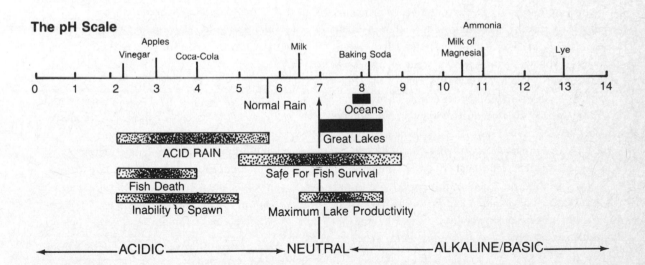

pH values of common acid and alkaline substances; a lower value denotes a higher acid content.

13. Acid Rain pH Diagram

"Acid Rain: Effects on Fish and Wildlife," page 1, Fish and Wildlife leaflet, Department of the Interior Fish and Wildlife Service, Washington, D.C., 1985. See Useful Resources.

PERSONAL HEALTH

The effect a particular climate may have on your health should not be overlooked. Hot, humid climates often aggravate asthma, allergies, hyperhidrosis, eczema, and other skin conditions. Those of you who are allergic to ragweed pollen should avoid southern New England, the Mid-Atlantic states, the southern Great Lakes area, and the northern and central states of the Midwest east of the Rockies.

Rheumatic and arthritic problems are increased in cold, moist areas. High altitudes cause shortness of breath and are undesirable for people with lung difficulties and cardiac conditions.

The rainfall in the coastal regions is considered healthier than that in the inland areas because of the salt air, and the dry air in general is healthier than humid air. These are among the reasons many older people move to Florida and Arizona. If you have health problems, consider the effect of climate carefully when selecting land and consult your doctor regarding your choice.

A FINAL WORD

I have discussed only a few of the major problems caused by weather, but there are many others. If you stay in an area awhile and study its climate history, you will know if you want to live there permanently. The most desirable areas of the country are those with the most temperate climate conditions, and land prices there are much higher than elsewhere. Rural costs generally decrease in proportion to the harshness of the winters. Do not be attracted to cheap land unless you are prepared to meet the exigencies of its climate. I have found that weather and its attendant problems have been major factors in causing people to leave their newly purchased country land and return to the cities.

USEFUL RESOURCES

Climate Maps, Tables, and Data

Complete climate information is available for every state and most major cities from the following agency:

National Climatic Data Center
Federal Bldg.
Asheville, NC 28801-2696

Available information includes a narrative climatic summary of the state; daily, monthly, and annual normals of maximum and minimum and mean temperatures; freeze dates; seasonal and annual precipitation and snowfall data; and heating- and cooling-degree days for each cooperative station in the state.

Also available is a wind energy resource atlas for every state with wind power maps, seasonal variations in wind resource availability, monthly average wind power and speed, and a lot of the major wind resource areas in the United States. A solar radiation energy resource atlas is available for every state, including direct and diffuse solar radiation data. An annual report is available for each state that charts the daily soil temperatures at certain depths of the soil, for various soil types. To get a complete catalogue of all available resources with current prices and ordering information, write to the National Climatic Data Center and request copies of their available publications, including *The Selective Guide to Climatic Data Services* and *Selective Climatological Publications*.

Examples of some of the data available from the National Climatic Data Center are the following:

Climate of Each State. Including a narrative climatic summary of the states; monthly and annual norms of maximum, minimum, and mean temperatures; precipitation, heating-degree days, and cooling-degree days; and freeze data. Specify state desired, and send $1.00 to the National Climatic Data Center.

Wind Energy Resources Atlas. Prepared for each state, identifying annual average wind power, wind power maps, major wind resource areas, and wind data sources.

Daily Means and Extremes of Temperature, Precipitation, and Snowfall (for each state).

Weekly Weather and Crop Bulletin.
Provides brief descriptions of crop and weather conditions important on a national scale.

National Thunderstorm Frequencies for the U.S.

U.S. Soil Temperature. Depth of soil temperature measurement, soil type, and daily measurement.

Interesting pamphlets on weather are being written and distributed annually by the Government Printing Office. Write for the current Weather Subject Bibliography from:

Superintendent of Documents
Government Printing Office
Washington, DC 20402

For example, the following are currently available for the specified prices:

Acid Rain and Transported Air Pollutants—
Implications for Public Policy
S/N 052-003-00956-1
$ 9.50

Climatic Change to the Year 2000—A
Survey of Expert Opinion
S/N 008-020-00738-2
$17.00

Wind Energy: Technical Information Guide
S/N 061-000-00656-7
$ 4.50

Satellite data are available from the Satellite Data Services Division located in Camp Springs, Maryland. The mailing address is:

National Climatic Data Center
Satellite Data Services Division
World Weather Bldg., Rm. 100
Washington, DC 20233

Literature on acid rain is becoming increasingly available. A good primer is *Acid Rain: Effects on Fish and Wildlife*, available from:

Publications Unit
U.S. Fish and Wildlife Service
Washington, DC 20240

Weather Bureau and Department of Commerce

In each state the U.S. Department of Commerce has a local weather bureau office with complete weather information for each county. You can get the local number from the telephone book under Weather or under United States Department of Commerce, National Oceanic and Atmospheric Administration (NOAA), National Weather Service, or by writing the Department of Commerce main office or any of the local offices listed at the end of this section.

U.S. Department of Commerce
Archival Services Branch E/CCLL
National Climatic Data Center
Federal Bldg.
Asheville, NC 28801-2696
(704) 259-0682

For satellite data write to:
National Climatic Center
Satellite Data Services Division
World Weather Bldg., Rm. 100
Washington, DC 20233
(301) 763-8111

Local Sources of Information

Local and county libraries have weather statistics, including information on disasters, such as floods and droughts. The county agriculture agent has weather charts and data on the variations of the growing seasons in your area.

The chamber of commerce has brochures containing local climate information. The local airport and fire department will have a weather station with a thorough record of the area's climate. They can be very helpful and often have the most accurate local statistics. The local board of health or county health department has pollen count statistics and other climate data that relate to health problems.

CHAPTER 4

Is There Enough Water on the Land?

Of all our natural resources, water has become the most precious.

—Rachel Carson in *Silent Spring*

Your land can have the most beautiful view in the world, but without water it is useless. Never buy land without a proven source of adequate water.

DRY LAND ISN'T ALWAYS IN THE DESERT

Most people buy land in the spring and early summer when creeks are full, springwater is bursting from the hills, and the meadows are green. In late August and September, the early buyer is often shocked to find that all of his water has dried up. If you have lived primarily in urban areas where water has always been just a turn of the tap away, you don't realize the work and expense involved in bringing water where you want it. Just to get running water into your house might involve installing a generator, pump, pipeline, holding tank, and well. You might see land with a beautiful creek and not realize that it is too far away from the nicest building site to be of any use.

If there is no water visible on the land, you will be told that everyone in the area uses wells and that if you dig deep enough you will find water. The facts are that not all land has underground water, finding any is often difficult, and drilling a well is expensive. A big creek or a good well on a neighboring property does not mean there is water on your land. Do not be fooled by such misconceptions.

To get a complete picture of the general pattern of water distribution throughout the United States you should read chapter 3, "Climate." Even if you have a year-round creek running through your land, you will be restricted in taking water from it by your state's water laws. A complete discussion of water rights is contained in chapter 10, "Water Rights."

TYPES OF WATER SOURCES

Water sources are either on the surface or underground. Surface waters include rivers, streams, creeks, lakes, ponds, bogs, marshes, mud flats, springs, and cisterns. Water is trapped underground in two types of areas: in aquifers, loose water-bearing materials such as gravel, sand, and clay; or in consolidated water-bearing rocks, notably limestone, basalt, and sandstone. In many cases, surface water sources are excellent for irrigation, livestock, fire fighting, ponds, and other uses, but cannot be utilized for drinking. Therefore, a well is often a necessity regardless of the presence of surface water.

The following sections cover the various aspects of each type of water source that you can have on land you buy.

SURFACE WATERS

Rivers, Streams, and Creeks

Rivers, streams, and creeks differ primarily in size and length. Rivers are large watercourses that are often navigable and public. Although you should have enough water available for your use, you may find that you have to share your river with motorboats, waterskiers, and swimmers, although swimming may be unpleasant because of the film of gas and oil left on top of the water by motorboats. Look upstream to see if there are factories, lumber mills, or other polluters that might make the river unpleasant to swim in and dangerous to drink. If you are interested in fishing, ask the local bait shop about the fishing potential of the river.

How much logging has occurred upstream? According to the Environmental Protection Agency, streams in logged areas contain up to seven thousand times more sediment after logging. The resulting siltation kills mature fish, smothers spawning beds, destroys stream vegetation, and clogs smaller creeks.

Check to be sure that there are no plans to build dams on the river that will flood your land. Get a copy of the master water plan for your area from your state water resources department. This is particularly important if you are buying along a major river. When dams are built, many homesteads along the river are condemned by the government and will become the bottom of a new lake. (See chapter 15, "Eminent Domain and Condemnation.")

Streams and creeks are much smaller than rivers, and often do not flow continuously throughout the dry season, especially in the arid West. The only way you can tell if your stream or creek will flow year-round is to see it flowing during the driest part of the summer, usually August or September. Don't accept the word of a real estate agent that a creek never goes dry. Even if he is not deliberately misleading you, he probably has never lived on the land and has no idea how much the flow decreases. If a creek is your only year-round source of water, your activities will be limited by the amount of water in it during its lowest period.

Check with the local farm advisor, health department, or U.S. Geological Survey office to see if the stream has ever been *gauged,* or measured. Talk to other people who live along the creek or stream to see what their experience has been. Look at their crops and those on the land you want to buy, if there are any, to get some idea of what the stream can support. If you are buying land that has never been lived on and nobody knows the performance of the stream, you should definitely see

31

the stream at its lowest point to determine if it will support your homestead.

You will probably want to know if you can fish in your stream. Many streams are classified as spawning grounds where fishing is prohibited. You can check the state fish and game code, which is usually obtainable in the local bait shop, to find out how your stream is classified. Often extremely heavy penalties are levied for fishing in spawning areas.

A unique problem along the coasts is the flow of salt water into inland streams and creeks. If you buy land near the ocean, be sure your stream does not have this problem. Salt water is bad for crops and drinking.

Lakes and Ponds

If you purchase land on a lake you will have many of the same problems you would on river land in terms of recreational disturbances and polluted water. Lakeside land is a very desirable place to live, but before you buy you should consider how crowded yours will become during the summer. Illustration 14 indicates the location of each type of lake property.

You might be lucky and find a parcel of land with a pond on it. If you do, find out the source of the water that feeds it. If a creek or spring feeds the pond, make sure the flow is sufficient to keep the pond full year-round. The presence of fish in the water is a good sign of a healthy pond. If they can live there, it probably doesn't get stagnant in the summer, but you should test the water before

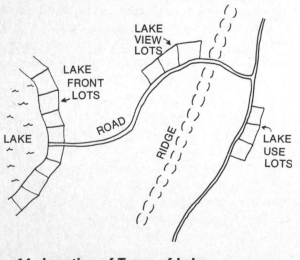

14. Location of Types of Lake Properties

assuming you can swim in it safely. Ask about the mosquito problem in the summer. This is often an undesirable side effect of a pond. If the pond is a good one, it is worth the extra money you will pay for the land.

It is much more likely a real estate agent will show you a possible "pond site" rather than a pond. He might show you some springs or creeks that could be used to feed a man-made pond and tell you that the site has already been researched. Never assume a pond can be built unless a reliable source, such as a geologist, your local farm advisor, or a Soil Conservation Service agent, investigates the site and determines its feasibility as a pond site. Ponds depend on the soil's ability to retain water, an adequate and continuous water flow, and proper geological conditions. I have seen ugly mud-holes where hopeful new landowners had put a lot of energy into creating beautiful ponds, only to find that their soil wouldn't hold water. Building a pond requires heavy-duty equipment, expensive building materials, and possibly a system to divert water to the pond from a water source. The mere presence of an "excellent pond site" should never be your primary reason for buying a piece of land. A "pond site" is a common sales gimmick used to make land seem more attractive and justify a high selling price. Don't be swayed by such tactics. I could go on any piece of land and point out a possible "pond site." So could you.

Bogs, Marshes, and Mud Flats

The presence of bogs, marshes, and large mud flats can present advantages or disadvantages. Occasionally the geographical layout will be such that you can build a dam and create a pond. Usually, however, these areas will be nonproductive breeding grounds for mosquitos and other pests. When they exist on the property, you are paying for land that cannot be used. Remember, too much water can be just as much of a problem as too little water. (See the section entitled "Drainage" in chapter 5.) Use this as one of your arguments when bargaining to lower the selling price.

Springs

In many areas, springs are the primary source of water. A spring occurs where water seeps to the surface from a crack in the rock formation or where a road cuts through a water vein. Artesian wells are like springs, except that the water is forced up by underground pressure.

Often a spring will be only a tiny trickle of water coming out of a hillside. Don't underestimate its value until you measure its rate of flow. If a spring produces 1 gallon of water a minute, which looks like a trickle, it produces 1,440 gallons every twenty-four hours. If you have a large holding tank to collect the water as it flows to the surface, this amount could support a small homestead. When you are looking at land with springs, take along a gallon jar and measure the flow per minute using a watch with a second hand. Multiply this amount by 60 to get the flow per hour, then multiply that result by 24 to get the flow per day. Of course, you will have to see the spring during the driest part of the year to be certain that the flow is still sufficient for your needs. (See "How Much Water Will You Need?" later in this chapter.) The rate of flow can often be increased if a spring is properly dug out and opened up. Never attempt to do this without the advice of an expert, because you might cut open too much and cause the spring to go underground.

If you want to locate a spring on some land, maps are available that indicate springs and groundwater sources. These can be good quadrangle maps or special water maps. You may obtain maps of your area from the local Soil Conservation Service or farm advisor. The U.S. Geological Survey and the Army Corps of Engineers might also have results of water studies done in your area. (See Useful Resources at the end of this chapter.) Even if you can't locate a water source on a map, you should go over the land on foot searching for new or undiscovered springs. Look for plants that indicate water is beneath the surface. Illustration 21 shows a few of these. Do some research to find out what the trees and shrubs are in your area that indicate water. Remember that the presence of springs on neighboring land does not mean that any exist on your land. Water may flow out of one side of a mountain and not the other.

Cisterns

Cisterns are large circular or rectangular storage tanks either completely open at the top to collect rainwater or open only enough to allow a pipe to enter and bring in water from roofs or fields. They are made of cement, wood, or metal. The collected water is rarely used for drinking due to the possibility of contamination. However, it can be used for swimming and irrigation.

Examine any cisterns on the land for leaks, holding capacity, connections to the water sources, and general condition of the structures and their enclosures. If a rain-gathering cistern is the only water source for the property, your activities will be limited by the amount of water gathered during the rainy time of year.

UNDERGROUND WATER

The two maps, Water Use by States and Water Resources Regions, and the accompanying chart will give you an idea of rural freshwater use in the United States in 1980.

Wells

Eighty percent of rural water in the United States comes from underground sources and is pumped to the surface through wells. Underground water, or *groundwater,* is preferred for drinking because it is purer than surface water. Groundwater can be brought up at any point and thus obtained close to where you need to use it. Because surface water flows away swiftly and is subject to tremendous evaporation, the fluctuation in a stream or creek varies more than the steady supply of groundwater. The primary difficulty with a well is the high cost of digging, casing, and sealing it and the necessity for a pump to bring the water to the surface.

If electricity is not available, you will have to use a generator to run your well pump. You might have a motor running several hours every day. This is a noisy, polluting, and expensive operation, and mechanical breakdowns can be frequent. If you can use a windmill or produce your own electricity with wind, solar, or water power, your life on the land might be more pleasant. See appendix J for information on windmills, pumps, and alternate sources of energy.

Problems

If you are going to use a well, find out the history of water problems in the area before you buy. When

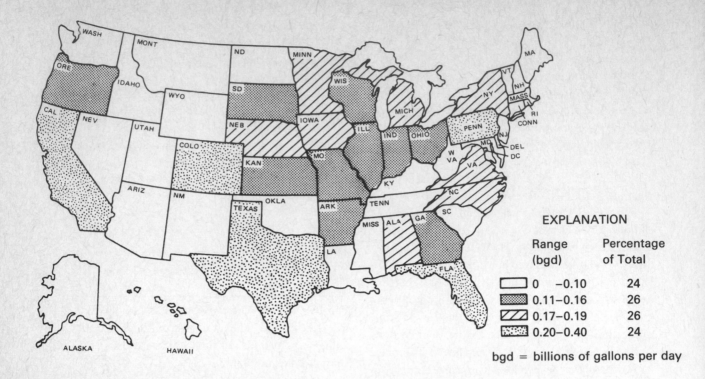

EXPLANATION

Range (bgd)	Percentage of Total
0 −0.10	24
0.11−0.16	26
0.17−0.19	26
0.20−0.40	24

bgd = billions of gallons per day

15. Water Use by State

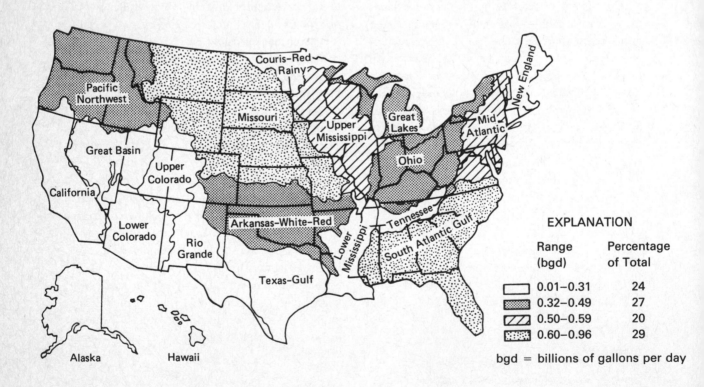

EXPLANATION

Range (bgd)	Percentage of Total
0.01−0.31	24
0.32−0.49	27
0.50−0.59	20
0.60−0.96	29

bgd = billions of gallons per day

16. Water Resources Regions

Rural freshwater withdrawals, by states and water resources regions, 1980.

17. Rural Freshwater Use, by Regions, in Million Gallons per Day, 1980

(Data generally are rounded to two significant figures; figures may not add to totals because of independent rounding.)

WATER RESOURCES REGION	DOMESTIC USE				LIVESTOCK USE				TOTAL DOMESTIC AND LIVESTOCK USE			
	Withdrawals			Consumptive use	Withdrawals			Consumptive use	Withdrawals			Consumptive use
	By source		Total		By source		Total		By source		Total	
	Ground-water	Surface water			Ground-water	Surface water			Ground-water	Surface water		
New England	130.0	1.1	130.0	63.0	4.5	4.7	9.2	9.2	140.0	5.8	140.0	73.0
Mid-Atlantic	430.0	2.4	430.0	110.0	79.0	32.0	110.0	86.0	510.0	35.0	550.0	190.0
South Atlantic–Gulf	720.0	0.4	720.0	440.0	130.0	110.0	240.0	240.0	850.0	110.0	960.0	670.0
Great Lakes	270.0	2.9	270.0	74.0	64.0	20.0	84.0	77.0	330.0	23.0	350.0	150.0
Ohio	290.0	21.0	310.0	200.0	63.0	90.0	150.0	140.0	360.0	110.0	470.0	350.0
Arkansas-White-Red	130.0	25.0	160.0	120.0	85.0	150.0	240.0	230.0	210.0	180.0	390.0	350.0
Texas–Gulf	120.0	0	120.0	120.0	78.0	120.0	190.0	190.0	200.0	120.0	310.0	310.0
Rio Grande	33.0	0.7	33.0	18.0	26.0	6.0	32.0	26.0	58.0	6.7	65.0	44.0
Upper Colorado	15.0	43.0	58.0	17.0	2.4	91.0	94.0	22.0	18.0	130.0	150.0	39.0
Lower Colorado	37.0	0.1	37.0	27.0	12.0	5.2	17.0	11.0	48.0	5.4	54.0	38.0
Tennessee	61.0	0	61.0	39.0	12.0	29.0	41.0	40.0	73.0	29.0	100.0	79.0
Upper Mississippi	290.0	10.0	300.0	190.0	220.0	51.0	270.0	270.0	510.0	61.0	570.0	460.0
Lower Mississippi	94.0	0.5	94.0	67.0	17.0	25.0	42.0	41.0	110.0	25.0	140.0	110.0
Souris-Red-Rainy	23.0	0	23.0	23.0	9.8	3.8	14.0	14.0	33.0	3.8	37.0	37.0
Missouri Basin	210.0	22.0	230.0	170.0	270.0	120.0	390.0	380.0	480.0	150.0	630.0	550.0
Great Basin	32.0	3.8	36.0	14.0	34.0	12.0	46.0	17.0	66.0	16.0	82.0	30.0
Pacific Northwest	230.0	32.0	270.0	200.0	21.0	34.0	55.0	49.0	250.0	66.0	320.0	250.0
California	130.0	9.4	140.0	84.0	36.0	50.0	86.0	47.0	170.0	60.0	220.0	130.0
Alaska	11.0	0.1	11.0	0.1	0.0	0.1	0.2	0.2	11.0	0.3	11.0	0.3
Hawaii	3.5	0.4	3.9	3.4	5.3	0.2	5.5	4.8	8.8	0.6	9.4	8.2
Caribbean	5.0	3.1	8.1	2.0	15.0	15.0	30.0	7.1	20.0	18.0	38.0	9.1
Total	3,300.0	180.0	3,400.0	2,000.0	1,200.0	980.0	2,200.0	1,900.0	4,400.0	1,200.0	5,600.0	3,900.0

large quantities of water are pumped, a *cone of depression* forms that lowers the water table underlying the land (see illustration 18). Sometimes too much water is pumped out to allow an adequate rate of water replenishment, and the shallower wells in an area may dry up as the water table gets lower. Once the water table is lowered it might take several years for it to be replenished, and all the wells in the area will have to be dug deeper, at great expense to the landowners. Surprisingly, this has been more of a problem in the eastern half of the United States, although it has occurred in some areas of the West. Often farming areas will experience a very bad underground water exhaustion problem for several years until a flood year replenishes the underground water basin.

A common problem in areas near salt water, especially on the East Coast, is saltwater seepage into wells, often caused by too many wells or faulty wells. Be very careful of this when looking at land near a body of salt water.

Wells Already on the Land

If you look at land that has a well on it, you should ask the seller to show you any records he has indicating the amount of water pumped at various times of the year. Examine his pumping setup to see if it is in good condition. Does it need a new pump or motor? Ask him to start up his pump and watch it operate for a few hours. Does the well need to be dug deeper to get a larger flow to meet your intended needs? Remember that the depth and size of a well do not necessarily coincide with its capacity to yield water. A well must have a watertight pump-mounting surface seal around the top

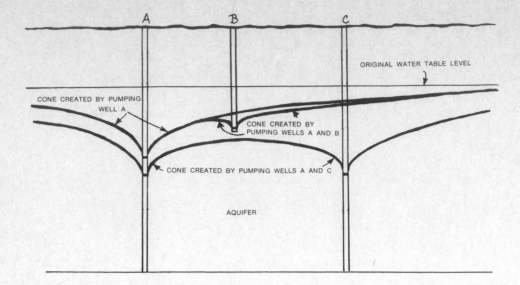

of it to prevent contamination from the entry of foreign matter into the well casing. This sanitary seal consists of a 12-inch concrete base above the surface of the ground and a 30-inch concrete casing that goes at least 30 inches below the ground level. Is the casing cracked or leaking?

A well must be located a safe minimum distance from any sewage disposal system before it will be approved by the county health department. If the well does not meet these requirements you may be prohibited from using it after you buy the land. Has the seller had his well approved and does he have the certificate of approval? (See chapter 13, "Building and Health Codes.")

The well *casing* is a metal or plastic pipe inserted into the well hole to prevent the sides from collapsing. It is perforated with holes or slits to allow water to seep in and be stored during the recharge period. Can you tell what condition it is in? Ask the seller what brand of pump he is using and what its capacity is. How old is the equipment, and when was it installed? Who drilled the well? Go to the well-driller and ask to see the drilling log or driller's report to read what information he has regarding the quality of the well and its capacity. Sometimes a driller will not show you this document without the owner's permission. If the seller will not grant you permission to inspect the report, you should be suspicious of the quality of the well. Illustration 19 is an example of such a report.

ANALYZING LAND WITH NO VISIBLE WATER

If there is no surface water on the land before you buy it, you must know whether you will hit a decent supply if you dig a well. Ninety percent of all water beneath the surface of the ground occurs in the top 200 feet, and the average depth of all domestic water wells in the United States is slightly less than 50 feet.

Groundwater exists only in the area called the *zone of saturation*. This is the area beneath the ground in which all the openings and pores in the soil, sand, gravel, or rock are filled with water. Developing a well involves drilling a hole into the zone of saturation, which allows water to drain by gravity from the saturated earth into the well, where it is pumped up to the surface, only to be replaced by other water flowing toward the well. (See illustration 20, page 38.) The rate at which this new water moves into the well, its *recharge rate,* determines the amount that can be withdrawn at any one time. Thus you will want to know not only if there is underground water present, but also its quantity and rate of flow. The total groundwater in an area is replenished every year by new precipitation, which controls the amount of water present in the zone of saturation. It is estimated that 95 percent of the total fresh water available is groundwater.

WATER WELL DRILLER'S REPORT
(Sections 7076, 7077, 7078, Water Code)

THE RESOURCES AGENCY OF

ORIGINAL
File Original, Duplicate and Triplicate with the
REGIONAL WATER POLLUTION

CONTROL BOARD No._____
(Insert appropriate number)

Do Not Fill In
Nº 117312

State Well No._____
Other Well No._____

(1) OWNER:
Name **Gabriel Stern**

Address **Anywhere**

U.S.A.

(2) LOCATION OF WELL:
County **Somewhere**   Owner's number, if any—

R.F.D. or Street No. **Section 21, Township 4 South, Range 2, East**

10 miles west of Eugene on south side of Hwy. 135

Riverside Ranch

(3) TYPE OF WORK (check):
New well ☒   Deepening ☐   Reconditioning ☐   Abandon ☐

If abandonment, describe material and procedure in Item 11.

(4) PROPOSED USE (check):
Domestic ☒ Industrial ☐ Municipal ☐

Irrigation ☐ Test Well ☐ Other ☐

(5) EQUIPMENT:
Rotary ☒

Cable ☐

Dug Well ☐

(6) CASING INSTALLED:
SINGLE ☒ DOUBLE ☐

From	ft. to	ft.	Diam.	Gage or Wall	If gravel packed Diameter of Bore	from ft.	to ft.
" 0	" 184		6 5/8	10	9	0	184
"	"	"		"	"	"	"
"	"	"		"	"	"	"
"	"	"		"	"	"	"
"	"	"		"	"	"	"

Type and size of shoe or well ring _____

Size of gravel: **1/2"**

Describe joint **Welded**

(7) PERFORATIONS:
Type of perforator used **Torch**

Size of perforations **6** in., length, by **3/16** in.

From	ft. to	ft.	Perf. per row	Rows per ft.
" 164	" 184	"	2	1
" 124	" 164	"	4	1
"	"	"		
"	"	"		
"	"	"		
"	"	"		

(8) CONSTRUCTION:
Was a surface sanitary seal provided? ☒ Yes ☐ No   To what depth **20** ft.

Were any strata sealed against pollution? ☐ Yes ☒ No   If yes, note depth of strata

From	ft. to	ft.
"	"	

Method of Sealing **Cement on pack**

(9) WATER LEVELS:
Depth at which water was first found _____ ft.

Standing level before perforating _____ ft.

Standing level after perforating **114** ft.

(10) WELL TESTS:
Was a pump test made? ☐ Yes ☒ No   If yes, by whom? **Bail**

Yield: **25** gal./min. with **30** ft. draw down after **1** hrs.

Temperature of water **Cool**   Was a chemical analysis made? ☐ Yes ☒ No

Was electric log made of well? ☐ Yes ☒ No

(11) WELL LOG:
Total depth **184** ft.   Depth of completed well **184** ft.

Formation: *Describe by color, character, size of material, and structure.*

0 ft. to	13 ft.	Brown clays
13 "	34 "	Clayee brn. & yellow sand (very soft)
34 "	44 "	Brown clays
44 "	45 "	Brown sandstone
45 "	49 "	Sandy grey clay
49 "	65 "	Fractured blue rock
65 "	67 "	Hard blue rock
67 "	69 "	Grey clay
69 "	90 "	Blue fractured rock w/streaks of clay
90 "	103 "	Brown rock w/streaks of brown clay
103 "	107 "	Brown clay w/rock
107 "	109 "	Fract. brn. rock w/stks. of clay
109 "	129 "	Fract. hard rusty grey rock
129 "	138 "	Very hard fractured greywackie
138 "	145 "	Blue and grey rock
145 "	151 "	Hard grey clay with rock streaks
151 "	157 "	Grey rock (rough)
157 "	162 "	Hard grey clay with rock streaks
162 "	167 "	Hard black and grey rock with fractures
167 "	174 "	Hard grey clay with rock streaks
174 "	176 "	Hard black rock
176 "	181 "	Hard grey clay with rock streaks
181 "	183 "	Hard black rock
183 "	184 "	Hard grey clay with rock streaks

Work started **9/20** 19 **73**   Completed **9/28** 19 **73**

WELL DRILLER'S STATEMENT:
This well was drilled under my jurisdiction and this report is true to the best of my knowledge and belief.

NAME **Wilcox Drilling & Pump Company**
(Person, firm, or corporation)   *(Typed or printed)*

Address **Anywhere**

U.S.A.

[SIGNED]_____

Well Driller

License No. **32890**   Dated **October 2**, 19 **73**

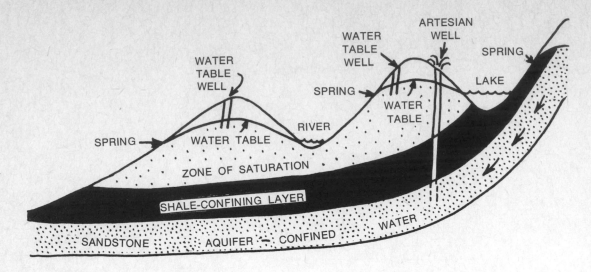

20. Sources of Groundwater

LOCATING UNDERGROUND WATER

Plants as Indicators of Groundwater (Phreatophytes)

One method used to locate underground water is to find those plants, called phreatophytes, that exist only when their root systems can reach the water table. (The name phreatophyte is derived from two Greek words meaning well plant.) Some phreatophytes indicate not only the presence of groundwater but also the quality and approximate depth of the water below the surface. For instance, in arid regions willows or cottonwood trees usually mean that good-quality water is available within 20 feet of the surface. Some species of birch, maple, sycamore, alder, bay, and live oak also indicate groundwater at shallow depths. Unfortunately, the value of these plants as indicators is reduced in humid regions where there is an abundance of water in the soil. Some of the principal plants that indicate groundwater in arid regions are shown and briefly described in illustration 21 (pages 39–41). Each area of the country has its own phreatophytes. Your local well-driller, farm advisor, agriculture experiment station, or other advisory agency (see Useful Resources) will know the ones to look for in your area.

Witching, Dowsing, and Divining to Find Groundwater

An ancient method used to find water that is still used today is witching or dowsing for water with a divining stick or rod. As far back as the sixteenth century, farmers walked across their land carrying a forked branch in front of them waiting for it to point down to the ground over a water source. A forked or straight twig from a peach, willow, hickory, dogwood, or cherry tree is the most common tool used by diviners. The twig is held between both hands facing out and up and is supposed to roll down or spin around when held over water. Almost every rural area has its well-known diviners. Some work for free and others charge a fee for their divining services. Some claim to be able to tell which way the water flows and how deep it is by the movement of the divining rod. However, the U.S. Geological Survey has concluded that not one scientifically conducted experiment using water witches to locate optimal sites for water-well location has ever yielded conclusive, reproducible support for water witches' claims. I would not buy land solely on the basis of their findings, but they might confirm some other appraisals made by a well digger or farm advisor. The National Water Well Association puts out a very informative pamphlet called "Before You Hire a 'Water Witch.'" (See Useful Resources, page 52.)

38

Rushes, sedges, and cattails indicate good-quality water at or just below the surface.

Reeds and cane indicate good-quality water within 10 feet of the surface.

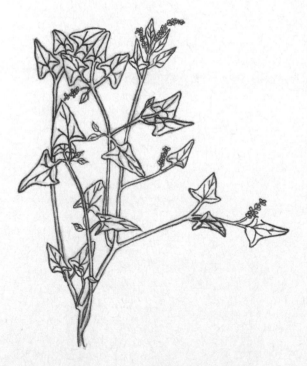

Saltbush is a reliable indicator of variable-quality water near the surface. It usually grows along the margins of salt flats.

Pickleweed indicates mineralized water near the surface. It usually grows on salt flats in soil that has between 1 and 2 percent salt content.

21. Phreatophyte Examples

Arrowweed indicates good-quality water 10 to 20 feet below the surface.

Elderberry shrubs and small trees indicate water within 10 feet of the surface.

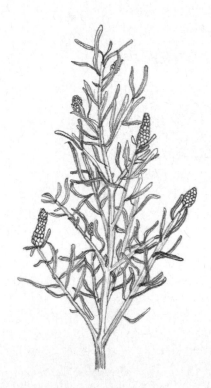

Rabbit brush indicates water within 15 feet of the surface.

Black greasewood indicates mineralized water 10 to 40 feet below the surface.

Mesquite indicates good quality water 10 to 50 feet below the surface.

Well-Driller's Appraisal of Groundwater

The local well-driller will probably give you the most complete and accurate appraisal of the availability of water on your land and the cost of pumping it. Get the appraisal from the driller you intend to hire to drill the well because all or part of his appraisal fee will be refunded when you finally hire the company to do the drilling. In our area, the appraisal fee is twenty dollars an hour, and there is a 50 percent refund if the well is put in within a year. The appraiser will compare your land to other property in the area where his company has drilled wells. Each company keeps accurate logs of drilling depths and of the quantity and quality of water that is finally pumped. They also examine the soil, vegetation, and geography to estimate the location of water.

Unfortunately, a company generally won't guarantee its appraisal but a test drilling can be done for a smaller charge than a complete well. If your decision to buy land is contingent solely on whether water is found, should a test drilling produce water, you can go ahead and drill the final well. When selecting the company to do the drilling, compare appraisal fees, refund provisions, costs for drilling methods, and the grade of casing to be used. Ask for recommendations from the local health department and people living in the area. A good well-drilling contractor will sign a written contract with you, operates well-maintained equipment, and provides insurance protection for the property owner. He estimates the cost of the job step by step, including a breakdown of unit prices, and gives the customer a specific drilling price in advance. When the job is completed, he provides a record of the strata penetrated by the well and a statement of work performed and materials used. Check to see if he is a member of the state and national associations of well-drilling contractors, evidence that he keeps abreast of the new developments in his field. Hire the driller with the best reputation, regardless of price. When it comes to well construction, like anything else, it's worth paying more for good quality.

TYPES OF WELLS

The following basic introduction to the types of

wells should help you estimate the costs of putting in a well on land that you intend to buy and evaluate wells already on the land.

Dug Well

The oldest type of well is the dug well. Usually 3 to 4 feet in diameter, it is dug with a pick and shovel to a maximum depth of 50 feet. These wells are dangerous and painstaking to dig, and they often go dry because they are so shallow. Their main advantage is the large storage area, but this permits contamination more easily than other wells because of seepage through the well walls and from the large opening on top. Dug wells are probably more common in Canada these days than in the United States. (See illustration 22.)

Bored Well

Bored wells are similar to dug wells except that they are often deeper and smaller in diameter. An auger bucket, either power or hand operated, is used to dig these wells, which often run to 100 feet and are cased all along the inside wall. The bored well is practically obsolete today because of the more efficient driven and drilled wells.

Jetted or Hydraulic Well

This type of drilling can be done only in soft, sandy soils as are found in some coastal areas. The well is drilled by applying a high-pressure stream of water that cuts through the earth and washes it out of the hole. As this is done, a 1½-inch pointed jetting tool is shoved down into the loose sand as far as it will go, and when it stops the well is complete. If you take a garden hose and jet the water into the ground, you do the same thing. This method is useless if rock or clay is reached.

Churn, Spud, or Percussion-Tool Drilled Well

To drill this type of well a large chisel-shaped bit is pounded into the ground over and over again by lifting it high into the air and dropping it. With each fall, the bit digs deeper into the ground. During this process, water is poured into the developing hole to transform the loosened dirt into mud, which is then drawn out of the hole. It takes a long time to drill a well in this manner, but it is still effectively done by commercial drillers.

Drilled Well

Drilled wells are the most common type of wells being used today. The method was first used when oil drillers built special power equipment to drill oil wells. The type of drill used is the rotary tool, which rotates like a drill into the earth rather than

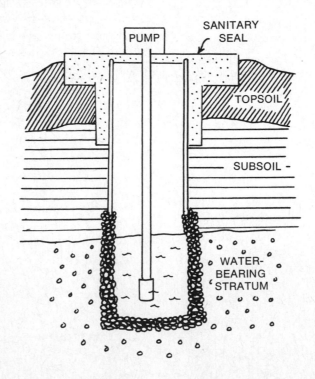

22. Dug Well

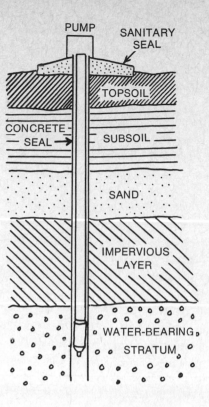

23. Drilled Well

pounding the surface as the percussion tool does. The drill has a sharp cutting bit on the end, and the shaft is hollow. As the drill turns into the earth, water is forced down into the drill stem, and the pressure of the water sends the cut dirt and rock to the top of the hole. As the drill goes deeper into the ground, additional sections of stem are screwed on to increase the length of the drill. (See illustration 23.)

Driven Well

A driven well is usually cheaper to construct than a drilled well. Pipe sections several feet long are screwed together with a sharp well-point and screen on one end. The pointed end is pounded into the ground until it reaches below the water-table level and a sufficient amount of water can enter the well through the screen. The ground must be soft enough to take a driven well, since hard rock and clay cannot be penetrated. The depth is limited to a maximum of 50 feet, and only a small flow of water will be attained. Occasionally several driven wells are joined together with a single pump to get a greatly increased flow. As with all wells, a driven well may be cut into the earth horizontally or vertically. (See illustration 24.)

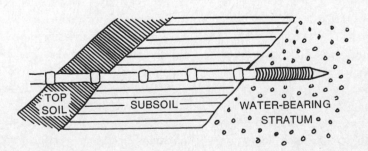

24. Driven Well (Horizontal)

THE COST OF WELL DRILLING

The cost of well drilling is based on the depth of the well in feet, the toughness of the earth, and the accessibility to the area. The usual cost for drilling into hard rock under normal conditions is $10 to $20 a foot, although this figure could vary greatly depending on the area and the competition among drillers. If you reach water before hitting rock, the price is usually cut in half. A drilled well can go to a depth of 1,000 feet. You can find out the normal well depth in your area from the local well-driller and thus estimate the approximate cost to you. In our area, wells are between 150 and 300 feet deep. At $15 per foot, a well can cost from $2,250 to $4,500. Drilled well construction includes lining the inside of the well with a steel or plastic casing to protect it from contamination and collapse, and pouring a concrete or grout seal around the top.

There is always a chance you will not hit water. No driller is going to guarantee water when he starts drilling. He just tells you his price per foot and then drills until he hits water or you can't afford to pay for another foot. You can pay several thousand dollars for a dry hole, and that is one of the biggest risks of buying country land. Even in areas where water is plentiful, drilling is successful only about 85 percent of the time. The people representing the other 15 percent are simply out of luck and money. You must be certain there is water before you buy.

IS THE WATER DRINKABLE?

If water is declared *potable* by the county health department, it is safe to drink. The safety is determined by examining the water at your source and the conditions around it. You will probably not be surprised to know that animal manure and soil bacteria are usually harmful to a water supply. Human sewage and poisonous sprays are the primary causes of contaminated water.

Drinking, tasting, or smelling water will tell you nothing about its potability since even clear, good-tasting water may be contaminated. However, your local county health or sanitation department will gladly conduct a free or inexpensive water analysis for you. A health inspector will come out to collect the sample and to examine the source and surrounding area. He will determine if an existing or intended septic tank, outhouse, or cesspool is too close to the water source. If the water flows through farmland or irrigated land, it can be tested for the presence of insecticides. Hazardous-waste disposal sites are an increasing source of groundwater contamination. If your land is very isolated, the health inspector will give you a sanitized bottle and tell you how to properly collect a water sample for testing. The basic water test includes a coliform bacterial count, which reflects the amount of human and other warm-blooded-animal excreta in it. If you want a more complete mineral and bacterial analysis, which is not usually necessary, you will have to pay to have it done by a commercial laboratory.

Underground well or spring water is usually safer than surface water. Underground water has been sifted through the porous earth, which purifies it, whereas contaminated surface water must travel a long distance to get the cleansing effect of underground sifting.

I recommend that you always get the basic water test done, no matter what the history of the drinking water on the land. The family living there may have been drinking the water for fifty years, but pollution can occur virtually overnight. Polluted water can cause cholera, typhoid fever, amoebic dysentery, infectious hepatitis, and possibly polio. Don't take any chances.

Groundwater Pollution

If you are relying on groundwater from a spring or well, you might also want to check the surrounding area for groundwater pollution, especially if there are any industries located in your area. More and more we are finding that toxic substances have been improperly stored and are leaking into the groundwater. For instance, about thirty square miles of a shallow acquifer were contaminated by aldrin and dieldrin, both toxic substances, at the Rocky Mountain arsenal and in the surrounding area. The wastes, by-products from the manufacture of pesticides and chemical warfare agents, had been stored in unlined holding ponds, and huge quantities of the waste had for years seeped from the ponds. Sixty-four domestic, stock, and irrigation wells had to be abandoned.

In heavily fertilized areas, such as farming communities, nitrates from decomposed ammonia fertilizer infiltrate the groundwater and pollute it. Nitrate-rich water leads to a serious disease in infants known as blue babies (methemoglobinemia).

Animal feedlots provide a huge volume of waste compared to their size. For example, a 10-acre feedlot with 1,000 head of cattle produces wastes equivalent to that of a town of 6,000 people. One public waste-supply well in northwestern North Dakota continued to be contaminated by livestock wastes more than 40 years after a nearby livery stable was abandoned. If you are buying in a farming or livestock area, always have the available drinking water tested before you purchase property there.

If you are looking at land that is in a floodplain, and if there are several other homes in that floodplain that use septic tanks and wells, it is very possible that the effluent from the septic tanks will pollute the groundwater. Check with the local health officials to see if there are periodic outbreaks of hepatitis due to an increase in coliform bacteria during times of high water.

If you suspect some kind of pollution of the groundwater in an area you are looking at, check with the local health department to see if it can give you any information.

Watch Out If the Land Is Too Cheap

A recent news article told of how a city in Florida sold seven acres that it knew to be saturated with toxic wastes to a virtually penniless veteran. He received a verbal warning that the land was contaminated. From 1958 to 1967 it had been the hazardous waste site for Allied Petroleum Products, Inc., to dump toxic sludge containing PBCs, heavy metals, and organic compounds. At one time a dike had broken and 200,000 gallons of poisonous sludge had oozed into a nearby creek, threatening the community's drinking water as PBCs leached into the groundwater. The city finally graded the site and covered it with sod in 1980. Then they offered it for sale for $992.74 in back taxes, and the veteran bought it.

When environmental officials arrived to study the site for a superfund cleanup, the owner first threw them off his land. The state then went to court to order him to clean up his land to the tune of $225 million. Now he is fighting back with a lawsuit, but meanwhile he has suffered a great deal and still has to cope with it.

Minerals in the Water

The quality of water is also affected by an excessive amount of calcium and magnesium, which cause it to become hard. Try to work up a lather with a bar of soap and a dish of water. The harder the water, the less suds you'll get. Hard water is less desirable for washing, cooking, and heating, but is generally not a serious detriment. Water-softening equipment can be purchased and installed at any time.

Other minerals may affect the quality and taste of the water. Iron in water affects the flavor of cooked vegetables, coffee, and tea. It stains clothes and water pipes and causes a reddish-brown sediment or oily scum to appear on the surface. Hydrogen sulfide gas and sulfate give water a rotten-egg odor and taste, which you will find highly objectionable. The water may also have silt suspended in it, which gives it a muddy or cloudy effect. These and other mineral problems can be corrected through the use of chlorination and filtration equipment, which will be an added expense to you and good cause for demanding a reduction in the purchase price.

HOW MUCH WATER WILL YOU NEED?

Without water you cannot cook, grow vegetables, flowers, and orchards, raise animals, bathe, wash, swim, fight fires, or quench your thirst. Although water needs differ depending on various factors, the U.S. Department of Agriculture lists the following daily water requirements:

Needed by:	Gallons Per Day
Each person (includes such activities as drinking, cooking, bathing, washing clothes and dishes,	20–80

Needed by:	Gallons Per Day
flushing toilets)	20–80
Each milk cow	35
Each horse	6–12
25 chickens	1–3
Each hog	2–4
Each sheep	2
Garden (1,000 sq. ft., say 50 × 20 ft.)	70 (or 700 every 10 days minimum)

The following are estimates of how much water is used for various domestic purposes:

Item:	Gallons
Taking a bath	30–40
Taking a shower	20–30
Running a washing machine (1 load)	20–30
Washing dishes	8–10
Flushing a toilet	4–6

If you intend to have a large garden or plant an orchard, berries, and flowers, you will need a much greater supply of water than you need for animals alone. If you must pump your water, you will not want to run your pump twenty-four hours a day, even if it is electric. Be sure that both the well and the pump have the capacity to deliver the amount of water you will need as quickly as you want it.

Always overestimate your water needs because after buying your land, your ability to develop it will be limited by the amount of water available.

THE WATER SUPPLY SYSTEM

If you are looking at undeveloped land, you must determine its suitability for a water supply system. The water supply system is the means by which you get the water from its source to your house, garden, trees, fields, and animals. The standard equipment includes pipe or hose, one or more holding tanks, a pump house, and various pieces of hardware such as valves and faucets. If you are looking at land that already has a developed water system, you will want to know if it was well designed and built and if it is still working properly.

The purpose of the following sections is not to tell you how to develop a water system, but to give you an idea of what to look for and think about in terms of developing or repairing a water system on land you might buy. Each type of water system has its own maintenance problems. Setting up an adequate water system can cost thousands of dollars. Before you buy a piece of land, estimate the costs required to develop a new water system or repair an existing one. If the expense is beyond your means, do not purchase that land.

Gravity-Flow System

The cheapest and easiest way to bring water where you need it is by using the force of gravity. To do this the water source must be higher in elevation than the place to which you want to bring the water, so that when you lay your hose or pipe the water will flow freely of its own accord to the lower point. However, because air is lighter than water, the hose between the two points must drop steadily downhill, or air bubbles will collect in the high spots of the hose and slow down or stop the flow of water. If you cannot avoid laying the hose over a high spot, you can prevent air from entering it by putting in the proper valves for bleeding the lines or by keeping both ends of the hose constantly submerged in water.

If a hill is situated above a building site but you cannot find a spring or other water source in it, you might consider drilling a horizontal well into the side of the hill to get water to flow out without using a pump. Ask a well-driller to appraise the possibility of finding water this way on land you might buy. It is difficult to determine different elevations over a long distance on a piece of land with the naked eye, and special meters are needed. The well-driller has this equipment, or you can rent it from a local surveying rental service and run your own test.

The only materials needed to set up a gravity-flow water system are a holding tank, which might be a springbox, lake, pond, or dammed up portion of a creek; the necessary pipe or hose; storage tanks; and various valves, faucets, and other hardware. This system is the cheapest and easiest to maintain because no pump is necessary.

Siphon System

The siphon system is similar to the gravity-flow system in that the source must be higher in elevation than the point to which you eventually want to bring the water. However, any rise in the ground that is higher than the source requires siphoning to get the water to flow over it. This is done by sucking the water up over the rise and far enough down the other side so that it begins to flow of its own accord. As long as you don't lose the siphon, the water will continue to flow. Every time the siphon is broken by air getting into the hose, you must suck the water to get it going again. You can use the same methods to prevent air from entering the hose as you would use in the gravity-flow system. The difference between these two systems is that in a pure gravity-flow system, none of the high spots in the hose are higher than the source, so no sucking is required to start the system.

If the rise is too high or the distance too great to begin the siphon by sucking with your mouth, you will need a pump to get it going. Otherwise, the siphon water system requires the same equipment as a gravity-flow system and costs the same to install and maintain.

Pumping Your Water Using Gas, Electricity, or the Wind

Unless you are fortunate enough to have a source positioned so that the water will flow by a gravity or siphon system, you will need a pump. The most common pump used for shallow wells and surface-water sources is the gasoline-powered centrifugal pump which sucks water up and pushes it out with great force. A two-horsepower pump of this type can suck the water to a height of only about 20 feet. However, if you can place the pump at the source, say along a stream or pond, it can push the water several hundred feet up a bank or hill.

If your source of water is a deep well, you will need an electric pump. The one-horsepower electric jet-pump can suck up water from a maximum depth of 110 feet. However, the electric submersible well-pump is more commonly used today. It is a long cylindrical pump that is placed at the bottom of the well, and it can push water up 450 feet. A one-horsepower submersible pump can push 10.2 gallons of water per minute up from 220 feet down.

Since these pumps require electricity, you will have to either bring it in or supply it by means of a generator. The most common generators are powered by gasoline or diesel fuel. There are also wind generators that look like windmills, and they produce electricity that recharges a set of storage batteries. If wind conditions are suitable, you can run an electric pump using this system without the noise and pollution of a gas or diesel generator. (See appendix J, "Alternative Energy Resources.")

You can also use a windmill to pump water directly from a source straight down, like a well. It is cheap, nonpolluting, and quiet compared to a gasoline-powered pump or generator. Today windmills are still widely used in place of the combustion engine or electric pumps in the southernmost parts of the country, notably Texas, and in parts of Pennsylvania. If one already exists on the land, find out if it still functions and what its capacity is. You will be fortunate if there is one on your land, but don't let its quaint but magnificent beauty persuade you to purchase land that is otherwise not what you want or pay a higher price for the land than it is really worth.

If you will need a pump and possibly a generator, find out the cost of buying and installing equipment sufficient to meet your needs before you buy the land. Since you can't do anything on the land until you have water, you should figure the cost of a motor and pump into the purchase price as part of your initial investment.

If a pump is set up on the land, ask the owner or real estate agent to start it up so you can see how well it works and how much water is pumped. Watch it pump for at least a half hour to be sure it operates well. Get the brand names and numbers of the motor or generator and pump so you can check with the local dealer to see how much they are worth and what their specifications are. Find out how long the owner has used the equipment and if he has had any problems with it. Does he have any repair bills, and does he still have a valid warranty for the equipment? (See Useful Resources at the end of this chapter for available pump information.)

Holding Tanks

Unless you have a lake, pond, or other large natural body of water situated higher than your homestead area, you will need at least one holding tank in your water system to keep a large quantity of water available. The greater your water needs, the larger the tank will have to be. If you want to irrigate an orchard and garden or grazing fields for your animals, you will need a large tank. For instance, if you plan to have a half-acre garden, it will require the equivalent of one inch of rain, or about 11,350 gallons, every ten days. If you want to water once every five days, you will need a tank that holds at least 5,675 gallons just to water your garden once. Fruit trees need to be watered less frequently than smaller plants, but they need a large amount of water when irrigated because their roots go extremely deep.

If there is a holding tank on the land, determine its capacity to be sure it is large enough for your intended needs. To figure out the volume in cubic feet of a cylindrical tank, multiply the area of the base in feet by its height in feet. (To refresh your memory, the formula is $3.1416 \times r^2 \times h$, where r is the radius of the base and h is the height of the tank.) The volume in cubic feet of a square or rectangular tank is figured by multiplying the length times the width times the height in feet. Once you get the volume in cubic feet, you have to transform the result into gallons. To do this, multiply the number of cubic feet by 7.4805, which is the number of gallons in 1 cubic foot. For example, assume you have a cylindrical tank with the following dimensions: the height is 10 feet, and the diameter of the base is 12 feet. Thus the radius is 6 feet. Plugging these numbers into the formula, we get $3.1416 \times 6^2 \times 10 = 3.1416 \times 36 \times 10 = 3.1416 \times 360 = 1,130.98$ cubic feet. To translate this figure into gallons of water, multiply $1,130.98 \times 7.4805 = 8,460.30$ gallons.

Check the tank to be sure it doesn't leak. Examine the structure that supports it to see if it is sturdy. The tank might be inside of a well-house. If so, is that in good shape? Holding tanks are expensive, and repairing or replacing a damaged one could be costly. Mention any necessary repair work to the owner, and either have him fix it before you buy the land or use this as another reason why he should lower his asking price. Price the tank on the land at the local supply house. Wooden tanks are always more expensive than metal ones. Ferrocement tanks are being used more frequently these days, and are usually very suitable for most places. If you have to develop your own water system,

figure in the cost of purchasing and installing a holding tank and its supporting structure.

Pipes and Fixtures

Check the pipeworks on the land to see if there are sufficient domestic and irrigation works to suit your needs. Look for leaks or evidence of recent repair. Has steel, concrete, or plastic pipe been used? Is it constructed so that water does not freeze in the winter? Each type of pipe has its own value.

The water system, if one exists, will be included in the selling price of the land, so you should evaluate its quality and value before buying. Often the system has been used for many years and the owner underestimates the depreciation in its value. Look for things that need improvement or parts that need replacement, and point out these things when bargaining to get the price down.

An Example to Help You Visualize Your Water System

Illustration 25 shows an example of possible ways to develop a water system. It is included to help you visualize how to look at a piece of land and consider its possibilities for water development. The three systems shown all use a large holding tank (5,000 gallons) situated on a high point of land above the house, garden, orchard, and animals, so that gravity flow can be used.

System 1 carries water from a holding box built around a spring that was exposed when a road was cut into the side of the hill. Since the spring is higher in elevation than the holding tank, a gravity flow brings a continuous flow to the tank. The spring produces only about 700 gallons a day in the driest part of the summer, which is not enough to support the needs of a family with a garden, orchard, and animals. The garden alone requires about 600 gallons a day. Since the young fruit trees, berries, flowers, animals, and people also need water, another method of getting more water must be developed.

System 2 illustrates the most inexpensive and logical next choice, which is to pump water from the nearest creek up to the holding tank.

System 3, which might be cheaper in the long run, requires drilling a well above the holding tank. A row of bay trees is growing up the side of the hill behind the holding tank, which indicates un-

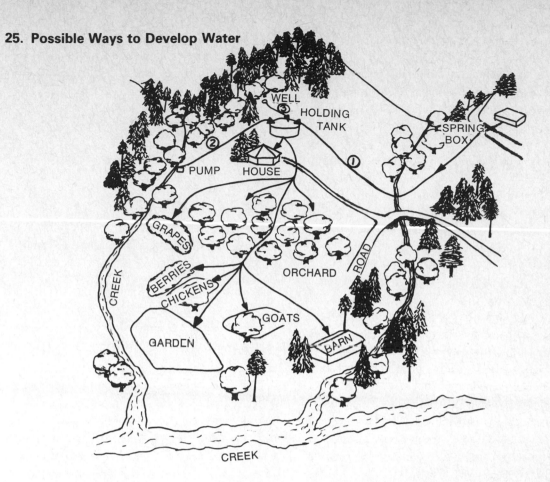

derground water. Since this is on the side of a hill, a horizontal well could be drilled, which would allow a gravity flow of water into the holding tank. Although this system would not require a pump, the amount of water this source would produce is unknown. After spending the money to drill a well, the rate of flow might not be sufficient to meet the needs of the family.

The three year-round creeks alone assure the family that they have a more than adequate water supply. If you plan your purchase carefully, you should always have enough water for your needs.

OUTSIDE WATER SUPPLY—PUBLIC UTILITY COMPANIES, PRIVATE WATER COMPANIES, AND PUBLIC WATER DISTRICTS

Some rural areas, especially those containing large farms in arid regions, have established irrigation companies, mutual water companies, and public or private utility companies that handle the task of supplying water within their service districts. The legal and operational setup is different for different agencies. If you have to purchase water from a private profit-oriented water company or a public utility company, you will pay rates regulated by the Public Utilities Commission. If you are supplied by a mutual water or irrigation company, you will have to join a private, nonprofit association of landowners who have organized to supply water to themselves.

Real estate ads will usually indicate if water is supplied by a private water company. The following are statements made in recent ads for land in Colorado: "good water shares available," "water line goes by property, irrigation dependent on classification by water users," "ditch irrigation, 500 water shares," and "35 tillable acres now ditch irrigated, 35 water shares with land."

The right to receive water is often based on ownership of shares of stock in the company. Instead of receiving monetary dividends, the shareholder receives water according to the amount of stock he owns. The price of stock can be quite high in areas where water is scarce. For instance, if you are buying land on which you intend to irrigate one acre and five shares of stock are needed to get enough water to irrigate that acre, you will have to buy those shares, either from the seller at the time of purchase or from the company after you own the land. If each share is worth $100 on the current market, it's going to cost you an extra $500 to get water to your land. If the owner includes shares of stock with the land, make sure you are not being overcharged for the water, since he will undoubtedly add the cost of the shares onto his asking price.

You should check with the company to find out how dependable it is, how many of your neighbors belong to it, and what the value of the shares is.

It is always better to buy the owner's water shares with the land, because sometimes shares are not easy to obtain. There may not be any surplus water available to a new farmer or, since these companies are private, the members may not like your life-style, and may refuse to sell shares to you under some pretext. The ad that says "irrigation dependent on classification by water users" means that the members of the water company have control over how much water, if any, will be sold to the landowner. Also, an ad that says "water shares available" doesn't mean that you will be able to get them. If shares do not come with the land, you had better be sure that you can purchase some or lease some before you buy, or have the seller buy what you need and then add the cost onto the price of the land. Don't buy on an assurance that you can get shares after the deal is closed. You might be left high and dry.

Public water or irrigation ditches are formed by state and local legislatures to provide water to their inhabitants. Each district has definite boundaries, local control, and, most importantly, the power to tax and assess property within the district. You are familiar with the idea of paying property taxes for school districts. Water districts operate the same way.

If your land is within the boundaries of a water district, you will want to know how you can get water and what the present and future tax assessment will be. Generally the value of land within such a district increases even if the land has its own independent source of water. Whether or not you use district water, you will have to pay assessments, just as you pay school taxes even if you don't have children. If you want to buy land but need to obtain your water from a district, you should be sure the land is within the district. Many districts will extend their services to land not previously within their boundaries if circumstances warrant. To obtain this service you will have to go before the county planning commission, board of supervisors, or water district board and petition them to allow your land into the service area. It will be easier to have the seller of the land do this before you buy. Accompany the seller to the hearings. If you cannot be serviced from the district and water is unavailable from any other source, the land is worthless, and you had better start looking somewhere else.

SHARING WATER WITH OTHERS

You will frequently encounter a situation where several parcels will be sharing one or more water sources. For example, the piece you are buying might have deeded water rights to take a percentage of water produced by a spring or creek on a neighbor's property, or the water right might be limited to taking a maximum number of gallons per day. This is a very tricky situation. You must go to the water source on the neighbor's land and determine the output. Often a land developer subdivides a single parcel into several smaller parcels and allots more water than is actually available. The fact that the county or local governing agency approves the subdivision does not mean there is an adequate water supply. Often the first people to develop their land have enough water, but as more development takes place, the water supply becomes inadequate. If your water source is being shared, talk to the persons you will be sharing the water with and determine what the history of usage is. It is a fact of life that people don't like to share water where water is scarce. You should find out before you buy what the situation is. If you are to share water, you will need deeded rights to install and maintain your water system on the neighbor's property, and you will need deeded rights to lay and maintain a pipeline to your property and possibly deeded access to drive to the water source to construct a tank and maintain a pump.

On the other hand, surrounding landowners might have the right to come onto your property and take water. Do you want land that one or more persons have the right to enter for purposes of constructing and maintaining pumping facilities?

I recommend that you never buy land in an area of scarce water unless you have your own water source on your own property free from interference by others. People are now moving into rural areas where homesteads may never have been developed, and as development starts, water starts to become a precious commodity. The legal battles in the future will be over water. Think about the future of your water before you buy.

THE WATER PROTECTION CLAUSE IN THE CONTRACT OF SALE

Never buy land without a written guarantee that a year-round source of water exists that is sufficient to meet your needs. Two guarantees are provided in the Model Contract of Sale in chapter 28. Clause 16(c) is a warranty by the seller that a visible water source delivers a specified minimum amount of water throughout the year. If the water dries up after you buy the property, the seller will be liable for a breach of this warranty. The fact that he makes this warranty, however, does not relieve you of the responsibility of examining the water situation during the critical dry months before you buy the land.

Clause 17(f) is a condition to the sale that should be used if no water source presently exists on the land. You want to have at least a test drilling and preferably a completed, productive well drilled before, not after, you finalize your purchase. The ideal situation is to have the seller pay to drill the well. If he locates a good water supply, he can add the price of the well to the purchase price. If he cannot locate water, you will not have to proceed with the purchase, the contract will be rescinded, and your money will be returned to you. If the seller resists such a condition, you can offer a compromise by agreeing to pay for half the drilling costs even if no water is found on the land. You should not agree to pay the entire costs if no water is found, since, if you do, you could spend a few thousand dollars drilling a dry well on land you do not own.

You do not want to make your land purchase on promises alone. If the seller is not willing to guarantee that there is water on the land, he does not care if he cheats you. You should never buy land without such a condition in the contract, unless you like gambling with high stakes.

Always read the documents that pertain to your water rights, or others' rights to take water from your land. If you have any questions about these documents or don't understand any portions of them, contact an attorney who is experienced in real estate matters so that he or she can explain them to you.

USEFUL RESOURCES

Publications on Water, Wells, Pumps, and Ponds

The following are available for the specified cost from:

ANR Publications
Division of Agriculture and Natural
    Resources
University of California
6701 San Pablo Ave.
Oakland, CA 94608-1239

California's Groundwater Resources	#21393	$ 1.00
California Water Resources	#21379	$ 1.00
Efficiency and Equity in Management of Agriculture Water Supplies	#1892	$ 1.00
Water Conservation: The Potential	#21382	$ 1.00
Water Wells and Pumps: Their Design, Construction, Operation & Maintenance	#1889	$ 4.50
Does Drip (and Other Low-Flow) Irrigation Save Water?	#21380	$ 1.00
Drip Irrigation	#2740	$ 1.00
Grading Land for Surface Irrigation	#2692	$ 2.00
Pumping Energy Requirements in California	#3125	$ 1.00
Irrigation Costs	#2875	$ 1.00
Irrigation on Steep Land	#2825	$ 1.00
Measuring Irrigation Water	#2956	$ 1.00
Saving Water in Landscape Irrigation	#2976	$ 1.00

Using Reclaimed Water on
   Farmland   #2931 $ 1.20

The following are available for the specified cost from:

    American Association for Vocational
       Instructional Materials
    120 Driftmier Engineering Center
    Athens, GA 30602

Planning for an Irrigation System $12.00
Planning for an Individual Water System $14.00

    Water Systems Council
    600 S. Federal St., Ste. 400
    Chicago, IL 60605

Order Your Water Well Done $ 2.00
Understanding Underground Water $ 2.00
Ground Water Heat Pump Brochure $ 2.00

    County of Mendocino
    Division of Environmental Health
    890 N. Bush St.
    Ukiah, CA 95482

Individual Water Supply Systems   free
Information About Contaminated Wells   free

Some excellent pamphlets are available for the specified price from:
    National Water Well Association
    500 W. Wilson Bridge Rd.
    Worthington, OH 43085

Ground Water Heat Pumps $ .50
Domestic Water Treatment for
   Homeowners $ .50
Before You Hire a "Water Witch" $ .50
Ground Water Pollution Control $ .50
Water Conservation in Your Home $ .50
America's Priceless Ground Water
   Resource $ .50
When You Need a Water Well $ .50
Catalogue of Available Publications   free

The following are available for the specified price from:
    Land Improvement Contractors of America
       Library (LICA)
    P.O. Box 9
    Maywood, IL 60053

Ponds $ .50
Level Basis Irrigation $ .50
Constructing Simple Measuring Flumes $ .50

The following is free from:
    State Water Resources Control Board
    Division of Water Rights
    P.O. Box 2000
    Sacramento, CA 95810

Water Well Standards: State of California

The following are free from:
    Soil Conservation Service
    U.S. Department of Agriculture
    Washington, DC 20250

Conservation and the Water Cycle
Ponds—Planning, Design, Construction
How to Control a Gully
What Is a Watershed?
Water Supply Sources for the Farmstead and Rural
   Home
Trout Ponds for Recreation
Catfish Farming
Trout Farming
Maintaining Subsurface Drains
Maintaining Watercourses
Small Watershed Projects
Trout in Farm and Ranch Ponds

Many pamphlets are available from the Superintendent of Documents. You can order a bibliography and price list of available materials. The following are some of those available on water and irrigation for the specified cost from:
    Superintendent of Documents
    Government Printing Office
    Washington, DC 20402

Treating Farmstead and Rural Home
   Water Systems
   S/N 0100-01421-0 $ 1.00
Ponds—Planning, Design and
   Construction
   S/N 001-000-04282-3 $ 5.00
Ground Water Regions of the United
   States
   S/N 024-001-03516-2 $ 4.95
Manual of Individual Water Supply
   Systems
   S/N 055-000-00229-1 $ 6.00
Warm-Water Fishponds
   S/N 0100-1455 $ .15
Design of Small-Diameter Variable-Grade
   Gravity Sewers
   S/N 001-000-04412-5 $ 1.25
Ground Water Manual
   S/N 024-003-00146-5 $14.00

The following is free from:
Deep Rock Manufacturing Company
5192 Anderson Rd.
Opelika, AL 38601

How to Drill Your Own Water Well

Regenerative Agriculture Society
222 Main St.
Emmaus, PA 18049

Water Safety Action Kit. This book will
help you find out if your water is unsafe
and explains what to do if it is. $ 2.95

Bulletins on water conditions in California from
1977 until now may be obtained by writing to:
State of California–Resource Agency
Department of Water Resources
P.O. Box 942836
Sacramento, CA 94236-0001

Ask for the publications list, and then select the
years you want. All of these bulletins are free. One
excellent bulletin is:

Water Wells and What You Should Know About Them

The following are available free from:
California Agricultural Extension Service
90 University Hall
University of California
Berkeley, CA 94720

Small Earth Dams—Circular 467
Soil and Water Management for Home Gardens—
AXT-111
What Does Water Analysis Tell You?—ATX-118

For a complete list of publications send for the
Agricultural Publications Catalogue from the above
address. You should also write for the publications
catalogue from your own state Agricultural Experiment Office. (See addresses in Useful Resources at the end of chapter 5.)

The following are free from any U.S. Geological
Survey Public Inquiries Office. See Useful Resources at the end of chapter 5 for addresses, or
mail to:
Public Inquiries Office
U.S. Geological Survey
503 National Center, Rm. 1-C-402
12201 Sunrise Valley Dr.
Reston, VA 22092

Ground Water
The Hydrologic Cycle
NASQAN: Measuring the Quality of America's
Streams
The National Stream Quality Accounting Network
(NASQAN): Some Questions and Answers
Rain: A Water Resource
Save Water . . . Save Money
State Hydrologic Unit Maps
Water Dowsing
Water in the Urban Environment: Erosion and
Sediment
What Is Water?
Water Use in the U.S., 1980
Ground Water: An Undervalued Resource
Ground-Water Contamination—No "Quick Fix" in
Sight
How Much Water in a 12-Ounce Can? A Perspective
on Water-Use Information
Toxic Waste—Ground-Water Contamination
What About Ground Water in Western North
Carolina: Are Large Supplies Feasible?
Map, Line & Sinker
A Primer on Water
A Primer on Ground Water
Estimated Use of Water in the United States in 1980

U.S. Geological Survey Water Resources Division

U.S. Geological Survey, under the U.S. Department of the Interior Water Resources Division, includes within it the following agencies:

HYDROLOGIC INFORMATION UNIT (HIU)

The Hydrologic Information Unit answers general
questions on hydrology, water as a resource, and
hydrologic mapping, as well as on the products,
projects, and services of the Water Resources Division. HIU offers free subscriptions to "National
Water Conditions," a monthly summary of water
resource conditions in the U.S. and Southern Canada.

Hydrologic Information Unit
U.S. Geological Survey
419 National Center
Reston, VA 22092

Questions related to water resources in a particular
area should be directed to the appropriate Water
Resources Division district office of the USGS.
(See pages 54–57 for addresses of all local offices.)

OFFICE OF WATER DATA COORDINATION (OWDC)

The Office of Water Data Coordination distributes a variety of free publications including:

> National Handbook of Recommended
> Methods for Water Data Acquisition
> Notes on Sedimentation Activities (yearly)
> Plans for Water Data Acquisition by Federal
> Agencies
> Guidelines for Determining Flood Flow
> Frequency

Additional publications on water data are available from OWDC at:

> Office of Water Data Coordination (OWDC)
> U.S. Geological Survey
> 417 National Center
> Reston, VA 22092

NATIONAL WATER DATA EXCHANGE (NAWDEX)

NAWDEX is a confederation of organizations working to improve access to water data. Its primary objective is to assist in the identification, location, and acquisition of water data. Toward this goal, the NAWDEX program office and its seventy-five assistance centers, which include the Water Resources Division district offices, provide a variety of services:

1. Identification of water-data collection sites. The NAWDEX Master Water Data Index identifies 460,000 water-data sites (collection of organizations, site locations, data types, measurement frequencies, and storage media).
2. Identification of water-data sources. The NAWDEX Water Data Source Directory identifies the more than 800 organizations that collect water data, the specific locations within the organizations that provide data, the organizations' geographic coverage and data types, and alternate sources of data.
3. Water-data search assistance. The NAWDEX program office and its seventy-five assistance centers help water-data users locate and obtain data. For instance, they will make bibliographic searches in the Water Resources Scientific Information Center's selected water resources abstracts for information on your specific water situation. Charges for services depend on the type of service requested and the organization fulfilling the request. Write to:

> National Water Data Exchange
> U.S. Geological Survey
> 421 National Center
> Reston, VA 22092

A publication entitled *NAWDEX: A Key to Finding Water Data* is available for free from the U.S. Geological Survey public inquiry offices listed above.

NATIONAL WATER DATA STORAGE AND RETRIEVAL SYSTEM (WATSTORE)

All types of water data are accessed through WATSTORE. The data in WATSTORE are grouped and stored in five files, depending on common characteristics and data collection frequencies: (1) Station Header File—an index for the 320,000 water-data storage sites; (2) Daily Values File—more than 240 million daily parameters such as streamflow, groundwater levels, specific conductance, and water temperatures; (3) Peak Flow File—460,000 records on annual maximum streamflow and gauge height valves; (4) Water Quality File—230,000 analytical results that describe biological, chemical, and physical water characteristics; and (5) Ground-Water Site-Inventory File—data on 850,000 sites.

Information on availability of specific types of data, on acquisition of data or products, and on user charges can be obtained from the Water Resources Division district offices listed below.

WATER RESOURCES DIVISION DISTRICT OFFICES

Specific information for each state is available from the local Water Resources Division district office. The address of each state office is located below. When writing to a state office, the first three lines of the address should read:

> Water Resources Division
> District Office
> U.S. Geological Survey
> (followed by the specific address for the
> state listed)

Alabama
520 19th Ave.
Tuscaloosa, AL 35401

Alaska
1515 E. 13th Ave.
Anchorage, AK 99501

Arizona
Federal Bldg., FB 44
301 W. Congress St.
Tucson, AZ 85701-1393

Arkansas
2301 Federal Office Bldg.
700 W. Capitol Ave.
Little Rock, AR 72201

California
Federal Bldg., Rm. W-2235
2800 Cottage Wy.
Sacramento, CA 95825

Colorado
Federal Center, Box 25046
Mail Stop 415
Denver, CO 80225

Connecticut
525 Ribicoff Federal Bldg.
450 Main St.
Hartford, CT 06103

Delaware
See listing for Maryland.

District of Columbia
See listing for Maryland.

Florida
Hobbs Federal Bldg., Ste. 3015
Tallahassee, FL 32301

Georgia
6481 Peachtree Industrial Blvd.
Doraville, GA 30360

Hawaii
300 Ala Moana Blvd., Rm. 6110
P.O. Box 50166
Honolulu, HI 96850

Idaho
230 Collins Rd.
Boise, ID 83702

Illinois
Champaign County Bank Plaza
102 E. Main, 4th Fl.
Urbana, IL 61801

Indiana
6023 Guion Rd., Ste. 201
Indianapolis, IN 46254

Iowa
264 Federal Bldg.
400 S. Clinton St.
P.O. Box 1230
Iowa City, IA 52244-1230

Kansas
1950 Constant Ave.–Campus West
University of Kansas
Lawrence, KS 66044

Kentucky
572 Federal Bldg.
600 Federal Pl.
Louisville, KY 40202

Louisiana
6554 Florida Blvd.
P.O. Box 66492
Baton Rouge, LA 70896

Maine
See listing for Massachusetts.

Maryland
208 Carroll Bldg.
8600 LaSalle Rd.
Towson, MD 21204

Massachusetts
150 Causeway St., Ste. 1309
Boston, MA 02114

Michigan
6520 Mercantile Wy., Ste. 5
Lansing, MI 48910

Minnesota
702 Post Office Bldg.
St. Paul, MN 55010

Mississippi
Federal Bldg., Ste. 710
100 W. Capitol St.
Jackson, MS 39269

Missouri
Mail Stop 200
1400 Independence Rd.
Rolla, MO 65401

Montana
301 S. Park Ave.
428 Federal Bldg.
Drawer 10076
Helena, MT 59626

Nebraska
406 Federal Bldg. and U.S. Courthouse
100 Centennial Mall, N.
Lincoln, NE 68508

Nevada
229 Federal Bldg.
705 N. Plaza St.
Carson City, NV 89701

New Hampshire
See listing for Massachusetts.

New Jersey
430 Federal Bldg.
402 E. State St.
Trenton, NJ 08608

New Mexico
720 Western Bank Bldg.
505 Marquette, N.W.
Albuquerque, NM 87102

New York
P.O. Box 1669
343 U.S. Post Office and Courthouse Bldg.
Albany, NY 12201

North Carolina
300 Fayetteville St. Mall
436 Century Station
P.O. Box 2857
Raleigh, NC 27602

North Dakota
821 E. Interstate Ave.
Bismarck, ND 58501

Ohio
975 W. Third Ave.
Columbus, OH 43212

Oklahoma
215 Dean A. McGee Ave., Rm. 621
Oklahoma City, OK 73102

Oregon
847 N.E. 19th Ave., Ste. 300
Portland, OR 97232

Pennsylvania
Federal Bldg., 4th Fl.
228 Walnut St.
P.O. Box 1107
Harrisburg, PA 17108

Rhode Island
See listing for Massachusetts.

South Carolina
1835 Assembly St., Ste. 658
Columbia, SC 29201

South Dakota
317 Federal Bldg.
200 Fourth St., S.W.
Huron, SD 57350

Tennessee
A-413 Federal Bldg and
U.S. Courthouse
Nashville, TN 37203

Texas
649 Federal Bldg.
300 E. Eighth St.
Austin, TX 78701

Utah
Administration Bldg., Rm. 1016
1745 W. 1700, S.
Salt Lake City, UT 84104

Vermont
See listing for Massachusetts.

Virginia
200 W. Grace St., Rm. 304
Richmond, VA 23220

Washington
1201 Pacific Ave., Ste. 600
Tacoma, WA 98402

West Virginia
3416 Federal Bldg. and
U.S. Courthouse
500 Quarrier St., E.
Charleston, WV 25301

Wisconsin
1815 University Ave.
Madison, WI 53705

Wyoming
4007 J. C. O'Mahoney Federal Center
2120 Capitol Ave.
P.O. Box 1125
Cheyenne, WY 82003

In addition to the above offices, you might be able to find the information you desire at any of the U.S. Geological Survey offices listed under Useful Resources at the end of chapter 5, "The Earth—Soil, Vegetation, Topography."

U.S. Topographic Maps

The U.S. Geographical Survey Topographic Maps indicate the following water features: perennial and intermittent seasonal streams, wells, and springs; intermittent lakes; marshes; inundated areas; dry lake beds; water tanks; dams; bridges; rivers; and perennial lakes.

Most real estate brokers keep such maps in their office. Local sporting-goods stores and bookstores usually sell them. You can also purchase the map for your area by following the instructions given in chapter 5.

The Local Well-Drilling Companies

If you look in the yellow pages in the area of the land and its surrounding communities, you will find one or more well-drilling companies. They are extremely helpful in determining the availability of water on your land. For a fee they will do a test drilling or surface appraisal. They can show you any available drilling logs and reports for wells already on the land or on neighboring land. The log indicates the depth of the well, the type of water-bearing material that has been drilled through, and the capacity and output of the well. Get the opinion of more than one company as to the possibility of water on your land. Ask them a lot of questions. Sometimes they may not release the information without the seller's consent. If the seller refuses to consent, he is hiding something.

Local Board of Health

You can locate the nearest health department through the telephone directory. They will have brochures on water testing and potability. You can arrange to have them test your water for you and give you a chemical analysis as well as a bacterial and coliform count. They have minimum standards for contamination of water and will tell you if your water is safe to drink. They do all of this as a public service, or, in some cases, for a slight fee.

Local Water, Irrigation, or Reclamation Districts, and Water Agencies

It is possible that your land will be within an area that is provided with water by a public or private water company, agency, or district. You should be able to find out if this is the case by asking the real estate broker or seller. Then go to the offices of the water facility and find out what their services are, how much water you can receive, and how much it will cost you. Even if your land is not covered by their operation, they might be able to give you information regarding the availability of water on your land.

WATER QUALITY

The following agencies are responsible for water quality protection programs.

Alabama
Water Quality
Environmental Management Department
1751 Federal Dr.
Montgomery, AL 36109

Alaska
Water Quality Section
Division of Environmental Quality
Environmental Conservation Department
Pouch O
Juneau, AK 99811

Arizona
Environmental Health Services Division
Department of Health Services
2005 N. Central, Rm. 202
Phoenix, AZ 85007

Arkansas
Department of Pollution Control and
Ecology
8001 National Dr.
Little Rock, AR 72209

California
Division of Water Quality
Water Resources Control Board
901 P St.
Sacramento, CA 95814

Colorado
Water Quality Control Commission
Department of Health
4210 E. 11th Ave.
Denver, CO 80220

Connecticut
Water Compliance Unit
Environmental Protection Department
165 Capitol Ave.
Hartford, CT 06106

Delaware
Division of Environmental Control
Natural Resources and Environmental
    Control Department
89 Kings Hwy., Box 1401
Dover, DE 19903

District of Columbia
Housing and Environmental Regulation
    Administration
Department of Consumer and Regulatory
    Affairs
614 H St., N.W.
Washington, DC 20001

Florida
Bureau of Water Quality Management
Environmental Regulation Department
2600 Blairstone Rd.
Tallahassee, FL 32301

Georgia
Water Protection Branch
Department of Natural Resources
270 Washington St., S.W.
Atlanta, GA 30334

Hawaii
Environmental Protection and Health
    Services Division
Department of Health
1250 Punchbowl St.
Honolulu, HI 96813

Idaho
Bureau of Water Quality
Department of Health and Welfare
450 W. State St.
Boise, ID 83720

Illinois
Environmental Protection Agency
2200 Churchill Rd.
Springfield, IL 62706

Indiana
Water Quality Branch
State Board of Health
1330 W. Michigan St., Rm. 388
Indianapolis, IN 46206

Iowa
Water, Air and Waste Management
    Commission
Wallace State Office Bldg.
Des Moines, IA 50319

Kansas
Division of Environment
Department of Health and Environment
Forbes Field
Topeka, KS 66620

Kentucky
Division of Water
Natural Resources and Environmental
    Protection Cabinet
18 Reilly Rd.
Frankfort, KY 40601

Louisiana
Office of Water Resources
Department of Environmental Quality
P.O. Box 44066
Baton Rouge, LA 70804-4066

Maine
partment of Environmental Protection
State House Station, #17
Augusta, ME 04333

Maryland
Water Management Administration
Health and Mental Hygiene Department
201 W. Preston St., 5th Fl.
Baltimore, MD 21201

Massachusetts
Water Pollution
Department of Environmental Quality
  Engineering
1 Winter St.
Boston, MA 02108

Michigan
Water Quality Division
Department of Natural Resources
P.O. Box 30028
Lansing, MI 48909

Minnesota
Division of Water Quality
Pollution Control Agency
1935 W. County Rd., #B-2
Roseville, MN 55113

Mississippi
Pollution Control Bureau
Department of Natural Resources
Southport Mall
Jackson, MS 39209

Missouri
Water Pollution Control Program
Division of Environmental Quality
Department of Natural Resources
P.O. Box 1368
Jefferson City, MO 65102

Montana
Water Quality Bureau
Health and Environmental Sciences
  Department
Capitol Station
Helena, MT 59620

Nebraska
Department of Environmental Control
301 Centennial Mall, S.
P.O. Box 94877
Lincoln, NE 68509-4877
  or
Environmental Engineering Division
Department of Health
P.O. Box 95007
Lincoln, NE 68509-5007

Nevada
Environmental Protection Division
Conservation and Natural Resources
  Department
201 S. Fall St.
Carson City, NV 89710

New Hampshire
Water Supply and Pollution Control
  Commission
Hazen Dr.
Concord, NH 03301

New Jersey
Division of Water Resources
Environmental Protection Department
1474 Prospect St., CN-029
Trenton, NJ 08625

New Mexico
Surface Water Quality Bureau
Department of Health and Environment
P.O. Box 968
Santa Fe, NM 87504-0968

New York
Department of Environmental Conservation
50 Wolf Rd.
Albany, NY 12233

North Carolina
Environmental Management
Natural Resources and Community
  Development Department
512 N. Salisbury St.
Raleigh, NC 27611

North Dakota
Water Supply and Pollution Control
  Division
Department of Health
1200 Missouri Ave.
Bismarck, ND 58501

Ohio
Wastewater Pollution Control
Environmental Protection Agency
361 E. Broad St.
Columbus, OH 43215

Oklahoma
    Water Quality Division
    Water Resources Board
    1000 N.E. 10th St.
    Box 53585
    Oklahoma City, OK 73152

Oregon
    Water Quality Division
    Department of Environmental Quality
    522 S.W. Fifth Ave.
    P.O. Box 1760
    Portland, OR 97207

Pennsylvania
    Bureau of Water Quality Management
    Environmental Resources Department
    Fulton Bldg., 11th Fl.
    Harrisburg, PA 17120

Rhode Island
    Division of Water Resources
    Department of Environmental Management
    83 Park St.
    Providence, RI 02903

South Carolina
    Environmental Quality Control
    Health and Environmental Control
    2600 Bull St.
    Columbia, SC 29201

South Dakota
    Division of Environmental Health
    Water and Natural Resources Department
    Foss Bldg.
    Pierre, SD 57501

Tennessee
    Office of Water
    Department of Health and Environment
    TERRA Bldg., 2nd Fl.
    Nashville, TN 37219

Texas
    Department of Water Resources
    Capitol Station, Box 13087
    Austin, TX 78711

Utah
    Bureau of Public Water Supplies
    Department of Health
    150 W.N. Temple, Rm. 435
    Salt Lake City, UT 84103

        or
    Water Pollution Control
    Department of Health
    150 W.N. Temple, Rm. 410
    Salt Lake City, UT 84103

Vermont
    Water Quality Division
    Department of Water Resources and
        Environmental Engineering
    Heritage II, 79 River St.
    Montpelier, VT 05602

Virginia
    State Water Control Board
    2111 N. Hamilton St.
    Richmond, VA 23230

Washington
    Office of Water Programs
    Department of Ecology
    Mail Stop PV-11
    Olympia, WA 98504

West Virginia
    Drinking Water Division
    Department of Health, Bldg. 3
    1800 Washington St., E.
    Charleston, WV 25305

Wisconsin
    Bureau of Water Resources Management
    Department of Natural Resources
    P.O. Box 7921
    Madison, WI 53707

Wyoming
    Water Quality Division
    Department of Environmental Quality
    Herschler Bldg.
    Cheyenne, WY 82002

WATER RESOURCES

The following agencies are responsible for water conservation, development, use, and planning in the state.

Alabama
    Soil and Water Conservation Committee
    1445 Federal Dr.
    P.O. Box 3336
    Montgomery, AL 36193

Alaska
  Division of Land and Water Management
  Department of Natural Resources
  Pouch 7005
  Anchorage, AK 99510

Arizona
  Department of Water Resources
  99 E. Virginia
  Phoenix, AZ 85004

Arkansas
  Soil and Water Conservation Commission
  1 Capitol Mall, Ste. 2-D
  Little Rock, AR 72201

California
  Department of Water Resources
  1416 Ninth St.
  Sacramento, CA 95814

Colorado
  Water Conservation Board
  Department of Natural Resources
  1313 Sherman St., Rm. 615
  Denver, CO 80203

Connecticut
  Water Resources Unit
  Environmental Protection Department
  165 Capitol Ave.
  Hartford, CT 06106

Delaware
  Soil and Water Conservation Division
  Natural Resources and Environmental
    Control Department
  89 Kings Hwy., Box 1401
  Dover, DE 19903

District of Columbia
  Housing and Environmental Regulation
    Administration
  Department of Consumer and Regulatory
    Affairs
  614 H St., N.W.
  Washington, DC 20001

Florida
  Water Management District
  Environmental Regulation Department
  2600 Blairstone Rd.
  Tallahassee, FL 32301

Georgia
  Water Resources Management Branch
  Department of Natural Resources
  270 Washington St., S.W.
  Atlanta, GA 30334

Hawaii
  Water and Land Development Division
  Land and Natural Resources Department
  1151 Punchbowl St.
  Honolulu, HI 96813

Idaho
  Department of Water Resources
  450 W. State St.
  Boise, ID 83720

Illinois
  Division of Water Resources
  Department of Transportation
  300 DOT Administration Bldg.
  Springfield, IL 62764

Indiana
  Water Division
  Department of Water Resources
  605 State Office Bldg.
  Indianapolis, IN 46204

Iowa
  Water, Air and Waste Management
    Commission
  Wallace State Office Bldg.
  Des Moines, IA 50319

Kansas
  Kansas Water Office
  503 Kansas Ave., #303
  Topeka, KS 66603

Kentucky
  Division of Water
  Natural Resources and Environmental
    Protection Cabinet
  18 Reilly Rd.
  Frankfort, KY 40601

Louisiana
  Office of Water Resources
  Department of Environmental Quality
  P.O. Box 44066
  Baton Rouge, LA 70804-4066

Maine
   Soil and Water Conservation Commission
   Agriculture, Food and Rural Resources
     Department
   State House Station, #28
   Augusta, ME 04333

Maryland
   Water Resources Administration
   Department of Natural Resources
   Tawes State Office Bldg.
   Annapolis, MD 21401

Massachusetts
   Division of Water Resources
   Department of Environmental Management
   100 Cambridge St., 13th Fl.
   Boston, MA 02202

Michigan
   Water Quality Division
   Department of Natural Resources
   P.O. Box 30028
   Lansing, MI 48909

Minnesota
   Water Resources Board
   55 Wabash St., Rm. 206
   St. Paul, MN 55102

Mississippi
   Soil and Water Conservation Commission
   410 Robert E. Lee Bldg.
   Jackson, MS 39201

Missouri
   Water Resources Planning Program
   Division of Geology and Land Survey
   Department of Natural Resources
   P.O. Box 250
   Rollo, MO 65401

Montana
   Water Resources Division
   Natural Resources and Conservation
     Department
   32 S. Ewing
   Helena, MT 59601

Nebraska
   Department of Water Resources
   301 Centennial Mall, S.
   P.O. Box 94676
   Lincoln, NE 68509-4676

   or
   Natural Resources Commission
   301 Centennial Mall, S.
   P.O. Box 94876
   Lincoln, NE 68509-4876

Nevada
   Water Resources Division
   Conservation and Natural Resources
     Department
   201 S. Fall St.
   Carson City, NV 89710

New Hampshire
   Water Resources Board
   37 Pleasant St.
   Concord, NH 03301

New Jersey
   Division of Water Resources
   Environmental Protection Department
   1474 Prospect St.
   Trenton, NJ 08625

New Mexico
   Water Rights Bureau
   Office of State Engineer
   Bataan Memorial Bldg.
   Santa Fe, NM 87503

New York
   Department of Environmental Conservation
   50 Wolf Rd.
   Albany, NY 12233

North Carolina
   Office of Water Resources
   Natural Resources and Community
     Development Department
   512 N. Salisbury St.
   Raleigh, NC 27611

North Dakota
   Water Commission
   State Office Bldg.
   900 East Blvd.
   Bismarck, ND 58505

Ohio
   Division of Water
   Department of Natural Resources
   Fountain Square, Bldg. E.
   Columbus, OH 43224

Oklahoma
Water Resources Board
1000 N.E. 10th St.
P.O. Box 53585
Oklahoma City, OK 73152

Oregon
Water Resources Department
555 13th St., N.E.
Salem, OR 97310

Pennsylvania
Bureau of Water Resources Management
Environmental Resources Department
P.O. Box 1467
Harrisburg, PA 17120

Rhode Island
Division of Water Resources
Department of Environmental Management
83 Park St.
Providence, RI 02903

South Carolina
Water Resources Commission
1001 Harden St., #250
Columbia, SC 29205

South Dakota
Department of Water and Natural Resources
Foss Bldg., 2nd Fl.
Pierre, SD 57501

Texas
Department of Water Resources
P.O. Box 13087
Capitol Station
Austin, TX 78711

Utah
Division of Water Resources
Department of Natural Resources and
   Energy
1636 W.N. Temple, Rm. 310
Salt Lake City, UT 84116

Vermont
Department of Water Resources and
   Environmental Engineering
Agency of Environmental Conservation
Heritage II, 79 River St.
Montpelier, VT 05602

Virginia
State Water Control Board
2111 N. Hamilton St.
Richmond, VA 23230

Washington
Office of Water Programs
Department of Ecology
Mail Stop PV-11
Olympia, WA 98504

West Virginia
Water Resources Division
Department of Natural Resources
1201 Greenbrier St.
Charleston, WV 25311

Wisconsin
Bureau of Water Resources Management
Department of Natural Resources
P.O. Box 7921
Madison, WI 53707

Wyoming
Water Development Commission
Herschler Bldg.
Cheyenne, WY 82002

Other Sources of Water Information

COUNTY AGRICULTURE AGENT OR FARM ADVISOR

LOCAL AGRICULTURAL EXPERIMENT STATION
   (See Useful Resources at the end of chapter 5.)

FOREST AND RANGE EXPERIMENT STATIONS
   (See Useful Resources at the end of chapter 5.)

SOIL CONSERVATION SERVICE
   (See Useful Resources at the end of chapter 5.)

ARMY CORPS OF ENGINEERS

THE STATE DEPARTMENT OF WATER RESOURCES
OR STATE ENGINEER

Address requests for information and inquiries, using this title, to your state capital, or get the address from the farm advisor or local health department. Every state has its own department or agency in charge of water resources, and you can get much useful information from the state office, usually located in the capital city of each state. (See addresses given above.)

LOCAL UNIVERSITIES AND COLLEGES

Various departments, such as the Department of Geology, conduct water surveys and investigations, and they might have some useful information.

THE COUNTY ENGINEER

Most counties have a civil engineer who is responsible for investigating and documenting water and flood conditions, drainage, and other geological problems. He might have some data you can use.

RESEARCH CENTERS DIRECTORY

Lists all agencies in each state involved in water research. (See Useful Resources at the end of chapter 5.)

For more information regarding using solar, wind, or water energy for pumping or any other application, see appendix J, "Alternative Energy Resources."

CHAPTER 5

The Earth—Soil, Vegetation, Topography

What then of the man who hears these words of mine and acts upon them? He is like a man who had the sense to build his house upon rock. The rain came down, the floods rose, the wind blew, and beat upon that house; but it did not fall, because its foundations were on rock.
—The Gospel of Saint Matthew 7:24–26

When a real estate agent shows you property, he emphasizes its best features. He is not going to walk you across the acre-long gully or tell you how the land turns into a giant undrained mud puddle for six months during the rainy season. He won't explain to you that the property is on a north slope and gets no sun all winter. He will show you some beautiful "home sites," but it will be up to you to determine if they can actually support buildings and gardens. Finding answers to questions about the condition of the soil, its drainage patterns, and its ability to grow things is essential in analyzing the land you intend to buy. If the soil is good, you will have abundant vegetation and few problems with erosion, drainage, slipping foundations, and flooding. You should inspect the geography, seek advice from experts, and study maps and photographs.

TOPSOIL

Topsoil is the loose upper layer of the soil. It is usually richer and darker than the subsoil because it contains humus, or decayed vegetable matter, which is almost black in color and rich in plant nutrients. A dark, thick topsoil rich in humus indicates high fertility. (See illustration 26.)

Almost 60 percent of the topsoil in the United States has been lost or destroyed by poor management. Heavy farming has depleted nutrients from the soil, and heavy grazing, logging, and fires have destroyed much of the cover vegetation that held the topsoil together. With the vegetation gone, erosion began. The action of water and winds removed the surface soil, washing it into the rivers and oceans. To get an idea of how much earth is carried off in a storm, fill a jar with water from the nearest creek the next time it rains and let the dirt settle to the bottom.

Good land should have at least 10 to 14 inches of loose topsoil. Ground that is rocky and hard lacks topsoil. If the earth is soft enough to poke a stick into easily, it has some topsoil. Generally, land near the ocean tends to be rocky and barren. The health and abundance of either natural or planted vegetation gives a good and simple indication of the soil quality. Land with too much vegetation on it is often better than land with not enough. Un-

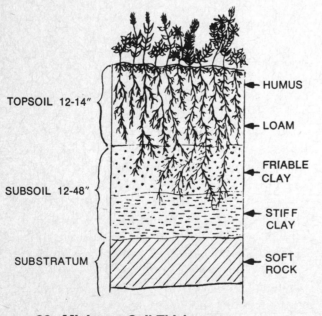

TOPSOIL 12-14"

SUBSOIL 12-48"

SUBSTRATUM

HUMUS

LOAM

FRIABLE CLAY

STIFF CLAY

SOFT ROCK

26. Minimum Soil Thicknesses for Good Land

desirable brush and weeds can be cleared quite easily with the right equipment, but bringing in lost topsoil that has been washed away because of poor ground cover is an enormous task. Uncleared brushy land will probably be cheaper to buy than land that has been cleared and is ready to build on. Ten of our eighty acres are flat land that is completely overgrown with thorny brush which could be cleared to make another home-site area. However, because this area can't be used as it is, instead of increasing the value of the land as flat land usually does, it did not affect the purchase price.

Although erosion is one of the easiest problems to spot, it is difficult to repair. In an eroded gully that has lost topsoil, plant roots will have a difficult time getting started in the hard subsoil. The gully makes a natural channel for excess rainwater to run off the land so that baby plants that do get a foothold quickly drown or are swept away by the force of the water.

Sandy soils, steep slopes with little vegetation, and land that has been logged by the clear-cut method are particularly susceptible to erosion. Not all land that has been logged is bad, however. If enough trees were left to hold most of the soil in place, it may be beautiful land that can be purchased at a much lower price than virgin timber land. You must carefully inspect the land for signs of erosion, though, and be wary if the land has been stripped of its trees.

If you are planning to farm for a living, you should carefully choose land with highly fertile soil. However, if you plan to have a family vegetable and flower garden and perhaps a small orchard, you might consider buying less fertile land with the idea of building up a rich topsoil. The process is a slow one and requires that you cart in loads of organic matter, such as spoiled hay, grass clippings, leaves, wet garbage, and dirt, but it is a rewarding process.

SOIL TEXTURE

The texture of the soil is important for healthy plants, good drainage, and building construction. There are four basic soil textures: gravel, sand, loam, and clay. Gravel and sand are made up of large particles, whereas clay consists of very tiny particles. Loam, the most common soil in the United States, consists of about equal parts of clay and sand. Because gravel and sandy soils are very loose, they quickly lose valuable nutrients, which are leached out in the water, and gain and lose heat rapidly, causing quick thawing and freezing. On the other hand, compact clay soil becomes mushy and sticky when wet, cutting off oxygen to the plant roots and making cultivation difficult. A loamy soil is preferred by most plants since it contains the best aspects of both sand and clay. To correct either a highly sandy soil or a heavy clay soil, you will have to build up the amount of humus in the soil.

The best way to determine the texture of the soil is to rub some in your hand and between your fingers. How does it feel? Sand is loose and gritty; clay is heavy and compact when dry and sticky and doughy when wet. It is usually gray or yellow. Loam will crumble in your hand and is black.

Dig some holes at different points of the land. Is it hard to dig? How soon do you hit rock? If you dig for several feet and still find a good loam and loose earth that is not too sandy, you have fine soil. If the whole area is rocky and hard, you will have problems. If a road has been put in, look at and feel the various layers of soil exposed where the road cuts into the earth.

DRAINAGE

Drainage refers to the amount of water that can be absorbed by the soil before it becomes saturated. At the saturation point, the water collects on the surface or runs off into the nearest creek or drainage ditch. Most plants will not grow where drainage is poor because their roots cannot tolerate being in more water than they can absorb. These plants actually "drown."

A layer of rock or other impervious material, such as hardpan or claypan, near the surface or a high water table can make drainage poor. A few types of soil, like adobe, have very poor drainage. When adobe gets wet, it swells up and prevents water from draining through it to deeper ground. Generally land in the humid eastern United States and in the northern central states is most likely to have drainage problems.

Water-loving plants like sedges, cattails, or rushes, or trees like willows, some maples, or bays dotting a meadow would indicate generally poor drainage, although those same plants located in a row or in a small clump would probably indicate the presence of an underground stream or spring.

Hardpan and Claypan

Hardpan (a compacted layer that is impenetrable by roots) and claypan (a hardpan consisting mainly of clay) occur naturally in the soil or result from years of intensive plowing. Poor plowing practices ruin the soil structure. The fine soil particles are compacted tightly together, which destroys the pore spaces in the subsoil and forms a dense, stonelike layer that cuts off the topsoil from the subsoil. These hard layers are usually impenetrable by plant roots or water. Plants trying to grow in the soil above the hardpan or claypan will have shallow roots that are easily injured by drowning and drought. The plant roots drown because water collects around them without being able to sink into the ground, and they dry up because they are so close to the surface that they cannot escape the hot sun by penetrating deeper into cooler, moist ground.

Drainage Tests

If little is growing on land that was once heavily farmed, be careful. Look at the land during and after a rainstorm. If the area becomes a huge mud puddle or the water runs off the surface without penetrating into the ground more than a few inches, the drainage is obviously bad, and the subsoil might be an impervious material.

A dry test involves digging six or more holes 4 to 12 inches in diameter and at least 3 feet deep at various places on the land, especially where your house and garden will be. Does the ground feel as if you are chopping into rocks? If so, you have an indication that the soil is bad. When you have finished digging, take a knife and scratch the sides of each hole. If the dirt crumbles easily, the soil is not impervious, but if the dirt is tightly compacted and hard to crumble, some kind of hardpan exists.

After you have examined the sides of the dry holes, you are ready to do a *percolation test*. (See illustration 27, page 68.) A percolation test determines how quickly and effectively water drains through a porous substance. First roughen the sides of each hole so that water can enter the soil easily, remove any loose dirt from the bottom, and add 2 inches of gravel to prevent sealing. Fill each hole with at least 12 inches of water. Keep the water level 12 inches above the gravel for four hours or more by adding water when needed. If you are doing this test during the dry season, keep the hole filled for at least twelve hours. The ground must simulate its condition during the wettest season of the year. When the dirt is thoroughly wetted, let the water level reach 6 inches above the gravel. Measure the drop in the water level every thirty minutes for four hours if the water drains out slowly. If the water drains out quickly, measure the drop in the water level every ten minutes for one hour. Add water after each measurement to bring the level back up to 6 inches above the gravel. Multiply the last measurement of the drop in the water level by 2 if you are measuring every thirty minutes or by 6 if you are measuring every ten minutes to get the percolation rate in inches per hour. If the percolation rate is less than 2½ inches per hour, the permeability of the soil is insufficient for good plant growth and sanitation. Water will collect after a heavy rain, drowning your plants and flooding your septic tank.

A faster test involves pouring several gallons of water on dry ground. Wait a few minutes and dig into the soil to see how far the water has penetrated. If the soil is still dry a few inches beneath the ground, the drainage could be a problem.

Ask your local health inspector if you can get a professional percolation test done. You may have to pay to have this test done by a licensed soil engineer or geologist in some places. For more information on drainage problems in your area and on how to test the soil, go to the state Agricultural Experiment Station or local office of the Soil Conservation Service. A soil map will also state the drainage qualities of each soil in the area. (See Useful Resources at the end of this chapter.)

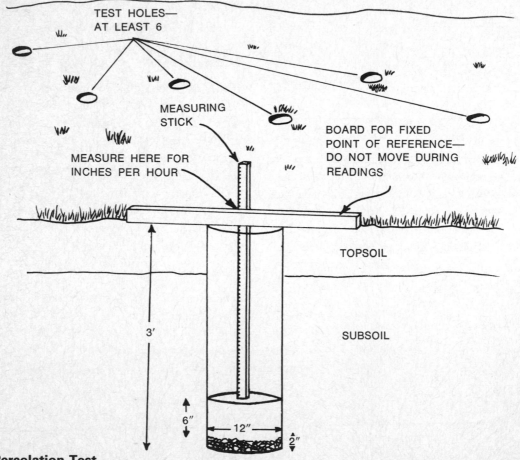

27. Percolation Test

68

Poor Drainage Affects Septic Tanks, Cesspools, Basements, and Building Foundations

Poor drainage often causes flooding in basements and septic tank systems. If there is a house with a basement on the property, go down and look at it carefully. Are there signs that it floods? Do the owners have a *sump pump* in the basement for pumping water out?

If you are planning to build a house on land with drainage problems, you can dispense with a basement but not with a sewage disposal system. If your soil will not allow proper drainage, building and health inspectors will not allow you to construct a dwelling if the building codes require the installation of a septic tank with a house. (See chapter 13, "Building and Health Codes.") If water will not drain properly, the water and sewage flushed into the septic tank and drained out by leach lines will float to the surface of the ground during a rainstorm. I have seen this happen in areas where drainage was poor, and it makes living conditions very unpleasant. The soil must be deep and permeable to effectively absorb the effluent, or discharge, from a septic tank. A rock layer or seasonal high water table in the upper 4 feet of the ground could make the area unsuitable for sewage disposal.

Where drainage is poor, you will also be required to construct special building foundations with extra stability. If water stands for a long period of time under a house, it will cause wood rot and mildew, which greatly decrease the value and the life of the house. It is important that you have the building and health inspectors view the land before you buy, so that you know you will have no problem obtaining permits afterward.

Correcting Drainage Problems

Correcting poor drainage is an expensive operation, requiring the construction of artificial drainage ditches or the laying of drainage tiles. Drainage tiles are pieces of tube with holes in them. The tiles are spaced closely together directly above the impervious layer of soil, and they collect and carry excess water out to a drainage area. (See illustration 28.) If the land has already been laid with tiles, be sure they are in perfect condition, because finding and correcting broken or separated tiles are expensive and time-consuming jobs. You should see the drainage system in full operation under the most

arduous water conditions before buying. The owner should show you a complete diagram of the tile pattern so that you can conduct a thorough investigation. Drainage ditches are usually made of concrete and are spaced farther apart than tiles. The ditches are above the ground, and water is carried in them to a creek or channel. They are also expensive to construct.

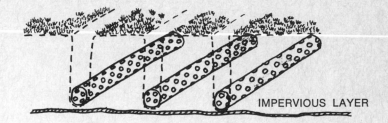

28. Drainage Tile

If proper drainage of land you want to buy requires a runoff system to deliver the water into a nearby creek or drainage ditch, you need a legal easement to cross neighboring lands. (See chapter 9, "Easement Rights.") If you divert water from your land onto adjoining lands, you may be held liable for damages unless you have the legal right by the laws of your state or by a written document to divert the water. (See chapter 10, "Water Rights.")

In areas where drainage is a problem, your land might be within a drainage district that was established to take water from all lands through a common system of canals. Membership in a drainage district is similar to membership in an irrigation district, except that the purpose of the organization is different. (See chapter 4, "Is There Enough Water on the Land?" to see how an irrigation district operates.) You should find out whether your land is within such a district and if so, whether the seller is already a member. How much are the assessments on the land? Before you buy, speak to the drainage district advisor about any drainage problems and about what will be involved in bringing the land within the district if it is currently excluded.

If you plan to buy land that will require the laying of drainage tiles or construction of ditches, you should add this cost into the purchase price because it is something that must be done before you can live on the land. If you buy land that has a drainage system already installed, the price will be higher because of this improvement. You should consider whether the added expense is really worthwhile, since it might be possible to find land in the area with good drainage for much less money. Occasionally the physical conditions of a particular parcel of land prevent good drainage regardless of what is attempted to alleviate the problem.

PLANNING TO INSTALL A SEPTIC TANK

If you are planning to have a septic tank, you may want to order a copy of an excellent pamphlet, entitled the *Manual of Septic Tank Practice*, from the Superintendent of Documents, U.S. Government Printing Office, Washington, D.C. 20402 for $1.05; it is listed in the Useful Resources at the end of this chapter. Also, pick up a copy of the sanitary regulations from the local health or pollution-control department.

The soil will have to be tested for permeability or percolation as specified above. According to the *Manual of Septic Tank Practice*, the groundwater level and bedrock should be at least four feet below the bottom of the trench field or seepage pit. Low areas should be avoided because after a rain, the water may collect there. Also avoid land that slopes more than 15 degrees because the water will flow too rapidly through the drainage pipes.

There should be enough room on the land to install a second drainage or leach area if the first one clogs up. The size of the drainage field depends on the soil's percolation rate and the number of bedrooms you will have in the house. The more trench you have above the minimum required, the better because the leach field will last longer. However, trenches shouldn't be any longer than 100 feet at most. The usual drainage field occupies 1,000 to 2,000 square feet. So you will want to have 2,000 to 4,000 square feet of space available for a leach field.

If you are going to obtain your water from a well, it should be 100 feet or more from the leach field and preferably uphill from it.

The minimum-size parcel for both a well and a septic tank is about one-half acre. If you are buying property on the edge of a town that has a sewage treatment system, and if it is possible that in a few years that system may be extended to include your property, try to see if you can put the leach field between the house and the street. That way it will be easier to connect to the public sewer if it becomes available. It will also be easier to reach with a septic-tank-cleaner's pumper truck. However, if the property is downhill from the street and will also have a well, you may have to locate the septic tank and leach field in the back and the well in the front near the street. In this case you may want to install an extra sewer connection in front if you are certain that a sewer will be available in the future.

The best septic tanks are made of concrete. Although there are wooden and steel tanks available, they are usually about the same price but last only ten years or so, whereas a concrete tank may last as long as the house does. Generally, for a one- or two-bedroom house the recommended tank size is 750 gallons; for three bedrooms, 1,000; four bedrooms, 1,250; five or six bedrooms, 1,500 gallons. These capacities take into account garbage disposals, automatic dishwashers, and washing machines. Most septic tank systems include a distribution box between the tank and the leach field to equalize the flow of effluent into the various pipes. When you lay out your leach field you may want to have the pipes interconnect if the ground is fairly level. That way, if one end of a pipe gets clogged up, effluent can still enter through the other end. See chapter 6 for more information on septic tanks.

ACIDITY AND ALKALINITY

The acidity or alkalinity of the soil has a tremendous effect on the vegetation. They are measured on a pH scale which goes from 0 to 14, 0 being extremely acid and 14 being extremely alkaline. A soil with a pH factor of 7.0 is neutral. Nearly neutral soils, testing in the range of 6.5 to 7.0, are best for most fruits, vegetables, field crops, and flowers. (See illustration 29.) Soil that is too acid or too alkaline locks valuable nutrients into the soil, making them unavailable for plant use. An extremely acid or alkaline soil may be difficult to remedy. To correct an acid soil requires the annual application of quantities of lime. An alkaline soil requires sulfur or gypsum. If you cannot correct

29. pH Scale

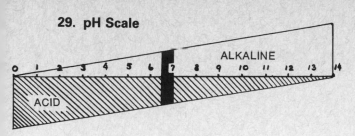

■ BEST pH RANGE FOR MOST FRUITS,
VEGETABLES, AND FLOWERS

the soil deficiency, you will be limited to growing only certain items. For example, the only crops that will grow on a heavily acid soil are berries, potatoes, peanuts, radishes, and watermelon.

For centuries farmers used to taste the soil to test for acidity or alkalinity. If the soil tasted sour, it was too acid; if it tasted bitter, it was too alkaline; but if it tasted sweet it was good for raising crops. Today there are two other simple ways you can test your soil to determine "sweetness." One uses reagents; the other uses litmus paper. For both tests you should collect moist soil samples from a depth of about 6 inches (where plant roots are) from various parts of the land, since different areas may have different pH factors.

The reagent test requires that you purchase an inexpensive soil-test kit. You can get one at any gardening supply house. Put a bit of the sample earth into a test tube or small clean container and mix in some of the liquid reagent that comes in the kit. The reagent is a chemical that changes color according to the pH factor. Look at the color that results from the mix and compare it with a color chart that comes with the kit to determine the acidity or alkalinity.

The cheaper test is done with litmus paper. You can purchase neutral litmus paper with a pH factor of 7.0 at a drugstore or garden supply center. Press a piece of litmus paper into the moist soil sample. If the paper remains the same color and just gets wet, the soil is neutral. If it turns blue, it's alkaline; if pink, it's acid.

After testing the soil, test the water source on the land to see if it is acid or alkaline. The water you use to irrigate your plants will affect them as much as the soil will.

You can get a more thorough test done by the local farm advisor, Soil Conservation Service, or college agricultural or soil department. After an-

alyzing your soil, they will tell you what kind of things you can grow on the land.

PESTICIDES IN THE SOIL

You may want to know if pesticides, herbicides, or other poisons have been used on the land or on neighboring land, since many of these poisons are very long-lived and can be carried by rainwater and irrigation water seeping through the soil to surrounding water supplies. If you are interested in organic gardening, you will want "pure" soil. Ask the owner what he has used on his plants. Look for poisons and spray containers in the barn, garage, basement, or greenhouse. The best insurance that you are getting unpoisoned soil is to buy land that has never been cultivated or lived on.

THE "BUILDING SITE"

Every real estate ad makes a point of mentioning that there is a building site on the land being sold. "Numerous building sites," "pretty building sites," "site to build a cabin or home," "excellent view home site," and "many level building sites" are examples of how this is advertised. When you evaluate so-called building sites, remember my warning about pond sites in chapter 4, "Is There Enough Water on the Land?" Just as anybody can point out a pond site, it is easy to call an area a building site. But it takes careful analysis to determine whether a place is truly suitable for the construction of a home. A favorite tactic used in selling rural land is to take prospective buyers to a spot on the property where there is a nice view or a fairly level clearing and call it a home site. The site looks beautiful, and its view overlooking the valley or lake captures the buyer. The person who buys this parcel may discover too late that the land is too steep to build on, that it is impossible to construct a road into the site, or that the drainage is insufficient for a septic tank.

Many considerations that don't apply to a city lot are necessary to determine the suitability of a country home site. The most important of these are the feasibility of building a road and getting utilities into the site and of getting water to it easily. For instance, if a home site is on a ridge high above a creek, which is the only source of water, you might find it impossible or very costly to bring water there, especially if no electricity is available. (Refer to chapter 4, "Is There Enough Water on the Land?" for the problems involved in getting water to the home site and garden areas.) If no road presently exists, you must get an estimate of the costs of constructing one before you buy. The terrain or the soil might make building a solid road to the site an impossible task. If an access road does exist but it is dirt, find out what the annual maintenance costs generally are to keep the road in good condition. You may find that the road becomes impassable in the winter, especially in snow country, which may mean a long walk from the country road with groceries. For heating, cooking, and lighting, you might want to use a large propane fuel storage tank, which must be filled periodically by a large tanker truck. Your road must be kept in good enough condition for the truck to get in and out, and your home site must have an area for the tank that will be accessible to the truck.

Consider the site's exposure to the elements. A house on a southern or southeastern slope will always be warmer because it gets the winter sun. A building site at the bottom of a hill facing north, on the other hand, will probably be cold and damp all winter long. (See illustration 30.) Another major decision is whether to buy on a mountaintop with a view or in a valley. On a ridge, you will probably be more exposed to high winds, a hot sun all day, and all the noises from the valley below. Valleys tend to be cooler, quieter, and closer to water sources. If you have your heart set on a spectacular view,

consider all the other aspects of the location too.

The ground on which you build your house is very important. You will have problems if it is either extremely hard or extremely soft. A rocky surface won't enable you to anchor your foundation well, and water runoff may be a problem. Soft dirt will be unstable and incapable of supporting a heavy structure, and will be susceptible to landslides and subsidence.

A major problem in areas of silty clay soil, commonly called adobe, is *soil creep*. This occurs when the earth slowly oozes downhill in wet-weather months. During the dry summer months, the soil shrinks as the water content decreases, and huge cracks may open up in the ground. When the winter rain comes, the unstable soil slips under the force of gravity until the particles settle into more stable positions. The greatest amount of soil movement occurs at the onset of the winter rains. Soil creep varies with the soil depth and pitch of the slope. Tests have shown that on a slope of only 8 degrees, soil 5 feet deep can move an average of half an inch each year at the surface. Soil creep can cause serious damage to foundations and walls. When examining an area, look for indications of poor soil stability, such as large cracks in the surface and leaning fence posts, power poles, and structures.

The possibility of land collapsing into *sinkholes* must be considered in many areas of the country. Sinkholes occur when the roofs of underground caverns, usually of limestone, suddenly collapse, leaving a huge pit in the ground. It is believed that this is caused by a natural or man-induced lowering of the water table. Where the necessary conditions exist, sinkholes are an extremely serious and frequent problem. For example, in Shelby County, Alabama, over one thousand sinkholes have oc-

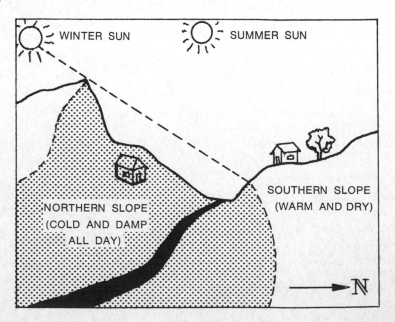

30. Site's Exposure to Sun

curred in the past twenty-five years. In fact, all of central and northern Alabama has soil that is very susceptible to cave-ins of this type. When investigating your soil, always ask about the occurrence of sinkholes and other regional soil problems.

With increasing frequency, large areas of swamp and marshland, riverbeds, and flooded areas are being filled in with dirt in an attempt to gain more land on which to develop housing and make a larger profit. Do not buy real estate where the building sites consist of landfill. You will have no end of troubles. Before buying, find out if the ground will support a house and other structures without creating excessive settling or cracking of the foundation.

The most common building problems are slipping and cracking foundations and walls, sliding hillsides, and flooded basements. The best ground to build on has soil at least five feet deep, allows good seepage of water, does not flood or lie over a high water table, and is level or moderately sloping. Steep slopes are generally poor building sites because they can slide and erode. The steeper the building site, the more difficult it will be to construct a solid foundation.

A level home site is an asset to a piece of property and always raises the land's value. (See chapter 19, ''Evaluating the Price of the Property.'') If you plan to have only a house, garden, and small family orchard, you only need a few level acres. Large stock animals, such as cows or horses, usually need at least one acre per animal for grazing. One way to get level land for a low price is to buy an area thickly covered with brush, since it is worth less than land that has already been cleared. Although considerable work may be required to clear the area, the soil is likely to be very rich, having been protected and fed by the brush for years. Be careful to protect the newly uncovered earth from erosion, and you will have some valuable land for very little money.

NATIVE BUILDING MATERIALS AND FUEL ON THE LAND

You will be very lucky if you find in this country land at a reasonable price with enough trees on it to construct a house. Such abundance is found mostly in Canada, where many people still construct their homes from standing timber on the land. In the United States, you will probably have to rely on such materials as rock and adobe rather than trees if you want to build from available resources.

In many areas where land has been logged, enough wood will be lying on the ground to use as fuel for cooking and heating your house for several years. Also, brush that must be cleared or dying trees that should be cut can be used for fuel. If you are buying in isolated country, wood fuel on the land is practically a necessity.

POISON OAK, POISON IVY, AND OTHER ALLERGIES

If you are sensitive to poison oak, ivy, or sumac, don't buy land that is covered with it. These prolific plants are very difficult to get rid of. They have to be dug up by the roots or continually sprayed with poisons. If you are allergic to them, you cannot do this yourself. Goats and donkeys will eat the stuff, but you will need quite a herd to make a dent.

Other allergies to plants, such as hay fever, can also make life in the country unpleasant. Try to avoid those plants that are particularly irritating to you. Visit the land in the worst season for your allergies, and if you start to wheeze and sniffle, look somewhere else. Ask a local health department official for information on local plant and pollen conditions.

EARTHQUAKE AND FAULT LINES

Although California and Alaska are most noted for their earthquakes, faults do exist in other regions of the country. A few major quakes have been recorded in New England; in South Carolina; in the Mississippi Valley region; and in the western mountain regions of Montana, Wyoming, Utah, northern Arizona, and New Mexico. In most areas of the country, earthquakes are a minor problem. Even if a major quake occurs, you will be safer in the country away from toppling buildings and the chaos of panicking people. Make sure that you don't build your house or access road on top of a fault line, since minor shifting of the earth will cause you endless problems. Check with your state division of mines and geology or your local farm advisor to determine whether fault lines exist in your area. They have maps showing where all the earthquake areas are located. Further information can be obtained from the National Center for Earthquake Research, U.S. Geological Survey Field Center, 800 Menlo Avenue, Menlo Park, California 94025, or from the U.S. Geological Survey, National Earthquake Information Center, Stop 967, Box 25046, Denver Federal Center, Denver, Colorado 80225. The latter primarily handles worldwide locations of recent earthquakes and puts out a catalogue of earthquake events within four months of their occurrence. The former is a research center primarily handling questions related to California and Alaska. If you write to one office and the other can answer better, it will forward your letter to the other office.

LANDSLIDES

If you are looking at a house built on a steep hillside or if you are planning to build your house on a hillside, check out the structure of the soil on the hill very carefully. You don't want to have your beautiful country house go sliding down the hill during an unusually heavy rainstorm.

Landslides occur during heavy rains on steep hills with surfaces of loose, fragile, or slippery rocks and soil. The term *landslide* includes slumps, earth flows, mud flows, rock slides, soil creep, and rock avalanches.

Often shallow surface flows of mud and debris will take a house in a landslide. But, in deep-soil areas, moisture will work its way down until it reaches layers of impervious clay or siltstone underneath the more porous rock and soil. The water accumulates to form a slick plane a few feet to many yards beneath the surface, and if more heavy rains occur, the entire block of hillside may slip away with the house or other structures on it.

If you are buying land in a subdivision, see if there is a soils and geology report or an environmental impact report available. Check with the U.S. Geological Survey (see Useful Resources at the end of this chapter for addresses) to see if any maps have been made of the land you are looking at. The USGS has prepared elaborate maps of many slide-prone areas in the United States. However, the less populated an area is, the fewer studies will have been done. Check with your local planning or zoning commission to see if they have any information.

If a house is built on a steep hill or the building site for your dream house is on a hill, you will want to put a contingency in your contract that the close of escrow is subject to your approval of an inspection and report prepared by a civil engineer, a registered geologist, or a soils engineer.

You will also want to find out how much it will cost to protect an existing house that is situated on a hill that might slide. The geologist or soils engineer may recommend that you build diversion walls or add deep piers to your foundation to anchor the house to solid bedrock, or he may recommend that you stabilize the hill. Some of these recommendations could be very expensive, and must be considered by you in the cost of your purchase.

MINERALS

I explain the importance of mineral rights and how to investigate them later, in chapter 11, "Mineral, Oil, Gas, Timber, Soil, and Other Rights." You may be shown land that does not have mineral rights. These rights will be in the possession of the seller, another party, or the United States government. Try to find out why the party in possession is holding onto the rights and investigate the geology of the area to determine the possibility of their ever wanting to exercise these rights.

You can do this by finding out what minerals are known to be on the land and in the general area. The same agencies that have earthquake information will have studies of the area's geology and facts on past and present mineral explorations in every part of the state. If it appears that the land does not have any minerals currently being used or sought after, you will probably be safe in buying it without mineral rights. Often the government or individuals will hold on to mineral rights without ever intending to use them. Sometimes the government will keep the mineral rights to a piece of land it sells as a matter of policy.

MAPS AND AERIAL PHOTOGRAPHS

When requesting information on the following maps and photos, include a description of the property you want covered. If it is within an area described by the U.S. Rectangular Survey, give the base and meridian, section, township, range, county, and state in which the parcel is located. (See chapter 8, "Land Descriptions and Surveys.") If the land is in another area, describe its location as precisely as possible under the particular survey system used.

Whenever ordering a map or photograph, ask for the most recent one available, since older maps and photos will not include new roads, highways, and buildings. In order to receive your map or photo in good condition, you must specifically request that it be sent in a mailing tube, so that it will not be folded by the sender or the post office.

Soil Maps and Other Soil Information

Every state is represented by a regional field office of the U.S. Forest Service (see Useful Resources at the end of this chapter), which has soil maps available to the public at little or no charge. A soil map, which breaks down the soil types throughout a given area, gives much information regarding the soil itself and what is growing on it (as you can see in illustration 31). Each map has an accompanying chart and leaflet explaining how to read the symbols. Before buying land, you should get all the maps you can find to help you really know the geography of the area. Soil information can be obtained from most of the resources listed at the end of this chapter.

Illustration 31 is a portion of a U.S. Forest Service soil map that covers our land. It is based on aerial photos and on-site inspection and classification. Each symbol details important aspects of the soil and vegetation of the area. For example, the symbols *D,T,M,* 812/5, and III represent the following information: *D* = Douglas fir; will not usually sprout if top is killed by fire; negligible browsing value for horses, cattle, sheep, goats, and deer. *T* = tan oak tree; will sprout following a fire; negligible browsing value for horses, cattle, sheep, goats, and deer. *M* = madrone tree; will sprout following a fire; negligible browsing value for horses and cattle, and poor to negligible value for sheep, goats, and deer. 812/5 = Hugo soil series; over four feet deep, loam texture, slightly acid, light grayish-brown in color; rolling to steep uplands topography; good permeability for movement of water, air, and roots through the soil; drainage good, no toxins present; annual rainfall is 65–75 inches; good to very good for commercial

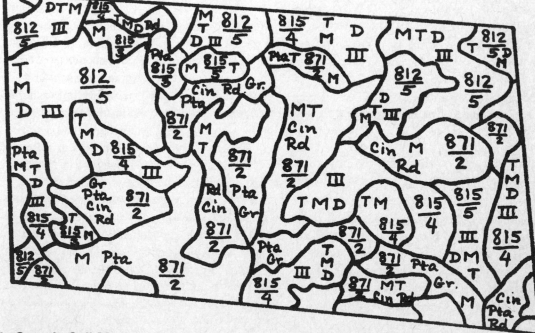

31. Sample Soil Map

timber, and fair for grasses. III = the height that the average Douglas fir tree reaches at the age of a hundred years on this soil is 140 feet.

Another source of soil maps and descriptions is the Soil Conservation Service (see Useful Resources at the end of this chapter), which publishes soil surveys for each state.

Included in the map and survey are soil/land capability groupings; productivity ratings for trees, farm, and horticultural crops; soil ratings and limitations; soil morphology; the relation of soils to their environment; principles of soil classification; and a general description of the climate and other features significant to soil problems of the area.

Vegetation and Timber Stand Maps

These maps are similar in style to soil maps. If an agency, such as the Forest Service, has soil maps for your area, it will probably also have timber stand and vegetation maps. Useful Resources at the end of this chapter contains information on where to get these maps.

Topographical Maps

The topographical map is an essential aid to understanding the lay of the land. The unique aspect of the "topo" map is the use of contour lines to indicate elevation. The distance between contour lines is usually 40 feet on the ground. Thus, the closer the lines, the steeper the terrain. These maps also show roads, railroads, cities, towns, and water features. By comparing aerial photographs of each area with actual ground inspections, the U.S. Geological Survey has prepared topographical maps for the entire United States.

Topographical maps are also called *quadrangle* maps because each unit of area surveyed is a quadrangle. You can get either 7½-minute or 15-minute quadrangle maps. Chapter 8, "Land Descriptions and Surveys," explains how an area is broken into quadrangles. The 7½-minute quadrangle map is drawn to a scale of 1:24,000, which means that 1 inch on the map equals 24,000 inches or 2,000 feet on the ground. Thus, 2 inches on the map equal approximately 1 mile. The 15-minute quadrangle map is drawn to a scale of 1:62,500, which makes 1 inch equal to about 1 mile on the ground. Thus, the 7½-minute maps give much greater detail.

The U.S. Geological Survey publishes an index to topographic maps for each state, which you can obtain free by writing the main office or visiting your nearest USGS office. Each index lists the map for each specific geographical region, or quadrangle, within the state by name and the year in which it was charted. The index also lists special maps available, the addresses of local map reference libraries, local map dealers, and federal map distribution centers. Order blanks and a list of prices are included. When you write for your state's index, also ask for the free booklet describing topographical maps and symbols.

Because of the popularity and importance of topographical maps, local sport shops, stationery stores, and dealers in civil engineering equipment usually sell them.

Aerial Photographs and Status Maps

Aerial photographs are taken with special automatic cameras that are held vertically while an airplane flies at a constant altitude above sea level along carefully laid-out sky trails. Each snap of the camera's shutter captures an area of ground that overlaps the ground covered in the last photograph by about 60 percent. Each strip of film covers a certain strip of ground. When the plane flies down the adjoining parallel strip of ground, the overlap between strips is from 30 to 50 percent. These photo strips are then laid out side by side to form a photo index showing the entire area.

Although aerial photography did not begin on a national basis until 1930, most areas of the United States have been covered. Some areas have been covered by more than one agency, and the quality of reproduction tends to vary according to who took the pictures and the date they were taken. A good photo can help you study the geography of the land, including the extent of erosion, vegetation, and timber growth.

An aerial photo can also be used to get an idea of the location of a parcel's boundaries if they have not been marked on the ground or if only the corners have been marked by a surveyor. Draw in the boundaries according to the description of the land on a topographical map, and compare it to an aerial photo done to the same scale. Since topographical maps are drawn using aerial photos, you should be able to locate and draw in the boundaries on the aerial photo quite easily. From the features shown in the photograph, you can then locate the boundaries on the ground fairly accurately.

The best way to look at an aerial photograph is with a set of paired stereoscopic prints. Placing two consecutive overlapping photos next to each other and using a stereo viewer or lens stereoscope, you can see the photo in 3-D. The effect is beautiful, and each feature sticks right at you as if you were hovering over the land in a helicopter. If you have ever looked at a 3-D movie or comic book using a red and green viewer, you know the effect. You can use a stereo viewer, or a similar device, at any of the agencies listed at the end of this chapter. You can buy one at stores that sell surveying or engineering equipment or from Forestry Supplies, Inc., 205 W. Rankin Street, P.O. Box 8397, Jackson, Mississippi 39204. Also, army surplus stores and scientific supply houses occasionally have them for sale. The folding pocket type is the least expensive.

Each agency that sells aerial photos issues free status maps showing what photos are available for your area. Each map indicates the area photographed, the date the photos were taken, the various sizes of photos available, the prices, and order blanks.

USEFUL RESOURCES

U.S. Geological Survey (USGS) and Public Inquiries Offices (PIO)

The USGS has offices around the country that can assist walk-in customers and also answer inquiries by mail or telephone.

In addition to assisting the public in the selection and ordering of all USGS products, the PIOs provide counter service for USGS topographic, geologic, and water-resources maps and reports. The offices furnish information about the USGS and its programs and are linked to information held by state and other federal offices. PIOs distribute catalogues, circulars, indexes, and leaflets, and provide bibliographic and geographic reference searches. Most PIOs maintain libraries of recent USGS book reports and are regional depositories for Open-File Reports. The USGS and PIOs function under the supervision of the U.S. Department of the Interior.

Listed below are PIO locations and the regions that each covers:

Alaska
Public Inquiries Office
U.S. Geological Survey
4230 University Dr., Rm. 101
Anchorage, AK 99508-4664

Earth Science Information and Sales
E-146 Federal Bldg., Box 53
701 C St.
Anchorage, AK 99508-4664
   (Covers: Alaska)

California
Public Inquiries Office
U.S. Geological Survey
7638 Federal Bldg.
300 N. Los Angeles St.
Los Angeles, CA 90012
   (Covers: Alaska, Arizona, California, Hawaii, Nevada, Oregon, and Washington)

Public Inquiries Office
U.S. Geological Survey
Bldg. 3, Rm. 122
Mail Stop 533
345 Middlefield Rd.
Menlo Park, CA 94025
   (Covers: Alaska, Arizona, California, Hawaii, Idaho, Nevada, Oregon, Utah, and Washington)

Public Inquiries Office
U.S. Geological Survey
504 Customhouse
555 Battery St.
San Francisco, CA 94111
   (Covers: Alaska, Arizona, California, Hawaii, Idaho, Nevada, Oregon, and Washington)

Colorado
Public Inquiries Office
U.S. Geological Survey
169 Federal Bldg.
1961 Stout St.
Denver, CO 80294
   (Covers: Alaska, Arizona, Colorado, Kansas, Montana, Nebraska, New Mexico, North Dakota, South Dakota, Utah, and Wyoming)

District of Columbia
Public Inquiries Office
U.S. Geological Survey
1028 General Services Administration Bldg.
19th and F Sts., N.W.
Washington, DC 20244
(Covers: All states)

Texas
Public Inquiries Office
U.S. Geological Survey
1-C-45 Federal Bldg.
1100 Commerce St.
Dallas, TX 75242
(Covers: Arkansas, Louisiana, New Mexico, Oklahoma, and Texas)

Utah
Public Inquiries Office
U.S. Geological Survey
8105 Federal Bldg.
125 S. State St.
Salt Lake City, UT 84138
(Covers: Arizona, Colorado, Idaho, Nevada, New Mexico, Utah, and Wyoming)

Virginia
Public Inquiries Office
U.S. Geological Survey
503 National Center
Rm. 1-C-42
12201 Sunrise Valley Dr.
Reston, VA 22092
(Covers: All states)

Washington
Public Inquiries Office
U.S. Geological Survey
678 U.S. Courthouse
W. 920 Riverside Ave.
Spokane, WA 99201
(Covers: Alaska, Idaho, Montana, Oregon, and Washington)

MAIN AND BRANCH LIBRARIES OF THE USGS

The library system of the USGS is open to the public. Most of the materials in the library system may be borrowed by the public through interlibrary loans initiated by local libraries. Holdings include 1.1 million monographs and serials; 385,000 maps; 355,000 pamphlets; and 340,000 reports and dissertations in microform, all relating to geological matters within the United States.

For more information write:

Arizona
Library, U.S. Geological Survey
2255 N. Gemini Dr.
Flagstaff, AZ 86001

California
Library, U.S. Geological Survey
Mail Stop 55
345 Middlefield Rd.
Menlo Park, CA 94025

Colorado
Library, U.S. Geological Survey
Mail Stop 914
Box 25046, Federal Center
Denver, CO 80225

Street Address:
Denver West Office Park, Bldg. 3
1526 Cole Blvd.
Golden, CO 80401

Virginia
Library, U.S. Geological Survey
950 National Center, Rm. 4-A-100
12201 Sunrise Valley Dr.
Reston, VA 22092

USGS PHOTOGRAPHIC LIBRARY

The photographic library contains a collection of over 250,000 photographs (mostly black and white) taken during USGS studies. The photographic library may be used by the public. Persons who wish to obtain prints or enlargements, copy negatives, or duplicate transparencies are encouraged to visit the library to make their selections. The library staff will prepare lists of selected photographs in response to specific requests. Photographs are indexed by subject and by geographic location and include aerial photographs of most areas within the United States.

For further information write:
Photographic Library
U.S. Geological Survey
Mail Stop 914
Federal Center, Box 25046
Denver, CO 80225

BOOK AND TEXT PRODUCTS SECTION OF THE USGS

The Book and Text Products Section distributes popular publications of general interest, such as leaflets, pamphlets, and booklets. Write for their catalogue from:

U.S. Geological Survey
Book and Open-File Reports
Federal Center, Bldg. 41
Box 25425
Denver, CO 80225

TOPOGRAPHIC MAPS AND OTHER USGS MAP PRODUCTS

The USGS Map Products Section sells over the counter and by mail geologic, hydrologic, topographic, land use, and land cover maps.

Mail Order

For maps of areas east of the Mississippi River, including Minnesota, write to:

Branch of Distribution
U.S. Geological Survey
1200 S. Eads St.
Arlington, VA 22202

For maps of areas west of the Mississippi River, including Alaska, Hawaii, and Louisiana, write to:

Branch of Distribution
U.S. Geological Survey
Federal Center, Box 25286
Denver, CO 80225

Residents of Alaska may order Alaska maps or an index for Alaska from:

Distribution Section
U.S. Geological Survey
Federal Bldg., Box 12
101 Twelfth Ave.
Fairbanks, AK 99701

Order by map name, state, and series. To obtain this information first write for a free index for your area of interest and a booklet describing topographic maps available. The indexes show available published maps. Index maps show quadrangle location, name, and survey data. Listed also are special maps and sheets, with prices, map dealers, federal distribution centers, map reference libraries, and instructions for ordering maps. Although the distribution offices described above provide counter service for their products, they are primarily mail-order outlets. For maps, PIOs are the main over-the-counter sales outlets of the USGS (see addresses above). In addition, the National Cartographic Information Center in Rolla, Missouri, sells over the counter topographic maps of the mid-continent region (see addresses below).

NATIONAL CARTOGRAPHIC INFORMATION CENTER

The National Cartographic Information Center (NCIC) exists to help the individual find maps of all kinds and much of the data and materials used to compile and to print them. NCIC collects, sorts, and describes all types of cartographic information from federal, state, and local government agencies and, where possible, from private companies in the mapping business. It is the public's primary source for cartographic information.

The NCIC staff can:

1. Inform you about maps and other cartographic information you can obtain from many government and private sources.
2. Take your orders for any of the full range of maps, map by-products, and other cartographic information produced by the U.S. Geological Survey, including millions of aerial photos and space images. Prepayment is required.
3. Search vast holdings of maps and other cartographic information to help you obtain quickly the information or products you may be seeking to meet a highly specific need.
4. If your question can be answered best by a leaflet or a simple handout, it will be sent to you free of charge. NCIC researchers may have to contact you for more details so they can find the best answer to your question. Most of NCIC's research services are free. If a charge is necessary, you will be informed before the research is started.

For more information on the services provided by the NCIC write to:

Alaska
Alaska Office, NCIC
U.S. Geographic Survey
4230 University Dr., Rm. 110
Anchorage, AK 99508-4664

California
Western Mapping Center, NCIC
U.S. Geographic Survey
345 Middlefield Rd.
Menlo Park, CA 94025

Colorado
Rocky Mountain Mapping Center, NCIC
U.S. Geographic Survey
Mail Stop 504
Federal Center, Box 25046
Denver, CO 80225

Mississippi
National Space Technology Laboratories
National Cartographic Information Center
U.S. Geographic Survey
Bldg. 3101
NSTL Station, MS 39529

Missouri
Mid-Continent Mapping Center, NCIC
U.S. Geographic Survey
1400 Independence Rd.
Rolla, MO 65401

Virginia
National Cartographic Information Center
U.S. Geographic Survey
507 National Center, Rm. 1-C-107
12201 Sunrise Valley Dr.
Reston, VA 22092

Eastern Mapping Center, NCIC
U.S. Geographic Survey
536 National Center, Rm. 2-B-200
12201 Sunrise Valley Dr.
Reston, VA 22092

State Affiliate National Cartographic Information Center (NCIC) Offices

State affiliate NCIC offices distribute free pamphlets, poster leaflets, and topographic map indexes. Many state affiliates sell maps of their respective states. The state affiliates also provide ordering assistance for custom cartographic products (including aerial photographs).

Alabama
Geological Survey of Alabama
P.O. Drawer O
University, AL 35486

Arizona
Arizona State Land Development
Information Resources Division
1624 W. Adams, Rm. 302
Phoenix, AZ 85007

Arkansas
Arkansas Geological Commission
Vardelle Parham Geology Center
3815 W. Roosevelt Rd.
Little Rock, AR 72204

Connecticut
Natural Resources Center
Department of Environmental Protection
State Office Bldg., Rm. 553
165 Capitol Ave.
Hartford, CT 06106

Delaware
Delaware Geological Survey
University of Delaware
101 Penny Hall
Newark, DE 19711

Georgia
Office of Research and Evaluation
Department of Community Affairs
40 Marietta St., N.W., 8th Fl.
Atlanta, GA 30303

Hawaii
Department of Planning and Economic
Development
Kamamalu Bldg.
250 South King St.
Honolulu, HI 96813

Idaho
Idaho State Historical Library
325 W. State
Boise, ID 83702

Illinois
University of Illinois at Urbana-Champaign
Map and Geography Library
1407 W. Gregory Dr.
Urbana, IL 61801

Kentucky
Kentucky Geological Survey
311 Breckinridge Hall
University of Kentucky
Lexington, KY 40506

Louisiana
  Office of Public Works
  Department of Transportation and
    Development
  Capitol Station, P.O. Box 44145
  Baton Rouge, LA 70804

Maryland
  Maryland Geological Survey
  The Rotunda, Ste. 440
  711 W. 40th St.
  Baltimore, MD 21211

Massachusetts
  University of Massachusetts
  Remote Sensing Center
  Hasbrouck Hall, Rm. 320
  Amherst, MA 01003

Michigan
  Division of Land Resources Programs
  Michigan Department of Natural Resources
  Steven T. Mason Bldg., Box 30028
  Lansing, MI 48909

Minnesota
  Minnesota State Planning Agency
  Land Management Information Center
  Metro Square Bldg., Rm. LL65
  Seventh and Roberts Sts.
  Saint Paul, MN 55101

Mississippi
  Regional Plannning Branch
  Mississippi Research and Development
    Center
  P.O. Drawer 2470
  Jackson, MS 39205

Missouri
  Missouri Department of Natural Resources
  Division of Geology and Land Survey
  P.O. Box 250
  Rolla, MO 65401

Montana
  Montana Bureau of Mines and Geology
  Montana Tech.
  Main Hall, Rm. 200
  Butte, MT 59701

Nebraska
  Conservation and Survey Division
  University of Nebraska
  Lincoln, NE 68508

Nevada
  Nevada Bureau of Mines and Geology
  University of Nevada, Reno
  Reno, NV 89557-0088

New Jersey
  Department of Environmental Protection
  New Jersey Geological Survey, CN-029
  Trenton, NJ 08625

New Mexico
  University of New Mexico
  Technology Applications Center
  2500 Central Ave., S.E.
  Albuquerque, NM 87131

North Carolina
  Geological Survey Section
  Division of Land Resources, DNRCD
  P.O. Box 27687
  Raleigh, NC 27611

North Dakota
  North Dakota State Water Commission
  State Office Bldg.
  209 E. Blvd.
  Bismarck, ND 58501

Oregon
  Oregon State Library
  Public Services
  Salem, OR 97310

Pennsylvania
  Department of Environmental Resources
  Bureau of Topographic and Geological
    Survey
  P.O. Box 2357
  Harrisburg, PA 17120

Rhode Island
  Sea Grant Depository
  Pell Marine Science Library
  University of Rhode Island
  Narragansett, RI 02882

South Carolina
  South Carolina Land Resources
    Conservation Commission
  2221 Devine St., Ste. 222
  Columbia, SC 29205

Tennessee
Tennessee Division of Geology
701 Broadway
Nashville, TN 37203

Texas
Texas Natural Resources Information Center
P.O. Box 13087
Austin, TX 78711

Utah
Utah Geological and Mineral Survey
606 Black Hawk Wy.
Research Park
Salt Lake City, UT 84108-1280

Virginia
Department of Conservation and Economic
Development
Division of Mineral Resources
Natural Resources Bldg.
Box 3667
Charlottesville, VA 22903

Washington
Washington State Library
Information Services Division
Olympia, WA 98504

West Virginia
West Virginia Geological and Economic
Survey
West Virginia Cartographic Center
P.O. Box 879
Morgantown, WV 26505

Wisconsin
State Cartographer's Office
144 Science Hall
550 N. Park St.
Madison, WI 53706

Wyoming
State Engineer
Barrett Bldg.
Cheyenne, WY 82002

Publications on Soil, Maps, and Aerial Photographs

The following are free from:
The U.S. Geological Survey main office or
Public Inquiries Offices (see addresses
above).

*Publications of the Geological Survey, 1962–
1970*
Publications of the Geological Survey, 1971
Publications of the Geological Survey, 1972
New Publications of the Geological Survey
(ask to be put on the list for future
monthly mailings)
Popular Publications of the U.S.G.S.
Information Sources and Services
The U.S. Geological Survey
Tools for Planning—Topographical Maps
Topographic Maps
United States Geological Survey Library
*Public Inquiries Offices of the U.S.
Geological Survey*
*Photographic Library of the Geological
Survey*
Pacific Coast Center
Geological Maps, Portraits of the Earth
Active Faults of California
*Elevations and Distances in the United
States*

Aerial Photography

Below is a list of sources for aerial photos and the names of the status maps you can order from them.

U.S. GEOLOGICAL SURVEY

Ask for *Status of Aerial Photography in the United States* and *Status of Aerial Mosaics*. These publications list the government agencies that have photographed each area of the country and the commercial aerial photographers who sell prints of their photos, and they tell how you can order the photos. Order these publications from the USGS offices listed above or from the Photographic Library and Distribution Service or Map Information Office at the following address:
Photographic Library
U.S. Geological Survey
Mail Stop 914
Federal Center, Box 25046
Denver, CO 80225
or
U.S. Geological Survey
Map Distribution
Federal Center, Bldg. 41
Box 25286
Denver, CO 80225

Ask for *Status of Aerial Photography*. This publication lists the photos of coastal areas and navigable rivers that you can order from them.

LOCAL COMMERCIAL AERIAL PHOTOGRAPHERS

Most areas have private businesses that engage in aerial photography. The cost of hiring a plane and photographer would be prohibitive, but in many cases they have already photographed your land, and for a small fee, you can purchase a copy of a picture of your land. Inquire at local photography stores and airports, and look in the telephone directory under Photographers—Aerial.

CITY HALL OR COUNTY COURTHOUSE

Many cities and counties have photographed large areas within their borders. Ask the Planning Commission if they have commissioned any aerial photographs of your area.

U.S. DEPARTMENT OF AGRICULTURE, ASCS

The D-1 packet gives information on what aerial photographs are available, sizes, types, scales, etc. The Aerial Photography Field Office (APFO) library includes photographs used by Agricultural Stabilization and Conservation Service (ASCS) and its predecessor agencies, the U.S. Forest Service (USFS) and Soil Conservation Service (SCS).

You can order a D-1 packet free from:
U.S. Department of Agriculture, ASCS
Aerial Photography Field Office
2222 W. 2300, S.
P.O. Box 30010
Salt Lake City, UT 84130-0010

Each ASCS county office has a photo index of the county or counties it serves. You may visit your state or county ASCS office, select the photo you need from this index, and obtain assistance in preparing an order.

If you are interested in an aerial photograph of a distant county you may wish to purchase a photo index for $5.00 or a line index for $4.00 of the area you are interested in and make your selection. Or you may send a legal description, including state, county, and township with section and range numbers or coordinate location, or a copy of a county or city map or USDS topographic map with

the area you are interested in outlined in red to the APFO address above.

ORDERING OLDER PHOTOS

Aerial photo negatives from 1941 and earlier were transferred to the National Archives. To order any of these older photos, write to:
National Archives and Records Service
Cartographic Archives Division
General Services Administration
Washington, DC 20408

U.S. Coast and Geodetic Survey (under the Department of Commerce)

This agency specializes in research of coastal areas and regions around navigable rivers. Send all inquiries regarding aerial photos to:
Director, Coast and Geodetic Survey
Attn: Photogrammetry Division
Washington Science Center
Rockville, MD 20852

U.S. Forest Service (USFS) Regional Field Offices (under the U.S. Department of Agriculture)

The USFS has information on soil studies in areas near the U.S. forests and also has aerial photographs.

Northern Region
(Covers: Idaho, Montana)
Federal Bldg.
P.O. Box 7669
Missoula, MT 59807

Rocky Mountain Region
(Covers: Colorado, Nebraska, South
Dakota, Wyoming)
11177 W. 8th Ave.
P.O. Box 25127
Lakewood, CO 80225

Southwestern Region
(Covers: Arizona, New Mexico)
Federal Bldg.
517 Gold Ave., S.W.
Albuquerque, NM 87102

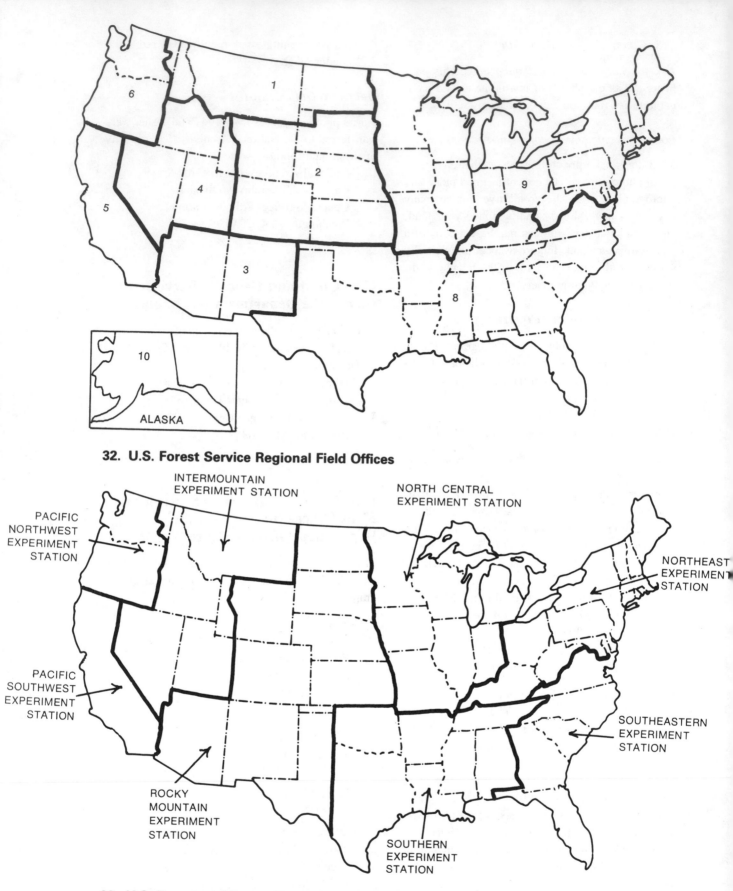

32. U.S. Forest Service Regional Field Offices

33. U.S. Forest and Range Experiment Stations

84

Intermountain Region
(Covers: Idaho, Nevada, Utah, Wyoming)
Federal Bldg.
324 25th St.
Ogden, UT 84401

Pacific Southwest Region
(Covers: California)
630 Sansome St.
San Francisco, CA 94111

Pacific Northwest Region
(Covers: Oregon, Washington)
319 S.W. Pine St.
P.O. Box 3623
Portland, OR 97208

Eastern Region
(Covers: Illinois, Indiana, Ohio, Michigan,
Minnesota, Missouri, New Hampshire,
Maine, Pennsylvania, Vermont, West
Virginia, Wisconsin)
310 W. Wisconsin Ave.
Milwaukee, WI 53203

Southern Region
(Covers: Alabama, Arkansas, Florida,
Georgia, Kentucky, Louisiana,
Mississippi, North Carolina, Puerto Rico,
South Carolina, Tennessee, Texas,
Virginia)
1720 Peachtree Rd., N.W.
Atlanta, GA 30367

Alaska Region
Federal Office Bldg.
P.O. Box 1628
Juneau, AK 99802

State and Private Forestry Offices

The state and private forestry offices are located in
the same buildings as the U.S. Forest Service regional field offices (see above) with the exception
of the following area:

Northeastern Area
(Covers: Connecticut, Delaware, Illinois,
Indiana, Iowa, Maine, Maryland,
Massachusetts, Michigan, Minnesota,
Missouri, New Hampshire, New Jersey,
New York, Ohio, Pennsylvania, Rhode
Island, Vermont, West Virginia,
Wisconsin)
6816 Market St.
Upper Darby, PA 19082

State Forestry Offices

The following state agencies manage and protect
the state's forest resources.

Alabama
Forestry Commission
513 Madison Ave.
Montgomery, AL 36130

Alaska
Division of Forestry
Department of Natural Resources
Pouch 7005
Anchorage, AK 99510

Arizona
State Parks Board
1688 W. Adams St., Rm. 106
Phoenix, AZ 85007

Arkansas
Forestry Commission
3821 W. Roosevelt Rd.
Little Rock, AR 72204

California
Department of Forestry
1416 Ninth St., 15th Fl.
Sacramento, CA 95814

Colorado
Division of Forestry
Colorado State University
Fort Collins, CO 80521

Connecticut
Forestry Division
Environmental Protection Department
165 Capitol Ave., Rm. 260
Hartford, CT 06106

Delaware
State Forester
Department of Agriculture
P.O. Drawer D
Dover, DE 19903

Florida
Division of Forestry
Agriculture and Consumer
Services Department
3125 Conner Blvd.
Tallahassee, FL 32301

Georgia
State Forestry Commission
P.O. Box 819
Macon, GA 31278

Hawaii
Division of Forestry and Wildlife
Land and Natural Resources Department
1151 Punchbowl St.
Honolulu, HI 96813

Idaho
Deptartment of Lands
Statehouse
Boise, ID 83720

Illinois
Department of Conservation
Lincoln Towers Plaza
524 S. Second St.
Springfield, IL 62706

Indiana
Forestry Division
Department of Natural Resources
613 State Office Bldg.
Indianapolis, IN 46204

Iowa
Forestry Division
Conservation Commission
Wallace State Office Bldg.
Des Moines, IA 50319-0034

Kansas
State and Extension Forestry
Kansas State University
2610 Claflin
Manhattan, KS 66506

Kentucky
Division of Forestry
Natural Resources and Environmental
    Protection Cabinet
627 Commanche Terr.
Frankfort, KY 40601

Louisiana
Office of Forestry
Department of Natural Resources
P.O. Box 1628
Baton Rouge, LA 70821

Maine
Forest Service
Department of Conservation
State House Station, #22
Augusta, ME 04333

Maryland
Forest, Park and Wildlife Services
Department of Natural Resources
Tawes State Office Bldg., B-2
Annapolis, MD 21401

Massachusetts
Division of Forests and Parks
Department of Environmental Management
100 Cambridge St.
Boston, MA 02202

Michigan
Forest Management Division
Department of Natural Resources
P.O. Box 30028
Lansing, MI 48909

Minnesota
Division of Forestry
Department of Natural Resources
500 Lafayette Rd.
St. Paul, MN 55146

Mississippi
Forestry Commission
908 Robert E. Lee Bldg.
Jackson, MS 39201

Missouri
Division of Forestry
Department of Conservation
P.O. Box 180
Jefferson City, MO 65102

Montana
Division of Forestry
Department of State Lands
2705 Spurgin Rd.
Missoula, MT 59801

Nebraska
Forestry, Fisheries and Wildlife
University of Nebraska, Lincoln
Plant Industry Bldg.–East Campus
Lincoln, NE 68503

Nevada
Division of Forestry
Conservation and Natural Resources
    Department
201 S. Fall St.
Carson City, NV 89710

New Hampshire
Forest and Lands Division
Resources and Economic Development
    Department
6 Loudon Rd.
Concord, NH 03301

New Jersey
Division of Parks and Forestry
Environmental Protection Department, CN-404
Trenton, NJ 08625

New Mexico
Forestry Division
Department of Natural Resources
Land Office Bldg.
Santa Fe, NM 87503

New York
Department of Environmental Conservation
50 Wolf Rd.
Albany, NY 12233

North Carolina
Forest Resources
Natural Resources and Community
    Development Department
512 N. Salisbury St.
Raleigh, NC 27611

North Dakota
School of Forestry
North Dakota State University
Horticulture Bldg.
Fargo, ND 58105

Ohio
Division of Forestry
Department of Natural Resources
Fountain Square, Bldg. C-3
Columbus, OH 43224

Oklahoma
Division of Forestry
Department of Agriculture
2800 N. Lincoln Blvd.
Oklahoma City, OK 73105

Oregon
Department of Forestry
2600 State St.
Salem, OR 97310

Pennsylvania
Bureau of Forestry
Environmental Resources Department
100 Evangelical Press Bldg.
Harrisburg, PA 17120

Rhode Island
Forest Environment
Department of Environmental Management
Old Hartford Pike
Scituate, RI 02903

South Carolina
Forestry Commission
P.O. Box 21707
Columbia, SC 29221

South Dakota
Division of Forestry
Department of Agriculture
Anderson Bldg.
Pierre, SD 57501

Tennessee
Division of Forestry
Department of Conservation
701 Broadway
Nashville, TN 37203

Texas
Forestry Service
Texas A&M University
302 Systems Administration Bldg.
College Station, TX 77843

Utah
State Lands and Forestry Division
Department of Natural Resources and
    Energy
3100 State Office Bldg.
Salt Lake City, UT 84114

Vermont
Forests, Parks and Recreation Department
Agency of Environmental Conservation
79 River St.
Montpelier, VT 05602

Virginia
Division of Forestry
Conservation and Historic Resources
Department
P.O. Box 3758
Charlottesville, VA 22903

Washington
Division of Forest Land Management
Department of Natural Resources
Mail Stop QW-21
Olympia, WA 98504

West Virginia
State Forester
Department of Natural Resources
1800 Washington St., E.
Bldg. 3, Rm. 729
Charleston, WV 25305

Wisconsin
Bureau of Forestry
Department of Natural Resources
P.O. Box 7921
Madison, WI 53707

Wyoming
Forestry Division
Public Lands Commission
1100 W. 22nd St.
Cheyenne, WY 82002

State Agricultural Experiment Stations

Mail all inquiries regarding land-related subjects such as soil conditions, water availability, and erosion problems to the local Agricultural Experiment Station listed below. Always request a list of available publications. The first line of each address is: State Agricultural Experiment Station.

Alabama
Auburn University
Auburn, AL 36849

Alaska
School of Agriculture and Land Resources
Management
University of Alaska
Fairbanks, AK 99701

Arizona
University of Arizona
Tucson, AZ 85721

Arkansas
University of Arkansas
Fayetteville, AR 72701

California
University of California at Berkeley
2120 University Ave., 7th Fl.
Berkeley, CA 94720

University of California at Davis
College of Agriculture and Environmental
Sciences
Davis, CA 95615

Citrus Research Center
College of Natural and Agricultural
Sciences
University of California
Riverside, CA 92521

Colorado
Colorado State University
Fort Collins, CO 80523

Connecticut
P.O. Box 1106
New Haven, CT 06504

University of Connecticut
Storrs, CT 06268

Delaware
University of Delaware
Newark, DE 19711

District of Columbia
University of the District of Columbia
4200 Connecticut Ave., N.W.
Washington, DC 20008

Florida
Institute of Food and Agricultural Sciences
University of Florida
1022 McCarty Hall
Gainesville, FL 32611

Georgia
University of Georgia
Athens, GA 30602

Georgia Station
Experiment, GA 30212

Coastal Plain Station
P.O. Box 748
Tifton, GA 31793

Hawaii
College of Tropical Agriculture and Human
Resources
University of Hawaii at Manoa
3050 Maili Wy., Rm. 202
Honolulu, HI 96822

Idaho
University of Idaho
Moscow, ID 83843

Illinois
University of Illinois
211 Mumford Hall
1001 W. Gregory Dr.
Urbana, IL 61801

Indiana
Purdue University
West Lafayette, IN 47907

Iowa
Iowa State University
Ames, IA 50011

Kansas
Kansas State University
113 Waters Hall
Manhattan, KS 66506

Kentucky
University of Kentucky
Lexington, KY 40506

Louisiana
Louisiana State University and A&M
College
University Station, Drawer E
Baton Rouge, LA 70893–0905

Maine
University of Maine
Orono, ME 04469

Maryland
University of Maryland
College Park, MD 20742

Massachusetts
University of Massachusetts
Amherst, MA 01003

Michigan
Michigan State University
East Lansing, MI 48824

Minnesota
University of Minnesota
St. Paul, MN 55108

Mississippi
Mississippi State University
P.O. Drawer ES
Mississippi State, MS 39762

Missouri
University of Missouri
Columbia, MO 65211

Montana
Montana State University
Bozeman, MT 59715-0002

Nebraska
University of Nebraska
109 Ag Hall
Lincoln, NB 65883

Nevada
University of Nevada
Reno, NV 89557

New Hampshire
University of New Hampshire
Durham, NH 03824

New Jersey
Rutgers University
P.O. Box 231
New Brunswick, NJ 08903

New Mexico
New Mexico State University
P.O. Box 3BF
Las Cruces, NM 88003

New York
Cornell University
292 Roberts Hall
Ithaca, NY 14853

State Station
Geneva, NY 14456

North Carolina
North Carolina Agricultural Research
Service
North Carolina State University
Box 7601
Raleigh, NC 27695-7601

North Dakota
North Dakota State University
State University Station
Box 5345
Fargo, ND 58105

Ohio
Ohio Agricultural Research and
Development Center
Ohio State University
Columbus, OH 43210

Ohio Agricultural Research and
Development Center
Ohio State University
Wooster, OH 44691

Oklahoma
Oklahoma State University
Stillwater, OK 74078

Oregon
Oregon State University
Corvallis, OR 97331

Pennsylvania
Pennsylvania State University
229 Agricultural Administration Bldg.
University Park, PA 16802

Rhode Island
University of Rhode Island
Kingston, RI 02881

South Carolina
Clemson University
Clemson, SC 29634-0351

South Dakota
South Dakota State University
Brookings, SD 57006

Tennessee
University of Tennessee
P.O. Box 1071
Knoxville, TN 37901

Texas
Texas A&M University System
College Station, TX 77843

Utah
Utah State University
Logan, UT 84322

Vermont
College of Agriculture and Life Sciences
University of Vermont
Morrill Hall
Burlington, VT 05405

Virginia
College of Agriculture and Life Sciences
Virginia Polytechnic Institute State
University
Hutcheson Hall
Blacksburg, VA 24061

Washington
Agricultural Research Center
Washington State University
Pullman, WA 99164

West Virginia
West Virginia University
Morgantown, WV 53706

Wyoming
University of Wyoming
University State, Box 3354
Laramie, WY 82071

Soil Conservation Service (under the U.S. Department of Agriculture)

This federal agency works with local soil and water conservation districts. Most rural areas contain one or more conservation districts and a local Soil Conservation Service. They have maps and conduct on-site inspections and evaluations of soil quality and water resources. To locate your local office look in the telephone book under U.S. Government, subheading U.S. Dept. of Agriculture, Soil Conservation District, or ask the local farm advisor.

You should request a list of published soil maps and surveys and other information for your state from the main office:

Soil Conservation Service
U.S. Department of Agriculture
Washington, DC 20250

Agricultural Stabilization and Conservation Service (ASCS)

This federal agency is under the U.S. Department of Agriculture. To locate the local office in your area write:

Agricultural Stabilization and Conservation
   Service
2222 W. 2300, S.
P.O. Box 3000
Salt Lake City, UT 84130-0010

State Soil Conservation Offices

The following state agencies coordinate programs
to conserve and protect the state's soil.

Alabama
   Soil and Water Conservation Committee
   1445 Federal Dr.
   P.O. Box 3336
   Montgomery, AL 36193

Alaska
   Division of Agriculture
   Department of Natural Resources
   P.O. Box 949
   Palmer, AK 99645-0949

Arkansas
   Soil and Water Conservation Commission
   1 Capitol Mall, Ste. 2-D
   Little Rock, AR 72201

California
   Land Resource Protection Division
   Department of Conservation
   1416 Ninth St.
   Sacramento, CA 95814

Colorado
   Soil Conservation Board
   Department of Natural Resources
   1313 Sherman St., Rm. 814
   Denver, CO 80203

Connecticut
   Environmental Protection Department
   165 Capitol Ave.
   Hartford, CT 06106

Delaware
   Soil and Water Conservation Division
   Natural Resources and Environmental
      Control Department
   89 Kings Hwy., Box 1401
   Dover, DE 19903

District of Columbia
   Housing and Environmental Regulation
      Administration
   Department of Consumer and Regulatory
      Affairs
   614 H St., N.W.
   Washington, DC 20001

Florida
   Soil and Water Conservation
   Agriculture and Consumer Services
      Department
   P.O. Box 1269
   Gainesville, FL 32602

Georgia
   Soil and Water Conservation Committee
   P.O. Box 8024
   Athens, GA 30603

Hawaii
   Board of Land and Natural Resources
   1151 Punchbowl St.
   Honolulu, HI 96813

Idaho
   Soil Conservation Committee
   Department of Lands
   801 Capitol Blvd.
   Boise, ID 83720

Illinois
   Dept. of Agriculture
   State Fairgrounds
   Springfield, IL 62706

Indiana
   Soil and Water Conservation
   AGAD Bldg., Rm. 7
   West Lafayette, IN 47907

Iowa
   Soil Conservation Department
   Wallace State Office Bldg.
   Des Moines, IA 50319

Kansas
   Conservation Committee
   217 S.E. Fourth St., 4th Fl.
   Topeka, KS 66603

Kentucky
Division of Conservation
Natural Resources and Environmental
    Protection Cabinet
605 Teton Terr.
Frankfort, KY 40601

Louisiana
Office of Forestry
Department of Natural Resources
P.O. Box 1628
Baton Rouge, LA 70821

Maine
Soil and Water Conservation Committee
Agriculture, Food and Rural Resources
    Department
State House Station, #28
Augusta, ME 04333

Maryland
Soil Conservation Committee
Department of Agriculture
50 Harry S. Truman Pkwy.
Annapolis, MD 21401

Massachusetts
Division of Conservation Services
Executive Office of Environmental Affairs
100 Cambridge St.
Boston, MA 02202

Michigan
Soil Conservation Division
Department of Agriculture
Basement, Lewis Cass Bldg.
Lansing, MI 48909

Minnesota
Soil and Water Conservation Board
Department of Agriculture
90 W. Plato Blvd.
St. Paul, MN 55107

Mississippi
Soil and Water Conservation Committee
410 Robert E. Lee Bldg.
Jackson, MS 39201

Missouri
Soil and Water Conservation Program
Division of Environmental Quality
Department of Natural Resources
P.O. Box 1368
Jefferson City, MO 65102

Montana
Conservation Districts Division
Natural Resources and Conservation
    Department
25 S. Ewing
Helena, MT 59620

Nebraska
Natural Resources Committee
301 Centennial Mall, S.
P.O. Box 94876
Lincoln, NB 68509-4876

Nevada
Soil Conservation Districts
Conservation and Natural Resources
    Department
201 S. Fall St.
Carson City, NV 89710

New Hampshire
State Conservation Committee
Sambornton, NH 03269

New Jersey
Soil Conservation Committee
Department of Agriculture, CN-330
Trenton, NJ 08625

New Mexico
Soil and Water Conservation Division
Department of Natural Resources
Villagra Bldg.
Santa Fe, NM 87503

New York
Department of Environmental Conservation
50 Wolf Rd.
Albany, NY 12233

North Carolina
Soil and Water Conservation
Natural Resources and Community
    Development Department
512 N. Salisbury St.
Raleigh, NC 27611

North Dakota
Soil Conservation Committee
Capitol Grounds, Highway Bldg.
Bismark, ND 58505

Ohio
Soil and Water Conservation Division
Department of Natural Resources
Fountain Square
Columbus, OH 43224

Oklahoma
Conservation Committee
20 State Capitol
Oklahoma City, OK 73105

Oregon
Soil and Water Conservation Committee
Department of Agriculture
635 Capitol St., N.E.
Salem, OR 97310

Pennsylvania
Soil and Water Conservation Bureau
Environmental Resources Department
P.O. Box 2357
Harrisburg, PA 17120

Rhode Island
Division of Agriculture and Marketing
Department of Environmental Management
22 Hayes St.
Providence, RI 02908

South Carolina
Land Resources Conservation Committee
2221 Devine St., #222
Columbia, SC 29205

South Dakota
Division of Conservation
Department of Agriculture
Anderson Bldg., Rm. 304
Pierre, SD 57501

Tennessee
Department of Agriculture
Ellington Agricultural Center
Nashville, TN 37204

Texas
Soil and Water Conservation Board
1002 First National Bank Bldg.
Temple, TX 76501

Utah
Division of Agricultural Development
Department of Agriculture
147 N. 200, W.
Salt Lake City, UT 84103

Vermont
Department of Water Resources
Environmental Engineering
Heritage II, 79 River St.
Montpelier, VT 05602

Virginia
Department of Conservation and Historic
Resources
1101 Washington Bldg.
Richmond, VA 23219

Washington
Conservation Committee
Mail Stop PV-11
Olympia, WA 98504

West Virginia
Soil Conservation Committee
Department of Agriculture
State Capitol Complex
Charleston, WV 25305

Wisconsin
Bureau of Land Resources
Agriculture, Trade and Consumer Protection
Department
P.O. Box 8911
Madison, WI 53708

Wyoming
Conservation Committee
Department of Agriculture
2219 Carey Ave.
Cheyenne, WY 82002

State Department of Agriculture

The following state agencies enforce agricultural laws and administer agricultural programs in each state.

Alabama
Agriculture and Industries Department
1445 Federal Dr.
P.O. Box 3336
Montgomery, AL 36193

Alaska
Division of Agriculture
Department of Natural Resources
P.O. Box 949
Palmer, AK 99645-0949

Arizona
Agriculture and Horticulture Committee
1688 W. Adams St., Rm. 421
Phoenix, AZ 85007

Arkansas
Livestock and Poultry Commission
1 Natural Resources Dr.
P.O. Box 5497
Little Rock, AR 72215
    or
Plant Board
1 Natural Resources Dr.
Little Rock, AR 72205
    or
Marketing Division
Industrial Development Commission
1 Capitol Mall, Rm. 4-C-300
Little Rock, AR 72201

California
Department of Food and Agriculture
1220 N St.
Sacramento, CA 95814

Colorado
Department of Agriculture
State Service Bldg., 4th Fl.
1525 Sherman St.
Denver, CO 80203

Connecticut
Department of Agriculture
165 Capitol Ave., Rm. 273
Hartford, CT 06106

Delaware
Department of Agriculture
P.O. Drawer D
Dover, DE 19903

Florida
Department of Agriculture and Consumer
    Services
The Capitol
Tallahassee, FL 32301

Georgia
Department of Agriculture
Capitol Square, Rm. 204
Atlanta, GA 30334

Hawaii
Department of Agriculture
1428 S. King St.
Honolulu, HI 96814

Idaho
Department of Agriculture
120 Klotz Ln.
P.O. Box 790
Boise, ID 83701

Illinois
Department of Agriculture
State Fairgrounds
Springfield, IL 62706

Indiana
Agriculture Division
Department of Commerce
1 N. Capitol
Indianapolis, IN 46204

Iowa
Department of Agriculture
Wallace State Office Bldg.
Des Moines, IA 50319

Kansas
State Board of Agriculture
901 Kansas Ave.
Topeka, KS 66612

Kentucky
Department of Agriculture
Capital Plaza Tower
Frankfort, KY 40601

Louisiana
Department of Agriculture
P.O. Box 94302
Baton Rouge, LA 70804-9302

Maine
Department of Agriculture, Food and Rural
    Resources
State House Station, #28
Augusta, ME 04333

Maryland
Department of Agriculture
50 Harry S. Truman Pkwy.
Annapolis, MD 21401

Massachusetts
Department of Food and Agriculture
Executive Office of Environmental Affairs
100 Cambridge St.
Boston, MA 02202

Michigan
Department of Agriculture
Lewis Cass Bldg.
Lansing, MI 48909

Minnesota
Department of Agriculture
90 W. Plato Blvd.
St. Paul, MN 55107

Mississippi
Department of Agriculture and Commerce
1601 Sillers Bldg.
Jackson, MS 39201

Missouri
Department of Agriculture
1616 Missouri Blvd.
P.O. Box 630
Jefferson City, MO 65102

Montana
Department of Agriculture
303 N. Roberts
Helena, MT 59620

Nebraska
Department of Agriculture
301 Centennial Mall, S.
P.O. Box 94947
Lincoln, NE 68509-4947

Nevada
Department of Agriculture
P.O. Box 11100
Reno, NV 89510

New Hampshire
Department of Agriculture
Prescott Park, Bldg. #1
105 Loudon Rd.
Concord, NH 03301

New Jersey
Department of Agriculture
John Fitch Plaza, CN-330
Trenton, NJ 08625

New Mexico
Department of Agriculture
New Mexico State University
P.O. Box 3189
Las Cruces, NM 88003

New York
Department of Agriculture and Markets
Campus, Bldg. #8
Albany, NY 12235

North Carolina
Department of Agriculture
1 W. Edenton St.
Raleigh, NC 27611

North Dakota
Department of Agriculture
State Capitol, 6th Fl.
Bismarck, ND 58505

Ohio
Department of Agriculture
65 S. Front St., 6th Fl.
Columbus, OH 43215

Oklahoma
Department of Agriculture
2800 N. Lincoln Blvd.
Oklahoma City, OK 73105

Oregon
Department of Agriculture
635 Capitol St., N.E.
Salem, OR 97310

Pennsylvania
Department of Agriculture
2301 N. Cameron St.
Harrisburg, PA 17110

Rhode Island
Division of Agriculture and Marketing
Department of Environmental Management
22 Hayes St.
Providence, RI 02908

South Carolina
Department of Agriculture
P.O. Box 11280
Columbia, SC 29211

South Dakota
Department of Agriculture
Anderson Bldg.
Pierre, SD 57501

Tennessee
   Department of Agriculture
   Ellington Agricultural Center
   Nashville, TN 37204

Texas
   Department of Agriculture
   Capitol Station, Box 12847
   Austin, TX 78711

Utah
   Department of Agriculture
   147 N. 200, W.
   Salt Lake City, UT 84103

Vermont
   Department of Agriculture
   116 State St.
   Montpelier, VT 05602

Virginia
   Department of Agriculture and Consumer
      Services
   1100 Bank St.
   Richmond, VA 23219

Washington
   Department of Agriculture
   406 General Administration Bldg.
   Olympia, WA 98504

West Virginia
   Department of Agriculture
   State Capitol Complex
   Charleston, WV 25305

Wisconsin
   Department of Agriculture, Trade and
      Consumer Protection
   P.O. Box 8911
   Madison, WI 53708

Wyoming
   Department of Agriculture
   2219 Carey Ave.
   Cheyenne, WY 82001

Hazardous Waste Management

The following agencies develop and maintain hazardous waste management programs.

Alabama
   Hazardous Waste Branch
   Land Division
   Environmental Management Department
   1751 Federal Dr.
   Montgomery, AL 36130

Alaska
   Air and Hazardous Waste Management
      Section
   Environmental Conservation Department
   Pouch O
   Juneau, AK 99811

Arizona
   Office of Waste and Water Quality
      Management
   Department of Health Services
   2005 N. Central
   Phoenix, AZ 85004

Arkansas
   Department of Pollution Control and
      Ecology
   8001 National Dr.
   Little Rock, AR 72209

California
   Waste Management Board
   Environmental Affairs Agency
   1020 Ninth St., Ste. 300
   Sacramento, CA 95814

Connecticut
   Hazardous Waste Management
   Environmental Protection Department
   165 Capitol Ave.
   Hartford, CT 06106

District of Columbia
   Housing and Environmental Regulation
      Administration
   Department of Consumer and Regulatory
      Affairs
   614 H St., N.W.
   Washington, DC 20001

Florida
   Bureau of Groundwater Protection and
      Waste Management
   Environmental Regulation Department
   2600 Blairstone Rd.
   Tallahassee, FL 32301

Georgia
    Industrial and Hazardous Waste Program
    Environmental Protection Division
    Department of Natural Resources
    270 Washington St., S.W.
    Atlanta, GA 30334

Hawaii
    Environmental Protection and Health
        Services Division
    Department of Health
    1250 Punchbowl St.
    Honolulu, HI 96813

Idaho
    Bureau of Hazardous Materials
    Department of Health and Welfare
    450 W. State St.
    Boise, ID 83720

Illinois
    Hazardous Waste Management
    Energy and Natural Resources Department
    325 W. Adams
    Springfield, IL 62704

Indiana
    Hazardous Waste Management Branch
    State Board of Health
    1330 W. Michigan
    Indianapolis, IN 46206

Kentucky
    Natural Resources and Environmental
        Protection Cabinet
    Capital Plaza Tower
    Frankfort, KY 40601

Louisiana
    Hazardous Waste Division
    Department of Environmental Quality
    P.O. Box 44066
    Baton Rouge, LA 70804
        or
    Division of Inactive and Abandoned
        Hazardous Waste Sites
    Department of Environmental Quality
    P.O. Box 44066
    Baton Rouge, LA 70804

Maryland
    Waste Management Administration
    Health and Mental Hygiene Department
    201 W. Preston St., Rm. 212
    Baltimore, MD 21201

Michigan
    Hazardous Waste Division
    Department of Natural Resources
    608 W. Allegan, South Tower
    Lansing, MI 48909

Minnesota
    Waste Management Board
    7323 58th Ave., N.
    Crystal, MN 55428

Mississippi
    Nuclear Waste Division
    Energy and Transportation Department
    510 George St.
    Jackson, MS 39202

Missouri
    Solid Waste Program
    Division of Environmental Quality
    Department of Natural Resources
    P.O. Box 176
    Jefferson City, MO 65102

New Hampshire
    Bureau of Hazardous Waste Compliance
        and Enforcement
    Division of Public Health Services
    Department of Health and Welfare
    Hazen Dr.
    Concord, NH 03301

New Jersey
    Division of Waste Management
    Environmental Protection Department
    32 E. Hanover St., CN-028
    Trenton, NJ 08625

New Mexico
    Hazardous Waste Section
    Environmental Improvement Division
    Department of Health and Environment
    P.O. Box 968
    Santa Fe, NM 87504-0968

New York
    Department of Environmental Conservation
    50 Wolf Rd.
    Albany, NY 12233

North Carolina
Solid and Hazardous Waste Management
   Branch
Division of Health Services
Department of Human Resources
P.O. Box 2091
Raleigh, NC 27602-2091

North Dakota
Division of Hazardous Waste Management
   and Special Studies
Department of Health
1200 Missouri Ave.
Bismark, ND 58501

Ohio
Division of Hazardous Material
Environmental Protection Agency
361 E. Broad St.
Columbus, OH 43215

Oklahoma
Waste Management Service
Department of Health
1000 N.E. 10th St.
Box 53551
Oklahoma City, OK 73152

Oregon
Department of Environmental Quality
522 S.W. Fifth Ave.
P.O. Box 1760
Portland, OR 97207

Pennsylvania
Division of Hazardous Waste Management
Environmental Resources Department
Fulton Bldg., 7th Fl.
Harrisburg, PA 17120

Rhode Island
Air and Hazardous Materials Division
Department of Environmental Management
75 Davis St.
Providence, RI 02908

South Carolina
Solid and Hazardous Waste Management
   Bureau
Health and Environmental Control
2600 Bull St.
Columbia, SC 29201

South Dakota
Air Quality and Solid Waste
Water and Natural Resources Department
Foss Bldg.
Pierre, SD 57501

Tennessee
Solid Waste Management Division
Department of Health and Environment
Customs House, 4th Fl.
Nashville, TN 37203

Texas
Texas Water Commission
1700 N. Congress
Austin, TX 78711

Utah
Bureau of Hazardous Waste Management
Division of Environmental Health
Department of Health
150 W.N. Temple, Rm. 426
Salt Lake City, UT 84110-2500

Vermont
Department of Water Resources and
   Environmental Engineering
Agency of Environmental Conservation
Heritage II, 79 River St.
Montpelier, VT 05602

Virginia
Solid and Hazardous Waste Management
   Department
Department of Health
101 N. 14th St.
Richmond, VA 23219

Washington
Office of Hazardous Substance and Quality
   Control
Department of Ecology
Mail Stop PV-11
Olympia, WA 98504

West Virginia
Solid Waste and Hazardous Waste
Water Resources Division
Department of Natural Resources
1201 Greenbrier St.
Charleston, WV 25311

Wisconsin
Bureau of Solid Waste Management
Department of Natural Resources
P.O. Box 7921
Madison, WI 53707

Other Sources of Soil Information

LOCAL BOARD OF HEALTH OR COUNTY HEALTH DEPARTMENT

Will test the soil for its suitability for septic tanks or other types of sewage systems. Some land is unsuited for sewage systems because of the poor drainage, and the health department will not issue the necessary permits, so get the soil checked before you buy.

LOCAL BUILDING INSPECTOR

Has information on soil types, drainage, and erosion as they pertain to the suitability for construction of a dwelling. Get the inspector to look at your land before you buy and tell you if you will be able to get a permit for your intended construction.

LOCAL UNIVERSITIES AND COLLEGES

Various departments study local soil and vegetation conditions. Check for information at such departments as forestry, soils, plant nutrition, geology, and mining.

STATE MINERAL AGENCIES

Every state has its agency in charge of mineral and geology studies within the state. For example, South Dakota has a state geological survey, Oregon has a Department of Geology and Mineral Industries, California has a Division of Mines and Geology, and Texas has a Bureau of Economic Geology. You can get the address of your state mineral agency from your local farm advisor, your nearest USGS office, or the Research Centers Directory.

RESEARCH CENTERS DIRECTORY

The reference section of most libraries will have a publication entitled Research Centers Directory, edited by Archie M. Palmer and published by the Gale Research Company. This book lists every agency involved in agricultural research and services in each state. By looking under your state in the Research Centers Directory you can find all the available sources of information and assistance in the evaluation of the land you are investigating.

Books and Pamphlets

The following are available from the:
Superintendent of Documents
Government Printing Office
Washington, DC 20402

Septic Systems and Ground-Water Protection Executive's Guide S/N 055-000-00257-6	$1.00
Utilization of Sewage Sludge Compost as a Soil and Fertilizer for Plant Growth S/N 001-000-04423-1	$2.25
Invite Birds to Your Home: Conservation Planning for the Northwest S/N 011-000-03307-7	$1.00
Assessing Erosion on U.S. Cropland S/N 001-019-00341-3	$1.50
America's Soil and Water: Conditions and Trends S/N 001-000-04313-7	$3.75
Wood as a Fuel S/N 001-000-04299-8	$2.25
Usual Planting & Harvesting Dates for United States Field Crops S/N 001-000-04416-8	$3.00
Drainage around Your Home S/N 001-000-03455-3	$1.00
Foresters Guide to Aerial Photo Interpretation S/N 001-000-03914-8	$5.00
Methods of Preventing Failure of Septic Tank	$ .25
Soils and Septic Tanks S/N 001-000-01023-9	$1.00
Making Land Produce Useful Wildlife S/N 001-000-00021-7	$1.00
Erosion and Sediment	$ .35
Manual of Septic Tank Practice (excellent)	$1.05
Insect Control in Farms—Stored Grain S/N 001-000-04088-0	$2.00
Field Crop Pests: Farmers Report the Severity and Intensity S/N 001-019-00377-4	$2.25

The following are free from:
Soil Conservation Service
U.S. Department of Agriculture
Washington, DC 20250

Soil Erosion—the Work of Uncontrolled
Water
Windbreaks for Conservation
Controlled Erosion on Construction Sites
Conservation Irrigation in Humid Areas
Environmental Do's & Don'ts on
Construction Sites
Farmers & Ranchers: Soil Surveys Can
Help You
Homebuyers: Soil Surveys Can Help You
Appraising Farmland: Soil Surveys Can
Help You
Soil Surveys Can Help You
Assistance Available from Soil Conservation
Service
List of Published Soil Surveys
Where to Get Information about Soil &
Water Conservation
Soil and Septic Tanks

The following are available for the specified price
from:

ANR Publications
University of California
6701 San Pablo Ave.
Oakland, CA 94608-1239

Forest Grazing Management		
in California	#21388	$1.00
Management of Small		
Pastures	#2906	$1.00
Guidelines for Managing		
California's Hardwood		
Rangelands	#21413	$5.00
Planning for Your Mountain		
Property	#21360	$1.00
What on Earth Is Soil?	#2637	$1.75
Generalized Soil Map of		
California	#4028	$2.00
Erosion Control on Bare		
Slopes around Your Home	#21137	$1.00
Soil and Water Management		
for Home Gardeners	#2258	$1.00
Applying Nutrients and Other		
Chemicals to Trickle-		
irrigated Crops	#1893	$1.75
Soil Physical Environment and		
How It Affects Plant		
Growth	#2280	$1.25
Compaction of Soil by		
Agricultural Equipment	#1881	free
Diagnosing Soil Physical		
Problems	#2664	$1.00

A Grower's Guide to Solving		
Salt Problems	#21350	$1.00
Gypsum and Other Chemical		
Amendments for Soil		
Improvements	#2149	$1.00
Managing Compacted and		
Layered Soils	#2635	$1.00
Forest Management		
Information Services: A		
Guide for California Forest		
Landowners	#21443	$1.25
Planting California Forest		
Land	#2925	$3.50
Developing Livestock Leases		
for Annual Grasslands	#21424	$1.00

The following pamphlet is available free from:
The National Water Well Association
500 W. Wilson Bridge Rd.
Worthington, OH 43085

Everything You Wanted to Know About
Septic Tanks . . . But Didn't Know Who
to Ask.

The following are available for the specified cost
from:
LICA (Land Improvement Contractors of
America) Library
P.O. Box 9
Maywood, IL 60153

Why LICA	free
What Is Land Improvement	free
Plant Materials	$ .65
Clearing of Land for Development	$ .50
The Corn Is Always Greener	free
Handbook of Earthmoving	$ .50
Soils and Septic Tanks	$ .50
Is Our Top Soil Being Railroaded?	$ .15
Install That Tile System	free
Facts and Septic Tanks	free

The following are free from:
In-Sink-Erator Division
Emerson Electric Co.
4700 21st St.
Racine, WI 53406

How a Septic Tank Works
The Effect of Garbage Disposers on the
Environment

The following book is available for the specified price from:

Whole Earth Access
2990 Seventh St.
Berkeley, CA 94710

Septic Tank Practices by Peter
Warshall   (postpaid) $6.95

The following is available for the specified cost from:

Canadian Mortgage and Housing
   Corporation
650 Lawrence Ave., W.
Toronto, Ontario, Canada M6A 1B2

CMHC Septic Tank Standards $3.00

For more information regarding minerals, see chapter 11, "Mineral Rights," and the Useful Resources at the end of that chapter.

For information on alternative energy resources, see appendix J, "Alternative Energy Resources," at the end of the book.

Recent Earthquake Data—National Earthquake Information Service (NEIS)

The National Earthquake Information Service computes and publishes epicenter locations for earthquakes worldwide and provides general information pertaining to the geographic location, magnitude, and intensity of recent earthquakes.

National Earthquake Information Service
U.S. Geological Survey
Mail Stop 967
Federal Center, Box 25046
Denver, CO 80225

CHAPTER 6

Evaluating the House, a Manufactured Home, and Other Structures

But what of the man who hears these words of mine and does not act upon them? He is like a man who was foolish enough to build his house on sand. The rain came down, the floods rose, the wind blew, and beat upon that house; down it fell with a great crash.

—The Gospel of Saint Matthew 7:26–27

Whether you want to find land with a house already on it or to build your own house is a basic decision. An existing house adds a considerable amount to the price of land. If you are willing to put in the necessary labor, building your own can be fairly cheap, and you can realize your dream house. Even if you hire a professional builder, you might save money in the long run buying undeveloped land and building the kind of house you want.

However, if you find a good piece of land with a house on it that is within your price range, you must be able to inspect the house to be sure it is soundly built and will be safe and comfortable to live in. If you want to refurbish an older house, you must determine how much work will have to be done and how much it will cost; the house might be too dilapidated to bring up to current building code standards. Faults in the structure that you find during your inspection can be used later in bargaining to get the purchase price down. (See chapter 19, ''Evaluating the Price of the Property,'' and chapter 20, ''Bargaining to Get the Seller's Asking Price Down.'')

This chapter will take you through every part of the house and tell you what to look for. Each item is listed to make it easier to refer to. Take this book with you on your inspection, along with a pencil, pad, flashlight, pocketknife, and some old clothes. Look at the house several times under good and bad weather conditions, in the daytime and at night, and you will have a good idea of how livable it will be for your family.

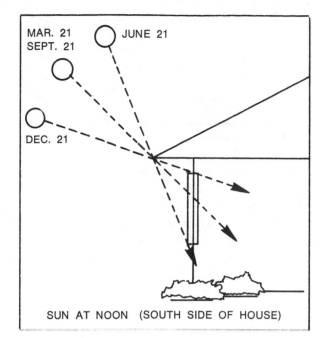

34. Exposure of the House to Summer and Winter Sun

THE NEIGHBORHOOD

If the property is in a populated area, the first thing you will notice is how the house looks in comparison to other houses in the neighborhood. If it looks shabbier than surrounding homes, the price might reflect the value of the community while the actual worth of the house may be much less.

PLACEMENT OF THE HOUSE

Before examining the structure itself, study the placement of the house in relation to both the surrounding area and the environment as a whole.

Is the house placed so you have the privacy you desire? Can you see other houses, and can you be seen by neighbors and passersby? If so, is the situation disagreeable to you and can it be easily remedied by constructing a fence or planting shrubs and trees?

What kind of view is there from the most frequently used rooms in the house? Is the view appealing to you? A good view increases the price of a house, but it makes life much more enjoyable.

Is the house placed so it receives the maximum amount of winter sun? The south side of the house should have the most windows and be where the most frequently used rooms are located. It should also have an overhanging roof or some other means of shading the inside of the house from direct sunlight in the summer. (See illustration 34.)

Does the vegetation around the house allow enough sunlight in, or is the house usually dark and damp? Many homes in the woods have a serious dampness problem because they are too well shaded by large trees. Some types of forests, such as redwood forests, are much damper than others. If you see the structure in the dry season, imagine what the conditions are like in the winter.

Is the house conveniently situated in relation to the rest of the property? For example, are the gardening and recreational areas near the dwelling? Are the outbuildings and other structures, such as the pumphouse, storage tank, and generator, nearby? Climbing up a steep and distant hill to fix the water pump in a pouring rain or snowstorm can be miserable.

Many of the above factors are given little consideration by builders despite their importance.

BLUEPRINTS AND ORIGINAL BUILDING CONTRACT

—Find out if the original blueprints of the house and other specifications are available for inspection.

—If the house was built by a contractor or someone hired to do the job, ask the seller if he has the original contract, which might have warranties in

103

it that guarantee against any defects in construction, including labor and materials.

FOUNDATION

The foundation is the supporting structure of the house. The house might be built on poles, on posts and concrete, on a concrete stone or brick perimeter foundation or concrete slab, or on a basement of stone, brick, or concrete.

Pole construction is used primarily where the building site is not level. Huge poles are sunk deep into the ground, and the house is built around them up in the air.

—If the poles are wooden, at least the buried part should be chemically treated to prevent them from rotting.

—Have they been treated against wood rot and termites? If so, when and by whom? Talk to the termite service that did the job, and ask them what they know about the house.

—Has there been a chemical coating applied to prevent dampness? If so, how long ago was this done? Are there any cracks in the dampproof coating? Does water ever stand under the house?

—If the house has a stone or brick foundation or is supported on masonry piers, check for cracks and crumbling mortar. Minor cracks can usually be repaired. More extensive deterioration may indicate that major repair or replacement will be necessary. If the house is built on posts sunk in concrete, the concrete might just be under each post or it might be under the entire perimeter of the house.

—Examine the concrete, either from the basement or from the crawl space, with your flashlight to see if there are any cracks. Minor cracks can usually be repaired. Large open cracks may get progressively worse and usually indicate a major problem.

—The concrete should show above the posts and not be completely buried under the earth, since the concrete protects the wood from rotting.

—Is the foundation sinking into the ground? Do all doors swing easily? Badly fitting doors are one of the first indications of sinking because the doorways are no longer square.

—Do the floor joists, or supports, sag?

—Have the posts separated from the floor at any point?

—Are there any irregularities in the foundation that you can see?

—Check for wood rot, termites, tunnels, and other indications of pests such as holes with fine sawdust under them. Has the foundation ever been chemically treated against termites? When and by whom? Talk to the termite service that did the job and ask them what they know about the house.

—Has a chemical coating been applied to the foundation to prevent dampness and water from getting beneath the house? When was it applied? Are there any cracks in the dampproof coating?

If the entire house is set on a concrete slab, examine it at all visible points. This kind of construction is often difficult to inspect.

—Does the slab appear to be tilting or sinking into the ground at any point?

—Has the floor become separated from the slab at any point?

—Can you see any large cracks in the cement? Hairline cracks are usually not important.

—Check for termites and wood rot. Take a screwdriver or some sharp tool and probe the wood. Does the tool enter easily, and does the wood break across the grain with little splintering?

—Slab construction offers greater protection to termites once they have invaded the wood. Is there any termite shielding around the house? Has the concrete been chemically treated? When and by whom? Talk to the termite service that did the job for information about the condition of the house.

CRAWL SPACE

The crawl space is the area under a house between the ground and the bottom of the house. Crawl space houses usually have a foundation wall or piers supporting the floor joists. Check for cracks and settlement of these supports.

If the house has foundation walls of poured concrete, minor hairline cracks have little effect on the structure. Open cracks indicate a failure that may get worse. It is difficult to tell without observing it over several months.

If the house is supported on wood posts and piers, check to be sure the wood posts are properly preserved and up off the ground on metal pedestals on adequate concrete supports. Wood should not be directly on or into the concrete as it absorbs moisture and rots at the contact point. Inspect posts for decay and insect damage. The bottom of the house must be a minimum of 18 inches from the ground. Walk around the house looking for vent openings into the crawl space. If none or an insufficient number exist, there will be excessive moisture from condensation under the house. This deteriorates the floors, foundation, and other parts of the structure and promotes wood rot. Vents are also necessary for safety if heating units are located within the crawl space and if gas and sewer lines run under the house.

You have to crawl into this space to see the foundation and the underside of the floor. (This is why you should wear old clothes.) Find the opening, take your flashlight, and crawl in.

—Has ground-cover paper or roofing paper been laid over the surface of the ground under the crawl space? This helps ventilation and insulation. What kind of condition is it in? Where this paper is used, vents are usually smaller. If the paper has deteriorated, the vents might be too small to prevent excessive moisture from forming.

—Is the heating unit located under the house? If so, inspect it as outlined below in "Heating System."

—Look at all visible pipes. Any leaks or corrosion?

—Look at the wiring. Do you see any loose, frayed, or broken wires?

—Inspect the foundation in the manner specified above.

THE BASEMENT

Many rural homes have a basement or cellar. It serves as an insulator for the house, and it may be used as a workroom, storage area, food and wine cellar, or recreation room. The most severe problems in basements are flooding and dampness. All basements are vulnerable to water at one time or another.

—A sump pump is turned on automatically or manually to pump water from a flooded basement. If you see one in the house, you know there are problems. Ask the owner why it is there, how often it is used, and why the basement floods. The prob-

lem might be corrected by placing drainage pipes or ditches around the house. It is more severe if the slope of the land itself is at fault. Talk to the building inspector about the problem and get an estimate of what has to be done to correct the problem.

—Other evidence of dampness are water stains on the walls and floors. Are there drainage holes in the floor? Are there signs of mud anywhere? Use your flashlight to inspect the basement carefully. Look for signs of water penetration such as rust at the base of the heater or steel posts, stains, discoloration or decay on wood partitions, wood posts, damaged floor tiles or mildewed carpeting, a white salt buildup (efflorescence) on foundation walls, stains or mildew on objects stored on the floor.

—If there is a drain, the floor should slope toward it.

—Even if the basement doesn't flood, it might have poor ventilation. Condensation causes moisture to form on basement walls unless there are open windows or vents where the weather is cool and dry. Are there sufficient vents or windows? Damp spots on walls or the floor could be due to condensation rather than water leaking in from outside.

—Are the basement walls and floor cement, wood, or dirt? A cement basement floor is the best kind. Do you see cracks in the walls or floor? Cracks cause water leaks and indicate structural defects. Has any kind of waterproofing been used on the walls and floors?

—If the basement is damp, it might require the installation of a dehumidifier. Is there one already installed? How old is it and what is its service history?

—In the basement you can inspect the foundation and look for evidence of termite infestation and wood rot.

Damp or leaky basement walls may require major repair. Possible causes of the dampness are clogged or broken downspouts, clogged drain tile, cracks in the walls, lack of slope of the finished grade away from the house foundation, or a high water table. Check for dampness by examining the basement a few hours after a heavy rain. Most of these problems can be remedied. However, a high water table is more serious and very difficult to remedy.

There are no miracle cures for a wet basement, so be very cautious if you see evidence of flooding.

TERMITES AND OTHER DESTRUCTIVE INSECTS

Regardless of the age of the house or the type of construction used, it can be infested by termites and other damaging insects. The most common and serious troublemaker is the subterranean termite. A heavily infested house can have 250,000 termites constantly eating away at it. Even if the seller has had the house fumigated recently, termites can return within a short time. The problem may be so serious that further fumigation is worthless. Although termites are found throughout the United States, they are particularly numerous in the South Atlantic and Gulf Coast states and California. (See illustration 35.) Termites inhabit over 200 million homes and cause $500 million damage a year.

Termites need two things to survive: wood and water. A termite will die in twenty-four hours if deprived of moisture. Good ventilation and dry ground under the house are essential in preventing termites. In heavily infested areas, a chemical bar-rier in the ground around the home is necessary.

There are several ways to detect termites:

The first is the presence of *termite highways*. Termites live in underground nests and burrow into the foundation and the rest of the structure. You can see paths along the foundation where they burrow up the wood. Look for veins or streaks along the wood.

The second is the *termite tube* or *tunnel*. These flattened tubes are made of mud suspended directly from underneath the floor to the earth. The termites travel through these tunnels to get from their nests in the moist ground to the wood. You will see these tubes in crawl spaces and basements. They are also built up the sides of the foundation, the walls, the water and drain pipes, and the chimney.

The third way to find termites is with a knife or screwdriver. Usually termite activity occurs inside wood that looks fine from the outside. Take your tool and make jabs at different parts of the house. If the wood is soft, you have termites or wood rot.

During your inspection, look for termites and discarded termite wings around anything that

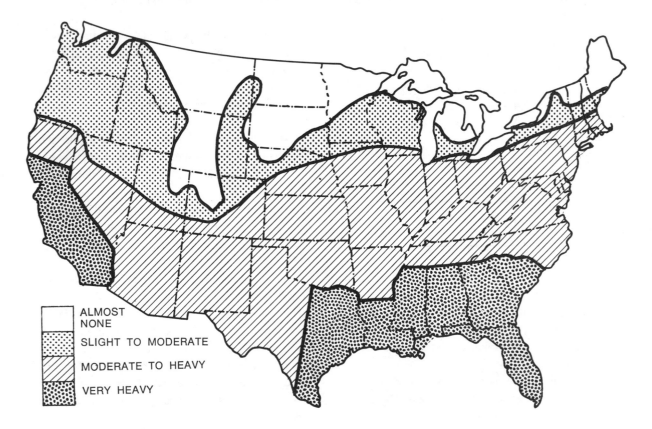

ALMOST NONE

SLIGHT TO MODERATE

MODERATE TO HEAVY

VERY HEAVY

35. Termite Incidence

touches, or is near, the ground, including the foundation, basement walls, floor joists, the underside of the floor, house beams and posts, window frames, porches, drain and water pipes, along chimneys, on the attic walls, roof beams, and the underside of the roof.

There are other insects that can seriously damage a building. Some of these include powder-post beetles, which occur throughout the United States; house borers, found in the eastern United States from Florida through Massachusetts; carpenter ants and bees; and two other types of termites. Your county building inspector can give you information on local pest problems and how to examine a structure for pest damage.

WOOD ROT (DRY ROT)

Wood rot is more damaging than termites. It is a major problem in the North. (See illustration 36.)

When wood becomes wet, either from direct contact with water or by condensation, a fungus grows, causing the wood to decay. These organisms cannot colonize or decay wood that has a moisture content of less than about 30 percent. A properly constructed and maintained home has a moisture content of under 15 percent. When this fungus occurs, the wood takes on the appearance of being dried out. This is why wet wood is often called "dry rot." Once wood rot sets in, the entire structure can become dangerously weakened, and the value of the house is greatly diminished. To prevent dry rot, the house must be dry and well insulated. Wood rot commonly occurs in attics, basements, crawl spaces, and under porches. As you inspect the house, maintain constant vigilance for wood rot. Use your flashlight to inspect every dark corner.

—When you see an area that looks rotten, take your pocketknife or screwdriver and scratch the wood. How easily does it break down? Stick the tool into the wood. If it sinks in easily, the condition is severe and probably too costly to repair.

SHADING INDICATES WHERE WOOD ROT IS A PROBLEM

36. Wood Rot Incidence

FLOOR SUPPORTS

Check the floor supports in the ceiling of the basement, or if there is no basement, from the crawl space under the house. Wood posts should not be embedded in a concrete floor. Examine the base of wood posts for decay even if they are set above the concrete.

Check wood girders for sag and also for decay at the exterior wall bearings. A small sag is not usually a problem unless parts of the house have obviously distorted.

Check the sill plates or joists and headers that rest on top of the concrete foundation. They are exposed to moisture and are subject to decay or insect attack.

Check at the framing of floor joists around stair openings. Some builders estimate that 50 percent of the houses built have inadequate framing around stairs. If floors are sagging you may have to relevel and reinforce them.

FLOORS

—Do the floors slope? A tilting floor indicates serious foundation problems.

—Loose and noisy floorboards also indicate foundation problems. Walk over the floor slowly to feel if there is any sagging or give.

—Are the wooden floors nicely sanded and finished?

—Look where the floors meet the walls. Are the joints tight, with no evidence of warping?

—If the floor is concrete covered with asphalt tile or wood flooring, are there any cracks in the covering?

—If the kitchen and bathroom floors are covered with linoleum or tile, look for cracks and chipped areas where water has entered and rotted the floor underneath. Is the tile or linoleum well laid and properly fitted around fixtures and along the walls? Has any of the covering come loose from the floor?

INTERIOR WALLS

Dry walls are wood, fiberboard, sheetrock, or gypsum wallboard nailed or taped onto the frame. Plastered walls are lath and plaster. Both types of walls might be painted or papered.

—Do the walls bulge or buckle?

—Is the plaster or paint cracking, or the paper peeling? Moisture, vapor, and condensation could cause these things to happen.

—Is a new paint job or wallpapering needed?

—Have the walls recently been painted or papered? If so, a defect may be hidden. Feel the walls and examine them closely. Wallpaper placed over the old covering might later peel.

—If you don't like the wall colors, you will have to figure in the cost of repainting or repapering.

—If there are water stains on the walls, the plumbing is deteriorating or the roof leaks.

CEILINGS

—Water stains on the ceiling also indicate a leaky roof or bad plumbing.

—Look for recent plastering, taping, or painting as a warning that the roof leaks or the ceiling is in a weak condition. It may have already begun to collapse in these places.

—Check the ceiling of the room directly underneath the bathroom for leaks.

DOORS

—Open and close all the doors. Are they snug without sticking? Is any warping evident? Examine the walls around the door, particularly over the top of the door. Cracks indicate a lack of proper bracing over and around the door opening.

—Is there weatherstripping on the doors leading outside? Is it in good condition or are there large cracks between the door and the door frame? Do you feel a draft when the doors are closed?

—Do all the doors latch properly?

—Are there screen doors? How is the screening?

—Are storm doors necessary?

—Do the doors need refinishing or painting?

—Are the doorways large enough for you to fit your furniture through?

WINDOWS

—Open and close all the windows to see if they are snugly installed. Is there a draft when they are closed?

—Is weatherstripping around the frames in good condition?

—Is there any broken or cracked glass?

—Are there warped sashes? (The sash is the frame holding the pane of glass.) Are windows loose, or is putty chipping badly?

—If any of the windows have been painted or nailed shut, find out why.

—Are storm windows or shutters needed?

—Is there screening on all the windows? Are there any holes in the screens?

—Are there shades or blinds?

—If any windows are covered by shades or curtains, look behind the coverings.

—Is there enough light in the house from properly sized and placed windows? Pay special attention to lighting in the kitchen.

—Are there any skylights? Look for evidence of leaking around the edges.

THE BATHROOM

—Is the bathroom conveniently located?

—Inspect floor and wall tiling for leaks, cracks, looseness, and sloppy workmanship.

—Is there any indication that water leaks from the shower, bathtub, sink, or toilet? Is caulking chipped or cracked?

—Is there a shower, and is it a good solid tiled or ceramic one, or is it a cheap metal semiportable type? If it is tiled, are any tiles buckling or cracked, indicating rot beneath the tiles?

—See ''Plumbing'' below.

THE KITCHEN

—Is the kitchen large enough for your needs and well laid out?

—If you are bringing in your own appliances, will they fit easily? If not, you will have to change the layout or buy a new appliance.

—An older kitchen might be less adaptable to modern conveniences, and this decreases the value of the house.

—Are appliances in the kitchen going to be included in the sale? For example, a stove, refrigerator, freezer, dishwasher, washing machine, clothes dryer, and microwave. See that each item is in good working order. Check the age, brand name, and original cost of each item. Have any been repaired or overhauled recently? If so, get a receipt of payment for the overhaul which indicates what work was done and whether there is a guarantee on it. Don't be afraid to ask questions.

—All appliances included with the home must be itemized in writing and included in the contract of sale.

WATER HEATER

—There are two kinds of water heaters: the instantaneous tankless type, and the storage tank type.

—The instantaneous type heats the water as it passes through small tubes in a combustion chamber, such as a firebox, and goes directly to the faucet.

—The storage tank type heats the water in an insulated tank, and the water remains in the tank until it is used. When the tank is emptied it takes time to heat up a new tank of water. Most houses use the tank type water heater.

—Examine the water heater. If it bears the label of the National Board of Fire Underwriters, it meets normal safety requirements.

—The manufacturer's label on the tank gives the size of the tank in gallons.

—If the heater operates on gas or oil, a family of four needs a tank with a capacity of 30 gallons.

—Electrical water heaters take longer to heat up and a minimum size of 50 gallons is recommended.

—A full load of clothes in an automatic washer takes 25 to 40 gallons of hot water; dishwashing and rinsing average 2 to 4 gallons; a tub bath takes 10 to 15 gallons; and a shower uses 9 to 12 gallons.

—Any evidence of leaks in the heating system? How old is it? Does the hot water appear rusty? This indicates a rusting heating system that needs replacing.

PLUMBING

—Faulty plumbing is the most expensive thing to repair in a home.

—Good water pressure is very important. Turn on all the faucets individually. Is there good pressure at each faucet? Turn on two or three faucets at the same time. With the water running at full force in the kitchen, is there adequate pressure in the bathroom? How is the pressure on the second floor?

—With the faucets on, flush the toilet and see if the water flow is affected. Poor plumbing will cause bursts of hot or cold water from a faucet when the toilet is flushed. This can be dangerous or unpleasant when taking a shower or washing.

—Is the pressure sufficient to permit you to install additional outlets or water facilities, such as another bathroom or a dishwasher?

—Do the faucets drip or leak? Look for water stains in the bathtub and sinks.

—Fill the sink and bathtub with water. Is the water rusty or clear? Old pipes or water heaters produce rusty water.

—Watch the water drain out. Is there good drainage, or are some drains plugged?

—Drop a fistful of toilet paper or a cigarette into the toilet and flush it. Does it flush well, refill quietly, and shut off completely?

—Do you like the fixtures: the sinks, tub, shower, toilet, faucets, etc? Generally, the older they are, the less value they add to the house. In older houses, the hot and cold faucets are separate units, which makes it difficult to wash.

—Are any of the fixtures chipped or scratched?

—Find out the cost of installing modern fixtures and figure it into the other expenses of bringing the house up to contemporary standards.

—Does a plumbing diagram exist showing where all the pipes are in the house?

—Is there a problem with freezing pipes in the winter? The building inspector will know the depth at which pipes should be buried in the area to prevent freezing under local winter conditions. Determine from blueprints, questioning the seller, and physical inspection that the pipes are situated to prevent freezing.

—How easy is it to make repairs on the system? There should be a main valve that shuts off the water supply to the house. Is it conveniently located? In addition, does each faucet have its own shutoff valve so that you can repair one outlet without shutting off all the water to the house?

—Is there a water softener or filtration system for improving the quality of the water? If so, does it serve its purpose well? Get the brand name and price it. How old a unit is it and what is its service history? When was the last time a plumber was called to make repairs? Get his name and talk to him about the condition of the plumbing.

If the house is over eighty years old, there is a possibility that the plumbing may still contain lead or lead alloy pipes. Check to see if the pipes are dull gray instead of copper. If so, they are probably lead.

Even if the house is newer and the pipes are copper, there may be a problem of contamination from lead solder, which until recently was used to join copper pipes. Contamination is most serious if the area has soft water, which is slightly acidic and therefore corrodes the lead solder, or if the copper pipes were installed using lead solder within the last five years because the lead dissolves most easily in the first five years. There are alternatives to lead solder, however. For instance, tin-antimony solder, a good alternative though more expensive than lead solder, may have been used in recently installed plumbing.

If you suspect lead contamination, call the local health department to see if they will test the tap water for lead and other contaminants. If they do not do the testing themselves, they can refer you to a private lab that will test the water.

As testing methods are becoming more sophisticated, it is becoming evident that lead is a highly toxic metal and that even the "maximum safe levels" of lead may not be safe enough. It can damage the nervous system, blood-forming process, kidneys, and reproductive system, and it can cause learning and behavioral disorders and stunted growth in young children and raise blood pressure in adults.

The seller may say that you can just put on a water filter. However, charcoal water filters won't remove lead. The only type recommended by the EPA is one with a reverse osmosis filtering process. But these are expensive, energy intensive, and difficult to maintain. Although cheaper initially, they may be more expensive than replacing the plumbing in the long run.

So if there is serious lead contamination, you should consider replacing the plumbing if you decide to buy the house. Find out how much it will cost to do and add that amount onto the price of the house.

See the Useful Resources at the end of this chapter for how to obtain an informative pamphlet entitled *Lead in Drinking Water: Should You Be Concerned?*

—See chapter 4, "Is There Enough Water on the Land?" for a discussion of wells, pumps, and other aspects of the plumbing system.

SEWAGE DISPOSAL SYSTEM

—If the house is connected to public sewage lines, is there any indication of broken pipes or bad connections?

—Does the house use a septic tank system installed on the property? A septic tank is a large wooden, steel, or concrete box with a filtration system in it that is buried underground. Leach lines carry the strained effluent from the tank through an underground absorption field where the fluid drains into the earth.

First find the tank. Oftentimes property owners don't even know where it is. Some people have a map, or there is one on record with the local health department. However, the tank shouldn't be too hard to find. Just look for where the sewer line exits the house, and the tank is usually 5 to 10 feet from the house and should be no more than a foot below ground. Poke into the ground with a strong stick or preferably an iron pole, and you should be able to locate it. Just hope that the owner hasn't built a beautiful patio or perhaps a lovely flower garden over it.

—The tank has a cover on it that is lifted off to pump it out. Find the cover and see if it is easy to remove. If it is covered with vegetation, that is a good indication that the tank has not been properly maintained.

—Is the septic tank an old wooden kind, a steel kind, or a new single-unit concrete one? The concrete ones are far superior to the others.

Try to find out the results of any percolation tests done on the property. Find out when the septic tank and leach field were installed and who did it. Find

out the type and location of the leach field. If the owner has a diagram of the system (see illustration 37), take a look at it, and go out and see if you can tell where the leach field is on the ground.

—There should not be any vehicles moving over this area or any deep-rooted vegetation growing there. If it appears this has occurred, the tank or leach lines might be damaged. If you see one area of the lawn that is much greener than the rest, it may be irrigated by leaking effluent. Inspect the ground for effluent or raw sewage. You should not smell any sewage in the area. If you do, you may not want to buy the house. Installing a new drainage field can cost as much as building a whole septic tank system for a new house and is usually much harder to do if there are landscaped gardens and yards to be careful of.

37. Septic Tank System Arrangements

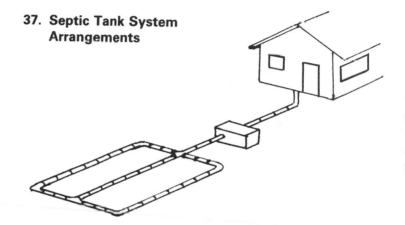

Closed or continuous tile septic tank system arrangement for level ground.

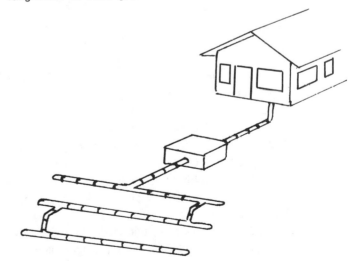

Serial distribution septic tank system arrangement for sloping ground.

—A septic tank should be cleaned periodically to remove the unfiltered material. This is done by a cleaning service that uses a tank truck, pump, and hose to pump the material from the septic tank. When was the tank last cleaned? Get the name and number of the cleaning company. Ask them to show you their service history of the tank and give you their opinion of its condition. Normal maintenance requires the tank to be inspected and cleaned every 3 to 5 years.

—What is the liquid capacity of the septic tank? The proper size is based on the number of people living in the house and the number of facilities hooked to the tank. If you have more people in your family than the previous owners or you intend to add more water-using equipment to the house, you must be sure the septic system can absorb the extra load. Get advice on this from the dealer who installed the tank or presently services it. The local health department also has this information.

If the system looks okay so far, challenge the system by flushing all the toilets three times in succession and filling up the bathtub with 5 or 6 inches of water and letting it drain. Then check the lowest drain in the house, like the basement laundry sink, to see if the water has backed up in it. If the system withstands this test, it may not matter when the owner had the system pumped.

Even if the water does back up due to your test, if you are still interested in the house, ask the owner to have a septic tank company come to see if the line from the tank to the leach field is blocked. That may cost as little as $20 to $40. You will want to be there when the work is done so you can ask the septic tank workers questions.

Ask the owner how the system is maintained. Are the owners careful not to overload the system by doing 3 or 4 loads of laundry in one day but instead to space them out over the week. Are they careful not to throw anything that isn't biodegradable into the septic tank, even filters from cigarettes? Also, bulky paper items like paper towels shouldn't be allowed to go in.

Caustic chemicals are very hard on septic systems, including those intended for septic systems that are supposed to soften solids. Flushing yeast or store-bought enzymes for septic tanks is totally unnecessary, though it usually isn't harmful. However, care should be taken not to destroy the anaerobic bacteria inside the tank that digest the sewage. Therefore, substances such as the salt so-lution used to recharge water softeners should be piped to a special seepage pit because salty water can shorten the life of a septic tank. However, moderate use of disinfectants, bleaches, and drain cleaners is not usually a problem.

—A cesspool is a hole or tank in the ground that simply collects the sewage. It does not contain a filter system or leach lines and is grossly inferior to a properly installed and maintained septic tank. Although a cesspool is regularly pumped, it is often smelly and prone to overflow in heavy rains because of its lack of an absorption field. You should not place much value on a cesspool. Figure in the cost of replacing it with a septic tank.

—Regardless of the sewage system, has it been approved by the local health department? (See chapter 13, "Building and Health Codes.")

ELECTRICAL SYSTEM

—Is there electricity in the house? If not, and you want to receive it, you will incur a major expense wiring the house. (For the expense involved in bringing in electricity to the land see chapter 7, "Amenities of the Area.")

—If there is electricity in the house, is it adequately wired to meet your needs? This will depend on the amount of electricity that the house is wired to accept and the availability of outlets. Older houses have thin wire incapable of safely conducting a large amount of amperes and usually have few outlets. Often there is no overhead lighting.

—Does each room have outlets? The kitchen is the most important room to check. Are there enough outlets for your appliances? If not, the wiring will probably not be sufficient because you should not overload the outlets.

—Are any wires loose or frayed?

—How many electrical appliances are presently being used around the house?

—The electrical system uses either a circuit breaker or fuse box. If a fuse blows or the circuit breaker is tripped, the electrical outlets on that line go dead. This often occurs when the system is overloaded or short-circuited. Does the house use fuses or a circuit breaker? Circuit breakers are used in modern systems.

—The local electric company can tell you how

much load the present system can carry. Does the present system meet building codes, and has it been approved?

—If the house has to be rewired to bring it up to current building code standards or to meet your needs, you should get an estimate of the costs involved from a local contractor. It is an expensive undertaking.

HEATING SYSTEM

Many different kinds of heating units are in use today. Central heating warms the entire house from one source either by blowing hot air through outlets, vents, and ducts in each room or by circulating hot water through pipes in the walls, floors, or ceilings of each room. The former is called conductive heating, the latter is called radiant heating. Instead of central heating, each room might have its own space heater such as a radiator, wall heater, fireplace, or other type of unit. The heating system might use electricity, oil, gas, coal, or wood fuel. The best way to eliminate drafts is to locate heating units along outside walls, under the windows. Baseboard heating is the most efficient draft eliminator.

—What heating system does the house have? Where are the individual outlets located?

—How much does it cost to run in the winter?

—Is heat supplied to each room in the house?

—Turn on the heating units to see how rapidly and effectively the house is heated.

—Does the heater make a lot of noise during operation?

—How old is the heating unit? What is the service history? Ask the local dealer what the life expectancy of such a unit is. Most heaters run trouble-free for only seven or eight winters.

—Look on the heater for the specifications. The *BTU output* is the amount of heat a furnace will emit. Write down the figure and see if its capacity is normal for the area.

—If the furnace is gas-fired, do you smell gas around it? The local gas company will inspect it free and tell you about its efficiency and cost of operation.

FIREPLACE AND CHIMNEY

—Your winter heating bills can be lowered considerably if you have an efficient fireplace, fireplace insert, or wood stove. A standard fireplace is extremely inefficient. As much as 90 percent of the heat value in the wood can be lost up the chimney. Fireplaces with heat exchangers are usually better, but they still do not solve the problem of air combustion. Airtight stoves or furnaces are the most efficient way to extract heat from wood. Modern wood-burning stoves approach the efficiency of modern gas or oil furnaces, with more than half of the heat energy in the fuel being converted into usable heat in the room or dwelling. Don't be sold automatically on a big old-fashioned fireplace. A good airtight stove or fireplace insert is far more valuable.

—A good one is worth paying a little more for. However, some fireplaces and wood stoves are poorly designed or improperly maintained and can cause many problems. Inspect it carefully.

—When was it last cleaned and by whom? They should be cleaned annually.

—Are the walls and floor around the fireplace or wood stove adequately protected? Do you see any smoke marks on the walls? There might be some draft problems.

—Have the owner show you how to operate the damper. Does it work easily? Does it open all the way?

—Are the bricks in good condition?

—Does the fireplace have vents on the side for extra heating efficiency?

—Is it large enough for good-size logs?

—Is it in a good location?

—Look where the chimney goes through the ceiling. Is it well protected? Any evidence of burning? If metal stovepipe is visible, tap the pipe. Do you hear flakes of creosote falling from the inside walls of the stovepipe? If so, it needs to be cleaned.

—When you go outside, examine the chimney. Any cracks, crumbling mortar, or missing bricks? Does the top extend far enough above the roof to be safe and to create a good draft? When you go up on the roof, examine the top of the chimney. Is the opening protected so that sparks don't escape? Does it need cleaning?

—The building inspector can tell you if the fireplace or wood stove is in good condition or what has to be done to bring it up to code.

—The best way to evaluate a fireplace or wood stove is to see it in action. Ask the owner to light a fire for you.

INSULATION

The house must have good insulation as well as heating. A house is insulated to prevent heat loss in the winter and to keep out heat in the summer. This is done by placing a layer of material between the inside and outside walls of the house to keep the air still. If a large airspace between the walls is the only insulation, the air will move and heat will escape by convection. Common types of insulating materials include foil, fill, slab, or board.

—Ask if there is any place in the house where you can see the insulating material. What kind is used? Older houses may have sawdust or newspaper, which are fire hazards.

—When the temperature outside falls, the inside surfaces of windows and exterior walls get colder. As the air within the house comes into contact with the cold windows and walls, it chills and settles to the floor, creating a draft as it moves across the floor. (As you walk through the house, does it feel well insulated? Is it uniformly warm? Do you feel cold drafts, especially on the floor?)

—If there is snow on the roof, how much of it is melted? Compare it with other houses in the area. Rapidly melting snow indicates heat is escaping through the roof because of poor insulation. (See illustration 38.)

—Extremely cold climates require up to 6 inches of fiberglass insulation in the walls, more in the roof, whereas temperate areas need only a thin layer. Ask the local building inspector or building supply store about the standards of the area.

—The roof, attic, basement, and crawl space are areas that affect insulation. (See below.)

VENTILATION

—As you walk through the house does the temperature seem too warm or too cold? Is the air clammy or stuffy? The first problem is caused by poor insulation, the second by improper ventilation.

—Proper ventilation allows good air circulation and is usually accomplished by opening windows on opposite sides of the house to create a slight breeze. If the openings on the cooler side of the house, usually the north side, are low and small and the openings on the hot side of the house, usually the south side, are high and large, the ventilation will be improved.

—Is the house comfortable in the summer?

—Ventilation in the winter when all the windows are closed is very important. In a properly constructed house the air will flow by its own conduction currents.

AIR-CONDITIONING

In most areas of the country, air-conditioning is a must for comfort. If the house you are looking at does not have air-conditioning, beware if you are told that it will be simple to install by using the existing forced warm air or other heating system. An efficient heating system will have ducts or vents near the floor because heated air rises. But because cooler air falls, if you use the heating ducts for air-

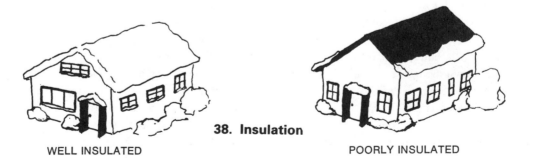

38. Insulation

WELL INSULATED　　　　　　　　POORLY INSULATED

114

conditioning, all the cool air will remain on the floor. Also, cool air needs larger vents, and if small heating vents are used, the cold air won't come into the room fast enough for comfort.

—For maximum efficiency, there should be separate, overhead air-conditioning properly sized for the house in which it is installed.

—If there is air-conditioning, what kind of a system is it?

—Where are the individual outlets located?

—How much does it cost to run in the hot months?

—Is cool air supplied to each room in the house?

—Turn on the system to see how rapidly and efficiently the house is cooled.

—Does the system make a lot of noise during operation?

—How old is the unit? What is its service history? Ask the local dealer what the life expectancy of such a unit is.

—If no air-conditioning system presently exists, will you want one? If so, what will be the cost of installing an adequate system?

THE ATTIC

Eighty percent of the heat lost from a house escapes through the roof. Therefore, an attic is very good for improving insulation because it creates an air pocket between the ceiling and the roof. The floor of the attic should also contain insulation.

—Is there an attic? If not, is the roof itself insulated?

—Is the attic insulated on the floor and under the roof?

—An attic must have good ventilation and air circulation. There should be louvered openings on the sides of the attic. A louver is a slatted opening with screen wire on the inside that aids ventilation. These vents should always remain open. If they are closed or if none exist, condensation occurs, and the moisture deteriorates the ceiling, walls, and roof.

—Does any light shine through the roof? If so, that could be a leaky spot.

—Take out your flashlight and look for water stains on the attic floor, walls, and underside of the roof. If you see any, the roof leaks or ventilation is poor.

—Look for dry rot and termite damage.

—Does the roof sag? Does the ceiling (the attic floor) look solid?

—Does it seem possible to convert the attic into another room? If not, is it a good storage area? It is always the hottest place in the house because heat rises. If it has already been converted into a room, what is the quality of the workmanship?

STAIRWAYS, BALCONIES, AND TERRACES

—Check the condition of all stairways in the house.

—Are they brick, wood, concrete, or steel?

—Do they have sufficiently safe railings? This is very important if you have young children or older people in the family who could fall easily.

—Are there any loose boards or cracks in the concrete?

—Examine the condition of the balconies and terraces.

—Are there good railings?

—Is the flooring solid?

—Are there any leaks in the protective coverings against rain and sun?

CLOSETS, CABINETS, BUILT-INS, AND STORAGE AREAS

—As you go from room to room, look in the closets and other compartments.

—Does each bedroom have a closet?

—Are the closets numerous enough and sufficiently roomy to meet the needs of your family?

—Well-designed built-ins are always used to impress a buyer and increase the value of a house, particularly built-in kitchens, where appliances are placed into the woodwork.

—Notice the quality of the design and construction of shelves, cupboards, and cabinets.

—Do they have glass, metal, or wooden doors that open and close easily?

—Are the joints solid?

A PORCH AND EXTRA ROOMS

An enclosed porch in some areas is an essential feature and will add value to the house.

—Check the condition and construction of both the inside and outside of the porch.

—Is the porch supported as well as the house itself?

—Is the crawl space underneath the porch well ventilated and dry?

—Check for termites and wood rot.

—Are the screens in good condition?

Any additional rooms, such as recreation and rumpus rooms, a laundry, workshop, darkroom, or storeroom, are going to increase the cost of the house, and you should evaluate their worth to you. If you plan to add on a room or two, is it feasible to do so? It might be cheaper to get a bigger house.

SIDING, EXTERIOR WALLS, AND TRIM

—Siding is the external covering of the house, whether boards, shingles, or some other material. How does it look? Are there any holes, cracks, or signs of patch jobs?

—Is any paint peeling? This can be caused by water getting into the walls or by condensation forming on the back of the siding due to moisture in the house and poor ventilation. Paint will also peel if it is an inferior or improper type or if too much repainting has been done. Talk to the local paint dealer about possible causes and the expense of correcting the condition. Find out when the house was last painted, what kind of paint was used, who did the job, and how much it cost.

—Examine the exterior trim for signs of wood rot or termites. Has it been painted recently? Is it fitted evenly?

—Do all the walls and doors square with each other, or is there sagging or sloping? These are signs of major structural defects.

ROOF GUTTERS AND DRAIN PIPES (LEADERS)

—Get up on the roof. What kind of roofing is used—shingles, tar paper, gravel, plywood, etc.? Are any shingles missing, curling, or broken? If any are distinctly lighter in color, they are newer. Ask when they were put on and why. Is the roof material fireproof?

—Is the tar paper ripping or cracking?

—When was the roof last worked on, what was done to it, and who did the work?

—Look at the places where the roof joins the chimney, at pipes, and at the connection where two roof slopes meet. Is there metal flashing installed in these places? Flashing is used to weatherproof joints and edges. Is it rusted and corroded? Are there cracks at any of these points?

—Is there any evidence of roof leaks?

—Does the roof extend out from the house sufficiently to prevent rain or snow water from running down the walls of the house? If it extends out far enough and you see water stains on the external walls, the roof might be leaking.

—Is there a complete gutter system around the roof? Any rust or corrosion?

—Are there drain pipes coming down from the roof? Are they in good condition and unclogged? Clogged pipes can cause water to back up and leak through the roof.

DRAINAGE

—Where does the water drain off the roof? If water stands around the house, it can seep through the foundation and cause wood rot and basement flooding.

—Look at the slope of the ground around the house. The ground should be graded so that water runs away from the house.

—Are there any drainage ditches or other drainage devices in the ground? Are they in good condition? (See chapter 5, "The Earth—Soil, Vegetation, Topography.")

WALKS AND DRIVEWAY

—Are the walkways in good condition? If they are cement, are there cracks anywhere?

—If there is a driveway, is it in good condition? Information on access roads is included in chapter 9, "Easement Rights."

FENCING

—If the house or garden area has a fence around it, is it beginning to lean to one side and fall apart in places, or does it look strong?

—Does it need a paint job?

—When was it built?

—If there is no fence and one is needed, what would it cost to erect one? Figure this into the house cost.

OUTBUILDINGS

The most common outbuildings in the country are garages, barns, and workshops. Often these buildings will be included in the deal at much less than their actual worth because they are used as extra selling points by the owner. Generally, these structures are not in as good condition as the house. The greater the emphasis the seller places on these buildings to justify his asking price, the more you should inspect them for defects.

Garage

—Is there any evidence that the roof leaks?

—Is it big enough to hold your car? Does it have a workshop or tool space in it?

—If it is connected to the house, give it as thorough an inspection as you give the house.

Barn

Many barns have not been maintained well and will be in poor condition.

—Is there any evidence that the roof leaks?

—Is the foundation sound?

—Is the wood rotting? Is there any evidence of termites?

—If you want horses, cows, or goats, is it big enough for them?

—Is it insulated? Heated? Are any utilities supplied to it?

—Does it have potential as a human dwelling?

—What has it been used for in the past?

Other Buildings

There might be any number of other assorted buildings on the land, including poultry houses, pigpens, rabbit hutches, feed storage sheds, and silos, granaries, game rooms, water tank housing, a tool and tack house, well-houses, greenhouses, and generator houses.

—What utilities are supplied to the buildings?

—Are these buildings worth whatever additional value the seller places on them? Find out how the seller breaks down the total asking price, what he thinks the house is worth, what the other buildings are worth. You should not hesitate to ask this question. Find out how the tax assessor has assessed the value of these buildings for tax purposes. (See chapter 17, "Property Taxes and Assessments.")

LANDSCAPING

Landscaping is always emphasized in real estate ads. Such things as "spacious lawn," "plenty of shade trees around house," and "numerous ornamental plantings in a beautifully landscaped setting" can raise the price of land considerably. You must decide whether these things are important enough to you to warrant the extra cost.

If the land is a small parcel and you have neighbors close by, trees and shrubs might afford needed privacy. Orchards and other land improvements that take many years to develop before producing are valuable assets if they are free from disease and have been well cared for. An orchard that has been neglected for many years, however, will take time and work to bring back to productivity, and you should not have to pay extra for it. Flowers and vegetables are nice but their value is minimal. It is easy to be swayed by a lovely garden and pay an inflated price for the property. If you are buying land that is carefully landscaped, be sure you estimate its true value by placing most of the emphasis on the house and land itself rather than the frills.

ADDED ATTRACTIONS—DON'T LET THEM BLIND YOU

The seller might try to entice buyers with many extras, such as animals, animal feed and maintenance equipment, a television antenna, carpets, drapes, furniture, air-conditioning, appliances of all kinds, tractors, compost shredders, plows, lawn mowers, gasoline pumps and generators, lawn and patio furniture, and almost anything else you can think of. Be very careful about letting these extras attract you to a deal which otherwise might not be what you want. I have heard people talk more about the extras that come with a home than about the home and land itself. Real estate agents often exploit this tendency by placing great emphasis on these added features to keep the buyer's mind off the important things.

If extras are included, note the condition of the items, their age and service history, and their brand names if applicable. Price the items yourself and then ask the seller how he computes the value in the total asking price. Have the seller operate each item for you. Is he overpricing the frills?

FINAL CONSIDERATION

Now that you have seen the house, the other buildings on the land, and the extras that come with the deal, think about the house again.

—How is the general quality of workmanship and materials?

—Would you feel comfortable living in it?

—Is it your idea of a relaxed home in the country?

—Does it blend in well with the land?

—Do you like the size of the rooms and the way they are laid out?

—Will your furniture fit in well?

—Is the house large enough for your present and future family needs?

—Will it lend itself well to any additions you might want to make? Can you get a building permit to construct additional rooms?

—Can the house be securely locked and sealed while you are away?

—If you are buying an old house and want to refurbish it, can you get the proper permits? Is it economically feasible to rebuild the structure?

—No house is perfect. There may be many things wrong with the house that can be fixed for only a few hundred dollars. Get estimates on the costs of repairing deficiencies. Armed with these figures you have three choices:

(1) Have the seller make the repairs before you buy the house.

(2) Bargain to have the price reduced at least by the amount needed to make the essential repairs.

(3) Do not buy the house because it is too dilapidated and the seller is not willing to cooperate with you.

USING A PROFESSIONAL INSPECTOR'S SERVICE

If you have decided that the land and the house are definitely what you want, you might like to get a professional evaluation of the house done to double-check your evaluation. Within the last twenty years or so, real estate inspector services have sprung up around the country to inspect and evaluate the present physical condition of a structure and estimate the current cost of making necessary repairs. (An inspector does not estimate the value of the house; that is done by an appraiser.) You can accompany the inspector when he goes over the house, and he will point out the defects to you. He will write up a detailed report that you can use when bargaining with the seller.

A good inspector can tell you whether those water marks in the basement indicate a chronic seepage problem or are the result of a single incident, and he can tell you if serious structural problems are hiding under a fresh coat of paint. All aspects of the house from top to bottom and from the heating and air-conditioning, electrical and plumbing systems to the foundation and insulation are covered by a professional inspection.

Especially if you are not willing to snoop around digging in every cranny of the house, a complete home inspection is well worth the price so that you can get a good idea of the condition of the house before you buy. However, even if you are willing to do your own inspection, it may be worth getting a professional inspection because the professional inspector has inspected hundreds, perhaps even thousands of homes in his career and can remain unbiased in his inspection—something you may not be able to do.

Shop around and compare inspection fees. Fees vary from one geographical area to another. Within one area fees can vary depending on where the house is located, how large it is, the age of the house, special structures or other features, and how long it takes to complete the inspection. The charge is usually somewhere between $150 and $350. House inspector services are an unregulated business, so you must carefully check reputations and qualifications before you hire one. You should try to hire an inspector who is also a licensed contractor or a licensed inspector. Be cautious in hiring anyone recommended by the seller or real estate agent. You could get recommendations from the county building inspector. Inspection services will be listed in the yellow pages of the phone book under Home Service or Building Inspection Service. A registered civil engineer is also qualified to inspect structures. One nationwide group, named the American Society of Home Inspectors, Inc. (ASHI), formed in 1976 is a nonprofit voluntary professional society. It has developed formal inspection guidelines and a professional code of ethics, and it gives homeowners an assurance of quality and professionalism. If you use an ASHI member you may be assured of a complete detailed inspection.

Rather than get a complete structural inspection, you may just want to get a termite and wood rot evaluation. This type of damage is the most destructive to a home and the most expensive to repair. A pest and fungus inspection costs less than a complete evaluation of the house and is considered essential by lenders and builders.

When selecting a pest control service, again be very careful. Membership in the National Pest Control Association or a state or local pest control association is a good sign that the company is established. Such associations usually have codes of ethics members agree to and members have access to the latest technical information on chemicals. Check with your local Better Business Bureau, chamber of commerce, county extension agents, or consumer office.

For a list of member firms of the National Pest Control Association write to National Pest Control Association, 8100 Oak Street, Dunn Loring, Virginia 22027.

When getting a pest inspection, ask what sanitary conditions might invite infestations, the extent and location of a pest problem found at the time of the inspection, what existing or potential avenues of entry there are for a pest infestation, and if there are structural deficiencies serving as actual or potential breeding sites for insects, rodents, and other pests.

I am including a sample Standard Structural Pest-Control Inspection Report.

39. STANDARD STRUCTURAL PEST-CONTROL INSPECTION REPORT

(WOOD-DESTROYING PESTS OR ORGANISMS)

This is an inspection report only—not a Notice of Completion.

ADDRESS OF PROPERTY INSPECTED	BLDG. NO.	STREET	CITY		DATE OF INSPECTION
			CO. CODE		

FIRM NAME AND ADDRESS

Affix stamp here on Board copy only

↓ A LICENSED PEST CONTROL OPERATOR IS AN EXPERT IN HIS FIELD. ANY QUESTIONS RELATIVE TO THIS REPORT SHOULD BE REFERRED TO HIM.

Telephone:

FIRM LICENSE NO.	CO.	STAMP NO.

Inspection Ordered by (Name and Address) _____

Report Sent to (Name and Address) _____

Owner's Name and Address _____

Name and Address of a Party in Interest _____

Original Report [X]   Supplemental Report [ ]   Limited Report [ ]   Reinspection Report [ ]   No. of Pages _____

YES	CODE	SEE DIAGRAM BELOW	YES	CODE	SEE DIAGRAM BELOW	YES	CODE	SEE DIAGRAM BELOW	YES	CODE	SEE DIAGRAM BELOW
	S	Subterranean Termites	X	B	Beetles—Other Wood Pests		Z	Dampwood Termites		EM	Excessive Moisture Condition
	K	Dry Wood Termites		FG	Faulty Grade Levels		SL	Shower Leaks	X	IA	Inaccessible Areas
X	F	Fungus or Dry Rot	X	EC	Earth-wood Contacts	X	CD	Cellulose Debris	X	FI	Further Inspection Recom.

1. SUBSTRUCTURE AREA *(soil conditions, accessibility, etc.)*   Sub basement—See #1 #2 #3 #4 & #5
2. Was Stall Shower water tested?   None   Did floor coverings indicate leaks?   -----
3. FOUNDATIONS *(Type, Relation to Grade, etc.)*   Concrete—See #6
4. PORCHES . . . STEPS . . . PATIOS   See #7 #8 #9 & #10
5. VENTILATION *(Amount, Relation to Grade, etc.)*   None
6. ABUTMENTS . . . Stucco walls, columns, arches, etc.   None
7. ATTIC SPACES *(accessibility, insulation, etc.)*   None
8. GARAGES *(Type, accessibility, etc.)*   None
9. OTHER   See #11

DIAGRAM AND EXPLANATION OF FINDINGS   (This report is limited to structure or structures shown on diagram.)

General Description _____ wood frame—occupied

_____ Inspection Tag Posted (Location) _____ In basement

Other Inspection Tags _____ None noted

The closed finished stucco and plastic walls, ceilings, areas beneath floor coverings, areas concealed by built-in cabinets, storage, and furnishings were inaccessible for inspection.

Since no visible evidence of infestation or damage was noted in the accessible portions except as set forth in this report, any further inspection of these areas would be impractical. We assume no liability for these areas.

Areas subject to moisture, except as outlined in this report, such as roofs, gutters, windows, shower enclosures, and plumbing leaks are to be maintained by homeowners. This Company assumes no liability for these areas. If work as outlined in this report is performed by others, and a building permit is posted, we will reinspect the property at an additional cost.

Reseating of toilets and caulking and sealing guaranteed for 60 days. Repairs and treating guaranteed for one year.

We assume no liability for damage, infection, or infestation in inaccessible areas, including sealed stucco walls and soffits. Further inspection of these areas will require openings and be performed on request with permission of authorized parties. No personal belongings, chattels, storage, or carpets were moved at time of inspection. Attics will be inspected when a release from possible damage is received and at additional cost.

State law requires that you be given the following information: CAUTION: PESTICIDES ARE TOXIC CHEMICALS. Structural Pest Control Operators are licensed and regulated by the Structural Pest Control Board, and apply pesticides which are registered and approved for use by the California Department of Food and Agriculture and the United States Environmental Protection Agency. Registration is granted when the state finds that based on existing scientific evidence, there are no appreciable risks if proper use conditions are followed or that the risks are outweighed by the benefits. The degree of risk depends upon degree of exposure, so exposure should be minimized.

If within 24 hours following application, you experience symptoms similar to common seasonal illness comparable to the flu: Contact your physician or poison control center and Comstock Termite and Pest Control immediately. For further information, contact any of the following: Comstock Termite Control 566-0600, County Health Department—588-2466, Poison Control Center—666-2845, County Agriculture Commission—558-3284, Structural Pest Control Board—1430 Howe Ave., Sacramento, CA. 95825 (916) 924-2291. The pesticide or pesticides proposed to be used are ☐ Chlordane ☐ Copper Napthanate ☐ Dursban (Chlorpyrifos)

1. Prior work has been performed. YES __X__ NO_____

2. Some windows and/or doors and surrounds in need of paint and maintenance or replacement. YES ___X___ NO_____ No cost for sash work as this work should be referred to proper trade.

3. Stall shower tested in presence of _____ and did not leak. We assume no liability for any leakage that may or may not appear in the future.

4. Bases of curtain walls and/or steps resting on/or slightly imbedded in concrete. YES_____ NO__X__

5. This is a reinspection of our original Report # _____ Stamp # _____ Dated_____

6. At the direction of _____ this inspection is limited to the areas as outlined and described below. No other inspection or representation is made or intended.

7. This is a supplemental to our original report # _____ Stamp # _____ Dated_____

8. All work as outlined in our original report has been completed by others. We assume no liability for work performed or permits procured or not procured by others. YES_____ NO_____

9. Sealing of stairs or decks to be performed by owner as part of general building maintenance.

10. No roofing work, inspection, or representation made by this company as we are not licensed in this field.

SUBSTRUCTURE:

1 & 2. Wood soil contact and infestation noted in window framing and under deck. B-F-EC on diagram.
RECOMMENDATION: Cut out all damage and repair as necessary. Treat all areas of infestation with Dursban.

3. Cellulose debris in sub area soil. CD on diagram.
RECOMMENDATION: Remove and dispose of all cellulose debris.

4. Wood soil contact at base of curtain wall. EC on diagram.
RECOMMENDATION: Cut off base of curtain wall and re-support as necessary.

5. Wood soil contact at base of studding and braces in front sub area. EC on diagram.
RECOMMENDATION: Remove and dispose of non-functional studding. Install new bracing supported on concrete.

Inspected by _____ License No. _____ Signature _____

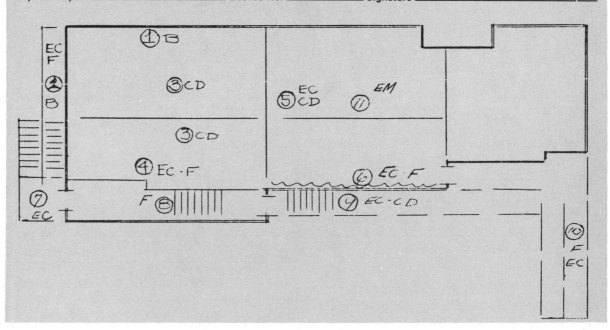

FOUNDATION:
6. Wood soil contact and damage at base of wall in area indicated. F-EC on diagram.
RECOMMENDATION: Cut out lower framing to remove all damage and to bring all framing above grade. Install new raised concrete footing.

STAIRS:
7. Wood soil contact at base of stairs. Area under lower landing and stairs is inaccessible, however, this appears to be newly built. EC-IA-FI on diagram.
RECOMMENDATION: Lower grade to clear stringers. Install access opening under lower landing for further inspection and recommendations.

STEPS:
8. Damage at base of stairway. F on diagram.
RECOMMENDATION: Cut off base of stairs and resupport as necessary.

STAIRS:
9. Wood soil contact and fungus under new stairway. EC-F on diagram.
RECOMMENDATION: Lift two stairs to gain access to this area. Remove and dispose of cellulose debris. Cut off support framing and resupport as necessary. Replace stairs used for access. (No paint.)

PORCHES & STAIRS:
10. Damage in stairs and ramp left from prior repairs. EC-F on diagram.
RECOMMENDATION: Cut out all damage and repair as necessary. Flash off joists at sidewalk.

OTHER:
11. The following conditions were found in units:
   UNIT #1—Lift brick around kitchen sink and repair framing. Reinstall brick. Remove tile around bathtub Install new waterproof Sheetrock. Retile around tub.

NOTE: A large section of front and rear sub areas has insufficient clearance to crawl. However, from the inspection that can be made of these areas, we find them to be clear and dry.

My Model Contract of Sale (see chapter 28) contains a warranty that the house is free of termite infestation and wood rot. (See Clause 16(e) and the accompanying explanation.) You can also condition the purchase on your approval of a complete or partial structural report. Clause 17(b) can be used for a complete inspection, and Clause 17(d) specifically provides for a pest and fungus report. You can thus sign a contract to buy the property, but the deal cannot be closed unless you approve the results of a structural and termite report. If you receive an unfavorable report, you can terminate the agreement to purchase or have the price reduced by the amount needed to make the repairs. (See Clause 17(a)).

If the seller is unwilling to warrant the condition of the house or allow the inclusion of these conditions, he might have something to hide. Actually, he should pay the inspection costs. You can compromise and pay half if you want. Sometimes if you demand a report, the real estate agent will pay for it if it will help him make the sale.

You can include other warranties of the condition of the property you are buying; for example, that the house is structurally sound, that all the appliances and machinery are in perfect working order, and that the livestock are in excellent health.

WILL YOU NEED TO RENOVATE?

If you basically like the house but will need to renovate it or modify it in some way to make it suit your needs, it still needs to be basically sound.

You will want to reject a house for renovation:

—If the foundation is poor and irreparable. It is occasionally possible to move a house onto a new foundation, but the rest of the house should be in extremely good condition to make this economically feasible.

—If the entire frame of the house is considerably out of square, or if the framing is infested with termites, wood rot, or something else.

—If there are so many repairs and replacements necessary that they make the job extremely uneconomical.

Be sure to check with the local building department. Sometimes what seems like a minor addition or repair may require a major revamping of the entire structure to comply with the building codes.

Remember, if the cost of buying and renovating the house does not exceed the fair market value of the houses in the area, it is probably a sound investment.

An excellent pamphlet on checking out a house

We converted it entirely ourselves. It used to be an 18th century windmill.

is available from the Government Printing Office. It is Home and Garden Bulletin No. 212, *Renovate an Old House*. See Useful Resources at the end of this chapter.

When you sign your contract, put in a condition that the deal is contingent on your getting a contractor to renovate the house for an amount that is within your budget.

PURCHASING A MANUFACTURED (MOBILE) HOME WITH THE LAND

Many of you will be looking to purchase a manufactured home already existing on the property. This is likely because in the last ten years one-third of all new single-family homes bought have been manufactured homes. This is a type of house that is constructed in a factory to comply with a building code developed by the Department of Housing and Urban Development (HUD). Some of these are also called mobile homes despite the fact that fewer than five percent of such homes are ever moved off the owner's original site. Many owner-built homes are now kits and are often good quality because quality control is maintained at the factory level. Manu-

factured homes can include prefab log or wood homes, domes, yurts, and other structures. However, in this section I will be referring to standard design manufactured homes.

Manufactured homes are cheaper to purchase than building a new home of the same size, but sometimes they do have problems. Metal mobile homes are certainly not as pleasing to have in a rural setting as a home built out of native materials. Many are poorly constructed and do not have the durability of frame construction or brick or stone dwellings. They are often small and lack adequate wiring and plumbing. Leaking is a problem, as is proper insulation. They are also far more prone to fire than a regular house.

But manufactured homes are easy to set up, have fairly low maintenance costs, and are taxed at a lower rate than regular-sized frame dwellings. They are often taxed on a special personal-property tax basis, rather than as part of the real estate. However, many states will tax them as part of the real estate if they are on permanent foundations.

You must check out the condition of a manufactured home as carefully as that of a conventional home. Test all the appliances, check all sockets with a light, and make sure the home is level. Ways to check to see if the home is level are to take a ball and place it on a floor with a hard surface to see if it rolls, and to open and close all interior and exterior doors. If any doors scrape against their jambs, the home may not be level. Turn on all faucets, and flush toilets. Look for the MHMA–TCA seal near the doorway or on the outside rear or side of the home. This is placed there to inform you that the Mobile Home Manufacturers Association–Traveler Coach Association (MHMA–TCA) building standards have been complied with. Have the seller show you all the warranties he has on the manufactured home, along with the purchase papers.

See what kind of foundation the home sits on and how it is secured. The home must be properly anchored to the ground to prevent severe winds and earthquakes from damaging it. If the home is two sections combined, a double wide home, carefully check the seams where they join together for evidence of leaking or loose-fitting areas. Proper leveling of the home is one of the most important aspects of setting up a manufactured home. If done improperly it could cause floors or walls to buckle. Even if it was installed properly when first placed on the site, over time foundation supports may settle unevenly and can cause serious damage.

You can obtain FHA–HUD and VA loans for the purchase of manufactured homes as well as real estate. See chapter 27, "Glossary of Financing Terms, Checklist for Evaluating a Loan, and Useful Resources," for all addresses of local offices that can supply you with current information on loan availability. Other conventional sources of financing are available.

An extremely important point to be aware of is that you usually need the consent of a lender to assume existing liabilities on a mobile home. Because it is sold like a car or personal property, the lender holds the "pink slip" until the home is paid for. You should always contact the lender regarding your assumption of an existing loan because lenders usually require that you qualify on your own to assume the loan. If you purchase the home without the lender's approval, the lender could accelerate the loan and call for it to be paid off immediately; the state will not recognize the transfer of ownership to you; nor will the insurance company put you on the policy as the insured owner.

If you are planning to purchase vacant land and then place a manufactured home on it, you should be aware of several points. For example, the zoning must allow placing a manufactured home in your location. Certain areas prohibit such homes or require a certain size and exterior appearance. Check the local planning and land use department for zoning restrictions.

Often in a subdivision, manufactured homes will be totally prohibited according to covenants, conditions, and restrictions on all parcels. You will know this if you request and read the restrictions before the close of escrow. If you intend to purchase a manufactured home, write into your purchase agreement a condition that your purchase and the close of escrow are contingent upon your obtaining a building permit to place a manufactured home on the property. The parcel of land must have a site accessible for the large truck that will have to haul the home to the site, the site must be as level as possible, the soil must be graded and sloped properly and compacted. This will have to be done by professionals, so you should figure that cost into your projections. In a rural area it is very important that you have an adequate access road for getting your home to the site.

There are dozens of styles of manufactured homes available, just like automobiles. For example, exterior siding can be made of hardboard, wood, vinyl, metal, or aluminum. You can have patios, carports, and decks. Home sizes can range from 2,500-square-foot multiple section units to a small single unit of only 400 square feet. Shop around for a home as you would for a car, comparing prices, options, extras, and warranties.

USEFUL RESOURCES

Publications to Help You Inspect a Home's Physical Condition, Construct a Home, and Learn about Energy-Efficient Home Construction

The following is available for the specified cost from:

R. Woods
Consumer Information Center, Y-6
P.O. Box 100
Pueblo, CO 81002

Subterranean Termites 143P	$2.50
Wood Heat: Is It Right for You? 439P	$ .50
Heating with Wood 131P	$1.00

The following is free from:
Extension Service
Mississippi State University
Box 5426
Mississippi State, MS 39762

Wood Heat

The following are available for the specified cost from:
National Pest Control Association
8100 Oak St.
Dunn Loring: VA 22027

How to Select and Use Pest Control Services	$ .15
The Uninvited Guests	$ .30
Buying or Selling a Home	$ .15

You can also write for a list of member firms. The following are available for the specified cost from:
Canadian Mortgage and Housing
    Corporation
650 Lawrence Ave., W.
Toronto, Ontario, Canada
M6A 1B2

Inspection Checklist for Maintenance and Repair	$1.00
Canadian Wood Frame House Construction	$5.00
New Life for an Old House	$2.50

You can also ask for a copy of their resource catalogue for other publications they offer.

The following are available for the specified cost from:

Small Homes Council-Building Research Council
University of Illinois at Urbana-Champaign
1 E. Saint Mary's Rd.
Champaign, IL 61820

Termite Control	#F2.5	$ .50
Moisture Condensation	#F6.2	$ .50
Heating the Home	#G3.1	$ .50
Maintaining the Home	#A1.5	$ .50
Plumbing	#G5.0	$ .50
Heat Pumps	#G3.4	$ .50
Chimneys and Fireplaces	#F7.0	$ .50

Write for a copy of their list of publications for a more complete list.

The following are available for the specified cost from:

ANR Publications
University of California
6701 San Pablo Ave.
Oakland, CA 94608–1239

Protecting Your Home against Wildfire	#21104	$1.00
Using Pesticides Safely in the Home and Yard	#21095	free
Mosquito Control on the Farm	#2850	$1.00
Ants and Their Control	#2526	$1.00
Termites and Other Wood-destroying Insects	#2532	$1.00
Heating Your Home with Wood	#21336	$1.00

The above pamphlets and other useful pamphlets are listed in the Agricultural Publication Catalogue, free from the above address, or from:

Cooperative Extension
U.S. Department of Agriculture
University of California
Berkeley, CA 94720

The following are free from:

U.S. Department of Housing and Urban Development (HUD)
451 Seventh St., S.W., Rm. B-258
Washington, DC 20410

or HUD regional area and services offices throughout the country.

(See addresses in Useful Resources at the end of chapter 26, "HUD/FHA- and VA-Insured Loans.")

Termites HUD-323-H
Wise Home Buying HUD-267-F
A Survey of Passive Solar Homes HUD-PDR-589
Homeowner's Glossary of Building Terms HUD 369-H

You can order the following at the specified cost from:

HUD User
P.O. Box 280
Germantown, MD 20874

Blueprint Catalogue. Includes 48 full-size working drawings of affordable and energy-efficient housing designs. Order "Blue Cat."	free
Guidance Manual for Sewerless Sanitary Devices and Recycling Methods: Summary PDR–739	$5.00

The following are available for the specified cost from:

Superintendent of Documents
Government Printing Office
Washington, DC 20402

Ants in the Home & Garden: How to Control Them S/N 001-000-03840-1	#SEA	$1.00
Controlling Household Pests S/N 001-000-03927-0	#SEA	$1.50
You Can Protect Your Home from Termites S/N 001-001-00420-1	#FS	$1.00
Finding and Keeping a Healthy House S/N 001-000-03263-1		$3.25
Subterranean Termites, Their Prevention and Control in Buildings S/N 001-000-04341-2		$2.50

Drainage Around Your Home
S/N 001-000-03455-3 $1.00

Protecting Residences from
Wildfires: A Guide for
Homeowners, Lawmakers,
and Planners
S/N 001-001-00579-7   #FS $4.75

Wood Decay in Houses: How to
Prevent and Control It
S/N 001-000-04096-1 $2.75

Principals for Protecting Wood
Buildings from Decay
S/N 001-001-00362-0 $1.05

New Life for Old Dwellings:
Appraisal and Rehabilitation
S/N 001-000-02988-6 $5.50

Use of Concrete on the Farm
S/N 001-000-03373-5 $ .45

Fireplaces and Chimneys
S/N 001-000-01520-6 $3.00

Roofing Farm Buildings
S/N 001-000-00465-1 $4.75

Renovate an Old House?
S/N 001-000-03505-3 $3.00

Wood-frame House Construction
S/N 001-000-03528-2 $7.50

The Energy-wise Home Buyer: A
Guide to Selecting an Energy-
efficient Home
S/N 023-000-00518-2 $5.50

In the Bank . . . or Up the
Chimney
S/N 023-000-00411-9 $3.00

Environmental Do's and Don'ts
on Construction Sites
S/N 0100-03298 $ .65

The following are available for the specified cost from:

    National Association of Brick Distributors
    1000 Duke St.
    Alexandria, VA 22314

Energy-efficient Fireplaces $ .85
Brick for Passive Solar Heating $ .85
Cold-Weather Construction $ .85
Building Residential Fireplaces $ .85
Build with the Sun $ .50
The All-Masonry Fireplace $ .25

The following are available for the specified cost from:

    American Society of Home Inspectors, Inc.
      (ASHI)
    1010 Wisconsin Ave., N.W., Ste. 630
    Washington, DC 20007

Maintaining Your Home (P-102) $1.00
Wet Basements (P-103) $1.00
The Home Inspection and You (P-104)   free

The following is free from:
    American Land Title Association (ALTA)
    1828 L St., N.W.
    Washington, DC 20036

Blueprint for Home Buying

The following is available for the specified price from:

    The American Association of Certified
      Appraisers
    Seven Eswin Dr.
    Cincinnati, OH 45218

Inspection of a Single-Family Dwelling $7.95

The following is free from:
    State Bar Pamphlets (H)
    Communications Division
    555 Franklin St.
    San Francisco, CA 94102

What Should I Know before I Buy a House?

The following is free from:
    Consolidated Dutchwest
    P.O. Box 1019
    Dept. 6ME9
    Plymouth, MA 02360-9990

The Stove Buyer's Guide

If you are interested in finding out information regarding toxic substances and pesticides, call the Environmental Protection Agency toll free:

    National Pesticide Telecommunications
      Network
    (800) 858-7378

    Toxic Substances Control Act
    Assistance Office
    (800) 424-9065

Log Homes

The North American Log Homes Council, a national organization with membership comprised of manufacturers of log homes, distributes information on manufactured log homes. You can obtain a free list of manufacturers and the information from:

Home Manufacturers Councils
North American Log Homes Council
National Association of Home Builders
15th and M Sts., N.W.
Washington, DC 20005

For a complete catalogue of available material on log home construction and maintenance, write to:
Log Home Guide for Builders and Buyers
P.O. Box 1150
Plattsburgh, NY 12901
or
1 Pacific
Ste.-Anne de Bellevue
Quebec, Canada H9X 1C5

Domes

For a list of companies that manufacture domes all over the country, write to:
Home Manufacturers Council
National Dome Council
National Association of Home Builders
15th and M Sts., N.W.
Washington, DC 20005

Individual manufacturers should be contacted for questions and information on designs, specifications, accurate prices and builder/dealers in a particular area.

Yurts

The national organization that promotes yurts as homes and seeks code approval for various designs is the Yurt Foundation. For free information on yurt plans sold by them and general information on yurt construction, write to:
The Yurt Foundation
Bucks Harbor, ME 04618

Manufactured Homes

The following is available for the specified cost from:
R. Woods
Consumer Information Center–A
P.O. Box 100
Pueblo, CO 81002

How to Buy a Manufactured
   (Mobile) Home   #418R $ .50

Send $.25 with a self-addressed stamped envelope to:
Council of Better Business Bureaus, Inc.
1515 Wilson Blvd.
Arlington, VA 22205

for the following pamphlet:

Mobile/Manufactured Homes

Write to the following agency for their current literature on manufactured home standards:
National Manufactured Housing
   Construction and Safety Standards
   Division
Department of Housing and Urban
   Development
451 7th St., S.W., Rm. 9156
Washington, DC 20410

The following book is available for the specified price from:
Caroline House, Inc.
55 250 Frontenac Rd.
Naperville, IL 60540

The Complete Guide to
   Factory Made Houses, $10.95
   A.M. Watkins   (postpaid)

Owner-Built Homes

Write to the following organization for their current list of publications, books, and information on building your own home.
Owner Builder Center
1516 5th St.
Berkeley, CA 94710

For more information on alternative energy, see appendix J, "Alternative Energy Resources," at the end of the book.

Many resource materials regarding the installation, operation, and maintenance of septic tanks and drainage tiles can be found in the Useful Resources at the end of chapter 5, "The Earth—Soil, Vegetation, Topography."

CHAPTER 7

Amenities of the Area

I don't mind on a given day—let's say a beautiful fall day or something—I can see getting into the car and driving up to the country and getting out and walking around and looking at the lake and leaves and that kind of thing and then getting back into the car and coming home. That I can see. To go and spend two hours, five hours in the country, something like that. I can't see bedding down in the country overnight. I see nothing in that.

I like to know, although I've never done it, I like to know that if at two o'clock in the morning, I get a sudden urge for duck wonton soup, that I can go downstairs, find a taxicab, go to Chinatown, get it and come back home. This is important to me.

I like the idea that it's a live, active city. I don't like to know that if I go outside, it's all trees and bushes and paths.

—Woody Allen

The life amenities desired by actor/director Woody Allen preclude him from living in the country. He is a city person through and through.

Amenities is a term often used by real estate agents to describe those aspects of an area that make it an attractive and enjoyable place to live. The amenities sought by people can differ greatly. Whether you are buying a permanent country residence or a second home for seasonal use, you want a place that meets your needs. The factors that might influence your choice of location are discussed in this chapter.

A good way to find out about an area is to talk to everyone you meet while visiting there. However, if you can rent a house or get a job as a caretaker, you will get a much deeper insight into whether you want to live there permanently.

HOW MANY PEOPLE IN THE AREA?

Be careful if you choose land in an area that is presently, or soon likely to be, experiencing a land boom. A few states and most small towns fairly near cities are gaining population rapidly. Watch for ads for recreational subdivisions or residential developments as indications that an area is being developed. Unless you are interested mainly in investing in a rapid growth area, you may not be prepared for some of the drastic changes your sleepy little town will undergo adjusting to its new growth. You may not recognize the place a few years after you buy. The area will be bustling with activity, taxes will go up, and zoning and building codes will be more stringently enforced.

On the other hand, if the population of an area is on the decline, land prices and taxes will be lower than in a developing area. However, it may be harder to find a job or open a business, and there may be a deficiency in available services.

According to government statistics, towns and cities with 2,500 to 10,000 people are the fastest-growing population centers in America. If you want to live in a place that will retain its rural qualities for a while, choose an area with fewer than 2,500 inhabitants and avoid areas in which packaged recreational or permanent-home subdivisions are being promoted. These developments are like small cities in the country. Between 1970 and 1980 the population of rural areas of all sizes grew, but the most rapid growth occurred in the relatively open country, outside the villages and hamlets recognized as separate entities.

The best source for statistical information about an area's population is the local field office of the Bureau of Census. These offices are listed in the Useful Resources section at the end of this chapter. Also see illustrations 42 through 57 at the end of the chapter (pages 146–56).

WHO ARE YOUR NEIGHBORS?

If you find a nice piece of land, meet your prospective neighbors and talk to them about your plans. They will probably be happy to meet you and proud to show you what they have done with their place. Spend an afternoon with them, and you will learn a lot about the community. You will want to be able to call on them occasionally to look after your place while you are away, to feed your animals or water your garden, and they will want the same from you. If you are moving to an isolated area, your neighbors might be more important to you than if you are living close to town.

If you have children, you will probably want neighbors with children in the same age group, particularly if you plan to live there permanently. On the other hand, if you don't have children, you may not want any children nearby who will climb your apple trees or adolescents who will race their cars. If most of your neighbors are young couples, you should expect an increase in the number of children in the area.

A unique problem with neighbors occurs in some areas where ranching is practiced. Many states still observe the "open range" law, which permits animal owners to let their livestock roam free. The burden of fencing in land is on the landowner who does not want the wandering herds to enter his property. Thus, if you buy a place next to a cattle ranch and you don't want cows wandering through your land, you will have to build a fence to keep them out. This is a costly project and should be figured into your purchase price.

EMPLOYMENT

Unless you are independently wealthy or interested in a vacation home only, you will have to decide how you want to support yourself. You may want to live near enough to the city so that you can continue to work at your present job, or you may intend to work in the country, either near or on your land. Your decision will depend to a great extent on what you do to make money and what area you pick to live in. Many artists and craftsmen have no trouble working in their homes in the country and traveling to the city occasionally to sell their wares. Some craftsmen set up their studios in nearby towns that have a tourist trade.

Since we bought our land several years ago, many individuals have opened successful businesses in town, including several women's, men's, and children's clothing stores, and including a used goods store, a shoe store, a bookstore, a movie theater, automobile repair shops, a health clinic, a veterinary office, a law office, several new restaurants, an ice cream parlor, real estate agencies, a restaurant and bar, a grocery store, a vitamin and herb store, an alternative energy store, a toy store, gift shops, a horseback-riding business, a canoeing and rafting business, a video rental store, and a motel. As rural areas become more populated with residents and tourists, business opportunities will increase, especially for service industries.

If you are thinking of opening a business in your area, consider the demand for your kind of service, the competition, and anticipated trends in the area before you decide. Does the area attract an ample tourist trade to support your business? If there are other businesses similar to yours already in existence, is there enough demand to support another one? If the community is growing rapidly, what new facilities are wanted and needed by the newer residents?

Talk to other businessmen in the community, ask questions at the local chamber of commerce, read the newspapers thoroughly, look in the yellow pages to see what businesses are already established, and keep your eyes and ears open to the needs of the business and residential community. Check the local taxes, zoning, and building codes, and talk with the supervisors from the Small Business Administration, a federal agency specializing in loans to businessmen, and the Farmer's Home Administration. (See Useful Resources at the end of this chapter.) These agencies will have information on how to start a business, what the chances of success are based on past results, and how to get financial assistance. The Small Business Administration (SBA) puts out a pamphlet entitled *Checklist for Going into Business* that is quite helpful. If you intend to buy an existing country business, thoroughly investigate it before purchasing, and find out why it's being sold. You may need the advice of a lawyer and an accountant to be safe.

Many people make part or all of their income in the country from home businesses such as raising animals; selling homemade clothing, pottery, weaving, furniture, or jewelry; running repair shops and other services; painting signs; selling antiques; and selling homegrown produce. The greater your imagination and abilities, the more likely you will think of a lucrative home business. You might have

to buy property on a well-traveled road if you want to operate a business from your home. Several of my clients are operating very successful mail-order businesses, selling records, children's cassettes and video tapes, rare books, alternative energy supplies, and musical instruments. The *Mother Earth News* is still the best source of inspirational stories of people making it in the country. (See appendix A for their address.)

Some of you are probably thinking about farming as a means of survival. The problems of setting up such an operation are far beyond the scope of this book, but the following government statistics reveal much about the current farm situation. The number of United States farms declined by more than half since 1950 from 5.6 million to 2.2 million in 1985. The number of farm failures is more than six times that of small-business failures. Small farms supply less than 8 percent of farm sales, whereas less than 1 percent of United States farms make almost 25 percent of all sales. The percentage of total population living on farms has decreased from 30.2 percent in 1920 to 15.3 percent in 1950 to 2.4 percent in early 1984; only about one person in forty lives on a farm now, as opposed to one in three in 1920.

The Farm Credit Administration summarized the farm situation in its 1986 report as follows:

The overall balance sheet of the farm sector shows significant deterioration. Land values have continued to fall; during 1984, nominal land values fell 13 percent nationwide, with far more drastic declines in many areas. Real estate values dropped 25 percent in the Corn Belt, 23 percent in the Northern Plains, and 21 percent in the Lake States. Since peaking in 1981, land values by early 1985 had declined almost 50 percent in Iowa and Nebraska and about 40 percent in Ohio, Illinois, Indiana, Minnesota, and Missouri. Land values in the Northeast were the only ones expected to remain stable. In Western areas, ranch land values showed some of the largest declines, with nonirrigated land values the second largest. Land values in 1986 in many areas have returned to mid-to-late 1970s levels. Farmland, like many other real assets in limited supply, has historically been viewed as a store of value against inflation, and it became a speculative investment for some [in the 1970s]. The expectation that land would continue to appreciate pushed values to levels that became unrelated to and inconsistent with the land's current income-generating capacity. Over the 1970s, farm real estate asset value tripled along with the debt. . . . This combination resulted in a negative return on equity for most highly leveraged farmland owners, and it was only a matter of time before land prices had to drop sharply. Between 1981 and 1985, farm real estate asset values declined $150 billion, with over $100 billion of that occurring during 1984. These huge losses of owner's equity and collateral value explain why many farmers and their lenders are facing their most serious crisis since the Depression.

Despite this extremely gloomy situation, I believe it is possible to generate at least part of your income by operating a small farm business. With the drop in land values, and the probable splitting-up of large ranches, the next decade could be a good time to begin farming on a smaller scale. There are several informative and inspirational magazines on setting up such an operation that are published regularly. The addresses of some of these publications are given in appendix A.

If you want to find employment in the country, try the small businesses, the farms and ranches, and the local industrial employers to see if anyone is hiring. Any rural area has a high rate of unemployment, so you must be realistic. However, those with special skills or credentials, such as teachers, nurses, doctors, lawyers, surveyors, and engineers, are usually in demand. Consult the publication put out by the federal government entitled *County Business Patterns* for the state and county you are interested in. It gives information for civilian jobs based on Social Security statistics, and lists what businesses are in the county, where they are located, what wages are paid, and how many people are employed. A new report for each state is issued every May. (See Useful Resources at the end of this chapter.)

Each state and county also operates its own employment research agency, which keeps vital statistics on employment within the state. In the Useful Resources at the end of the chapter, I list agencies in each state you can write to for statistical information and answers to any questions on employment. You can get more detailed information about local conditions from the nearest Department of Human Resources Development (HRD) or employment agency. Try calling on some employers when you visit the area and ask about work opportunities. You might be surprised at what is available.

If you want to live in a rural area and continue to commute to a city job, you can do so in most parts of the country. Most cities are relatively com-

pact, and the country is not far away. Figure out how long it would take to get home from your place of employment in the city. It may take a half hour to go the first five miles, but then once you are out of the city, you may be able to go another thirty miles in the next half hour. Many people are now moving to rural areas and getting to work by driving to a commuter train or bus station, parking there for the day, and taking the commuter run into the city, thus avoiding the daily traffic jam. Decide how much time you are willing to spend commuting each day, get a map of your area, pinpoint your place of work, and draw a circle around that point which covers those areas within a commuting distance within your desired time limit. You then have a large area to choose from. Don't make your circle too small. If you become too concerned about your commuting time you might end up looking at suburban property instead of real country land. Another ten minutes and you might find yourself in the heart of the backwoods. It's much closer than you think. Illustration 40 is an example of how to plot the distances from the land to the places that are important to you.

Basically, this idea simply reverses the usual trend, which has been to live in the city and commute to a vacation home in the country. With the ever-increasing ease of mass transportation this will become an option for a greater number of people who will realize they can have their city income and their country relaxation simultaneously.

UTILITIES—WATER, SEWAGE, GAS, GARBAGE, ELECTRICITY, PHONE, MAIL DELIVERY, AND CABLE TELEVISION

In most areas of the country, you will have to take care of your own utility provisions. The local town will not furnish water and other services beyond its limits.

Setting up a water system and a sewage disposal system are standard country procedures, and you must determine the costs involved before buying your land. (See chapter 4, "Is There Enough Water on the Land?" and chapter 13, "Building and Health Codes.") If you want gas or liquid fuel, most rural

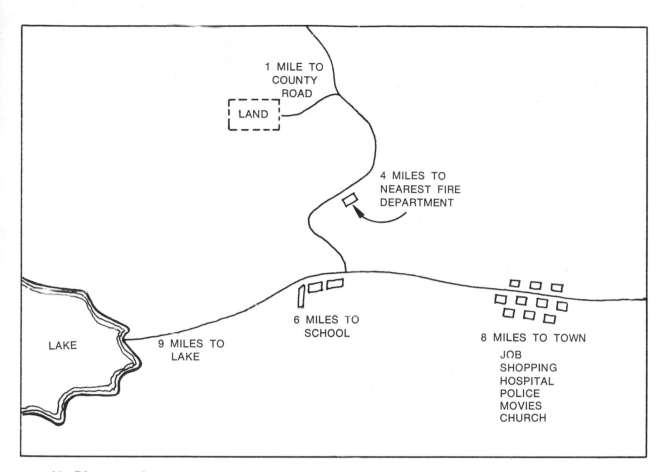

1 MILE TO COUNTY ROAD

LAND

4 MILES TO NEAREST FIRE DEPARTMENT

6 MILES TO SCHOOL

LAKE

9 MILES TO LAKE

8 MILES TO TOWN
JOB
SHOPPING
HOSPITAL
POLICE
MOVIES
CHURCH

40. Distances from Land to Places Important to You

areas have companies that will install a large tank behind your house which is refilled periodically by a tanker truck. You can usually get propane or diesel in this manner. Talk to the local propane dealer about charges for setting up and servicing the system. You will then have to get appliances that use these fuels.

Do not expect a garbage man to come by your home unless you are living in town. Most people use county and town dumps, for which there may be a small fee. In the country, you will probably recycle most of your garbage anyway.

Electricity seems to be the one thing most people can't do without. If you think you don't need it, try living without any for a while before buying land. Can you do without electric lights, a record player, television, and modern appliances, including power tools? If not, you will need land near existing electric lines. Electricity is extremely expensive to bring in from far away, and for most people a gas or diesel generator is too expensive, noisy, and polluting to be practical for full-time use. Before you buy, be sure you have an easement

to bring in utility lines, and check into the costs involved. Only the electric company office nearest to the land can give you a complete estimate. Electric rates are determined by the number of appliances you have and the number of feet of line that will have to be brought in from the nearest available source. You will get credit for each type of appliance. For example, in our area, Pacific Gas & Electric (PG&E) gives 300 feet free for lighting, 275 feet for an electric hot-water heater, 75 feet for an electric refrigerator, 150 feet for an electric range, etc. These credits are cut for second homes. The company brings in lines free to homes within 800 feet of an existing line. Beyond that range the cost is computed by the foot. PG&E charges $8.34 for each foot minus the amount of credit received for each appliance. This is for above-ground pole-strung wires. If you want the line buried, you will have to pay two to three times more, even if you dig your own trench. If other people living nearby want to join you in bringing in electrical lines, the cost can be shared among you. There is always a maximum distance the electric company will string lines even if the customer is willing to pay the entire costs involved. For example, in some areas of Maine service will not be extended farther than a quarter of a mile, and in our area after 2,000 feet the cost jumps drastically.

You also might consider installing your own photovoltaic cells or water or wind generators to generate your own electricity if you are beyond the reach of the local electric company. Breakthroughs are occurring rapidly now in photovoltaics. The price of photovoltaic cells dropped from approximately $40 per watt in the 1970s to between $5 and $10 per watt in 1985, and there have been new discoveries that may drop the price even further. One new chip, known as the point-contact photovoltaic cell, "shows potential to provide electricity at costs comparable to conventional power plants, such as those burning fossil fuels, in sun-rich areas like the southwestern United States," a report prepared by the Electric Power Research Institute said. (See Useful Resources at the end of chapter 4 for information on alternative energy.) In our home 90 percent of our electricity is produced by solar panels and a water turbine hydropowered unit in our creek.

Phone lines are often extended into areas where electricity is not provided. But you should check with your local phone company to see where service is given and how much it will cost to bring in phone lines to your intended home.

Mail is usually delivered to mailboxes along the public county roads, so that should not be a problem. Ask about the mail service at the nearest post office.

Cable television is often available in small towns but not usually beyond the town boundaries. Check with the local cable television company listed in the yellow pages if you are interested in this.

FIRE AND POLICE PROTECTION

Many small towns do not have their own fire and police departments. Often fire protection is maintained on a community volunteer basis. The greatest danger of fire exists in western mountainous areas where forest fires are an annual disaster. If you intend to buy forest land you should learn something of the history of forest fires in your area and how quickly and successfully they were con-

tained. The local forest ranger station or farm advisor, as well as old-time residents, will have this information. In most areas, fire stations are manned only during the critical summer months. If possible, you should have a large reserve water supply and pump on your land if your area is susceptible to fires. Also trim the lower branches off trees near your house, and keep fire hazards in mind when building a house or planting near your house.

You shouldn't have much cause to call the police if you live outside the cities and suburbs. However, if you are going to be absent from your home or land for a large part of the year, the local law enforcement may be able to keep an eye on your place for you. If you want to keep hunters or trespassers off your land, or if your land is too inaccessible for normal police protection, sometimes you can hire permanent residents to patrol it for a small fee. Your neighbors might be willing to help you also.

ROAD MAINTENANCE

Frequent maintenance of public roads is a necessity in the country. You will have endless difficulties where heavy snowfalls occur if the roads are not swiftly cleared each day. You might be late for work often, and you could be prevented from leaving your house for a long time. Where rainfall is heavy, roads need frequent attention and may need frequent repair, depending on the type of soil under the road. Notice how the roads look as you drive around. Ask old-time residents in the area about the quality and frequency of roadwork. You might not want to purchase a home so far away that it is the last area to be cleared each day. Consider the problems involved if you have only a dirt access road. Check with your local department of roads to see what kind of service is provided for private roads. Usually a fee is charged for private road maintenance.

EDUCATIONAL FACILITIES AND CULTURAL ATTRACTIONS

If you have children, you will want to know about the schools in the area. Most children in the country are bused to a centrally located public school, and you will want to buy near a bus pickup point. Usually the schools are small and have fewer facilities and teachers than city schools, but that does not mean they are not as good. Many country schools are excellent. A few private schools and "alternative schools" are appearing in the country, but they vary widely in quality. Never depend on such a school unless you determine its stability, cost, and quality of education. The chamber of commerce and local board of education can tell you the location of the schools in your area and the busing routes. Visit the school, talk to the teachers, and see what facilities they have. Take your children with you.

If you are interested in going to school yourself, many colleges sponsor basic extension courses in rural secondary schools. If you want an extensive variety of courses, or you want to attend concerts, movies, or amateur theatrical and sports events, you might buy in an area near a college or university. Excellent new colleges have been built near rural towns in the last twenty years. Visit the college to see what it offers before you buy in the area. Land is usually more expensive in areas where large schools and colleges are located.

MEDICAL FACILITIES

Local doctors, hospitals, and veterinarians are always an asset in the country. If you are in need of ongoing medical treatment, you must be sure that good service is available in your area from doctors you can trust. Ask your present doctor if he knows a good area in which to settle where the medical facilities are reputable and not overly expensive. Don't be surprised at the informal, relaxed atmosphere in a country clinic. This does not necessarily mean the treatment is inadequate.

SHOPPING AREA

If you have a large family, a nearby shopping center or general store may be a requirement. Check out the shopping facilities in your area, particularly

grocery and drug stores and laundromats. How are the prices? Remember that prices for nearly everything will be higher in the country.

If you are fifteen miles away from the nearest store, it is a thirty-mile drive to pick up groceries. In the winter this can seem like a very long distance.

CHURCHES AND OTHER SOCIAL ORGANIZATIONS

Many of you will want to have the church or synagogue of your choice in your new community. Look in the phone book and local newspapers for local churches and synagogues. Attend a religious service, and talk to the religious and lay leaders and members of the congregation.

If you are interested in social groups, ask the chamber of commerce about clubs in the area, such as bridge, gardening, and service groups. Your children may want to know about local scouting groups, agricultural clubs, and athletic teams. You can visit meetings and functions of such organizations to get a feeling about the kinds of things they are doing and their receptivity to newcomers.

RECREATIONAL FACILITIES

If you intend to buy a vacation home, the recreational facilities of the area will be a major consideration. The local chamber of commerce will have maps and brochures detailing the area's vacation resources. If you are interested in water sports, such as fishing, boating, and swimming, be sure you buy where public water facilities are available. Whether you are interested in hunting, golfing, skiing, mountain climbing, horseback riding, bowling, spas, movies, or good restaurants, recreational facilities are rapidly expanding in rural areas, particularly where the number of seasonal residents is increasing. You do not have to buy land in a massive, expensive, planned "recreational development" in order to satisfy your needs. Buy yourself a piece of land centrally located to the facilities you want. You will save a lot of money and have a true feeling of living in the country.

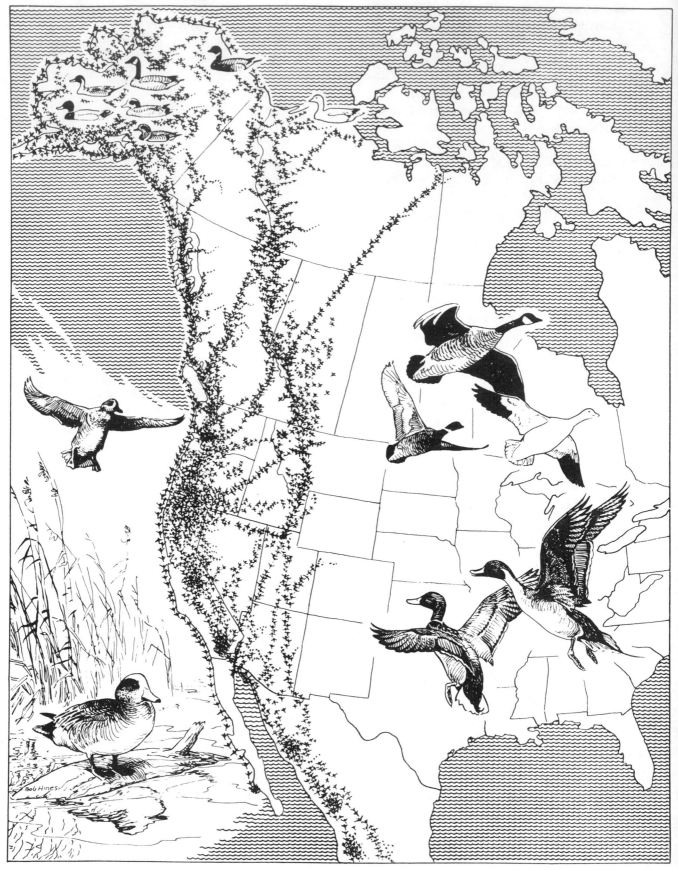

U.S. DEPARTMENT OF THE INTERIOR • FISH AND WILDLIFE SERVICE

For more on the disadvantages of "package-deal" subdivisions, see chapter 14, "Subdivisions and Condominiums."

THE GOVERNMENT AS A NEIGHBOR

Many real estate agents use the fact that land is located next to federal or state land as a selling point. You will frequently see ads stating that "property borders national forest," "property sits next to U.S. government land," or "adjoining BLM land will provide thousands of acres of recreation." Be very careful when buying such land. Any federal land under Bureau of Land Management (BLM) control can be used for grazing, logging, mining, and removal of oil and gas, and industrial and recreational development under the Multiple Use Classification system.

The Bureau of Land Management, an agency of the U.S. Department of the Interior, controls the use of over 450 million acres of public lands. Before buying property adjoining any of these holdings, go to the local BLM office (see appendix B for addresses) or office of the Department of the Interior and ask for a full report on the present and intended future use of that government land. They will have a map indicating all uses planned for the land for the next five years. You should examine it thoroughly. What kind of activities are planned in the area near your land? Logging, mining, or a large influx of tourists can destroy your peace and quiet. But if the land is to be preserved and presents no problems as a neighbor, you may actually find yourself with a backyard of thousands of acres in which to play.

The same problems exist if your land adjoins a national park or other public lands. You must be extremely careful in investigating privately owned land for sale within the boundaries of federally or state-owned land. The government may have offered to buy or trade the property for government land located elsewhere in order to unify its holdings. Eventually the owners of that land could be forced to sell through condemnation. (See chapter 15, "Eminent Domain and Condemnation.")

LOCAL POLITICS

You can get a good sense of the political climate in a community by reading the local newspaper, by listening to the nearest radio station, and by attending a board of supervisors meeting. These meetings are open to the public and announced in advance in the local paper and at the local courthouse or city hall. They are informative and a change of pace from big-city politics. The board legislates and approves the county budget, local improvements, and appeals for zoning changes and variances. The governing bodies and local media are better indicators of the flavor of life in the community than anything else.

A SAMPLE REPORT ON THE AREA

See the Sample Final Subdivision Public Report (illustration 77) in chapter 14, "Subdivisions and Condominiums," to get an idea of what kind of information on the location of the land you should look for. The report includes facts on geological conditions, water, fire protection, electricity, gas, telephone service, sewage disposal, streets and roads, public transportation, schools, and shopping facilities.

NOISE

Many people buy land without realizing they are near enough to a road to pick up the sound of every car and truck that passes by all night. Heavy trucks, particularly industrial or logging trucks, often run only on weekdays or late at night, so if you look for land on holidays and weekends and don't spend at least one night on the property before you buy, you may not realize the full impact of the traffic.

Every sound in the country is greatly magnified—it comes out of the silence like a roar. If you live near a steep grade, the big trucks will be downshifting as they crawl up the hill. If your house is on the outside of a curve in a road, it might be directly in the path of oncoming headlights. When you look at property, stop to listen for sounds and see how the place is situated in relation to nearby roads.

If you live on a mountaintop, you will hear everything that goes on for miles around—traffic, chain saws, and construction noises. Valleys, by comparison, are relatively quiet because the mountains or hills on either side muffle the sounds. The noise factor is a major disadvantage to living on top of a ridge in a populous rural area.

Even if no road is close enough to bother your sleep now, one may be planned for the near future. Most areas have official county and city maps that indicate future street and road development. Talk to the planning department and the department of public roads in your county or the state highway commission to determine where new construction will take place. With the increasing rural population, new road construction is proceeding at a rapid pace and represents a threat to the land buyer in terms of greater noise and possible condemnation. (See chapter 15, "Eminent Domain and Condemnation.")

Living in snow country exposes you to the new menace of the snowmobile's roar. Unless you intend to have one, you probably will not want to be anywhere near a snowmobile road. Many such roads are being developed throughout the country, officially and unofficially, and you might want to determine if any will be in the neighborhood of your new home.

Not until I spent some time as a caretaker on a large ranch did I realize the importance of avoiding a home under an airplane flight path. Every evening as I was quietly enjoying the beautiful sunset, a jet would roar directly overhead and spread its dirty exhaust across the sky. I made certain when we bought our land that no flight paths existed overhead. Most maps will tell you where military bases and public and private airports are located. You will have to determine how their presence affects your land.

You should also be aware of private landing strips on nearby farms and ranches. Many wealthy landowners now have their own planes and runways. Don't think this isn't much of a problem. An airplane is a toy in the hands of many private pilots. Even when used only for business, a low-flying plane that is flown directly over your place several times a day could make your life miserable.

Ask your future neighbors if planes or jets are a problem.

Never buy land within sight or sound of a gravel extracting operation, or a rock-crushing business.

SMELLS AND SMOKE

Lumber mills, paper mills, factories of all kinds, asphalt plants, garbage dumps, and rendering plants are some of the air polluters that you do not want as country neighbors. Legislation controlling air pollution is slow in coming, so don't buy land under the false hope that the local mill will be forced to close down. I have seen rural areas with worse smog than any city I have been in. When we bought our land, we made certain that the two local lumber mills that had recently been closed down had no intention of reopening. During the period when they were going full blast, a clear blue sky was rarely seen.

Look at local maps to determine where such polluting agents exist in your community. Find out from the chamber of commerce or planning commission where new industries intend to locate, and check the zoning to see if industrial development is permitted in the area. (See chapter 12, "Zoning Laws.")

CROP DUSTING

Crop dusting is a method of spraying insecticides from small planes flying low over field crops. The poisons are easily carried in the wind to neighboring lands and can be a threat to the health of members of your family, particularly the very young, the very old, the ill, and childbearing women.

USEFUL RESOURCES

The following are available from the
Superintendent of Documents
Government Printing Office
Washington, DC 20402

*U.S. Cropland, Urbanization, and
Landownership Patterns*
S/N 001-019-00366-9 $ 1.50

*Farm Population Trends by Farm
Characteristics*
S/N 001-019-00333-2 $ 2.00
A Profile of Female Farmers in America
S/N 001-019-00378-2 $ 1.50
*Getting Started in Farming on a Small
Scale.* Discusses financing, farm
selection, planning, training, and crop
selection.
S/N 001-000-04259-9 $ 3.25
*Patterns of Change in the Metro and
Nonmetro Labor Force, 1976–82.*
Measures differences between
metropolitan and nonmetropolitan areas
in the growth of the labor force,
employment, and unemployment.
S/N 001-019-00358-8 $ 2.00
Managing the Family Forest in the South
S/N 001-001-00591-6 $ 2.75
*Minifarms: Farm Business or Rural
Residence*
S/N 001-019-00360-0 $ 1.50
*Living on a Few Acres: 1978 Yearbook of
Agriculture*
S/N 001-000-03809-5 $13.00
*What Attracts New Residents to Nonmetro
Areas*
S/N 001-019-00430-4 $ 1.00
Farm Population of the United States 1985
S/N 003-001-91103-5 $ 1.50
*Population Profile of the United States
1984/85*
S/N 803-005-10003-1 $ 2.75

The following are available for the specified price
from:

ANR Publications
University of California
6701 San Pablo Ave.
Oakland, CA 94608-1239

*Are There Ways to Earn More
from Your Small Farm?*   #2215 $ 1.00
*Can You Earn a Living on a
Small Farm?*   #2213 $ 1.00
*Do You Want a Home in the
Country?*   #2210 $ 1.00
*So . . . You Want a California
Farm?*   #2291 $ 1.00
Management of Small Pastures #2906 $ 1.00
*Trout and Salmon Culture
(Hatchery Methods) Fish
Bulletin 169*   #4100 $ 5.00

*Demographic Shifts, Trends,
and other Factors Affecting
Demand; and New Product
Development for California
Agriculture*   #A1CR1   free
*Handbook for the Small-Scale
Pork Producer*   #21435 $ 2.00

The following are available for the specified price
from:

R. Woods
Consumer Information Center, A
P.O. Box 100
Pueblo, CO 81002

*Financial Management: How to
Make a Go of Your Business* $ 2.50
*Starting and Managing a
Business from Your Home* $ 1.75
Opportunities in Franchising $ 1.00

For the following pamphlet, send a self-addressed
stamped envelope to:

Council of Better Business Bureaus, Inc.
1515 Wilson Blvd.
Arlington, VA 22209

Work-at-Home Schemes $ .25

For a copy of the following 100-page book prepared by the editors of *Mother Earth News,* write
to:

Nissan Guide to Bootstrap Businesses
P.O. Box 7055
North Hollywood, CA 91609-7055

*Financial Independence:
Nissan Guide to Bootstrap Businesses* $ 2.00

For a list of publications written especially for small-
scale farm producers, write to:

The Small Farm Center
University of California, Davis
Davis, CA 95616

Some of those available free are:

California Small Farm Profile
Sources of Help for Family Farmers
Should You Try Farming?
*Marketing for the Small Farmer: Direct
Marketing and Quality Control*
*Marketing for the Small Farmer: Marketing
Cooperatives*

*The Marketing Situation and Opportunities
for Low-Income Growers of Fresh
Produce
Marketing for the Small Farmer: Choices in
Marketing Fresh Fruits and Vegetables
How to Determine if It Is Profitable to
Harvest Your Crop*

You can also get a free subscription to *Small Farm
News* by writing to the above address.

If you are thinking of retiring to the country, an
excellent free booklet can be ordered from:

    American Association of Retired Persons
    Consumer Affairs, Program Department
    1909 K Street, N.W.
    Washington, DC 20049

*Your Home, Your Choice: A Workshop for Older
People and Their Families*

The following are available for the specified cost
from:

    National Association of Home Builders
    15th and M Sts., N.W.
    Washington, DC 20005

Land Buying Checklist	$10.00
Buying a New Home: A Step-by-Step Guide	$ 1.50
Condominium Buyers Guide	$ .75

The following is available for free from:

    S. James
    Consumer Information Center, Y-6
    P.O. Box 100
    Pueblo, CO 81002

    *Checklist for Going into Business
    Women's Handbook*

The following is available for $12.50 plus $2.00
postage and handling from:

    The Conservation Foundation
    1255 Twenty-third St., N.W.
    Washington, DC 20037

The Market for Rural Land-Trends, Issues, Policies by
Healy and Short

Employment Services

The following state offices provide job counseling,
testing, and placement services.

Alabama
    Employment Services Division
    Department of Industrial Relations
    649 Monroe St.
    Montgomery, AL 36130

Alaska
    Division of Employment Services
    Department of Labor
    P.O. Box 37000
    Juneau, AK 99802

Arizona
    Employment and Rehabilitation Services
        Division
    Department of Economic Security
    1717 W. Jefferson
    Phoenix, AZ 85007

Arkansas
    Employment Security Division
    Department of Labor
    Capitol Mall
    Little Rock, AR 72201

California
    Employment Development Department
    800 Capitol Mall, Rm. 5000
    Sacramento, CA 95814

Colorado
    Division of Employment and Training
    Department of Labor and Employment
    251 E. 12th Ave.
    Denver, CO 80203

Connecticut
    Employment Security Division
    Department of Labor
    200 Folly Brook Blvd.
    Wethersfield, CT 06109

District of Columbia
    Department of Employment Services
    500 C St., N.W., Rm. 600
    Washington, DC 20001

Florida
    Division of Labor, Employment and
        Training
    Labor and Employment Security Department
    300 Atkins Bldg.
    Tallahassee, FL 32301

Georgia
  Employment Services Division
  Department of Labor
  501 Pulliam St., S.W.
  Atlanta, GA 30312

Hawaii
  Employment Services Division
  Labor and Industrial
    Relations Department
  1347 Kapiolani Blvd., 4th Fl.
  Honolulu, HI 96814

Idaho
  Department of Employment
  317 Main St.
  Boise, ID 83735

Illinois
  Employment Security
  Department of Employment Security
  Consolidated Office, S.
  923 S. Sixth St.
  P.O. Box 5236
  Springfield, IL 62705
    or
  Employment Security
  Department of Employment Security
  Consolidated Office, S.
  924 E. Adams St.
  P.O. Box 1888
  Springfield, IL 62705

Indiana
  Employment Security Division
  10 N. Senate Ave., Rm. 331
  Indianapolis, IN 46204

Iowa
  Merit Employment Department
  Grimes State Office Bldg.
  Des Moines, IA 50319

Kansas
  Department of Human Resources
  401 S.W. Topeka Blvd.
  Topeka, KS 66603

Kentucky
  Examination and Recruitment
  Department of Personnel
  Capitol Annex
  Frankfort, KY 40601

Louisiana
  Office of Labor
  Department of Labor
  P.O. Box 94094
  Baton Rouge, LA 70804-9094

Maine
  Bureau of Employment Security
  Department of Labor
  State House Station, #54
  Augusta, ME 04333

Maryland
  Job Training and Placement Administration
  Department of Employment and Training
  1123 N. Eutaw St., Rm. 700
  Baltimore, MD 21201

Massachusetts
  Bureau of Human Resources Development
  Department of Personnel Adminstration
  1 Ashburton Pl., Rm. 519
  Boston, MA 02108

Michigan
  Bureau of Employment Relations
  Department of Labor
  1200 Sixth St., 14th Fl.
  Detroit, MI 48226

Minnesota
  Employment Programs Division
  Department of Economic Security
  390 N. Robert St.
  St. Paul, MN 55101

Mississippi
  Employment Security Commission
  1520 W. Capitol
  Jackson, MS 39203

Missouri
  Division of Employment Security
  Labor and Industrial Relations Department
  421 E. Dunklin, Box 59
  Jefferson City, MO 65104

Montana
  Job Service Division
  Department of Labor and Industry
  Capitol Station
  Helena, MT 59620

Nebraska
Job Training Program
Department of Labor
P.O. Box 94600
Lincoln, NE 68509-4600

Nevada
Employment Security Department
500 E. Third St.
Carson City, NV 89710

New Hampshire
Bureau of Employment Services
Department of Employment Security
32 S. Main St.
Concord, NH 03301

New Jersey
Division of Employment Services
Department of Labor
John Fitch Plaza
Trenton, NJ 08625

New Mexico
Employment Security Department
401 Broadway, N.E.
Albuquerque, NM 87102

New York
Department of Labor
Campus State Office Bldg.
Albany, NY 12240

North Carolina
Employment Security Commission
Department of Commerce
700 Wade Ave.
Raleigh, NC 27605

North Dakota
Job Service of North Dakota
P.O. Box 1537
Bismarck, ND 58502-1537

Ohio
Bureau of Employment Services
145 S. Front St.
Columbus, OH 43215

Oklahoma
Division of Employment Services
Employment Security Commission
203 Will Rogers Bldg.
Oklahoma City, OK 73105

Oregon
Employment Division
Department of Human Resources
875 Union St., N.E.
Salem, OR 97301

Pennsylvania
Office of Employment Security
Department of Labor and Industry
1720 Labor and Industry Bldg.
Harrisburg, PA 17120

Rhode Island
Department of Employment Security
24 Mason St.
Providence, RI 02903

South Carolina
Employment Security Commission
1550 Gadsden St.
P.O. Box 995
Columbia, SC 29202

South Dakota
Division of Job Services
Department of Labor
116 W. Missouri Ave.
Pierre, SD 57501

Tennessee
Field Operations
Department of Employment Security
504 Cordell Hull Bldg.
Nashville, TN 37219

Texas
Employment Commission
101 E. 15th St.
Austin, TX 78778

Utah
Job Service
Department of Employment Security
174 Social Hall Ave.
Salt Lake City, UT 84147

Vermont
Department of Employment and Training
Green Mountain Dr.
Montpelier, VT 05602

Virginia
Employment Commission
703 E. Main St.
Richmond, VA 23219

Washington
   Division of Employment Services
   Department of Employment Security
   212 Maple Park
   Olympia, WA 98504

West Virginia
   Department of Employment Security
   112 California Ave., Rm. 608
   Charleston, WV 25305

Wisconsin
   Job Service Division
   Industry, Labor and Human Relations
   P.O. Box 7903
   Madison, WI 53707

Wyoming
   Employment Service Division
   Employment Security Commission
   P.O. Box 2760
   Casper, WY 82602

Write to the following agencies for information on jobs, employment, and population trends. These agencies are responsible for the overall regulation and growth of the state's economy.

Alabama
   Alabama Development Office
   135 S. Union St.
   Montgomery, AL 36130

Alaska
   Department of Commerce and Economic
      Development
   Pouch D
   Juneau, AK 99811

Arizona
   Department of Commerce
   1700 W. Washington, 4th Fl.
   Phoenix, AZ 85007

Arkansas
   Industrial Development Commission
   1 Capitol Mall, Rm. 4-C-300
   Little Rock, AR 72201

California
   Department of Commerce
   1121 L St., Ste. 600
   Sacramento, CA 95814

Colorado
   Division of Commerce and Development
   Department of Local Affairs
   1313 Sherman St., Rm. 523
   Denver, CO 80203

Connecticut
   Department of Economic Development
   210 Washington St.
   Hartford, CT 06106

Delaware
   Department of State
   Townsend Bldg.
   Dover, DE 19901

District of Columbia
   Office of Business and Economic
      Development
   1350 Pennsylvania, N.W., Rm. 208
   Washington, DC 20004

Florida
   Department of Commerce
   510-C Collins Bldg.
   Tallahassee, FL 32301

Georgia
   Department of Industry and Trade
   230 Peachtree St., N.W.
   Atlanta, GA 30301

Hawaii
   Department of Commerce and Consumer
      Affairs
   1010 Richards St.
   Honolulu, HI 96813

Idaho
   Department of Commerce
   Statehouse
   Boise, ID 83720

Illinois
   Department of Commerce and Community
      Affairs
   620 E. Adams St., 3rd Fl.
   Springfield, IL 62701

Indiana
   Department of Commerce
   1 N. Capitol
   Indianapolis, IN 46204

Iowa
 Commerce Community
 Lucas State Office Bldg.
 Des Moines, IA 50319

Kansas
 Department of Economic Development
 503 Kansas Ave., 6th Fl.
 Topeka, KS 66603

Kentucky
 Commerce Cabinet
 Capital Plaza Tower
 Frankfort, KY 40601

Louisiana
 Department of Commerce
 P.O. Box 94185
 Baton Rouge, LA 70804-9185

Maine
 State Development Office
 Executive Department
 State House Station, #59
 Augusta, ME 04333

Maryland
 Office of Business and Industrial
  Development
 Economic and Community Development
  Department
 45 Calvert St.
 Annapolis, MD 21401

Massachusetts
 Department of Commerce and Development
 Executive Office of Economic Affairs
 100 Cambridge St., 13th Fl.
 Boston, MA 02202

Michigan
 Department of Commerce
 Law Bldg., 4th Fl.
 P.O. Box 30004
 Lansing, MI 48909

Minnesota
 Department of Energy and Economic
  Development
 150 E. Kellogg Blvd., 9th Fl.
 St. Paul, MN 55101

Mississippi
 Department of Economic Development
 1201 Sillers Bldg.
 Jackson, MS 39201

Missouri
 Division of Community and Economic
  Development
 Department of Economic Development
 Truman Bldg., Box 118
 Jefferson City, MO 65102

Montana
 Department of Commerce
 1424 Ninth Ave.
 Helena, MT 59620

Nebraska
 Department of Economic Development
 301 Centennial Mall, S.
 P.O. Box 94666
 Lincoln, NE 68509-4666

Nevada
 Department of Commerce
 201 S. Fall St.
 Carson City, NV 89710

New Hampshire
 Division of Economic Development
 Resources and Economic Development
  Department
 105 Loudon Rd.
 Concord, NH 03301

New Jersey
 Department of Commerce and Economic
  Development
 1 W. State St., CN-820
 Trenton, NJ 08625

New Mexico
 Department of Economic Development and
  Tourism
 Bataan Memorial Bldg.
 Santa Fe, NM 87503

New York
 Urban Development Corporation
 1515 Broadway
 New York, NY 10036

North Carolina
 Department of Commerce
 430 N. Salisbury St.
 Raleigh, NC 27611

North Dakota
Economic Development Commission
Liberty Memorial Bldg.
Capitol Grounds
Bismarck, ND 58505

Ohio
Department of Commerce
2 Nationwide Plaza
Columbus, OH 43215
    or
Department of Development
30 E. Broad St., 25th Fl.
Columbus, OH 43215

Oklahoma
Department of Economic Development
4024 N. Lincoln Blvd.
Oklahoma City, OK 73105

Oregon
Department of Commerce
428 Labor and Industries Bldg.
Salem, OR 97310

Pennsylvania
Department of Commerce
433 Forum Bldg.
Harrisburg, PA 17120

Rhode Island
Department of Economic Development
7 Jackson Walkway
Providence, RI 02903

South Carolina
State Development Board
1301 Gervais St.
P.O. Box 927
Columbia, SC 29202

South Dakota
Department of Commerce and Regulations
State Capitol
Pierre, SD 57501

Tennessee
Department of Economic and Community
    Development
320 Sixth Ave., N.
Nashville, TN 37219

Texas
Governor's Office of Economic
    Development
Capitol Station
P.O. Box 13561
Austin, TX 78711

Utah
Department of Community and Economic
    Development
6290 State Office Bldg.
Salt Lake City, UT 84114

Vermont
Department of Development
Agency of Development and Community
    Affairs
109 State St.
Montpelier, VT 05602

Virginia
Office of Commerce and Resources
607 Ninth St. Office Bldg.
Richmond, VA 23219

Washington
Department of Trade and Economic
    Development
101 General Administration Bldg.
Olympia, WA 98504

West Virginia
Department of Commerce
State Capitol Complex
Charleston, WV 25305

Wisconsin
Department of Development
123 W. Washington Ave.
P.O. Box 7970
Madison, WI 53707

Wyoming
Department of Economic Planning and
    Development
Herschler Bldg.
Cheyenne, WY 82002

Other Sources of Information on the Area and Its Facilities

Chamber of commerce or visitors bureau
The county or city agency in charge of promoting the area's assets is one of the first places you should visit for information on employment, recreational

143

facilities, schools, cultural and social activities, shopping and medical facilities, and churches. Take a bunch of their free brochures.

Local newspapers and the yellow pages
These will give you an idea of the types of businesses in the area and a feel for what the local attitudes and social life are like.

Utility company
Only the local power company can give you accurate information on the availability and cost of supplying electricity and gas. They also have their own studies of population growth in the area and can give you some predictions on where the future growth is to occur and how soon.

Telephone company
Information on available installation and costs.

Board of education
Information on educational facilities and busing service of public and private schools.

Forest ranger station and farm advisor
Information on available fire protection service.

Department of roads
The county, city, and state road departments have information on when roads are cleared and whether private roads can be cleared by the public road crews.

Small Business Administration
This is a federal agency in charge of providing information on how to commence and operate a small business. It also makes loans available for this purpose. Write for the address of your local office (see below) or look in your local telephone directory for SBA field offices under United States Government. Almost any type of business you can think of is covered in their pamphlets. Write and request a list of available pamphlets in the following series:

Small Business Bulletins
Small Business Management Series
Management Research Summaries
Starting and Managing Series Aids Annuals

Some of those available are listed below:

Locating or Relocating Your Business	$ .50
Problems in Managing a Family-owned Business	$ .50
Checklist for Going into Business	$ .50
Thinking about Going into Business	$ .50
Feasibility Checklist for Starting a Small Business	$ .50
The Business Plan for Home-based Business	$ .50
Starting and Managing a Small Business of Your Own S/N 045-000-00212-8	$4.75
Starting and Managing a Small Service Business S/N 045-000-00207-1	$4.50
Starting and Managing a Small Business from Your Home S/N 045-000-00232-2	$1.75
Small Business Incubator Handbook: A Guide for Start-up and Management S/N 045-000-0237-3	$8.50

Address all requests and inquiries to:
    U.S. Small Business Administration
    Washington, DC 20416

U.S. Small Business Administration field offices are located in the following cities:

Albany, NY	Biloxi, MS	Charleston, WV	Concord, NH
Albuquerque, NM	Birmingham, AL	Charlotte, NC	Coral Gables, FL (Miami)
Anchorage, AK	Boise, ID	Chicago, IL	Corpus Christi, TX
Atlanta, GA	Boston, MA	Cincinnati, OH	Dallas, TX
Augusta, ME	Buffalo, NY	Clarksburg, WV	Denver, CO
Austin, TX	Camden, NJ	Cleveland, OH	Des Moines, IA
Bala Cynwyd, PA	Casper, WY	Columbia, SC	Detroit, MI
(Philadelphia)	Cedar Rapids, IA	Columbus, OH	Eau Claire, WI

144

Elmira, NY	Knoxville, TN	Oakland, CA	Shreveport, LA
El Paso, TX	Las Vegas, NV	Oklahoma City, OK	Sikeston, MO
Fairbanks, AK	Little Rock, AR	Omaha, NE	Sioux Falls, SD
Fargo, ND	Los Angeles, CA	Phoenix, AZ	South Bend, IN
Fort Worth, TX	Louisville, KY	Pittsburgh, PA	Spokane, WA
Fresno, CA	Lubbock, TX	Portland, OR	Springfield, IL
Grand Prairie, LA	Madison, WI	Providence, RI	Springfield, MO
Greenville, NC	Marquette, MI	Reno, NV	Statesboro, GA
Harlingen, TX	Marshall, TX	Richmond, VA	Syracuse, NY
Harrisburg, PA	Melville, NY	Rochester, NY	Tampa, FL
Hartford, CT	Memphis, TN	Sacramento, CA	Towson, MD
Helena, MT	Middletown, CT	Saint Louis, MO	Tucson, AZ
Holyoke, MA	Milwaukee, WI	Salt Lake City, UT	Tulsa, OK
Honolulu, HI	Minneapolis, MN	San Antonio, TX	Washington, DC
Houston, TX	Montpelier, VT	San Diego, CA	West Palm Beach, FL
Indianapolis, IN	Nashville, TN	San Francisco, CA	Wichita, KS
Jackson, MS	Newark, NJ	San Jose, CA	Wilkes-Barre, PA
Jacksonville, FL	New Orleans, LA	Santa Ana, CA	Wilmington, DE
Kansas City, MO	New York, NY	Seattle, WA	

You can get any information about the results of census activities in each state from any of the Regional Information Services of the Census Bureau listed below. They also have resources you can use in the office or purchase that will give you just about any kind of information you desire, from the history of the population growth to the age of the residents.

Census Bureau—Regional Information Services

California
11777 San Vicente Blvd., Rm. 810
Los Angeles, CA 90049

Colorado
7655 W. Mississippi Ave.
P.O. Box 26750
Denver, CO 80226

Georgia
1365 Peachtree St., N.E., Rm. 625
Atlanta, GA 30309

Illinois
55 E. Jackson Blvd., Ste. 1304
Chicago, IL 60604

Kansas
1 Gateway Center
4th and State Sts.
Kansas City, KS 66101

Massachusetts
441 Stuart St., 10th Fl.
Boston, MA 02116

Michigan
Federal Bldg. and
    U.S. Courthouse
231 W. Lafayette St., Rm. 565
Detroit, MI 48226

New York
Federal Office Bldg.
26 Federal Plaza, Rm. 37130
New York, NY 10278

North Carolina
230 South Tryon St., Ste. 800
Charlotte, NC 28202

Pennsylvania
William J. Green Jr. Federal Bldg.
600 Arch St., Rm. 9244
Philadelphia, PA 19106

Texas
1100 Commerce St., Rm. 3-C-54
Dallas, TX 75242

Washington
Lake Union Bldg.
1700 Westlake Ave., N.
Seattle, WA 98109

42. States Ranked by Total Population: 1980

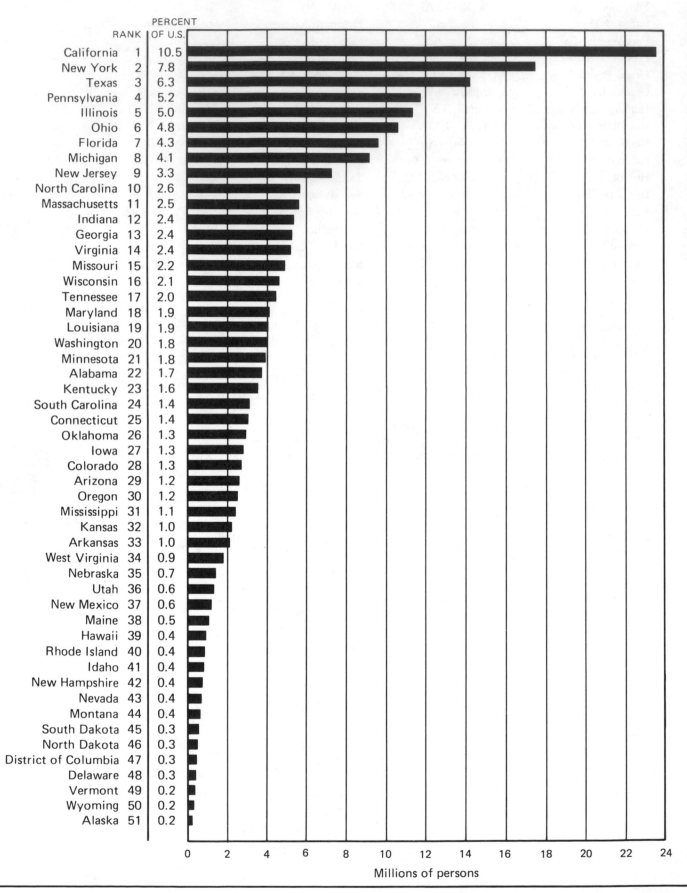

	RANK	PERCENT OF U.S.
California	1	10.5
New York	2	7.8
Texas	3	6.3
Pennsylvania	4	5.2
Illinois	5	5.0
Ohio	6	4.8
Florida	7	4.3
Michigan	8	4.1
New Jersey	9	3.3
North Carolina	10	2.6
Massachusetts	11	2.5
Indiana	12	2.4
Georgia	13	2.4
Virginia	14	2.4
Missouri	15	2.2
Wisconsin	16	2.1
Tennessee	17	2.0
Maryland	18	1.9
Louisiana	19	1.9
Washington	20	1.8
Minnesota	21	1.8
Alabama	22	1.7
Kentucky	23	1.6
South Carolina	24	1.4
Connecticut	25	1.4
Oklahoma	26	1.3
Iowa	27	1.3
Colorado	28	1.3
Arizona	29	1.2
Oregon	30	1.2
Mississippi	31	1.1
Kansas	32	1.0
Arkansas	33	1.0
West Virginia	34	0.9
Nebraska	35	0.7
Utah	36	0.6
New Mexico	37	0.6
Maine	38	0.5
Hawaii	39	0.4
Rhode Island	40	0.4
Idaho	41	0.4
New Hampshire	42	0.4
Nevada	43	0.4
Montana	44	0.4
South Dakota	45	0.3
North Dakota	46	0.3
District of Columbia	47	0.3
Delaware	48	0.3
Vermont	49	0.2
Wyoming	50	0.2
Alaska	51	0.2

Millions of persons

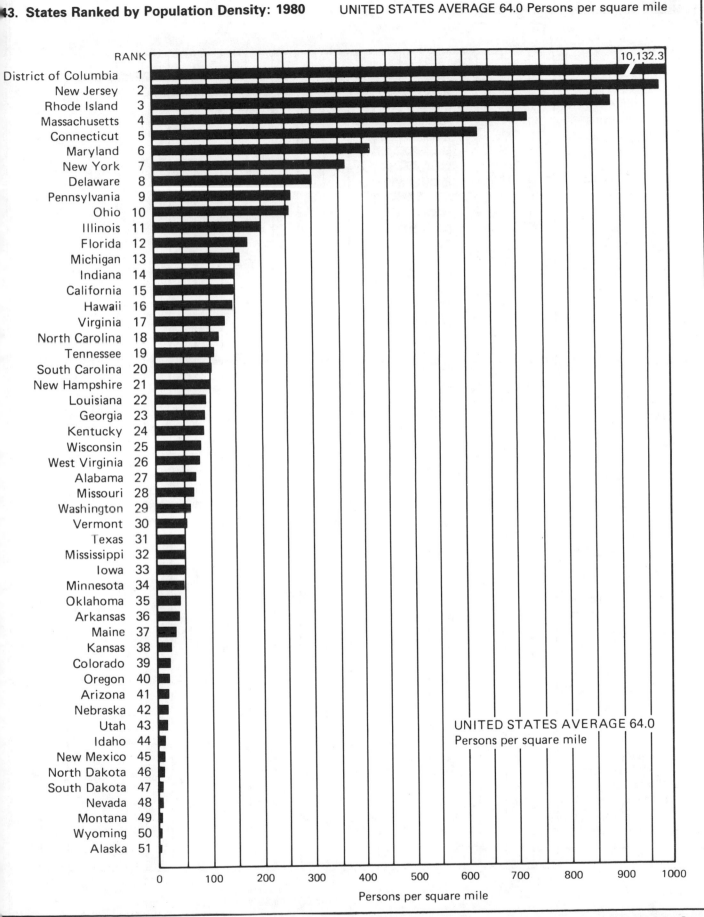

RANK		
District of Columbia	1	10,132.3
New Jersey	2	
Rhode Island	3	
Massachusetts	4	
Connecticut	5	
Maryland	6	
New York	7	
Delaware	8	
Pennsylvania	9	
Ohio	10	
Illinois	11	
Florida	12	
Michigan	13	
Indiana	14	
California	15	
Hawaii	16	
Virginia	17	
North Carolina	18	
Tennessee	19	
South Carolina	20	
New Hampshire	21	
Louisiana	22	
Georgia	23	
Kentucky	24	
Wisconsin	25	
West Virginia	26	
Alabama	27	
Missouri	28	
Washington	29	
Vermont	30	
Texas	31	
Mississippi	32	
Iowa	33	
Minnesota	34	
Oklahoma	35	
Arkansas	36	
Maine	37	
Kansas	38	
Colorado	39	
Oregon	40	
Arizona	41	
Nebraska	42	
Utah	43	
Idaho	44	
New Mexico	45	
North Dakota	46	
South Dakota	47	
Nevada	48	
Montana	49	
Wyoming	50	
Alaska	51	

UNITED STATES AVERAGE 64.0
Persons per square mile

0   100   200   300   400   500   600   700   800   900   1000

Persons per square mile

44. States Ranked by Amount of Population Change: 1970–1980

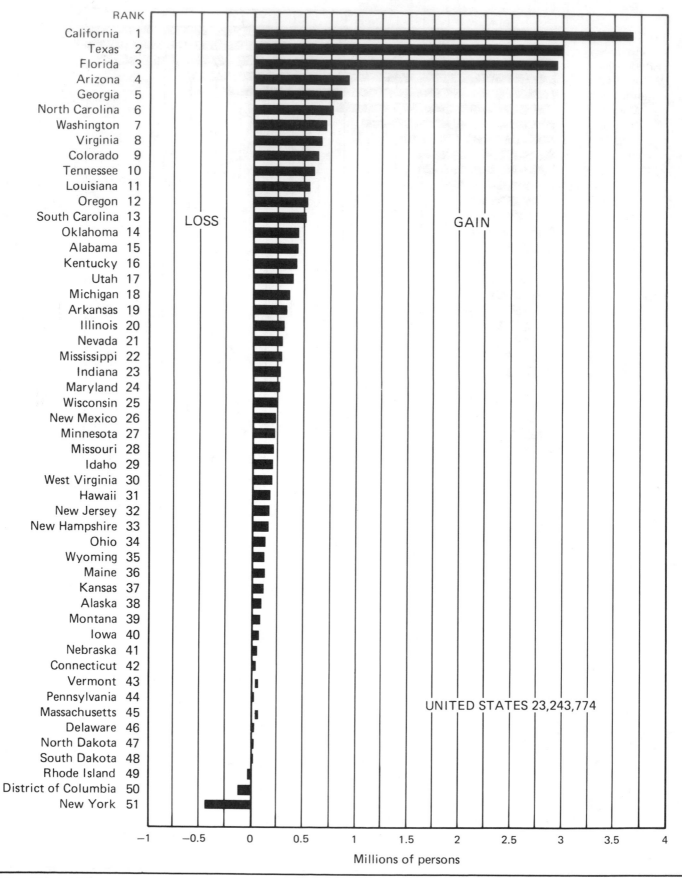

RANK

State	Rank
California	1
Texas	2
Florida	3
Arizona	4
Georgia	5
North Carolina	6
Washington	7
Virginia	8
Colorado	9
Tennessee	10
Louisiana	11
Oregon	12
South Carolina	13
Oklahoma	14
Alabama	15
Kentucky	16
Utah	17
Michigan	18
Arkansas	19
Illinois	20
Nevada	21
Mississippi	22
Indiana	23
Maryland	24
Wisconsin	25
New Mexico	26
Minnesota	27
Missouri	28
Idaho	29
West Virginia	30
Hawaii	31
New Jersey	32
New Hampshire	33
Ohio	34
Wyoming	35
Maine	36
Kansas	37
Alaska	38
Montana	39
Iowa	40
Nebraska	41
Connecticut	42
Vermont	43
Pennsylvania	44
Massachusetts	45
Delaware	46
North Dakota	47
South Dakota	48
Rhode Island	49
District of Columbia	50
New York	51

LOSS   GAIN

UNITED STATES 23,243,774

−1   −0.5   0   0.5   1   1.5   2   2.5   3   3.5   4

Millions of persons

U.S. Department of Commerce

Bureau of the Census

1–18 UNITED STATES SUMMARY

NUMBER OF INHABITANTS

45. States Ranked by Percent of Population Change: 1970–1980

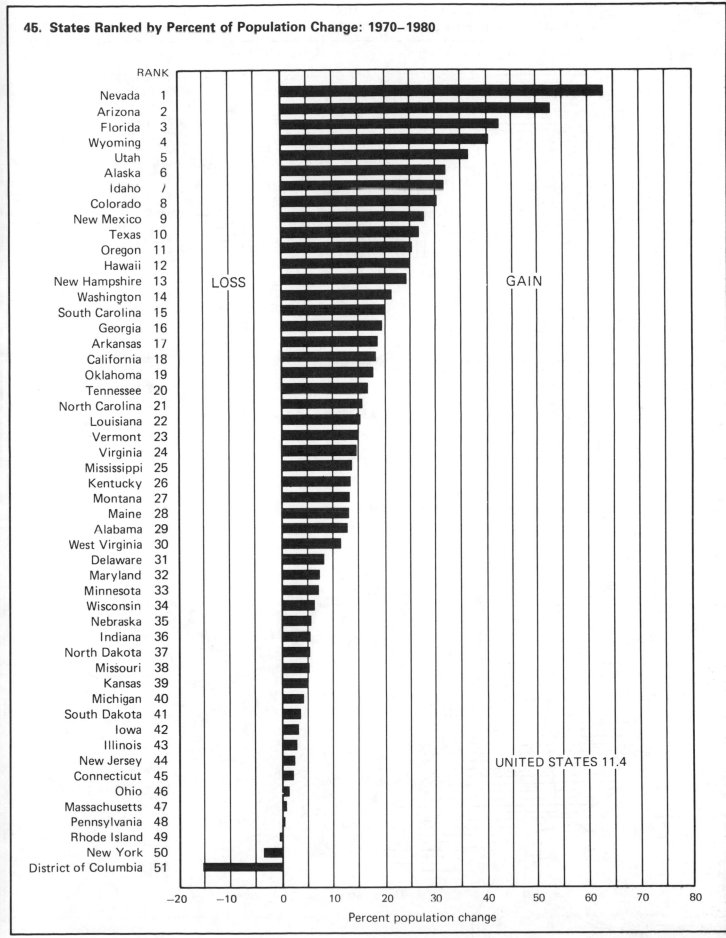

RANK	
Nevada	1
Arizona	2
Florida	3
Wyoming	4
Utah	5
Alaska	6
Idaho	7
Colorado	8
New Mexico	9
Texas	10
Oregon	11
Hawaii	12
New Hampshire	13
Washington	14
South Carolina	15
Georgia	16
Arkansas	17
California	18
Oklahoma	19
Tennessee	20
North Carolina	21
Louisiana	22
Vermont	23
Virginia	24
Mississippi	25
Kentucky	26
Montana	27
Maine	28
Alabama	29
West Virginia	30
Delaware	31
Maryland	32
Minnesota	33
Wisconsin	34
Nebraska	35
Indiana	36
North Dakota	37
Missouri	38
Kansas	39
Michigan	40
South Dakota	41
Iowa	42
Illinois	43
New Jersey	44
Connecticut	45
Ohio	46
Massachusetts	47
Pennsylvania	48
Rhode Island	49
New York	50
District of Columbia	51

LOSS GAIN

UNITED STATES 11.4

Percent population change

−20 −10 0 10 20 30 40 50 60 70 80

46. Percent Change in Total Population by States: 1970–1980

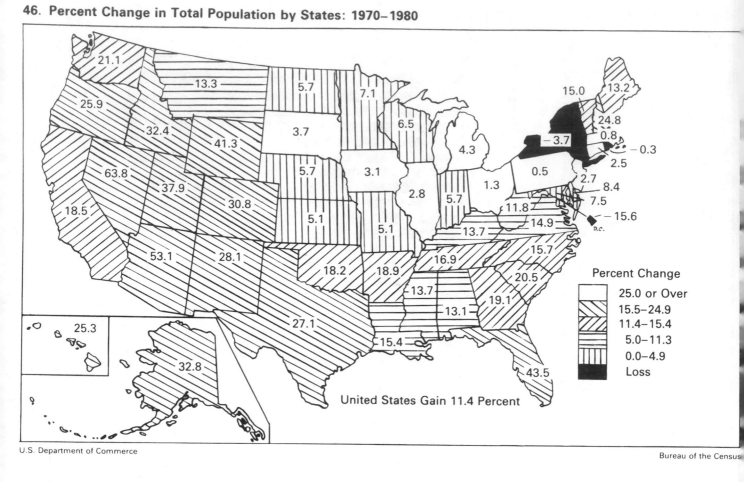

Percent Change

- 25.0 or Over
- 15.5–24.9
- 11.4–15.4
- 5.0–11.3
- 0.0–4.9
- Loss

United States Gain 11.4 Percent

U.S. Department of Commerce

Bureau of the Census

47. Percent Change in Urban Population by States: 1970–1980

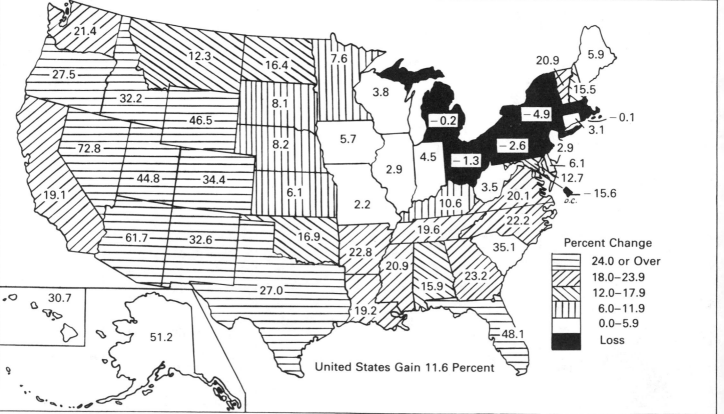

Percent Change

- 24.0 or Over
- 18.0–23.9
- 12.0–17.9
- 6.0–11.9
- 0.0–5.9
- Loss

United States Gain 11.6 Percent

U.S. Department of Commerce

Bureau of the Census

48. Percent Change in Rural Population by States: 1970–1980

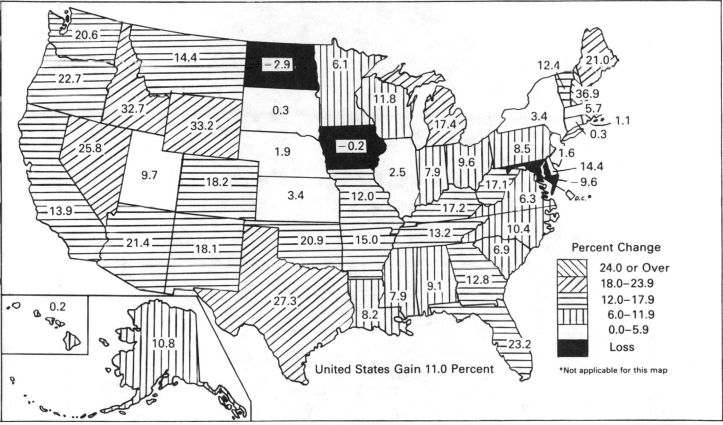

Percent Change

	24.0 or Over
	18.0–23.9
	12.0–17.9
	6.0–11.9
	0.0–5.9
	Loss

*Not applicable for this map

United States Gain 11.0 Percent

Source: PC80-1-A1 U.S. Summary, Table 13 U.S. Department of Commerce

Bureau of the Census

49. Population Density by Counties: 1980

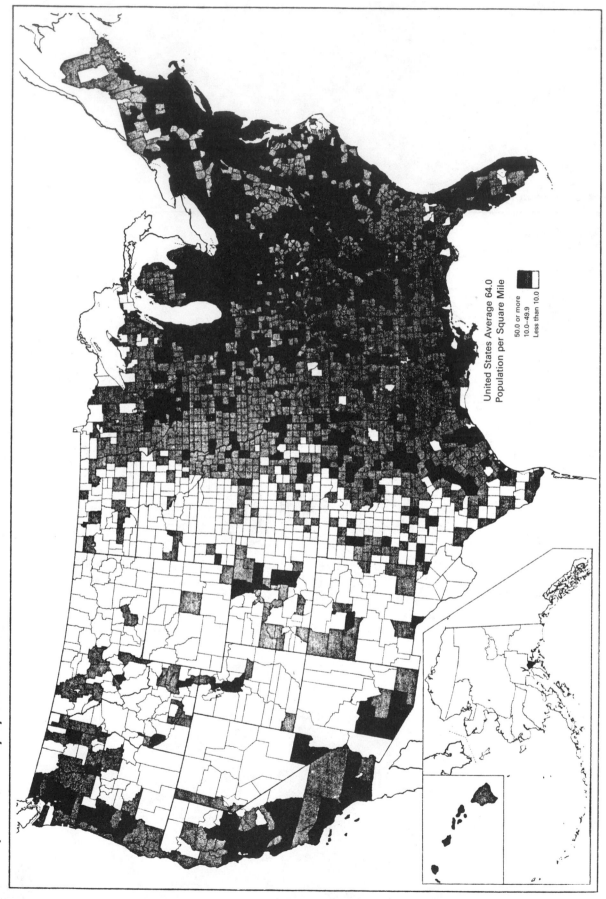

United States Average 64.0
Population per Square Mile

50.0 or more
10.0–49.9
Less than 10.0

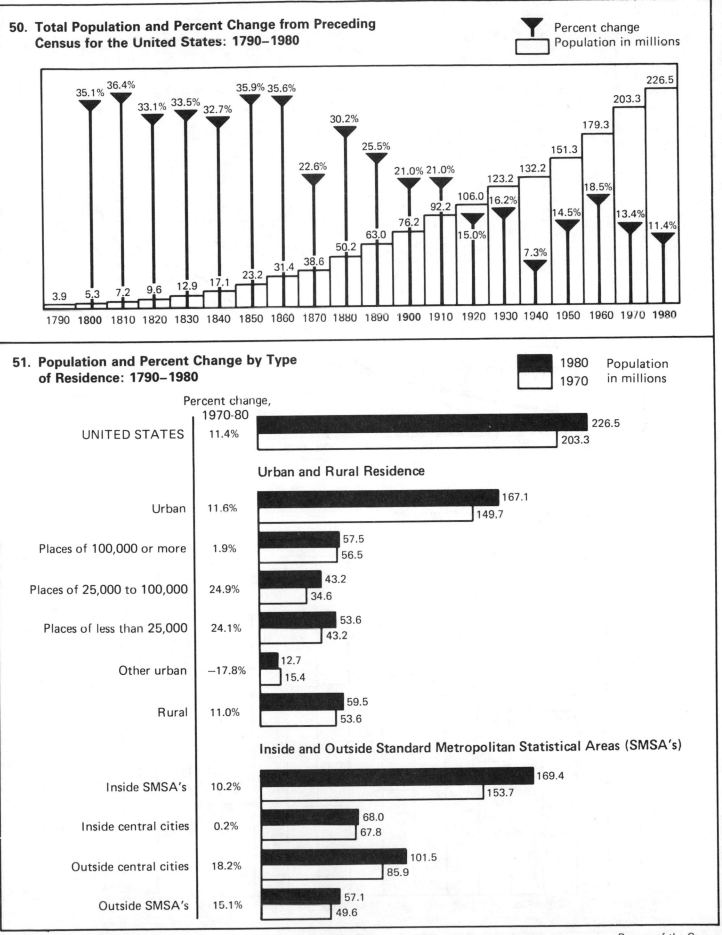

50. Total Population and Percent Change from Preceding Census for the United States: 1790–1980

▼ Percent change
☐ Population in millions

Year	Population (millions)	Percent change
1790	3.9	
1800	5.3	35.1%
1810	7.2	36.4%
1820	9.6	33.1%
1830	12.9	33.5%
1840	17.1	32.7%
1850	23.2	35.9%
1860	31.4	35.6%
1870	38.6	22.6%
1880	50.2	30.2%
1890	63.0	25.5%
1900	76.2	21.0%
1910	92.2	21.0%
1920	106.0	15.0%
1930	123.2	16.2%
1940	132.2	7.3%
1950	151.3	14.5%
1960	179.3	18.5%
1970	203.3	13.4%
1980	226.5	11.4%

51. Population and Percent Change by Type of Residence: 1790–1980

■ 1980   Population
☐ 1970   in millions

	Percent change, 1970-80	1980	1970
UNITED STATES	11.4%	226.5	203.3

Urban and Rural Residence

	Percent change, 1970-80	1980	1970
Urban	11.6%	167.1	149.7
Places of 100,000 or more	1.9%	57.5	56.5
Places of 25,000 to 100,000	24.9%	43.2	34.6
Places of less than 25,000	24.1%	53.6	43.2
Other urban	−17.8%	12.7	15.4
Rural	11.0%	59.5	53.6

Inside and Outside Standard Metropolitan Statistical Areas (SMSA's)

	Percent change, 1970-80	1980	1970
Inside SMSA's	10.2%	169.4	153.7
Inside central cities	0.2%	68.0	67.8
Outside central cities	18.2%	101.5	85.9
Outside SMSA's	15.1%	57.1	49.6

52. Population of Regions: 1790–1980

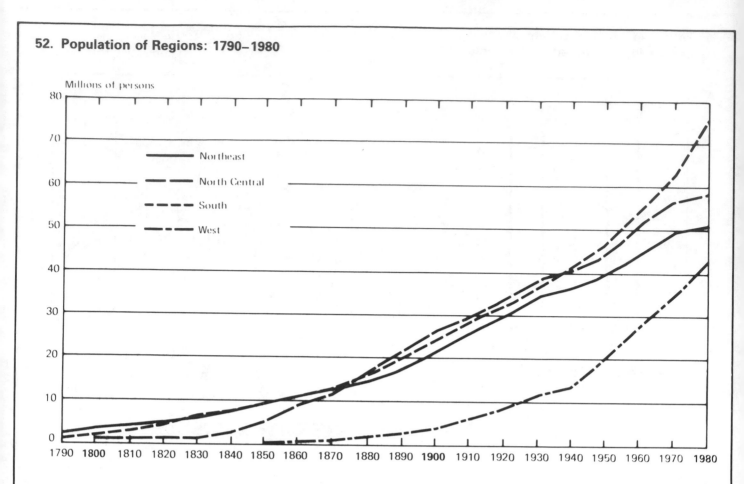

Millions of persons

Northeast
North Central
South
West

53. Percent Distribution by Regions: 1790–1980

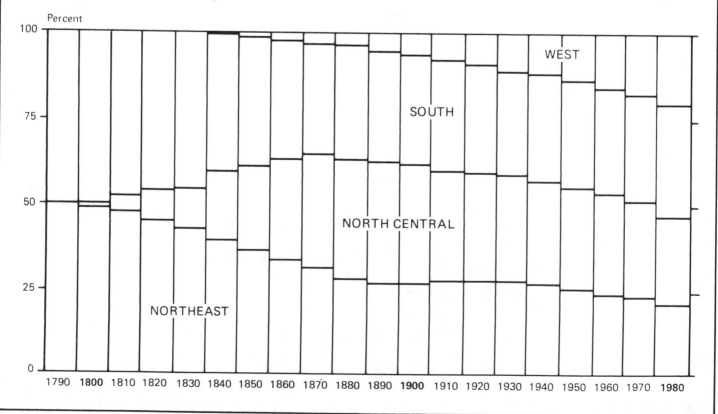

Percent

WEST

SOUTH

NORTH CENTRAL

NORTHEAST

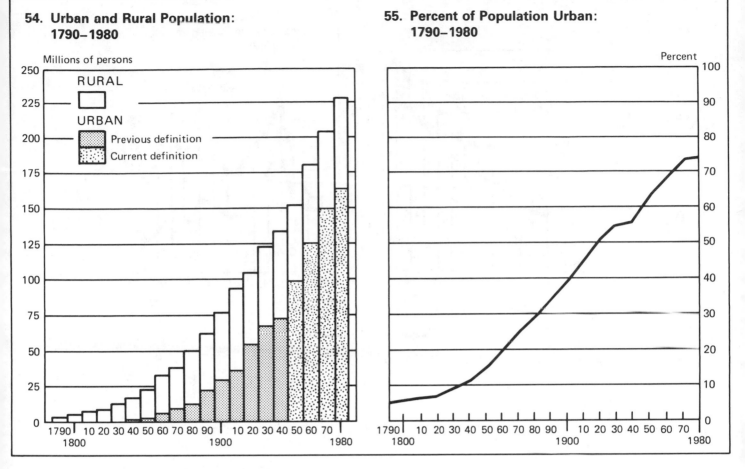

54. Urban and Rural Population: 1790–1980

Millions of persons

RURAL

URBAN
Previous definition
Current definition

55. Percent of Population Urban: 1790–1980

Percent

56. Changes in Farming: 1950–1984

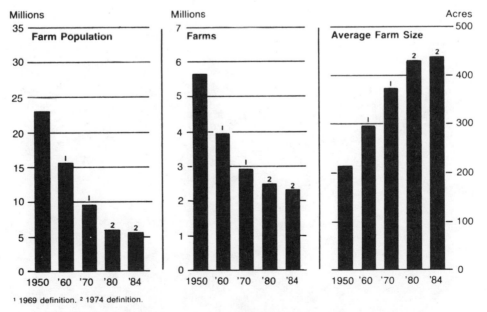

Millions — Farm Population

Millions — Farms

Acres — Average Farm Size

1950 '60 '70 '80 '84

¹ 1969 definition. ² 1974 definition.

Source: Chart prepared by U.S. Bureau of the Census. For data, see tables 1115 and 1120.

Over time, the Bureau of the Census has used varying definitions of a farm. In the Census of Agriculture for 1974 and later, a farm was defined as any place from which $1,000 or more of agricultural products were sold, or would have been sold, during the census year. Between 1959 and 1969, places of less than ten acres were counted as farms if estimated sales of agricultural products for the year amounted to at least $250, and places of ten or more acres if such sales amounted to at least $50. In 1950 and 1954, places of three or more acres were counted as farms if the annual value of agricultural products, exclusive of home garden products, amounted to $150 or more. Places of less than three acres were counted as farms only if annual sales amounted to $150 or more.

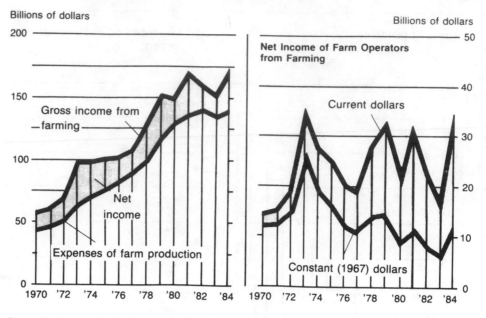

Billions of dollars

Billions of dollars

200

50

Net Income of Farm Operators from Farming

40

150

Gross income from farming

Current dollars

30

100

Net income

20

50

Expenses of farm production

Constant (1967) dollars

10

0

0

1970 '72 '74 '76 '78 '80 '82 '84

1970 '72 '74 '76 '78 '80 '82 '84

Source: Chart prepared by U.S. Bureau of the Census. For data, see table 1144.

57. Farm Income and Expenses: 1970–1984

III

THE LAND AND THE LAW

CHAPTER 8

Land Descriptions and Surveys

Cursed be he that removeth his neighbor's landmark. And the people shall say, amen.

—Deuteronomy

Remove not the ancient landmark which thy fathers have set.

—Psalms

Throughout history most problems of landownership have arisen from boundary disputes. Surveying was begun by the Egyptians nearly seven thousand years ago, and several references to boundary marking can be found in the Bible, but even today most land has not been accurately surveyed, and boundary disputes continue to be a major problem for the landowner. The three most common areas of litigation for rural property owners are easements, boundary lines, and water rights.

Laws require only that a deed contain a legal "description" of the land, which defines the parcel in such a way that it cannot be confused with any other piece of land. However, this description does not tell you accurately where the boundaries are located on the ground. That is done by a survey, based on the land description. Because surveys are expensive, many rural parcels are sold without them, despite their importance to the buyer. I will explain why you should demand to have a survey taken on land before you buy after I explain some of the principles involved in land descriptions and surveys.

159

In the United States parcels are legally described in one of the following three ways:

1. By reference to a section, township, and range that are part of the U.S. Government Survey or Rectangular Survey System.
2. By metes and bounds,
3. By reference to a recorded map, plat, or tract system.

DESCRIPTIONS BY REFERENCE TO A SECTION, TOWNSHIP, AND RANGE

The United States government, under the direction of the U.S. Surveyor General, began to survey its original public lands in 1784 using the Rectangular Survey System (the Cadastral System), dividing the lands into sections, townships, and ranges. Large portions of land were broken up into rectangles on a map and then located and marked on the ground by a survey team. By using these marked points, any parcel within a rectangle can be described and located today.

The U.S. Rectangular Survey System is the most common form of land description used in the country today. Twenty-nine states use it, including all the states west of the Mississippi except Texas and Hawaii. It was the form used when we purchased our land, and I will use it throughout this book.

The description in our deed states that we own:

The South Half of the Northwest Quarter of Section 21, Township 4 North, Range 2 East, Humboldt Meridian.

The government started its survey by dividing its land into portions, each of which was given a vertical line running north and south called the *principal meridian* and a horizontal line running east and west, perpendicular to the principal meridian, called its *base line*. There are thirty-six principal meridians in different parts of the country. (See illustration 58.) Each meridian is individually named; for example, Mt. Diablo Meridian, Indian Meridian, and Second Principal Meridian. A description including the name of the principal meridian locates the area in which the land is situated. You then work backward in the description.

58. Principal Meridians in the U.S. Rectangular System

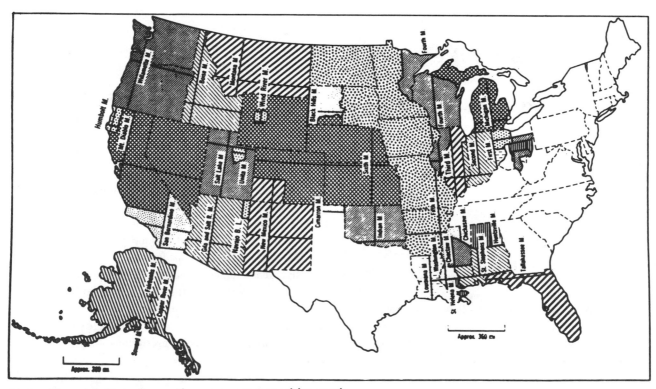

Note: The shading shows the area governed by each
principal meridian and its base line.

On both sides of the principal meridian line, the land is cut into equal strips 6 miles wide called *ranges*. (See illustration 59.) On both sides of the base line, the land is cut into equal strips 6 miles wide called *townships*. (See illustration 60.) Together these strips form a "land checkerboard." Each square of the "checkerboard" is called a *township* and has boundary lines 6 miles long on all four sides. (See illustration 61.) The range and township strips are numbered outward from the meridian and base lines and can be used in the same way you use a highway map or atlas to find any township.

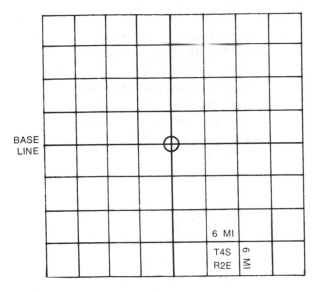

61. Resulting Townships

In illustration 61, I indicate which township contains our land. It is a square located two ranges to the east of the principal meridian and four townships to the south of the base line. Thus, it is described as "Township 4 South, Range 2 East."

Since a township is a square 6 miles on a side, it contains 36 square miles. (Area equals length times width.) Thus, each township is divided into 36 square-mile *sections*, each containing approximately 640 acres and having sides about 1 mile long. (See illustration 62.) (An acre is a square approximately 208.71 feet long on each side with an area of 43,560 square feet or 4,840 square yards.) Due to the primitive methods used for the original surveys, many sections may actually be severely distorted and contain much less, or much more, acreage than 640 acres, which is the theoretical number of acres in a section. The sections in each township are numbered, starting in the northeast corner and moving alternately right to left, then left to right, concluding in the southeast corner. Illustration 62 indicates how Township 4 South, Range 2 East is divided into 36 sections. Section 21, in which our land is located, is shaded.

Each 640-acre section is then quartered into 160-acre parcels, called *quarter sections*, which are designated as the northeast, southeast, northwest, and southwest quarters. Quarter sections are then quartered into parcels, called forties or *square* forties," since each one contains approximately 40 acres. A square forty can then be quartered into four 10-acre parcels, which might be subdivided

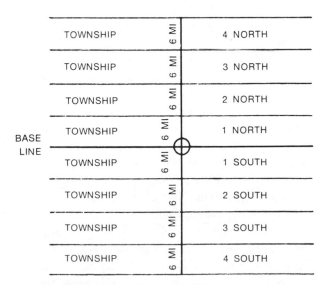

59. Dividing into Ranges

60. Dividing into Townships

further into four 2½-acre parcels, and so forth. Illustration 63 indicates the possible subdivisions of section 21. The location of our 80 acres is the shaded portion of the section.

When we found the land we wanted to buy, the real estate agent gave us a copy of its description as it would appear in our deed. Using a large quadrangle map, based on the U.S. Rectangular Survey that covered the proper meridian and township, we

62. Dividing Townships into Sections

63. Dividing a Section into Quarters and Smaller Parcels

located section 21. Taking a pencil, we quartered the section and then halved the northwest quarter horizontally. Thus, we located the south half of the northwest quarter of section 21. The map depicted geographical land features, and we could see what roads and creeks went through the land parcel. (Illustration 53 in chapter 9, ''Easement Rights,'' is a copy of what we saw on the map.) Thus, without actually finding the corners and walking the boundaries, we got an approximate idea of what we would be buying. By superimposing the map over an aerial photograph of the same scale, we saw a more accurate picture of the land.

You will notice that section 21 in illustration 53 in chapter 9 is not a perfect rectangle. Because of the curvature of the earth or inaccurate measurements at the time of the original survey, the sections may not be equal in acreage. For instance, our land seems to include 80 acres. In fact, on the ground the area covers only 78½ acres. With large parcels, often slightly more acreage will be advertised than will actually be sold. You can find out the true amount by referring to a legal survey of the land. A survey might already exist and be filed in a volume entitled Record of Surveys, Book of Maps, or Official Records in the county or local recorder's office, or the seller might have a copy of a survey. In cases where no survey presently exists, you will need to be protected in the contract of sale if a subsequent survey shows that less land is present than is advertised. (See Clause 2, Clause 3, and Clause 17(b) of the Model Contract of Sale in chapter 28.) If you are buying land advertised as 40 acres at $1,000 an acre, and in fact you are only receiving 38½ acres, such a safety clause could save you $1,500. Most sellers cover themselves by indicating that the acreage is approximate, for example, 40 ± acres.

In the 1800s, the government land office (now known as the Bureau of Land Management) surveyed in each area of the United States where the Rectangular Survey System exists. The purpose of these surveys was to compile township maps. The maps were first divided into townships and sections on the drawing board. Then the government land office contracted out to surveyors who went throughout the country and established and marked corners, generally every one-half mile around the perimeter of sections. They did this until they completed a survey of each township. They then completed a township plat which was returned to the United States government. Once approved it was then the basis for issuing land patents to the original homesteaders.

These numbered and lettered markers are the starting points for private surveyors hired to locate and subdivide parcels within the sections. The surveyors from the Government Land Office took thorough survey notes, called *field notes*, which are used by subsequent surveyors to find section corner markers.

You can get a copy of the original survey maps and notes indicating the location of section markers in your area from the BLM office in the state. (See appendix B for addresses of BLM offices.) You might also be able to get a copy of these notes and maps from the county surveyor or county engineer. However, you will probably need only the latest survey on which would be indicated the location of monuments and how they are marked or *scribed;* for example, a blaze in a tree or a metal pipe in the ground.

DESCRIPTIONS BY METES AND BOUNDS

Although most of the United States is within the U.S. Rectangular Survey System, many deeds describe land using the method of *metes* and *bounds*. *Metes* are measures of length, such as inches, feet, and yards. *Bounds* are natural and artificial boundaries, such as rivers and roads, or previously established boundaries. This system, which has been described as a treasure hunt, follows a course from a fixed point, called a monument or marker, to other fixed points until the area of land is entirely enclosed.

In a description by metes and bounds, a fixed starting point is found on the ground that can be easily identified, such as an unusual tree, a pile of rocks, a creek, the mouth of a stream, a known and fixed point, or some other object. If a unique object cannot be found, the position is identified by a measurement from the nearest government land corner, or some other accepted property control. Other similarly identified objects must be found at various points around the land so that a boundary line can be formed that encloses the area. Often the markers are highly variable, such as rivers or

dirt roads, or impermanent, such as rock piles or trees. You may have heard stories of a landowner moving boundary markers to increase the size of his land. It is easy to get away with such tactics under this kind of a system. For this reason, a metes and bounds description should be used only as a last resort. The system is usually used when irregular land shapes are sold and in areas that have not been laid out according to the U.S. Rectangular Survey.

Below is an example of a metes and bounds description:

Beginning at a point that is 500 feet South and 200 feet East of the Northwest corner of Section 5, Township 2 South, Range 3 West;

Thence North 100 feet, thence East 200 feet to the West boundary of Jim Jones's property described in Book 60 of Deeds, page 102 of the Official Records of Bloomingdale County;

Thence South along said line 100 feet;

Thence West 200 feet to the point of beginning.

The tract as described contains approximately 200 acres.

Regardless of how the parcel is described, you must be able to find the boundaries to your land on the ground by using the description. The description must describe a boundary that totally encloses the parcel. That is, it must start and end at the same point on the ground. If this is not the case, do not buy the land until the description is legally perfected.

MAP, TRACT, OR PLAT SYSTEM

The third common method used to describe a parcel of land is by reference to another recorded instrument that identifies the land and usually contains a survey. You will probably not encounter this type of description unless you purchase land as part of a large rural or second-home subdivision or a minor subdivision or parcel-split. In that case, all the lots should already be surveyed and recorded with the county recorder in a final parcel map, subdivision map, tract map, or plat. (Illustration 76 in chapter 14, "Subdivisions and Condominiums," is an example of a parcel map.) Each parcel within the subdivision is described by referring to its location on the recorded map. For example:

The real property in the County of Goshen, State of Arkansas, described as Lot 80, Happy Home Subdivision (per map recorded July 2, 1988, at page 46 of Book 8 of Maps), Office of the County Recorder of Goshen County.

If you look up page 46 in Book 8 of Maps you will find a map of the subdivision divided into parcels or lots. Be sure the lot number on the map corresponds to the lot you think you are purchasing. The subdivision map will show the location of markers on the ground that delineate the boundaries of each parcel. Using the map, locate the markers for your lot, and you will see what you are buying. You should purchase a copy of the recorded map from the local office where it is recorded.

If your land is described by reference to another document, the document should be properly recorded with the county recorder and must correctly identify your parcel of land.

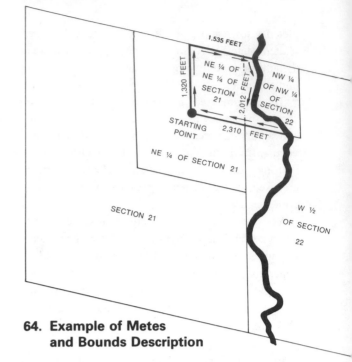

64. Example of Metes and Bounds Description

along the southerly line of the Northwest quarter of the Northwest quarter of Section 22 a distance of 2,310 feet to the point of beginning.

LEGAL SURVEYS

A legal survey is made by a team of licensed surveyors who carefully lay out in *bearings* (angles) and distances the exact location of the property on the ground. The survey is based on the description of the parcel given in the deed. So that you will have no delusions as to where your boundaries lie, be sure that they are accurately surveyed and marked on the ground by a legal survey.

An example of a metes and bounds description is shown in illustration 64. Trace out the boundary line in the illustration by following the description. The parcel of land taking in the northeast quarter of the northeast quarter of section 21 goes to the road, giving it an irregular shape. A description by metes and bounds of this land could read like this:

Beginning at the Southwest corner of the Northeast quarter of the Northeast quarter of Section 21, Township 4 South, Range 2 East, Mt. Diablo Meridian; proceed a distance of 1,320 feet north along the western line of said Northeast quarter of the Northeast quarter of Section 21 to the Northwest corner of the Northeast quarter of the Northeast quarter of Section 21 a distance of 1,535 feet to the paved county road, the County Road; thence southerly along the road a distance of 2,012 feet to the southern line of the Northwest quarter of Section 22; thence west

THE SURVEY AND YOUR LAND PURCHASE

If the seller or real estate agent has a copy of a survey in his possession that he claims identifies the boundaries of the land for sale, check these points:

1. Was the survey conducted by a licensed surveyor?

2. Is it recorded in the recorder's office as an official survey of the land?

3. By using it, can you locate on the ground exactly where the boundaries are? Have permanent markers been placed in the ground by the surveyor, and/or have the boundary lines been flagged?

In most cases, only the corners of the property are marked with permanent stakes. Sometimes, a line will be *flagged,* that is plastic ribbons will be tied on trees or bushes, or spiked into the ground all along the line. If you can locate all the corners, you might be able to estimate the boundary lines fairly accurately yourself with a compass, a tape, a flag on a tall post, and the help of a friend or two. However, if an important part of the property you are buying, such as a spring, creek, road, or house, appears to be close to a boundary line, you should definitely get a licensed surveyor to run the line between the two corner points before you buy.

If no survey of the land exists, you can only estimate from a map where the boundaries lie. When an inch on a map equals 1,000 feet on the ground, it takes only the thickness of a pencil lead to put a valuable stream either on or off the property.

Surveys are expensive. The average fee in our area is $600 a day for a two-person crew. The rates vary across the country from $75–150/hour for a two-man crew, which is the most common crew used for private surveys. The total cost depends on the amount of time it takes to find the corners, run the boundaries, and complete the office research, calculations, and mapping as well as other technical details. If no surveys have been done in the area around the land and if the locations of marked section corners or other starting points are far away, the job could take a week or more and cost over $5,000. Often large sections of land in rural areas have been sparsely or inaccurately surveyed. The job will also take longer if the terrain is rugged, if the parcel is large, or if you want the surveyors to run and mark the entire length of the boundary lines rather than just stake out the corners. Always go to the local surveyor and ask him what he knows about the land. You can find the surveyors by looking in the telephone book yellow pages under Surveyors—Land. The local surveyor will give you an estimate of what a total survey would cost, or the cost of just flagging a line. He can calculate the acreage you are buying once the survey is complete. He will tell you if any surveys have been done on the total property, or along any of its boundary lines. You might also need a road easement surveyed, and he can give you the cost of that service as well.

If you want a guarantee that you are getting what you are paying for, you must demand a legal survey before you buy a parcel of land. If you have a choice between a civil engineer and a licensed sur-

veyor, I recommend using a licensed surveyor because they are specialists in their field. The seller should pay to have a survey done if one does not already exist. Naturally, he will be reluctant to provide you with a survey if it will cost him any money. But sometimes he has already added the estimated cost of a survey into his asking price, anticipating that the buyer will demand a survey. Thus, in reality, you are already paying for it.

In many cases, the seller will state that the price will have to be increased if you want a legal survey. If you are certain that you want the land and the purchase price is otherwise satisfactory, you should insist on a survey and pay the seller the cost involved. You will get your money back when you sell the land, since property is more valuable when it is surveyed. It is also easier to sell. But don't give in to the seller without a fight. At least, try to get him to pay half of the survey cost.

I have encountered instances where the real estate agent paid for a survey in order to make a sale to a demanding buyer. An agent would rather make half a commission than none at all. If the seller is hesitant, never hesitate to ask the agent to get the survey done.

A few states have laws prohibiting a seller from conveying land without a legally recorded survey. Most subdivision laws governing the creation of new parcels require surveys of each parcel to be sold. My Model Contract of Sale has protective clauses in it that make the closing of the deal subject to buyer's approval of a legal survey so you will know how much land you are acquiring and where the boundary lines are. See Clause 2, clause 3, Clause 16(b), and Clause 17(b) of the Model Contract and the accompanying explanation in chapter 28.

You will undoubtedly encounter real estate agents who will tell you that it is not customary to get land surveyed in the area and that your neighbors agree on where the property lines are. For such an agreement to be legally binding, there must be a recorded boundary line agreement in the county

recorder's office. The agent will point out to you where the approximate boundaries of the property are. Unfortunately, many people who buy land on this basis find out later that the boundaries are not where the agent "thought they were." Several years ago in our area a highly publicized lawsuit was initiated against a well-established real estate agent in town who sold the same waterfall to three different land buyers. Had the buyers demanded surveys before they bought, this could not have happened. As a general rule, never buy land without a condition in the contract giving you the right to approve a survey prior to the close of escrow, and then see that you have a survey done if there is any question in your mind about the location of essential features of your intended purchase, such as a house site, creek, spring, or grove of trees.

MEASUREMENTS

A List of Measurements Used in the Rectangular Survey

Township = 36 square miles = 6 miles on each side.
Section = 1 square mile = 640 acres = 5,280 feet on a side = 80 chains.
Quarter section = 160 acres = 2,640 feet on a side = 40 chains.

A List of Measurements That Might Be Used in Any Type of Survey

1 link = 7.92 inches.
1 rod = 16.5 feet = 25 links = 5.5 yards.
1 chain = 66 feet = 4 rods.
1 pole = 1 rod.
1 mile = 5,280 feet = 80 chains = 52.8 engineer's chains = 320 rods.
1 furlong = 40 rods.
1 acre = 10 square chains = 1/640 of a square mile = 43,560 square feet = 4,840 square yards = 160 square rods. If it is a square acre, it will be 208.71 feet on a side.

These measurements are used in old surveys. More recent surveys are conducted with a steel tape and electronic measuring instruments rather than a chain.

Even more recently, modern technology has replaced the more traditional measuring tapes, com-

passes, and solar transits with electronic instruments. Microwave, light wave, laser beam, photogrammetry, and gyroscopic orientations are among the new, high-tech equipment bringing changes to an occupation dating back to biblical times. A surveyor today often goes out into the field with thousands of dollars' worth of equipment in order to make the most accurate survey possible.

Measurements are taken on the ground without regard for height variations in the earth's surface. Thus if the measurement is a line 500 feet long, it is taken as if measuring along a flat level water surface.

In illustration 65, the 800-foot walking distance is measured as 500 feet because the measurement is taken as though it were along a flat level water surface. If it were not done this way, surveys and land descriptions would be even more ambiguous and fluctuating than they are at the present time.

COMMON SURVEYING TERMS

BEARING TREE. A marked tree used as a corner accessory, its distance and direction from the corner being recorded. Bearing trees are identified by prescribed marks cut into their trunks; the species and sizes of the trees are also recorded.

CORNER. A point on the earth, determined by the surveying process, that defines an extremity on a boundary.

FIELD NOTES. The official written record of a survey conducted by any surveyor and used by him to draft his final map, which becomes the official record of the survey. In many areas this map will be recorded with field notes on it at the county recorder's office.

MEANDER LINE. A traverse of the margin of a permanent natural body of water or any line that meanders, such as along a road, creek, or lake.

MONUMENT. The physical object that marks the location of a corner point.

ORIGINAL SURVEY. A cadastral survey that creates land boundaries and marks them for the first time.

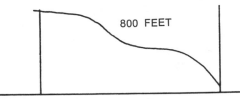

65. Measurements Taken as though Ground Were Flat

PLAT. A graphic representation drawn to scale depicting the actual survey as described in the official field notes.

RESURVEY. Cadastral survey to identify and remark the boundaries of lands that were established by an earlier survey.

TRAVERSE. A sequence of lengths and directions of lines connecting a series of stations that are field points on the ground.

WITNESS CORNER. A monumented point usually set back on the true line survey near a corner point that cannot be physically occupied or that falls at a place subject to destruction by the elements. The witness corner is then a reference to the true corner point.

USEFUL RESOURCES

The following are available from:
Superintendent of Documents
Government Printing Office
Washington, DC 20402

Specifications for Descriptions of Tracts of Land Map Data Catalog. Explains how to order cartographic holdings from U.S. Geological Survey, as well as other federal, state, and private agencies
S/N 024-001-03522-7 $4.00

Map Projections Used by the United States Geological Survey
S/N 024-001-03497-2 $8.00

Restoration of Lost or Obliterated Corners and Subdivision of Sections
S/N 024-011-00012-7 $4.25

U.S. Department of the Interior
Bureau of Land Management
Denver Federal Center, Bldg. 50
Denver, CO 80225

Public Land Surveying: A Profession

National Cartographic Information Center

The National Cartographic Information Center (NCIC) of the USGS provides a nationwide information service for U.S. cartographic data. NCIC gives the public, as well as federal, state, and local government agencies, easier access to information about maps and charts, aerial and satellite photographs and imagery, map data in digital form, and geodetic control data obtained by more than thirty different federal agencies. Information and assistance in placing orders can be obtained from any of the offices.

NCIC–Headquarters
U.S. Geological Survey
507 National Center
Reston, VA 22092

NCIC–Mid-Continent
U.S. Geological Survey
1400 Independent Rd.
Rolla, MO 65401

NCIC–Rocky Mountain
U.S. Geological Survey
Federal Center, Box 25046
Mail Stop 504
Denver, CO 80225

NCIC–NSTL Station
U.S. Geological Survey
Bldg. 3101
NSTL Station, MS 39529

NCIC–West
U.S. Geological Survey
345 Middlefield Rd.
Menlo Park, CA 94025

NCIC–Alaska Office
U.S. Geological Survey
4230 University Dr.
Anchorage, AK 99508-4664

The following are available from any of the above offices:

Map Accuracy
Looking for an Old Map

This office also has a large number of historical topographic maps dating from 1879. If you are interested in obtaining a photographic reproduction of a particular map, send a description of the area that you want the map to include. You may be able to obtain a beautiful historical map of your land.

The article *Surveying Your Own Land* can be found in *Mother Earth News*, Issue No. 101, which can be ordered for $3.00 from:
Mother Earth News
P.O. Box 70
Hendersonville, NC 28793-9989

167

CHAPTER 9

Easement Rights

Most of the country land we looked at was located some distance away from a public road. Usually one or more people owned land between the property and the road. This is true of the land we bought, which is a mile in from the public county road, with access to it by a single private dirt road. The dirt access road passes through three individually owned parcels. Before we signed any papers we wanted to be guaranteed that we would have a legal right to cross the private land from the county road to our place. In legal language, we wanted a *deeded easement* for ingress and egress.

Easement conflicts frequently cause legal disputes in and out of court, but there is no reason why you should have any problems if you do a thorough job of investigating and negotiating before you buy. When you are shown a piece of land with no direct access to a public road, the first thing you should do is ask the agent if there are deeded easements to it. Ask him to show you a map that identifies all intervening parcels and their owners. If he tells you there are no existing deeded easements to the land, then it is presently worthless. What value is land if you don't have a legal right to get to it? As foolish as it may seem, people have unknowingly bought such land in the past and will continue to do so.

An agent may tell you that it is okay; there is a prescriptive easement to the land or some other type of unrecorded easement, like an easement by necessity. These kinds of easements are not binding until after they have been granted by a court of law and then the judgment granting such an easement will appear in the public records. If your agent cannot show you a written recorded easement, then none presently exists legally. Getting one of these types of easements granted in a court of law is not automatic. You should never rely on an agent's promise that you can get one. Even if you could eventually get one, you will have to spend many months, perhaps even years, involved in costly litigation. I discuss these types of easements in more detail later in this chapter under the heading "Unrecorded Easements."

In my law practice the most frequent litigation involving rural property arises over easement disputes.

ACQUIRING AN EASEMENT

In most cases, the seller will already have a proper easement. If he does not, then you should demand that he, or the real estate agent, get a legal right of way from each owner of the intervening prop-

erties. Once you have a recorded easement in your deed, it will last forever in your favor unless stated otherwise in the description. A landowner will probably charge for the right to cross his land with a vehicle. If the seller has to pay for the easement, he will undoubtedly add that cost onto the total purchase price. Sometimes the real estate agent will urge you to buy the land, assuring you that he can get the right-of-way permission you need at a later date. However, you should buy only after you get the easement, not before.

HOW TO CHECK THE DEEDED ACCESS ON A MAP

You will understand the concept and importance of an easement if you study the following maps. I will use our own situation to show you how to check an easement description against a quadrangle map. Illustration 66 is a portion of the quadrangle

66. Easement Example

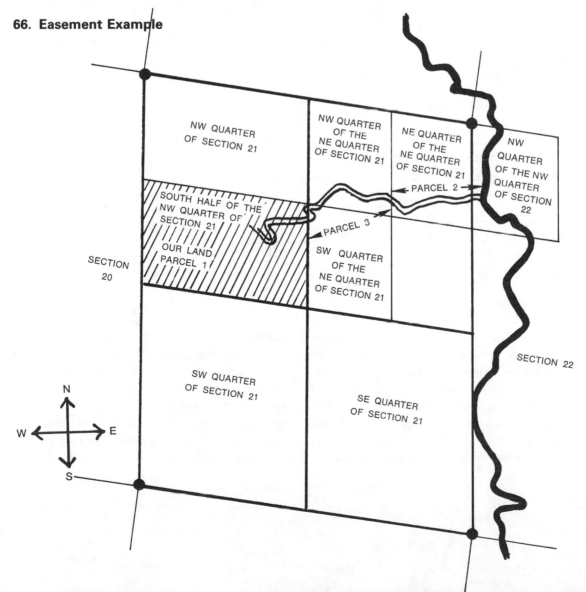

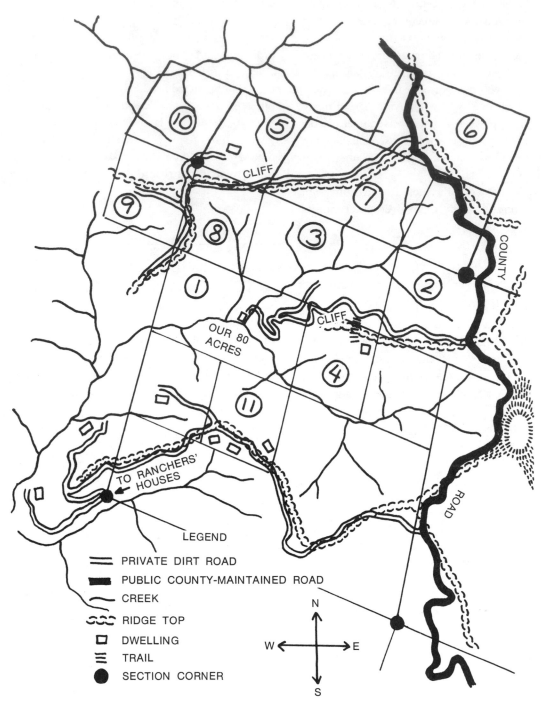

LEGEND

≡ PRIVATE DIRT ROAD

▬ PUBLIC COUNTY-MAINTAINED ROAD

∿ CREEK

ᵒᵒᵒ RIDGE TOP

▢ DWELLING

≣ TRAIL

● SECTION CORNER

67. Easement Problems

map of our area and is the type of map found in any real estate agent's office. (If you read chapter 8, "Land Descriptions and Surveys," you will understand how this quadrangle map was created.) Illustration 67 shows the same area as illustration 66, but land features, roads, and houses are indicated. The numbered areas in illustration 67 are parcels of land owned by private parties. These

parcels do not necessarily follow the regular section and quarter divisions in illustration 66, since land parcels are split in many different ways. Before signing anything, we asked the real estate agent to type up a description of the easement we were to get exactly as it would appear in our purchase contract and deed. According to what he typed we were purchasing:

That real property situated in the County of Humboldt, State of California, described as follows:

PARCEL ONE:

The South Half of the Northwest Quarter of Section 21, Township 4 South, Range 2 East, Humboldt Meridian.

PARCEL TWO:

A nonexclusive easement 60 feet in width over the existing road located in the Southerly portion of the Northeast Quarter of the Northeast Quarter of Section 21 and in the Southerly portion of the Northwest Quarter of the Northwest Quarter of Section 22, in Township 4 South, Range 2 East, Humboldt Meridian, and extending from the West line of said Northeast Quarter of the Northeast Quarter, Easterly to the West line of the County Road, together with the right to convey said easement to others.

PARCEL THREE:

A nonexclusive easement 60 feet in width over the existing road located in the Southerly portion of the Northwest Quarter of the Northeast Quarter and the Northerly portion of the Southwest Quarter of the Northeast Quarter of Section 21, Township 4 South, Range 2 East, Humboldt Meridian, and extending from the West line of said Southwest Quarter to the Northeast Quarter, Easterly and Northerly to the East line of said Northwest Quarter of the Northeast Quarter, together with the right to convey said easement to others.

Follow the above descriptions on the maps. Parcel 1 is our 80 acres. It is shaded on illustration 66 and marked 1 on illustration 67. Numbers 2, 3, and 4 on Map B indicate land parcels owned by three different individuals. You can see that the dirt road that runs from the county road to our 80 acres crosses through these parcels.

Parcel 2 in the deed includes the dirt road starting at the western side of the county road and running to the western edge of the northeast quarter of the northeast quarter of Section 21. This area is marked 2 on illustration 67, and labeled as Parcel 2 on illustration 66.

Parcel 3 then brings the easement through the area marked 3 and 4 on illustration 67, and labeled Parcel 3 on illustration 66, to the point where the dirt road touches our land and remains on it.

It may take you a while to completely understand the above description, but once you do, you will have no problems when you go to make your own purchase. It is essential that you understand how to determine what your easement description in-

cludes. The above-described parcels assure us that we own a right of way from the county road all the way to our building site. You should check your easement against a quadrangle map in a similar fashion to ensure that you are getting unquestionable access rights.

TERMS DEFINING THE EASEMENT

"Nonexclusive" Easement

You will notice in the preceding description of our easements that they are specified to be "nonexclusive." This means that we are not the only people permitted to use this road; neighboring property owners share this easement with us. It is important to know what this means in actual practice. I talk about the mutual problems of road maintenance later in this chapter.

"60 Feet in Width"

It is also specified that the easement is to be "60 feet in width." Actually the road is not this wide. The right of access is set at 60 feet because there is always a possibility that the road might wash out and have to be reconstructed next to the previously existing road. Since the road is only 20 feet wide now, we have a 40-foot leeway. A minimum 60-foot allowance is necessary as a safety clause in any easement.

"Over the Existing Road"

The phrase "over the existing road" means that our access route follows the dirt road in existence at the time of purchase rather than some other route not yet developed. If there is a road already constructed into your land and it is satisfactory for your needs, then be sure that your deed includes the phrase "over the existing road" so there is no misunderstanding at a later date as to which route your easement is to take. If the road itself has been specifically surveyed, then the survey description should be used because of its precision. It is often preferable to have the road surveyed so there is no question of its location in the future, and because the easement is then insurable by a title company.

"The Right to Convey Said Easement to Others"

The clause in our deed that allows us "the right to convey said easement to others" is important since we might wish to sell our eighty acres in the future. Although most courts have ruled that an easement that benefits the easement holder in the use of his land automatically goes with the land, the inclusion of the right to convey, in writing, makes it specific. It is always best to express the full intent of an agreement in the purchase contract and deed. If we choose to subdivide our land there is always a question of whether we could pass the easement on to two or more parcels. A property owner is not allowed to overburden an easement, and litigation often arises over such issues. It is best to have language in the easement allowing you to grant it to subdivisions of your parcel.

MAKE SURE YOUR ACCESS DESCRIPTION INCLUDES THE ENTIRE ROUTE

One land buyer I interviewed has a serious problem caused by his failure to examine his easement carefully enough before his purchase. He discovered too late that he did not have the access he thought he had. Although his land is actually several hundred miles from my property, for example purposes only I indicate his parcel as 5 on illustration 67. When he bought his land there was already a road running from the county road to his building site. In his deed, the easement was described as the road going through parcels 6 and 7, leading to his boundary line. You can see that the dirt road hits his land just above the lower left corner of parcel 7. But notice that the access road then crosses through his land at the lower right corner, goes off his land, courses through three other people's property, 8, 9, and 10, and then circles back onto his land, terminating at his house.

Because this road was already in existence when he purchased his land, he assumed that his easement covered the entire route. The real estate agent told him only that he had "deeded access to his land." The title company did a title search before closing and insured him for the access outlined in his deed, which went only from the county road

to his boundary line. But at the point where the road enters his land is a cliff, which makes it impossible for him to build a road from there to his house. The cliff is indicated on the map.

Thus he is now negotiating with the owners of 8, 9, and 10 for easement rights across their property. He will probably have to pay a large sum of money for those rights, should they decide to give them to him. They are not bound to do so. This landowner does not have a case against the agent or title company since they only guaranteed him access to his land, which he had. The easement just didn't go all the way to his house as he had assumed. It was the landowner's fault because he failed to check his easement description against a map and survey of his property prior to purchase.

EASEMENTS WHERE NO ROAD EXISTS AT THE TIME OF PURCHASE

If you are buying land that does not have an access road already built, you must carefully examine the easement you are to be given in terms of its suitability for a road. Ideally you should get the seller to put in the road before you buy. He will probably add this cost to the selling price, but since constructing a road involves many problems, it is better to have the seller assume the risks.

If you wish to put the road in yourself, you should insert the following condition, or safety clause, for your protection in the Model Contract of Sale (see chapter 28):

The Buyer shall make a diligent effort to construct a permanent access road along the route designated by the Easement in the Contract of Sale and the Deed. The road shall be no less than 20 (twenty) feet in width, and shall extend from the most accessible public road to the Buyer's building site. The road shall be adequate for ingress and egress of heavy-duty vehicles. The Buyer shall construct the road by any means of his choosing and the maximum cost the Buyer is willing to assume is $_____. If the Buyer cannot locate and develop an adequate access road for his needs, as specified herein, and he has performed all of the conditions herein, then this Contract is rescinded immediately and the Buyer shall receive all money he has paid to the Seller, and the Buyer shall suffer no further liability under this Contract. Furthermore, Seller shall reimburse the Buyer for the total amount the Buyer has expended in his attempt to construct an access road.

Have a local contractor, construction company, or road builder examine the area and determine the best route to your land before you purchase. They will probably do this for free, as well as give you an estimate of costs, because they anticipate being hired for the job. Give the contractor's written report to the seller, and tell him that you want an easement that covers every part of that route because it is the most feasible access route to your land. If he cannot deliver easement coverage over that area, then you should not buy the land. If you do not take the above precautions you might discover too late that you have been given an easement unfit for the construction of a low-cost permanent road.

KNOW WHERE YOUR ACCESS ENTERS YOUR PROPERTY

When you get an easement be sure it goes to the most desirable place for entry, to serve your proposed building site. A difficult situation developed for some people we know in a neighboring county. Although their property is 100 miles from my property, for example purposes only I show their property as number 4 on illustration 67. They use a dirt road to get to their property. But notice where it hits their property line in the upper left-hand corner of 4. Since their only good building sites were on the upper right-hand side of their land, they built their house there, as indicated on the map. Directly below the house is a trail which the owners find much more convenient to use than coming up from the point where the access road meets their property. However, you can see that the trail leaves the access road and crosses part of the property belonging to 3. Thus they are trespassing at that point. Legally they need another easement to cross that small portion of their neighbor's land.

Instead of asking the owner of parcel 3 for an easement, the owners went ahead and built a trail up the cliff to their house. The man who owns parcel 3 was very upset about the trespassing and

the trail across his property. He could sue the owners of parcel 4 for trespassing and damage to property. He may win in court, and the trespassers will be forced to enter their land far from their house where their right-of-way first touches their land. They may also have to pay some money for damages.

DETERMINING THE VALIDITY OF YOUR EASEMENT

Since an easement is a property right, it should be documented in writing in a grant or deed and shown in an abstract of title or title report. This is very important. Easements should also be filed with the county recorder. When you get a title search before closing, easement rights will be shown if they are to be included in your deed or title. If no easements show on your title report stop the deal and question the title company or abstracter about your easement rights.

PRELIMINARY EASEMENT CHECK

You can do your own preliminary easement check. Find out from the real estate agent who owns each parcel between your land and the public road. If he doesn't have this information, you can get it from the local tax assessor. If possible find out the year each landowner, including the person you are buying land from, purchased his property. Copies of all recorded deeds are kept in the county recorder's office which is usually in the county courthouse or local city hall. Look in the deed index or grantee index, which is often filed by year, under the name of the present owner to see where to find a copy of his deed. In his deed you should usually find a description of the easement to his property. For a thorough discussion on searching the records, see chapter 31, "The Title Search, Abstract of Title, and Title Insurance Policy." Easements are often conveyed by documents separate from a deed so that you will be able to determine them only by ordering a title report.

SHARING AND MAINTAINING AN EASEMENT

In the usual nonexclusive easement, where several people have the same easement rights over a single road to their respective properties, there is often no indication of who will be responsible for the upkeep of the access road. Usually this responsibility is shared by the people who hold the easement. Here is our situation.

You can see that three other landowners, numbered 2, 3, and 4 in illustration 67, share the easement with us. These owners help us repair the road each summer. We share the cost on a pro rata basis, with ourselves paying the largest share since we are at the end of the road. Thus, we and three neighbors share the $400 annual expenses.

When other people are using the same easement access that you are going to use, you should speak to some of them before you buy. Ask about the average cost of road repairs and who pays for them. If you find out this information beforehand you may foresee future difficulties with noncooperative neighbors. Many states have laws that a person who shares an easement is responsible for a proportionate share of road maintenance according to his use.

If you are the only person who has an easement over a road, you alone will be responsible for maintenance. The landowner of the parcel through which your easement runs cannot interfere with your use of the road, but he does not have to maintain your access. If both of you use the same access, legally you are each responsible for upkeep. This maintenance cost will be greater the farther you are from the public road. Before you buy your land, be sure you can afford your isolation.

When examining your access road, notice how much permanent improvement has been made that will decrease yearly maintenance expense. Look for culverts, which are steel or concrete pipes placed under the road surface to drain water away from the road. Culverts are essential in preventing a dirt road from becoming impassable due to large ruts and puddles resulting from winter rain or snow. They are expensive items, and if other landowners use your road, you will want all of them to cooperate when it comes to upkeep and improvement.

One large culvert in our road cost $300, and a dump truck of rock costs $60.

GETTING THE COUNTY TO MAINTAIN YOUR EASEMENT

Real estate agents will sometimes tell a prospective buyer that the road he will be using will be taken over and maintained by the county after the buyer purchases the land. Be very skeptical of such claims. There are always stiff requirements that must be met before public tax money is spent on any road. For example, in California if a group of property owners want their road to be taken into the county system, they first must bring the road up to county standards at their own expense. This requires ditching, putting in culverts, and laying a minimum amount of surface gravel or asphalt, which is a very costly job. And once this work is done and the county takes over maintenance of the road, by law it becomes permanently open to the public.

EASEMENTS OVER PUBLIC LANDS

Each year thousands of individuals apply to the Bureau of Land Management and state governments to obtain a right-of-way. The federal government charges an application, monitoring, and annual rental fee. They grant easements only by permit and generally will not grant permanent easement rights. If you sell your property and if it is served by an easement over public lands, you must obtain permission to assign your easement rights. If you are purchasing land served by a road over government land that is not a general public road, check with the government agency about your access rights before the close of escrow. A good pamphlet discussing easements over federal property is *Obtaining a Right-of-Way on Public Lands*, available free from the U.S. Department of the Interior, Bureau of Land Management, Washington, D.C. 20240.

DOES A NEIGHBOR HAVE AN EASEMENT OVER YOUR LAND?

Easement problems also occur if an access is owned across your land by other landowners. Then it is your land that is being crossed, and it is said to be *encumbered* by or subject to an easement. You can often determine if your land is subject to an easement by personally examining it. Obviously if a road runs through your place continuing onto another person's land and you can see that someone is using it, you should suspect that an easement exists. Others' rights to cross your land will usually show up in a title report or abstract of title, unless such rights are unrecorded.

UNRECORDED EASEMENTS

How does an unrecorded easement become legally binding and "of record"?

There are three situations whereby an unrecorded easement might be able to be proven to exist in a court of law. Such an easement will not show up in a title search nor will it be protected by a policy of title insurance until such time as the easement is declared to exist by a judge in a court case and a judgment is recorded in the public records. Obtaining a judgment can be very expensive and often difficult to prove because essential witnesses may be dead or hard to locate. These easements usually physically exist but a title search will not reveal them. If you see evidence of a road that does not show up in your title search, you should suspect that there may be one of the following three types of unrecorded easements: an easement by prescription, an easement by implication, or an easement by necessity.

Easement By Prescription

If a person openly crosses someone else's land continuously for a prescribed number of years as if he has a right to do so, but in fact the owner has not given him permission, the user might be able to get an *easement by prescription*, commonly called a *prescriptive easement*. The use of the easement must be open, hostile, notorious, continuous for the specified period of time, and under a claim of right. The time period required varies in each state. In California it takes five years to establish, whereas it takes ten years in New York, Louisiana, and Oregon; fifteen years in Minnesota; twenty years in Illinois, Maine, and Wisconsin; and twenty-one years in Ohio. British Columbia, on the other hand, has abolished the right to prescriptive easements. Regardless of where you are, a prescriptive easement cannot be gained over government property.

Easement By Implication

If one piece of land is divided into two or more parcels, and if the owner sells one of the parcels, A, without reserving an easement across his own parcel, B (see illustration 68, page 176), but a road exists to parcel A across parcel B which the new owner of parcel A uses openly and obviously with the owner B's knowledge, the court might grant an easement by implication to the owner of parcel A even though parcel A may have another way out to a public road. This type of easement is often very difficult to obtain because such an easement would burden parcel B and the courts do not like to create a burden on property unless necessary.

Easement By Necessity

An easement by necessity is similar to an easement by implication except that an easement by necessity is granted when parcel A is completely landlocked by the property of the original seller B. The expressed intentions of the parties is very important in this type of case.

All of these types of easements are complicated and difficult to prove. If you suspect that an unrecorded easement exists on land you are looking at but you are still sufficiently interested in the property, be sure to consult an attorney who specializes in easement law to see what you will be getting involved in. If it turns out that you have another recorded easement so that you do not need to pursue one of these types of easements in court, you will be able to purchase the land with peace of mind. If, on the other hand, the lawyer tells you that you will face costly litigation and possibly years of hassling, you will be glad that you can back out of the deal now and look for something else.

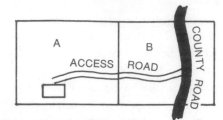

68. Easement by Necessity

IT IS YOUR DUTY TO INSPECT THE PARCEL

The implied easement, prescriptive easement, and easement by necessity will not appear in the county records and will not be covered by your policy of title insurance. For this reason it is very important that you personally walk over and examine your land in its entirety. Make a thorough investigation of any roads or paths that cross the land, whether or not they appear to be well traveled. Perhaps the road is used only at certain times of the year. The burden is placed on you to inspect the premises before you purchase in order to determine the existence of unrecorded easements. Once you have taken title you will have little chance in court of preventing someone from crossing your land if he possesses a legally sound unrecorded easement and if he can prove the elements necessary to win his case.

IS THE EASEMENT OVER YOUR LAND GOING TO BOTHER YOU?

When one or more landowners have the right to cross your land at any time, such activity could seriously interfere with your peace and quiet. The burden will be greater if the road runs next to your best building site than if it merely crosses the corner of the land far from the living area. Also your own access problems could be greater due to the number of people using the access road. If an encumbering easement breaks up the unity of some land you are interested in, you should use this to get the price down. However, you should evaluate the situation carefully before you buy. The following fictional story illustrates the importance of predicting the future impact of an easement on the enjoyment of your land.

Some neighbors, who live on the ridge above our valley, bought 40 acres that were originally part of a large ranch which now extends to the south and southwest of them. Their land is numbered 11 on illustration 67. When the ranchers sold the 40 acres, they reserved easement rights for themselves and others along the dirt road that crosses the neighbor's land. You can see the road running along the ridge of the mountain from the county road to the rancher's houses. The only available building site on the 40 acres is next to the dirt road, which is where the owners built their dwelling. Now the quiet days are frequently interrupted by jeep, truck, and car traffic as ranch hands enter and leave their ranch.

In addition, the ranchers use heavy-duty vehicles on the road, which inevitably produce huge ruts during the winter rains. This makes winter access difficult for the family, which has only lightweight two-wheel-drive vehicles. When the ruts get too deep, the owners have to walk into their land until the road can be repaired the following summer because they cannot afford to repair it themselves and the ranch won't help out. They could file an action in the courts since they are being prevented from using their legal access road, but such action is costly and time consuming. So they have learned to live with this encumbering easement. But would you want to?

You cannot know the use patterns of an easement unless you spend some time on the land before buying it. I would never buy any land that has an easement within eyesight of the homestead area.

EASEMENTS IN GROSS

An *easement in gross* is one that does not serve a specific parcel of land but is a generalized easement for crossing a parcel; i.e., for log hauling or hunting. If an easement in gross has been reserved over your land, together with the right to grant it to others, you could have an unlimited number of persons crossing your property in the future. If the easement is in gross, the deed will normally state that.

UTILITY LINE EASEMENT

Easements are not restricted solely to personal access. The right to bring utility lines along the easement route can be included. Your easement should provide for "ingress and egress and public utilities." Even if you don't want electricity brought in yourself, it is helpful to have this in your deed if you ever decide to sell your land. A future buyer might want his easement to specifically include utilities.

You will also want to be aware of a utility easement across your land. Although you might be willing to see a car go by a few times a day, you might not enjoy the sight of telephone and electrical poles and wires strung across your property, particularly if they are large distribution lines constructed on huge towers.

PIPELINE EASEMENTS

A person who has the right to take water off your land will also have a pipeline easement over your land to transport the water. If you are receiving water rights from another parcel, make sure you have an easement for "laying and maintaining a pipeline" from the water source to your property.

"THE LAND HAS FRONTAGE ON COUNTY ROAD"

You will frequently see the above phrase in real estate advertisements. Don't make the assumption that road frontage necessarily means direct road access. The side of the property that borders the county road might be a cliff or a ravine. In such cases, entrance must be gained by crossing a neighbor's land. Illustration 69 shows road frontage with easement access required.

AN EASEMENT WARRANTY— YOUR BEST INSURANCE

An excellent means of obtaining extra easement protection if there is any question in your mind

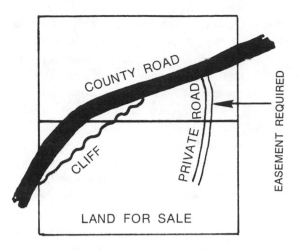

69. Road Frontage Deception

about access is to include a warranty clause in the contract of sale. I have done so in the Model Contract of Sale which is in chapter 28. Clause 18(a) states that the seller warrants the buyer that he will receive legal access, or easements, over the most accessible route between the public road and his building site. This warranty covers the problems discussed in this chapter and assures you of legal recourse against the seller if any undisclosed easement problems arise after the deal is closed. Clause 18(k) keeps the warranty binding even after you receive the deed to the property. If your purchase is subject to your prior approval of a title report or abstract, you will have the opportunity to review the easements shown in the report prior to closing. If they are not adequate, stop the deal until the seller can make them sufficient.

A FINAL WARNING

The importance of understanding easements and knowing when and where they are located cannot be overstressed. Beware of the real estate agent who tells you, "Don't worry about getting an easement. The former owner of this land has been using this land for years. Everybody is real friendly. Nobody around here ever gets easements." Tell him that if nobody cares if you use the road, then he should have no problem getting the landowners to sign deeds granting such an easement formally.

Think about the future. The people who now

own the land you cross might not care whether you do so, but the next owner might not be so gracious. Or the present owner might not like your looks and decide that he's not going to treat you as he did the last owners. All he has to do is put up a gate and tell you not to cross his land if you don't have deeded access. These situations are very common in the history of real estate disputes.

You must also protect yourself against easements that could interfere with your use of the land. A thorough personal inspection of your prospective purchase is mandatory for uncovering evidence of easements. It is helpful to discuss the situation with the seller and his neighbors. Question the real estate agent thoroughly on the matter.

A deeded easement should be described as pre-cisely as possible, in terms of location and purpose. Remember that an easement may not always be revealed by a title search. Thus a comprehensive general warranty is necessary. Easements crossing the seller's land should be used to your advantage when negotiating the selling price if it depreciates the land value by diminishing the peace and quiet of the country isolation you would like.

Prior to the close of escrow, you should order copies of all documents referred to in the title report or abstract and read through them to see what the easement situation is all about. Finally, never buy land that does not have deeded recorded adequate easement rights from a public road all the way to the parcel. If you do, you are almost assured of eventually getting into litigation.

"We didn't know a damn thing about the right-of-way until after we had the pool put in."

CHAPTER 10

Water Rights

The water right is a property right. It is a valuable right. And it is real estate. . . . The holder of a water right in an area in which the competition for water is keen needs to be constantly on guard to protect his right against infringement or loss. It is said that eternal vigilance is the price of a good water right.

—Wells A. Hutchins,
leading water rights
expert

The importance of having water on your land has been pointed out in great detail in an earlier chapter. The mere presence of water on your property, however, does not necessarily insure that you have unfettered rights to use it. Every state has specific and detailed laws regarding water rights and how they may be obtained and lost that apply to all users of the water. It is impossible for me to detail all of the water laws in each individual state, but I will explain the basic theories and their applications to different types of water sources. Contact your state department of resources or your local farm advisor to find out how you can get a pamphlet detailing the water laws of the state where your land is located. For example, in California you can write to the California State Water Resources Control Board in Sacramento for a pamphlet entitled *General Information Pertaining to Water Rights in California*. (See Useful Resources at the end of this chapter.) Similar guides are put out in other states.

THE PURPOSE OF WATER LAWS

All water is classified as either surface water or underground water. These waters are regulated by different laws, as enacted by state legislatures and interpreted by the state and federal courts. The primary aim of the water laws is to prevent the waste of water and to use what is available in the most beneficial manner possible.

SURFACE WATERS

Surface waters include lakes, rivers, streams, springs, ponds, marshes, and any other visible water. Most rivers and lakes are considered to be *navigable* public waters, and the federal government has control over them. If your land abuts on or includes navigable waters, you have water rights as long as they do not interfere with public use.

However, if your land has surface water on it, it is more likely that it will be a *nonnavigable* stream, spring, or pond. Whether navigable or not, all surface water in the United States is subject either to riparian laws, prior appropriation laws, or combinations of the two.

These two separate areas of water law, *riparian rights* and *prior appropriation rights,* developed because the water needs in the arid West are very different from those in the humid East. Generally, east of the one-hundredth meridian west longitude line, rainfall is abundant throughout the year, whereas west of that line rainfall is sparse and nearly all of it falls during the winter months. (See chapter 3, ''Climate.'') Illustration 70 shows the distribution of the types of rights to surface water used by each state.

Riparian Rights

Water laws, like the rest of our laws, evolved from the English common law brought here by the early settlers. Since these settlers first established themselves in the humid eastern portion of the country

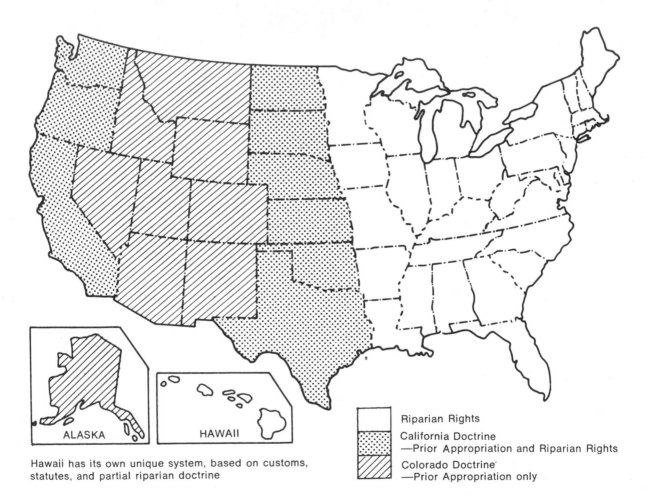

ALASKA   HAWAII

Hawaii has its own unique system, based on customs, statutes, and partial riparian doctrine

Riparian Rights

California Doctrine
—Prior Appropriation and Riparian Rights

Colorado Doctrine
—Prior Appropriation only

70. Acquisition of Surface Water Rights

where water is plentiful, the riparian laws of England, itself a humid country, were nicely suited to the region. Thus it was logical that we accepted them as our first water laws.

A riparian landowner is one whose land is directly adjacent to the water source. The amount of land actually touching the water is usually irrelevant. The majority of land for sale with surface water contains springs rather than a definable stream. If a spring does not pass beyond the boundary of the land on which it is located, the owner of the land has sole rights to use the water as he wishes. But if the spring is the source of a natural stream that flows across other lands, it falls within the laws of riparian rights. Where many riparian landowners have property adjacent to a single stream or lake, riparian laws are used to determine how much water each is allowed to use.

Originally this country followed the doctrine, inherited from English law, that required that each riparian landowner must let the stream flow in its "natural state" to lower lands. Thus the flow could not be diminished in quantity or impaired in quality by a riparian user, and any water diverted must be returned to the stream before leaving the user's property. The purpose of this rule originally was to insure the free passage of water downstream from one mill wheel to the next. As of this writing, eight states still follow this natural flow method of allocating water. They are Georgia, Maine, Mississippi, Missouri, New Jersey, Pennsylvania, South Dakota, and West Virginia. Since this method results in the wasteful loss of much water into the sea, today the majority of state courts and legislatures more often follow the *reasonable use* rule in determining riparian rights.

Reasonable use is a priority system that follows the rule that a riparian landowner can use all the water he needs for "ordinary" or "domestic" purposes without regard to the effect of such use on the water flow to lower riparian landowners. Domestic uses include taking water for washing, cooking, drinking, and watering domestic stock animals and gardens. Often a state will fix a maximum quantity considered reasonable for domestic use. For example, some states permit 18.5 gallons per day per 100 square feet of home gardens for irrigation. For a house with a sink and flush toilet, each person is permitted a maximum of 40 gallons per day. *Extraordinary* uses, often referred to as *artificial* uses, include taking water for irrigation

of commercial crops, manufacturing, mining, and other commercial uses. All domestic uses by all riparian landowners on the stream must be fulfilled before any one of them can use surplus water for artificial uses. Sometimes an upper riparian landowner in using water only for domestic purposes takes all the available water and none flows to lower riparian landowners. This is allowed as long as the use is "reasonable." You should be aware of use patterns upstream when buying land with the expectation of receiving a good steady flow of water.

In determining which artificial uses take priority after all domestic uses have been fulfilled, many facts are considered, including the length of the stream, the volume of water, the extent of riparian land ownership, and the purpose and extent of the use. Using water for aesthetic and recreational purposes, such as swimming and fishing, is far down on the list of preferred uses. Taking water out of a stream to store for use later is usually not allowed under the riparian system. Only if every other riparian owner has enough for domestic and artificial uses can water be taken and stored. Fortunately, the riparian system predominates in the eastern half of the United States where water is plentiful and storage is usually not necessary. The states that follow the reasonable use riparian laws exclusively are: Alabama, Arkansas, Connecticut, Delaware, Florida, Illinois, Indiana, Iowa, Kentucky, Louisiana, Maryland, Massachusetts, Michigan, Minnesota, New Hampshire, New York, North Carolina, Ohio, Rhode Island, South Carolina, Tennessee, Vermont, Virginia, and Wisconsin. Those states discussed later that follow a combined *riparian appropriation* system generally recognize the reasonable use concepts with regard to riparian rights.

Riparian rights can go with the land itself and cannot be lost because of disuse. They always remain with the land adjoining the water unless specified otherwise. Illustration 71 shows an effect of a sale of riparian land.

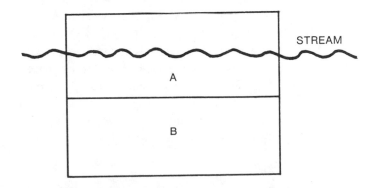

71. Sale of a Riparian Right

Both parcels A and B were originally one unit of land owned totally by A. When parcel B was sold, the buyer did not automatically get riparian rights to the stream because his parcel does not adjoin the stream. However, if A included riparian rights and access rights in the deed to B, then B can use the stream and his rights run with the land. This is legal because B is in the watershed and was originally a part of the riparian land. The sale simply divided the riparian land into two parcels whereas previously it had all been one parcel owned by one person. But some states might reclassify B as an *appropriator* with rights secondary to those of a riparian owner.

Once a riparian right is lost, however, the loss is permanent and can never be regained. If B, in the above example, did not get riparian rights reserved in his deed, parcel B can never regain those rights unless it is resold to A and reunited as one parcel of land adjoining the stream. If you are buying land that is being severed from a riparian piece of land, riparian rights will attach to your land only if expressly reserved in writing in your deed.

If you buy land with a stream or other surface water on it, you will be paying for that water since it increases the value of the land. A seller who reserves for himself or for the buyer of another parcel riparian rights and easement rights to cross your land and use the stream should greatly reduce his asking price since such a reservation means you must share the stream on your land with others. The seller may try to reserve these rights for other parcels he is selling because it makes any property not adjoining the water a better sales prospect. Carefully evaluate the effect on your home if other property owners have the right to come onto your land, run water lines to their property, and take water from your land. Generally, you should not buy land under such circumstances.

When you buy riparian land or land with riparian rights granted in the deed, you can be sold only those rights the seller possesses already. Therefore, you must find out what his rights include. Be certain that the seller has not previously granted his riparian rights to another user, leaving him with no rights to give you. Because this information may not show up in the deed, be sure that it is covered in your title search. Courts are destroying riparian rights in legal disputes where they cannot absolutely be shown to exist, so if there is any doubt about your rights, resolve them before taking title to the land.

As a riparian landowner your right to have an adequate water flow includes a right to pure water. Lawsuits between riparian owners over the issue of pollution are fairly common. However, a private action is not as effective as an action by a state agency to prevent pollution. If you want adequate relief you should file a complaint with the appropriate state agency as well as with the court. Upstream polluters are also liable for damages and possible criminal charges. In some areas, pollution that occurs as a result of bathing or watering stock animals is permissible.

In many states, you are not free to stock and take fish from some streams or lakes that are adjacent to your land. We cannot fish in our creek under any circumstances because it is classified as a "spawning creek" by the state Department of Fish and Game. The fines for fishing illegally are often several hundred dollars. You should look up your stream's classification in the state fish and game regulations before you buy your land if fishing is a major reason for your move to the country. You might also want to check the local rules regarding fish stocking. You generally need a permit to stock your stream or lake, and the type of fish you can use is selected by state officials to protect nearby public waters.

As a riparian landowner you own the rocks in the stream bed and may remove them for use on your land as long as you do not disturb the flow of the water to lower riparian users, although you may need a permit from your state fish and game or wildlife office.

Although the property line of land bordered by a nonnavigable stream generally extends to the middle of the stream, it is wise to have this written into your deed if a creek or stream is used as a boundary line of the land. The property line of land on a navigable stream or lake extends to the low-water mark. On a nonnavigable stream, as the course of the water gradually shifts through the years, the property lines shift with the stream. The soil that is slowly deposited on your land during the shifting process is your gain and your opposing neighbor's loss. This process is called *accretion*. However, if the stream changes course as a result of a sudden storm or flood rather than by a gradual process of change, the rule of accretion does not apply, and the boundary lines do not change.

All riparian owners are eligible to take and use the water only on land within the *watershed,* which is that area that drains into the stream, river, or lake. (See illustration 72.) If you buy a large piece of land on a stream and want to pump water from the stream over a hill to use on a section of your property that is in another watershed, you will be appropriating the water and thus subject to *appropriation* laws rather than riparian laws. Legal action could be taken against you by other riparian owners lower than you on the stream and by *prior appropriators* because you are illegally depriving them of stream water.

Prior Appropriation Rights (Alone or with Riparian Rights)

In 1849 gold was discovered in California, and people swarmed into the West. Mining towns, army camps, and trading posts grew up around major water routes. At first gold was mined directly from the streams in the Sierra Mountains by using the naturally flowing stream water to wash the sand out of the sifting pans, leaving the gold on the bottom. As gold processing became more advanced, however, long ditches were dug to create more water pressure to separate the gold, and tremendous amounts of water were required. It became necessary also to store huge quantities of water in large reservoirs so that mining could continue during the long dry summer months. New laws were needed to define who could use the limited supplies of water, and prior appropriation laws were adopted.

The basic principle involved in the law of prior appropriation is "first in time is first in right." The first user, often called the *prior* or *senior appropriator,* is permitted to take all the water in the stream he can put to a reasonable and beneficial use to the exclusion of all others higher or lower on the stream who want to take water after him. This rule came into being to avoid wasting water in dry periods. The feeling was that it was preferable to let one individual water user take all the available water needed in a drought rather than to distribute the water in amounts inadequate for each of several users.

As the amount of gold gradually dwindled, many miners and new settlers turned to farming. They began to construct ditches to divert water from streams for a new purpose, to carry it to their lands for irrigation. By 1880, the feasibility of raising large crops by irrigation had been proven, and intensive land development in the West began. Many of the prior appropriation laws developed by miners carried over to this new use of the water resources.

Prior appropriation rights specified that the first settler in an area could choose the land he wanted and build irrigation ditches from the nearest stream to his fields. It was irrelevant whether his land was contiguous, or riparian, to the stream, since nobody else was using the water. The next settler to come to the area had second choice of the land and secondary rights to appropriate the available water to irrigate his land. This pattern was repeated with subsequent settlers.

Thus, because of the scarcity of water and the needs of mining and agriculture, the original riparian laws that the humid East had adopted from

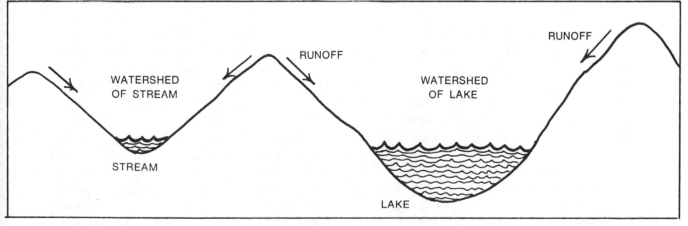

72. Watershed

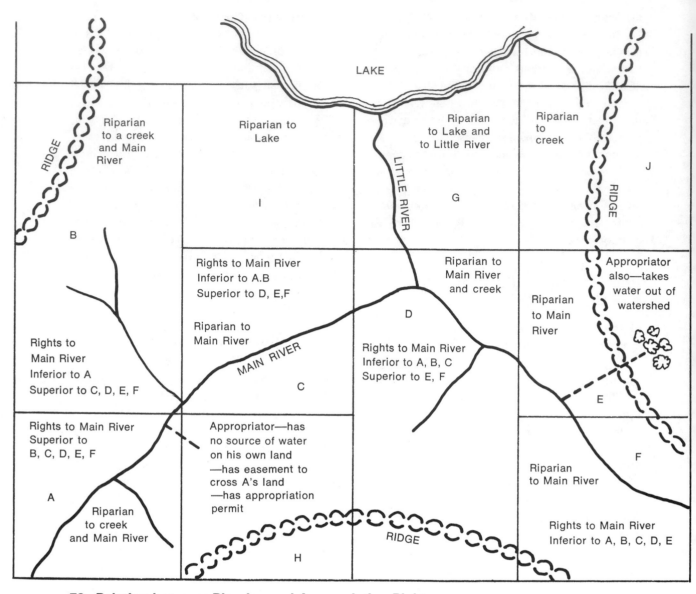

73. Relation between Riparian and Appropriation Rights

(LETTERS REFER TO INDIVIDUAL PARCELS)

England gave way to the new doctrine of prior appropriation. Nine of the most arid western states now follow the *Colorado doctrine* which recognizes only prior appropriation laws and does not differentiate between riparian and nonriparian lands. These states are Alaska, Arizona, Colorado, Idaho, Montana, Nevada, New Mexico, Utah, and Wyoming.

The other nine western states follow the *California doctrine* which does distinguish riparian lands but also has coordinated the principle of prior appropriation into the laws. These states are California, Kansas, Nebraska, North Dakota, Oklahoma,

Oregon, South Dakota, Texas, and Washington. In these states, appropriators are nonriparian users only. Riparian users always have priority over appropriators. (See illustration 73 to see the relationship between riparian rights and appropriation rights.) Hawaii has a unique system derived from custom and ancient rights which is beyond the scope of this discussion.

The appropriator in every prior appropriation state except Montana must apply to the state for a permit and license to take water. The time of appropriation and priority to use the water dates from the time formal application is made to the state and actual

184

use is begun under an appropriation permit. When buying land in one of these states, you should investigate the history of water applications on your stream. Not only should you determine what legal steps have been taken to secure water rights on the seller's land, but you should also investigate similarly other lands adjoining the stream. If you intend to divert a large amount of water and expect to invest a substantial sum of money in diversion equipment, you would be wise to have a survey taken by a local engineer who knows the river. You should establish where diversions have already been made, how much water is taken out of the river by prior appropriators, and whether there will be enough left for your use. You can write to the state resources agency or state engineer and ask if any permits have been sought or licenses issued to appropriate water on your stream or river.

This research for prior appropriators is difficult and often inconclusive, but at least make some preliminary investigations since the standard policy of title insurance does not guarantee water rights. You do not want to find your stream dry in August because your upstream neighbor is pumping out all the water before it reaches your property line and you can do nothing about it because he has a ten-year permit from the state to do so. If you are in an appropriation state that does not recognize riparian rights, you have no recourse. If you are in one of the nine appropriation states that do recognize riparian rights, you might be able to force the appropriator to allow enough water through to meet your water requirements, but only after engaging in expensive litigation.

Obtaining a Permit

The procedure for obtaining an appropriate permit is similar in each state. I have reprinted a typical application form. (See illustration 74, pages 186–88.) You can obtain the application forms and rules for filing in your state from your state resources agency or state engineer in charge of water allocation. The procedure I describe below is only an example and may not be applicable in your state.

As you can see, the application is quite detailed and specific. It calls for a description of the diversion works including location and amount of water to be diverted, a schedule of when the work is to be completed once you have your permit, a description of the proposed use, and information on the effect of the appropriation on fish and wildlife and how you are prepared to deal with such effects. You are also required to pay filing fees and include copies of a project map.

You should file for a permit as soon as possible since the filing date is the one used to determine who is prior in time. After you have filed your application, notice of the filing is issued and posted in public places and at the stream so that anybody else who may be prior in time to you or who may have objections can protest. Persons wishing to object to your application have to submit a written protest to the agency and to you, the applicant, within a specified time period. You then have fifteen days to answer the protest and must reply to the specific complaints. You must file this answer with the agency and send a copy to the complainant.

A hearing is then held before a division of the state water resources agency, which has the authority to grant permits. At this time witnesses and any other evidence regarding the case is heard. If the agency feels the information is insufficient, it may order a field investigation at which you and the protestor may be present. The data obtained from this investigation are used to help the agency make a final determination. If it approves your intended diversion, a permit is issued, and you can begin to take the water. Approval by the agency does not insure water rights. It only indicates that you have been granted permission by the state to use water, and this permission establishes a priority date for you. If others have prior permission and use up all the water, there is nothing you can do.

Once the permit is granted you must act with reasonable diligence to begin diverting and putting the water to good use. After you begin doing this, the agency grants you a license. You can keep this license forever as long as there are not three successive years in which no use is made of the diversionary works, in which case you would lose your appropriation rights. Whenever requested, you must report to the agency on what you are doing so that it can be sure the water resources are being put to "the best and most efficient use possible."

Dams and Reservoirs

If you wish to dam up your stream, you should be acquainted with any regulations in your state regarding dams. Generally, even though you are ri-

State Water Resources Control Board
DIVISION OF WATER RIGHTS

APPLICATION to APPROPRIATE WATER

Application No. _____

1. APPLICANT

I, _____
(Name of Applicant)

_____
(Telephone Number where you may be reached
between 8 a.m. and 5 p.m.—include area code)

_____
(Address)   (City or Town)   (State)   (Zip Code)

do hereby make application for a permit to appropriate the following described waters of the State of
SUBJECT TO VESTED RIGHTS

2. SOURCE

a. The name of the source at the point of diversion is _____
(If unnamed, state nature of source and that it IS unnamed)

tributary to _____

b. In a normal year does the stream dry up at any point downstream from your project? YES ☐ NO ☐. If Yes, during what months
is it usually dry? _____

3. POINT of DIVERSION and REDIVERSION

a. The point of diversion will be in the County of _____

b.

List all points giving coordinate distances from section corner or other tie as allowed by Board regulations	Point is within (40-acre Subdivision)	Section	Township	Range	Base and Meridian
	¼ of ¼				
	¼ of ¼				
	¼ of ¼				

c. Does applicant own the land at the point of diversion? YES ☐ NO ☐.

d. If applicant does not own land at point of diversion, state name and address of owner and state what steps have been taken to obtain right
of access: _____

4. PURPOSE of USE, AMOUNT and SEASON

a. State the purpose(s) for which water is to be appropriated, the amounts of water for each purpose and dates between which diversions will
be made in the table below. Use gallons per day if rate is less than 0.025 cubic feet per second (approximately 16,000 gallons per day).

PURPOSE OF USE	DIRECT DIVERSION				STORAGE		
	AMOUNT		SEASON OF DIVERSION		AMOUNT	COLLECTION SEASON	
	RATE (Cubic feet per second or gallons per day)	Acre-feet per year	Beginning Date (Mo. & Day)	Ending Date (Mo. & Day)	Acre-feet per year	Beginning Date (Mo. & Day)	Ending Date (Mc. & Day)
Irrigation							
Domestic							
		_____ (TOTAL)			_____ (TOTAL)		

b. Total combined amount taken by direct diversion and storage during any one year will be _____ acre-feet.

74. Application to Appropriate Water

5. JUSTIFICATION OF AMOUNT

a. IRRIGATION: Maximum acreage to be irrigated in any one year will be _____ acres.

CROP	ACRES	METHOD OF IRRIGATION (Sprinklers, flooding, etc.)	ACRE-FEET (per year)	NORMAL SEASON	
				Beginning Date	Ending Date

b. DOMESTIC: The number of residences to be served _____. Separately owned: YES ☐   NO ☐

The total number of people to be served _____. Estimated daily use per person _____.
(gallons per day)

The total area of domestic lawns and gardens _____.
(square feet)

Miscellaneous domestic uses _____.
(Dust control area. Number and kind of domestic animals, etc.)

c. STOCKWATERING: Kind of Stock _____. Maximum Number _____. Describe type of operation (feed lot, dairy, range, etc.)
_____

d. RECREATIONAL: Type of recreation: Fishing ☐,   Swimming ☐,   Boating ☐,   Other ☐.
(Submit "Supplement to Application", form SWRCB 1-1, for justification of amount for uses not listed above.)

6. DIVERSION WORK

a. Diversion will be by pumping from _____. Pump discharge rate _____. Horsepower _____.
(sump, offset well, channel, reservoir, etc.)   (cfs/gpd)

b. Diversion will be by gravity by means of _____.
(pipe in unobstructed channel, pipe through dam, siphon, gate, etc.)

c. Estimated total cost of the diversion works proposed is _____.
(Give only cost of intake, or headworks, pumps, storage reservoirs, and main conduits.)

d. Main conduit from diversion point to first lateral or offstream storage reservoir:

CONDUIT (Pipe or channel)	MATERIAL (Kind of Pipe or channel lining)	CROSS SECTIONAL DIMENSION (Pipe diameter or ditch depth and top and bottom width	LENGTH (feet)	TOTAL LIFT OR FALL		CAPACITY (estimated)
				(feet)	(+ or −)	

e. The following applies to storage reservoirs: (For reservoirs having a capacity of 25 acre-feet or more, complete supplemental form SWRCB 1-1.

Name or number of reservoir, if any	DAM				RESERVOIR		
	Height of dam from streambed to spillway level (ft.)	Material construction	Dam Length (ft.)	Freeboard Dam height above spillway crest (ft.)	Approximate surface area when full (acres)	Approximate capacity (acre-feet)	Max. water depth

f. If water will be stored and the reservoir is not at the diversion point, the maximum rate of diversion to offstream storage will be _____ cfs.
Diversion to offstream storage will be amde by pumping ☐;   gravity ☐.

7. PLACE OF USE

a. Applicant owns the land where the water will be used: YES ☐   NO ☐. Land is in joint ownership: YES ☐   NO ☐.

All joint owners should include their names as applicants and sign the application. If applicant does not own land where the water will be used, give name and address of owner and state what arrangements have been made with the owner.

_____

_____

USE IS WITHIN (40-acre Subdivision)		SECTION	TOWNSHIP	RANGE	BASE AND MERIDIAN	IF IRRIGATION	
						State Number of Acres	Presently cultivated (Yes or No)
¼ of	¼						
¼ of	¼						
¼ of	¼						
¼ of	¼						
¼ of	¼						
¼ of	¼						

If area is unsurveyed, state the location as if lines of the public land survey were projected. If space does not permit listing all 40-acre tracts, include on another sheet or state sections, townships and ranges, and show detail on map. For public districts or other extremely large areas, see Page 16 of instruction booklet "How to File an Application to Appropriate Water in California".

8. COMPLETION SCHEDULE

a. What year will work start _____? b. What year will work be completed _____?

c. What year will water be used to the full extent intended _____? d. If complete, year of completion _____?

9. GENERAL

a. What is the name of the post office most used by those living near the proposed point of diversion? _____

b. Does any part of the place of use comprise a subdivision on file with the State Department of Real Estate? YES ☐ NO ☐. If Yes, state name of subdivision _____ If No, is subdivision of these lands contemplated? YES ☐ NO ☐.
Is it planned to individually meter each service connection? YES ☐ NO ☐. If Yes, when? _____

c. Have you consulted the California Department of Fish and Game concerning this proposed project? YES ☐ NO ☐. If Yes, state the Department's opinion concerning the potential effects of your proposed project on fish and other wildlife and state measures required for mitigation _____

_____

If No, state the effects on fish and other wildlife you foresee as potentially arising from your proposed project. _____

_____

d. Please name other public agencies, if any, from which you have obtained or are required to obtain approvals regarding this project: _____

_____

e. What are the names and addresses of diverters of water from the source of supply downstream from the proposed point of diversion? _____

_____

f. Is the source used for navigation, including use by pleasure boats, for a significant part of each year at the point of diversion, or does the source substantially contribute to a waterway which is used for navigation, including use by pleasure boats? _____

_____

10. EXISTING WATER RIGHT

Do you claim an existing right for the use of all or part of the water sought by this application? YES ☐ NO ☐

If yes, complete table below

Nature of Rights (riparian, appropriative, groundwater,)	Year of First Use	Purpose of use made in recent years including amount, if known	Season of Use	Source	Location of Point of Diversion

11. AUTHORIZED AGENT (Optional)

With respect to: ☐ All matters concerning this water right application, ☐ those matters designated as follows: _____

_____

Name _____ Address _____

_____ Zip Code: _____

is authorized to act on my behalf as my agent.   (Telephone No. of agent between 8 a.m. and 5 p.m.)

12. SIGNATURE of APPLICANT

I (we) declare under penalty of perjury that the above is true and correct to the best of my (our) knowledge and belief.

Dated _____ 19 _____ , at _____ , California

Ms. Mr.
Miss, Mrs. _____
(Signature of applicant) (Refer to Section 671 of the Board's regulations

If applicants are members of the same family (i.e., husband, wife, mother, father, son, brother, sister, etc.) or reside at the same address, please indicate their relationship:

Ms. Mr.
Miss, Mrs. _____
(Signature of applicant) (Refer to Section 671 of the Board's regulations

188

parian to a stream, if you build a dam for the purpose of storing water for swimming, fishing, or irrigation, you are appropriating that water and must meet the regulations regarding water appropriation in your state. However, mere regulation of the flow of a stream is not an appropriation if it only detains, but does not reduce the flow of, the water. For instance, dams that are built to create enough head on a stream to drive a power plant do not diminish the actual flow.

Many states have standards set for dam and reservoir construction. Usually a dam must exceed certain specified limits before it qualifies for state control. For example, although California does regulate dams, it does not supervise any dams that are less than 6 feet high or hold less than 15 acre-feet of water. For any larger construction the builder must file for a permit and pay set fees. You can find out your state's requirements, if any, from the same agency that supervises the water uses described above. If an upstream user builds a dam that endangers your water supply, you should file a written complaint to the appropriate department in your county or state.

Thirteen states have enacted Mill Acts which permit a dam to be built by an upper riparian landowner for the purpose of supplying water power regardless of any detrimental effects on lower riparian users as long as they are compensated for damages. The states that have this stipulation for water are Connecticut, Georgia, Kentucky, Nebraska, New Hampshire, North Carolina, North Dakota, Rhode Island, South Dakota, and Virginia.

Lakes

If you buy property on or near a lake, find out the rights and regulations regarding lakes in your state. A lake, like a river, can be navigable or nonnavigable but the same rules apply in most cases. In most states, the government owns the beds of navigable lakes, but the owner cannot prevent the public from freely using the lake and taking water from it as long as the public has access to it. In all states, the ownership of the shore goes with the adjoining property, and the public may be prevented from using that part of the shoreline.

You may have more rights if you are on a nonnavigable lake. As a riparian landowner you own the bed of the lake along with all other riparian owners. You have the right to use the entire surface of the lake for recreation although your property may adjoin the lake for only a small distance along the shoreline. A minority of states, including Illinois, require that ownership of the lake bed be specified in your deed before you may use the water, and some states restrict your use within the boundaries of your part of the lake bed.

If you are buying property that is not directly on a lake, but the seller assures you that you have a right to use it, investigate his assurances. You will probably need an easement across someone's land to get to the lake, and you may need separate rights reserved in writing in your deed to use the lake. If you desire docking facilities for a boat, you will need written permission from the person who owns the docks. The permission should be permanent, otherwise you might be charged an excessive fee to renew the right at a later date. All of these rights are valuable assets to the property and must be recorded in the public records and in your deed to be legally binding. Your title search should investigate your rights to use a lake if you expect to do so after you purchase your land.

UNDERGROUND WATER

Wells capturing underground waters provide most rural landowners with their own water supply. Underground waters, usually called groundwater or percolating waters, form from the rain or snow runoff that drains beneath the surface rather than over it and is held in aquifers, porous earth formations such as gravel and sandstone. Some states divide underground waters into several categories, such as underground streams, underflow of streams, and percolating water, and apply different laws to each type of water.

Whereas numerous surface water laws had been enacted centuries ago, only a handful of laws relating to underground water had been passed prior to World War II. This was due to the fact that large-scale development of groundwater resources did not occur prior to that time. Underground water laws are extremely confusing, partly because legislation has not kept up with scientific research on the patterns of underground water movement. In this chapter I can give you only a general idea of the types of laws in force today. The variables are so great throughout the country that you must investigate your state's particular laws in order to gain a complete knowledge of your rights and liabilities.

As with surface waters, different types of water rights laws have developed for underground waters. These are the English common-law doctrine of absolute ownership, the American rule of reasonable use, the California rule of correlative rights, and the prior appropriation doctrine.

The Doctrine of Absolute Ownership

The original rule established in England drew no distinction between underground water and the soil around it. Thus no rights to groundwater as a separate entity were recognized. The owner of a parcel of land owned the water within it as part of the land. He could extract as much water as he desired, even if he drained all the water from the soil of adjoining landowners. This rule of unlimited withdrawals is now the prevailing doctrine in all the states of the humid Midwest and East, although statutes have been passed modifying the rule to various degrees in many of these states. The main reason for the lack of advancement in underground water laws in the East is that water shortages are not as much of a problem as in the states of the arid West. Texas is the only arid state that still follows the law of absolute ownership and unlimited withdrawal.

The Rule of Reasonable Use

A few arid states employ the American rule of reasonable use, which is simply a variation of the English rule of absolute ownership. It holds that a landowner can pump water from beneath his land, even if he draws water from a neighbor's land, as long as the amount he takes is reasonable in relation to the rights of surrounding landowners. Of course, "reasonableness" is difficult to determine, and therefore the reasonable use rule has not been applied in many states. Only Arizona, Nebraska, and Oklahoma continue to use it today.

The Rule of Correlative Rights

California is the only state that recognizes the rule of correlative rights. Under this rule, if the source of water for two or more neighboring landowners

is the same acquifer and if they both use their water reasonably and beneficially, both must share a shortage according to their respective ownerships. No priorities exist between them. One landowner cannot use more than his share if the rights of another neighboring landowner will be injured thereby. The purpose of this doctrine is to insure that all landowners get some water as long as any is available, regardless of how little.

The Prior Appropriation Doctrine

Priority between appropriators of underground water is based on the same "first in time is first in right" rule that is used for surface waters. All of the western states, except Nebraska and Texas, have some form of prior appropriation law for underground water. Often this law is applied in combination with another doctrine for particular types of underground sources. The sixteen states that use prior appropriation are Alaska, Arizona, California, Colorado, Idaho, Kansas, Montana, Nevada, New Mexico, North Dakota, Oklahoma, Oregon, South Dakota, Utah, Washington, and Wyoming.

Thirteen of these states require a permit for all groundwater extractions, regardless of whether the appropriator is an overlying owner, unless the water is to be used only for domestic purposes or for watering stock, lawns, or gardens. The other three states, Arizona, California, and Montana, only require the landowner to apply for a permit to pump water in a few designated areas, although all states require a permit to drill a well. Arizona has a new groundwater statute under which groundwater may not be used and wells may not be drilled in statutorily designated active management areas, except pursuant to a previously established water right or permit. This is to prevent further development in areas of water shortages.

As with surface-water prior appropriation, the date of issue of a permit determines one's priority in time of shortage. Once a permit is issued, it can be revoked if no water is used for a period of two to five years, depending on the state's requirements.

Investigating Potential Well Disputes

Even in areas of plentiful water, pumping can sometimes lower the water table sufficiently to cause problems. Many cases of water depletion due to an overabundance of wells in one water basin area have been recorded. When the basin dries up, all well owners suffer. Legal battles often arise between overlying owners because one of them causes the water level to drop below the well depth of the adjacent user. For example, the first landowner pumps from a 100-foot well. A second landowner constructs a 200-foot well and pumps twice as much water as the first well owner. There is still water available for the latter's use, but he will have to extend his well deeper to get it. (See illustration 18 in chapter 4, "Is There Enough Water on the Land?") The courts have arrived at various solutions to such problems. The second well owner may be ordered to diminish pumping in hopes that the water level will rise, or he may be required to pay the costs of lowering the first landowner's well to the new depth of the lowered water table. A court might consider any use that lowers the natural water table to be unreasonable and enjoin such use. If the first user had a permit, the second user might be prohibited from drilling a well in the first place.

When you are looking for land, be sure enough water is available for your intended needs, because if you deplete the water source or lower its level, you could be liable for damages or enjoined from pumping. Ask adjacent landowners how much water they use and if they know the extent of the underground waters and the level of the water table. In prior appropriation states, check the county recorder's office, state engineer's office, or state water agency for permits that have been filed and approved that affect the extent of current pumping and the priorities of other well owners.

Many states regulate well drilling, and certain requirements must be met by both the landowner and the well-driller. You might be required to file a statement of intent and file for a permit if you plan to dig a new well, dig one deeper, or repair an old one. The work may have to be inspected by a county or state official, and a permit fee may be demanded. The well-driller might be required to file reports, or logs, with the state engineer, geologist, or surveyor. The water's potability might have to meet certain legal standards. If you are buying land that already has a well on it and if the state or county has any ordinances governing wells, you will want to be sure the seller has complied with all the regulations. (See chapter 13, "Building and Health Codes.")

LOSING WATER RIGHTS BY PRESCRIPTION

The necessary elements for prescriptive water rights are the same as those for adverse possession. The prescriptive user must take and use the water in a hostile, actual, notorious, exclusive, and continuous manner under a claim of title. (These elements are explained in chapter 16, "Adverse Possession.") A prescriptive use of water can extinguish a riparian right in some states. For example, if a riparian user diverts more water than he is entitled to for the prescribed period of time, he can obtain a permanent right to take the water. Because of the difficulties involved in a water user's knowing that an upstream user is taking more than his share and challenging his action before the prescribed period of time elapses, most states no longer recognize prescriptive water rights.

DIFFUSED SURFACE WATER

In some areas diffused surface water, produced by rain, snow, or spring runoff, creates serious problems. Often a landowner will try to protect his land from flooding by diverting a large amount of runoff away from his house or fields and, in the process, damage neighboring property. If such a situation is likely to occur on land you might buy, find out the laws regarding diffused surface waters for your area.

A majority of states permit a landowner to pave or regrade his land in order to alter the flow of surface runoff only if he does so reasonably, with little danger of harm to adjoining lands.

Twelve states, Arizona, Arkansas, Hawaii, Indiana, Missouri, Nebraska, New York, North Dakota, Oklahoma, Virginia, West Virginia, and Wisconsin, follow the *common enemy doctrine,* which takes the view that flood and runoff waters are an enemy a landowner may combat by any means necessary even if his self-defense creates increased dangers for his neighbors. In other words, your neighbor can divert flood waters onto your land, you can divert them onto the next adjacent land, and so on. Although this may seem ridiculous and unreasonable, it was the original approach taken by the courts. If you are buying land in one of these twelve states, you must inspect the land for signs that it has been flooded or is in danger of being inundated by runoff from a neighbor's land. Since you will probably be a newcomer to the neighborhood, older residents might attempt to take advantage of you. Talk to them before you buy about the problems, if any, that result from excess water runoff. This is most important where your parcel is small and is surrounded by many other parcels.

A few states have formulated an approach to runoff surface water exactly opposite to the common enemy doctrine. This rule, called the *natural flow doctrine*, prohibits a landowner from interrupting or affecting the flow of water even if he is harmed by his inaction. The theory is that fewer people will be harmed this way. The states that follow this doctrine are Alabama, California, Georgia, Illinois, Kansas, Kentucky, Pennsylvania, and Tennessee.

Sometimes farmers approach drainage problems on a large scale with the combined help of many landowners. Since large areas of flat fertile land would be useless without adequate drainage or flood control, many areas have formed drainage districts. A *drainage district* is created when landowners in an area petition the state for permission to erect an extensive system of drains and ditches across large areas for the purpose of protecting valuable land. A vote is held in the affected area, and if the issue passes, a district is organized. Private lands can be purchased for easements to lay drainage title and ditches, and if the owners refuse to sell, their lands may be condemned and taken by the government's right of eminent domain. (See chapter 15, "Eminent Domain and Condemnation.") Tax assessments increase in the area because of the additional benefits afforded by the efficient large-scale drainage organization, and the price of land within the district generally increases. If your land is within a drainage district, find out what your assessments will be and how your land will be serviced by the district.

WATER SUPPLY DISTRICTS AND COMPANIES

Water companies and districts are organized to supply water to landowners where large areas need irrigation and the available water resources are inadequate.

Irrigation districts are organized in the same manner as drainage districts except that the irrigation district brings water to land rather than removing water from the land. Water costs in a district are regulated by the state public utilities commission. Sometimes a special assessment will be levied by the district on each property owner to pay for the water development.

Occasionally, instead of forming an irrigation district, farmers band together and organize their own mutual irrigation, or water, company. Each farmer owns shares in the company. The company purchases, stores, and distributes water to its shareholders. These private, nonprofit associations of landowners pool their separate water rights into the company and work together for the purpose of helping each other.

More common today are private commercial water companies that sell water as their "product." The amount of water to be received by a landowner is determined by a contract between the landowner and the company or by the amount of corporate stock bought by the purchaser. If the landowner has stock, his "dividends" are in water rather than money. In most cases, stock can be used only on the land for which it was issued. If you purchase land being serviced by a mutual or private water company, be sure you are to receive stock or a contract to get water as part of your purchase.

A public utility water company may be set up to sell water to anyone requesting it within its service area. This kind of water company operates like any other public utility company that serves a large city. You will be charged a rate established by state regulations according to the amount of water you use.

A FINAL CAUTION

You now have a basic knowledge of the potential problems that can arise among water users. You can take steps before purchasing land to protect yourself. The seller may not be aware of many potential problems regarding the water on his land. He may never have used the water for purposes for which you intend to use it. He may have been appropriating water without getting a permit, and you will fail to have seniority. You should understand what your rights will be before you buy the land, lest you be unable to get what you need when it's too late. You should also know about the water problems explained in chapter 4, "Is There Enough Water on the Land?"

If after you take title you ever do have a water problem that you can't settle by dealing with your fellow water users on a personal level, you may have to hire an attorney. He will probably initiate legal actions of quieting title and declaratory relief to settle boundary and water usage disputes. If immediate relief is sought, he will file a temporary restraining order (TRO) and a permanent injunction to prevent you from having your supply completely cut off. He might also file an action for damages. These expensive actions can be avoided by careful planning before you complete your purchase.

The various laws discussed throughout this chapter are subject to change at any time. Legislatures are constantly enacting new laws and eradicating old ones. Courts are always coming up with new decisions. It is your responsibility, unless you want to pay a lawyer to do the work, to investigate current water rights laws in your state and to determine the potential for future problems.

Without a doubt, the legal battles of the twenty-first century will be over water, the one commodity we can't live without. You should expect to see water rights mentioned in the press and on television with greater frequency in the years to come. Many rural places where folks are now settling have never had developed homesites at any time in the past, with people using water on a daily basis for all their needs. There is no question that the population is expanding in many rural areas where the water supply is insufficient to meet the needs of all the landowners. Where I live, I am getting clients into my office practically every week complaining about water hassles they are having with their neighbors. You cannot be too cautious in evaluating the water situation for any property you are thinking of buying.

USEFUL RESOURCES

Local Farm Advisor, Agricultural Experiment Station, State Department of Resources, and State Engineer

Any of these sources should have information re-

garding your state's water laws and how the land you want to buy is affected by them. The addresses of the experiment stations are given in Useful Resources in chapter 5, "The Earth—Soil, Vegetation, Topography."

Every state has a department of resources. There is usually an agency within the department which has specific control over water resources and which issues water regulations and oversees all water use. The director of this agency is usually called the state engineer or water commissioner. If you write to your state's water agency, it will send you complete information on the laws for your state with an application form for a permit to appropriate where applicable.

The following are available free from:
U.S. Geological Survey
Department of the Interior
Washington, DC 20240

or from any local office listed in Useful Resources for chapter 5, "The Earth—Soil, Vegetation, Topography."

*Water Law with Special Reference to
Ground Water—Circular 117
Water Rights in Areas of Ground Water
Mining—Circular 347
Interpretation and Current Status of Ground
Water Rights—Circular 432
Ground Water and the Law—Circular 446
Water Laws and Concepts—Circular 629*

Although the following pamphlets and application forms apply only to California, they are good examples of the types of information you can obtain from any state you are in. The following are free from:
State Water Resources Control Board
Division of Water Rights
P.O. Box 2000
Sacramento, CA 95810

*General Information Pertaining to Water
Rights in California
Statements of Water Diversions and Use
Regulations and Information Pertaining to
Appropriation of Water in California
Application to File for an Appropriation
Permit*

How to File an Application to Appropriate Unappropriated Water in California

The following is available for the specified price from:

Publications Department, 86
World Wildlife Fund/The Conservation
  Foundation
1255 Twenty-third St., N.W.
Washington DC 20037

Water Rights and Their Transfer in the Western United States $6.00
(postpaid)

CHAPTER 11

Mineral, Oil, Gas, Timber, Soil, and Other Rights

When we decided on the property we wanted to buy we were surprised during our preliminary investigation after receiving our preliminary title report to discover that our deed would include a reservation of mineral rights in favor of the federal government. The reservation read:

The Seller grants said land to the Buyer excepting therefrom all coal, oil, gas, and other hydrocarbon rights and mineral rights in said land together with the right to prospect for, mine, and remove the same as reserved by the United States of America in Patent recorded June 8, 1928, in Book 24, page 214 of Patents in the Office of the County Recorder of said County.

Mineral rights, oil and gas rights, timber rights, rights to take water, crops, and anything else in or near the earth can be reserved in a deed when the seller of a piece of land wants to keep a right to take these things. Once these rights have been legally reserved, they become encumbrances on the land title regardless of who buys the land. The right to take something from another's land is called a *profit* or *reservation*. In our case, the federal government retained, or reserved, a profit to take oil and natural gas when it originally sold the land to a private buyer on June 8, 1928. The original deed was recorded in the patents books, which are on public file in the county recorder's office, and thus it is binding on us and anyone else who buys the

195

land after us. When the government first deeded land out of the public domain it used a patent, which is like a deed. Every patent usually reserved mineral rights as standard procedure, without regard to whether or not useful minerals actually existed. There is now a procedure so that landowners may be able to reacquire the mineral rights to their own land provided the government determines that there are no minerals likely to be found on the land. (See Part X, ''Protecting Your Land after Purchase.'')

INVESTIGATING A RESERVATION

You are probably wondering why we bought the land knowing the government could come in and extract minerals at any time. Before we bought, we conducted a full-scale investigation of the history of mineral exploration in our area. We first went to our state Division of Mines and Geology, cornered an official, and spent the day with him going over technical mineral maps of our area and discussing the possibility of the government ever exercising its reservation rights. Tracing the history of oil exploration in our area, we found that in 1861 the first producing oil wells in California were drilled in a town just 20 miles north of us. The first shipment of oil came out of the area in 1865 when 100 gallons of oil were carried out of the hills in goatskin bags on the backs of mules. Drilling continued for only four months at that location, and a total of 100 barrels of oil were pumped. In the late 1800s and early 1900s, oil rigs were put up in three other towns, which are all within 15 miles of our place. None of those derricks produced a substantial amount of oil, and pumping was terminated. That activity was the sum total of oil drillings in our area. There was no evidence that large-scale mining of coal or other minerals had occurred, although during World War II nitrates had been mined about 10 miles from us for a short period of time. We also checked with the federal Office of Minerals and found no new information.

Thus we knew that our land was not another Alaskan oil field, and it was the unofficial opinion of the government official that the reservation would probably never be exercised. The federal government always reserves oil and mineral rights when it sells its land, and although it could always sell its profit to some enterprising company that might drill on pure speculation, we decided that the chances of that happening during our ownership of the land were not very high. We also took into consideration the fact that the government had held the profit since 1928 without using it. This reservation of oil and natural gas was the only defect or encumbrance on the title, so we decided to take the risk and buy the land since everything else about the deal was excellent.

In general I don't recommend buying land that has a reservation or a profit in the deed. However, after a thorough investigation, if you think that the reserved right will not be exercised during your ownership and if everything else in the deal is perfect, you might consider buying the land, although the price should reflect the fact that there is a reservation of rights against the title. I have told you about our investigation to give you an idea of the kind of search you should conduct to ascertain the potential danger of a reservation of the right to remove something from the land. You should consider the length of time between the reservation and your purchase, and whether the profit has ever been exercised. Another important consideration is the potential damage that would be done to the land if the profit is ever used. For example, if oil is extracted, rigs would be used until all the oil was removed. They would then be removed. If the right to take gravel is reserved, a whole river bottom might be dug up. If timber rights are reserved, all the trees on your land can be cut. One of the most frequently reserved, and potentially dangerous, rights is the right to cut and remove timber.

TIMBER RIGHTS

If your deed includes a reservation of timber rights, the owner of the profit can come onto the property to remove the trees at any time. When this reservation exists, the real estate agent or seller might say that the land has already been logged once and there cannot possibly be another cutting for a hundred years. Depending on how extensive the last cutting was and on how fast the trees grow, this may or may not be true. Even if it is, you will have a harder time selling the land to someone else as the time approaches for the trees to be cut, and you can never cut any of the trees yourself without incurring potential liability to the timber owner.

As with mineral rights, if the timber rights have previously been sold separately from the land, this sale is recorded in the county recorder's office. You should be aware of the special meanings of the words used to reserve the right to cut timber. If the original sale specified only that "timber is reserved," the holder can cut only the timber growing at the time he received the profit. Thus, if trees have been cut once by the person who reserved the timber on your land and the cutting was done after the date of the reservation, that person no longer holds any right to cut trees. You will own the timber rights. If the timber was already cut, the land might look so bad that you wouldn't want it anyway. If it is represented to you that the timber is no longer subject to the right to be cut, then you should request that a deed be obtained clearing this encumbrance from the land title.

Timber that has been cut and is lying on the ground does not automatically pass with the land. Once a tree is cut it becomes personal property, losing its status as real property. If trees have recently been cut on your land, you should be sure that the deed specifically states that you will acquire the fallen timber with the land and that the seller has not already sold the fallen timber to anyone else.

HOW TO FIND OUT IF THERE IS A RESERVATION IN THE DEED

Even if the seller or real estate agent does not inform you that you are not getting clear title to the entire land, you will know the truth when you receive an abstract of title, or preliminary title report. Any profit given in a transaction prior to the sale to you will be recorded in the public records and thus will be uncovered by a title search. If it is not recorded, and you do not know about it, then it will not be legally binding on you. When you become aware of the presence of a prior reservation, you should go to the county recorder's office and examine the original document that contains the reservation so you will know all the details of the encumbrance. This will help you conduct your

investigation to determine the probabilities of the profit's being exercised in the future. It is very easy to look up the document when you know the book and page number.

RIGHT OF ENTRY

If someone has been granted the right to extract something from your land, implied in that right is the right of entry, unless it is specified otherwise. When the holder of a profit has the right of entry, he can use the surface of the land in any reasonable manner to perform drilling or other operations for the purpose of extracting the materials that are the subject of the profit.

You will be in a much safer position regarding a reservation if it is specified that the holder does not have a right of entry. For example, the reservation in the deed might read like this:

The Seller grants the land to the Buyer reserving all oil, mineral, gas, and other hydrocarbon substances below a depth of 500 feet under the real estate described in the deed, without the right of surface entry.

If the holder of the profit does not have the right of entry to your land, you can refuse him entrance to your property or you can charge him a fee for this privilege. In the above example, if you refuse entry, the holder of the profit can only dig on an adjoining parcel and take whatever is lower than 500 feet under your land. This type of reservation is used mainly for gas and oil, for which the right of entry is not essential because a well dug on someone else's land can pump the gas and oil that flows beneath your land to the well.

RIGHT TO REMOVE CROPS

If you are buying farm land that has crops growing on it, you will want to ascertain whether the crops have been sold by the owner to another party before you buy the land. If that is the case, then the price of the land should be reduced accordingly. The crops on the land the season you buy might be all that have been sold or the owner might have a long-term contract with a buyer that will be binding on you if you purchase the land. Read any such contracts extremely carefully to ascertain their terms.

GRAZING RIGHTS

If your land is subject to someone else's rights to graze livestock on it, you probably don't want the property. Livestock can cause considerable damage to land and seriously disrupt your quiet enjoyment of your property. If there are cattle grazing on your land when you are inspecting it prior to purchase, inquire as to why they are there, how they will be removed, and what rights, if any, the livestock owner has to have his livestock there. Grazing and wandering horses, cattle, and sheep are a serious problem in many areas of the country, particularly where open grazing is allowed.

ROYALTY RIGHTS

If the title is subject to a profit that was sold by the present owner or someone prior to him, the person who sold the profit probably retained royalty rights to take part of the income arising from a future taking of any materials. Try to determine from the recorded documents, the real estate agent, or the seller if any royalty arrangements have been made. If so, and you are considering buying the land, you should attempt to have such royalty rights transferred to you with the property. Then if the property is disturbed by oil drillers or anyone else, you will reap some benefit from the situation.

IF THE SELLER WANTS TO RESERVE A PROFIT

If your seller wishes to reserve the right to take something from the land after he sells it to you, then the situation is different from that which we confronted when we bought our land. It is one thing when the government reserved mineral rights as a

matter of policy fifty years ago and has never exercised the right. But it is much different when your seller wants to hold on to some rights when he sells you the land. You should be extremely cautious in such a situation. Why does the seller want to reserve a profit? When he sells the land, he should sell all of his rights in it. If he refuses to sell the land without reserving the right to remove something, I recommend that you start looking somewhere else.

GETTING A LOAN WHEN PROFITS ARE RESERVED

If you intend to borrow money with your land as collateral, some lending agencies might be reluctant to help you if it seems likely that excavations will occur on the land. They may feel that you and your land are not a very good risk because your ownership might be interfered with at a later date. You can determine the effect of any reservation in your deed on possible loans by talking to a few lending agencies before you buy. Obviously if a reservation prevents you from getting the loan you need to buy the land, you had better look for another piece of land.

PROFITS BY PRESCRIPTION (PRESCRIPTIVE PROFITS)

I have already talked about prescriptive easements in chapter 9, "Easement Rights." Profits can also be gained by prescription. The requirements are the same as for adverse possession (see chapter 16) except that the situation is different. To gain a prescriptive profit, the person who is claiming the right must have been removing the materials for the legally prescribed length of time, which is set by the statute of limitations. For example, if an adjoining landowner has been taking fruit from trees on the seller's land under the conditions required for adverse possession, and he has done so for the required amount of time, he can claim a prescriptive profit to take the fruit for as long as he wants to continue to do so.

You can discover a prescriptive user only by inspecting the land. If you see evidence that rocks, soil, water, timber, crops, or other materials are being removed, find out what the situation is. A title search or abstract of title will not detect a prescriptive use.

RESERVATION OR PROFIT IN THE CONTRACT OF SALE

All recorded reservations in the deed and against the title will show up in a title report or abstract of title, which should be shown to you for your approval prior to the close of escrow. You should have a copy of any reservation before you close escrow or approve of it so that you know what is not included in the title to the property.

If you find that a reservation exists and you don't want to buy the property unless it is cleared from the title, then you should disapprove of the title report or abstract of title and demand that it be removed before the close of escrow. You can write your objection in the following manner:

Buyer disapproves of the condition of title and demands the removal of the existing reservation which states that

_____

_____ .

This reservation must be removed as an encumbrance on the title to said property, by an appropriate document recorded with the County Recorder, before the time scheduled for closing of escrow. If the condition is not satisfied, Buyer has the right at his election to terminate the agreement or waive the condition.

USEFUL RESOURCES

U.S. Geological Survey Earth-Science Information and Sales

Questions about all aspects of geology can be directed to the Geologic Inquiries Group. This office answers questions on topics such as earthquakes, energy, and mineral resources, the geology of specific areas, and geologic maps and mapping.

Information on geologic map indexes for the states

is also available. Contact:

Geologic Inquiries Group
U.S. Geological Survey
907 National Center
Reston, VA 22092

or any local USGS office listed in Useful Resources of chapter 5.

State Geoscience Agencies (SGA)

Many state geoscience agencies sell USGS products (book reports, maps, etc.) that pertain to their region or state. Some state geoscience agencies are also affiliated with the National Cartographic Information Center. (See NCIC under Useful Resources of chapter 8, ''Land Description and Surveys.'') The USGS cooperates with state geoscience agencies in a variety of projects; publications resulting from these projects are commonly available from both organizations.

In addition to selling USGS products, many state geoscience agencies maintain reference collections that include USGS materials. State geoscience agencies allow the public to consult, but not borrow, these materials. Certain state geoscience agencies are also designated as depositories of specific USGS Open-File Reports.

If you are interested in finding out about minerals in your state, contact one of the SGA offices listed below or one of the state USGS offices listed in chapter 5, Useful Resources.

Alabama
Geological Survey of Alabama
P.O. Drawer O
University, AL 35846

Alaska
Division of Geological and Geophysical Survey
3001 Porcupine Dr.
Anchorage, AK 99701

Arizona
Bureau of Geology and Mineral Technology
845 N. Park Ave.
Tucson, AZ 85719

Arkansas
Arkansas Geological Commission
3815 W. Roosevelt Rd.
Little Rock, AR 72204

199

California
California Division of Mines and Geology
1416 Ninth St., Rm. 1314
Sacramento, CA 95814

Colorado
Colorado Geological Survey
1313 Sherman St., Rm. 715
Denver, CO 80203

Connecticut
Department of Environmental Protection
Natural Resource Center
165 Capitol Ave., Rm. 553
Hartford, CT 06106

Delaware
Delaware Geological Survey
University of Delaware
101 Penny Hall
Newark, DE 19711

Florida
Bureau of Geology
903 W. Tennessee St.
Tallahassee, FL 32304

Georgia
Georgia Geologic Survey
19 Martin Luther King Dr., S.W., Rm. 400
Atlanta, GA 30334

Hawaii
Department of Land and Natural Resources
Division of Water and Land Development
P.O. Box 373
Honolulu, HI 96809

Idaho
Idaho Geological Survey
University of Idaho
Moscow, ID 83843

Illinois
Illinois State Geological Survey
615 E. Peabody Dr., Rm. 121
Champaign, IL 61820

Indiana
Indiana Geological Survey
Department of Natural Resources
611 N. Walnut Grove
Bloomington, IN 47401

Iowa
Iowa Geological Survey
123 N. Capitol St.
Iowa City, IA 52242

Kansas
Kansas Geological Survey
University of Kansas
1930 A Ave., Campus West
Lawrence, KS 66044

Kentucky
Kentucky Geological Survey
University of Kentucky
311 Breckinridge Hall
Lexington, KY 40506

Louisiana
Louisiana Geological Survey
Department of Natural Resources
Box G, University Station
Baton Rouge, LA 70813

Maine
Maine Geological Survey
Department of Conservation
State House Station, #22
Augusta, ME 04330

Maryland
Maryland Geological Survey
The Rotunda
711 West 40th St., Ste. 440
Baltimore, MD 21211

Massachusetts
Department of Environmental Quality
  Engineering
1 Winter St., 7th Fl.
Boston, MA 02108

Michigan
Geologic Survey Division
Michigan Department of Natural Resources
Mason Bldg., 4th Fl.
P.O. Box 30028
Lansing, MI 48909

Minnesota
Minnesota Geological Survey
2642 University Ave.
St. Paul, MN 55114-1057

Mississippi
  Mississippi Geological, Economic and
    Topographical Survey
  P.O. Box 5348
  Jackson, MS 39216

Missouri
  Department of Natural Resources
  Division of Geology and Land Survey
  P.O. Box 250
  Rolla, MO 65401

Montana
  Montana Bureau of Mines and Geology
  Montana College of Mineral Science and
    Technology
  Butte, MT 59701

Nebraska
  Conservation and Survey Division
  University of Nebraska
  Lincoln, NE 68588

Nevada
  Nevada Bureau of Mines and Geology
  University of Nevada
  Reno, NV 89557-0088

New Hampshire
  Department of Resources and Economic
    Development
  University of New Hampshire
  117 James Hall
  Durham, NH 03824

New Jersey
  New Jersey Geological Survey, CN-029
  Trenton, NJ 08625

New Mexico
  New Mexico Bureau of Mines and Mineral
    Resources
  Campus Station
  Socorro, NM 87801
    or
  Resources Development and Management
    Division
  Department of Energy and Minerals
  525 Camino de los Marquez
  Santa Fe, NM 87501

New York
  New York State Geological Survey
  State Science Center, Rm. 3140
  Cultural Education Center
  Albany, NY 12230

North Carolina
  North Carolina Geological Survey Section
  P.O. Box 27687
  Raleigh, NC 27611

North Dakota
  North Dakota Geological Survey
  University Station
  Box 8156-58202
  Grand Forks, ND 58201

Ohio
  Ohio Division of Geological Survey
  Fountain Square, Bldg. B
  Columbus, OH 43224

Oklahoma
  Oklahoma Geological Survey
  University of Oklahoma
  830 Van Vleet Oval, Rm. 163
  Norman, OK 73019

Oregon
  Department of Geology and Mineral
    Industries
  1005 State Office Bldg.
  Portland, OR 97201

Pennsylvania
  Bureau of Topographic and Geological
    Survey
  Department of Environmental Resources
  P.O. Box 2357
  Harrisburg, PA 17120

Rhode Island
  Statewide Planning Program
  265 Melrose St.
  Providence, RI 02907

South Carolina
  South Carolina Geological Survey
  Harbison Forest Rd.
  Columbia, SC 29210

South Dakota
South Dakota Geological Survey
Science Center
University of South Dakota
Vermillion, SD 57069

Tennessee
Department of Conservation
Division of Geology
701 Broadway
Nashville, TN 37203

Texas
Bureau of Economic Geology
University of Texas at Austin
University Station, Box X
Austin, TX 78712

Utah
Utah Geological and Mineral Survey
606 Black Hawk Wy.
Salt Lake City, UT 84108

Vermont
State Geologist
Agency of Environmental Conservation
79 River St.
Montpelier, VT 05602

Virginia
Virginia Division of Mineral Resources
P.O. Box 3667
Charlottesville, VA 22903

Washington
Division of Geology and Earth Resources
Department of Natural Resources
Mail Stop PY-12
Olympia, WA 98504

West Virginia
West Virginia Geological and Economic
Survey
P.O. Box 879
Morgantown, WV 26507

Wisconsin
Wisconsin Geological and Natural History
Survey
University of Wisconsin Extension
1815 University Ave.
Madison, WI 53705

Wyoming
Geological Survey of Wyoming
University Station
P.O. Box 3008
Laramie, WY 82071

Federal Office of Minerals (Minerals Exploration Field Offices)

These offices can supply you with reports and maps covering the extent of mineral exploration in your area. The main office and four regional offices are under the direction of the U.S. Geological Survey. Their addresses are below.

MAIN OFFICE

Office of Minerals Exploration
U.S. Geological Survey
Washington, DC 20242

REGION 1
(Covers: Idaho, Montana, Oregon, Washington)

Office of Minerals Exploration
W. 920 Riverside Ave., Rm. 656
Spokane, WA 99201

REGION 2
(Covers: Alaska, California, Nevada, Hawaii)

Office of Minerals Exploration
Bldg. 2
345 Middlefield Rd.
Menlo Park, CA 94025

REGION 3
(Covers: Arizona, Colorado, Kansas, Nebraska, New Mexico, North Dakota, Oklahoma, South Dakota, Texas, Utah, Wyoming)

Office of Minerals Exploration
Denver Federal Center
Bldg. 53, Rm. 203
Denver, CO 80225

REGION 4
(Covers: All other states)

Office of Minerals Exploration
Post Office Bldg., Rm. 11
Knoxville, TN 37902

Information can also be obtained from the U.S. Geological Survey offices listed in chapter 5, ''The Earth—Soil, Vegetation, Topography.''

State Office of Minerals

Each state has its own department of minerals. Ask the local farm advisor, Agricultural Experiment Station, or building inspector, or write to the federal USGS office (addresses given above) for your state and ask for the address of your state office.

CHAPTER 12

Zoning Laws

Zoning is one of the public rights to regulate the individual land use, without compensation to the owner, for the health, safety, and general welfare of everyone. Building and health codes and subdivision laws are also included in this public regulatory power. Depending on your reasons for buying land, zoning laws can be either excellent protection or a damper on your freedom. An investigation of the zoning in your area is an essential aspect of your purchase.

Over four-fifths of the three thousand counties in the United States have zoning power. Each county is first divided into districts, or zones, according to a master plan created by the local planning or zoning commission. The basic zones are industrial, business, residential, and agricultural. But there can be many other types. The following list of some of the common types of zones is a good example of how land use can be broken down.

After the county has formed the zones, the specific regulations for each division limit the dimension of the buildings, the size of the building lots and subdivision limits, the density of the population and the number of houses permitted, and the purposes for which the buildings and land can be used.

Zone Symbol	Description
A	Agriculture
A1	Agriculture; residential-agriculture; single-family
A2	Agriculture; poultry and rabbit raising
A3	Heavy agriculture; floriculture
AC	Arts and crafts
AE	Agriculture; agriculture-exclusive
AL	Limited agriculture

AR	Agriculture-residential; administrative-research	RE	Residential estate
AV	Airport	RF	Recreation-forestry
B	Buffer	RR	Rural residential; resort-recreation; residential-resort
C	Business; commercial	RRB	Restricted roadside business
C1	Limited commercial; retail	RT	Recreational-tourist; residential transitional
C1S	Shopping center	RWY	Railway
C2	General commercial; limited commercial; neighborhood shopping	SR	Recreation; scientific research
C3	General commercial; regional shopping; community shopping	T	Trailer park
C4	Unlimited commercial; service stations	U	Unclassified; hog ranch
CA	Commercial-agriculture	WA	Watercourse area
CH	Highway commercial	WR	Watershed-recreational
CM	Commercial manufacturing		
CO	Commercial-office; professional office		
CR	Restricted commercial; recreational-commercial; community reserve		
D2	Desert-mountain		
E2	One-family residence; estate; executive; small farms		
E3	One-family residence; estate; mountain estate		
FP	Flood plain		
FR	Forestry-recreation		
GA	General agriculture		
GR	Guest ranch		
H1	Highway		
IA	Intermediate agriculture		
IR	Industrial-recreational; industrial-administrative research		
LI	Light industrial		
M	Industrial; manufacturing		
M1	Light manufacturing; residential-manufacturing		
M3	Heavy industrial		
O	Open space; official		
P	Parking; parks		
PC	Planned community		
PF	Public facilities		
PR	Park and recreation		
Q	Quarries		
R1	Single-family residential		
R1H	Residential hillside		
R2	Duplex; multiple-family		
R3A	Multiple-family; mountain resort		
R4	High-density multiple-family; suburban residential		
R5	Tourist accommodations		
R15	Single-family, low density		
RA	Residential-agriculture		

FIND OUT THE ZONING LAWS IN YOUR AREA BEFORE YOU BUY

Because zoning is not covered in an abstract of title or title insurance policy, you will have to do some research on your own to insure that the land you want to buy is in an area that permits the specific activities you want and prohibits those you want to avoid.

All zoning regulations for a particular area are kept by the county board of supervisors, the zoning commission, the planning commission, or the building inspector. Ask to see the master plan of the entire area so you can determine the direction of future development. To determine the zoning for a specific parcel of land you should have its legal description, which you can get from the seller or real estate agent. You might then have to see the tax assessor and get the tax or parcel number for the land if that is how it is listed in the planning books for your community. If the area you are looking at has been incorporated into a town or city, it will be regulated by town or city ordinances; otherwise, separate county ordinances will apply. In some areas, no zoning ordinance will exist at all.

If your area has not been zoned yet, you will have to exercise extreme care in the selection of your country home. After you purchase the land somebody might come along and establish a bar, junkyard, rendering plant, chicken farm, shopping center, recreation center, second-home subdivision, trailer park, or factory. You can't predict the future in an unzoned area. Don't assume that just because the land is far away from a town or city no ordinances exist. A piece of land can be very isolated and still be in an industrial zone where any big business can put up a factory and you might not be allowed to build a residence, or you might not want to. I had a recent case where a homesite was along a beautiful river that turned out to be a gravel extraction area, and there was nothing the landowner could do to stop daily rock crushing.

COMMON ZONING RESTRICTIONS TO WATCH FOR

Zoning law enforcement is usually carried out by the building inspector and health inspector. They will refuse to issue a permit if a proposed building or use of the land violates the zoning restrictions of the area. The penalties for violating these laws are very harsh, and enforcement in the more populated areas is relatively efficient. (See chapter 13, "Building and Health Codes.")

There are a few zoning restrictions that commonly hinder rural land buyers who want to live on their land. Among these are the following:

Seasonal Dwelling Restrictions

Some secluded areas are zoned for second-home summer use only. You will not be permitted to live on the land the entire year.

Number of Homes Permitted

Most rural areas restrict the number of homes that can be built in an area. For example, only one dwelling will be permitted for every 20 acres of land, or one dwelling per parcel, regardless of size.

Minimum Size of a Parcel for a Dwelling

No home can be built on a parcel of less than a specified minimum area.

Prohibition of Further Subdividing

Your parcel might already be at a size that prohibits further dividing. If you are planning to split a parcel off to sell to raise money to pay for your remaining parcel, be sure the zoning will allow this. Also be aware of this if you buy with partners and intend to split up the land among you at a later date. You might not be able to do so.

Floodplain Zoning

An area with a history of flooding might be zoned as a floodplain where all home construction is prohibited.

Trailers and Mobile Homes

Zoning laws often prohibit the use of mobile homes, trailers, buses, and vans for dwellings. Mobile homes and trailers, if permitted, are usually restricted to a specified area to prevent them from "cheapening" the value of surrounding houses.

VARIANCES AND USE PERMITS

If you want to use your land in a way prohibited by the zoning regulations, you must seek a variance or nonconforming use permit. The purpose of issuing such permits is to retain flexibility in the zoning laws so that land may be used for activities that are compatible with the surrounding area or are only temporary. For example, if a trailer is prohibited as a dwelling, you could apply for a use permit to live in a trailer on your land while you are building a permanent residence.

An application must be made to the board of appeals, board of supervisors, or planning commission for a variance. The petition application must show that the intended use will not detrimentally affect the surrounding area or create problems for the regular uses permitted in the zone.

Variances are not issued automatically. If they were, the whole purpose of zoning would be defeated. If a real estate agent tells you to go ahead and buy the property because getting a variance will not be a problem, don't listen to him. Always get a necessary variance before you buy. Clause 17(c) of the Model Contract of Sale in chapter 28 can be used to condition the closing of the deal on your ability to get a use permit. If the permit has not been granted by the close of escrow, you can either terminate the contract or extend the closing date.

ZONING WARRANTY

Clause 16(d) in the Model Contract of Sale is a warranty stating what the zoning is at the time the contract is signed and that it will continue to be so zoned at the close of escrow. This is to prevent the situation where a rezoning occurs before escrow closes that could prohibit your intended use of the land. If the zoning is changed, the contract can be terminated or you can sue the seller for breach of warranty.

Clause 16(f) is a warranty by the seller that there are no violations of any zoning ordinances resulting from any activity on his property at the time of sale, whether or not he has actually been cited by the county for a zoning violation.

USEFUL RESOURCES

The following pamphlet is available free from:
U.S. Department of Agriculture
Office of Information
Washington, DC 20250

Zoning for Rural Areas L 510

The following are available for the specified price from:
Superintendent of Documents
Government Printing Office
Washington, DC 20402

Why and How of Rural Zoning
A 1.75:196/2 $ .40
Zoning for Small Towns and Rural Counties
C 46.8:Z7 $ .50

Free information is available from the following national planning and zoning organization, including a catalogue of available books:
American Planning Association
1313 E. 60th St.
Chicago, IL 60637

Information on local zoning in your area can be obtained from the county planning commission, the county zoning commission, the board of supervisors, or the county building inspector.

Coastal Zone Management

The following state agencies plan and implement programs for the orderly development of coastal zones.

Alabama
Coastal Area Program
Environmental Management Department
3263 Demetropolis Rd., #10
Mobile, AL 36609

Alaska
Division of Land and Water Management
Department of Natural Resources
Pouch 7005
Anchorage, AK 99510

California
Coastal Commission
631 Howard St., 4th Fl.
San Francisco, CA 94105

Connecticut
Planning and Coastal Area Management
Environmental Protection Department
165 Capitol Ave.
Hartford, CT 06106

Delaware
Coastal Management Program
P.O. Box 1404
Dover, DE 19903

Florida
Coastal Zone Management
Environmental Regulation Department
2600 Blairstone Rd.
Tallahassee, FL 32301

Georgia
Coastal Resources Division
Department of Natural Resources
1200 Glynn Ave.
Brunswick, GA 31523-9990

Hawaii
Planning Division
Planning and Economic Development
    Department
P.O. Box 2359
Honolulu, HI 96804

Illinois
Division of Water Resources
Department of Transportation
310 S. Michigan, Rm. 1606
Chicago, IL 60604

Louisiana
Office of Coastal Management
Department of Natural Resources
P.O. Box 44124
Baton Rouge, LA 70804-4124

Maine
State Planning Office
Executive Department
State House Station, #38
Augusta, ME 04333

Maryland
Tidewater Administration
Department of Natural Resources
Tawes State Office Bldg.
Annapolis, MD 21401

Massachusetts
Coastal Zone Management
Executive Office of Environmental Affairs
100 Cambridge St.
Boston, MA 02202

Michigan
Great Lakes Shoreland Section
Department of Natural Resources
P.O. Box 30028
Lansing, MI 48909

Minnesota
Water Division
Department of Natural Resources
500 Lafayette Rd.
St. Paul, MN 55146

Mississippi
Bureau of Marine Resources
Department of Wildlife Conservation
University of Mississippi, Gulfport Campus
Long Beach, MS 39560

New Hampshire
Office of State Planning
2½ Beacon St.
Concord, NH 03301

New Jersey
Division of Coastal Resources
Environmental Protection Department
John Fitch Plaza, CN402
Trenton, NJ 08625

New York
Department of Environmental Conservation
50 Wolf Rd.
Albany, NY 12233

North Carolina
Coastal Management Division, Natural
Resources and Community Development
Department
512 N. Salisbury St.
Raleigh, NC 27611

Ohio
Division of Water
Department of Natural Resources
Fountain Square, Bldg. E
Columbus, OH 43224

Oregon
Policy Division, Land Conservation and
Development Department
1175 Court St., N.E.
Salem, OR 97310

Rhode Island
Coastal Resources Management Council
60 Davis St.
Providence, RI 02903

South Carolina
Coastal Council
1116 Bankers Trust Tower
Columbia, SC 29201

Virginia
Council on the Environment
Ninth Street Office Bldg.
Richmond, VA 23219

Washington
Division of Marine Land Management
Department of Natural Resources
Public Lands Bldg.
Olympia, WA 98504

Wisconsin
Coastal Management Section
Department of Administration
P.O. Box 7864
Madison, WI 53707

CHAPTER 13

Building and Health Codes

I sometimes think men do not act like reasonable creatures, when they build for themselves combustible dwellings in which they are every day obligated to use fire.
—Benjamin Franklin in his letter of 1787 entitled Building Acts Anticipated

Building and health codes, like zoning ordinances, are included in the right of the government to regulate individual land use for the health, safety, and general welfare of the people. The county may also regulate the construction of private roads that lead onto public county roads in order to protect those public roads. In this chapter I discuss building codes, permits, and enforcement; health codes and per-mits; road encroachment permits; and how to protect yourself to be sure no code violations exist on the property you are buying in the contract of sale.

BUILDING CODES

The first recorded building code was passed in New York (then called New Amsterdam) in 1625. The law specified types of roof coverings and locations of dwellings to prevent roof fires. In 1648, New York prohibited wooden or plastered chimneys, and inspections by firemasters were initiated. By 1656, straw and reed roofs were prohibited and ordered removed from all houses. Philadelphia went a step further in 1701 by passing a law providing that any person whose chimney caught on fire would be prosecuted and fined. From the very beginning building laws were enacted only after a disaster had occurred. Although fire prevention was the primary issue in the first building codes, today all aspects of construction are regulated.

Building laws are designed to protect people's financial investment as well as to insure their personal safety. Often the appearance of a structure will be regulated, and unusually designed houses will be discouraged. (I talk more about this later in this chapter.)

Today most building regulations throughout the United States are based on the Uniform Building Code, which was established by the International Conference of Building Officials (ICBO) in 1927. The Uniform Building Code's stated purpose is to prevent people from being hurt physically or financially by providing minimum uniform standards of building construction.

The Uniform Building Code sets standards for foundations, building materials, design, size and location of rooms, means of exit, windows and ventilation, fireproofing in construction, load and stress of materials for particular purposes, chimneys, stairways and guards, sanitary equipment, plumbing, and electricity. Reprinted here are some requirements from the Uniform Building Code that are a good example of the kind of details covered by the codes.

1. With each application for a building permit, two sets of plans for construction shall be submitted.
2. Plans shall be drawn to scale upon substantial paper and shall be of sufficient clarity to indicate the nature and extent of the work proposed and show in detail that it will conform to the provisions of the uniform building codes.
3. Plans shall include a plot showing the location of the proposed building and of every existing building on the property.
4. Minimum room sizes:
   a. At least one room of 120 sq. ft.
   b. Rooms used for both cooking and living or living and sleeping at least 150 sq. ft.
   c. Rooms used for sleeping two persons—90 sq. ft. Each additional person—50 sq. ft.
   d. Kitchen at least 50 sq. ft.
5. Minimum horizontal dimension of any habitable room shall be 7'0". Minimum ceiling height in habitable rooms, service rooms, and toilet rooms shall be 7'6". Where sloping ceilings occur, the required ceiling height shall be provided in at least 50% of the room and no portion of any room having a ceiling height of less than 5' shall be considered as contributing to the minimum required areas.

Minimum ceiling height in hallways, corridors, and closets shall be 7'0".

6. No water closet (toilet) space shall be less than 2'6" wide and shall have a minimum of 2'0" clear space in front of the water closet.
7. Required window area and opening:
   a. Bathrooms and water closet compartments not less than 3 sq. ft. nor ⅛ of the floor area, ½ openable.
   b. Kitchens, rooms used for living, dining or sleeping purposes not less than 12 sq. ft. nor ⅛ of the floor area, ½ openable.
8. Every dwelling shall be provided with a kitchen. No kitchen shall be used for sleeping purposes.
9. Every dwelling shall have the following minimum sanitary facilities: water closet, lavatory, tub or shower and kitchen sink. All kitchen sinks shall be provided with hot and cold water. All of the above items shall be properly trapped, vented, and connected to an approved sewage disposal system.
10. There shall be no opening from a room in which a water closet is located into a room in which food is prepared or stored.
11. The specifications on this sheet are for conventionally framed dwellings, and persons wanting unusual type construction should consult a professional designer.

Two thousand of the three thousand counties in the country follow the ICBO (International Council of Building Officials) standards, although some areas make changes when necessitated by climatic or topographical conditions and local administrative procedures. The local building inspector's office will have copies available of the area's building requirements, including standards for building construction, electrical wiring, and plumbing.

PERMITS AND FEES

Before you build or renovate a structure, you must submit your plans to the local building inspector for approval and pay the applicable permit fees. If the building is a standard-construction "conventionally framed dwelling" of stud wall or masonry construction, you can submit your own plans. The inspector will examine the plans for compliance with the codes. If they are suitable, they will be approved. Then you pay a permit fee based on the number of square feet in the building. There is a standard-fee list for each area that you can see before paying a fee. At the time plans are approved, one-half of the stated building fee must be paid.

Other permits must be obtained for plumbing and electrical facilities and additional fees paid. These fees are based on the number of outlets to be built into the dwelling.

INSPECTIONS AND CERTIFICATION OF OCCUPATION

Once your plans are approved and a permit is issued, you can build the house yourself. The law does not require you to hire professional builders. During construction many building departments make four inspections. The first is to look at the foundation before it is laid. The second is a frame inspection after the roof framing and basing are in place and pipes, chimneys, and vents are complete. The third is the wall inspection before plastering and siding are commenced. The fourth and final inspection comes after the building is completed and ready for occupancy. Many rural areas require only a single inspection after the house is completed.

Before a house can be lived in and after the final inspection, the building department will often be required to issue a certificate of occupancy. If you are buying a newly constructed house, be sure it has been certified properly.

GETTING AN UNCONVENTIONAL STRUCTURE APPROVED

If you intend to build an unusually designed dwelling, you will be required to write to the International Conference of Building Officials (see Useful Resources at the end of this chapter) to see if they have any approved standard plans for such a structure. They have approved standard plans for common unconventional designs, such as domes, yurts, and round houses. In most areas, you must have specific plans drawn up by a licensed engineer or contractor.

TEST FOR STRUCTURAL STRENGTH

The Uniform Building Code provides that if a structure does not meet normal code requirements, the local building inspector may conduct a test for structural strength on the building before it can be approved. In many cases, you will have to hire a structural engineer to conduct these tests to the satisfaction of the building department. Because of the growing popularity of domes, some companies have conducted strength tests on plywood domes. If you plan a dome, write for the results of tests undertaken by any of the members of the Home Manufacturers Council's National Dome Council. The HMC's National Dome Council is a national organization with membership comprised of manufacturers of dome buildings. Yurts are also growing in popularity and have their own national organization, the Yurt Foundation, which sells plans and distributes free information. See the Useful Resources at the end of chapter 6 for addresses of various dome manufacturers and of the above yurt and dome organizations.

You can contact these manufacturers for answers to questions and information on designs, specifications, prices, and builders/dealers in your particular area. These companies sell sets of dome and yurt plans that may get automatic approval from any building inspector working under the Uniform Building Code. The reason for this is that the ICBO has already tested these designs and approved them. Most building inspectors have not had the experience of dealing with a dome, yurt, or other atypical design and thus won't accept anything other than ICBO approved plans. But you must check with your local department to see what their attitude is. If you can convince an inspector you know what you are doing, you may be able to get approval for a dome, yurt, or other unconventional design.

TEMPORARY DWELLINGS

If you want to buy land but don't have the money to put up a house right away, most counties will allow you to live in temporary dwellings while building a permanent dwelling. In some areas, the building inspector does not have jurisdiction to regulate any temporary dwellings or canvas structures, such as tents or tepees. A tent usually means that 25 percent or more of the walls and roof are covered by canvas or other fabric.

If you have a bus, van, camper, or trailer, you can usually live in it on isolated land indefinitely except where zoning and building restrictions are strictly enforced. A fee is charged for a temporary dwelling permit, and a limit is placed on the length of time you can house yourself temporarily. Many subdivisions have restrictions against living in any temporary facility, even while constructing a permanent dwelling. Read the subdivision covenants, conditions, and restrictions to see if this is the case in your area.

LAND THAT HAS STRUCTURES ON IT

If you want to purchase land with a structure already on it, you should be sure that it has been approved and that it meets current building and health code standards.

Two problems arise when you buy an older house. The first occurs if the structure was built to code but is now substandard because the code has since been revised. Fortunately new codes do not apply retroactively to buildings already approved in previous years. However, if it is determined that the structure is a fire or health hazard, or substandard because of revised code requirements after it was built, no permits will be issued for repairs, enlargements, or modernization of the building. The theory is that if you are unable to touch the house as it is, you will tear it down and rebuild according to contemporary standards. This situation is usually encountered in areas close to urban centers.

The more frequent problem in rural areas occurs if a house was built prior to the institution of building codes in that locality and thus was never built to any set of standards. Whether you can live in it as it is or must first have it brought up to code will depend on your local building inspector. I have encountered inspectors who would take no pity in such a situation.

HOW TO FIND OUT IF A BUILDING IS UP TO CODE STANDARDS

To discover whether a building meets the current

standards, you should visit the county building inspector and see what he has on file with regard to the structure. You will have to give him the name of the current owner and the location of the land. Don't tell him what you think is wrong with the place until you see what he has on it. He should have a paid permit with all approvals having been granted. If you are talking to the official who inspected the house, ask him his opinion of the structure. Then tell him what you are going to pay for it and observe his reaction. He might reinforce your opinion or open your eyes to some defects in the property you had not considered.

APPEALING A DENIAL OF A BUILDING PERMIT

Every county that has building codes will have an established process for appealing decisions of building inspectors. The first level of appeal is often within the building codes department itself where a board of appeals will hear your request for a modification of a specific ordinance. You must present your situation and explain why it is impractical for you to comply with the code. For example, you might have to completely rebuild an older house to meet the codes, or you might be located far from any other buildings and thus your structure will not decrease the value of surrounding buildings. In most cases, it will be difficult to convince the board why it is not practical for you to comply with the ordinance, but it is always worth a try if you feel you are being harassed. You should use the same method for preparing your case as that used for a tax appeal. (See chapter 17, "Property Taxes and Assessments.") If the appeal fails, you will probably have to go to court, which involves the expenditure of time and money.

Some people choose to ignore the codes and permit requirements altogether. I have been in many places where enforcement is insignificant. However, every area of the country is gradually becoming more efficiently regulated on all levels. Even if you manage to avoid the building inspector now, when you decide to sell your property in five or ten years, your buyers might not be willing to pay a good price for a structure that was not approved. Meeting code requirements in rural areas is often so easy that it is really only a matter of paying the fees.

PENALTIES

The Uniform Building Code establishes penalties for violation of the code in the following manner:

Any person, firm, or corporation violating any of the provisions of this Code shall be deemed guilty of a misdemeanor and each such person shall be deemed guilty of a separate offense for each and every day or portion thereof during which any violation of any of the provisions of this Code is committed, continued, or permitted, and upon the conviction of any such violation such person shall be punishable by a fine of not more than $300, or by imprisonment for not more than 90 days, or by both such fine and imprisonment.

In addition:

Where work for which a permit is required by this Code is started or proceeded with prior to obtaining said permit, the fees required by said permit shall be doubled, but the payment of such double fee shall not relieve any persons from fully complying with the requirements of this Code in the execution of the work nor from any other penalties prescribed herein.

ENFORCEMENT

Most local laws permit an inspector to enter your property at any reasonable hour to enforce the provisions of the local ordinances. If you refuse him permission to enter, as some do, he may leave and return with a search warrant and an entire squadron of enforcers, including policemen, police dogs, sheriffs, and deputies. Sometimes the county agencies use small aircraft and helicopters that scan the countryside in search of new and illegal constructions. By checking the records they know if permits have been taken out on any new construction they spot from the air. If none have, they will pay the builder a visit.

Sometimes the building inspector will go to great lengths to enforce the regulations. In one place I visited, the building inspector used a helicopter to fly low over an area where many young people had recently immigrated and dropped smoke bombs over the sites of illegal structures. A crew on the ground then followed the smoke to the buildings and issued citations. Obviously every county is not this efficient. But when large numbers of new residents move in, the authorities usually keep an eye on their activities.

The salary of the building inspector is dependent on how much money he takes in for permits. If he manages to increase local revenue, he will not only have a better chance of keeping his job, but he also has a good argument for a salary increase. Much of the activity of building inspectors and other bureaucrats with a smattering of power is dependent on local politics.

HEALTH CODES AND PERMITS

Regardless of where you buy land, you will have to deal with the local health authorities. They are empowered to make sure that you have proper water and sewage facilities and to issue permits and collect fees. A small fee buys a permit for the construction of an outhouse and later installation of a septic tank. Contrary to popular belief, outhouses are not outlawed by many health departments. In many areas, if you do not have adequate running water under pressure to your house and the outhouse is not located within 200 feet of an adjacent residence, you are permitted to use an outhouse (privy). The following are standard health requirements for outhouses:

1. It shall be unlawful to erect or maintain a privy or outhouse unless a suitable shelter be provided to afford privacy and protection from the elements. The door thereof shall be so constructed as to close automatically by means of a spring or other device.
2. The vault shall not be permitted to become filled with excreta nearer than two feet from the surface of the ground and such excreta shall be regularly and thoroughly disinfected.
3. The privy building shall be made flyproof.
4. The pit privy shall be at least 4 feet deep.
5. The pit privy shall be at least 75 feet from well or stream.
6. All privy buildings shall be kept in a clean and sanitary condition at all times.

Most areas today require that permanent septic tanks and leach lines be installed when a residence is constructed. This is often a costly venture requiring a machine operator to come in with a backhoe to dig your septic tank hole. The required minimum capacity of a septic tank is usually 750 gallons for a two-bedroom house. If you are purchasing land with a house already on it, be sure that the waste disposal system has been approved by the county and is functioning properly. You will save yourself a lot of trouble and expense if you discover inadequacies at an early stage in the proceedings. In most counties, cesspools and sewer wells are strictly prohibited, and even where they are allowed, they are an inferior method of waste disposal. Since these facilities are very common in many parts of the country, be sure that the local regulations have not rendered such systems obsolete if they are in use on the land you are buying.

If no septic tank exists on the property and you desire to construct a home, never buy the property without first completing a percolation test and having the local health department approve the property for sewage disposal. If you buy the property without approval you might not be able to obtain a permit later, and you will not be able to build on the land, making it worthless. I have seen this occur dozens of times over the last fifteen years in my law practice. See chapter 5, ''The Earth—Soil, Vegetation, Topography,'' for information on percolation tests.

Health codes also regulate the construction of water facilities, particularly wells. Sanitary seals of concrete are required around the tops of wells to prevent seepage, and a coliform potability test is taken of all running water before it receives health department approval.

ROAD ENCROACHMENT PERMITS

Some counties are touchy about how private roads encroach, or lead onto, a county road since these adjoining roads, if not constructed and maintained properly, could cause damage to public roads. Problems include automobiles tracking mud from a dirt road onto a paved county road, washouts of dirt roads, and dirt washing down onto paved roads.

Some counties regulate the construction of private roads and require permits and fees before construction of a dirt road that will encroach onto a public road can be commenced. The private owner is required to bring his road up to the standards of the public road at the point where the two roads meet. To do this the costs vary but often run up to $300 or $500, which includes grading materials, culvert pipe, paving, and labor. If you are required to construct a road to get onto your land, you should figure this cost into the purchase price and adjust the figures accordingly. If there is a good road into the property you will pay for this ''extra.''

Check on all road and encroachment requirements by talking to the local department of public works. Often they will have a special office for roads called the road division. Find out if the seller has obtained the proper permits for his road and if it meets current county standards.

Many counties also have minimum requirements for unimproved roads that must be met before a building permit will be issued. For instance, there must be minimum road widths of 20 feet so emergency vehicles can pass each other on the road, a certain number of turnouts must be available, and a minimum layer of gravel and rock must be in place.

WARRANTY THAT NO CODE VIOLATIONS EXIST

Clause 16(f) of the Model Contract of Sale (see chapter 28) is a warranty by the seller that no codes are being violated by his use of the property or by the construction of any improvement on it. This warranty means that no building, health, road encroachment, zoning, or other codes are being violated and that all permits have been issued and fully paid for. The fact that the seller signs this warranty as part of the contract should not relieve you of going to the local departments to determine if the seller has met the required statutes and codes.

CONDITION THE PURCHASE ON YOUR ABILITY TO OBTAIN NECESSARY PERMITS

If you intend to build a house on the land you are buying, you should speak to all the various inspectors about the local codes and have them look at the land to determine if there will be any problems with the building site that could prevent the issuance of the necessary permits. You should know before you buy that you can put a road in, build a house, and have adequate site conditions for sewage disposal. If there is any doubt about your ability to obtain a permit, you should insert the type of permit being sought in Clause 17(c) of the Model Contract of Sale. If you cannot get approval by the close of escrow, you can terminate the purchase and have your money returned or postpone the close of escrow. You must make a reasonable attempt to obtain the permit by submitting appropriate forms.

HOW ONE HOMEOWNER GOT RID OF THE BUILDING INSPECTOR

Many people in the country deal with the myriad bureaucratic hassles, permits, and fees by ignoring them and hoping they don't get caught. A good friend of mine named Paul chose the exact opposite tactic in dealing with his local building inspector, who was one of the toughest I have met. When Paul bought his place, the largest structure on the land was a big beautiful red barn which he wanted to convert into his family dwelling. Because a barn in the eyes of the law is not meant to be a house, many problems were involved in meeting the requirements of the building codes.

Knowing in advance that he would meet the building inspector sooner or later, Paul went to his office and told him what he was going to do. He drew up some fairly sketchy but basic plans, submitted them for approval, and paid the first part of his fees. Then he began to modify the barn and make it his home. The inspector came to make an inspection and then began appearing on a regular basis. Each time, he hassled Paul about some aspect of his remodeling job until he really got on Paul's nerves. So Paul decided to give him some of his own medicine.

Any time he began a new part of his remodeling, like a new wall, floor, beam, ceiling, or fireplace, he called up the building inspector and asked him what kind of materials he should use, how much

he should buy, what kind of nails or cement he should get, and how he should do the job. After several weeks of constant phone calls, the inspector had had enough. In complete exasperation he told Paul, "Dammit, I'm not your architect or contractor. Stop calling and bothering me." Paul then sent in the rest of his fees and never saw the building inspector again.

As long as you know that your house is going to have to be built to code and be inspected by someone who's being paid with your fees, you might as well get your money's worth. Bug the inspector. Maybe he'll leave you alone. If you're way off in the hills, all he probably cares about is getting those fees. As long as nobody is going to see your house and complain about it and his job will not be jeopardized, he will probably leave you alone. On the other hand, the building inspector can be very helpful to you in answering questions you might have regarding the home you are building. Inspectors have different philosophies and outlooks on their job, and many of them can be useful advisors. I hope you find an enlightened building official in your area.

USEFUL RESOURCES

All local codes and sample plans can be obtained at your local inspector's office. Check with the building inspector, department of roads, and health inspector.

The three national organizations that make up the various codes will send you any information you want on any aspect of the requirements for house construction. Write to the following:

(Uniform Building Code)
International Conference of Building
  Officials
5360 S. Workman Mill Rd.
Whittier, CA 90601

(Uniform Plumbing Code)
International Association of Plumbing and
  Mechanical Officials
5032 Alhambra Ave.
Los Angeles, CA 90032-3490

(The Electric Code)
The National Fire Protection Association
Batterymarch Park
Quincy, MA 02269

Although local building inspectors usually distribute the required building regulations and sample construction plans, you can obtain a copy of the latest edition of *Dwelling Construction under the Uniform Building Code* by sending $10.75 to the ICBO. The complete set of the Uniform Building Code costs $50.75.

To receive a copy of the latest National Electric Code, updated every three years, write to the National Fire Protection Association, attention: Publications, at the above address. The code was revised in 1987 and costs $18.50.

For the complete Uniform Plumbing Code, also updated every three years, write to the International Association of Plumbing and Mechanical Officials at the above address. The code was revised in 1985 and costs $35.70 for the soft cover, $39.90 for the loose leaf.

The following agencies establish and enforce standards of construction, materials, and occupancy for all buildings in their respective states. Not all states have a central agency devoted to this.

Alabama
Building Commission
800 S. McDonough St.
Montgomery, AL 36104

California
Division of Codes and Standards
Housing and Community Development
Department
6007 Folson Blvd., Ste. A
Sacramento, CA 95819

Colorado
Division of Housing
Department of Local Affairs
1313 Sherman St.
Denver, CO 80203

Connecticut
Office of State Building Inspector
Department of Public Safety
294 Colony St., Bldg. 3
Meriden, CT 06450

District of Columbia
Building and Land Regulation
Administration
Consumer and Regulatory Affairs
Department
614 H St., N.W.
Washington, DC 20001

Florida
Building Codes and Standards Section
Department of Community Affairs
Howard Bldg.
Tallahassee, FL 32301

Georgia
Technical Assistance Division
Department of Community Affairs
40 Marietta St., 8th Fl.
Atlanta, GA 30303

Idaho
Building Division
Labor and Industrial Services Department
317 Main St.
Boise, ID 83720

Illinois
Housing Development Authority
130 E. Randolph, Ste. 510
Chicago, IL 60601

Indiana
State Building Commission
1099 N. Meridian St.
Indianapolis, IN 46204

Iowa
Building Code Division
Department of Public Safety
Wallace State Office Bldg.
Des Moines, IA 50319

Kentucky
Housing, Buildings and Construction
The 127 Bldg.
U.S. 127, S.
Frankfort, KY 40601

Maryland
Building Codes Administration
Economic and Community Development
Department
45 Calvert St.
Annapolis, MD 21401

Massachusetts
Building Inspections
1 Ashburton Pl., Rm. 1301
Boston, MA 02108

Michigan
Shelter Environment Section
Department of Public Health
P.O. Box 30035
Lansing, MI 48909

Minnesota
Building Code Division
Department of Administration
408 Metro Square Bldg.
St. Paul, MN 55101

Montana
Building Codes Division
Department of Administration
1218 E. Sixth Ave.
Helena, MT 59620

New Jersey
Division of Housing and Development
Department of Community Affairs,
CN-804
Trenton, NJ 08625

New Mexico
Construction Industries Division
Regulation and Licensing Department
Bataan Memorial Bldg.
Santa Fe, NM 87503

New York
Division of Housing and Community
Renewal
2 World Trade Center
New York, NY 10047

North Carolina
Building Inspection Services Division
Department of Insurance
P.O. Box 26387
Raleigh, NC 27602

North Dakota
Office of Intergovernmental Assistance
Office of Management and Budget
State Capitol, 14th Fl.
Bismarck, ND 58505

Ohio
Board of Building Standards
Department of Industrial Relations
2323 W. Fifth Ave.
Columbus, OH 43204

Oregon
Division of Building Codes
Department of Commerce
401 Labor and Industries Bldg.
Salem, OR 97310

Rhode Island
State Building Code Commission
Department of Community Affairs
1270 Mineral Spring Ave.
North Providence, RI 02904

South Carolina
State Housing Authority
2221 Devine St., #540
Columbia, SC 29205

Tennessee
Department of Finance and Administration
James K. Polk Bldg., 17th Fl.
Nashville, TN 37219

Utah
Division of Contractors
Department of Business Regulation
160 E. 300, S.
Salt Lake City, UT 84145-0801

Vermont
Department of Labor and Industry
7 Court St.
Montpelier, VT 05602

Virginia
Housing and Community Development
205 N. Fourth St.
Richmond, VA 23219

Washington
Building Construction
Safety Inspection Services
Department of Labor and Industries
520 Water St., Mail Stop AX-31-BC
Olympia, WA 98504

West Virginia
  Office of State Fire Marshal
  2000 Quarrier St.
  Charleston, WV 25305

Wisconsin
  Bureau of Code Development
  Industry, Labor and Human Relations
  P.O. Box 7969
  Madison, WI 53707

CHAPTER 14

Subdivisions and Condominiums

Friends, you are now in Coconut Manor, one of the finest cities in Florida. Of course, we still need a few finishing touches. But who doesn't? This is the heart of the residential district. Every lot is a stone's throw away from the station. As soon as they throw enough stones, we're going to build a station. Eight hundred beautiful residences will be built right here. . . . You can have any kind of home you want to. You can even get stucco—oh how you can get stucco. . . . And don't forget the guarantee—my personal guarantee. If these lots don't double in value in a year, I don't know what you can do about it.

—Groucho Marx portraying a land hustler in the movie *The Coconuts*

BEWARE OF VACATION AND RECREATIONAL LAND DEVELOPMENTS

You have seen ads in periodicals and heard commercials on the radio and television about "planned recreational subdivisions." You are enticed with talk and photos of golf courses, swimming pools, other recreational activities of various types, and "modern" homes in a country setting. Finally you are told that if you buy early, you will make a small fortune when you sell in a few years. Do not fall for the Madison Avenue come-ons that offer you free vacations, traveling expenses, drinks, and assorted sucker bait. Let them keep their presents, for they are borne by Trojan horses.

Here's how the developers make a fortune off of you. A group of wealthy businessmen combine finances and organize themselves into a partnership or syndicate for the purpose of buying and subdividing land for a profit. They scout the country to locate a rural area they think is ''ripe for development.'' When they find a large piece of undeveloped land, their eyes begin to see houses, streets, Sold signs, and dollar signs. They purchase the land for a mere pittance compared to what they will sell it for.

For example, in New Mexico a land corporation bought 86,200 acres for $3 million and subdivided it into 86,176 lots. Without building any homes, they began reselling the land for ten times what they had paid for it. Profits from land sales and interest, by the time the last lot is sold, will be $112 million. Their expenses for advertising and meeting federal requirements are relatively minimal.

COMMON LAND FRAUDS

I have nothing against somebody making a profit, but not when it's done through fraudulent means, and particularly when the people who are defauded are those who can least afford it. Buyers in sub-

Reprinted with permission of *The San Francisco Examiner* copyright © 1975 *The San Francisco Examiner.*

divisions rely largely on what they are told through the media and by the real estate salesmen, and exercise little caution because they are not required to part with a large sum of money at once, but rather pay in low monthly installments. In most cases, the information is misleading because of what is left unsaid or because what is stated is a half-truth. Since this type of misrepresentation does not meet the legal requirements for fraud, it is often difficult to bring a developer to court.

The most common fraud is the failure of developers to construct promised amenities, such as lakes, recreation centers, swimming pools, golf courses, stables, and the like. In small print, the contract they use states that the developers do not have to construct these things until 90 percent of the lots have been sold. After they sell 80 percent of the lots, more than enough to give them a healty profit, they simply stop advertising and move their operation to a new development. Thus, they have not violated the terms of the contract, and you are stuck with a lot in the middle of a thousand other lots with nothing to show for your "investment" of thousands of dollars.

Another scheme is the promise, which is never made in writing, that streets and other facilities will be installed by the county or municipality once the development gets built up. Most of these developments, however, are built in unincorporated areas outside of town boundaries. The lots are sold, and the streets, sidewalks, utility lines, and other expected facilities are never constructed. The average rural county cannot afford to build facilities for three thousand new homeowners, even with the initial tax gain from property taxes, and many rural areas do not welcome large subdivisions intruding into their quiet communities, destroying the ecology and small-town mood of the area. In an example of a variation on this scheme, developers truthfully told buyers that the water table under the development was enough to supply one million people for five hundred years. They forgot to mention that the utility company that was the only water supplier in the area had facilities for only eight thousand homes, whereas there were over sixty thousand lots for sale in the development.

Often subdivision lots are put up for sale before they have actually been surveyed into parcels and staked out on the ground, or if they have been surveyed, no roads have been put in. Salesmen will take prospective buyers to a hill overlooking the development and point out in the distance the lots that are for sale. The buyer never sets foot on the parcel he buys. When the time comes to put in a driveway and a house, the buyer discovers that his lot is steep, inaccessible, and without a decent building site. Never forget that the developers' idea of a "building site" might be a mountain goat's idea of heaven. A lot advertised as "readily accessible" might be reached only by foot or four-wheel drive.

Often salesmen will fail to mention that maps of a development are available. They will try to get people to buy lots already earmarked for a future public road. Since this information is part of the public records, the buyer's ignorance is no defense. Anything that can be discovered from the records is held to be "constructive notice" to a land buyer.

Sometimes developers will try to create a sense of urgency in prospective buyers by using two-way radio systems to give the impression that huge volumes of property are being sold, when actually this is not the case. Although these radios are also used for legitimate purposes of communication, be wary if you feel pressured.

Misleading advertising is rampant. A development might be advertised as "10 miles from town," which is true if you are a crow. For people, it's 40 miles by car. Phony photographs and artist's "conceptions" of what a development will eventually look like are frequently used in ads. Small-print advertising is another common technique that, though legal, should be carefully scrutinized. One of my favorite examples of this technique is a brochure distributed by the Lakeworld Corporation for its "environmental project" called "Tahoe Donner" at Lake Tahoe, California. In large print, the colorful pamphlet states that "when the first snowfall comes, you'll head for Tahoe Donner's own private* ski resort, planned for family skiing. . . . Because Tahoe Donner is a private* ski resort, it's one of the few uncrowded places in the area." If you look for the asterisk, you will find it at the end of the brochure, where the following statement is printed in the smallest type used in the advertisement: "Lakeworld reserves the right to open the Tahoe Donner Ski Bowl to the public at any time."

Several years ago the California attorney general brought suits against eighty individuals and firms for a scheme involving "vacation certificates" given by companies in league with land promoters. California firms sell inexpensive tickets to Las Vegas, and while the "vacationers" are in Nevada, they are confronted by hard-sell land salesmen peddling desert and swampland worth a dollar or less an acre for $1,000 or more an acre. Over 2 million vacation certificates were sold for the undisclosed purpose of selling subdivisions in Nevada that would be illegal under California law.

The Federal Trade Commission clamped down on seven land sales companies because they were telling customers that their company's main interest was to provide real estate training when they were actually trying to sell land. These companies were also saying that adverse economic conditions don't affect land values.

Many subdivisions are sold that include a "Lot Owners Association," which is supposed to maintain roads and other facilities in the development. These associations often sound better on paper than they work in actual practice. The administrator for HUD's Interstate Land Sales Full Disclosure Act (discussed later in this chapter) has stated: "Too often, the Lot Owners Association is a smoke-screen established and controlled by the developer." You must read the conditions and agreements of any association before buying in a subdivision.

Many land promoters make a huge amount of money by selling land they don't have clear title to themselves. The promoter gets together enough cash to make a down payment on a large piece of land, and he gives the seller a mortgage for the rest. Then he subdivides the land and sells the parcels under *land contracts* whereby he doesn't have to deliver title for many years. He uses the payments from his buyers to make his own mortgage payments. This is a dangerous situation for the buyers because if for any reason the promoter's loan gets foreclosed on, they will never get title to the land. Other reasons why you should never buy land under a land contract are discussed in chapter 21, "Types of Financing: Land Contract, Mortgage, Deed of Trust."

A point continually stressed by subdivision salesmen is the profit the buyer can anticipate when he resells the parcel. The buyer will be told that the developer will buy back the lot if it doesn't make a profit as an investment. Of course, this promise is never put in writing. It doesn't occur to the buyer that he can't resell at a profit until the developer has sold every single lot; otherwise he will be competing with the developer's own salesmen and prices. Even when the developer is out of the picture, the buyer is in competition with thousands of other lot owners, all selling basically the same product. Look in the want ads of your local paper if you want an idea of how many people are trying to sell their lots. It's ridiculous. It has been estimated that the average minimum amount of time a lot owner must wait before he can make any profit on a resale is ten years.

Every lot buyer figures that all the other buyers will build houses on their lots and that this will increase the value of his lot, which he can leave undeveloped and sell at a profit when the surrounding land is built up. The trouble is, every other buyer is thinking the same way. For example, in California the *build-out rate,* the percentage of lots on which homes are actually erected, is only 1 percent in recreation land developments. For these reasons and because land in a development is often so overpriced, you may find out too late that your "investment" has turned into a financial liability.

If you are interested in making a good land investment, you would be much better off buying a nice-sized piece of undeveloped land for the same price you would have paid for that tiny lot in a development. You can hold on to it for a few years and then sell it as a whole piece or subdivide it yourself to make a larger profit.

To buy land strictly as an investment and actually make any money you will have to spend a little more time planning your purchase than you would by simply sending a check to a large developer for one of his lots. It's not that easy to make money. You will have to research the local subdivision laws in your area to see if your scheme is possible and profitable. But if you are interested in making an investment, you should be willing to spend some time and energy to make it a good one. You will always be better off buying a parcel of land in an area near the recreational facilities you want rather than in a planned "recreational community." Most areas in the country now have golf courses, swimming facilities, riding stables, bowling alleys, ski slopes, and the other amenities most people desire. In the country, 10 acres for $20,000 is almost always going to be a better investment than a 1-acre lot for $20,000 in a "recreational subdivision."

TYPES OF FRAUDS PROSECUTED BY THE FEDERAL GOVERNMENT

The federal government's Office of Interstate Land Sale Registration in the last ten years has taken action against land developers in hundreds of cases. The following areas are some of the more interesting and flagrant examples of land frauds the government has pursued. Various developers have been caught:

Painting grass to look green and tying pinecones on trees to make the land more desirable for promotional movies.

Not revealing that raw sewage had been dumped into a pit in the development, and that a building advertised as the golf and pro shop contained no golf equipment and had no golf pro.

Failing to disclose that it could cost owners up to $12,000 to have electricity extended to their lots.

Giving a figure for installing wells and septic tanks that was one-third of actual cost.

Misrepresenting to buyers that the Army Corps of Engineers was building a canal connecting the subdivision property in Florida with the Gulf of Mexico.

Harassing property owners who complained to the federal agency about land frauds.

Handing out brochures stating that two Florida subdivisions were conveniently located near shopping centers, hospitals, and beaches, when in fact the facilities were 40 miles away.

Failing to state that lots were not accessible by ordinary automobile.

Showing roads on maps that were in fact unmarked open fields.

Failing to disclose that the developer was in foreclosure at the time parcels were being sold.

Failing to reveal that lots would need fill before structures could be built on them.

Failing to reveal that the state department of health had closed the subdivision swimming pool.

Failing to reveal that many of the lots in a Florida subdivision are covered with tidal waters.

Failing to reveal that the water in the subdivision was not potable.

Falsely representing that purchase of a lot was a way to achieve financial security and representing that prices were increasing without disclosing that the increase may be the result of the developers' pricing, not related to actual changes in the value of the land.

Promising buyers that a swimming pool was built for use by all property owners without revealing that the pool was a small backyard type that soon closed.

Failing to reveal that the lake for boating and swimming was too shallow for either activity.

Presenting maps to customers showing many recreational amenities that did not exist.

Failure to reveal that lots in a Nevada subdivision were not accessible by any vehicle because of deep arroyos and fences, and that some lots were located in a floodplain.

Failing to inform purchasers of homesites that local laws prohibited the construction of homes on individual lots of the size they bought.

Telling purchasers that the property in the subdivision would remain in a natural wooded state for use as a recreation and retirement community, when in fact they had leased coal rights to an oil company that would permit the company to surface-mine coal in the subdivision.

Routinely giving buyers a "fast shuffle" closing, after which they left the sales office without copies of contracts, notes, property reports, or any other important documents.

Falsely promising purchasers a twenty-acre lake would be built when, in fact, the developer had no plans for a lake and had never applied for a state permit to build one.

The above examples of fraudulent land sales techniques are only a few of the many that have been used by land promoters. You might think that a defrauded buyer always has the remedy available of suing the developer or salesman, but this is often impossible because the corporation or syndicate that sold the land has since disbanded or has gone bankrupt by means of slick legal maneuvering. Even if the developer is available to be sued, a lot of money is needed to hire a lawyer and proceed with a civil suit in court. Most lawyers require fairly large retainers, which the average land buyer can't afford since he has already spent much of his money on the land. Of course, developers usually have several experienced and slick lawyers ready at their defense. Since recourse in the courts is expensive and there is certainly no guarantee of success, your best insurance, if you insist on buying land in a promotional subdivision, is to use every resource and method of investigating subdivisions—which I will now discuss.

LAWS REGULATING SUBDIVISIONS

The first law regulating land subdivisions was passed in the late 1800s and required uniform land surveys. Then, in the 1920s, tremendous land swindles swept the country and more control was assumed by local governments. Many of the laws passed since then are full of loopholes, but the federal, state, and local governments are closing the loopholes and getting tougher as time goes on.

Generally the purpose of subdivision laws is to prevent the creation of lots of inadequate size and poor design; to prevent the creation of building sites in areas where the topography, floods, or other factors make safe and beneficial land use impossible; to prevent the creation of badly built roads; to prevent hazards from sewage effluent and inadequate drainage; to prevent the lowering of property values and loss of opportunity for a good overall development of neighborhoods caused by successive, uncontrolled, and haphazard land divisions; to prevent excessive cost to taxpayers of the county for providing services within the subdivision; and to prevent fraudulent land sales practices.

Not all subdivisions are large planned developments. Any land that is broken up into two or more parcels of any size is "subdivided." Many state and local laws apply to all types of subdivision— a two-hundred-acre parcel being split into four pieces as well as a two-thousand-acre parcel being split into four hundred lots. If you are planning to buy any land that has been subdivided for the purpose of reselling it, read this chapter carefully and check into all the laws that apply in your state and county.

THE FEDERAL INTERSTATE LAND SALES FULL DISCLOSURE ACT

This act, passed by Congress in 1968, now regulates all land promoters who offer twenty-five or more undeveloped lots for sale through the mail or by advertising from one state to another in any kind of interstate commerce. The seller must first submit a statement of record with the Office of Interstate Land Sales Registration, an agency within the United States Department of Housing and Urban Development (HUD). The statement must include required information about the ownership of the land, the state of its title, its physical nature, the availability of roads and utilities, and other matters. All prospective buyers must receive a printed property report containing extracts from the statement of record at least forty-eight hours before signing a contract of sale. The sample Final Subdivision Public Report later in this chapter is an example of the information that must be included in the property report.

Every buyer shown a property report has a "cooling off" period of seven days after signing in which to cancel the agreement, get out of the deal, and get a full refund. If the property report has not been given to the buyer before the time of signing the contract, the buyer may revoke the agreement within two years of the date of signing.

If you want to receive a public report or any information on an interstate land promotion, write to the address given in Useful Resources at the end of this chapter.

THE BIG BUST OF 1972

In 1972, HUD came down on 450 land developers nationwide for alleged violations of the Interstate Land Sales and Full Disclosure Act. One of the biggest subdivison frauds attacked involved Lake Havasu Estates in Arizona. It all began in 1964, when the McCulloch Corporation developed Lake Havasu City in the Arizona desert on the edge of Lake Havasu, one of the rare lakes in the arid Southwest. Since that time, the subdivision has become a self-contained city of over ten thousand, famed for its purchase and reconstruction of the London Bridge.

This boom of Lake Havasu City prompted a group of unscrupulous investors to purchase 10,000 acres of desert 40 miles to the north, subdivide it, name it Lake Havasu Estates, and promote it in a national sales campaign. The sales brochures contained pictures of lake recreation and implied the land was near water and would soon have all types of facilities just like Lake Havasu City. Potential buyers were shown a copy of the magazine *Arizona Highways,* which contained an article about the fine accomplishments at Lake Havasu City. Salesmen described Lake Havasu Estates as a great city of the future, although it has no known water supply, no electricity, telephone lines, or paved streets, no sewage disposal system, no garbage collection, no hospital, shopping areas, or schools. The only buildings it has are a large geodesic "dinesphere" that has never opened for dining and a portable sales office.

The developers of Lake Havasu Estates easily sold the plots sight unseen to buyers in other states by setting the price of each lot at $3,000 to $5,000 with a down payment of $165 and monthly payments of $57.29. Buyers were given a year to get a refund if desired. Although many buyers did request refunds, none were given.

In response to complaints by the victims of this white collar crime, a federal grand jury indicted nine of Lake Havasu Estate's officers and salesmen on charges of mail fraud, misrepresentation in selling and advertising, and failure to register lots and provide property records to purchasers as required by the Interstate Land Sales and Full Disclosure Act.

THE FEDS CATCH A FORMER U.S. ATTORNEY

One of the major convictions by the federal prosecutors was of one of their own people. A former Pennsylvania assistant U.S. attorney was convicted of 33 counts of violating federal law in connection with a land development in the Pocono Mountains in Pennsylvania. A federal jury found the defendant guilty of 21 counts of violating the Interstate Land Sales Full Disclosure Act and 12 counts of mail fraud.

Among many false representations made by the defendant, the following were the most flagrant:

—He gave completion dates for installing sewage disposal systems and paving roads, knowing the facilities could not be finished on schedule.

—He promised to put funds from the sale of each lot into an escrow account to cover the installation costs of roads and water and sewer lines with full knowledge the funds were insufficient.

—He asserted the subdivision had been surveyed and the lots were staked so they could easily be identified. Actually, most of the lots were unmarked.

—He promised to build a heated swimming pool and tennis courts. The promises were not kept, despite the developers' claims in his reports.

—He said it was unnecessary to drain surface water or use fill to build on the lots. In fact, some of the lots are subject to flooding and need drainage or fill to make them fit for construction.

—He withdrew more than $15,000 from an escrow account set up to build a bathhouse. The facility was not built. Similarly, money was taken from an escrow account for swimming pool work not performed.

After conviction, the former U.S. attorney was sentenced to four years in prison and fined $11,550. The following statement was issued by the prosecutor's office after the conviction: "The conviction is part of the federal government's program to protect consumers from dishonest land developers. In far too many instances, people invest their life savings in land for retirement or other purposes, only to see their dreams go down the drain. We urge the public to look at the land firsthand before buying it. Buyers should ignore gaudy pamphlets describing fancy facilities that may never be built. Would-be purchasers of unimproved land cannot be too careful in checking the credibility and business methods of some developers who offer land for sale. Although it is the duty of the developer to provide the buyer with a copy of the required report, this action is meaningless unless the consumer reads the report and fully understands its contents before signing the contract."

STATE AND LOCAL SUBDIVISION LAWS

State and local governments have authority founded in the Constitution to regulate and direct the future growth patterns of their communities. Therefore, they should shoulder their share of the responsibility to protect their land resources from profit-minded developers who not only bilk the buying public, but devastate the land in the process.

—George K. Bernstein, former head of the Office of Interstate Land Sales Registration

Most state and local governments are also concerned with the regulation of land splits or subdivisions and have enacted their own laws, usually referred to as subdivision laws. Different laws are required for various types of subdivisions, which are distinguished on the basis of the size of the parcels and the number of parcels created. The legal requirements for land divisions vary among the states and areas within the states. However, these laws are becoming standardized, based on the federal laws. You will have to check with your local planning commission, board of supervisors, and building inspector to find out the laws that control your area. (See Useful Resources at the end of this chapter.)

Local governments usually control subdivisions in all stages of their development. Before a development can begin, the promoters must file a preliminary map or *plat* for approval by the public authorities. After the land is subdivided, they must get approval from the building inspector, health department, department of public works, and other agencies before construction can begin on dwellings, if any are to be built, or land improvements. Before the selling of the land and homes can begin, a sales permit must be issued. Finally, before anyone can live in any houses on the land, a certificate of occupancy must be issued for each dwelling by the local authorities. (See chapter 13, "Building and Health Codes.") Some states also require that a bond be furnished as a guarantee that the developers will complete all the improvements promised to the buyers. The problem is that only the county can sue on the bond if the developers don't follow through on their promises. In general, the more parcels there are, the more regulations apply to the development.

THE LOCAL PLANNING COMMISSION

The city and county planning (or zoning) commissions throughout the country play a major role in what happens to real estate in their areas. The planning commission prepares a comprehensive long-term general plan for the development of land in the area of its jurisdiction. Once its conception of the area has been composed on paper, the group must approve all proposed land developments, using the plan as its guide.

The planning commission controls such matters as the location and extent of land use; the placement of roads, streets, and utilities; the density of the population and intensity of building construction; and zoning variances and use permits. When a plan for a subdivision is submitted to the planning commission for approval, in order to be approved it is supposed to conform to the master plan. Since projected plans are never permanent, rezoning, waivers, or variances are often permitted for the purpose of allowing the proposed subdivision to go ahead with its plan.

You may become involved with the planning commission if you seek a variance of the zoning or a use permit to conduct certain activities on your land. If their meetings are open in your area, you will learn much about the future plans and present attitudes of the local government by attending a commission hearing. More information on the planning commission is contained in chapter 12, "Zoning Laws."

PLATTING THE SUBDIVISION

Platting is the term used for the process of mapping out the planned development and plotting on paper the manner in which the land is to be divided. The plat must show the surveyor's layout of the parcels in relation to survey marks actually in the ground. Each lot must be numbered, its size indicated, and the length of all boundary lines and the location of all streets, easements, open areas, and facilities designated. Any aspect of the surrounding area affecting the subdivision must be shown.

Many states now require that a preliminary plat

"... Scientists in Pasadena were stunned by the latest Viking photographs of Mars, where previously it had been believed there were no signs of life as we know it ..."

of a proposed subdivision be submitted and tentatively approved by the planning commission. Illustration 75 is an example of a preliminary, or tentative, plat submitted for approval of a four-parcel land split, called a *minor division*. Once the plat is approved, the subdivision will almost certainly progress to completion. The plat will include a separate document containing any protective restrictions and covenants that are part of the development, including the types of dwellings permitted in terms of style and quality and restrictions, if any, on businesses, fences, and maintenance of open space. The plat and any accompanying reports must indicate the extent of utilities, streets, curbs, gutters, sidewalks, storm and sanitary sewers, fire hydrants, street lighting, and other facilities to be provided.

Often if the parcels are several acres or more in size, the developer is required to indicate only a few things on his plat. It must show that each parcel has been surveyed and laid out on the ground. Easements from each parcel to the public road must be shown; a soil report indicating the adaptability

of the area to proper installation of sewage facilities, usually septic tanks, must be included; and the available water supply must be located on the plat.

Plats may not be required for all land splits. For example, in California, only land splits in which any resulting parcel is less than 60 acres may require complete surveying and the submission of a subdivision plat for approval by the planning commission and board of supervisors. Therefore, if a seller splits up a 130-acre piece of land into two parcels of 65 acres each, he will not have to file a plat for approval.

Those states that require the filing of a preliminary plat also require a final plat to be submitted after approval of the former. This second filing is really just a formality. After it is approved and recorded, the building inspector must give his approval of any proposed buildings. He investigates whether the proposed plans meet the present zoning regulations with regard to the size of the parcels and houses. If the plans do not meet these requirements, the planning commission will consider a

227

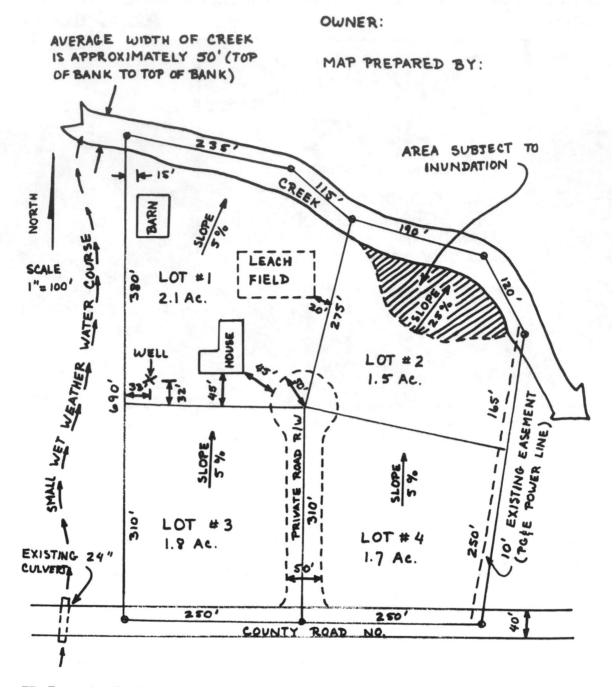

OWNER:

MAP PREPARED BY:

AVERAGE WIDTH OF CREEK IS APPROXIMATELY 50' (TOP OF BANK TO TOP OF BANK)

AREA SUBJECT TO INUNDATION

NORTH

SCALE 1" = 100'

CREEK

235'

115'

190'

120'

15'

BARN

SLOPE 5%

LEACH FIELD

LOT #1 2.1 Ac.

380'

SLOPE 25%

26'

275'

LOT #2 1.5 Ac.

WELL

HOUSE

45'

690'

33'

32'

45'

SMALL WET WEATHER WATER COURSE

165'

10' EXISTING EASEMENT (PG&E POWER LINE)

SLOPE 5%

SLOPE 5%

310'

PRIVATE ROAD R/W

310'

LOT #3 1.8 Ac.

LOT #4 1.7 Ac.

250'

EXISTING 24" CULVERT

50'

250'

250'

40'

250'

COUNTY ROAD NO.

75. Example of a Minor Division Tentative Map

request for rezoning or a variance for the development. Assuming the okay is given, the building inspector must then approve the buildings.

All required plats must be placed on file with the local planning commission and recorded with the local government's recorder. There you can examine the submitted plats, if there are any, for the land you are interested in. You should be absolutely certain they have been approved and recorded since you can be refused building and health permits if your land is part of an unapproved subdivision. Always examine where your parcel will be in relation to the rest of the subdivision as indicated on the plat.

228

PARCEL MAPS

In some states, land splits containing fairly large parcels, usually 40 acres or more, require only parcel maps, which are much less detailed than full-scale plats or subdivision maps.

The parcel map must be drawn up by a licensed surveyor or registered civil engineer and submitted to the county surveyor or engineer for approval before filing. Usually the map need indicate only the location of boundary lines for each parcel and easements from each parcel to the public road. Illustration 76 is an example of a parcel map submitted for a subdivision of ten parcels approximately 44 acres each.

THE FINAL SUBDIVISION PUBLIC REPORT

Due to increasing fraudulent activities of large-scale land developers, several states now require promoters to submit a public report covering all aspects of the planned subdivision. This is similar to the Federal Property Report required under the Federal Interstate Land Sales Full Disclosure Act.

I have included the entire contents of a final subdivision public report here (see illustration 77). It indicates what a public report of this type must cover in order to meet the legal requirements of providing the buyer with essential information concerning his proposed purchase although the specific information in this report may not apply to yours. For instance, in this report the mineral rights have been reserved whereas in yours they may not be. If you are buying in a state that does not require such a report, it will be up to you to make your own report to satisfy yourself that your purchase is a wise one. You will see after examining this final subdivision public report that it covers exactly those questions about land that I am detailing throughout this book. Of course, you should double-check the contents of any report, but if you can get a public report, much of your work will already be done for you. All you will have to do is read and analyze the report to understand what is involved in your purchase.

Unfortunately, many land developers don't file these reports even when they are required. The state

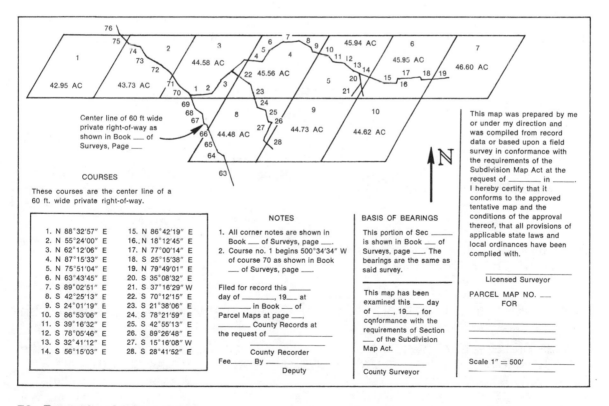

76. Example of a Parcel Map

real-estate enforcement agencies are usually understaffed and underfinanced and are unable to force the submission of such reports for many years until after much damage has already been done.

You must always demand a public report from the seller or real estate agent handling the sale of subdivided land. If he says there is none, then go to the county planning commission and find out if one is required. You might uncover an illegal subdivision in the process.

Any legitimate land development's advertising brochure will contain the following language: "Obtain the property report required by federal law and read it before signing anything. No federal or state agency has judged the merits or value, if any, of this property." The ad should also direct you as to how to obtain a public offering statement in those states where one is required. I cannot overemphasize the need to read these public reports and offering statements. They have been required by the federal and state governments for your protection.

that his market will be increased by prospective buyers who need FHA-insured and VA-guaranteed home loans, the subdivision must meet certain government standards. There are requirements on such things as housing design, taxes and assessments, restrictive covenants, physical plans for the area, housing needs, accessibility to public facilities, and other essentials of a good loan risk. For more information on this, see Useful Resources at the end of this chapter.

PROPERTY OWNERS' ASSOCIATIONS AND COVENANTS, CONDITIONS, AND RESTRICTIONS

One of the major problems in subdivision and condominium development is the fact that these operations are supposed to be run by all the property owners banded together in an owners' association. This association is initially formed by the developer, who usually drafts articles of incorporation, the bylaws, and the general rules.

Each property owner automatically becomes a member of the association, and the owner or owners of each parcel are entitled to one vote per parcel in the decision-making. The association normally

FHA AND VA APPROVAL

If a subdivider wants FHA and VA approval so

DEPARTMENT OF REAL ESTATE

OF THE

STATE OF _____

_____, Real Estate Commissioner

In the matter of the application

(SELLER'S NAME)

for a final subdivision public report on
(NAME OF THE SUBDIVISION)
COUNTY,

FINAL SUBDIVISION
PUBLIC REPORT

FILE NO. _____

ISSUED: ____(DATE)____
EXPIRES: ____(DATE)____

THIS REPORT IS NOT A RECOMMENDATION OR ENDORSEMENT OF THE SUBDIVISION BUT IS INFORMATIVE ONLY.

BUYER OR LESSEE MUST SIGN THAT HE HAS RECEIVED AND READ THIS REPORT. THIS REPORT EXPIRES ON DATE SHOWN ABOVE OR UPON A MATERIAL CHANGE.

77. Example of a Final Subdivision Public Report

SPECIAL NOTES

PROSPECTIVE PURCHASERS ARE URGED TO VISIT AND INSPECT THIS PROPERTY BE-FORE ENTERING INTO AN AGREEMENT TO PURCHASE.

THIS TRACT IS BEING OFFERED FOR SPECULATION ONLY.

THIS MEANS THE SUBDIVIDER HAS NOT BEEN REQUIRED TO MAKE ANY SHOWING THAT THE LOTS MAY BE USED FOR ANY OTHER USE, SUCH AS RESIDENTIAL.

SINCE NO PROVISIONS HAVE BEEN MADE FOR ANY OTHER USE THAN SPECULATION OF RAW LAND, THE SUBDIVIDER HAS NOT MET REQUIREMENTS FOR WATER, ROADS, UTILITIES, SEWAGE DISPOSAL, OR OTHER USUAL REQUIREMENTS FOR A RESIDENTIAL SUBDIVISION.

PURCHASERS WHO MIGHT CONTEMPLATE THE EVENTUAL DEVELOPMENT OF THEIR LOTS SHOULD CONSIDER THAT SUBSTANTIAL COSTS COULD BE INCURRED TO MAKE THE PROPERTY SUITABLE FOR ANY PROPOSED USE.

PURCHASERS SHOULD ALSO UNDERSTAND THAT WITHOUT THE COOPERATION OF OTHER PROPERTY OWNERS, INDIVIDUAL LOT OWNERS MIGHT FIND IT DIFFICULT AND EXPEN-SIVE TO DEVELOP THE PROPERTY.

ANY PERSON WHO PURCHASES FIVE OR MORE LOTS IN A SUBDIVISION WITH THE IN-TENT OF OFFERING THE LOTS FOR RE-SALE MUST OBTAIN A SUBDIVISION FINAL PUB-LIC REPORT FROM THE REAL ESTATE COMMISSIONER. IF THE LOTS ARE TO BE OF-FERED FOR SALE FOR RESIDENTIAL OR OTHER USAGE, IT WILL BE NECESSARY THAT THEY BE SUITABLE FOR SUCH USE BEFORE THE COMMISSIONER CAN ISSUE SUCH A PUBLIC REPORT.

IN A SUBDIVISION SUCH AS THIS, THE SUBDIVIDER'S PROMOTIONAL AND SALES COSTS ARE GENERALLY GREATER THAN IN OTHER TYPES OF DEVELOPMENT. A PERSON CON-TEMPLATING PURCHASE OF A PARCEL IN THIS SUBDIVISION WITH THE IDEA OF RESALE SHOULD CAREFULLY CONSIDER THE DIFFICULTIES OF RESELLING AT A PROFIT WITH-OUT A PROMOTIONAL CAMPAIGN OR A SALES ORGANIZATION. HE SHOULD ALSO REAL-IZE THAT IN ATTEMPTING TO RESELL, HE MAY BE IN AN UNFAVORABLE COMPETITIVE POSITION WITH THE SUBDIVIDER AND OTHER PROSPECTIVE SELLERS OF PARCELS IN THE SUBDIVISION AND IN THE VICINITY.

PURCHASERS WHO WISH TO RE-SUBDIVIDE THEIR LAND INTO FOUR PARCELS FOR SALE OR LEASE, MAY BE REQUIRED TO COMPLY WITH THE SUBDIVISION MAP ACT PROVI-SIONS REGARDING ROADS AND SHOULD CONTACT THE COUNTY DEPARTMENT OF PUB-LIC WORKS FOR THEIR REQUIREMENTS AND ESTIMATED COSTS OF FILING A PARCEL MAP.

THE ASSESSED VALUATION OF THIS LAND PRIOR TO SUBDIVIDING AND IMPROVING OF THE LAND IN CONNECTION WITH SUBDIVIDING IS $5.00 PER ACRE. ASSESSED VALUA-TION OF REAL PROPERTY IS 25% OF FULL CASH VALUE AS DETERMINED BY THE COUN-TY ASSESSOR. THIS MEANS THAT THE FULL CASH VALUE OF A 20-ACRE PARCEL OF THE LAND BEFORE IMPROVEMENTS ACCORDING TO THE ASSESSOR IS $400. THE ONLY IMPROVEMENTS OF THE LAND TO BE MADE IN CONNECTION WITH THE SUBDIVIDING ARE DIRT-GRADED ROADS. THE SUBDIVIDER IS OFFERING 20-ACRE PARCELS OF THE LAND AT PRICES RANGING FROM $9,500 TO $17,500.

THERE IS LITTLE OR NO DEVELOPMENT IN THE SUBDIVISION TO DATE. THERE IS NO ASSURANCE OF SUBSTANTIAL DEVELOPMENT IN THE NEAR FUTURE.

THE SUBDIVIDER HAS NOT DEMONSTRATED TO THE DEPARTMENT OF REAL ESTATE THAT HIS PROPERTY AS SUBDIVIDED HAS INVESTMENT MERIT OR PROFIT POTENTIAL TO OWNERS OF PARCELS THEREOF.

LOCATION AND SIZE: In _____ County. Twelve (12) miles southwest of ___(TOWN)___, on County Road.

Approximately 400 acres divided into 20 lots or parcels.

TITLE: A title report shows title, among other things, to be subject to: A non-exclusive right of way for ingress and egress over the existing road lying within the North Half of the North Half of Section 24, and within the South Half of the Northeast Quarter and the Southeast Quarter of the Northwest Quarter of Section 13, Township 3 South, Range 2 East, _____ Meridian, as granted in the Deed dated January 4, 1971, executed by ___(GRANTOR'S NAME)___ to _____(GRANTEE'S NAME)_____, and recorded March 17, 1971, in Book 895, Page 60, Official Records, under Recorder's Serial No. 12663, in the Office of the County Recorder of said County.

The above referred to Deed also contains the following: "The above right of way is conveyed on the condition that it shall be used only for normal ranch use, and there shall be no commercial hauling over said right of way."

EASEMENTS: Easements for utilities, drainage, ingress and egress, roads, rights of way, pipelines, transmission lines and other purposes are shown on the title report and parcel map recorded in the Office of the _____ County Recorder, Case 5, Drawer 12, Page 68.

USES AND ZONING: Zoned for 20 acre minimum (Upland-Recreation).

RESTRICTIONS There are no recorded restrictions, however, this subdivision is subject to the provisions of all applicable county ordinances.

TAX ESTIMATES: If the subdivider is unable to give you the current tax information for your lot, you may approximate your taxes as follows:

Take 25% of the sales price, divide by 100, and then multiply by the total tax rate. The tax rate for the 19___-19___ fiscal year is $9.046. The tax rate and assessed valuation may change in subsequent years. For example, any bonded debt or special district assessment approved after the above tax rate had been set could increase the future rate.

MINERAL RIGHTS: You will not own the mineral, oil and gas rights of every nature and kind under your land. These have been reserved to previous owners in a deed recorded in Book 3 of Official Records, Page 104, and by Correction Deed under Recorder's File No. 3124, _____ County Records.

The right to surface entry has not been waived, and the owners of the mineral rights may enter upon the land at some future date to extract minerals, etc. This right could affect your ability to obtain financing for building on your property.

INTERESTS TO BE CONVEYED—CONDITIONS OF SALE: Grant deed will include non-exclusive right of way for ingress and egress, water pipe lines and public utilities.

PURCHASE MONEY HANDLING: The subdivider must impound all funds received from you in an escrow depository until legal title is delivered to you. (Refer Section 11013.2(a), Business and Professions Code.)

GEOLOGIC CONDITIONS: The State Division of Mines and Geology reports: "Some parts of this area are underlain by relatively soft rock formations. In this rural area we assume that development will be concentrated on the more favorable sites avoiding the steeper slopes. However, if construction is planned on steep terrain in the area, precautions should be taken during site development to minimize slope-stability problems."

WATER: The subdivider does not intend to install any water system or wells in this subdivision.

Existing springs and private water wells are the only source of water in this tract and you will be required to pay all costs to have a well installed.

The subdivider's well driller has submitted the following information:

"Ample water for domestic use should be obtained in this area by drilling small diameter deep wells or, in some cases, through the development of existing springs.

"The small diameter deep wells, in which rock will have to be penetrated, could cost between $3,000 and $5,000, with the pressure system costing between $1,000 and $1,500.

"Some existing springs could be developed with a cost of from $300 to $500. In most cases, a pressure system for this type of well would cost less than $500.

"Well depths will vary from area to area with the deep wells averaging from 150 to 300 feet. The springs should be able to be developed within 8 to 20 feet."

232

However, there is no guarantee of the quality or quantity or availability of water on each lot or parcel.

The State Water Code requires every person who digs, bores, or drills a water well to file a notice of intent prior to commencement of work and a report of completion within thirty days after the work has been completed. Said notice and report are to be filed with the district office of the Department of Water Resources administering the area in which the well is located. Forms will be furnished upon request by any district office of the Department of Water Resources.

FIRE PROTECTION: Furnished by Forestry Service if equipment is available, from May 15 to November 1. No fire protection is available from approximately November 1 to May 15 of each year.

ELECTRICITY: There are no electric facilities within the subdivision. The nearest Pacific Gas and Electric Company electric facilities are approximately 15,300 feet to the farthest parcel in the tract and the cost to reach that parcel would be approximately $153,000.

GAS: Natural gas service is not available.

TELEPHONE: The local Telephone Company reports that the extension of existing phone service lines to the farthest parcel in this tract (about 37,000 lineal feet) would be approximately $3,750, based on a cost of $10 per each 100 lineal feet of line (with no charge for the first 300 feet). A decrease in these amounts would be made in the event additional orders for service were received along this distribution route.

SEWAGE DISPOSAL: Septic tanks will be used for sewage disposal. You must pay for your septic tank. Prior to commencing construction, you should contact the local health department for specifications, requirements and any local problems.

A General Contractor estimates that the cost of septic tank installation would be $500 for a 2-bedroom, 1-bath home and $600 for a 3-bedroom, 2-bath home.

STREETS AND ROADS: The roads within this subdivision are private. No provision for their repair and maintenance has been made by the developer, and it is not contemplated that he will do so. All repair and maintenance of these private roads will be your responsibility and expense individually and collectively proportionately to the use of the road easement by you.

If you and your neighbor cannot agree on pro rata shares or upon the need or extent of repair and maintenance, it will be necessary for you to appeal to the proper superior court for the appointment of an impartial arbitrator or for the determination of the court as to the pro rata shares.

An engineer estimates it will cost lot owners $40,000 per mile to bring roads to county standards and that the annual cost for maintaining roads as existing at time of sale will be $350 per lineal foot.

Purchasers should be aware and should fully investigate the possibility that the development of the ground and roads in this subdivision may alter the terrain so as to affect access to the building site and the views for particular lots in the subdivision.

PUBLIC TRANSPORTATION: Bus service is approximately 12 miles from the subdivision at the nearest town.

SCHOOLS: County Unified School District. You should contact the school district for information concerning schools, class schedules, and bus service.

SHOPPING FACILITIES: In Wilco, 12½ miles southeast of the subdivision with limited facilities.

performs such tasks as maintaining the private roads in the subdivision, maintaining the shared facilities like the swimming pool, tennis courts, golf course, boat ramp facilities, clubhouse, and hiring and firing employees of the association.

The association is run by a board of directors, a president, vice president, secretary, and treasurer. It is a small government set up to manage the owners' affairs. It often suffers the same problems as any government: lack of sufficient funds, good leadership, experienced personnel, and longevity. When it is initially formed by the developer, he owns all the properties so he runs the show. Once the developer is out of the picture, chaos often occurs. Because most of the owners are absentee, the few permanent residents tend to manage everything. They don't like to do anything that will "upset the waters" because they have to live with one another. Generally it is difficult to get anything done.

I prosecuted a lawsuit a few years ago against a property owners' association on behalf of an owner whose house was destroyed in a landslide caused by water running off a road above her house because of a lack of proper road maintenance, such as ditching and placement of rocks and culverts. For six months before her house was destroyed she had written to her association and attended every meeting demanding that they repair the road above her house. The directors declined to do anything because they said they lacked the funds to hire a road contractor. Fortunately for my client, every meeting was taped and the evidence was there loud and clear when her house was destroyed. We sued the association, and the insurance company bought my client a new house. The association was lucky it had insurance, or it would have paid from its own account.

The association has the power to levy assessments against each property owner for funds to operate the subdivision. These assessments become liens against the property, like property taxes. The problem is that the directors hate to raise the assessment level to meet their needs because they take so much heat from their neighbors who don't want their "taxes" raised. As a result, most associations operate on a shoestring, and the turnover of officers and directors is very high because nobody wants the responsibility of being in charge of such an operation.

One of the most difficult jobs for the association leaders is to enforce the covenants, conditions, and restrictions (CC&Rs) that bind each property owner. Almost every subdivision and condominium has a set of regulations that are binding upon each owner. Those rules can include the following:

1. Prohibit commercial activities on the property.
2. Before constructing a house, the owner must receive prior approval of the directors, or of an architectural, design, or environmental control committee for the house plans.
3. Prohibit occupancy of a trailer, mobile home, or temporary structure.
4. Prohibit keeping boats or cars parked in the street.
5. Prohibit keeping of horses, dogs, and other livestock.
6. Prohibit shooting, hunting, or cutting of trees.
7. Prohibit the construction of outbuildings.
8. Prohibit renting of the home or condominium unit.
9. Require a certain level of maintenance of ground areas.

Generally, any individual property owner can bring a suit to enforce the CC&Rs, but usually the enforcement is left to the association. Often the rules look good on paper when you buy your parcel, but if they are not enforced they are meaningless. Generally nobody likes to take on the job of enforcer, so the enforcement becomes very lax and the rules are often forgotten.

If you intend to purchase in a subdivision or condominium and you care about how things are run, then you had better be prepared to take an active role in the association and to spend a large part of your time in the country playing politics. If the thought of meetings and rules turn you off, then do not buy land in a subdivision or purchase a condominium.

While you are investigating the property, demand to see a copy of the articles of incorporation, the bylaws, the operating rules, and the covenants, conditions, and restrictions, and read them thoroughly to see if you want to be part of such a project (see sample form, right).

GETTING AROUND SUBDIVISION LAWS

Of course, land developers have found ways of getting around existing subdivision laws. Some go ahead and subdivide without even attempting to comply with the laws, but there are "legal" ways

Declaration of Covenants,
Conditions, and Restrictions

CHUCK EDWARD and JERRY HERBERT, hereinafter called "Developers," are the owners of the following described real property, situated in the County of _____, State of _____:

> Lots 1 through 90 of Tract No. 109, The
> Pines, as per Map recorded in Book 116,
> Pages 116 through 124, of Maps, in the
> office of the County Recorder.

It is the desire and intention of Developers to sell the real property described above and to impose on it mutual, beneficial restrictions, covenants, and conditions, under a general plan or scheme of improvement for the benefit of all of the real property in the tract and the future owners thereof;

THEREFORE, Developers hereby declare that all of the property described above is held and shall be held, conveyed, hypothecated or encumbered, leased, rented, used, occupied, and improved, subject to the following restrictions, covenants, and conditions, all of which are declared and agreed to be in furtherance of a plan for the subdivision, improvement, and sale of the real property and are for the purpose of enhancing and protecting the value, desirability, and attractiveness of the real property and every part thereof.

All of the restrictions, covenants, and conditions shall run with the land and shall be binding upon all parties having or acquiring any right, title, or interest in the described real property, or any part thereof.

1.   Land Use and Building Type

No lot shall be used except for residential or church purposes. No building shall be erected, altered, placed, or permitted to remain on any lot other than one detached single family dwelling not to exceed two and one-half stories in height and a private garage for not more than three cars, with the exception that attached quarters may be used as a guest house, for the housing of hired help, or similar uses, but such quarters may not be rented or leased as separate units. Houses may be rented while waiting for a sale, but not to exceed 24 months. Lots 1 through 25, 34 through 36, 51 through 54, and 63 through 109 may have double wide mobile homes, provided a concrete foundation and a roof similar to a conventional home is provided. Garages and carports must be of wood construction with suitable roofing material to complement the proposed mobile home. The Developers' approval of all designs and location of improvements on a given lot must be obtained before obtaining a County permit. Permission to install a particular unit should be obtained before purchase, by submitting for Developers' approval the brochure of the manufacturer showing the unit that the applicant proposes to install.

2.   Architectural Control

No building or mobile home shall be erected, placed, or altered on any lot until the construction plans and specifications and a plan showing the location of the structure have been approved by Developers, as to quality of workmanship and materials, harmony of external design with existing structures, and as to location with respect to topography and finish grade elevation. No fence or wall shall be erected, placed, or altered on any lot nearer to any street than the minimum building setback line unless similarly approved. Frontage fences shall be of a redwood product unless another design is specifically approved. Cyclone type fence, of a maximum height of 48 inches, with wood palings, will be considered equal to redwood.

Developers' approval or disapproval, as required herein, shall be in writing. If such written approval or disapproval is not accomplished within 30 days after submission of a plan and/or specification, then it shall be deemed approved and in compliance with this document.

3. Dwelling Cost, Quality, and Size.

No dwelling shall be permitted on any lot at a cost of less than $45,000, based upon cost levels prevailing on the date these covenants are recorded. It is the intention and purpose of this covenant to assure that all dwellings shall be of a quality of workmanship and materials substantially the same or better than that which can be produced on the date these covenants are recorded at the minimum cost stated herein for the minimum permitted dwelling size. The ground floor area of the main structure, exclusive of one-story open porches and garages, shall be not less than 800 square feet for a one-story dwelling, nor less than 800 square feet for a dwelling of more than one story. All buildings and mobile homes will meet County Building Department Standards for High Density Subdivisions.

4. Building Location

(a) No building or mobile home shall be located on any lot nearer than 30 feet to the front lot line, nor nearer than 20 feet to any side street line. However, these front and side setbacks may be reduced to a minimum of 20 feet and 10 feet, respectively, by obtaining the prior written approval of Developers and a variance from the County Planning Commission.

(b) No building shall be located nearer than 10 feet to any interior lot line. No dwelling or mobile home shall be located on any interior lot nearer than 10 feet to the rear lot line.

(c) For the purpose of this covenant, eaves, steps, and open porches shall not be considered as a part of the building, provided, however, that such eaves, steps, and open porches shall not be located nearer than 5 feet to any lot line.

5. Re-subdivision Prohibited

No lots shall be re-subdivided.

6. Easements

Easements for installation and maintenance of utilities and drainage facilities are reserved as shown on the recorded plat. Within these easements, no structure, planting, or other material shall be placed or permitted to remain which may damage or interfere with the installation and maintenance of utilities, or which may change with the direction of flow of drainage channels in the easements, or which may obstruct or retard the flow of water through drainage channels in the easements. The easement area of each lot and all improvements on it shall be maintained continuously by the owner of the lot, except for those improvements for which a public authority or utility company is responsible. All natural drainages shall be kept free flowing.

7. Nuisances

No noxious or offensive activity shall be carried on upon any lot, nor shall anything be done thereon which may be or may become an annoyance or nuisance to the neighborhood.

8. Temporary Structures

No structure of a temporary character, trailer, basement, tent, shack, garage, barn, or other outbuilding shall be used on any lot at any time as a residence either temporarily or permanently, except that a travel trailer with proper sanitation facilities may be used as temporary housing during the construction of a home but not to exceed twelve months.

9. Signs

No sign of any kind shall be displayed to the public view on any lot except one professional sign of not more than two square feet, one sign of not more than three square feet advertising the property for sale, or signs used by a builder to advertise the property during the construction and sales period. Professional people operating their businesses within their homes may use the above sign limitations.

10. Livestock and Poultry

No animals, livestock, or poultry of any kind shall be raised, bred, or kept on any lot, except that dogs, cats, or other household pets, poultry not exceeding 10 in number, and sheep not exceeding 6 in number may be kept, provided that any such animals or poultry, other than household pets, must be contained not less than 50 feet from any frontage street. All dogs, animals, and poultry must be confined to their owner's lot at all times. Horses or cattle may be kept on parcels 1 through 11, 21, 22, 23, 68, and 69, provided adequate fencing is provided and conditions are provided for the animals to minimize flies and odors to neighbors. Additionally, this paragraph is subject to, and limited by, paragraph 7, above.

11. Garbage and Refuse Disposal

No lot shall be used or maintained as a dumping ground for rubbish. Trash, garbage, or other waste shall not be kept except in sanitary containers. All incinerators or other equipment for the storage or disposal of such material shall be kept in a clean and sanitary condition.

12. Water Supply

No individual water system shall be permitted on any lot unless such system is located, constructed, and equipped in accordance with the requirements, standards, and recommendations of the County Health Department. Approval of such system as installed shall be obtained from such authority.

13. Sewage Disposal

No individual sewage disposal system shall be permitted on any lot unless such system is designed, located, and constructed in accordance with the requirements, standards, and recommendations of the Country Health Department. Approval of such system as installed shall be obtained from such authority.

14. Term

These restrictions, covenants, and conditions are to have a term of thirty-five years from the date this document is recorded. After thirty-five years the term shall be automatically extended for successive periods of 10 years, unless an instrument signed by a majority of the then owners of the lots has been recorded, agreeing to change said term or otherwise modify the provisions of this document.

15. Enforcement

Enforcement shall be by proceedings at law or in equity against any person or persons violating or attempting to violate any restriction, covenant, or condition. The remedy sought may be to restrain violation or to recover damages.

16. Severability

Invalidation of any one of these restrictions, covenants, or conditions, by judgment, or otherwise, shall in no way affect any of the other provisions which shall remain in full force and effect.

17. Mortgages and Deeds of Trust

Nothing herein contained shall defeat or impair the lien of any mortgage or deed of trust made in good faith and for value, but title to any property obtained through sale in satisfaction of any mortgage or deed of trust shall be held subject to all of the measures and provisions hereof.

18. Enviromental

The beauty of this subdivision is in its mixture of trees and open space. Trees (defined as having a minimum trunk diameter of six inches, measured two feet above ground level) may only be cut if the following conditions are met: They must be dead or dying trees; or removal of the trees must be required to clear for building sites, access roads, or to enable installation of utilities. In any event, no trees may be cut without obtaining the prior approval of Developers.

DATED:

_____

CHUCK EDWARD

_____

JERRY HERBERT

to avoid them as well, if the government is not watching.

Let's assume that your state subdivision law applies only to land splits of more than four parcels. A seller wants to sell to eight separate buyers but he doesn't want to create eight parcels because then he would be obligated to meet the standards of the subdivision laws, which would mean added expense and bother to him. So he makes four parcels and pairs the eight buyers. Each member of a pair of buyers will "own" half of a parcel as specified in a contract between the two "partners" as drawn up by the seller. Since there are only four parcels, only four deeds will be issued, one for each pair of buyers. Thus each buyer pays for his interest as if he were getting his own separate parcel, but in fact, each person is a *tenant-in-common* in relation to the others and will suffer the problems of such a relationship. The developer sells the land for as much as he would have made had he sold eight separate and independent parcels, and he has legally avoided his legal responsibilities and the legal safeguards for the buyer.

A variation on this scheme is the creation of a *campsite community*. A developer with a large piece of land advertises that each buyer will join with other buyers as tenants-in-common on a beautiful large piece of property and will have the right to have his own campsite on a spot of his choice on a first come, first served basis. Often a certain amount of land will be designated as open space. Thus the buyer is one owner sharing his land with many other people under the pretext that he is buying into a "community," when in fact, the developer has bought a large parcel of land at a reasonable price and resold it to many buyers, at a tremendous profit.

The above plan is often not considered a subdivision under the legal definitions of many states, and therefore there are no regulations that must be met. In a few areas of the country, state and local laws decree that where "five or more undivided interests" are sold, the development must comply with all normal subdivision requirements, such as plat approval and issuance of public reports.

CONDOMINIUM DEVELOPMENTS

A condominium development is an apartment arrangement surrounded by open land and recreational areas owned in common by all persons who buy the apartment units. The promotional literature emphasizes the ecological aspects of preserving open space. Aside from the fact that this "preserved" space includes golf courses, swimming pools, horse-riding trails, and hundreds of people tramping across it, the investment is often a poor one since the extremely high price really buys only an apartment. The buyer could take his $50,000 to $250,000, which is what one of these fancy apartments in the "country" costs, and get 50 or more beautiful acres of land near the recreational facilities he enjoys, and still have enough money left over to construct a comfortable house.

If you are nevertheless interested in a vacation or rural resort condominium, there a few important things to know. Most of the people who buy into such projects use their condos for weekends and holidays. Therefore, you would not want to buy one for year-round occupancy because your needs will likely be very different. You will not have full-time neighbors, and you may require a greater level of daily upkeep than the absentee owners.

The costs to you can become very high: First, you buy the condominium unit, then you pay monthly assessments to maintain the common property, as well as paying regular local property taxes. Always look at the operating budget of the development. It is available for public inspection. Study to see if the developer retains ownership of the common area. For example, the developer will hang onto ownership of the recreational facilities and lease them back to the buyer. The sales pitch is that the lease arrangement means lower-priced condominiums. What often happens though is that the owners get burdened with high rental charges which get higher every year. All of this information is available to you if you ask for it.

If you are buying into a new development, you will have to use your best estimate in projecting the future costs of ownership. If the condominium is several years old, look over the past records, see the cost increases, and project them into the future. Often the condominium will be managed by a professional management firm, and that increases the costs. This is a necessity for vacation condos. The firm will also handle rental of your condo to third persons when you are not using it. This can help pay for the condo, but it also results in considerable wear and tear on the unit.

"Here you can have the unique distinction of being the first on your block to be the first on your block."

Because the development is managed by a board of directors, you should ask permission to sit in on a board meeting before you purchase to judge for yourself how the project is run. These are your neighbors, and since you will all be living extremely close to one another, you should determine how compatible you are with other owners, not only in personality, but in life-style and matters of taste.

The federal government recently completed an evaluation report called *Planned Unit Developments, Condominiums and Homeowner Associations*, which concluded:

The most startling finding of this report is not how badly the Homeowners Associations are faring in the . . . condominium developments studied, but how they have even managed to survive, given the obstacles and barriers to their viability. It is indeed surprising to see haphazard groupings of . . . homeowners with little or no assistance from developers, HUD, mortgagees, local governments, or each other who have learned how to manage and care for what are in essence mini-governmental jurisdictions.

SOME FINAL ADVICE

The Office of Interstate Land Sales has issued a list of warnings regarding the purchase of rural property, including the following:

1. Don't buy land like you buy TV sets, buy it like the serious real estate purchase that it is.
2. Don't buy land without first seeing it in person.
3. Buy scared—don't buy on the spot on the first visit, or at a free dinner, or when under pressure from a salesman.
4. Don't buy before asking for and reading the property report or, preferably, before showing it to an attorney or real estate authority.
5. Know your rights in buying land.
6. Look into the background of the developers—what other projects have they done?
7. Know the special risks involved, such as the chance that the land may not appreciate in value and the possibility that resale of the land may be subject to restrictions.

240

8. Know how to deal with high-pressure sales tactics.
9. Do your homework.

As a general rule, your money will be better spent purchasing your own piece of land outside of a subdivision. You will not have to deal with petty internal politics, you will be in control of your environment, and your property will appreciate faster in value. The more promises made to you in the slick brochures of the land and condominium developers, the more cautious you should be. If it sounds too good to be true, it is. Don't be swayed by low-money-down deals. Money is money, and it should be spent as productively as possible, or not at all.

USEFUL RESOURCES

The Office of Interstate Land Sales Registration

This is under the U.S. Department of Housing and Urban Development (HUD). The addresses of the local HUD offices are given in Useful Resources at the end of chapter 26, "HUD/FHA- and VA-/Insured Loans." If you want information on any subdivision you should also write the main office:

Land Sales Registration Division
Assistant Secretary for Housing
Federal Housing Commissioner
Department of Housing and Urban
Development
451 7th Street, S.W., Rm. 6278
Washington, DC 20410

Send them the name and location of the subdivision you are interested in and ask them for any information they have on the project; write to them for any information on the current federal laws or on their study entitled *Subdividing Rural America*. You should also write to them if you feel you have been cheated in a deal.

The following are available free from the above HUD office:

Financing Condominium Housing
HUD-77-H
HUD/FHA Non-Assisted Program for Condominium Housing HUD-227-H
Questions about Condominiums
HUD-365-H

Better Business Bureaus

Listed below are all the Better Business Bureaus in the United States and Canada. You can check with the one nearest the subdivision or condominium you are interested in for any information they have available on real estate promotions and buying property. Not all states are represented.

UNITED STATES BUREAUS

NATIONAL HEADQUARTERS

Council of Better Business Bureaus
1515 Wilson Blvd.
Arlington, VA 22209

LOCAL BUREAUS

Alabama
1214 S. 20th St.
Birmingham, AL 32503

108 Jefferson St.
Huntsville, AL 35801

707 Van Antwerp Bldg.
Mobile, AL 36602

Union Bank Bldg.
Commerce St., Ste. 810
Montgomery, AL 36104

Alaska
417 Barrow
3605 Arctic Blvd., #BB
Anchorage, AK 99503

Arizona
4428 N. 12 St.
Phoenix, AZ 85013

100 E. Alameda St., Ste. 403
Tucson, AZ 85701

Arkansas
1216 S. University
Little Rock, AR 72204

California
705 18th St.
Bakersfield, CA 93301

1265 N. La Cadena
Colton, CA 92324

5070 N. Sixth St., Ste. 176
Fresno, CA 93720

639 S. New Hampshire Ave., 3rd Fl.
Los Angeles, CA 90005

508 16th St., Rm. 1500
Oakland, CA 94612

1401 21st St., Ste. 305
Sacramento, CA 95814

Union Bank Bldg., Ste. 301
San Diego, CA 92101

4310 Orange Ave.
San Diego, CA 92105

2740 Van Ness Ave., #210
San Francisco, CA 95109

1505 Meridian Ave.
P.O. Box 8110
San Jose, CA 94125

20 N. San Mateo Dr.
P.O. Box 294
San Mateo, CA 94401

111 N. Milpas St.
P.O. Box 746
Santa Barbara, CA 93102

1111 N. Center St.
Stockton, CA 95202

17662 Irvine Blvd., Ste. 15
Tustin, CA 92680

Colorado
524 S. Cascade, Ste. 2
Colorado Springs, CO 80903

1780 S. Bellaire, Ste. 700
Denver, CO 80222

140 W. Oak St.
Fort Collins, CO 80524

Connecticut
Fairfield Woods Plaza
2345 Black Rock Turnpike
Fairfield, CT 06430

100 S. Turnpike Rd.
P.O. Box 2068
New Haven, CT 06473

630 Oakwood Ave., Ste. 223
West Hartford, CT 06110

Delaware
20 S. Walnut St.
P.O. Box 300
Milford, DE 19963

1901-B W. 11th St.
P.O. Box 4085
Wilmington, DE 19807

District of Columbia
1012 14th St., N.W.
Prudential Bldg., 14th Fl.
Washington, DC 20005

Florida
3969 Ulmerton Rd.
Clearwater, FL 33520

8600 N.E. 2nd Ave.
Miami, FL 33138

3080 Tamiami Trail, N.
Naples, FL 33940

608 Gulf Dr., W., Ste. 3
New Port Richey, FL 33552

132 E. Colonial Dr.
Orlando, FL 32801

P.O. Box 1511
Pensacola, FL 32597-1511

3015 Exchange Ct.
West Palm Beach, FL 33409

Georgia
100 Edgewood Ave., Ste. 1012
Atlanta, GA 30303

624 Ellis St., Ste. 106
P.O. Box 2085
Augusta, GA 30903

8 13th St.
Columbus, GA 31901

6822 Abercorn Extension
P.O. Box 13956
Savannah, GA 31406

Hawaii
677 Ala Moana Blvd., Ste. 614
Honolulu, HI 96813

Idaho
409 W. Jefferson
Boise, ID 83702

Illinois
35 E. Wacker Dr.
Chicago, IL 60601

109 S.W. Jefferson St., Ste. 305
Peoria, IL 61602

3 W. Old Capitol Plaza, Rm. 14
Springfield, IL 62701

Indiana
118 S. Second St.
P.O. Box 405
Elkhart, IN 46515

133 S.E. Fourth St.
Evansville, IN 47708

1203 Webster St.
Fort Wayne, IN 46802

4231 Cleveland St.
Gary, IN 46408

22 E. Washington St., Ste. 310
Indianapolis, IN 46204

204 Iroquois Bldg.
Marion, IN 46952

Ball State University
Whitinger Bldg., Rm. 192
Muncie, IN 47306

Iowa
Alpine Center
2435 Kimberly Rd., N., Ste. 110
Bettendorf, IA 52722

3 Irvine Bldg.
417 First Ave., S.E., Ste. 3
Cedar Rapids, IA 52401

615 Insurance Exchange Bldg.
Des Moines, IA 50306

318 Badgrow Bldg.
Sioux City, IA 51101

Kansas
501 Jefferson, Ste. 24
Topeka, KS 66607

300 Kaufman Bldg.
Wichita, KS 67202

Kentucky
629 N. Broadway
Lexington, KY 40508

844 S. Fourth St.
Louisville, KY 40203

Louisiana
1407 Murray St., Ste. 101
Alexandria, LA 71306

2055 Wooddale Blvd.
Baton Rouge, LA 70806

300 Bond St., Box 9129
Houma, LA 70360

804 Jefferson St.
P.O. Box 3651
Lafayette, LA 70501

1413 Ryan St., Ste. C
P.O. Box 1681
Lake Charles, LA 70602

141 De Siard St.
ONB Bldg., Ste. 114
Monroe, LA 71201

301 Camp St., Ste. 403
New Orleans, LA 70130

1407 N. Market St.
Shreveport, LA 71107

Maryland
401 N. Howard St.
Baltimore, MD 21201

6917 Arlington Rd.
Bethesda, MD 20814

Massachusetts
8 Winter St.
Boston, MA 02108

106 State Rd., Ste. 4
Dartmouth, MA 02747

1 Kendall St., Ste. 307
Framingham, MA 01701

Federal Bldg., Ste. 1
78 North St.
Hyannis, MA 02601

316 Essex St.
Lawrence, MA 01840

293 Bridge St., Ste. 324
Springfield, MA 01103

32 Franklin St.
P.O. Box 379
Worcester, MA 01601

Michigan
150 Michigan Ave.
Detroit, MI 48226

1 Peoples Bldg.
Grand Rapids, MI 49503

Minnesota
1745 University Ave.
St. Paul, MN 55104

Mississippi
502 Edgewater Gulf Dr.
Bldg. C, Ste. 10
Biloxi, MS 39531

105 Fifth Ave.
Columbus, MS 39701

510 George St., Ste. 107
P.O. Box 2090
Jackson, MS 39225

601 22nd Ave., Ste. 313
Meridian, MS 39301

Missouri
306 E. 12th St., Ste. 1024
Kansas City, MO 64106

Mansion House Center
440 N. Fourth St.
St. Louis, MO 63102

205 Park Central, E., Ste. 312
Springfield, MO 65806

Nebraska
719 N. 48th St.
Lincoln, NE 68504

1613 Farnam St., Rm. 417
Omaha, NE 68102

Nevada
1829 E. Charleston Blvd., Ste. 103
Las Vegas, NV 89104

372-A Casazza Dr.
P.O. Box 2932
Reno, NV 89505

New Hampshire
1 Pillsbury St.
Concord, NH 03301

New Jersey
836 Hadden Ave.
P.O. Box 303
Collingswood, NJ 08108

690 Whitehead Rd.
Lawrenceville, NJ 08648

34 Park Pl.
Newark, NJ 07102

2 Forest Ave.
Paramus, NJ 07652

1721 Route 37, E.
Toms River, NJ 06753

New Mexico
4520 Montgomery, N.E., Ste. B-1
Albuquerque, NM 87109

308 N. Locke
Farmington, NM 87401

Santa Fe Division
227 E. Palace Ave., Ste. C
Santa Fe, NM 87501

New York
775 Main St.
Buffalo, NY 14203

266 Main St.
Farmingdale, NY 11735

257 Park Ave., S.
New York, NY 10010

1122 Sibley Tower
Rochester, NY 14604

200 University Bldg.
Syracuse, NY 13202

209 Elizabeth St.
Utica, NY 13501

158 Westchester Ave.
White Plains, NY 10601

120 E. Main
Wappinger Falls
White Plains, NY 12590

North Carolina
29½ Page Ave.
Asheville, NC 28801

202 N. Tryon St.
Charlotte, NC 28202

2608 W. Friendly Ave.
Greensboro, NC 27410

Northwestern Bank Bldg.
11 S. College Ave., Ste. 203
Newton, NC 28658

P.O. Box 95066
3120 Poplarwood Dr., Ste. G-1
Raleigh, NC 27625

2110 Cloverdale Ave., Ste. 2-B
Winston-Salem, NC 27103

Ohio
P.O. Box F-596
Akron, OH 44308

1434 Cleveland Ave., N.
Canton, OH 44713

898 Walnut St.
Cincinnati, OH 45202

1720 Keith Bldg.
Cleveland, OH 44115

527 S. High St.
Columbus, OH 43215

40 W. Fourth St., Ste. 280
Dayton, OH 45402

P.O. Box 1706
130 W. Second St.
Mansfield, OH 44901

405 N. Huron St.
Toledo, OH 43604

Mahoning Valley
P.O. Box 1495
Youngstown, OH 44501

Oklahoma
606 N. Dewey
Oklahoma City, OK 73102

4833 S. Sheridan, Ste. 412
Tulsa, OK 74145

Oregon
520 S.W. Sixth Ave.
Portland, OR 97204

Pennsylvania
528 N. New St.
Dodson Bldg.
Bethlehem, PA 18018

53 N. Duke St.
Lancaster, PA 17602

511 N. Broad St.
Philadelphia, PA 19123

610 Smithfield St.
Pittsburgh, PA 15222

601 Connell Bldg.
N. Washington Ave.
Scranton, PA 18503

Rhode Island
270 Weybosset St.
Providence, RI 02903

South Carolina
1338 Main St., Ste. 500
Columbia, SC 29201

608 E. Washington St.
Greenville, SC 29601

Tennessee
Park Plaza Bldg.
1010 Market St., Ste. 200
Chattanooga, TN 37402

124 W. Summit Hill Dr.
P.O. Box 3608
Knoxville, TN 37902

1835 Union, Ste. 312
P.O. Box 41406
Memphis, TN 38104

506 Nashville City Bank Bldg.
Nashville, TN 37201

Texas
Bank of Commerce Bldg., Ste. 320
Abilene, TX 79605

1008 W. 10th St.
Amarillo, TX 79101

1005 American Plaza
Austin, TX 78701

476 Oakland Ave.
P.O. Box 2988
Beaumont, TX 77704

202 Varisco Bldg.
Bryan, TX 77803

109 N. Chaparral, Ste. 101
Corpus Christi, TX 78401

2001 Bryan St., Ste. 850
Dallas, TX 75201

6024 Gateway, E.
El Paso, TX 79905

709 Sinclair Bldg.
106 W. 5th St.
Fort Worth, TX 76102

2707 N. Loop, W., Ste. 900
Houston, TX 77008

910 E. Marshall St.
Longview, TX 75601

1015 15th St.
P.O. Box 1178
Lubbock, TX 79401

Air Terminal Bldg., Rm. 216
P.O. Box 6006
Midland, TX 79711

115 S. Randolph
San Angelo, TX 76903

1800 Northeast Loop 410, Ste. 400
San Antonio, TX 78217

608 New Rd.
P.O. Box 7203
Waco, TX 76714-7203

1106 Brook Ave.
Wichita Falls, TX 76301-5009

Utah
1588 S. Main St.
Salt Lake City, UT 84115

Virginia
105 E. Annandale Rd., Ste. 210
Falls Church, VA 22046

2019 Llewellyn Ave.
P.O. Box 11133
Norfolk, VA 23517

701 E. Franklin, Ste. 100
Richmond, VA 23219

151 W. Campbell Ave., S.W.
Roanoke, VA 24011

Washington
2200 Sixth Ave.
Seattle, WA 98121

S. 176 Stevens St., Ste. A
Spokane, WA 99204

1101 Fawcett Ave., #222
Tacoma, WA 98401

424 Washington Mutual Bldg.
Yakima, WA 98907

Wisconsin
740 N. Plankinton Ave.
Milwaukee, WI 53203

CANADIAN BUREAUS

NATIONAL HEADQUARTERS
1231 Yonge St., Ste. 208
Toronto, Ontario M4W 2T8

LOCAL BUREAUS

Alberta
630 8th Ave., S.W., Ste. 404
Calgary, Alberta T2P 1G6

10240 124th St., Ste. 600
Edmonton, Alberta T5N 3W6

600 Guardian Bldg.
10240 124th St.
Grande Prairie, Alberta

Red Deer, Alberta

British Columbia
788 Beatty St., Ste. 404
Vancouver, B.C. V6B 2M1

635 Humboldt St., Rm. M-37
Victoria, B.C. V8W 1A7

Manitoba
365 Hargrave St., Rm. 204
Winnipeg, Manitoba R3B 2K3

New Brunswick
348 King St., 3rd Fl.
Fredericton, New Brunswick E3B 1E3

Box 1002
236 St. George St., Ste. 110
Moncton, New Brunswick E1C 8P2

400 Main St.
St. John, New Brunswick E2K 4N5

Newfoundland
360 Topsail Rd.
P.O. Box 516
St. John's, Newfoundland A1C 5K4

Nova Scotia
1731 Barrington St.
P.O. Box 2124
Halifax, Nova Scotia B3J 3B7

Ontario
170 Jackson St., E.
Hamilton, Ontario L8N 1L4

365 Richmond St., Ste. 404
P.O. Box 2153
London, Ontario N6A 4E3

58 Scott St.
Kitchener, Ontario N2H 2R1

71 Bank St., Ste. 503
Ottawa, Ontario K1P 5N2

215 Mavety St.
Toronto, Ontario M6P 4C6

500 Riverside Dr., W.
Windsor, Ontario N9A 5K6

Quebec
2055 Peel St., Ste. 460
Montreal, Quebec H3A 1V4

475 rue Richelieu
Quebec City, Quebec G1R 1K2

Saskatchewan
2049 Lorne St.
Regina, Saskatchewan S4P 2M4

Consumer Fraud

The following state agencies investigate and mediate consumer complaints of deceptive and fraudulent business practices.

Alabama
Consumer Protection Division
Office of the Attorney General
138 Adams Ave.
Montgomery, AL 36130

Alaska
Consumer Protection Section
Department of Law
1031 W. Fourth Ave., Ste. 110
Anchorage, AK 99501

Arizona
Financial Fraud Division
Office of the Attorney General
1275 W. Washington, #259
Phoenix, AZ 85007

Arkansas
Consumer Protection Division
Office of Attorney General
Justice Bldg.
Little Rock, AR 72201

California
Department of Consumer Affairs
1020 N. St., Rm. 516
Sacramento, CA 95814

Colorado
Antitrust/Consumer Protection
Department of Law
1525 Sherman St., 2nd Fl.
Denver, CO 80203

Connecticut
Consumer Protection Department
165 Capitol Ave.
Hartford, CT 06106

Delaware
Department of Community Affairs
156 S. State St.
Dover, DE 19901

District of Columbia
Office of Consumer Education and
Information
Consumer and Regulatory Affairs
Department
614 H St., N.W., Rm. 108
Washington, DC 20001

Florida
Division of Consumer Services
Agriculture and Consumer Services
Department
Mayo Bldg.
Tallahassee, FL 32301

Georgia
Office of Consumer Affairs
Office of Planning and Budget
205 Butler St., S.E., Plaza E
Atlanta, GA 30334

Hawaii
Office of Consumer Protection
Commerce and Consumer Affairs
Department
1010 Richards St.
Honolulu, HI 96813

Idaho
Office of the Attorney General
Statehouse
Boise, ID 83720

Illinois
Attorney General
500 S. Second St.
Springfield, IL 62706

Indiana
Division of Consumer Protection
Office of Attorney General
215 State House
Indianapolis, IN 46204

Iowa
Consumer Protection Division
Office of Attorney General
Hoover State Office Bldg.
Des Moines, IA 50319

Kansas
Consumer Protection Division
Office of Attorney General
Judicial Center
Topeka, KS 66612

Kentucky
Attorney General
State Capitol
Frankfort, KY 40601

Louisiana
Office of Consumer Protection
Urban and Community Affairs Department
P.O. Box 94455
Baton Rouge, LA 70804-9455

Maine
Bureau of Consumer Credit Protection
Business, Occupational and Professional
Regulations Department
State House Station, #35
Augusta, ME 04333

Maryland
Consumer and Investor Affairs Division
Office of Attorney General
7 N. Calvert St.
Baltimore, MD 21202

Massachusetts
Executive Office of Consumer Affairs
1 Ashburton Pl.
Boston, MA 02108

Michigan
Regulatory and Consumer Affairs
Department of Commerce
P.O. Box 30221
Lansing, MI 48909

Minnesota
Consumer Division
Office of Attorney General
117 University Ave.
St. Paul, MN 55155

Mississippi
Consumer Protection Division
Office of Attorney General
Gartin Bldg., 5th Fl.
Jackson, MS 39201

Missouri
Department of Economic Development
Truman Bldg.
P.O. Box 1157
Jefferson City, MO 65102

Montana
Consumer Affairs Unit
Department of Commerce
1424 Ninth Ave.
Helena, MT 59620

Nebraska
   Consumer Fraud Section
   Office of the Attorney General
   P.O. Box 94906
   Lincoln, NE 68509-4906

Nevada
   Division of Consumer Affairs
   Department of Commerce
   2501 E. Sahara Ave., #202
   Las Vegas, NV 89518

New Hampshire
   Attorney General
   208 State House Annex
   235 Capitol St.
   Concord, NH 03301-6397

New Jersey
   Division of Consumer Affairs
   Department of Law and Public Safety
   1100 Raymond Blvd., Rm. 504
   Newark, NJ 07102

New Mexico
   Consumer Protection and Economic Crimes
      Division
   Office of Attorney General
   Bataan Memorial Bldg.
   Santa Fe, NM 87503

New York
   Consumer Protection Board
   Twin Towers
   99 Washington Ave.
   Albany, NY 12210

North Carolina
   Consumer Protection Division
   Department of Justice
   Justice Bldg., Box 629
   Raleigh, NC 27602

North Dakota
   Consumer Fraud Division
   Office of Attorney General
   State Capitol, 17th Fl.
   Bismarck, ND 58505

Ohio
   Office of Consumers Counsel
   137 E. State St.
   Columbus, OH 43215

Oklahoma
   Consumer Credit Department
   2101 N. Lincoln Blvd.
   Oklahoma City, OK 73105

Oregon
   Division of Consumer Protection and
      Services
   Department of Justice
   520 S.W. Yamhill
   Portland, OR 97204

Pennsylvania
   Bureau of Consumer Protection
   Office of Attorney General
   Strawberry Square, 14th Fl.
   Harrisburg, PA 17120

Rhode Island
   Consumers Council
   365 Broadway
   Providence, RI 02902

South Carolina
   Department of Consumer Affairs
   2221 Devine St.
   P.O. Box 5757
   Columbia, SC 29250-5757

South Dakota
   Division of Consumer Affairs
   Office of Attorney General
   State Capitol
   Pierre, SD 57501

Tennessee
   Division of Consumer Affairs
   Department of Commerce and Insurance
   206 State Office Bldg.
   Nashville, TN 37219

Texas
   Division of Consumer Affairs
   Office of Attorney General
   P.O. Box 12548
   Austin, TX 78711

Utah
   Consumer Services Committee
   Department of Business Regulation
   160 E. 300, S.
   Salt Lake City, UT 84110-5802

Vermont
   Public Protection Division
   Office of Attorney General
   109 State St.
   Montpelier, VT 05602

Virginia
   Consumer Affairs Office
   Agriculture and Consumer Services
      Department
   1100 Bank St.
   Richmond, VA 23219

Washington
   Office of Consumer Protection
   Office of Attorney General
   Dexter Horton Bldg.
   Seattle, WA 98104

West Virginia
   Consumer Protection Division
   Office of Attorney General
   1204 Kanawha Blvd., E.
   Charleston, WV 25305

Wisconsin
   Trade and Consumer Protection Division
   Agriculture, Trade and Consumer Protection
      Department
   P.O. Box 8911
   Madison, WI 53708

Wyoming
   Office of the Attorney General
   State Capitol
   Cheyenne, WY 82002

The following is available for the specified cost
from:
   R. Woods
   Consumer Information Center, A
   P.O. Box 100
   Pueblo, CO 81002

Buying Lots from Developers. What you're
   entitled to know—and should ask—
   before you sign a contract.
   S/N 023-000-00694-4 128R $2.50

The following is available for the specified cost
from:
   Superintendent of Documents
   Government Printing Office
   Washington, DC 20402

*Condominiums—Their Development and
   Management,* Catalog Number HH 1.2:C
   75/3 $1.25

The following are free from:
   U.S. Department of Housing and Urban
      Development (HUD)
   451 Seventh St., S.W., Rm. B-258
   Washington, DC 20410

Questions about Condominiums HUD-365-F
*HUD/FHA Comparision of Condominium and
   Cooperative Housing* HUD-256-F

FHA and VA

The FHA and VA have information on their own
specifications for a proper subdivision. They also
have separate reports on projects that they have
approved, and you can ask for them at any local
office. The addresses of regional offices of FHA
and VA are given in Useful Resources at the end
of chapter 26, "HUD/FHA- and VA-Insured
Loans."

   You can get a free copy of *Neighborhood Standards* at any FHA office.

State Real Estate Commissioner

Your state real estate commissioner has local offices throughout the state, and they can give you
any information they have on a subdivision. Ask
any real estate agent or planning commissioner for
the address of the commissioner.

County Agencies

The best place to start any investigation about a
land purchase, and particularly a subdivision development, is at the county offices overseeing land
use in the area.

   The following officials can give you the specified
information:

Planning Commission (Director of Planning)—is
   the primary agency in charge of processing subdivision applications, plats, and reports. It controls zoning and land use in general, and its
   information is available to the public.
Building Inspector—information on the use of the
   land as a homesite; specifically grading, stability, erosion, drainage, and building quality design for homes already constructed.

Health Officer or Department—information on water supply, sewage disposal, and health facilities.

Road Commissioner—information on the quality of road construction in the subdivision; specifically surface materials and grading, and easement provisions.

County Engineer—must approve geological, drainage, and flooding conditions of the subdivision.

County Surveyor—processes all surveys, plats, and maps submitted for a subdivision. You can copy any maps in his office.

Fire Officer—can give you information on fire protection in the area.

County or District School Superintendent—information on education facilities.

County Sheriff—home protection and public safety information.

CHAPTER 15

Eminent Domain and Condemnation

Federal, state, city, and county governments, improvement districts, public utilities, and similar public and semipublic organizations have the power of *eminent domain*. This right permits them to take private property for a public benefit by *condemning* it. Private lands have been condemned for such things as public irrigation systems, railroads, electric power plants, parks, government buildings, airports, streets, highways, roads, and sewer plants.

A TRUE CONDEMNATION STORY

The following story is condensed from an article originally published in the *Mother Earth News*.

A young married couple purchased 760 acres of fine farm land that was bordered on two sides by federal land controlled by the Bureau of Land Management (BLM). The BLM is responsible for managing 400 million acres of government land. Like many land buyers, this couple falsely assumed that it was an advantage to buy next to government land.

One month after they moved onto their farm, a neighbor told them that the BLM was preparing to construct two logging roads across their land in order to reach the timber on the federal land bordering their farm. Although the couple found this hard to believe, they checked with the local BLM office and, much to their astonishment, found out the sad truth. One road was to run behind their house and right through the source of their water supply. The other road was to start at their driveway and continue on a path between their barn and house, cross over their pasture, and enter the BLM land. (See illustration 79.) Once constructed, these roads would be traveled by huge diesel trucks carrying cut logs from the BLM's "preserved" and "protected" woodlands.

The couple immediately registered a protest against the proposed plans and later prevented entry by a government surveying team that wanted to survey the exact location for the roads. The government was forced to go to federal court to formally request condemnation actions against that part of the property needed for the road. They argued that they had to cross the farm rather than choose an alternative route because "the proposed roads are the easiest and cheapest routes for the logging companies." The court granted the BLM "the right to enter, survey and mark on the ground the location of an easement in relation to estab-

lished property corners, and to appraise the market value of such an easement." In addition, "the United States of America, acting through the Bureau of Land Management of the Department of the Interior, its representatives, agents, or contractors [is allowed] to remove, sell, or otherwise dispose of any trees necessary to [do] such survey work."

The owners hired an attorney who forced the BLM to comply with some legal requirements they had ignored, and this postponed immediate action on the road. But after the government has complied with the regulations, the court will probably grant a permanent easement for the two logging roads. When this is done, the couple will be compensated an amount of money equal to the "appraised value" of the "condemned" land. But their farm will no longer be the quiet and private place they had longed for.

The previous owner who sold this farm probably knew of the proposed plans for the logging roads and was aware of the diminished value the land would have after their construction. He was not legally required to inform the buyers of this fact, and they, unfortunately, did an inadequate job of researching the land before they purchased it. Had they spent only an hour at the nearest BLM office

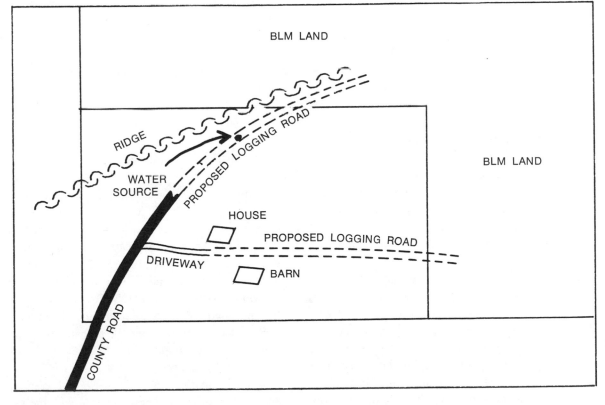

79. Example of a Condemnation

they might have discovered what was in store for their land.

No private property is exempt from the government's power of eminent domain. However, the landowner can protest such action in court, in which case the government will have to bring a condemnation proceeding against him to prove that taking the land will benefit the general public and is required for public necessity. Since it is usually easy to prove to a court that the proposed action is for the "benefit of the public," the primary dispute in almost all condemnation or eminent domain cases is over the amount of "just compensation" to be paid the property owner.

"JUST COMPENSATION" UPON CONDEMNATION

If the entire property is condemned, the owner will be paid its "fair market value." (See chapter 19, "Evaluating the Price of the Property.") This is called the owner's "just compensation" for the taking of his property. The amount of just compensation does not include expenses involved in moving and relocation, personal inconvenience, the necessity to buy more expensive land if nothing else is available in the area, and loss of profits to any business conducted on the land. Generally, the person whose property is condemned will not be happy about it, particularly when the entire parcel is not taken.

Most condemnations take only a part of a person's land. For example, in the condemnation story earlier, the government took only an easement for the logging roads across the couple's land. Therefore, the government has to pay them only the fair market value of the strips of land they condemn and an amount of money for *severance damages*. Severance damages are the loss in value of the land as a whole caused by a condemnation and taking of only a portion of it. The damages are usually figured as the difference between the original market value of the entire parcel and its reduced market value after the roads are put in. Although this might be a large sum of money, it will not be enough to allow the couple to buy a comparable piece of land, and no amount of money can make life satisfying in a home next to a logging road.

Even though none of your land is condemned, when property next to or near yours is condemned and you are injured in the process, you can be compensated for noise, smoke, and loss of privacy. Since the value of such things is hard to determine, the affected person is rarely satisfied with his amount of "just compensation."

MY FAVORITE EMINENT DOMAIN WAR STORY

I was fortunately able to help an elderly couple fight their local sewer district in Superior Court during a two-week jury trial. My clients, in their early seventies, had a beautiful redwood-covered parcel of land with a small cabin and an orchard that had been in the wife's family for over fifty years. They were good citizens and always believed the things that happened to them would never happen in America, where property rights are sacred. That is, until they became the defendants in the case of *The Miranda Community Services District* v. *Arnold and Helen Cooper*.

The service district, represented by its board of directors, was interested in putting in a sewer system for their town, which had reached its limit for permissible septic tank installations. The town fathers decided that the sewer plant would fit nicely right in the middle of the Coopers' family retreat.

But the Coopers liked their property just the way it was and were not interested in selling at any price.

The district hired a lawyer and filed a condemnation action to take forcibly the Coopers' property by eminent domain. The Coopers could not stop this action, so their option was to fight to get fair compensation for their land. In a condemnation case the trial becomes the battle of the appraisers, and this case was no exception. The government district had two appraisers who testified that the property was worth only $25,000. The Coopers had one appraisal of $58,000 and one of $52,000.

But what emerged during the preparation of the case was that one of the service district's appraisers had originally independently appraised the Cooper property at approximately $55,000. The district, not wanting to pay that price, agreed with the appraiser to destroy parts of that appraisal and to lower the value. Sections of the original appraisal were then burned in the appraiser's fireplace, never to be seen again. The value was then reduced to $25,000.

Fortunately, a jury of twelve good citizens decided that the Coopers should receive $58,000 for their property and rendered their verdict in less than two hours, after a two-week jury trial. But the Coopers lost their property, for which no amount of money could truly compensate. Mrs. Cooper had been vacationing at her family retreat since she was born and had a lifetime of fond memories.

The point of this story is not that the good guys won, which they did, but that the eminent government, successor to the Crown, has almost unlimited power to exercise its right to take back its "domain," if it is for the "general welfare" of its subjects. Never assume it can't happen to you. Be aware of any potential eminent domain possibilities in the area where you are looking at property. Going through a condemnation case in court takes thousands of dollars and years of aggravating time.

INVESTIGATING THE POSSIBILITY OF FUTURE CONDEMNATION OF YOUR LAND

When you are ready to buy some land, search out every possible plan for future construction and development in your area. If the land is bordered by public lands of any kind, check with the agency controlling those lands. (The addresses of the BLM offices in charge of federal lands and the state agencies in charge of state lands are located in appendix B.) Look at their official maps, and see what is planned for the land adjoining your property. City and county land offices will be located in the city hall. The local planning commission and road department can give you much information and will show you the maps of proposed projects. The local and state water resources agencies and the local

office of the Soil Conservation Service will have information on proposed water and irrigation projects. Also read the local newspapers. Don't be afraid to ask a lot of questions.

You should be looking for the most common causes of condemnation: roads, water and drainage canals, utilities, and dams. By doing a little investigating you can discover all the plans for the area that can affect your land. Look for proposals that have not yet been approved but that can cause problems if they are.

Of course, there is nothing you can do to prevent future actions by the government that have not yet been discussed. Regardless of your thorough investigation, your land might someday be threatened by eminent domain. If this happens, you may have to retain an attorney to fight against the condemnation or for a just compensation.

THE WARRANTY FOR CONDEMNATION AND EMINENT DOMAIN

In many cases, longtime residents of rural areas will have inside information on future condemnation actions to be levied against their property, and they will sell out before this occurs. The unsuspecting buyer is left to suffer the consequences of eminent domain. The Model Contract of Sale in chapter 28 has a warranty in Clause 16(h) to protect you in such a case. After you take title, if the land is condemned you can win a legal action against the seller by proving he had knowledge of the impending condemnation.

Clause 13 of the Model Contract of Sale deals with the possibility that the land may be taken by eminent domain after the signing of the contract and before the closing of escrow. If this occurs, the buyer may choose either to terminate the purchase or to get the purchase price reduced by the amount its value is reduced by the condemnation.

CHAPTER 16

Adverse Possession

"SQUATTER'S RIGHTS"

Under certain circumstances you can lose title to part or all of your land by a legal device known as *adverse possession*. This has been referred to as "squatter's rights" and is one of the legal traditions that gave rise to the expression, "Possession is nine-tenths of the law." Buyers who purchase land as investors and never use it often don't keep track of their property and finally lose their title by adverse possession. The law was established to encourage use of land and to clear up confusing title conflicts arising most often between owners of adjoining land.

For a person to take your title away from you, his use of your land must be: (1) hostile, (2) actual, (3) open and notorious, (4) exclusive, (5) continuous, and (6) under a claim of title; and he must (7) pay the property taxes for a specified period of time. Each of these elements must be satisfied by the person, or "squatter," who seeks to adversely possess your land.

1. The possessor must use your land without your permission and must deny the fact that you are the true owner. Thus, if you give the person permission to, or specific orders not to, use the land, he can never gain title by adverse possession. His use must be *hostile* to you. Where there is no written proof of the permission, it is difficult to defeat a claim of adverse possession. (See chapter 38, "How to Be a Nice Neighbor without Paying for It in the End.")

2. The person must be making *actual use* of your land. He must be living or working on the land in some fashion. Some activities that have led to ad-

verse possession of portions of land in the past include clearing brush, cutting trees, planting crops, putting in ditches, erecting a building, fencing off a section of the land, and living on the land.

3. The user must be *open and notorious* in the manner in which he is on the land. He cannot sneak around the owner's property in such a manner that he could not be discovered, and his activities must be visible to the owner if he were to examine the land.

4. *Exclusive possession* means that the user must be on the land alone. If he is there with the owner, he cannot get title to the land.

5. Use of the land must be *continuous* from the beginning of the prescribed time period to the end, although seasonal use for the prescribed number of years is generally permissible.

6. The possessor must claim that he owns the land, even if he is wrong. His actions will speak for themselves in this regard. If he is acting as if he believes he owns the land, he is taking the property under a *claim of title*. He must also pay the property taxes on the land during the period of occupancy.

7. The time limit for acquiring adverse possession is called the *statute of limitations*. All of the above elements must occur for a minimum length of time before adverse possession "ripens" into title. The minimum period varies among the states; for example, California (5 years); Louisiana, New York, and Oregon (10 years); Minnesota (15 years); Colorado (18 years); Maine and Wisconsin (20 years); Ohio and Pennsylvania (21 years). It runs from the time the possessor begins to use the property and continues running even if the property is sold by the actual owner. Each person's use can "tack on" to his predecessor's use to make up the statutory time period.

ACQUIRING THE LAND

The most common instance of acquiring land by adverse possession occurs when a neighbor unknowingly puts up a fence that encloses a portion of an adjoining landowner's property. If he meets all the above requirements and has his fence up for the prescribed period of time, when he discovers that he has fenced in the neighboring land, he can go to court and get a court order, or *declaratory judgment,* stating that he now owns the land he has enclosed.

Another common situation that leads to adverse possession is when a part of a building, a section of an orchard, or another improvement encroaches on a neighbor's land, and this mistake is not discovered before the prescribed time period has elapsed. Usually the person whose fence, building, or other improvement is on a neighbor's property by mistake has been paying taxes on this property for years. This fact helps to prove his case in court.

The willingness of the courts to award title by adverse possession varies among the states. For example, some states require that the possessor have a document, such as a faulty deed, that appears to give good title but actually does not. This is referred to as possession under *color of title*. Other states simply require possession by the adverse user for any purposes.

PRECAUTIONS

A title report or abstract of title will not indicate that a person has met the requirements to adversely possess a piece of land, because the possessor's ownership will not be part of the public records until he makes a claim. A standard owner's policy of title insurance will not insure the buyer against adverse possession because such activity can be discovered only by a correct legal survey and/or by inspection of the property. This shows the importance of having your land legally surveyed before you buy in order to discover where your boundaries are. (See chapter 31, "The Title Search, Abstract of Title, and Title Insurance Policy.")

If you are looking at land and discover that an adjoining landowner or anyone else is occupying the land, you must not close the deal until you determine on what basis the user is occupying the land. Go talk to him and ask him. Tell him you are buying the property and want to find out what his intentions are. You might find out you are walking into a potential lawsuit by purchasing the property. Tell the seller you want the trespassing squatter off the property prior to the close of escrow. Never decide to buy the property first and then to evict the squatter. You might end up in a very expensive battle that will ruin your dream of a peaceful life in the country.

If you encounter a situation like this before your purchase and you are still interested in buying the property, seek out the advice of a good local real estate attorney, preferably one who has experience with adverse possession and prescriptive easement litigation.

Adverse possession involves taking title to a piece of land. There is a similar legal right that can be gained to allow a person to take substances, such as water, minerals, and timber, from another person's land. This is called a *prescriptive profit* or *prescriptive right*. (See chapter 10, ''Water Rights,'' and chapter 11, ''Mineral, Oil, Gas, Timber, Soil, and Other Rights.'') An individual can also gain a legal right to cross over another person's land by a method called a *prescriptive easement* or *easement by prescription*. (See chapter 9, ''Easement Rights.'')

CHAPTER 17

Property Taxes and Assessments

YOU CAN'T LIVE ON THE LAND FOR FREE, EVEN IF IT'S PAID FOR

The tradition of taxing a person on the basis of the land he owns began toward the end of the Middle Ages. The idea was that taxes should be paid by those who could afford them. Up until the last one hundred years most people earned the greatest part of their income from agriculture, and the amount and quality of land a person owned was the most visible and reliable measurement of his wealth. Since land is difficult to hide, unlike stocks, bonds, money, and other personal property, it became an easy target for governments needing to raise money to run their operations.

REAL ESTATE TAXES ON LAND AND IMPROVEMENTS

The purpose of taxes is to pay for services provided to people living within the taxed area. The police and fire departments, hospitals, schools, libraries, street and sidewalk maintenance, recreational facilities, local government, and other public services are supported largely by property taxes. There is no doubt that these taxes will continue to increase in the future.

Fewer government services are provided the farther you are from large population centers, and the taxes drop accordingly. A recent study by the U.S. Department of Agriculture found that taxes on agricultural land in counties with a major city are three times higher than in the nearest neighboring counties and seven times higher than in the next group of counties. (See illustration 80.)

Your local taxes may include a tax on real property (land and structures), a tax on personal property (appliances, machinery, etc.), special assessment liens, special district taxes, and possibly some others. There is no federal real property tax. The county tax assessor maintains all the tax records in each county and can give you information on all local taxes you will be responsible for. The assessor also determines the value of each parcel of property for purposes of levying taxes on it. The county tax collector. treasurer. or other officer is responsible for collecting the tax. State laws specify when tax installments are due and what exemptions will be allowed.

APPRAISED VALUE (FAIR MARKET OR FULL CASH VALUE)

The tax appraiser must appraise the *fair market value* or *full cash value* of land in his county each year for the purpose of levying taxes on it. This value is supposed to represent the amount of cash or its equivalent that the property would bring if it were put up for sale on the current market under conditions in which a willing buyer and seller knew all the facts of the situation. The assessor uses the same general standards for appraising the property as I outline in chapter 19, "Evaluating the Price of the Property." The basic method is the comparison analysis.

The assessor knows what property is sold each year by using the county recorder's deed index. He determines the sale price from tax stamps and the amount of transfer taxes paid, questionnaires filed when the deeds are recorded or sent to new buyers after the deed is recorded, and personal interviews with real estate agents. If he knows what a parcel sells for, he knows what its fair market value is. If surrounding property is similar, then it will be assumed that the unsold land has the same value as the sold land.

For example, if a 20-acre parcel with a $60,000 house on it sells in 1988 for $80,000, a similar 20-acre parcel with a $60,000 house on it that is located a half-mile away, and that has not changed hands in ten years, will be appraised at, or near, $80,000 under the comparison test. Of course, this is a very simple example, but it approximates the method used. Appraising property is not an exact science, but uniformity is supposed to be the goal of every appraiser.

In areas where most of the land is undeveloped, the assessor looks at current market conditions and establishes a set market value of an acre of land. For instance, all land in a 100-square-mile area might be appraised at $1,500 per acre. Then the improvements on each parcel are examined and given separate appraisals. Conventional buildings are appraised higher than unusual structures, and

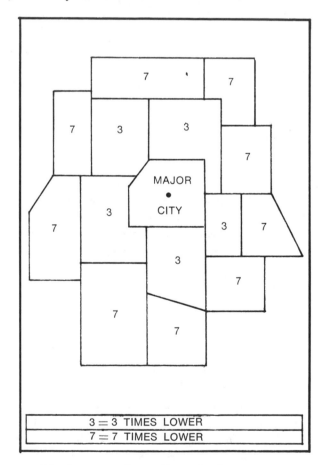

80. Amount Taxes Drop in Counties Surrounding Large Cities

260

older houses have a depreciated value placed on them. Since the assessor cannot look at all land each year, a parcel might have the same appraisal for several years regardless of improvements. But in many areas, the appraiser is notified every time a construction permit is issued and he makes it a point to visit the land and reassess its value based on the new improvements being constructed.

After the tax assessor appraises the property, your final tax is determined according to the property's assessed value and the current tax rate.

ASSESSED VALUE

The assessed value is some percentage of the appraised value, usually 20–50 percent, although it can be 100 percent. The percentage is called the *assessment ratio*. For example, in a county that bases its property tax on an assessment value of 25 percent, if the tax assessor determines that a piece of land has a fair market value of $60,000, the tax levied on it will be based on 25 percent of that figure, or $15,000.

THE TAX RATE

The *tax rate,* or *mill rate,* is the percentage of assessed value that is levied in taxes. It is usually described as the tax rate per $100 of assessed valuation.

The county government determines the tax rate each year by first drawing up a budget of proposed expenses for the coming year. Let's assume your county budget requires $30 million. The treasurer then figures out how much money the county will receive from sources other than property taxes. Assume this income equals $6 million. This amount is subtracted from the total budget figure, and the remaining amount must be collected in the form of property taxes. This would be $24 million. The tax assessor adds up the appraised fair market value of all taxable land in the county and from this sum derives the total assessed value. Assume the fair market value of the land in your county is $2.4 billion. Assuming that the assessment ratio of assessed value to appraised value is 25 percent, the

total assessed value of the land will be $600 million.

The $24 million needed by the county then is divided by the $600 million total assessed value. The result is the tax rate, which is .04 or 4 percent. Thus your county will charge $4 on every $100 of assessed value. If your property is appraised at $60,000 and then assessed at 25 percent of that, or $15,000, you will be charged $600 in taxes that year.

A Decrease in the Tax Rate Does Not Always Mean Lower Taxes

Be careful when the county declares it is lowering the tax rate. This does not automatically mean your taxes will be lowered. If the percentage used to determine assessed value increases at the same time the tax rate decreases, your taxes may actually be greater. This is a common tax ploy. Compare these two examples:

1. Tax rate in 1987   12% ($12 per $100 of assessed value)

   Assessment Ratio (assessed value to the appraised value)   20%
   True value of property $80,000
   Assessed value (20%) $16,000
   Tax Rate times assessed value ($16,000 × .12) $1,920 in taxes will be due

2. Tax rate (lowered) in 1988   10% ($10 per $100 of assessed value)

   Assessment Ratio (assessed value to appraised value)   25%
   True value of property $80,000
   Assessed value (25%) $20,000
   Tax rate times assessed value ($20,000 × .10) $2,000 in taxes will be due

Even though the tax rate is lowered, taxes increase by $80 because the assessment ratio is increased.

PROPERTY TAXES ON TIMBER, MINERALS, AND WATER RIGHTS

Your real property tax will be based on the value of the minerals, standing timber, water, and other permanent fixtures on the land as well as the land itself. The value of each of these things is often determined separately and then added to the value of the bare land to find the overall worth of the property.

Standing Timber

To determine the value of standing timber on land for tax purposes, a survey, often called a *county cruise*, is made of the trees on the property. Sometimes the survey will group several parcels together and evaluate the timber in a large geographical area. In that case, the timber tax assessment for each separate parcel is based on the value of the timber on the area as a whole, with no consideration given to the physical condition and accessibility of the timber. Usually, however, tax assessors rely on information supplied by the timber owners themselves, which is then corroborated by aerial photos and field sampling.

Only merchantable timber, mature trees capable of being cut and sold at the time of assessment, are considered. The definition of a mature tree varies, depending on the state's law. In some places, a stand of trees can be declared mature forty years after the time of planting or removal of the original timber growth, or when its average quality and volume per acre are at least equal to the quality and volume of those timber stands in the area that are being converted into wood products. Values are usually determined by analyzing timber sales in the general area of the land.

Many landowners are forced to cut their trees to eliminate the excessive tax burden, which is the reason timber is taxed. If every rural landowner left his trees standing to provide beauty, preserve the soil, and maintain the water table, the lumber industry would have a diminished source of timber. Although lumber companies own much of their own land, once it is logged it is worthless to them for many years until the second or third growth develops sufficiently to be logged again. Often after their land is logged, they subdivide and sell it. Forty years later, when the trees are ready to be cut again, the government begins taxing for marketable timber, regardless of whether the owner is cutting the trees. If the landowner cannot afford to pay the increased real property tax, the lumber companies are back in business with that same piece of land, or the subdivision developers take it over.

The factors of taxation in this situation are analogous to those that are causing vast farm acreage to be sold to developers by farmers who can no longer pay the exorbitant taxes. This is the main reason some states have enacted preferential assessment systems, which I discuss later in this chapter. As timber supplies diminish further in the future, the value of timber will increase and many more property owners will be forced to log in order to be able to pay the increasing taxes on their land.

In some states, timber is only taxed when it is cut. Ask the local tax assessor how timber is taxed in your county. He should show you a copy of the law regarding valuation of timber for tax purposes. Find out if your state allows an *immature forest trees exemption,* which I discuss later in this chapter.

Fruit and nut trees may also assessed as part of the real property. If they are planted on a noncommercial basis, they increase the value of the property from the time they are planted. If they are part of a systematic planting in an orchard for commercial purposes, they may be exempt from taxation for a specified number of years. For example, in California fruit- and nut-bearing trees that have been planted less than four years are tax exempt.

Minerals

The value of minerals on your property will probably be slight and, therefore, have little effect on the real property tax. However, where the land has some proven mining value, the added tax assessment might be very high.

Water Rights

In states that recognize *riparian* rights, the real property tax assessment will usually include the value of any riparian rights that go with the land. In *appropriation* states the value of the right to take the water might be assessed differently. However it is done, the right of a landowner to take and use water on his land increases the value and, therefore, the property taxes. If water rights are shared with others, the value and taxes should be diminished somewhat. (See chapter 10, ''Water Rights.'')

PERSONAL PROPERTY TAXES

Over half the states in the country levy a tax on

personal property. Although this tax affects mainly businesses, certain household items and farm animals may be taxed in your area. However, most household furnishings and personal effects are exempt from the tax, as are automobiles. Although many states exempt intangible property such as stocks, bonds, and other "paper" assets, many areas do not exempt such intangibles as notes, deeds of trust, and mortgages.

SCHOOL TAXES

School taxes, like the general real property tax, are levied according to the value of your land. The tax rate may be different from the tax rate used for the general real property taxes, however. Every school district has its own methods, but it is common to include school taxes within the general property tax bill. Check with the tax assessor's office for information on school taxes in your county.

These taxes support the schools in each district in the county and are levied regardless of whether the landowner has children in school. If the schools are old or inadequate for the growing rural population in your area, you can expect increased school taxes to finance new school construction.

SPECIAL TAX ASSESSMENTS

Property taxes pay the general expenses of running the local government and providing necessary services for the county's residents. Some services that are provided only to a particular group within the county are paid for by that group through another type of tax called a special assessment. These usually include water and irrigation systems, drainage and sewer systems, road construction, and sidewalk and curb improvement. These projects can be initiated by the landowners who will benefit by the completion of such construction, or the city or county in which the area is located may have an election to set up a special improvement district. The cost of providing these services is usually split up among the landowners according to the amount of benefit to be received. A separate tax bill may be issued by the special district, or the special assessment

may be included as part of the county tax bill. If the tax is collected by the special district itself, you can go to the district office to determine the tax status of land you intend to buy.

Special assessments really hurt when your land is within a district that is providing sewers, water lines, new roads, and other improvements for a new, or soon-to-be-built, housing development. Your land may be several miles away from the development, but if you are within the district, you must pay for the subdivision's improvements. Check with the tax assessor's office to find out what properties are included in your district and what the district's boundary lines are.

Assessments are usually levied over a period of several years. For example, if a sewage district is installing sewer lines to replace septic tanks, each property owner's share in this improvement might be $300, payable over a period of three years at the rate of $100 annually.

Because special assessments support projects that increase the value of your land, you cannot deduct these taxes from your income tax as is possible with general property taxes. If you are thinking about buying in an area that is developing rapidly, you should expect future special assessments, which will be an added burden on your funds.

The Seller Should Pay the Entire Special Assessment Lien

A problem often arises when a seller has not completely paid off a special assessment tax, or lien, at the time he sells the property. For example, suppose the county has begun paving all the dirt roads in one section of the county. The value of this land increases immediately upon the announcement that the roads are to be paved, although the paving cannot be completed for three years. All the affected property has a special assessment levied against it. You want to buy land in this area, and the seller is going to get a better price for his property than he could have received before the road paving began. Thus when you buy the land, you are in effect paying the assessment by paying a higher price. If you are also to assume payment of the assessment upon taking title to the land, you are paying for the improved roads twice. Therefore, a condition of the sale should be that the seller pay off all assessment liens before the closing of escrow.

The seller will probably resist this condition. A traditional solution of the conflict is that the seller pay for special assessments levied on work started before the buyer made his offer to buy. The buyer then pays for work started after he made his offer. I do not like this remedy. Rather, I would insist that the seller pay the entire assessment before the close of escrow or subtract the amount due from the purchase price. Clause 10 of the Model Contract of Sale in chapter 28 provides for this. But if the seller absolutely refuses to pay the entire assessment, of course you will have to pay it after you purchase the property.

TAX LIENS

When taxes are declared each year, the county has a lien, or claim, on the property until they are paid. Taxes are so important to the state and local governments that laws have been passed giving tax liens precedence over all other claims by creditors of the property owner. When property is foreclosed, taxes are always the first debts paid.

Each county has its own remedy for collecting unpaid taxes. The most common method is by a *tax sale*. At the end of the year, if you have not paid your taxes, the county will sell your land at a tax sale to get its money. This is not usually as serious as it sounds. Often a municipality, and sometimes a private party or commercial investor, purchases a certificate of tax sale which gives the buyer the right to take title and get a deed to your land if you do not pay the back taxes within a specified redemption period. The redemption period varies among the states, but is usually up to a year. Occasionally no redemption period is allowed.

If you pay your taxes within this period, you will be charged penalty payments and interest on the unpaid taxes, and the county will cancel the lien on your land. You will be issued a redemption certificate showing that payment has been made and that title has been redeemed. The person who "bought" your land at the tax sale then gets his money back, plus interest, and the county gets its taxes plus a penalty charge. If you fail to pay the back taxes within the redemption period, the purchaser of the land at the tax sale receives title to the property. Always keep the redemption certificate, and when you buy land, get any that may be in the possession of the seller before escrow closes.

Before the close of escrow you should examine the tax records book in the tax collector's office to see if any back taxes are due on the land. If so, find out if the seller can still redeem the property. If he can, he must pay the taxes before the close of escrow and thus clear the title to the land. This is stated in Clauses 6 and 10 of the Model Contract of Sale in chapter 28. If you buy land with any tax lien on it other than the current year's, which is a lien but not yet due and payable, be sure that the seller clears the record before escrow closes, using your deposit if necessary. If he needs your deposit and part of the down payment to pay back taxes, the escrow holder will pay them and obtain a redemption certificate before giving the seller his money. (See Model Escrow Instructions in chapter 30, "Opening and Closing of Escrow and the Role of the Escrow Holder.")

In some states, the property taxes can be past due for a specified number of years before the property owner loses his land by a tax sale; in California you will not lose your land for nonpayment of taxes until you are five years in arrears.

PRORATION OF TAXES

Prorating taxes divides the obligation to pay them between yourself and the seller according to your respective periods of ownership during the tax year that you buy the land. The proration date is usually the close of escrow. However, any date you and the seller agree on may be used. Because the owner of the property at the time the taxes became due will be responsible for paying the entire amount, provisions are made in the contract of sale to reimburse the party who pays the taxes for the period in which he does not own the property. (See Clause 8 in the Model Contract of Sale, chapter 28). Tax periods usually extend from January 1 to December 31 or from July 1 to June 30. However, the term used varies from state to state, and you should check with the local tax assessor for the dates used in your area.

Here's an example of how a proration is figured. Assume the taxable year is from July 1 to June 30 and escrow is to close on February 15. The seller will own the property from July 1 to February 15, or seven and a half months of the taxable year. If the total taxes for the year are $750, the taxes each month would be $62.50. Figuring thirty days in a month, the taxes come to $2.08 per day. The seller will owe $437.50 for seven months and $31.20 for the fifteen days of February, equaling $468.70 as his share of the proration. The buyer then owes $281.30 to make the total tax of $750. Thus, if the seller has already paid the taxes for the entire year, the buyer will be charged $281.30 at the close of escrow.

Usually the escrow holder computes the proration, but you should always double-check his figures.

SEGREGATION OF TAXES

When a landowner subdivides his property for sale, the taxes for the year in which he sells the land will be based on the value of the original parcel. By filing for a *segregation* of taxes, the year's taxes will be apportioned among the new pieces of land according to their respective values. Do not confuse this with a *proration* of taxes, discussed above.

Here's an example of how a segregation is worked out. Assume a seller subdivides 120 acres into three 40-acre parcels. His taxes for the year of sale on 120 acres are $3,720. This amount must be divided among the three parcels. One of the "forties" has a house on it, and the other two are unimproved land. The tax assessor has appraised the fair market value of the land itself at $800 per acre and the value of the house at $90,000. Therefore the appraised value of each of the two unimproved pieces of land is $32,000. The appraised value of the 40 acres with the house on it is $32,000 plus $90,000, or $122,000. In this particular county, the assessed value (assessment ratio) is 20 percent of the appraised value, and the tax rate is 10 percent. Thus, the assessed value of each of the two unimproved "forties" is $6,400, and the tax on each of them is $640. The assessed value of the remaining "forty" with the house is $24,400, and the tax on it is $2,440. Adding $2,440, $640, and $640 gives the total of $3,720 owed for the year.

Thus, when taxes become due on a parcel before segregation takes place, the buyer and seller will prorate on the basis of an agreed amount. Using our example, if you are buying the parcel with the house on it, you and the seller will prorate on the basis that your parcel represents 33⅓ percent of the land tax and the total tax on improvements, since your house is the only improvement on the 120 acres. If when the taxes are finally assessed after escrow closes the proportions by which you agree to segregate are different, then the seller and you are to make reimbursements accordingly.

The best way to find out how the property taxes will be segregated is to talk to the tax assessor before the close of escrow and get an estimate of how the taxes will probably break down after the segregation takes place. Let him know exactly what you are buying so he can segregate the values correctly. Be absolutely certain that he understands where the boundary lines are for the new parcels and which parcels contain the improvements, or you could end up paying taxes on a house that is not on your land. Since his assessment will be based partly on what you are paying for the property, he will probably ask you for the figure. When you get your tax statement, check the assessments to see if they are in accordance with the agreement between you and the seller.

You and the seller must apply for segregation immediately on closing by filing all the necessary forms with the tax assessor. The reason a segregation cannot be obtained before the close of escrow is that the title must be transferred to the buyer before a legal segregation can occur. The tax assessor always segregates parcels automatically when he gets a copy of a newly recorded deed, but often a deed might not be sent to the tax assessor by the county recorder for several months. To avoid this delay, file for segregation immediately on closing.

TAX IMPOUNDS BY LENDERS

If you give a mortgage or deed of trust when purchasing land, the lender will take the responsibility for paying your property taxes on time each year until the loan is paid off. If he left the responsibility to you and you failed to pay your taxes, the land could be sold at a tax sale, and he would lose his only security for the loan. So that he can pay the taxes when they become due, he must collect the money from you in advance. This is done by having you pay impounds with your regular payments of principal and interest. Thus you pay the taxes to the lender, and he pays them to the government.

Almost all commercial lenders collect impounds. However, if the seller finances the sale himself, he usually provides in the loan agreement that you are to pay the taxes yourself. Since he holds a mortgage or deed of trust, he might tell the tax collector to notify him if you fail to pay the taxes. If that occurs, under the terms of most loan agreements, the seller can foreclose.

ESTIMATING YOUR FUTURE TAXES

Although taxes on the land you are buying may be low now, they will not necessarily stay that way. The more land being sold in the area, the faster the taxes will increase.

The best way to get an idea of what your future taxes might be is to determine how much taxes have been increasing in the past few years. Go to the tax assessor's office, find your land on the tax parcel map, and get its parcel number. Sometimes part of the land will be included in one tax district and the rest will be in another. If so, the property will have two parcel numbers. Look up the property's tax statements in the tax file or index. Check all parcel number records that cover the property. The tax records will indicate the amount of past property taxes (county, school, city, special districts, etc.), when the property was last appraised, the breakdown of appraised value between improvements and the land itself, the ratio of assessed value to appraised value, the assessed value, the tax rate, and the existence of any tax liens, tax sales, and other delinquencies. Reprinted here is a typical tax statement with all the information you will find in the tax file or tax rolls. (See illustration 81.)

Compare the current appraised value to the price you are planning to pay for the land. If the difference is great, you should expect an immediate substantial increase in the taxes, because when you buy the land, one of the factors the tax assessor will use when reappraising the property is the price

you paid for it. The tax assessor's office is informed when property is sold and often sends out a questionnaire to the new owner asking the price paid for the property. The next year when the tax bills are sent out, the new price you paid will be the value placed on the property.

Trace the records back at least five years to see how much the taxes increased each year. Any changes in the appraisal of the property, in the ratio of assessed value to appraised value, or in the tax rate will affect the amount of the tax. Note the assessments made on improvements. Are there any improvements that have not yet been assessed? If so, you can expect a tax increase the next time the property is reappraised.

Don't be afraid of the tax assessor or his office. All files are open to the public, and the chances are that the person who appraised your land will be in the office and available for discussion. Ask him what factors he considered in appraising the property, including improvements, recent sales in the area, and the price being asked by the seller for the property. He can give you a rough estimate of how much your taxes will probably increase based on the amount you intend to pay for the land.

In a subtle way, ask him if he thinks the seller's asking price is reasonable. His answer and analysis of the property might give you some valuable information to use when negotiating the purchase price. (See chapter 19, ''Evaluating the Price of the Property,'' and chapter 20, ''Bargaining to Get the Seller's Asking Price Down.'') Do not rely completely on the tax assessor's opinion, however, because these officials are often behind on current market values.

KEEP THOROUGH TAX RECORDS

Generally, taxes are collected in installments during the year to ease the burden on the landowner. Different taxes might be due at different times of the year. Get a list of due dates for all taxes from the local tax collector. There is a penalty for late payment, and some states reduce your tax as a reward for early payment.

The majority of tax delinquencies occur during the first year of property ownership. This is due to the following circumstances:

IMPORTANT INFORMATION

1. Examine this bill carefully. The Tax Collector cannot be responsible for payments on wrong property.
2. ASSESSED VALUATIONS are established by the County Assessor at an announced ratio of 25% of full cash value. Questions regarding valuation should be addressed to the County Assessor,   Courthouse,
3. PAYMENT OF TAXES should be made by mail by returning the appropriate stub or stubs with your payment in the return envelope.
   a. The Tax Collector acts only as the taxpayer's collecting agent and assumes no responsibility for the loss of any such items or the proceeds thereof in transit or for losses resulting from the failure of any bank used as a collection agency.
   b. IF A CHECK OR DRAFT WAS GIVEN IN PAYMENT OF A TAX BILL THE RECEIPT GIVEN SHALL BE VOID AND OF NO EFFECT SHOULD SAID CHECK OR DRAFT BE NOT PAID ON PRESENTATION. (Revenue and Taxation Code.)
4. THE FIRST INSTALLMENT IS DELINQUENT AFTER DECEMBER 10, 19 , 6% PENALTY ADDED THEREAFTER. THE SECOND INSTALLMENT IS DELINQUENT AFTER APRIL 10, 19 , 6% PENALTY PLUS $3.00 COSTS ADDED THEREAFTER.
5. If you find "SOLD FOR TAXES" on your tax bill, it is an indication of delinquent taxes for a previous year and thereafter, as provided by law, additional penalties will be charged. To ascertain the amount necessary to redeem, write directly to Treasurer-Tax Collector,   Courthouse,
6. TAXES ARE LEVIED ON BOTH REAL AND PERSONAL PROPERTY as it exists the first day of March. Subsequent removal or change of ownership does not relieve the real estate of the personal property lien, and the tax collector cannot credit payments for real property taxes unless the personal property tax has been paid or is tendered.
7. Tax Statements are mailed only to addresses appearing on the Assessment Rolls of the County Assessor as of the First of March.
8. If you no longer own this property, please return this tax bill, giving the name and address of new owner, if known.

YOUR CANCELLED CHECK IS YOUR BEST RECEIPT   Complete the following information for your records:

1st Inst. Paid By Check No._____Date____ 2nd Inst. Paid By Check No._____Date_____ or Total Tax Paid Check No._____Date_____

81. Example of a Real Property Tax Statement

1. A new owner not reading or understanding the title report or escrow papers as they pertain to taxes paid and taxes "subject to," meaning that the taxes are due but have not been paid prior to or at the close of escrow.
2. Not knowing tax due dates and delinquent dates on real property taxes.
3. Misunderstanding who is to pay the taxes—the property owner or his lending agency.
4. Erroneously believing the property is not subject to taxes or penalties unless a tax bill is rendered.
5. Not inquiring about taxes until billed.
6. A new owner not receiving a tax bill because it is sent to the previous owner. Nonreceipt of a tax bill does not prevent the imposition of penalties after the delinquent date. It is the new owner's responsibility to see that the tax assessor has the new address to mail the future tax bills to the new owner.

		LAND		IMPROVEMENTS		STATE and/or COUNTY TAXES		CITY TAXES		EDUCATION (SCHOOL) and/or SPECIAL ASSESSMENTS		PERSONAL PROPERTY and/or OTHER TAXES	
YEAR	TAX DATE	Full Cash (True) Value	Assessed Value	Full Cash (True) Value	Assessed Value	Amount Due	Date Paid	Amount Due	Date Paid	Amount Due	Date Paid	Amount Due	Date Paid

82. Sample Method of Maintaining Tax Records

Illustration 82 is an example of how you might set up your tax records. By keeping the chart up to date, you can have all your tax information readily available.

USEFUL RESOURCES

The following is available for the specified cost from:

National Technical Information Service
U.S. Department of Commerce
5285 Port Royal Rd.
Springfield, VA 22161

Agriculture and the Property Tax—A Forward Look Based on a Historical Perspective PB 291812 $10.00

Farm Real Estate Taxes, 1979 PB 81-214876 $ 8.50

Farm Real Estate Taxes, 1981 PB 84-121987 $ 7.00

The following is available for the specified cost from:

National Association of Home Builders
15th and M Sts., N.W.
Washington, DC 20005

Tax Savings for Home Buyers $ .50

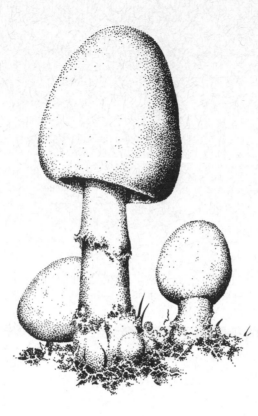

CHAPTER 18

Insuring Your Property for Yourself and Your Creditors

Even if you don't want to pay to have your property insured, you might not have a choice. Institutional lenders always require that insurance against loss by fire be taken out by the borrower to protect a mortgaged home. Most sellers who take back a mortgage or deed of trust will also want the house insured during the payment period. These creditors are concerned that if they don't require you to insure your house, and it burns down and you default on your payments, it will be difficult to collect the money you owe them even if they foreclose, since

the value of the property will have greatly decreased.

If your property is not being held as security, your decision on whether to get insurance will depend mainly on your philosophy and pocketbook. Throughout this book I have strongly advised that you do many things to protect yourself about buying land, and I also recommend that you be properly insured.

Shop around to find the kind of coverage you want at the lowest price. Insurance premiums for the same amount of coverage differ among companies by as much as 20 percent. Never buy insurance from a mail-order company or from someone who sells insurance as a sideline. Avoid taking out a policy through the real estate agent who handles your deal until you have compared the cost of his coverage with similar insurance that is available through other companies. Go to reputable insurance companies and individual insurance brokers, preferably in the area of your rural home. Ask around for recommendations. Compare types of coverage being offered and the cost of premiums being charged.

FIRE INSURANCE AND THE LENDER'S INSURANCE REQUIREMENTS

If your lender requires that you get insurance, the amount and type of coverage will be dictated by his demands. The standard condition in a loan agreement states that:

The Buyer agrees to keep all buildings now on, or that may hereafter be placed on, said property insured in the name of the Lender (or Seller) against loss by fire in an amount not less than the fair replacement value thereof, and in no event for less than _____ Dollars ($_____), the policies to be in a form and in a company or companies satisfactory to the Lender (or Seller). The Lender (or Seller) may require that the Buyer deposit said policies with him.

If you fail to get insurance according to the lender's condition or maintain the premium payments, most loan documents allow the lender to make the payments and then add the amount onto the total debt owed, making it subject to interest. Normally, however, the lender will start to foreclose on you for failing to abide by the mortgage conditions. Most creditors require only that the property be insured against loss by fire, although some might require extended coverage. A single policy covering both yourself and your creditor can often be obtained at no greater cost than if just one of you was named as the beneficiary. Both you and your creditor will keep copies of the policy.

If you are in a rural area where water is scarce and fire protection is not readily available, you should assume that in case of fire your house will suffer a total loss. Therefore, you would probably want to, and may be required to, insure it to its maximum value. When figuring its value, for instance, rather than use the price you paid for the house, you must determine the replacement value, or the amount that would be necessary to rebuild the house. When calculating the replacement value,

do not figure in the value of the land, since most policies will not cover land. You would normally increase the coverage over the years to keep up with inflation.

Insurance companies usually require that you get a minimum coverage of 80 percent of the replacement value of the house. The coverage can be extended upward for relatively little money above the minimum premium amount. Therefore, you should probably get the maximum coverage that you can afford up to 100 percent coverage for fire.

The coverage cost is usually based on a certain dollar-per-square-foot value based on local costs of construction. For example, if your house has 1,500 square feet and building costs in your area are $40 per square foot, it would cost $60,000 to rebuild your house, so that would be the amount of insurance coverage you would buy. Local insurance brokers have the current values for your area.

Insurance policies generally run for one year and then are renewed annually. The premium payment schedule can be arranged with the insurance agent, but the most common schedule is three annual payments. If the seller is financing your purchase, you will probably be responsible for paying the insurance premiums yourself, rather than paying through an impound fund, and your seller will order the insurance company to inform him if you do not make the required payments. If your loan is from a commercial lender, you will usually pay monthly *impounds* with your regular loan payments, which cover the cost of the insurance premiums. The lender will make the premium payments when they become due from the money you have prepaid in the impounds. (See chapter 23, "Buying Property That Is Encumbered by a Loan Agreement.")

Most policies include a *deductible* clause, which requires that in case of loss you must pay the deductible amount and the insurance company pays the rest up to the amount of the coverage. The deductible amount is usually a few hundred dollars. For example, when you have a $500-deductible clause, if your house sustains $800 worth of damages from a fire, you pay $500, and the insurer pays $300. Most policies reduce the deductible amount as the total coverage increases. Before taking out a policy, be sure you understand all the terms regarding deductible items and have the insurance agent explain anything you don't understand until it is completely clear. If the policy does not seem worth the price, go somewhere else.

If you suffer a partial loss of your home through a fire, the check issued for the loss is written in the name of you and your lender. Normally the lender would endorse the check over to pay for the repairs to the home. If the house is totally destroyed by fire, the lender can keep the entire loan proceeds up to the amount remaining due under your note, in which case he will reconvey the property to you free and clear or he can allow you to use the funds to rebuild your home and continue to use it as security for the mortgage or deed of trust.

EXTENDED COVERAGE

For a small additional cost you can get extended coverage, which protects you against losses caused by hailstorms, tornados, wind, erosion, riots, aircraft damage, vehicle damage, and smoke damage from cooking or heating units. Read the policy, because smoke damage from fireplaces may not be covered. A maximum amount to be paid for broken windows, such as $50, may be specified. If you want coverage for vandalism and malicious mischief or for earthquake damage, specify that it be included in your policy. An extended policy never covers loss or damage to personal property, only to the structures. Theft must be covered by a separate policy, which I discuss later.

THE "RISK OF LOSS" RULE AND PROPERTY INSURANCE

If you take possession of your future home after the contract of sale is signed but before escrow closes, your insurance should cover you from the time you take possession rather than the time title is transferred to you. Consider the following possibility:

A family is buying a house in the country and is very anxious to move in. The contract of sale is signed, and the deal looks as if it is going to go through to everybody's satisfaction. Two weeks before closing of escrow, the seller allows the buyer and his family to move into the house. A week before escrow closes, the house burns down in a fire of unknown origin while the buyer's family is away for the weekend. Does the buyer still have to complete the purchase? The seller does not want the property now that it is destroyed, and the buyer doesn't want to make payments for ten years on a pile of ashes. Most states have now adopted the standard Vendor and Purchaser Act, or Risk of Loss Rule, which places the loss on the party in possession before title is transferred. Thus, in this example, the buyer will be legally required to proceed with the deal. He did not get insurance covering him from the time he took possession, and the seller's insurance company is going to deny liability because its insured party, the seller, was not in possession of the property at the time the loss occurred.

If you are going to take over the seller's insurance policy, get him to place your name with the company as an insured beneficiary as of the date you are to take possession and get a certificate from the company stating you are insured, as well as a copy of the policy with your name as a coinsured. If the seller cannot put you on his policy, you must get your own.

If you are not going to take possession early, your policy should insure you as of the date of the closing of escrow, whether or not you move onto the property at that time. Once you receive title to the land, the responsibility for any loss will always fall on you because you are then the owner, unless the destruction is caused by the seller's actions after you take title. Prior to the close of escrow, you should have a binder in your hands guaranteeing you that you will be insured the moment escrow closes. You get this from the insurance agent who is selling you your insurance.

PERSONAL LIABILITY INSURANCE

Insurance covering injuries to other people while they are on your property is the most important type of coverage to have in the country, whether or not you have a house on the land. The possibilities for accidents are numerous. Someone's child could fall out of a tree, someone could slip in your creek or fall into your well, get bitten by your dog or kicked by your horse. When you invite someone onto your land, you are under a legal duty to exercise care to prevent injury to that person, and you could suffer great losses if a person were to sue you because of an injury suffered on your property.

Liability, or indemnity, insurance protects you up to the amount of coverage if legal action is taken against you for personal injury. The usual policy, costing several hundred dollars a year, can cover you for up to $300,000 for injuries to each person or $300,000 damages per incident or any other amount for which you purchase coverage. If you intend to invite many people to your land, you might want greater coverage, because $300,000 is not much when you see the kinds of awards juries sometimes give to seriously injured plaintiffs.

This type of policy does not cover injuries to yourself or your family. Those injuries are covered under your own medical insurance plan.

THEFT INSURANCE

If you are buying a country home you intend to occupy only part of the year, you might want theft insurance. The country, too, has burglaries, although they are not as prevalent as in the city. The type of coverage varies widely as does the maximum amount of coverage available.

A new program has been started by the federal government called the Federal Crime Insurance Program. The government provides crime insurance at a low rate in any state that does not have ready crime insurance available for homeowners. The insurance is sold through licensed insurance agents and brokers and through private insurance companies acting as servicing companies for the Federal Insurance Administration. Coverage includes loss from burglary, larceny, and robbery. A licensed insurance broker should be able to provide you with the current information on this program and the appropriate application forms. Your local office of Housing and Urban Development (HUD) will also have this information (see chapter 27 for addresses), or write to the Federal Insurance Administration, U.S. Department of Housing and Urban Development, Washington, D.C. 20410.

THE HOMEOWNERS INSURANCE POLICY

The most common type of policy today is the *standard* or *homeowners policy*, which combines the features of fire, personal liability, and theft insurance at a cheaper rate than they would cost if purchased individually. The policy covers the home, garage, and other structures on the land as well as personal property. The policy should state the type and the value of the property covered, the maximum amount that will be paid in case of loss, and the kinds of losses covered. Generally, damage to buildings other than the house and personal property outside the home will not be covered to their full replacement value. Find out what kind of proof you will have to provide as evidence of your loss. You should keep a list of all your personal property and its value in case of loss. I also advise having the inside and outside of your home videotaped in detail with the videotape stored off your property so you will have a visual record of your home and its contents in the event of a fire or theft loss.

The types of coverage and costs vary greatly throughout the insurance industry, so you will have to shop around for the best deal.

Most states now have Workers Compensation laws that require you to provide insurance coverage for persons working on your property for you, e.g., carpenters, gardeners, painters, and housesitters. If they are injured while engaged in employment for you, they are entitled to have their medical bills paid, to receive disability payments, and a sum of money for any permanent disability. If you are not insured, you can be sued, and your insurance may not cover you unless you specifically have Workers Compensation coverage. This is normally added to your standard homeowners policy for an additional premium. I advise getting this additional coverage if you intend to employ any persons to work on your property.

THE NATIONAL FLOOD INSURANCE PROGRAM

The standard insurance policies never cover structural damage due to floods or mud slides. Because of the great losses that occur annually, the federal government decided to offer federally subsidized flood insurance, through the private insurance industry, to homeowners in areas that have met land use and flood control requirements and have been approved for this type of subsidy by the U.S. Department of Housing and Urban Development.

Any local property and casualty insurance agent or broker should have information regarding the availability of flood insurance in your area, or write to the Federal Emergency Management Agency (FEMA), U.S. Department of Housing and Urban Development, Washington, D.C. 20410, or to the National Flood Insurance Program, Box 450, Lanham, Maryland 20706. Ask if your state is in the subsidy program and if so, where the nearest office is that offers such coverage.

MORTGAGE LIFE INSURANCE

This is a unique form of life insurance which provides that in the event of the death or disability of the head of a family, the insurance company will continue to make mortgage payments until the amount due is completely paid. The cost of the premium will depend on the age of the insured and the amount of the mortgage. Some lenders and sellers might require you to carry this type of insurance. Any reputable insurance broker can give you complete information.

ASSUMING THE SELLER'S INSURANCE POLICY

The seller may already have the property insured, and you might find it to your advantage simply to take over his policy. Ask him to show you a copy of his policy with the schedule of premium payments. Sometimes an insurance company will want to increase the premium rates for the person assuming an existing policy. Find out if they intend to do so in your case. Then investigate to see if

you can get a better deal elsewhere.

If you decide to assume the seller's insurance, you must agree to do so in writing. This is specified in Clause 8(b) of the Model Contract of Sale. (See chapter 28.) The policy does not transfer automatically with the sale of the property; the insurance company must consent in writing to your assuming it. The local insurance broker or escrow holder can handle the problems involved in transferring the policy to you.

Prorating the Prepaid Insurance Premium When You Assume a Policy

If you assume the seller's insurance policy, the premium will have to be prorated according to the time you are to take possession of or title to the property. The seller will probably have paid the premium in advance, so you will have to reimburse him for the amount of the premium that will cover your ownership of the property. Sometimes the insurance company will reimburse the seller for the amount, write a new policy for you, and have you pay them immediately.

The following example illustrates how such a proration is done. Assume that the seller has a one-year extended coverage fire insurance policy and that he paid a premium of $600 on July 1, 1988, covering the next year from July 1, 1988, to June 30, 1989. The policy will expire on June 30, 1989, but the buyer is to take title on May 1, 1989. We want to figure out how many days the seller will have used the insurance, and how many days the buyer will benefit from it. Dividing the premium of $600 by 12, we get the monthly rate of $50.

The seller was covered from July 1, 1988, to May 1, 1989, a period of ten months. Since the premium is $50 per month, he used $500 worth of insurance for the ten months. Thus $500 out of the $600 premium will have covered the seller. Since the buyer will be covered for the rest of the insuring period, he must reimburse the seller for the remaining amount of the premium covering the two months of May and June, 1989. Subtracting $500 from $600 leaves $100, which the buyer is to pay to the seller at the closing of escrow. (See chapter 30, "Opening and Closing of Escrow and the Role of the Escrow Holder.") This is the method of proration specified in Clause 8(b) of the Model Contract of Sale. (See chapter 28.)

USEFUL RESOURCES

The following are available free from:

U.S. Department of Housing and Urban Development
451 Seventh St., S.W., Rm. B-258
Washington, DC 20410

or HUD Regional Area Offices throughout the country listed in chapter 27.

Home Mortgage Insurance HUD-43-F
Programs for Home Mortgage Insurance HUD-97-F

The following pamphlet is available for 25 cents and a self-addressed stamped envelope from:

Council of Better Business Bureaus, Inc.
1515 Wilson Blvd.
Arlington, VA 22209-2450

Homeowners Insurance

IV

DECIDING ON A FAIR PRICE

CHAPTER 19

Evaluating the Price of the Property

All principles of appraisal ethics stem from the following central fact: The primary goal of a monetary appraisal is the determination of a numerical result which is *objective* and unrelated to the desires, wishes, or needs of the client who engages the appraiser to perform the work.
—American Society of Appraisers,
Statement of Ethics

When you find some land that is right for you, that meets all your requirements and feels like home, you will want to evaluate what that land is worth and compare your results with the seller's asking price. Then you can begin the bargaining game described in the next chapter.

To evaluate the price of the land you want to buy, regardless of where it is located, you can do a number of things without employing a professional appraiser. This chapter will tell you how to make your own appraisal of the property and how to hire a professional if you decide you need one. Finally, I explain how the seller establishes his asking price.

WHAT DETERMINES THE VALUE OF A PIECE OF PROPERTY?

Determining the value of a piece of land is a complex and ambiguous process. If there is any such thing as a formula for finding land value, it would have to be: Value is determined by the law of supply and demand. Although the supply of land is ultimately finite, its availability is constantly fluctuating as large ranches, farms, and other land parcels are split up for sale to the public.

In 1970 there were approximately 2,949,000 farms in the United States. By 1984, there were only 2,328,000. Although many of these, more than 600,000 farms, were absorbed by larger commercial farmers, known as "agrimonoliths," a large amount of acreage was subdivided and sold to the general public.

The U.S. Department of Commerce, Bureau of the Census, has released its study of land values for farmland from 1970 to 1985. The average value of land per acre for farmland and buildings in the U.S. (excluding Alaska and Hawaii) in 1970 was $196 per acre. The value rose quickly and steadily to a peak of $823 per acre in 1982, then gradually dropped to $679 per acre in 1985. In many parts of the country, the values are again rising.

The Bureau of the Census has taken a special survey to determine where the average person prefers to have his primary residence. The results are shown below:

Where do you

Residential Location and Preferences

	Where do you live now? (percent)	Where would you prefer to live? (percent)
Open Country	12	34
Small Town or City	33	30
Medium-sized City or Suburb	28	22
Larger City or Suburb	27	14
Total	100	100

Sixty-four percent of the people questioned expressed a desire to live in a nonurban setting. Only 45 percent of the interviewees now live in this type of area. If you combine the 19 percent who wish to make a permanent move away from the cities and suburbs with the increasing number of second-home land buyers, it is clear that there is a tremendous demand for rural and semirural property.

All indications are that the rate of interested land buyers will continue to increase at a faster rate than land will become available and prices will continue to rise at varying rates in all parts of the country.

A LIST OF VALUE FACTORS

Many elements must be considered in deciding whether the price of a piece of property is "worth it." A general list of the basic factors includes the following:

—Supply.

—Demand.

—Usability, e.g., level land is more valuable.

—State of the title, e.g., what *clouds,* or defects, exist?

—Location, e.g., neighbors, schools, shopping, public transportation, church, recreational facilities.

—Directional growth of the area, e.g., industrial, commercial, recreational, or residential.

—Population and economic growth in the area.

—Aesthetics, e.g., nice view, landscaping, beautiful house.

—Road frontage.

—Accessibility to the property, e.g., condition of the roads.

—Water: quality and quantity.

—Soil and drainage, e.g., for agricultural and building purposes.

—Orchards and gardens, e.g., have they been well cared for?

—Amount of timber and type of vegetation.

—Availability of utilities.

—Zoning and building codes.

—Public health measures and regulations.

—Condition and age of the house and other structures.

—Size of the parcel, e.g., the larger the parcel, the smaller the price per acre.

—Any stigma attached to the property.

—Personal property included in the sale.

—Climate.

—Exposure to the land, e.g., north slope versus south slope.

—Timing of the sale, e.g., the owner must sell quickly because he is being transferred to a different location in his job.

Each of these elements has its own effect on the value of a parcel of land. For example, the closer property is to a populated area, the more desirable and expensive it will be. If it is close to employment, if it is accessible by a paved road, if utilities are supplied, if a house and other improvements are on the land, it will be more expensive than land without these features.

Potential Use

One of the main determinants of value is the land's potential for development, meaning that it is valuable not for its own qualities, but as a possible site for future activities of a profitable nature. Thus, if large numbers of people are moving into the area and the land is level or nearly so, more intensive use of the land may be expected, and this potential increases the value of the land considerably. This is because level land can be subdivided into more usable parcels than steep land. The real estate agent may play up the land's suitability for subdivision to lure you with the thought of future profits, and thus make the present asking price seem more reasonable. If large timber is standing on the land, the price will be higher because you can cut and sell the trees. It is irrelevant whether you actually want to do so. The fact is that the potential is there.

When you evaluate the land, look at the potential uses for it and how soon the property will be in demand for such uses. How close is the nearest subdivision, and how well is it selling? Are any large industries planned nearby that might foretell a growing population? These things indicate the extent of the land's potential in determining the price.

HOW THE TAX ASSESSOR EVALUATES THE LAND AND ITS IMPROVEMENTS

A good place to start when determining the value of the land and its improvements is by checking the county tax assessor's records for the appraised market value. (The appraisal of land for tax purposes is discussed in chapter 17, "Property Taxes and Assessments.") First you must know how current the appraisal is. Talk to a tax assessor to see how recently he has been to your area. Usually several assessors work in the office, and you can ask to talk to the one who appraised the seller's land. He will tell you what he thinks it is worth,

which is usually somewhat more than he appraises it for taxes. You can tell him what the seller's asking price is and get his opinion of it.

You can also ask his opinion of any improvements on the land, their condition and value, independent of the land itself. He will take into consideration factors of depreciation and appreciation.

The assessor will be familiar with prices of surrounding land, and he can tell you what kind of prices land has been going for in your area. He will also know about developments being planned in the area and their possible effect on land values. This information is used in the most important and common of all appraisal techniques used by tax assessors and land appraisers, the comparison test.

The Comparison Test

A parcel of land is compared to other parcels in the area that have recently been sold to determine its current value on the market, often called the *fair market value*. You must find out the purchase prices of two or three separate pieces of land nearby that have been sold recently and that are similar in size and major features to the land you are interested in. For instance, if you are looking at land along a creek, try to find out the price of the creek land above and below your prospective place.

Since each parcel of land is unique, you must be careful in comparing prices. Any improvements and other features, such as buildings, orchards, ponds, and equipment, will raise the value of the property, so take these things into consideration. Two pieces of land that are basically similar except for the fact that one has a house on it and the other doesn't may be difficult to compare because of the added value of the house.

Where tax stamps are required on deeds, they can be used to find the purchase price of a piece of land. Prior to January 1, 1968, federal law required the placing of Internal Revenue Documentary Tax Stamps on every deed used to transfer property. Although there is no longer a federal land sale tax, many states have enforced their own tax stamp, or real property transfer tax, laws. If your state imposes a transfer tax, you can find out how the tax is computed from the county recorder and look up the deed of any land parcel to find out the purchase price from either the stamps affixed to it or the stated amount of taxes that were paid. (See chapter 33, "Deeds and Recording.") For example, under the old federal tax, $.55 worth of tax stamps were required for every $500 or fraction thereof of the purchase price. Thus property that sold for $49,850 would have $53.90 worth of documentary stamps on the deed. To figure out the sale price from the stamps, divide the amount of the stamps by $.55, then multiply that quotient by $500. The basic procedure can be used to determine the selling price whenever taxes are required.

After looking at recent selling prices of comparable land, you will be able to price the land currently for sale. The more land you look at, the better idea you will have as to whether the land you like is priced high or low for the area. Ask other real estate agents who show you land if they are familiar with the land you are interested in. Tell them what the asking price is to see their reaction. Of course, you should not rely on their appraisal, but it will be interesting to hear what they say about it. When you compare the asking price of other land for sale, remember that asking prices are almost always inflated.

As you compare the price of similar parcels to the land you are interested in, try to determine if there is justification for any difference in price. If a large discrepancy exists with no justification that you can see, keep it in mind to bring up during the bargaining and negotiations with the seller when you are pointing out why the price is too high.

If the seller bought the land within the past few years, try to find out the price he paid for it. You can simply ask him, although he may be reluctant to tell you, especially if he is making a large profit. You can look up his deed and determine the purchase price by the amount of transfer taxes paid or the number of tax stamps if they are required. Also compare the tax assessor's appraised value of his land the year before he bought the property with its appraised value after he took title. The increased amount reflects the amount he paid for it.

You should ask everyone familiar with the property his or her opinion of the reasonableness of the asking price. This includes the building inspector, tax assessor, other real estate agents, people living in the area, and the farm advisor.

HIRING A PROFESSIONAL APPRAISER

A professional appraiser does not have access to

any information you cannot get to, but experience is on his or her side. The appraiser who works in one section of the country for many years should be thoroughly familiar with property values in the area and how they are set. But if you do a thorough job of comparing land prices and getting the opinions of people who have been in the area a long time, I believe you can efficiently appraise the value of the land yourself. Even professional appraisals vary.

Unfortunately real estate appraisers are not usually regulated by any state laws, so you must be careful whom you select. Anybody can call himself an appraiser, and in fact, most real estate agents will do an appraisal if asked, usually for about $75 to $300. However, appraisers belonging to one or several national organizations are supposed to abide by a code of ethics and pass some accreditation standards. If you look in the local telephone book under Appraisers, those with memberships in a professional organization will be so designated. The group that seems to be preferred by professional lenders is the American Institute of Real Estate Appraisers (AIREA), sometimes identified as MAI which means Member, Appraisal Institute or RM which means Residential Member. Other groups include the Society of Real Estate Appraisers (SREA), the American Association of Certified Appraisers, Inc. (AACA), the American Society of Appraisers (ASA), and the American Society of Farm Managers and Rural Appraisers, Inc. (AFM–ARA). In Useful Resources at the end of this chapter you will find the addresses of these organizations. If you write them, they will send you a list of where their appraisers are located. Always use a registered appraiser if at all possible.

Appraisal fees are usually based on the amount of time needed to complete the job, and that depends on how thoroughly a job must be done. Undeveloped land will not take as long to evaluate as land that has a house on it. Costs vary throughout the country, but the minimum is usually around $75. A good report includes an evaluation of the house and other structures, the availability of utilities and other services, the value of the location, the potential for resale at a profit, present zoning and possible future rezoning, recorded restrictions, the expected economic and population growth in the community, and comparison figures on other similar sales in the area. The result of this research will be a figure that is the appraised fair market value of the property in question.

Never use the real estate broker who is selling the land as your appraiser, because his or her commission depends on how much money the property sells for. You must also be careful that the appraiser you hire does not have a personal friendship with the broker handling the deal, which might sway the evaluation.

If you are a veteran, you can apply for a loan, and the Veterans Administration will appraise the property for a small fee as part of the loan. You must fill out a form called Request for Determination of Reasonable Value. You do not have to go through with the loan, but you will know, if it is approved, whether the asking price is reasonable. The Veterans Administration should also tell you what their appraisal is. (See chapter 26, "HUD/FHA- and VA-Insured Loans.")

You can also apply for a regular commercial or FHA loan to get an inexpensive appraisal, but they generally do not tell you the results of the appraisal. They will tell you only whether they accept or reject the application for the loan.

The seller might have had a professional appraisal done. If he presents you with an appraisal that equals his asking price, go to the appraiser yourself, talk to him, and try to get a sense of how honest he is.

HOW THE SELLER SETS HIS ASKING PRICE

The seller usually arrives at his asking price by combining four factors: (1) the value of the property and the improvements; (2) the costs of selling the land; (3) the bargaining margin and the profit; (4) the psychology of numbers.

The Value of the Property and the Improvements

The seller may determine the value of the property and improvements by using the same methods as those explained above. However, he naturally will tend to estimate the value higher than you, the buyer, because of his sentimental attachment to the property. He will tend to emphasize appreciation due to a greater demand to live in the area or to improvements made on the land, and overlook depreciation due to physical deterioration of the land

and improvements, the obsolescence of structures because of stylistic trends and technological advances, or the decline in the demand to live in the area. The seller usually considers the price he paid for the land and adds on whatever he spent to get its actual value. But it is possible he paid too much, especially if he bought in the early 1980s, so don't assume you automatically have to pay him at least whatever he paid. As land values decrease after the inflationary period of the late 70s and early 80s, some people are selling at a loss in various parts of the country.

The Costs of Selling the Land

Once the seller determines what he believes the actual value of the property to be, he will add on the costs involved in selling the land. These could include the real estate agent's commission; attorney's fees; escrow charges; taxes; and survey, appraisal, and title insurance costs. By figuring them into the asking price, the seller passes these costs onto the buyer. This is standard procedure, and brokers generally advise sellers to set their prices in this manner.

The Bargaining Margin and the Profit

The seller then adds on a bargaining and profit margin figure, usually anywhere from 10 to 50 percent of the property's value as he sees it. Part of the purpose of this additional figure is to give the seller room to negotiate with the buyer. When the buyer offers a low figure the seller can "compromise" by coming down in his asking price and still realize a profit. He might allow the buyer to talk him down in price several times, giving the buyer the illusion that he is getting a "steal." If the seller finances the purchase himself, he will realize an additional profit in the interest over the years, so he might reduce his initial profit margin by quite a bit. (See chapter 22, "Terms of the Loan Agreement and Their Effect on the Total Price.") You will see how this works in the negotiations in chapter 20, "Bargaining to Get the Seller's Asking Price Down."

The real estate agent often plays an important role in setting the price because sellers rely on his appraisal and judgment. One practice is for the agent to set the price high in order to convince the seller to give him an exclusive listing. He makes a few attempts to sell the property, then tells the seller the market is bad and he should lower the price. The seller almost invariably follows the agent's advice. Then the agent tries to get a quick sale and commission. He will lower the price according to how desperately he needs a sale. Competition is sometimes so cutthroat in the rural real estate business that some agents would rather sell the property and take a small commission than risk losing the seller to another agent when his contract expires. You might come along at just the right time.

A real estate agent is usually torn between trying to get as high a price as possible for land, since his commission is based on a percentage of the sale price, and making a sale. This often means trying to convince a seller to accept a lower offer than he would like, so the broker can make a sale and a commission before he loses the listing to another broker.

The Psychology of Numbers

Often a seller, or agent, will use a figure that seems much lower than it actually is. For example, instead of setting the price at $47,000, he will ask for $46,950. This is an old device that was first used by J. C. Penney and is now widely employed as a sales technique. The psychology of the odd price gives the buyer the feeling that he is getting a bargain and that the price has been cut as far as possible.

THE APPRAISAL AS A SAFETY VALVE IN THE CONTRACT OF SALE

A common safety valve put in buyers' contracts by attorneys is the condition that the purchase may be terminated if the buyer has the property appraised and he is dissatisfied with the results. Clause 17(b) in the Model Contract of Sale in chapter 28 allows this type of condition to be inserted. You should always write in the parenthetical part that you are having an appraisal conducted on the property. You can use anyone you want as an appraiser. If you obtain an appraisal and you decide sometime after the seller has signed the contract and made it binding that you want out of the deal, all you have to do is write the seller a letter saying you do not approve the results of the appraisal you had done if it is lower than the price you agreed upon.

USEFUL RESOURCES

You can get appraisal information and a directory of appraisers throughout the United States from each of the following professional appraiser organizations:

Society of Real Estate Appraisers (SREA)
645 N. Michigan Ave.
Chicago, IL 60611

American Institute of Real Estate Appraisers (AIREA)
430 N. Michigan Ave.
Chicago, IL 60611-4088

American Society of Appraisers (ASA)
P.O. Box 17265
Washington, DC 20041

American Association of Certified Appraisers, Inc. (AACA)
Seven Eswin Dr.
Cincinnati, OH 45218

In addition to the pamphlets that you will receive when writing for appraisal information, the following brochures are available free from the professional appraisers organizations.

From the AIREA listed above ask for:

Guide to Real Estate Services
Estimating Home Value
Planning Home Improvements
Analyzing Rehab Potential
Statement of Purpose
Understanding the Appraisal
Membership Qualifications
Selecting the Residential Appraiser
The Appraisal Institute—Organization & Services
Directory of Members

The following are available free with a stamped, self-addressed business envelope from the ASA listed above:

Appraisal Publications
Information on the Appraisal Profession
About the American Society of Appraisers
Directory of Certified Professional Personal Property Appraisers

282

Directory of Certified Business Appraisers
ASA Principles of Appraisal Practice Code
of Ethics
Career Opportunities in Appraising
The Public and Appraisers

The following items are available for the specified price from the ASA listed above:

Market Approach to Basic Rural Appraisal
    Valutape No. 32 Audiocassette $ 5.00
Ad Valorem Taxes and Real Property
    Valutape No. 46 Audiocassette $ 5.00

Guides for professional property appraisers are available for the specified price from:
    AIREA Book Sales
    c/o Gateway Distributing
    940 N. Shore Dr., Dept. 6-LI-8
    Lake Bluff, IL 60044

The Appraisal of Rural Property
    ISBN 0-911780-66-1 $28.50
The Appraisal of Timberland
    ISBN 0-911780-81-5 $ 6.00
Rural Property in Transition: Nonagricultural Uses
    ISBN 0-911780-82-3 $ 6.00

The following is available for the specified price from:
    National Technical Information Service
    U.S. Department of Commerce
    5285 Port Royal Rd.
    Springfield, VA 22161

Effects of Small Watershed Developments
    on Land Values PB 282547 $ 8.50

The following is available free from:
    U.S. Department of Housing and Urban
    Development
    451 Seventh St., S.W., Rm. B-258
    Washington, DC 20410

Questions and Answers on FHA Home Property
    Appraisals HUD 38-H

The following is available for the specified price from:
    Publications Department, 86
    World Wildlife Fund/The Conservation
    Foundation
    1255 Twenty-third St., N.W.
    Washington, DC 20037

The Market for Rural Land: Trends,
    Issues, Policies $12.50

CHAPTER 20

Bargaining to Get the Seller's Asking Price Down

THE RULES OF THE GAME AND ORDER OF THE MOVES

The game of bargaining is an ancient one, and the rules and moves are well established. Because each piece of land is unique, uniform prices cannot be set, and bargaining has survived as the most common means of buying and selling land. The seller usually sets his price higher than he hopes to re-ceive because he expects to bargain. Naturally, you and the seller will each be acting in your individual self-interest. Your job is to lower the price so that it is fair to you, which means keeping the seller's profit as low as possible. Don't worry about a seller losing money on the deal. It rarely happens.

I have outlined in the previous chapter, "Evaluating the Price of the Property," how the seller determines his asking price and how you can appraise the land to see if that price is fair. Usually it will be higher than you want to pay, and you will want to negotiate the price down. Bargaining is a game of endurance and coolness. I have isolated seven factors that influence all negotiations and affect the nature of your bargaining and the final purchase price. They are (1) the willingness of both parties to play the game, (2) the seller's anxiety to sell the property and your anxiety to find a home, (3) the length of time the property has been up for sale, (4) the current market for the property, (5) your ability to point out deficiencies of the property versus the seller's ability to point out its desirable features, (6) your ability to come up with more cash and the seller's desire to take more than he originally asked for, and (7) your ability to know when you are getting a fair deal.

The Willingness of Both Parties to Play the Game

The game is bargaining. If you and the seller are going to play, you must both be willing to make compromises. Unless you and the seller are willing to change your positions, the game cannot be played.

The seller usually sets his asking price higher than he expects to get for the specific purpose of establishing a position from which to bargain. His expectation of bargaining is implicit in the words *asking price*. In other words, he intends to play the game, and he will be very surprised if you don't play along by making a low offer in return. You will then bargain back and forth until either a stalemate or a common agreement is reached.

Unfortunately, every seller is not a game player. There are occasions when a seller sets his price with no intention of bringing it down regardless of the circumstances. He intends to sit and wait until he gets a buyer at his price, even if it takes four or five years. I have known such people, but there are not many. You should assume, until you have found out otherwise, that the seller will come down in his price and that you will have to come up from your original offer. In other words, be prepared to play the game.

Needless to say, the real estate agent will play his part in the game. He has a vested interest in the results: his commission is based on the final selling price, but he doesn't get his commission until the property is sold. This places him in a curious position. Although he will favor the seller because he works for him, he will attempt to get the seller and you to compromise your positions so that the property gets sold and he receives his commission. The average rural town agent dislikes a stubborn seller as much as an unwilling buyer. The longer he has to spend showing the property and dealing with buyers, the less monetary return he will get for his time. So he will be right there in the middle pushing you and the seller, trying to get you to sign a contract. This is the essence of the bargaining game.

The Seller's Anxiety to Sell the Property and Your Anxiety to Find a Home

This factor is closely related to the previous one. The less anxious a seller is to get rid of his property, the less bargaining and compromising he will do. He may be holding the land as an investment and can afford to wait until he can "make a killing." All he has to do is make the payments, pay the annual taxes, and wait as long as necessary to get a buyer at his nonnegotiable price. You cannot negotiate with this type of landowner, and the real estate agent won't try very hard to sell his property.

However, if the owner does not live on the land and he is obviously an investor, this does not necessarily mean that he is not anxious to come down in his price. You do not know what the situation is. He might have to sell because he needs fast money for an emergency or new investment, or land values in the area might not be increasing as fast as he thought they would.

An owner who is presently living on the land, or has recently moved from it, will usually want to sell as soon as possible. He may have a job waiting for him in another area, his family may have outgrown the house, he may not be able to make payments or keep up with the taxes, or he may be involved in a bankruptcy or divorce. Sometimes land is sold at very reasonable prices when an owner dies and his beneficiaries want to sell as fast as possible in order to settle the estate. The greater the pressures on the seller to sell, the better the circumstances are for getting the price down.

It may be difficult for you to determine the seller's anxiety. One of the first things you should do is ask the owner or the real estate agent why the land is for sale. You may not get an honest answer if the truth might dissuade you from buying the land or encourage you to drive a hard bargain. You should verify what you are told by speaking to surrounding landowners and other real estate agents in the area. Often local agents know the facts about a piece of property even if it is not listed with them. If you can discover the seller's situation, you may feel more confident when bargaining with him.

You should be conscious, too, of the fact that your own urgency can work to the seller's advantage. "Buyer's fever" has caused many to buy land at inflated prices simply because they were tired of looking for a place. Often a real estate agent can scare people into believing that a land boom is on, that property is going fast, and that prices are soaring. This is his job. If he can convince you that the land won't be there tomorrow and thus increase your anxiety to buy, you will not be very hard-nosed when it comes to bargaining. Notice as you look at land how many times you hear a phrase like "Someone else might beat you to the bargain if you delay." The real estate agent attempts to play on your insecurity in order to soften you up.

If you are unusually itchy to buy land because you have been looking for a long time, or you need to get settled quickly, do not fail to exercise your full bargaining power anyway. Be cool. Don't let on how long you have been looking and how tired and anxious you are to find a home. The seller may be willing to go much lower than you realize. You will always be in a more secure position than he is because you can usually look at a lot of land for as long as you want until you find what you like, but he has to patiently wait and hope that he gets a purchaser at his price.

If the agent and seller know that you are anxious to move out of the city or get a second home as soon as possible, they will plan their sales pitch with that in mind. For the sake of bettering your bargaining position, therefore, you should assume that any landowner who puts his property up for sale is anxious to sell, and you should never reveal your own desperation to buy.

The Length of Time the Property Has Been Up for Sale

The longer a parcel of land has been on the market, the more realistic the seller tends to become in his demands. The seller is at a disadvantage when his property does not sell for a long time because he knows that prospective buyers will wonder if something is wrong with it. It is natural to assume that if property is worth the price, it will sell reasonably quickly. If it stays on the market for an excessive amount of time, the assumption is that it's overpriced or seriously deficient.

Ask the real estate agent how long the property has been for sale, not just how long he personally has listed it. Ask if the price has been reduced since it was first put on the market and if so, how

many times and by what amounts. This is another time when you should verify the answers you get with other agents and neighboring landowners.

If the property has just been placed on the market, you will not have the bargaining advantage of time on your side. However, if the land has been listed for a long time, try to find out why it hasn't sold. It is possible that the market for such land, especially if it is very rugged, is very small. Point out the fact that something must be wrong if the land hasn't brought any acceptable offers in such a long time. Tell the seller, or agent, you are willing to pay a fair price and then make your offer. If the agent is anxious to get the owner to sell, your arguments and persistence might get him to increase his pressure on the seller to lower his demands.

I have watched the attitudes of property owners trying to sell their property over a long period of time. They always start out with tremendous demands and a great amount of optimism that they will get a buyer at their price. The longer their property stays on the market, the more nervous and malleable they become. For example, I know of 40 acres that was put up for sale at $80,000. In the first year, six offers were made in the range of $35,000 to $40,000. Then six months went by with no offers. The seller and agent began to get pessimistic and decided they would take the next reasonable offer. They did, and the land sold for $45,000. The owner and agent were glad to get rid of it after two years of trying, even at that price.

The Current Market for the Property

Since the beginning of the 1900s, the demographic trend has been for most people to move from country farms to the city, although there have been a few back-to-the-land movements during this time. The last one was in the late forties. The present land rush started in the late sixties and is still going on. Conditions in the cities and suburbs are getting worse, and the emigration to more rural areas increases annually. In addition, the idea of a second home is increasingly more inviting to the urban resident who finds himself with more leisure time.

When looking at different areas you would like to live in, remember that the more people there are moving into an area, the higher the prices will be due to the old rule of supply and demand. You may feel more comfortable in an area where there

Do you know that even the little woman who waxes my legs has 200 acres somewhere?

are other people like yourself who are moving away from the city to begin a new life in the country or are discovering the pleasures of owning a vacation home. In those places, your bargaining powers will be diminished because buyer competition will be high. However, if you venture into those parts of the country that have not yet become popular (and there are many), the market will be very small, and prices will be lower and negotiable. As land buying spreads to new areas, the buyers in the first rush always get the best deals. They buy when competition is low, before the demand for land increases. We bought our land just before our area

started to attract a steady stream of homesteaders. Land selling for $200 an acre when we bought is now going for five to ten times that much, and may be even more expensive by the time you read this book.

Regardless of the area, if you are looking for extremely isolated and undeveloped land, the demand will always remain small. There are still very few people willing to build their own houses, live without electricity, develop their own water systems, haul their own garbage, and live many miles from the nearest towns. Such areas will have the cheapest land and a relatively small market of purchasers. Undeveloped backwoods land for sale is usually a buyer's market.

However, you can find land with more conveniences that is not yet affected by the inflated prices of a large market if you avoid obviously popular and publicized areas. Some of the nicest areas of the country have not yet been touched by the second-home boom, and if you shop wisely you may find an undiscovered area that suits you.

Your Ability to Point Out Deficiencies of the Property vs. the Seller's Ability to Point Out Its Desirable Features

As a prospective purchaser, you are on the offensive in the bargaining game. This is a strong tactical advantage when you begin to point out the deficiencies of the property. If you have read the first part of this book, you should be an expert at this. Every piece of property has some deficiencies—your job is to find and use them to get the price down when you bargain with the seller. Certain defects will be much costlier than others, and these major items are the ones you should emphasize.

For instance, when downgrading a house your first comments should be directed at structural weaknesses, such as a cracked foundation, dry rot, termites, a leaky roof or basement, poor plumbing, old wiring, and faulty electricity. Emphasize the serious and expensive items first. Then bring in the smaller items like broken windows, cracked tile, peeling paint, and torn screens.

While you point out the bad points, the seller will counter with such desirable features as a beautiful fireplace, the isolation of the house, the gardens, the redwood shake exterior, and other things that are plus factors to most people. If any of these factors is not a positive feature to you, let the seller know it. Since the real estate agent represents the seller, he will probably raise a vigorous defense to your criticisms.

Your complaints do not have to deal solely with the structures or land features. You can point out that the land is in a poor location or that there are no utilities available or anything else you can think of. If you can afford to get a complete house inspection and land appraisal, you can use these professional analyses in your bargaining, but you have enough information from reading this book to do these things yourself. Take notes on what you learn, and get estimates of what it will cost

you to correct existing defects in the property. At least try to decrease the asking price by the estimated amount needed to repair the major defects in the property. In the seller's defense, the real estate agent will tell you that all the deficiencies were taken into account when the asking price was set. You should then ask him to break down the asking price to indicate just how these deficiencies were figured into it. How do his figures compare to yours? What are his estimates to correct the existing structures and other defects of the property? He might have an appraisal and inspection for the property. This appraisal will probably be different from yours, or he wouldn't show it to you. Read it carefully to find out when it was conducted and what items are covered. Was the appraiser a member of a professional organization? Even if the seller's appraisal concludes the property is worth more than your own appraisal does, yours is just as valid as his and you should continue to press its results, assuming they are in your favor. If the seller's inspection report has underestimated the defects, say so. Use your evidence for all it's worth when bargaining. Don't worry about being repetitive. Let the seller know you are a careful buyer.

There might also be clouds, or defects, on the title, such as a reservation of an easement across the property or a reservation of a right to take minerals or water. The structure might not have been properly approved by the building inspector or there might be a restrictive covenant in the deed that diminishes the future uses of the property.

If you can't find any deficiencies in the land, the improvements, the location, or the title, you haven't looked hard enough.

Your Ability to Come Up with More Cash, and the Seller's Desire to Take More than He Originally Asks

After you have made several offers and have brought the price down as far as possible, there is a final move left that you can make. You can offer a larger down payment or full cash in exchange for a lower price.

When a seller finances the sale, he generally asks for a cash down payment with monthly payments to continue until the principal and interest are paid. The requested down payment is usually 10 to 33⅓ percent of the total asking price. However, the seller is often grateful to get more immediate cash than he asks for, even if it means he will get less money in the long run. If you think this doesn't seem likely, listen to our case.

When we were bargaining for our land, I got the seller down to what he claimed was his rock-bottom price. Then I asked him how much of a discount he would give us if we paid the entire purchase price immediately in cash. He offered to reduce the price by an additional 30 percent. We got a loan, at the same interest rate as our mortgage to the seller would have been, and paid cash. Thus, not only did we reduce the price by 30 percent, but we reduced the total amount of interest we would have to pay because the amount of the principal was cut.

If you have to borrow the money at a higher interest rate, you will have to figure out if you are actually saving by paying cash. Here are two simple illustrations of how this works:

Suppose the asking price of a parcel of land is $40,000 with a $10,000 down payment and monthly installments at the rate of 9 percent on the remaining $30,000. You already have $10,000, and you can borrow another $20,000 at 12 percent interest from the bank. The seller offers to cut his price down to $30,000 if you give him the entire amount in cash. If you accept this offer, you will pay 12 percent interest on the remaining $20,000 owed the bank. The question is whether this is cheaper than paying 9 percent on $30,000. Figuring the interest for the first year you get:

9 percent interest $\times$ $30,000 = $2,700

whereas

12 percent interest $\times$ $20,000 = $2,400

The $2,400 interest is less at 12 percent than the $2,700 interest at 9 percent because the total price is less, so you should take the offer for $30,000 and finance it through the bank.

Now look at this example. The asking price for some land is again $40,000 with a down payment of $10,000 and monthly installments at the rate of 9 percent on the remaining $30,000. You again offer to give the seller a total price of $30,000 cash since you can borrow $20,000 at 12 percent interest from the bank. The seller offers to cut his selling price by only $5,000, making it $35,000. You will

have to give the seller a second mortgage for $5,000 at 9 percent in addition to the first mortgage to the bank at 12 percent. Figuring the first year's interest, you get:

9 percent interest $\times$ $30,000 = $2,700

whereas

12 percent interest $\times$ $20,000 = $2,400
plus 9 percent interest $\times$ $5,000 = $450

so that

$2,400 + $450 = $2,850 is $150 more
than $2,700

Although this time the interest is higher by $150 the first year, there will be a smaller difference in succeeding years. In fact if you pay off the loan over ten years, you will actually pay about $3,000 less by taking out a loan from the bank because your purchase price has been cut by $5,000. You can figure this out by using the table in chapter 22 to figure out the monthly payments assuming a ten-year payoff period. Using the table to amortize a $1,000 loan, locate the factor in the column under 9 percent and in the row for 10 years. This factor is 12.6676. Multiply this number by 30 since the loan is for $30,000 not $1,000. Monthly payments for 9 percent on $30,000 are approximately $380.10. Do the same thing for 12 percent on $20,000 and 9 percent on $5,000. The monthly payments for 12 percent on $20,000 are $287 plus the monthly payments for 9 percent on $5,000 are $63.35; these total $350.35. Multiplying 12 payments per year times 10 years equals 120 payments. $380.10 $\times$ 120 payments = $45,612. $350.35 $\times$ 120 payments = $42,042. You should do this type of analysis on your own deal if you are in a position of being able to make a higher down payment than is asked for.

The seller will have a down payment established as part of the purchase price when he places the land on the market, and you should just tell him that you think you will be able to meet it if you decide to buy the land. Never reveal to the seller that you have a larger amount of cash available until the last minute, because you want to get his price as low as possible by the other methods before offering him your final enticement.

Sometimes this strategy might not get you anywhere because there are landowners who don't want a larger down payment or full cash for their land because of their tax situation or because they prefer to make more money in the long run by the accrual of interest. But usually when the possibility of more cash is presented to the seller, he will make adjustments in his price to get it.

Your Ability to Know When You Are Getting a Fair Deal

This is the most subtle part of effective bargaining. You must realize when you have pushed the price down as far as it is going to go. The buyer who continues haggling beyond the point where a fair deal has been reached often loses the property because another buyer comes along and makes a better offer which the seller accepts. Don't be greedy. The price is right when the seller stands to make a little money and you get a good piece of land at a reasonable sum. You will make your profit when you decide to sell. This is not to say that the seller always makes a profit, but he usually does, and you should approach the negotiations with that in mind. Bargain strongly on your own behalf but also be willing to compromise. Temper your self-interest just when the price is right and you can't go wrong. Don't hesitate to finalize the deal if you feel you have bargained wisely and you are getting a good deal.

Now that you understand the interacting elements, or "rules," affecting the bargaining process, you are ready to begin making "moves," which consist of offers, rejections, counteroffers, and finally acceptance.

YOUR FIRST MOVE—YOUR OFFER

First, you should decide if you can afford to purchase the property you are looking at. A common formula states that a family should not buy a home that exceeds more than two times their annual family income. Another approach is that a homeowner usually should not pay more than 38 percent of income after federal tax for monthly housing expenses (payment on the mortgage loan plus average cost of heat, utilities, repair, and maintenance).

You should also have the cash necessary to meet the down payment and closing costs, such as title insurance, tax prorations, and escrow fees. Once you have determined that the property you want is within your affordability, you are ready to start bargaining.

Your first move in the bargaining process is your offer to the seller to buy his property. Your offer should be made in a contract of sale that states all the terms you want and the price you are offering to pay. If you are dealing through a real estate agent, he must relay your offer to the owner. Just as the asking price is set high to give the seller room to bargain, your offer should be much lower than you expect to pay. You can always go up when the seller rejects your offer, but if you start high and your offer is accepted, it is too late then to bargain for a lower price. You never know how badly the seller wants to dispose of his property. Disregard any statements by the agent that the seller does not intend to reduce his price.

How low should your first offer be? In my experience the best way for you to begin bargaining is to offer somewhere between 50 to 80 percent of the asking price. Don't offer more than 80 percent initially unless you know for sure that the asking price is fair already and that the property may be sold immediately. You might think this is ridiculous and will offend the seller. The agent may imply that you are crazy and attempt to dissuade you from "wasting everybody's time." But do not give in. Tell him you have looked at a lot of land and feel your offer is a reasonable one.

The agent has a fiduciary duty to relay your offer to the seller. The worst thing that can happen is that the seller will reject your offer. Since you already expect him to do so, you should not feel embarrassed. It is all part of the game. If you suspect that the broker hasn't relayed your offer, ask him for a written rejection from the seller.

Because you start low you will have ample room to come up in later offers, giving the impression that the seller is forcing you higher. Being in this position gives you a psychological edge over the seller, particularly in the later stages of the negotiations.

Never tell the broker how high you will go. If you offer $50,000 against a $70,000 asking price, but tell the broker you will be willing to raise your offer to $60,000 if the seller doesn't accept the first offer, you can be sure the seller will find this out and know your $50,000 offer is meaningless. Always remember the broker works for the seller because he is paid by the seller and he has a legal duty to disclose all information to the seller. He cannot keep information you tell him confidentially from the seller. It is hard to be discreet with the broker because often you will develop a friendly relationship with him or her as the broker spends some time with you showing various properties.

But, as hard as it is, never discuss your personal financial arrangements in front of the broker. Don't show any positive emotion when looking at properties and try to remain passive, nonchalant, and noncommittal. Never let on that underneath your cool exterior you are burning up with buyer's fever.

THE SELLER'S REJECTION, COUNTEROFFER, OR FINAL ACCEPTANCE

The seller will respond to your offer in one of three ways. First, he might accept it, and then you can move to close the deal. However, this is unlikely. Second, he might simply reject it and say it is not enough money and that he cannot afford to let the property go at your price and that you're too far apart to even negotiate. Or third, he might start bargaining by rejecting your offer and making a counteroffer. His counteroffer will either be a new price lower than his original one, or it will be some added or deleted terms in the contract of sale. This is the usual response, and it means that he is willing to bargain with you. He might split the difference with you and go to the halfway point, but usually he will reduce his price only by 5 or 10 percent. There is usually a 10 to 15 percent difference between the asking price and final selling price.

After the seller sends this new price to you through the agent, you can bring out the various deficiencies in the property that you have been accumulating. You will then make your second offer, which will be slightly higher than your first one. He may reject it and make a new counteroffer. If you feel this is as low as he will go, then you can offer a larger down payment or full cash (if you can get it) if he will cut more off the price. Eventually you will force him to his lowest position, and he will bring you to your highest one. If your compromises are mutually satisfactory, then a deal has been made. If not, you had better start looking somewhere else.

Frequently during the bargaining process something occurs that can bring things to a head faster than anticipated. For example, another interested buyer might enter the picture and force you to compete with him for the land. A well-known sales trick used by some real estate agents is to tell you that your offer has been surpassed by another prospective buyer, although this is actually not true. A variation on this trick is for the seller to arrange to have a friend or his broker telephone while he is showing the house to you. The call presumably is another interested buyer. Don't rush your decision unless you are certain you are getting what you want. Ask to meet the other buyer or see his offer.

There are a few tricks you can use yourself. Pick out a piece of property that another agent in town is handling under a completely different deal and

TRAVELS WITH FARLEY/Phil Frank

announce to your original agent that you are preparing to buy the other property if the seller does not accept your present offer, which is your final one. This might scare the seller or make him more willing to compromise with you if he is anxious to sell and does not want to lose you as a prospective buyer.

YOUR DEPOSIT OR EARNEST MONEY BINDER WITH THE CONTRACT OF SALE

When you make your first and subsequent offers to the seller, you will do so using the Model Contract of Sale in chapter 28, which you will adapt to your own situation, or you will use a form presented to you by the broker. When you present him with the contract, which is also an offer to purchase, you will include a small deposit in order to show your seriousness and to whet the seller's appetite for more. This is usually called a deposit, or earnest money payment. (See chapter 28, "The Model Contract of Sale.")

Sometimes the seller or real estate agent gives the buyer a *deposit receipt* containing no contingencies to be signed before the final sales contract is drawn up. This is deceptive. The deposit receipt

becomes a legally enforceable contract for the purchase of land as soon as both you and the seller sign it, if it contains the date, names of the parties, and description of the property. *Nothing you are told verbally is legally binding.* Nothing that is not in writing is legally binding. If you agree to some condition orally with the seller and if you then make a cash deposit and sign a binder or contract or deposit receipt without the condition written into it, that condition is not binding on the seller, and he does not have to write it into a more complete contract of sale later on. One of the most frequent complaints made to the local real estate departments comes from buyers who demand the return of their deposits. The buyer usually suffers because he did not get his terms or agreements with the real estate agent or seller put in writing. Do not make the mistake of assuming, as many buyers do, that anything not called a contract will not be important. Often contracts for the sale and purchase of land are given such names as Conditional Sales Agreement, Offer to Purchase, Preliminary Sales Agreement, Deposit Receipt, Sales Deposit Receipt, Agreement for Sale of Real Estate, Binder, Installment Contract, and Contract of Sale.

Instead of signing the usual deposit receipt, I recommend that you submit your deposit and your offer to purchase with all the terms of the sale in a single document called the contract of sale, which is explained in detail in chapter 28.

V

FINANCING YOUR PURCHASE

CHAPTER 21

Types of Financing: Land Contract, Mortgage, Deed of Trust

When you find land you want to buy, you must decide how you are going to pay for it. Unless you have enough money to pay cash, you will have to pay off your purchase gradually. Country land sales, particularly of undeveloped properties, are usually financed by the seller, since it is generally difficult to get a loan from a commerical lender. If the seller extends you credit, you will pay him a down pay-

ment and pay off the rest of the purchase price gradually under the terms of either a *land contract*, *mortgage*, or *deed of trust*. If you are able to borrow money from a third party to combine with your own money, you can pay the seller cash for the land and give the lender either a mortgage or a deed of trust.

Each type of financing is diagramed in illustration 88 at the end of this chapter. As you read each of the following sections, you should refer to this illustration.

THE LAND CONTRACT

Financing by land contract is the riskiest way to buy rural land. Do not confuse the land contract

295

with the contract of sale. The contract of sale is the document that contains the terms and conditions of the sale. (See the Model Contract of Sale in chapter 28.) The land contract only details the financial arrangements of the purchase and the rights and obligations of the seller and buyer during the payment period.

A land contract may also be called an *installment sale contract, second contract, land sale contract, land contract of sale,* or *conditional sales contract.* Regardless of the name used, the principle of *buying on contract* remains the same.

You give the seller a cash down payment and then make regular payments until the purchase price and interest are paid off. What makes buying on contract risky is that during the payment period the seller gives you only *possession* of the land. You will not get a deed until after all the payments have been made. (This is what differentiates this plan from a *mortgage* or *deed of trust,* as you will see below.)

The seller holds title to the land during this entire period. If you do not properly record the land contract, the seller can encumber the land with easements, mortgages, and other liens that will seriously affect the title you are to eventually receive. Often a seller will convey land under a land contract while still paying for it himself. If he fails to make his payments, his loan is foreclosed, and he loses the land, then you will also lose the land. If you go to court at that time you may get your payments back, but it is very unlikely that you will get the land since the seller no longer has it. The situation is similar if the seller goes bankrupt while owing money on a prior mortgage on the property.

Sellers like land contracts because of the great advantages they offer if you are unable to make your payments. Under the *strict foreclosure action* generally used for land contracts, the seller simply asks you to leave the premises. Since he already has title to the land, he does not have to go through a regular court foreclosure. At the end of the foreclosure, the seller not only has the land but he has all the money you have already paid him.

Although you can sue him for the value of improvements you made on the land, such as buildings, septic tanks, and water systems, you must hire a lawyer and initiate a costly court action. If you refuse to leave the property, the seller will be forced to go to court and obtain an *action for ejection* or *writ of possession* against you. He might

be willing to make a settlement with you out of court to avoid this expense, in which case you can demand that he reimburse you for the improvements you have made on the land. You should also ask for the money you have paid him under the land contract. You may get at least some of your money back in this manner. Never leave the land voluntarily unless the seller makes a deal.

Because of the nature of the land contract, sellers often require an extremely small down payment and low monthly terms. This might be the only way some of you can buy a piece of country land because of your poor financial condition. I recommend that you never buy on contract unless you have no alternative. If you have no other choice, at least be sure you have the following essential protections written into the land contract:

—The land contract should state that the seller is to put the title to the land in trust with an escrow holder, or third party trustee, until you complete your payments or default on them.

—Have the seller write out a deed to you and place it with the trustee with instructions to give it to you upon the completion of your payments. This will ensure that a deed is ready to be delivered to you as soon as you have completed your payments.

—The land contract should state that your payments are to go to the trustee, who is to use the money to pay all taxes and other liens on the land, such as the seller's mortgage, before he forwards any money to the seller. This will prevent a foreclosure by the seller's creditor or a tax sale if your payments are sufficient to meet the sums due.

—Require that the land contract be recorded immediately with the county recorder so that the world is put on notice that you are buying that parcel, and the seller will not be able to encumber or sell the property.

—The land contract must specifically forbid the seller from encumbering the title in any way, so he can make no loans against the property.

—Get the seller to include a clause in which he promises to convey all or part of the title to you after you have completed a certain amount of the total payments. For example, after you have made half the payments, he will give you full title to the land and you can give him back a mortgage or trust deed for the remaining amount due. The earlier you get title to the land the better.

—Never allow the seller to put a *prepayment penalty clause* into the land contract penalizing you for paying off the balance at an earlier date than scheduled. For example, if your payments are to be $300 a month, you should be permitted to pay ''$300 or more per month.'' (See chapter 22 for more on this.)

—You will be required to keep the property in good repair and to pay for fire and hazard insurance on the property under terms to be approved by the seller. Be sure you are a named insured or beneficiary under the policy, as well as the seller.

—Have the seller state, in detail, the conditions under which he can force you off the land. Make sure you understand them.

—Use the information in chapter 22 on the terms and elements of amortization to get the best financing arrangement possible.

THE MORTGAGE (PURCHASE MONEY MORTGAGE) AND DEED OF TRUST

Unlike the land contract, when you give a *mortgage* or *deed of trust* in exchange for a cash down payment and credit, you receive title to the land immediately. The property is always held as security, or collateral, for the loan so that the lender has sufficient protection if you default on your payments.

A mortgage is technically called a *purchase money mortgage* when it is used for the specific purpose of buying land. (The term mortgage used throughout this book actually refers to a purchase money mortgage.) If the seller finances the deal himself, he does not actually give you money to buy the land. Instead he allows you to pay off the purchase price over a period of time. He is giving you credit, which is like lending you the money.

When you borrow money from a third party, e.g., a bank, in return for a mortgage or deed of trust, you actually receive cash to give to the seller for the land. You then pay back the lender* over a period of time.

---

*Throughout this and subsequent chapters, when I refer to the *lender* I am talking about either the seller who finances the sale himself or a third party lender, unless I specify otherwise. It is assumed that the *borrower* is the buyer. A *creditor* is a person to whom money is owed. A *debtor* is the person who owes the money.

THE TITLE THEORY OF MORTGAGES

Seventeen states use the title theory of mortgages. Under this financial arrangement you do not keep the title to the land during your payment period. For example, if the seller finances the sale, he delivers title to you at the close of escrow. Because you receive title at that time you can get the standard title protections, such as a title search and title insurance. You receive a deed specifying ownership in your name. Then, when you give the mortgage to the seller, it is as if you are giving the seller back your title to the land. He then holds title as security only, until you complete your payments. During that time, you have the right to the possession of the land. When you complete the required payments of principal and interest, the seller makes a new deed and redelivers the title to you. If you default on your payments, the seller merely keeps the title to the land. VA loans operate this way.

If you give a mortgage under this system to a third party lender, the seller delivers title to you and then you deliver it to the lender with a mortgage in exchange for cash, which you give to the seller. The terms of a title theory mortgage must specify that the creditor not alter the title in any way from the time you give it to him as security with the mortgage until he redelivers it to you on your last required payment, by recording a *satisfaction of mortgage*.

The difference between this system and a land contract is that in the latter form of financing you never receive title until you have completely paid for the property. With a title mortgage you receive title immediately and then give it back to the seller in the form of a mortgage. You have much greater protection under a title theory mortgage than with a land contract.

The states that use this title theory of mortgages are Alabama, Arkansas, Connecticut, Illinois, Maine, Maryland, Massachusetts, Mississippi, New Hampshire, New Jersey, North Carolina, Ohio, Pennsylvania, Rhode Island, Tennessee, Vermont, and West Verginia. If your land is in any of these states you should determine whether the title theory is still observed at the time of your purchase. (Illustration 83 is a sample mortgage form.)

SAMPLE MORTGAGE FORM

THIS MORTGAGE, made this _____ day of _____, 19_____.

BETWEEN _____ (name of borrower) _____, herein called Mortgagor,

Whose address is _____,

and _____ (name of lender) _____, herein called Mortgagee;

WITNESSETH: That Mortgagor hereby mortgages to Mortgagee, all that property located in the City of _____, County of _____, _____, described as:

(Legal Description of the Property)

TOGETHER WITH all the tenements, hereditaments, and appurtenances thereunto belonging or in any wise appertaining thereto, the reversions, remainders, rents, issues, and profits thereof, and also all the estate, right, title, and interest, homestead or other claim or demand, in law and in equity, which Mortgagor now has or may hereafter acquire, in and to said property, or any part thereof, as security for the payment of the indebtedness evidenced by a promissory note, of even date herewith, executed by Mortgagor in the sum of _____ Dollars, ($_____), in favor of Mortgagee, for any additional sums and interest thereon which may hereafter be loaned to the Mortgagor or his successors or assigns by the Mortgagee, and for the performance of each agreement herein contained. Additional loans hereafter made and interest thereon shall be secured by this Mortgage only if made to the Mortgagor while he is the owner of record of his present interest in said property, or to his successors or assigns while they are the owners of record thereof, and shall be evidenced by a promissory note reciting that it is secured by this Mortgage.

A. TO PROTECT THE SECURITY OF THIS MORTGAGE, MORTGAGOR AGREES:

Maintenance and Repair

1. To keep said property in good condition and repair; not to remove or demolish any building thereon; to complete or restore promptly and in good and workmanlike manner any building which may be constructed, damaged, or destroyed thereon and to pay when due all claims for labor performed and materials furnished therefor; to comply with all laws affecting said property or requiring any alterations or improvements to be made thereon; not to commit or permit waste thereof; not to commit, suffer, or permit any act upon said property in violation of law; to cultivate, irrigate, fertilize, fumigate, prune, and do all other acts which from the character or use of said property may be reasonably necessary, the specific enumeration herein not excluding the general.

Fire Insurance

2. To provide, maintain, and deliver to Mortgagee fire insurance satisfactory to and with loss payable to Mortgagee. The amount collected under any fire or other insurance policy may be applied by Mortgagee upon any indebtedness secured hereby and in such order as Mortgagee may determine, or at the option of Mortgagee the entire amount so collected or any part thereof may be released to Mortgagor. Such application or release shall not cure or waive any default or Notice of Default hereunder or invalidate any act done pursuant to such notice.

Defense of Security

3. To appear in and defend any action or proceeding purporting to affect the security hereof or the rights or powers of Mortgagee, and to pay all costs and expenses, including cost of evidence of title and attorney's fees in a reasonable sum, in any such action or proceeding in which Mortgagee may appear, and in any suit brought by Mortgagee to foreclose this Mortgage.

83. Sample Mortgage Form

Payment of Liens and Taxes

4. To pay the following: (a) all taxes and assessments affecting said property, including assessments on appurtenant water stock, at least _____ days before delinquency; (b) when due, all encumbrances, charges, and liens, with interest, on said property or any part thereof, which appear to be prior or superior hereto; and (c) all costs, fees, and expenses of this Mortgage. Should Mortgagor fail to make any payment or to do any act as herein provided, the Mortgagee, but without obligation so to do and without notice to or demand upon Mortgagor and without releasing Mortgagor from any obligation hereof, may do the following: (a) make or do the same in such manner and to such extent as he deems necessary to protect the security hereof (Mortgagee being authorized to enter upon said property for such purposes); (b) appear in and defend any action or proceeding purporting to affect the security hereof or the rights or powers of Mortgagee; (c) pay, purchase, contest, or compromise any encumbrance, charge, or lien which in the judgment of Mortgagee appears to be prior or superior hereto; and (d) in exercising any such powers, pay necessary expenses, employ counsel, and pay his reasonable fees.

Reimbursement of Costs

5. To pay immediately and without demand all sums so expended by Mortgagee, with interest from date of expenditure at the amount allowed by law in effect at the date hereof, and to pay for any statement provided for by law in effect at the date hereof regarding the obligation secured hereby any amount demanded by the Mortgagee not to exceed the maximum allowed by law at the time when said statement is demanded.

Condemnation Awards

6. That any award of damages in connection with any condemnation for public use of or injury to said property or any part thereof is hereby assigned and shall be paid to Mortgagee who may apply or release such moneys received by him in the same manner and with the same effect as above provided for disposition of proceeds of fire or other insurance.

Waiver of Late Payments

7. That by accepting payment of any sum secured hereby after its due date, Mortgagee does not waive his right either to require prompt payment when due of all other sums so secured or to declare default for failure so to pay.

Release and Subordination

8. That at any time or from time to time, without liability therefor and without affecting the personal liability of any person for payment of the indebtedness secured hereby, or the effect of this mortgage upon the remainder of said property, Mortgagee may: (a) release any part of said property from this Mortgage; (b) consent to the making of any map or plat thereof; (c) join in granting any easement thereon; or (d) join in any extension agreement or any agreement subordinating the lien or charge hereof.

Satisfaction of Mortgage

9. When all sums secured hereby have been paid in full; the lien created hereby shall cease and become void, and Mortgagee shall cause a satisfaction of mortgage to be entered of record stating that all sums secured thereby have been fully paid, satisfied, and discharged, and that said property has been released from the lien of this Mortgage. At such time, Mortgagee shall also cancel the note secured hereby and shall return this Mortgage and said note to the Mortgagor.

Assignment of Rents

10. That as additional security, Mortgagor hereby gives to and confers upon Morgagee the right, power, and authority, during the continuance of this Mortgage, to collect the rents, issues, and profits of said property, reserving unto the Mortgagor the right, prior to any default by Mortgagor in payment of any indebtedness secured hereby or in the performance of any agreement hereunder, to collect and retain such rents, issues, and profits as they become

due and payable. Upon any such default, Mortgagee may at any time without notice, either in person, by agent, or by a receiver to be appointed by a court, and without regard to the adequacy of any security for the indebtedness hereby secured, enter upon and take possession of said property or any part thereof, in his own name sue for or otherwise collect such rents, issues, and profits, including those past due and unpaid, and apply the same, less costs and expenses of operation and collection, including reasonable attorney's fees, upon any indebtedness secured hereby, and in such order as Mortgagee may determine. The entering upon and taking possession of said property, the collection of such rents, issues, and profits and the application thereof as aforesaid, shall not cure or waive any default or Notice of Default hereunder or invalidate any act done pursuant to such notice.

Default and Foreclosure

11. That upon default by Mortgagor in payment of any indebtedness secured hereby or in performance of any agreement hereunder, Mortgagee may declare all sums secured hereby immediately due and payable by instituting legal proceedings for judicial foreclosure of this Mortgage, in which case the net proceeds from the sale under the direction and decree of a court of competent jurisdiction shall be applied to the indebtedness secured hereby.

Inurement

12. That this Mortgage applies to, inures to the benefit of, and binds all parties hereto, their heirs, legatees, devisees, administrators, executors, successors, and assigns. In this Mortgage, whenever the context so requires, the masculine includes the feminine and/or neuter, and the singular number includes the plural.

The undersigned Mortgagor requests that a copy of any Notice of Default and of any Notice of Sale hereunder be mailed to him at his address hereinbefore set forth.

The promissory note secured hereby is given as a part of the purchase price of the property herein described.

Signature of Mortgagor

_____

Acknowledgment

State of _____ } ss
County of _____

On _____, 19___, before me, the undersigned, a Notary Public in and for said county and state, personally appeared ____(name of mortgagor)____ known to me to be the person(s) whose name(s) is(are) subscribed to the within instrument and acknowledged to me that he (she or they) executed the same.

WITNESS my hand and official seal.

NOTARIAL

SEAL

_____
Notary Public in and for said County and State

_____
Type or Print Name of Notary
My Commission expires _____

THE LIEN THEORY OF MORTGAGES

All of the other states, except trust deed states mentioned below, follow the lien theory of mortgaging property. When you give a mortgage, you do not give up title to the land but simply promise, in writing, that you will repay the lender or complete payments to the seller. The mortgage becomes a lien on the property, which means that a foreclosure action can be taken if payments are not made. Title and possession rights remain with you, the buyer, during the entire period. The seller's, or lender's, lien on the land will be removed upon completion of all payments. Because you always keep the title in your possession, it is much harder to have your land taken from you if you default on your payments than under the title theory of mortgages where the lender already has title to the land if you default.

Under both mortgage theories, the buyer who gives the mortgage is called the *mortgagor*. The lender or seller who receives the mortgage is called the *mortgagee*.

THE DEED OF TRUST (TRUST DEED)

Thirteen states prefer the system where the borrower, or *trustor*, delivers a deed of trust to the seller rather than giving a mortgage to the lender or seller. Under this system, the lender is the beneficiary under the deed of trust. The third party trustee is usually a commercial institution such as a bank, title company, or escrow company. The trustee in essence holds title to the property in trust with the power to foreclose on the buyer if there is a default in payments. The buyer still owns the property and has full rights of ownership, subject to the conditions of the deed of trust. For example, the property cannot be logged or the improvements removed until the note and deed of trust are paid off. (See chapter 30, "Opening and Closing of Escrow and the Role of the Escrow Holder.")

The trust is established in the following manner. The seller delivers title to you, the buyer, by giving you a deed to the land. If the seller is your creditor, you give him a down payment on the land and sign a note and deed of trust. If you borrow the money from a third party, you pay the seller the entire purchase price and sign a note and deed of trust to the lender. You then make your payments and pay the taxes and other liens on the land and keep the improvements insured, with the lender as coinsured. When the loan has been completely paid off, the trustee delivers clear title to you by recording a deed of reconveyance.

If you fail to make payments, the trustee has the right to sell the land at a foreclosure sale and deliver the title to the new purchaser or back to the seller if nobody bids at the foreclosure sale. Any money owed to the seller or lender including interest and other expenses the seller has incurred as a result of the foreclosure action is paid from the money received from this sale. The balance goes to you. This method of disposing of the title to the land upon default makes the deed of trust the preferred security instrument from the seller's point of view, because he does not have to hire a lawyer or go to court for a judicial foreclosure.

Do not confuse a *deed* with a *deed of trust*. A deed is evidence of ownership of the property. The deed of trust, sometimes called the trust deed, is a method of financing and securing a sale of land. It is slowly being accepted throughout the country, although the mortgage remains the primary means of securing property for a loan. Either method is fine. The one you use will depend on which method is customary in your state.

The District of Columbia, California, Colorado, Idaho, Illinois, Mississippi, Missouri, Nevada, New Mexico, Tennessee, Texas, Virginia, West Virginia, and Utah use deeds of trust. (Illustration 84, pages 302–305, is a sample deed of trust form.)

THE PROMISSORY NOTE OR BOND

The mortgage or deed of trust is always accompanied by a promissory note or bond, which is the document that actually specifies the debt and how it is to be paid. A mortgage and deed of trust only specify the security for the debt. In the note the borrower makes an unconditional promise in writing to the lender that he will pay the loan according to a specified plan. Illustration 85, page 306, is a

DEED OF TRUST

This Deed of Trust, made this _____ (Date) _____ day of _____, 19___,
Between _____ (Name of Borrower) _____

Whose address is _____ (Address of Borrower) _____
                      (Number and Street)   (City)   (State)

herein called Trustor, _____ (Name of Trustee) _____, a ____ (State) ____ corporation, herein called Trustee,
and _____ (Name of Seller or Lender) _____

_____ herein called Beneficiary,

Witnesseth: That Trustor irrevocably GRANTS, TRANSFERS AND ASSIGNS to TRUSTEE IN TRUST, WITH POWER OF SALE, that property in _____ (City where land is located) _____
County of _____ (County where located) _____, _____ (State) _____, described as

(Legal Description of the Property)

TOGETHER WITH the rents, issues and profits thereof, SUBJECT, HOWEVER, to the right, power and authority given to and conferred upon Beneficiary by Paragraph 5 of Part B of the provisions incorporated herein by reference to collect and apply such rents, issues and profits, For the Purpose of Securing payment of the indebtedness evidenced by a promissory note, of even date herewith, executed by Trustor in the sum of _____ (Amount of Loan) _____

_____ Dollars, ($_____).
any additional sums and interest thereon which may hereafter be loaned to the Trustor or his successors or assigns by the Beneficiary, and the performance of each agreement herein contained. Additional loans hereafter made and interest thereon shall be secured by this Deed of Trust only if made to the Trustor while he is the owner of record of his present interest in said property, or to his successors or assigns while they are the owners of record thereof, and shall be evidenced by a promissory note reciting that it is secured by this Deed of Trust.

By the execution and delivery of this Deed of Trust and the note secured hereby the parties hereto agree that there are adopted and included herein for any and all purposes by reference as though the same were written in full herein the provisions of Section A, including paragraphs 1 through 6 thereof, and of Section B, including paragraphs 1 through 10 thereof, of that certain fictitious Deed of Trust recorded in the official records in the offices of the County Recorders of the following counties ___
(List of counties in state) _____

    A copy of said provisions so adopted and included herein by reference is set forth on the reverse hereof.
    The undersigned Trustor requests that a copy of any notice of default and of any notice of sale hereunder be mailed to him at his address given above.

(Name of Borrower) _____

(Signature of Borrower) _____

State of
County of _____ } ss.

    On this _____ day of _____ (Date this agreement is signed) _____, 19___,
before me, the undersigned, a Notary Public in and for said _____ (Name of County) _____
County, personally appeared _____ (Name of Borrower) _____

known to me to be the person(s) whose name(s) _____ subscribed to the within instrument, and acknowledged that _____ executed the same.
WITNESS my hand and official seal.
(SEAL)

(Signature of Notary) _____

Notary Public in and for said County & State
My Commission Expires: _____ (Date of Expiration) _____   (Name of Notary) _____

Type or Print Name of Notary

84. Sample Deed of Trust

The following is a copy of the provisions of Section A, including Paragraphs 1 through 6 thereof, and of Section B, including Paragraphs 1 through 10, thereof, of that certain fictitious Deed of Trust recorded as set forth on the reverse hereof:

A. TO PROTECT THE SECURITY OF THIS DEED OF TRUST, TRUSTOR AGREES:

Maintenance and Repair

1. To keep said property in good condition and repair; not to remove or demolish any building thereon; to complete or restore promptly and in good and workmanlike manner any building which may be constructed, damaged or destroyed thereon and to pay when due all claims for labor performed and materials furnished therefor; to comply with all laws affecting said property or requiring any alterations or improvements to be made thereon; not to commit or permit waste thereof; not to commit, suffer or permit any act upon said property in violation of law; to cultivate, irrigate, fertilize, fumigate, prune and do all other acts which from the character or use of said property may be reasonably necessary, the specific enumerations herein not excluding the general.

Fire Insurance

2. To provide, maintain and deliver to Beneficiary fire insurance satisfactory to and with loss payable to Beneficiary. The amount collected under any fire or other insurance policy may be applied by Beneficiary upon any indebtedness secured hereby and in such order as Beneficiary may determine, or at the option of Beneficiary the entire amount so collected or any part thereof may be released to Trustor. Such application or release shall not cure or waive any default or notice of default hereunder or invalidate any act done pursuant to such notice.

Defense of Security

3. To appear in and defend any action or proceeding purporting to affect the security hereof or the rights or powers of Beneficiary, or Trustee; and to pay all costs and expenses, including cost of evidence of title and attorney's fees in a reasonable sum, in any such action or proceeding in which Beneficiary or Trustee may appear.

Payment of Liens and Taxes

4. To pay: at least ten days before delinquency all taxes and assessments affecting said property, including assessments on appurtenant water stock; when due, all encumbrances, charges and liens, with interest, on said property or any part thereof, which appear to be prior or superior hereto; all costs, fees and expenses of this Trust.

Reimbursement of Costs

5. To pay immediately and without demand all sums expended by Beneficiary or Trustee pursuant to the provisions hereof, with interest from date of expenditure at seven percent per annum.

Right to Protect the Security

6. Should Trustor fail to make any payment or to do any act as herein provided, then Beneficiary or Trustee, but without obligation so to do and without notice to or demand upon Trustor and without releasing Trustor from any obligation hereof, may: make or do the same in such manner and to such extent as either may deem necessary to protect the security hereof, Beneficiary or Trustee being authorized to enter upon said property for such purposes; appear in and defend any action or proceeding purporting to affect the security hereof or the right or powers of Beneficiary or Trustee; pay, purchase, contest or compromise any encumbrance, charge or lien which in the judgment of either appears to be prior or superior hereto; and, in exercising any such powers, pay necessary expenses, employ counsel and pay the reasonable fees.

B. IT IS MUTUALLY AGREED THAT:

Condemnation Award

1. Any award of damages in connection with any condemnation for public use or injury to said property or any part thereof is hereby assigned and shall be paid to Beneficiary who may apply or release such moneys received by him in the same manner and with the same effect as above provided for disposition of proceeds of fire or other insurance.

Waiver of Late Payments

2. By accepting payment of any sum secured hereby after its due date, Beneficiary does not waive his right either to require prompt payment when due of all other sums so secured or to declare default for failure so to pay.

Release and Subordination

3. At any time or from time to time, without liability therefor and without notice, upon written request of Beneficiary and presentation of this Deed and said note for endorsement, and without affecting the personal liability of any person for payment of the

indebtedness secured hereby, Trustee may: reconvey all or any part of said property; consent to the making of any map or plat thereof; join in granting any easement thereon; or join in any extension agreement or any agreement subordinating the lien or charge hereof.

Full Reconveyance

4. Upon written request of Beneficiary stating that all sums secured hereby have been paid, and upon surrender of this Deed and said note to Trustee for cancellation and retention and upon payment of its fees, Trustee shall reconvey, without warranty, the property then held hereunder. The recitals in any reconveyance executed under this deed of trust of any matters or facts shall be conclusive proof of the truthfulness thereof. The grantee in such reconveyance may be described as "the person or persons legally entitled thereto."

Assignment of Rents

5. As additional security, Trustor hereby gives to and confers upon Beneficiary the right, power and authority, during the continuance of these Trusts, to collect the rents, issues and profits of said property, reserving unto Trustor the right, prior to any default by Trustor in payment of any indebtedness secured hereby or in performance of any agreement hereunder, to collect and retain such rents, issues and profits as they become due and payable. Upon any such default, Beneficiary may at any time without notice, either in person, by agent, or by a receiver to be appointed by a court, and without regard to the adequacy of any security for the indebtedness hereby secured, enter upon and take possession of said property or any part thereof, in his own name sue for or otherwise collect such rents, issues and profits, including those past due and unpaid, and apply the same, less cost and expenses of operation and collection, including reasonable attorney's fees, upon any indebtedness secured hereby, and in such order as Beneficiary may determine. The entering upon and taking possession of said property, the collection of such rents, issues and profits and the application thereof as aforesaid, shall not cure or waive any default or notice of default hereunder or invalidate any act done pursuant to such notice.

Default and Foreclosure

6. Upon default by Trustor in payment of any indebtedness secured hereby or in performance of any agreement hereunder, all sums secured hereby shall immediately become due and payable at the option of the Beneficiary. In the event of default, Beneficiary shall execute or cause the Trustee to execute a written notice of such default and his election to cause to be sold the herein described property to satisfy the obligations hereof, and shall cause such notice to be recorded in the office of the recorder of each county wherein said real property or some part thereof is situated.

Notice of sale having been given as then required by law, and not less than the time then required by law having elapsed after recordation of such notice of default, Trustee, without demand on Trustor, shall sell said property at the time and place fixed by it in said notice of sale, either as a whole or in separate parcels and in such order as it may determine, at public auction to the highest bidder for cash in lawful money of the United States, payable at time of sale. Trustee may postpone sale of all or any portion of said property by public announcement at such time and place of sale, and from time to time thereafter may postpone such sale by public announcement at the time and place fixed by the preceding postponement. Trustee shall deliver to the purchaser its deed conveying the property so sold, but without any covenant or warranty, express or implied. The recitals in such deed of any matters or facts shall be conclusive proof of the truthfulness thereof. Any person, including Trustor, Trustee, or Beneficiary, may purchase at such sale.

After deducting all costs, fees and expenses of Trustee and of this Trust, including cost of evidence of title and reasonable counsel fees in connection with sale, Trustee shall apply the proceeds of sale to payment of: all sums expended under the terms hereof, not then repaid, with accrued interest at seven per cent per annum; all other sums then secured hereby; and the remainder, if any, to the person or persons legally entitled thereto.

Inurement

7. This Deed applies to, inures to the benefit of, and binds all parties hereto, their heirs, legatees, devisees, administrators, executors, successors and assigns. The term Beneficiary shall mean the holder and owner of the note secured hereby; or, if the note has been pledged, the pledgee thereof. In this Deed, whenever the context so requires, the masculine gender includes the feminine and/or neuter, and the singular number includes the plural.

Acceptance by Trustee

8. Trustee accepts this Trust when this Deed, duly executed and acknowledged, is made a public record as provided by law. Trustee is not obligated to notify any party hereto of pending sale under any other Deed of Trust or of any action or proceeding in which Trustor, Beneficiary or Trustee shall be a party unless brought by Trustee.

304

Substitution of Trustees

9. Beneficiary may, from time to time, as provided by statue, or by a writing, signed and acknowledged by him and recorded in the office of the county recorder of the county in which said land or such part thereof as is then affected by this deed of trust is situated, appoint another Trustee in place and stead of Trustee herein named, and thereupon, the Trustee herein named shall be discharged and Trustee so appointed shall be substituted as Trustee hereunder with the same effect as if originally named Trustee herein.

Cotrustees

10. If two or more persons be designated as Trustee herein, any, or all, powers granted herein to Trustee may be exercised by any of such persons, if the other person or persons is unable for any reason, to act, and any recital of such inability in any instrument executed by any of such persons shall be conclusive against Trustor, his heirs and assigns.

DO NOT RECORD

To obtain either a partial Reconveyance or a Subordination Agreement, this Deed of Trust, together with the note secured hereby, must be presented to the Trustee for endorsement, accompanied by either a Request for Partial Reconveyance or a Subordination Agreement, as the case may be, and Trustee's fee.

To obtain a full Reconveyance of this Deed of Trust present to the Trustee this request properly executed, the Deed of Trust, the original note secured by said Deed of Trust and any other evidence of indebtedness secured thereby, together with reconveyance fee.

REQUEST FOR FULL RECONVEYANCE

To_____, Trustee.   Date: _____
　　　(name of trustee)　　　　　　　　　　　　　　　　　　　　　　　　　(date)

The undersigned is the legal owner and holder of the note in the amount of $_____and all other indebtedness secured
　　　　　　　　　　　　　　　　　　　　　　　　　　　　　　　　　　　(loan)
by the foregoing Deed of Trust, which was recorded in Book_____Page_____of_____Official Records of
the_____ County of_____,_____,_____
　　(name of office where document recorded)　　　　　　　　　　　　(name of county)

You are hereby notified that said note and all other sums and indebtedness secured by said Deed of Trust have been fully paid and satisfied; and you are hereby requested and directed upon surrender to you of said note, Deed of Trust, and evidence of any other indebtedness secured thereby, for cancellation and retention, and upon payment to you of any sums owing to you under the terms of said Deed of Trust, to reconvey, without warranty, to "the person or persons legally entitled thereto," the estate now held by you thereunder.

Mail reconveyance to this address:

_____   Signed:_____
　　　　　(address of borrower)　　　　　　　　　　　　　　　　　　　　　(signature of lender)

Received reconveyance: _____   Signed:_____
　　　　　　　　　　　　　　　　　　　　　　　　　　　　　　　　　　　(signature of borrower)

_____   _____

305

DO NOT DESTROY THIS NOTE

When paid, this note, if secured by Deed of Trust, must be surrendered to Trustee for cancellation, before Reconveyance will be made.

Form 41

INSTALLMENT NOTE
(Combined Principal and Interest in Equal Installments)

$ (Amount of Loan) (City) (State) _____ (Date) , 19_____

FOR VALUE RECEIVED, I promise to pay in lawful money of the United States of America,

to _____ (Name of Lender) _____

_____, or order at

(Address of Seller or Institution that will collect the payments)

the principal sum of (Amount of Loan) _____ (Interest Dollars,

with interest in like lawful money from (Date loan is made) , 19_____ at Rate) per cent

per annum on the amounts of principal sum remaining unpaid from time to time.

Principal and interest payable in (monthly, quarterly, annual) installments of

____ (Amount of Payment to be made with each installment) Dollars,

or more each, on the (Day of Payment) day of each and every (Payment Period)

beginning (The date payments must start to be made on the loan)

_____

_____

_____

Each payment shall be credited first, to the interest then due; and the remainder to the principal sum; and interest shall thereupon cease upon the amount so paid on said principal sum. AND I agree that in case of default in the payment of any installments when due, then the whole of said principal sum then remaining unpaid, together with the interest that shall have accrued thereon, shall forthwith become due and payable at the election of the holder of this note, without notice. AND, I agree, if action be instituted on this note to pay such sum as the Court may fix as Attorney's fees. THIS NOTE IS secured by a deed of trust of even date herewith to (Name of Trustee) a (State)Corporation, as TRUSTEE.

(Name of Borrower) _____

(Signature of Borrower) _____

85. Sample Installment Note

sample note, titled Installment Note, which would be used in the case of a deed of trust. (A note for a mortgage would include the same elements, only all references to the lien would be to a mortgage rather than to a deed of trust.) The note or bond is signed and sometimes recorded with the county recorder at the same time as the mortgage or trust deed, which are always recorded.

Most notes are negotiable, which means they are as good as money and the holder of the note can sell or transfer it to another person and "order" the debtor to make all future payments to the new holder of the note.

A few states use a bond rather than a note as evidence of the debt. A bond generally contains the same information as a note and has the addi-

tional protection of a formal seal by a notary public. You might also encounter a document that incorporates both the security of the debt and the evidence of the debt. That is, the element of a mortgage or trust deed and a note or bond are combined in the same form. Read every word and thoroughly understand the provisions of any document you sign. Always keep a copy.

A SECOND, OR "JUNIOR," MORTGAGE AND DEED OF TRUST

If you have more than one mortgage on your land,

one is always junior to the other, which means that under a foreclosure action, the senior lender collects first and any surplus goes to the junior lender.

For example, say you want to buy some property for $60,000, but the seller wants 75 percent cash down payment and you have only $15,000. You find you can get a loan from a bank for $30,000 to make the $45,000 down payment, but then you must give the seller a *second mortgage* on the remaining $15,000 owed for the land. The seller will have to agree to *subordinate* his mortgage to the bank's mortgage in order for the bank to make the loan. Commercial lenders always insist on having a lien on the property that is superior to all other credit liens. If you fail to make your payments either to the bank or to the seller, the loan will be foreclosed, and the bank will get to collect its money first. Any money left over goes next to the seller holding the second mortgage up to the amount of his lien. If any money is left, it goes to you. If the seller takes a second mortgage, he runs a greater risk of not being able to collect the money owed him if a foreclosure becomes necessary. Therefore, he might charge you a higher rate of interest on his mortgage. You will usually have to repay both mortgages simultaneously.

You might want a loan to obtain money to construct a house or other improvements on the land after you take title. If you give the seller a mortgage on the land, you might want him to subordinate it to enable you to obtain a bank loan to build a house. If you plan to do this, you must have a subordination clause in the note and mortgage you give to the seller so you can either get a construction loan prior to closing or at a later date. Since a house increases the value of the property and, therefore, the potential selling price of the land, the risk of losing money in the event that a foreclosure becomes necessary diminishes for both the commercial lender and the seller. However, the seller might not want to run the risk of having to take back the property and pay off the construction lender, and might refuse to subordinate. In that case, you will have to do a total refinancing of the property. If it is essential that the seller subordinate, it should be a condition in your contract of sale.

When you have satisfied the loan by completing all your payments, you must request that your creditor issue a *certificate of satisfaction* or, if you have a title theory mortgage or deed of trust, a *deed of reconveyance*. (Illustration 86 is a sample deed of reconveyance that would be used with a deed

DEED OF RECONVEYANCE

_____, a corporation, as TRUSTEE under the Deed of Trust executed _____, 19___ by

and recorded in Liber _____ of Official Records of _____ County, State of _____, at page _____ (Recorder's Serial No._____) pursuant to the written request of the beneficiary, does hereby GRANT AND RECONVEY unto the PERSON OR PERSONS LEGALLY ENTITLED THERETO, without warranty, all the estate and interest derived to said TRUSTEE by or through said Deed of Trust, in the lands therein described.

_____, Trustee,   Dated _____, 19 ___

By _____   By _____
          Its Vice President   *Its Vice President*

STATE OF _____, *County of* _____
On _____, *19___ before me, the undersigned, a Notary Public, in and for said County and State, personally appeared* _____
known to me to be the Vice Presidents of the corporation that executed the within instrument, and also known to me to be the persons who executed it on behalf of such corporation and acknowledged to me that such corporation executed the same.

_____ *Notary Public*
          Type or Print Name of Notary

86. Sample Deed of Reconveyance

of trust.) This document must be recorded immediately with the county recorder. Once it is recorded, your title becomes clear of the lien against it. The original mortgage or deed of trust and the note or bond must be returned to the trustee by the beneficiary in order to have the property title cleared. That is why the original note should never be destroyed.

RELEASE CLAUSES

Release clauses in mortgages or deeds of trust come into play in two special circumstances.

Often a subdivider will purchase a large parcel of land and then subdivide it, selling off several parcels. When the subdivider purchases his large piece, he gives his seller a note and mortgage on the entire parcel. This will be a much larger sum than the price he will be selling each subdivided parcel for. If he has financed his property, as he sells off each parcel his seller will release each parcel from the overlying mortgage and either be paid off a set sum of money by the subdivider or take back a separate smaller note on the piece.

Some developers do not have a proper release clause and will attempt to sell you the parcel subject to a substantially larger mortgage that affects your parcel and the other parcels in the subdivision. It is extremely risky to buy land in that manner. If the payments are not made by your seller to his mortgage holder, you and the other parcels owners could be foreclosed upon even though you have made all your payments to your seller.

Thus you should never buy property which is subject to a mortgage that is a lien upon other property as well as your own. If you are tempted to do so, you must see an attorney for advice on how best to protect yourself.

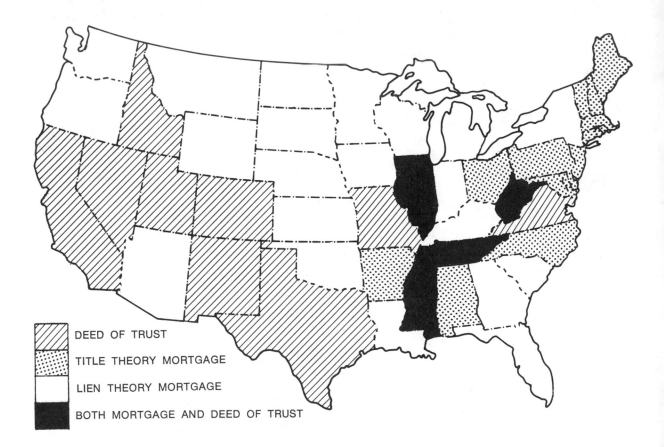

DEED OF TRUST

TITLE THEORY MORTGAGE

LIEN THEORY MORTGAGE

BOTH MORTGAGE AND DEED OF TRUST

87. Common Financing Arrangements by States

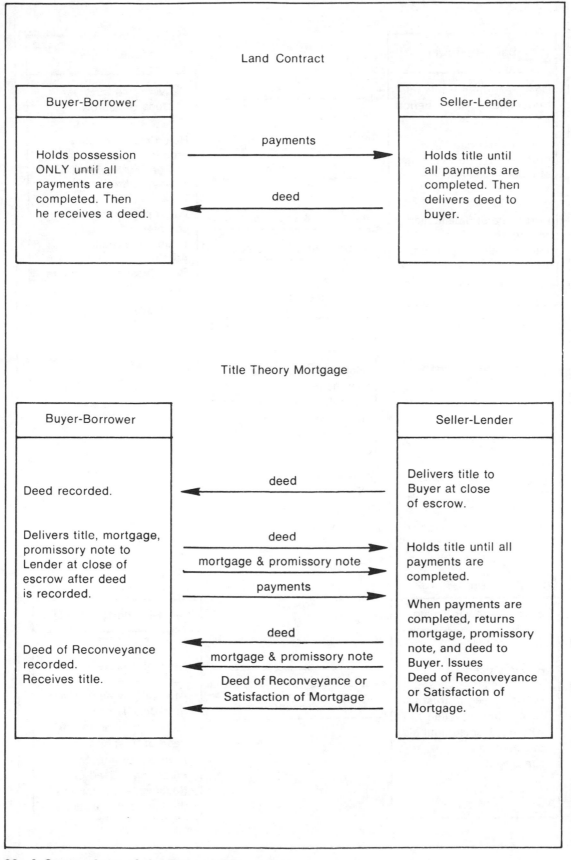

88. A Comparison of the Types of Financing

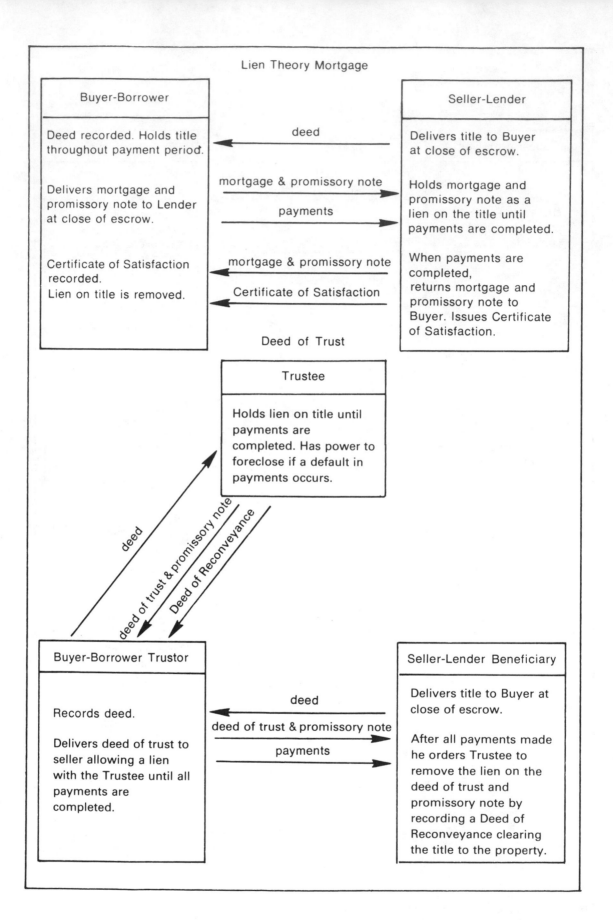

Lien Theory Mortgage

Buyer-Borrower

Deed recorded. Holds title throughout payment period.

Delivers mortgage and promissory note to Lender at close of escrow.

Certificate of Satisfaction recorded.
Lien on title is removed.

Seller-Lender

Delivers title to Buyer at close of escrow.

Holds mortgage and promissory note as a lien on the title until payments are completed.

When payments are completed, returns mortgage and promissory note to Buyer. Issues Certificate of Satisfaction.

deed ←

mortgage & promissory note →

payments →

mortgage & promissory note ←

Certificate of Satisfaction ←

Deed of Trust

Trustee

Holds lien on title until payments are completed. Has power to foreclose if a default in payments occurs.

deed

deed of trust & promissory note

Deed of Reconveyance

Buyer-Borrower Trustor

Records deed.

Delivers deed of trust to seller allowing a lien with the Trustee until all payments are completed.

Seller-Lender Beneficiary

Delivers title to Buyer at close of escrow.

After all payments made he orders Trustee to remove the lien on the deed of trust and promissory note by recording a Deed of Reconveyance clearing the title to the property.

deed ←

deed of trust & promissory note →

payments →

The second manner in which release clauses are important is if you purchase land with the intention of subdividing. You will want to have a clause in your note and deed of trust to your seller allowing you to release each parcel from your note upon each sale by paying some cash or you can have the seller, in essence, split your note among each of the parcels you will be selling so that each buyer will make payments directly to the seller.

This is a complex matter, and if it is your intention to do this, you must consult an attorney to draft the appropriate release clause.

ILLUSTRATIONS COMPARING TYPES OF FINANCING AND WHERE THEY ARE USED

Illustration 87 shows which forms of financing are most common in each state. Illustration 88 shows the different operations of the four types of financing: land contract, title theory of mortgage, lien theory of mortgage, and deed of trust. By following this diagram as you read the text you will readily understand the different methods used.

CHAPTER 22

Terms of the Loan Agreement and Their Effect on the Total Price

The terms of a loan include the amount of the loan, the interest rate being charged, the length of time in which the loan is to be paid off, the amount of each payment, and the payment plan (when each payment is to be made).

THREE DIFFERENT TYPES OF AMORTIZATION

Regardless of the type of financing you arrange, you will be making payments at regular intervals for a set length of time. This method of paying off a debt is called *amortization,* and each installment you make will usually consist of principal and interest.

The *principal* is the amount of money you borrow or owe. The *interest* is the price you are charged for the privilege of being allowed to pay the principal over a period of time. Interest is charged as a percentage of the unpaid principal and should always be quoted to you on a *per annum,* or yearly, rather than monthly or quarterly basis.

The three types of loan are the *unamortized,* the *partially amortized,* and the *fully amortized loan.* Each type results in differing costs to the borrower. To illustrate how to figure out the different financial aspects of each kind of loan, I will use one simple example. Say you are buying 40 acres of undeveloped land for $40,000. You are to give the seller a down payment of 25 percent of the purchase price, or $10,000, and he will take back a note and mortgage for the remaining $30,000. The $30,000 is to be paid off in ten years with 10 percent interest due per year on the outstanding principal. Here are the figures for easy reference:

Total price	$40,000
Cash down payment	$10,000
Principal (to be paid off in ten years)	$30,000
Interest rate	10 percent

FIGURING INTEREST DUE

It is very useful and easy to be able to calculate interest on an annual, monthly, and daily basis. It helps to use a calculator in making the calculations in this chapter.

Interest rates are usually quoted on a per annum basis. To calculate the annual interest due on a principal amount, multiply the principal amount, P, times the annual interest rate, R. $P \times R =$ Annual Interest. Using our example, $P = \$30,000$; $R = 10$ percent or .10, so $\$30,000 \times .10 = \$3,000$ interest per annum.

If you want to know how much interest is due monthly, calculate the annual amount and divide it by 12 months. So $(P \times R) \div 12$ months = the monthly amount of interest. Using our example again $(\$30,000 \times .10) \div 12$ months $= \$3,000 \div 12$ months $= \$250$ interest per month.

If you want to know how much interest is due daily, calculate the monthly amount and divide it by 30 days (the commonly accepted number of days in a month). Using our example $\$250 \div 30 = \$8.33$ interest per day.

Unamortized Loan

Since *amortize* means to pay off a loan in installments, under an unamortized loan the entire principal is paid in a lump sum at the end of a specified period of time. Interest on the principal is paid at regular intervals. The total amount of interest you will pay using this type of payment plan is large due to the fact that the principal does not decrease as the interest is paid. Using our example, the principal of $30,000 is to be paid in one sum at the end of ten years. During those ten years, interest may be paid once a year. Ten percent of $30,000 is $3,000 interest due each year. Interest of $3,000 per year for ten years will amount to $30,000 interest for the entire period of the loan. At the end of ten years, the principal amount of $30,000 is due. The total cost of the loan is $60,000. Because this is an interest only payment loan, it is rarely used, but it is still possible to obtain such a loan under certain circumstances.

Partially Amortized Loan

The partially amortized method of paying off a loan is rarely used, but is much cheaper than the unamortized method. By this method you pay a fixed amount of the principal plus interest in regular installments. The amount of principal paid each time is always the same, but the amount of interest due gets progressively smaller as the debt is paid.

Say the $30,000 principal is to be paid in equal annual installments of $3,000 for ten years. At the end of the first year the amount of interest is 10 percent of the full $30,000, since none of the loan has been paid yet. Ten percent of $30,000 is $3,000. Thus the first payment will consist of $3,000 principal and $3,000 interest or a total of $6,000. Subtracting the $3,000 payment of principal from the total borrowed leaves $27,000 of the loan left unpaid. The interest due at the end of the next year will be 10 percent of $27,000, or $2,700, and that year's payment will be $3,000 principal plus $2,700 interest, or $5,700. This leaves $24,000 of the principal unpaid. The interest the next year will be 10 percent of $24,000, or $2,400, so the payment will be $3,000 principal plus $2,400 interest, or $5,400.

As the amount of interest due gets smaller, each payment gets smaller, until the last year's payment will consist of only $300 interest plus $3,000 principal, or $3,300. By adding up the interest paid each time, the total amount of interest for ten years is $16,500, considerably less than the $30,000 interest paid on the unamortized loan.

Fully Amortized Loan

A fully amortized loan is the most common payment method used today. This loan plan, like the partially amortized method, combines paying principal and interest in each installment, but the amount of each payment is always the same. Since interest is charged as a percentage of the unpaid principal, the portion going to pay the interest is quite large in the first payments. As you pay off the loan, the portion of each payment allotted to the principal gradually increases, while the amount going to pay the interest gradually decreases. You will see how this works below.

Because payments are almost always made in

monthly, rather than annual, installments, I will do the following example using a monthly payment plan. An *amortization table* (see illustration 89) is very helpful in figuring out various aspects of the payment schedule.*

1. Figuring the amount of each payment

To figure the amount of each monthly payment using our example, first look at illustration 89 under *years* for 10 years. Then move to the right under the 10 percent column, which is the interest rate. Insert a decimal point after the first two digits of the number there. This amount, $13.2151, is what you must pay per month for each $1,000 due on the mortgage. Since you owe $30,000, you multiply this figure by 30. The result, $396.453, should be rounded up to the nearest penny, or $396.46. This is the amount of each monthly payment to pay off a loan of $30,000 at 10 percent interest over a period of ten years. When the seller or lender tells you what his terms are, you can plug in the figures to determine what each monthly payment will be.

2. Figuring the length of the amortization period

If the seller or lender tells you what your monthly payments will be but not how long you will be paying, you can determine this by working backward in illustration 89. Using the same example, if you are told that each payment is to be $396.46 per month, divide that figure by 30, since your principal is $30,000, ($396.46 ÷ 30 = 13.2153). Look down the 10 percent column until you find the figure closest to the result; $13.2151 is closest

to $13.2153. The chart shows that for this monthly payment you will be paying ten years.

3. Figuring the total amount of interest on the loan

Once you know what your monthly payments will be and how long you have to pay off the loan, you can easily determine how much the total interest will be. Continuing our example: The payments will extend for ten years. Twelve monthly payments per year for ten years makes a total of 120 monthly payments. By multiplying the $396.46 of each monthly payment by 120 payments, you get the total amount of principal and interest you will pay on your loan over ten years, which is $47,575.20. Since the principal amount of the loan is $30,000, subtract that amount to see how much the total interest will be. $47,575.20 minus $30,000 is $17,575.20. This is the amount of interest on the loan, and represents the true cost of your loan. This is the number that usually shocks the first-time property purchaser. It is expensive to pay interest on a loan. However, loan interest on a primary or secondary residence is deductible on your federal income tax.

4. Figuring how much of each payment is allocated for principal and interest

You will want to know how much of each monthly payment goes toward paying off the principal and how much goes toward paying the interest. Using our example (see illustration 90, page 319): At the time of the first payment, the unpaid balance is the total loan amount of $30,000. Since the interest rate is 10 percent per year on the unpaid principal, 10 percent of $30,000 is $3,000. Since $3,000 is the interest for the entire year, divide this figure by 12 to get the amount due the first month: $3,000 divided by 12 equals $250. Thus, out of a $396.46 payment, $250 will go to pay interest, and $396.46 minus $250, or $146.46, will go to pay off the principal.

To figure the next month's ratio between interest and principal, subtract the $146.46 of the principal already paid from $30,000, which leaves $29,853.54. Multiply that figure by 10 percent, getting $2,985.35 interest for the next year (.10 × 29,853.54 = 2,985.35). Dividing that figure by 12 (months), the amount of interest in the second installment is $248.779, or $248.78 rounded off

---

*For those of you interested in mathematics, the formula for getting those numbers is

$$mp\ (\$) = \text{loan}\ (\$) \times mir \times \left[\frac{(1 + mir)^n}{(1 + mir)^n - 1} \right]$$

where *mp* ($) is monthly payment in dollars, loan ($) is loan value in dollars, *mir* is monthly interest rate (i.e., annual interest rate divided by 12), and *n* is number of months over which the payments are to be made. For example, 9 percent means 9/100 = .09, so that if the annual interest rate is 13 percent, say, then mir = 13/100 ÷ 12 = 13/1200 = 0.01083333. If you have a calculator that has an x^y key, this formula is very easy to calculate. However, without such a function it would be difficult to compute $(1 + mir)^n$ where *n* is a large number like 120, the number of monthly payments in a 10-year loan term.

89. Table of Monthly Payments Required to Amortize $1,000 Loan

Year	6¾%	7%	7¼%	7½%	7¾%	8%	8¼%	8½%	8¾%	9%	9¼%	9½%	9¾%	10%	10¼%	10½%	10¾%	11%
1	86.4116	86.5268	86.6421	86.7575	86.8729	86.9885	87.1041	87.2198	87.3356	87.4515	87.5675	87.6836	87.7997	87.9159	88.0323	88.1487	88.2651	88.3817
1½	58.5715	58.6850	58.7987	58.9124	59.0263	59.1403	59.2545	59.3688	59.4832	59.5977	59.7124	59.8272	59.9421	60.0571	60.1723	60.2876	60.4030	60.5186
2	44.6594	44.7726	44.8861	44.9996	45.1134	45.2273	45.3414	45.4557	45.5702	45.6848	45.7996	45.9145	46.0297	46.1450	46.2604	46.3761	46.4919	46.6079
2½	36.3184	36.4320	36.5457	36.6597	36.7739	36.8884	37.0030	37.1179	37.2329	37.3482	37.4637	37.5794	37.6953	37.8115	37.9278	38.0444	38.1611	38.2781
3	30.7630	30.8771	30.9916	31.1063	31.2212	31.3364	31.4519	31.5676	31.6836	31.7998	31.9163	32.0330	32.1500	32.2672	32.3847	32.5025	32.6205	32.7388
3½	26.7993	26.9143	27.0295	27.1450	27.2609	27.3770	27.4935	27.6102	27.7272	27.8446	27.9622	28.0801	28.1983	28.3169	28.4357	28.5548	28.6742	28.7939
4	23.8305	23.9463	24.0625	24.1790	24.2958	24.4130	24.5305	24.6484	24.7666	24.8851	25.0040	25.1232	25.2427	25.3626	25.4829	25.6034	25.7243	25.8456
4½	21.5249	21.6416	21.7588	21.8763	21.9942	22.1125	22.2311	22.3502	22.4696	22.5894	22.7096	22.8302	22.9511	23.0725	23.1942	23.3162	23.4387	23.5615
5	19.6835	19.8012	19.9194	20.0380	20.1570	20.2764	20.3963	20.5166	20.6373	20.7584	20.8799	21.0019	21.1243	21.2471	21.3703	21.4940	21.6180	21.7425
5½	18.1798	18.2985	18.4178	18.5374	18.6576	18.7782	18.8993	19.0208	19.1428	19.2653	19.3882	19.5116	19.6354	19.7597	19.8845	20.0097	20.1354	20.2615
6	16.9293	17.0491	17.1694	17.2902	17.4115	17.5333	17.6556	17.7784	17.9018	18.0256	18.1499	18.2747	18.4001	18.5259	18.6522	18.7790	18.9063	19.0341
6½	15.8735	15.9944	16.1158	16.2377	16.3602	16.4832	16.6068	16.7309	16.8556	16.9808	17.1065	17.2328	17.3596	17.4870	17.6149	17.7433	17.8722	18.0017
7	14.9708	15.0927	15.2152	15.3383	15.4620	15.5863	15.7111	15.8365	15.9625	16.0891	16.2163	16.3440	16.4723	16.6012	16.7307	16.8607	16.9913	17.1225
8	13.5097	13.6338	13.7585	13.8839	14.0100	14.1367	14.2641	14.3922	14.5209	14.6503	14.7803	14.9109	15.0423	15.1742	15.3068	15.4401	15.5740	15.7085
9	12.3801	12.5063	12.6333	12.7611	12.8895	13.0188	13.1487	13.2794	13.4108	13.5430	13.6758	13.8094	13.9437	14.0787	14.2145	14.3509	14.4881	14.6259
10	11.4825	11.6109	11.7402	11.8702	12.0011	12.1328	12.2653	12.3986	12.5327	12.6676	12.8033	12.9398	13.0771	13.2151	13.3540	13.4935	13.6339	13.7751
12	10.1511	10.2839	10.4176	10.5523	10.6880	10.8246	10.9621	11.1006	11.2400	11.3804	11.5216	11.6638	11.8069	11.9508	12.0957	12.2415	12.3881	12.5356
15	08.8491	08.9883	09.1287	09.2702	09.4128	09.5566	09.7015	09.8475	09.9945	10.1427	10.2920	10.4423	10.5937	10.7461	10.8996	11.0540	11.2095	11.3660
20	07.6037	07.7530	07.9038	08.0560	08.2095	08.3645	08.5207	08.6783	08.8372	08.9973	09.1587	09.3214	09.4852	09.6503	09.8165	09.9838	10.1523	10.3219
21	07.4335	07.5848	07.7375	07.8917	08.0473	08.2043	08.3627	08.5224	08.6835	08.8459	09.0095	09.1744	09.3405	09.5079	09.6764	09.8460	10.0168	10.1888
22	07.2811	07.4343	07.5890	07.7452	07.9028	08.0618	08.2223	08.3841	08.5473	08.7118	08.8776	09.0447	09.2130	09.3825	09.5532	09.7251	09.8981	10.0723
23	07.1442	07.2992	07.4558	07.6139	07.7735	07.9346	08.0970	08.2609	08.4262	08.5927	08.7606	08.9298	09.1002	09.2719	09.4447	09.6187	09.7939	09.9701
24	07.0208	07.1776	07.3361	07.4961	07.6576	07.8206	07.9850	08.1509	08.3181	08.4867	08.6566	08.8278	09.0003	09.1739	09.3488	09.5249	09.7020	09.8803
25	06.9092	07.0678	07.2281	07.3900	07.5533	07.7182	07.8846	08.0523	08.2215	08.3920	08.5639	08.7370	08.9114	09.0871	09.2639	09.4419	09.6210	09.8012
26	06.8080	06.9684	07.1305	07.2941	07.4593	07.6260	07.7942	07.9638	08.1349	08.3073	08.4810	08.6560	08.8323	09.0098	09.1885	09.3683	09.5493	09.7313
27	06.7161	06.8782	07.0420	07.2074	07.3744	07.5428	07.7128	07.8843	08.0571	08.2313	08.4068	08.5837	08.7617	08.9410	09.1215	09.3031	09.4858	09.6696
28	06.6323	06.7961	06.9616	07.1287	07.2974	07.4676	07.6394	07.8125	07.9871	08.1630	08.3403	08.5189	08.6987	08.8797	09.0618	09.2451	09.4294	09.6148
29	06.5559	06.7214	06.8885	07.0573	07.2276	07.3995	07.5729	07.7478	07.9240	08.1016	08.2806	08.4608	08.6422	08.8248	09.0086	09.1935	09.3794	09.5663
29½	06.5202	06.6864	06.8544	07.0240	07.1951	07.3679	07.5421	07.7177	07.8948	08.0732	08.2530	08.4340	08.6162	08.7996	08.9842	09.1698	09.3565	09.5442
30	06.4860	06.6531	06.8218	06.9922	07.1642	07.3377	07.5127	07.6892	07.8671	08.0463	08.2268	08.4086	08.5916	08.7758	08.9611	09.1474	09.3349	09.5233

Years	11¼%	11½%	11¾%	12%	12¼%	12½%	12¾%	13%	13¼%	13½%	13¾%	14%	14¼%	14½%	14¾%	15%	15¼%	15½%
1	88.4984	88.6151	88.7319	88.8488	88.9658	89.0829	89.2001	89.3173	89.4347	89.5521	89.6696	89.7872	89.9048	90.0226	90.1404	90.2584	90.3764	90.4945
1½	60.6343	60.7501	60.8660	60.9821	61.0983	61.2146	61.3311	61.4476	61.5643	61.6812	61.7981	61.9152	62.0324	62.1498	62.2672	62.3848	62.5026	62.6204
2	46.7240	46.8404	46.9569	47.0735	47.1904	47.3074	47.4245	47.5419	47.6594	47.7771	47.8949	48.0129	48.1311	48.2495	48.3680	48.4867	48.6056	48.7246
2½	38.3953	38.5127	38.6303	38.7482	38.8662	38.9845	39.1029	39.2216	39.3405	39.4596	39.5789	39.6984	39.8181	39.9381	40.0582	40.1786	40.2992	40.4199
3	32.8573	32.9761	33.0951	33.2144	33.3339	33.4537	33.5737	33.6940	33.8145	33.9353	34.0564	34.1777	34.2992	34.4210	34.5431	34.6654	34.7879	34.9107
3½	28.9139	29.0342	29.1548	29.2757	29.3969	29.5183	29.6401	29.7621	29.8845	30.0071	30.1301	30.2533	30.3768	30.5006	30.6247	30.7491	30.8738	30.9988
4	25.9671	26.0891	26.2113	26.3339	26.4568	26.5800	26.7036	26.8275	26.9518	27.0764	27.2013	27.3265	27.4521	27.5780	27.7042	27.8308	27.9577	28.0849
4½	23.6847	23.8083	23.9323	24.0566	24.1813	24.3064	24.4319	24.5577	24.6839	24.8105	24.9374	25.0647	25.1924	25.3205	25.4489	25.5777	25.7068	25.8363
5	21.8674	21.9927	22.1184	22.2445	22.3710	22.4980	22.6254	22.7531	22.8813	23.0099	23.1389	23.2683	23.3981	23.5283	23.6590	23.7900	23.9214	24.0532
5½	20.3881	20.5151	20.6426	20.7706	20.8990	21.0278	21.1571	21.2868	21.4170	21.5476	21.6787	21.8102	21.9422	22.0746	22.2074	22.3407	22.4744	22.6086
6	19.1624	19.2912	19.4205	19.5502	19.6805	19.8112	19.9425	20.0742	20.2063	20.3390	20.4722	20.6058	20.7399	20.8745	21.0095	21.1451	21.2811	21.4175
6½	18.1317	18.2623	18.3933	18.5249	18.6570	18.7897	18.9228	19.0565	19.1907	19.3254	19.4606	19.5964	19.7326	19.8694	20.0066	20.1444	20.2827	20.4215
7	17.2542	17.3865	17.5194	17.6528	17.7868	17.9213	18.0564	18.1920	18.3282	18.4649	18.6022	18.7401	18.8784	19.0174	19.1568	19.2968	19.4373	19.5784
8	15.8436	15.9794	16.1158	16.2529	16.3906	16.5289	16.6678	16.8073	16.9475	17.0882	17.2296	17.3716	17.5141	17.6573	17.8011	17.9455	18.0904	18.2360
9	14.7645	14.9037	15.0437	15.1843	15.3256	15.4676	15.6103	15.7536	15.8977	16.0424	16.1877	16.3338	16.4804	16.6278	16.7758	16.9244	17.0737	17.2236
10	13.9169	14.0596	14.2030	14.3471	14.4920	14.6377	14.7840	14.9311	15.0789	15.2275	15.3767	15.5267	15.6774	15.8287	15.9808	16.1335	16.2870	16.4411
12	12.6840	12.8332	12.9833	13.1342	13.2860	13.4386	13.5921	13.7463	13.9014	14.0572	14.2139	14.3713	14.5295	14.6885	14.8483	15.0088	15.1701	15.3321
15	11.5235	11.6819	11.8414	12.0017	12.1630	12.3253	12.4884	12.6525	12.8174	12.9832	13.1499	13.3175	13.4858	13.6551	13.8251	13.9959	14.1675	14.3400
20	10.4926	10.6643	10.8371	11.0109	11.1857	11.3615	11.5382	11.7158	11.8944	12.0738	12.2541	12.4353	12.6172	12.8000	12.9836	13.1679	13.3530	13.5389
21	10.3618	10.5358	10.7109	10.8870	11.0642	11.2422	11.4213	11.6012	11.7820	11.9637	12.1463	12.3297	12.5139	12.6989	12.8847	13.0712	13.2585	13.4464
22	10.2475	10.4238	10.6011	10.7794	10.9587	11.1390	11.3202	11.5023	11.6853	11.8692	12.0538	12.2393	12.4256	12.6127	12.8005	12.9890	13.1783	13.3682
23	10.1475	10.3259	10.5053	10.6857	10.8671	11.0494	11.2327	11.4168	11.6018	11.7877	11.9743	12.1618	12.3500	12.5390	12.7287	12.9190	13.1101	13.3018
24	10.0597	10.2401	10.4215	10.6039	10.7872	10.9715	11.1567	11.3427	11.5296	11.7173	11.9058	12.0951	12.2851	12.4758	12.6673	12.8593	13.0521	13.2454
25	09.9824	10.1647	10.3480	10.5323	10.7175	10.9036	11.0906	11.2784	11.4671	11.6565	11.8467	12.0377	12.2293	12.4217	12.6147	12.8084	13.0026	13.1975
26	09.9144	10.0985	10.2836	10.4696	10.6565	10.8443	11.0330	11.2225	11.4128	11.6038	11.7956	11.9881	12.1813	12.3752	12.5697	12.7648	12.9604	13.1567
27	09.8543	10.0401	10.2269	10.4145	10.6031	10.7925	10.9828	11.1738	11.3656	11.5582	11.7514	11.9454	12.1400	12.3352	12.5310	12.7274	12.9244	13.1219
28	09.8013	09.9886	10.1770	10.3662	10.5563	10.7472	10.9389	11.1314	11.3246	11.5185	11.7132	11.9084	12.1043	12.3008	12.4978	12.6954	12.8936	13.0922
29	09.7543	09.9432	10.1330	10.3236	10.5151	10.7075	10.9005	11.0944	11.2889	11.4841	11.6800	11.8764	12.0735	12.2712	12.4693	12.6680	12.8672	13.0669
29½	09.7328	09.9225	10.1130	10.3043	10.4965	10.6895	10.8832	11.0777	11.2728	11.4686	11.6651	11.8621	12.0597	12.2579	12.4566	12.6558	12.8555	13.0556
30	09.7127	09.9030	10.0941	10.2862	10.4790	10.6726	10.8670	11.0620	11.2578	11.4542	11.6512	11.8488	12.0469	12.2456	12.4448	12.6445	12.8446	13.0452

Years	15¾%	16%	16¼%	16½%	16¾%	17%	17¼%	17½%	17¾%	18%	18¼%	18½%	18¾%	19%	19½%	20%	20½%	21%
1	90.6126	90.7309	90.8493	90.9677	91.0862	91.2048	91.3235	91.4423	91.5611	91.6800	91.7991	91.9182	92.0374	92.1556	92.3954	92.6346	92.8740	93.1138
1½	62.7384	62.8565	62.9747	63.0931	63.2115	63.3301	63.4489	63.5677	63.6867	63.8058	63.9251	64.0444	64.1639	64.2835	64.5231	64.7633	65.0039	65.2450
2	48.8438	48.9632	49.0827	49.2024	49.3223	49.4423	49.5625	49.6829	49.8034	49.9242	50.0450	50.1661	50.2873	50.4087	50.6519	50.8959	51.1404	51.3857
2½	40.5409	40.6621	40.7835	40.9052	41.0270	41.1490	41.2713	41.3937	41.5164	41.6392	41.7623	41.8856	42.0091	42.1328	42.3808	42.6296	42.8793	43.1298
3	35.0338	35.1571	35.2806	35.4044	35.5285	35.6528	35.7773	35.9021	36.0272	36.1524	36.2780	36.4038	36.5298	36.6561	36.9094	37.1636	37.4189	37.6751
3½	31.1240	31.2496	31.3754	31.5015	31.6279	31.7546	31.8816	32.0089	32.1365	32.2643	32.3924	32.5209	32.6496	32.7785	33.0374	33.2973	33.5584	33.8206
4	28.2125	28.3403	28.4685	28.5971	28.7259	28.8551	28.9846	29.1144	29.2446	29.3750	29.5058	29.6370	29.7684	29.9002	30.1647	30.4304	30.6974	30.9657
4½	25.9662	26.0964	26.2270	26.3580	26.4894	26.6210	26.7531	26.8855	27.0183	27.1514	27.2849	27.4188	27.5530	27.6875	27.9577	28.2293	28.5024	28.7768
5	24.1855	24.3181	24.4511	24.5846	24.7184	24.8526	24.9872	25.1223	25.2577	25.3935	25.5297	25.6663	25.8032	25.9406	26.2165	26.4939	26.7729	27.0534
5½	22.7432	22.8782	23.0136	23.1495	23.2859	23.4226	23.5598	23.6974	23.8354	23.9739	24.1128	24.2521	24.3918	24.5320	24.8135	25.0968	25.3817	25.6682
6	21.5545	21.6919	21.8298	21.9681	22.1069	22.2462	22.3859	22.5261	22.6667	22.8078	22.9494	23.0914	23.2339	23.3768	23.6639	23.9529	24.2436	24.5360
6½	20.5607	20.7005	20.8408	20.9816	21.1228	21.2646	21.4068	21.5496	21.6928	21.8365	21.9807	22.1254	22.2705	22.4161	22.7088	23.0034	23.2998	23.5981
7	19.7200	19.8621	20.0048	20.1479	20.2916	20.4359	20.5806	20.7258	20.8716	21.0179	21.1647	21.3120	21.4598	21.6081	21.9062	22.2062	22.5083	22.8123
8	18.3821	18.5288	18.6761	18.8240	18.9725	19.1215	19.2711	19.4213	19.5720	19.7233	19.8751	20.0275	20.1804	20.3339	20.6425	20.9533	21.2661	21.5811
9	17.3741	17.5253	17.6771	17.8295	17.9826	18.1362	18.2905	18.4454	18.6009	18.7569	18.9136	19.0709	19.2287	19.3871	19.7057	20.0266	20.3496	20.6749
10	16.5959	16.7514	16.9075	17.0643	17.2217	17.3798	17.5386	17.6979	17.8579	18.0186	18.1798	18.3417	18.5042	18.6673	18.9953	19.3256	19.6583	19.9932
12	15.4948	15.6583	15.8225	15.9874	16.1530	16.3193	16.4863	16.6539	16.8223	16.9912	17.1609	17.3312	17.5021	17.6737	18.0187	18.3661	18.7159	19.0681
15	14.5131	14.6871	14.8617	15.0371	15.2133	15.3901	15.5676	15.7458	15.9247	16.1043	16.2845	16.4653	16.6467	16.8288	17.1948	17.5630	17.9335	18.3062
20	13.7254	13.9126	14.1005	14.2891	14.4782	14.6681	14.8585	15.0495	15.2410	15.4332	15.6258	15.8190	16.0127	16.2069	16.5967	16.9883	17.3816	17.7765
21	13.6351	13.8244	14.0143	14.2049	14.3961	14.5879	14.7802	14.9732	15.1666	15.3606	15.5551	15.7501	15.9455	16.1415	16.5347	16.9295	17.3260	17.7239
22	13.5587	13.7500	13.9418	14.1342	14.3272	14.5208	14.7149	14.9096	15.1048	15.3004	15.4966	15.6932	15.8902	16.0877	16.4839	16.8816	17.2808	17.6814
23	13.4942	13.6871	13.8807	14.0748	14.2695	14.4647	14.6604	14.8566	15.0533	15.2505	15.4481	15.6461	15.8446	16.0434	16.4423	16.8426	17.2442	17.6470
24	13.4394	13.6340	13.8291	14.0247	14.2209	14.4176	14.6147	14.8123	15.0104	15.2089	15.4078	15.6072	15.8069	16.0069	16.4081	16.8106	17.2144	17.6192
25	13.3929	13.5889	13.7855	13.9825	14.1800	14.3780	14.5765	14.7753	14.9746	15.1743	15.3744	15.5749	15.7757	15.9769	16.3801	16.7846	17.1901	17.5967
26	13.3535	13.5508	13.7486	13.9469	14.1456	14.3448	14.5444	14.7444	14.9448	15.1456	15.3467	15.5481	15.7499	15.9520	16.3571	16.7632	17.1704	17.5784
27	13.3199	13.5184	13.7173	13.9167	14.1166	14.3168	14.5175	14.7185	14.9198	15.1216	15.3236	15.5259	15.7286	15.9315	16.3382	16.7458	17.1543	17.5637
28	13.2913	13.4909	13.6909	13.8913	14.0921	14.2933	14.4949	14.6968	14.8990	15.1015	15.3044	15.5075	15.7109	15.9146	16.3226	16.7315	17.1412	17.5517
29	13.2670	13.4675	13.6684	13.8698	14.0715	14.2735	14.4759	14.6706	14.8816	15.0848	15.2884	15.4922	15.6963	15.9006	16.3098	16.7198	17.1306	17.5419
29½	13.2562	13.4572	13.6585	13.8603	14.0624	14.2648	14.4675	14.6706	14.8739	15.0776	15.2814	15.4856	15.6899	15.8945	16.3043	16.7148	17.1260	17.5378
30	13.2462	13.4476	13.6494	13.8515	14.0540	14.2568	14.4599	14.6633	14.8670	15.0709	15.2751	15.4795	15.6841	15.8890	16.2993	16.7102	17.1219	17.5341

Years	21½%	22%	22½%	23%	23½%	24%
1	93.3540	93.5944	93.8352	94.0764	94.3178	94.5596
1½	65.4866	65.7287	65.9713	66.2144	66.4580	66.7022
2	51.6316	51.8782	52.1254	52.3734	52.6219	52.8711
2½	43.3811	43.6333	43.8862	44.1400	44.3946	44.6500
3	37.9323	38.1905	38.4497	38.7098	38.9709	39.2329
3½	34.0840	34.3484	34.6140	34.8807	35.1485	35.4173
4	31.2353	31.5061	31.7782	32.0515	32.3261	32.6019
4½	29.0526	29.3298	29.6084	29.8883	30.1696	30.4523
5	27.3354	27.6190	27.9040	28.1905	28.4785	28.7680
5½	25.9563	26.2461	26.5375	26.8305	27.1251	27.4213
6	24.8302	25.1262	25.4238	25.7232	26.0242	26.3269
6½	23.8982	24.2002	24.5039	24.8095	25.1168	25.4258
7	23.1182	23.4260	23.7357	24.0472	24.3606	24.6759
8	21.8981	22.2171	22.5382	22.8612	23.1862	23.5132
9	21.0024	21.3320	21.6636	21.9974	22.3331	22.6709
10	20.3304	20.6697	21.0112	21.3548	21.7005	22.0481
12	19.4224	19.7790	20.1377	20.4984	20.8612	21.2259
15	18.6809	19.0576	19.4362	19.8167	20.1989	20.5828
20	18.1729	18.5706	18.9698	19.3701	19.7716	20.1741
21	18.1231	18.5237	18.9254	19.3283	19.7322	20.1371
22	18.0832	18.4861	18.8901	19.2952	19.7011	20.1079
23	18.0510	18.4560	18.8620	19.2689	19.6766	20.0850
24	18.0250	18.4318	18.8395	19.2480	19.6571	20.0670
25	18.0042	18.4125	18.8216	19.2313	19.6418	20.0528
26	17.9873	18.3969	18.8072	19.2181	19.6296	20.0416
27	17.9737	18.3844	18.7958	19.2076	19.6200	20.0328
28	17.9627	18.3744	18.7866	19.1993	19.6124	20.0259
29	17.9539	18.3664	18.7793	19.1926	19.6064	20.0204
29½	17.9501	18.3630	18.7762	19.1899	19.6038	20.0181
30	17.9467	18.3599	18.7734	19.1874	19.6016	20.0161

1. Locate the monthly payment factor for the desired interest rate and term of years.

2. Multiply this number by the loan amount divided by $1,000 to obtain the MONTHLY PAYMENT. For instance, for a $75,000 Loan amount, multiply the factor by $75 ($75,000 ÷ $1,000 = $75).

3. Round up to the nearest penny.

The monthly payment of principal and interest for a $75,000 loan at 12% for 30 years is 10.2862 × $75 = $771.465 or $771.47.

(2,985.35 ÷ 12 = 248.779 = 248.78). The amount going to pay the principal is $396.46 (the monthly payment) minus $248.78 (the amount allocated to interest), resulting in a payment toward principal of $147.68 ($396.46 − $248.78 = $147.68). Each succeeding monthly payment can be computed in this same way.

You see that in this example (see illustration 90) the amount of interest paid when you first start to make payments is larger than the amount of principal being paid. However, as the principal is paid off, the portion of the payment going to pay interest will drop steadily. By the time you have paid off half the principal, the amount of interest in each payment will be much lower than the amount going to the principal. Figuring 10 percent of $15,000, half the principal, amounts to $1,500 interest for a year. Dividing this figure by 12, you get $125 interest due for one month. Out of the $396.46 payment now, only $125 goes to the interest and

$396.46 minus $125, or $271.46, goes to pay the principal, a considerable increase in the ratio of principal to interest. By the time three-quarters of the loan is paid off, the interest portion will be quite low, amounting to only $62.50 out of the $396.46 payment.

THE BALLOON PAYMENT

Sometimes a balloon payment will be due during the period of a loan, usually at the end. It is ballooned because it is much larger than the regular installment amount. For example, you may have amortized your loan over a 15- or 20-year period to keep the monthly payments lower, but the loan is due and payable in 10 years. After 10 years the remaining principal due at that time must be paid

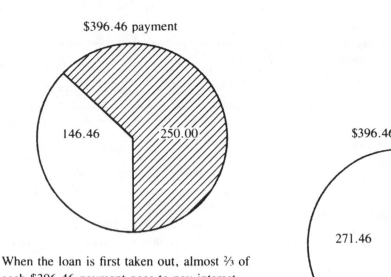

$396.46 payment

146.46   250.00

When the loan is first taken out, almost ⅔ of each $396.46 payment goes to pay interest.

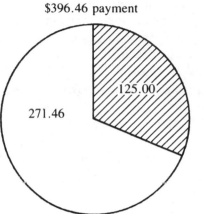

$396.46 payment

271.46   125.00

When ½ the loan is paid off, almost ⅓ of each $396.46 payment goes to pay interest.

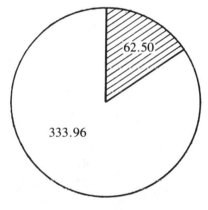

$396.46 payment

62.50

333.96

When ¾ of the loan is paid off, only about ⅙ of each $396.46 payment goes to pay interest.

Portion of payment that goes to pay principal.

Portion of payment that goes to pay interest.

90. Relationship between Principal and Interest during Payment Period

in a lump sum along with any interest due, usually only that which is due for that month.

Occasionally a loan will have one or more balloon payments periodically during the loan. For instance, your seller may allow you to amortize your loan over a 20-year period to keep your monthly payments down, but then may want you to pay, in addition to your regular monthly payments, a balloon payment at the end of, say, 5 years and another final balloon payment at the end of 10 years, so that the loan is paid in full in 10 years. These balloon payments will be credited almost entirely toward the principal.

For instance, if you were paying off a loan with an interest rate of 12 percent and monthly installments of $300, and the principal balance is $20,000 before paying a set balloon payment, the usual monthly payment would consist of ($20,000 × .12) ÷ 12 months which equals $200 interest, leaving $100 to go toward principal. If, however, you paid a $5,000 balloon payment at this time, the same $200 would be credited against interest, and $4,800 would be credited against principal, leaving a principal balance on the loan of $15,200. Your next monthly installment of $300 would then break down as follows: ($15,200 × .12) ÷ 12 months equals $152 toward interest and $148 toward principal.

THE LOAN FEES

Generally, if the seller is financing your loan, no loan fees will be charged other than the interest rate. However, if you are financing your purchase through a commercial financial institution, there will be various charges, including an application fee, charges for credit checks, property appraisal, points that are generally calculated as a percentage of the total loan, and charges for drawing up and recording the loan documents. Loan fees may be called a *debt service fee, loan brokerage fee, new loan fee, placement fee, origination fee,* or *loan installment fee.* They are not standard from lender to lender, so it is possible to save hundreds, even thousands, of dollars by shopping around for a lender and comparing interest rates, loan fees, and points charged. This will be discussed further in

chapter 25, "Borrowing from Third Party Lenders."

HOW TO GET A COMPUTERIZED LOAN AMORTIZATION SCHEDULE

Although knowing how to compute all the aspects of your loan yourself is essential, for a slight fee a computer company in Santa Monica, California, will compute everything for you and send you a computer printout of your entire payment schedule. You must send the following information: the amount of the loan, the interest rate, the term of the loan in years and months, the amount of each payment, and the payment schedule (monthly, quarterly, annually, etc.). You can omit either the term of the loan or the amount of each payment, and they can still compute your loan. Indicate if the interest is to be paid as part of each installment. If you are to make monthly payments and escrow closes in the middle of the month, the first payment will not be due for a full thirty days. Give the number of days accounted for in that first month.

A loan amortization schedule costs $12 for a straight loan schedule with a term of 19 years or less. If the term is more than 19 years or if there are any changes, such as a change in interest rate or balloon payments, the charge is $24. The printout they send you gives the terms of the loan, including the number of payments, the amount of each payment, the breakdown of how much of each payment goes toward interest, the amount of the principal still unpaid at the end of each payment, and the sum of the entire loan. For an additional $18 you can also buy a Truth in Lending Law Disclosure Statement, which states the full amount of any finance charges the lending institution may attach and the full interest charged on the loan. Lending institutions are required to furnish you with this information. However, if you are financing your purchase through the seller, a loan amortization schedule might be very informative. The company responds to requests immediately.

Send your name and address and the information required with a check to: Delphi Information Sciences Corporation, P.O. Box 3066, Santa Monica, California 90403. The telephone number is (213) 828-5541. (See Useful Resources in chapter 27 for a pamphlet on truth in lending.)

You should, however, try to get the seller or real estate agent to furnish this essential information for you. Many brokers now have computer software that can give you a partial printout with the essential loan information you will need, as described above.

FACTORS THAT AFFECT THE COST OF A LOAN

The Effect of the Interest Rate on the Cost of the Loan

When a loan is being paid off over a long period of time, a variation in the interest rate of even one percent can make quite a difference in the total amount you pay. The figures below show the effect of one percent increases in the interest rate on a $40,000 loan over a period of ten years:

Interest Rate (%)	Monthly Payment of Principal and Interest	Total Interest for 10 years
9	$506.71	$20,805.20
10	528.61	23,433.20
11	551.01	26,121.20
12	573.09	28,770.80
13	597.25	31,670.00
14	621.07	34,528.40
15	645.34	37,440.80

The Effect of the Amount of the Down Payment on the Cost of the Loan

The more cash you can afford for a down payment, the cheaper your loan will be in the long run. The figures below show the amount of interest paid in proportion to various down payments made on a $60,000 purchase at 12 percent interest paid off in monthly installments for ten years:

% of $60,000	Down Payment	Principal Amount to be amortized	Monthly Payments of Principal and Interest for 10 years	Interest for 10 years
	0	$60,000	$830.83	$43,299.12
10% =	$ 6,000.00	54,000	774.74	38,968.80
15% =	9,000.00	51,000	731.70	36,804.25
20% =	12,000.00	48,000	688.66	34,639.29
25% =	15,000.00	45,000	645.62	32,474.34
30% =	18,000.00	42,000	602.58	30,309.38
40% =	24,000.00	36,000	516.50	25,979.47

The Effect of the Payment Period on the Cost of the Loan

Although the total amount of interest will be lower if you pay off your loan fast, most buyers like to spread their payments over a long period of time in order to keep the monthly payments at a level easy to meet. However, to give you an example of the effect of the payment period on the cost of a loan, the figures below show the size of each payment and the total amount of interest on a $40,000 loan at 10 percent interest for four different payment periods.

Payment Period (years)	Monthly Payment of Principal and Interest	Total Interest Paid
5	$849.89	$10,993.40
10	528.61	23,433.20
15	429.85	37,373.00
20	386.01	52,642.40

THE ADVANTAGES OF PREPAYMENT WITHOUT PENALTY OR PROHIBITION

You can cut down on the total amount of interest you will ultimately pay by making larger payments early in the payment schedule, since interest is figured as a percentage of the unpaid principal. You can do this only if your loan agreement includes a statement that "the principal and interest are payable in installments of _____ dollars *or more.*" (See illustration 85 in chapter 21.) I have always been able to add this clause to a loan agreement where it was not already included. Often it is.

Your creditor may not want you to pay off your loan early because that would deprive him of interest. Another reason for prohibition of early payment is that the creditor does not want to take in more money than expected because it would push him into a higher income tax bracket. He might put a *prepayment penalty clause* in the note that specifies that you are to be penalized if you pay off any part of the loan in advance. This penalty makes up for the interest lost by the early payment. Or the lender might put in a clause totally prohibiting prepayment, or early payoff, of the loan. Always fight to have such a penalty clause removed from the loan agreement and note. It is harder to have this clause removed from a commercial loan than from one financed by the seller. Also the longer the term of the loan the harder it is to get it removed. Some states have laws allowing prepayment after the first year of sale for residential property. Check with the bank or mortgage company, title or escrow company or lawyer to find out the laws in your state.

If you decide to sell your land before it is fully paid for, you will be in a better position if you can offer the buyer title free of encumbrances. If you are allowed to prepay your debt, when your buyer pays you for the land you can pay off your creditor to get clear title. If you are not permitted to prepay your debt, you will be unable to clear the title for your buyer, and you might have trouble selling the land.

Sometimes a lender would be very happy to receive a large amount of cash early, and you might save some money. If you come into some money, you can offer to prepay the total remaining due if your creditor gives you a discount on the remaining unpaid balance. It might be that the lender could really use the extra cash and is anxious to have the mortgage paid off early in exchange for a discount. Such a situation occurs frequently when the seller finances the sale himself. Professional mortgage companies that purchase notes generally discount them for cash by as much as 40 percent. For example, if your seller holds a note with a balance of $40,000, a mortgage company might pay him $30,000 cash for the note. Certainly your seller would give the same discount to you if he was interested in getting paid off early. Never offer to pay off a loan early without asking your lender to discount the note. You might easily save a few thousand dollars.

ADJUSTABLE RATE MORTGAGES WITH VARIABLE INTEREST RATES

Adjustable rate mortgages (ARM) with variable interest rates are sometimes also called variable rate loans or floating loans. Shopping for a mortgage used to be a relatively simple process. Most home mortgage loans had interest rates that did not change over the life of the loan. Choosing among these *fixed rate* mortgage loans meant comparing interest rates, monthly payments, fees, prepayment penalties, and due-on-sale clauses.

Today, many loans have interest rates (and monthly payments) that can change from time to time. To compare one ARM with another or with a fixed rate mortgage, you need to know about indexes, margins, discounts, caps, negative amortization, and convertibility. You need to consider the maximum amount your monthly payment could increase. Most important, you need to compare what might happen to your mortgage costs with your future ability to pay.

With a fixed rate mortgage, the interest rate stays the same during the life of the loan. But with an ARM, the interest rate changes periodically, usually in relation to an index, and payments may go up or down accordingly.

Lenders generally charge lower initial interest rates for ARMs than for fixed rate mortgages. This makes the ARM easier on your pocketbook at first than a fixed rate mortgage for the same amount. It also means that you might qualify for a larger loan because lenders sometimes make this decision on the basis of your current income and the first year's payments. Moreover, your ARM could be less expensive over a long period than a fixed rate mortgage—for example, if interest rates remain steady or move lower.

Against these advantages, you have to weigh the risk that an increase in interest rates would lead to higher monthly payments in the future. It's a trade-off—you get a lower initial rate with an ARM in exchange for assuming more risk. Be aware that if interest rates skyrocket as they did in the late 70s, the mortgage payments could increase beyond your capacity to make the payments. Over the course of a variable rate loan, the payments could increase $500 per month or more. This is why you always want an interest rate cap on your loan.

An *interest rate cap* places a limit on the amount your interest rate can increase. ARMs with caps may cost more than ARMs without them. Caps are of two types: *periodic caps*, which limit the interest rate increases from one adjustment period to the next; and *overall caps*, which limit the interest rate increase over the life of the loan.

Some ARMs include *payment caps*, which limit the monthly payment increase at the time of each adjustment. For example, a 5 percent cap would mean that a mortgage payment of $400 could increase to no more than $420 during the first adjustment period and no more than $441 in the second.

With most ARMs, the interest rate and monthly payment change every six months, every year, every three years, or every five years. However, some ARMs have more frequent interest and payment changes. The period between one rate change and the next is called the *adjustment period*. So a loan with an adjustment period of one year is called a one-year ARM, and the interest rate can change once every year.

Most lenders tie ARM interest rate changes to changes in an *index rate*. These indexes usually go up and down with the general movement of interest rates. If the index rate goes up, so does your mortgage rate in most circumstances, and you will probably have to make higher monthly payments. On the other hand, if the index rate goes down, your monthly payment may go down.

Sometimes the initial interest rate offered for ARMs is several points below the current market rate. In this case, you can be sure that unless market rates drop substantially your interest rate and your monthly payment will rise the maximum amount allowed in the next few adjustment periods until your interest rate reaches current market rates.

Lenders base ARM rates on a variety of indexes. Among the most common are the rates on one-, three-, or five-year Treasury securities, or the national or regional average cost of funds to savings and loan associations. A few lenders use their own cost of funds, over which—unlike other indexes—they have some control. You should ask what index will be used and how often it changes. Also ask how it has behaved in the past and where it is published.

An ARM loan with a *variable interest rate* may be valuable if interest rates are exceedingly high at the time you take out a loan. Usually, however, only institutional lenders offer ARMs because calculating a varying interest rate is somewhat complicated.

In recent years, whenever interest rates have been very high, many commercial lenders have offered only variable rate loans and have deleted their fixed rate loans on real property.

You will see mortgages advertised that look extremely attractive. Ads will feature low initial interest rates without disclosing that substantial increases could occur over the course of the loan.

(See information on truth in lending in chapter 25.) Every lender should give you in writing the factors that will cause your rate to increase; what the effects of the increase will be; and limitations, if any, on the increases.

When comparing adjustable rate mortgages, obtain the following information:

> ARM annual percentage rate
> Adjustment period
> Index used and current rate
> Margin
> Initial payment without discount
> Initial payment with discount (if any)
> How long will discount last?
> Interest rate caps: periodic
>   overall
> Payment caps
> Negative amortization
> Convertibility or prepayment privilege
> Initial fees and charges
> *Monthly Payment Amounts*
> 1.   What will my monthly payment be after twelve months if the index rate
>   a.   stays the same?
>   b.   goes up 2 percent?
>   c.   goes down 2 percent?
> 2.   What will my monthly payment be after three years if the index rate
>   a.   stays the same
>   b.   goes up 2 percent per year
>   c.   goes down 2 percent per year

Take into account any caps on your mortgage, and remember that it may run as long as thirty years.

NEGATIVE AMORTIZATION

Many commercial lenders are now offering a feature called negative amortization, usually in conjunction with variable interest rate loans. Negative amortization means that your monthly payment is not sufficient to pay the total amount of monthly interest due, and therefore your loan balance will actually increase. For instance, say you have a loan balance of $65,000 and your interest rate is 14 percent.

($65,000 $\times$ .14) $\div$ 12 months = $758.34 interest due per month.

If, however, your monthly payment is $700, it wouldn't even pay the interest due, and the $58.34 left owing would be added to the principal. The next month's interest would be calculated: ($65,058.33 × .14) ÷ 12 months = $759.02. Notice that the amount of interest due is increasing too. If your payments stay the same, you keep adding the extra interest to the principal each month, and you are then charged interest on the interest.

If interest rates are high, commercial lenders sometimes offer negative amortization on some variable rate loans for the first six months or one year to keep the payments lower and therefore more attractive to prospective borrowers. However, after the time period of negative amortization is up, you may find that your monthly payments are much higher than you can afford.

Or a lender might offer a fixed interest rate for the first six months, and then beginning with the seventh month the interest rate begins to vary, while the payments stay the same for the rest of the year. If the interest rates go up, your payments may not cover the interest due. Then every twelve months thereafter the payments are adjusted to an amount sufficient to pay the unpaid balance in full by the maturity date. Again, you may find that your payments have increased so much that you cannot afford them.

If you cannot afford payments that at least pay the interest due, you cannot afford the loan. Always check to be sure there isn't a negative amortization clause buried in the text of your loan. And always check your monthly loan statement if you have a variable rate loan to be sure that the payment has covered both interest and some portion of principal, even though very small at first.

LOAN INTEREST IS TAX DEDUCTIBLE

You are permitted to deduct any interest you pay on a loan from your state and federal income tax obligation. This, along with the right to deduct property taxes and to depreciate real property from your income taxes, makes land ownership easier for the average-income family.

MAINTAINING A PAYMENT SCHEDULE

It is important to maintain an accurate schedule of your loan payments and the terms of your loan. Illustration 91 can be used as a model when you set up your payment schedule. You can figure out what portion of each payment goes to principal and to interest by using the methods explained at the beginning of this chapter.

Amount of Principal Indebtedness _____

Interest Rate of _____ % Payable _____ (e.g., monthly, quarterly) _____

Payments Made _____ (e.g., the first day of each month) _____ Beginning _____

Date	Amount of Full Payment	Amount of Interest Paid	Amount Going Towards Principal	Principal Balance Still Owed

91. Sample Payment Schedule

CHAPTER 23

Buying Property That Is Encumbered by a Loan Agreement

TAKING SUBJECT TO OR ASSUMING A LOAN

When you buy land, if the seller still owes money under a loan agreement that he cannot pay off before conveying title to you, you will either take the land subject to the loan or you will assume the loan.

If you buy *subject to* a loan, the seller continues to be personally responsible for making the payments until his loan is fully paid. You make a separate loan agreement with the seller. You then pay him, and he pays his creditor. When he pays off his loan, he will get clear title to the land. When you finish paying your seller, he will give you clear title. During this time, if the seller fails to make his payments, his creditor can foreclose on his loan and you will lose the land unless you jump in and take over the payments yourself. If you have to do this, you will stop making payments to your seller. The problem is you might have to make larger payments than you expected. Here is an example of a case I was hired to deal with:

Seller A buys a 120-acre piece of property for $120,000, pays $30,000 down, and gives back to the seller a note and mortgage for $90,000, payable

$1,000 per month. Seller A then divides the property into three 40-acre parcels and sells two of them for $80,000 each to buyers B and C. Buyers B and C pay cash for their property, so the seller receives $160,000, and he pays his lender $30,000 cash for each of the two parcels he sells to B and C, and the lender releases those parcels from the $90,000 mortgage. Thus, the mortgage is reduced to $30,000, but the payments are still $1,000 a month.

Seller A then sells Buyer D the third parcel for $60,000 because it is worth less than the other two. He takes $15,000 down and a mortgage for $45,000 payable $500 per month from Buyer D. Therefore, Buyer D would be paying Seller A $500 a month, and Seller A has to add another $500 to it to make his $1,000 a month mortgage payments.

By this time Seller A has already received $175,000 from Buyers B, C, and D, and he has paid his lender only $90,000. So he is now $85,000 ahead. He then either gets in financial trouble and cannot make his $1,000 per month payments, or he simply walks away, leaving Buyer D holding the bag for the $1,000 per month payments. Buyer D is greatly distressed when his land starts to be foreclosed on, because he then has to come up with $1,000 per month to save his land.

How could this unfortunate situation have been avoided? When Buyer D bought his parcel for $60,000, giving back his seller a mortgage for $45,000, he should have found out that the seller still had his own mortgage against the property for $30,000. He would have known this from a title report or abstract. Buyer D then should have demanded a full disclosure from Seller A as to the existing mortgage. When Buyer D found out that the existing mortgage had payments of $1,000, either he should not have gone ahead with the deal, or he should have had Seller A renegotiate the terms of his loan so that Buyer D's payments covered the loan.

Or Buyer D could have made Seller A open a special collection account in the local bank and put in enough money to cover the extra $500 per month loan payments for the balance of the seller's loan. The money would be placed in an account where the seller could not withdraw it. Thus, so long as Buyer D made his $500 per month payments on time, he would be sure the other $500 was available to make the seller's $1,000 per month mortgage payments. The bank with this type of account makes the payments directly to the mortgage holder, so no money goes through the hands of Seller A.

On the other hand, if you *assume* the loan, you replace the seller and become personally liable to his creditor for the remaining debt. You pay your seller a sum of money in cash and get the property, with the remaining obligation on the loan. You are then primarily responsible for paying the loan. If you fail to make your payments, the creditor can foreclose on your loan. He can also sue your seller if he seeks a deficiency judgment, unless your seller gets the creditor to sign a document relieving him of liability under the loan once you assume it.

Most commercial loan agreements have a clause that prohibits transferring the debt without the written approval of the lender. If you are to assume a loan, be certain that the seller has his creditor's approval to transfer the property to you. Often a creditor will allow the debtor to transfer his obligation only if you qualify as a borrower and if the interest rate can be raised. If it will be raised before you are to assume the loan, you should shop around to see if you can get a new loan on better terms from someone else. If you can, borrow the money and pay for the land in cash, and give a mortgage to your lender under the terms you have received. If you cannot get a better deal than the loan you are to assume and you still want to purchase the land, try to get the seller to reduce his asking price by the amount of the increased interest you will be bound to pay.

THE WRAPAROUND OR ALL-INCLUSIVE MORTGAGE

It is always better to *assume* a loan than to take *subject to* it. If the seller will allow you to take title to the land only if you take subject to his loan rather than assume it, he may be planning to charge you a higher interest rate in his loan agreement with you than he is paying his lender so he can make a profit on the extra interest. This type of *secondary loan agreement* is taken subject to the seller's loan and is called a *wraparound* or *all-inclusive* loan agreement because your mortgage with your seller "wraps around," or includes, the loan agreement the seller has with his lender. Find out what the seller's interest rate is and whether he intends to overcharge you if you buy subject to his loan. Do not let him get away with this. Even if his increased interest rate is no larger than you would get under a new loan agreement, you are always better off assuming a loan than taking subject to it because you can deal directly with the creditor.

Wraparound mortgages are becoming more frequent, so you should be sure you understand how they work. The following illustration shows how the mechanics operate.

Seller takes back a $40,000 mortgage from buyer, at 12 percent interest, payable $450 per month which wraps around his existing mortgages.

Seller → Owes $20,000 to 1st mortgage holder A at 9 percent interest, payable $200 per month.

Seller → Owes $10,000 to 2nd mortgage holder B at 10 percent interest, payable $180 per month.

Therefore, buyer pays seller 12 percent on a $40,000 mortgage which wraps around the seller's preexisting mortgages at 9 percent and 10 percent. Seller thus makes extra money by charging buyer 12 percent to pay his loans at 9 percent and 10 percent. The buyer would be better off simply assuming the existing loans of $20,000 at 9 percent and $10,000 at 10 percent, giving the seller back a third mortgage for $10,000 at 12 percent. Then the buyer is paying 12 percent only on a $10,000 mortgage, rather than on a $40,000 mortgage.

If the seller insists on a wraparound or all-inclusive mortgage, then you must be sure that you and the seller open a special collection account at the local bank, whereby the bank takes your payment of $450 every month and pays the $200 first mortgage and $180 second mortgage automatically before any money goes to your seller. It then pays the $70 due the seller under his third mortgage.

This way, you know that as long as you make your monthly payment, the mortgage holders will be paid. Never rely on the seller himself to make these payments. If he is lax in making them and

foreclosure starts, you will have problems. Always open a special collection account in the local bank or savings and loan. The charge for this is minimal, usually a few dollars per month. The extra protection and security are well worth it.

If you do take title subject to a loan agreement, be sure the seller has permission from his lender to sell the property. Many loan agreements contain an *acceleration clause,* or *due-on-sale clause,* which is activated if the borrower sells or encumbers the land without permission. If the land is sold to you without permission from the lender, he can demand immediate payment of the entire remaining principal and interest. If your seller cannot pay this amount, the loan can be foreclosed on, and you could lose the land. Under these provisions, the only way a seller can convey his land is by paying the remaining money due before the sale. The due-on-sale provision is always contained in the note and deed of trust or mortgage.

The contract of sale should specify if you are to take title subject to or by assuming an existing loan. Either way, you should receive an offset statement or beneficiary statement from the creditor specifying the amount of interest and principal remaining on the loan, the amount of each payment, and how much longer payments must be made. This is very important. Never assume a loan without getting written confirmation from the lender as to the balance due on the loan. If you are assuming a loan held by a commercial lender, a fee will be charged for the necessary paperwork to transfer the documents.

Prorating the Loan Agreement if You Assume the Obligation

If you assume the responsibility of paying off the seller's loan on the property, you will have to prorate the seller's payment during the month that escrow closes. For instance, say escrow is to close on the thirteenth day of the month, and payments are made on the first. If the monthly payments you are to assume are $450 including principal and interest, divide this figure by 30, the commonly accepted number of days in a month, to get the amount of the payment due per day, in this case $15. Multiply the $15 owed per day by the seventeen days that you will own the land that month.

You will credit the seller with this amount, in this case $255, since he paid the entire month's payment on the first. To see how this fits into the pattern on closing of escrow, see chapter 30, "Opening and Closing of Escrow and the Role of the Escrow Holder."

Getting the Seller to Remove the Lien at the Time of Purchase

If you want title to the property free of an existing loan agreement, Clause 6 of the Model Contract of Sale (chapter 28) takes care of this. When you place your money in escrow, you should instruct the escrow holder to pay the lender the money due him and request that a certificate of satisfaction or deed of reconveyance be recorded clearing the mortgage lien from the title to the property.

Assignment of the Loan Agreement

During the time you are making payments, your creditor might *assign* his rights to receive your payments to a third party in exchange for cash. Some commercial businesses buy loan agreement notes for an amount of cash that is less than the amount due on the loan. A person who needs money might be willing to sell his note at a loss for immediate cash. This frequently occurs with sellers who finance their own sales.

When an assignment occurs, a document is executed between your creditor and the buyer of your note which is recorded with the county recorder. When the recording takes place, you will be notified and bound to make all further payments to the new holder of the note. You might be required to sign a document, called an owner's estoppel certificate or debtor's statement, which certifies the amount of money you still owe on the loan and states that you are personally bound to pay the remaining amount. This document is executed to protect the person who is buying the right to receive your payments.

If you want to be able to sell your land before paying off your loan, you will also want the right to assign your obligation to your buyer. Your mortgage or trust deed and note will usually automatically be assignable, unless it is stated otherwise. Be sure to ask about this when you are in escrow.

PAYING THE INSURANCE, TAXES, AND ASSESSMENTS ON THE LAND —IMPOUNDS

Since the basic security for a loan is the property, your creditor wants to be certain that nothing happens to endanger his security. Therefore, he may require that you pay him the money for insurance, taxes, and assessments in advance, and he can then pay them as they become due. These additions to your normal payments are called *impounds*. Generally, in each payment you will be charged a portion of the annual insurance premiums and taxes for that year. The insurance premium and taxes are divided equally into twelve monthly installments if that is how you pay your mortgage or deed of trust. Commercial lenders usually require advance impound payments for the property taxes and insurance.

If the seller, rather than a financial institution, is your creditor, you may be responsible for paying these expenses yourself. But the tax collector will be instructed to notify him of any lapses in tax payments so that he can have a chance to pay them before the land is subjected to a tax sale. If you fail to pay the taxes or premiums, the creditor can legally foreclose on you.

If there is a house on the land, your creditor will probably require you to carry a basic policy of property insurance protecting the property against fire and other hazards. You will have to name the lender as a beneficiary in the policy too and deliver a copy of the insurance coverage to him. If the house burns, you will negotiate with the lender as to whether the insurance will be used to rebuild the house or cover your debt to the lender. The loan agreement will specify the amount of insurance coverage you must buy. These impounds may increase your monthly payments by $100 or more per month over the principal and interest due.

RECORDING A REQUEST FOR NOTICE OF DEFAULT

When a seller sells a parcel to you and you assume

an existing mortgage and give a new mortgage to the seller, the seller wants to be sure that he has notice if you fail to make your payments to the first mortgage holder. If the first mortgage holder starts to foreclose on you and the seller doesn't know it and the foreclosure goes through and you lose the land, your mortgage to the seller is wiped out. Therefore, the seller will always want to record a request for notice of default. This insures him that if you start to get foreclosed, he will know about it. He will then make the payments to the first mortgage holder himself and start to foreclose on you. In order to stop the foreclosure, you will have to reimburse the seller for any payments he made to the first mortgage holder. The next chapter tells you more about the process of foreclosure.

CHAPTER 24

Default, Foreclosure, and Redemption

DEFAULT

When you purchase your property and give a mortgage or deed of trust back to the seller or lender, you have certain obligations to meet during the term of the loan. You must keep the payments current on all your mortgages; you must keep the property taxes and fire insurance current; and you must not "commit waste" or damage the property or cause it to deteriorate, causing a lessening of the value of the property as security. For example, you will not be permitted to do a large-scale logging operation on forest land before the loan is substantially or totally paid off.

If you fail to meet any of your obligations out-lined above, then you are in *default* on your loan, and the lender or seller can immediately start to foreclose on you. This is usually started by his recording a *notice of default* and sending it to you and to all other persons who have an interest in the property, such as other mortgage holders, at the address specified in your security agreement. Be sure the lender or seller always has your current address. If you are not the current mortgage holder but you want to know if foreclosure proceedings start, you will want to record a *request for notice of default* with the county recorder. You can find out about this document through an attorney or a title or escrow company.

FORECLOSURE

Once the default has occurred, and foreclosure has begun, you will lose your land if you don't redeem your loan or cure the default.

Most states require a court or judicial foreclosure, which means that a notice of default must first be filed with the county recorder and a copy mailed to those interested in the property stating that the buyer has not made the required payments or paid the taxes or is otherwise in default. The buyer is then given from one to three months to make up the missed payments or otherwise cure the default. If the payments are not made, the creditor can file a petition to foreclose in the county court. The court evaluates the creditor's claim, determines its validity, declares the amount of money that is due him, and orders a foreclosure.

Then the creditor usually publishes a notice in the local newspaper that the property is to be sold to the highest bidder at a public auction. The sale is supervised by the court and often handled by a court-appointed commissioner. The proceeds from the sale are used to pay the creditor any money due on the land sale. If any surplus money remains, it goes to the defaulting buyer. This may not be a bad deal for the buyer if the land sells for a good price, but usually the lender bids in his note and simply takes the property back. It is rare that any money will be left over for the defaulting owner.

Under other policies, such as the *foreclosure without sale, strict foreclosure,* or *foreclosure by entry and possession,* the creditor takes the entire property and can do with it as he wishes.

When executing a loan agreement, you should understand the type of foreclosure the creditor can use if you default. These vary depending on the type of transaction involved. For example, if you are buying under a land contract, the seller can simply come onto the property and retake it without any court proceedings. If you are buying with a mortgage, it might take as long as four or five months for the seller to foreclose. Ask your title company or attorney about the proceedings in your case.

The Dangerous Acceleration Clause

A clause creditors usually put into the loan agreement states that the creditor can immediately demand, or accelerate, the entire amount of the remaining principal and interest if you miss a payment. You cannot prevent foreclosure simply by making up back payments. The entire amount due must be paid. Although this is a standard clause in most loan agreements, you should negotiate to have a grace period put in your loan with a late-payment penalty, just in case you get behind in payments. Even though the note has an acceleration clause, foreclosures are subject to state law. State laws often require a redemption period. Ask your title company, escrow company, bank, or lawyer if laws in your state allow for a redemption period.

CURING THE DEFAULT AND THE RIGHT OF REDEMPTION

Most states have laws allowing the debtor a certain period of time after foreclosure proceedings have begun to make up his payments, cure the default, and keep the land. This grace period is referred to as the *right of redemption* or *equity of redemption.* To redeem after a foreclosure is begun, the owner must make up all back payments due plus penalties plus interest; pay all property taxes to bring them current; pay all insurance premiums; pay the costs of foreclosure, which are often between $500 and $1,500; pay all legal fees incurred by the lender. There is a period of time after foreclosure commences when the payment of all of the above can stop a foreclosure. But after a certain time, according to state law, the foreclosure can be stopped only by the owner paying off the entire amount due on the loan, not just the back payments.

In some states, the redemption period extends until the time of the sale by foreclosure, which might be anywhere from two months to a year after the buyer defaults. If you make up defaults and pay the penalties, no further action can be taken against you by the creditor, and the foreclosure is stopped. If you do not make up your payments by the time the foreclosure sale is initiated, you have no further chance of keeping the land.

Some states allow a right of redemption even after a sale or repossession of the land by foreclosure. When the land is sold at a foreclosure sale, the new buyer does not take full title to it but gets an *equitable right to the title* during the period of redemption. He will get full legal title only if the debtor does not make up his payments by the end of the redemption period. During this time, the debtor still retains the right of possession of the land.

See chapter 42, "What to Do if You Are Having Trouble Making Payments," for valuable information on what to do if you can't make your payments. If you get into a serious bind leading to a foreclosure, you should immediately consult a real estate attorney.

THE DEFICIENCY JUDGMENT

Sometimes the lender has a right to sue the borrower to get a deficiency judgment if an insufficient amount of money is obtained from a foreclosure sale to make up the amount of money due him. However, most states and courts will not permit a deficiency judgment when the loan is made for the purchase of a home or land. Such a loan is called a *purchase money mortgage*. Since the loan was made on the basis of the value of the security, the creditor cannot complain if it later results that the property is worth less than the loan. If enough money is not obtained at a resale of the land, the court assumes that the buyer probably paid too much for it in the first place and should not have to suffer further because of that circumstance.

For instance, the seller sells you his land for $60,000, you pay off $10,000 worth of principal, and then default. You still owe $50,000. The seller forecloses the loan and resells the land for only $40,000. In most states, he cannot then obtain a deficiency judgment against you for the remaining $10,000.

ADVANTAGES OF A PARTIAL RECONVEYANCE OR PARTIAL RELEASE CLAUSE

If you purchase a large parcel of property, or two or more adjacent parcels, you can have a clause inserted that calls for a partial release of land with clear title after you make a specified number of payments. You can use the released portion of land as security for a new loan to finance construction of a house or meet other financial needs. Since you will have clear title to part of the land, if you find it necessary, you may be able to sell that portion not encumbered by liens to finance the remaining portion.

For example, if you purchase two 20-acre parcels and give the seller one mortgage secured by both parcels, and if you make a down payment of 30 percent of the purchase price at the close of escrow, you can have a release clause in the note stating that after you have paid off 35 percent of the remaining principal you can have one of the parcels released from the mortgage lien, i.e., reconveyed to you. That way you will have one of the 20-acre parcels free and clear of any liens so that you can sell it or borrow against it.

CHAPTER 25

Borrowing from Third Party Lenders

Most commercial lenders do not lend money on remote improved or unimproved rural land because they consider remote country property to be a speculative security. Values on such land are not easily determinable since fluctuations in the supply and demand are great. Whereas a lot in a town or city with an $80,000 house on it is apt to sell quickly at a predictable price if a foreclosure becomes necessary, it is much harder to sell 20 acres of land 100 miles from the nearest big city, especially if the land has no structures, commercial electricity, running water, or paved access.

If you are interested in rural land that has a house and basic amenities and is located in a developed rural area, your chances of getting a loan are improved because the lender's risk is reduced. If your country property is to be a second home and you have a mortgage on your first home, a commercial lender assumes that if you ever get into financial difficulty, you will default on your country property before defaulting on your regular home. When second-home loans are made, the lender often prefers to insure his loan by taking a first or second mortgage on the borrower's city house. These mortgages are called *homeowner's loans* or *home equity loans*, and many lending agencies, particularly mortgage specialists, offer them. Since nearly 65 percent of the householders in the United States own the houses they occupy, homeowner loans are becoming a major method of financing. The loan is based on the amount of equity the owner has in his house. Equity is calculated as the difference between the current fair market value of the house and the remaining balance owed on the mortgage, if there is one. For example, if your house and lot is appraised by the lender at $180,000 and you still owe $60,000 on the existing mortgage, you have an equity of $120,000, and the amount of money you can borrow for a second home is based on this amount. Interest rates are usually higher on homeowner loans than on conventional first mortgages. However, the interest is deductible on your taxes.

If you are buying a working farm, the commercial lender wants assurance that the income to be derived from it is enough to pay your family and business expenses as well as your loan. As with most country land, productive farm property is usually financed by the seller.

When a commercial lender does give a loan for purchase of country property, the terms are stricter than usual. The standard loan rule is: The greater the risk to the lender, the higher will be the interest rate, the shorter the maturity date, and the lower the ratio of loan to value. The ratio of loan to value is the percentage of the appraised value of the property that will be given as a loan. For instance, if the appraised value of a parcel is $80,000 and the loan-to-value ratio is 75 percent, you can get a maximum loan of $60,000. You generally get a lower loan-to-value ratio for rural property than for urban property because if the lender has to foreclose on you and sell the property to get his money back, he will generally have a harder time in rural areas than in urban areas. In urban areas, loan-to-value ratios may be as high as 90 percent.

When seeking a loan, go to as many different sources as possible and try to get the best terms you can. Because lending agencies located near the land you intend to buy will probably be familiar with the land and the local conditions, you should go to them first, unless you have established credit with, and are trusted by, an institution in your city.

Speak to the real estate agent handling the sale to see if he can offer some leads. Agents often have close ties with local banks and other lenders and can help you get a loan. However, be cautious. Lenders often offer kickbacks or commissions to agents who bring them business, and these are ultimately charged to the borrower indirectly through the loan fees. This problem is so rampant in the lending industry that the federal government submitted a proposal to Congress several years ago to deny FHA approval to any lender engaged in such practices. See what the agent can do for you, and then try to find a loan on better terms. You always have the absolute discretion to choose your own lender, so never give in to pressure from the agent. Only if he has the best deal should you go through him, but get an accounting of the loan fees first (see below).

Your chances of obtaining a loan depend to a great extent on whether money is "tight" or "easy" at the time you are making your purchase. Lending agencies constantly change their loan policies depending on the national and local economic situations and on the changes in the real estate market. Every lending agency has its own policies. For example, many lenders prefer loans underwritten by the government and prefer to lend money for home purchases. It is never easy to get financing on rural property, except from the seller, but if a commercial lender thinks your credit is very good, he might place more emphasis on this aspect than on the property value, and lend you some money. This chapter tells you what is available on the loan market. Never assume you can't get a loan without trying, particularly if the property has a house on it and your credit is good.

Each year the number of second-home buyers continues to increase. With this increasing demand for country property, there is every reason to believe that lending policies will continue to become more liberal with regard to the purchase of rural land.

YOUR FINANCIAL HISTORY AND CREDIT RATING

When you apply for a loan, you will be asked to fill out an application in which you are to give complete details of your financial condition and credit history, and you will be requested to produce documents relating to this information. Although the maximum amount of your loan will never be as much as the appraised value of the property, the lender is always concerned about your ability to repay the loan. Foreclosures are an expensive and time-consuming procedure. It is much easier for a creditor to work out feasible monthly payments than to go through an expensive foreclosure and the process of advertising and selling the property in order to have the loan repaid. Commercial lenders do not want to foreclose on a borrower. They want the borrower to make the mortgage payments because they make their profits on the interest collected.

When answering questions, be as truthful as possible. The computerization of bank and credit accounts is becoming so thorough that any dishonest answers are likely to be uncovered when the lending institution does its independent investigation. If you have had some problems in the past repaying debts, you should explain this to the loan officer handling your case rather than misstate the facts and have the lender discover the truth in some other manner.

The following information is required by all major lending institutions:

1. How much cash and how many liquid assets do you own at the time you are applying for the loan? Liquid assets are those things that can easily be converted to a known amount of cash, such as bonds and stocks, as opposed to real estate, which is a nonliquid asset. The lender will combine separate bank accounts of a married couple. He will request a copy of your checking account balance, savings account balance, and an accounting of your stocks and bonds. You will also have to produce current and past state and federal income tax returns.

2. What type of employment do you and your spouse have and what is your current income?

3. How many current debts do you have? All current debts in your family will be considered, as well as possible future debts, such as schooling and common necessities. The lender will determine whether you have too many debts for the size of your income, which would prevent you from being capable of paying further debts. A common formula used to determine the borrower's ability to repay a loan for the purpose of buying land is: The borrower's combined total monthly income minus the payments due on other loans must be at least four to four and a half times greater than the amount of the monthly payments that will be required on principal, interest, taxes, assessments, and insurance premiums.

4. What type of credit history do you have? This involves an investigation of your entire past with regard to loans and buying on credit. The lender will be looking to see whether you have always paid your bills on time, whether you borrow constantly for everything you buy, how many different persons you owe money to, whether you have ever declared bankruptcy, how often you move, whether you change jobs often, and how long you have had your present job.

5. What is your past banking experience? Here you will be asked to list your bank(s). They will be contacted for information regarding the size of your account, the length of time you have been banking with them, the average amount of money you have on hand, and any other information they can supply.

6. Do you have adequate personal and credit references? You will be required to bring in letters from creditors and acquaintances regarding your reliability and integrity. The amount of stress placed on these letters varies from lender to lender.

7. How old are you and your spouse? Age is often a relevant factor because your earning potential usually declines as you get older. A common formula used in lending institutions is the *rule of seventy,* which states that the length of time you will be given to pay back the loan must not extend beyond the date when you will reach the age of seventy. Thus, if you are forty-five years old at the time you apply for a loan, the maximum time you will be permitted to repay the money is twenty-five years.

8. You will be asked to state the amount of money you wish to borrow and the repayment schedule you desire.

THE FAIR CREDIT REPORTING ACT

In investigating your credit history, prospective lenders often use the services of a consumer reporting agency. This agency will issue a consumer report or investigative consumer report showing how you pay your bills; if you have ever been sued, arrested, or declared bankrupt; what your neighbors' and employer's opinions are of your character, general reputation, and manner of living; and any other information relating to your reliability as a borrower.

Sometimes obsolete or inaccurate information is given by an agency which prevents you from obtaining a loan. Under the Federal Fair Credit Reporting Act of 1971, you can discover the type of information being distributed about you and your activities.

You have the right to be told the name and address of the agency which prepared the report that led to the denial of credit to you. Within thirty days of the denial of credit, you can approach the agency and discover the nature and sources of their information without paying a fee. You can request a reinvestigation of incomplete or incorrect information and have the revised information sent to your prospective lender. If you desire, you may include in your file your own version of any dispute with the agency and have it included in any future consumer reports. An agency is not permitted to report adverse information seven years after the occurrence unless it is a bankruptcy, which may be reported up to ten years later.

If you want more information about your rights under the Fair Credit Reporting Act, see Useful Resources in chapter 27 for sources of pamphlets on the Act, and for the addresses of the Federal Trade Commission, which oversees enforcement of the Fair Credit Reporting Act.

THE APPRAISAL OF THE PROPERTY

Lending institutions often employ their own property appraisers to evaluate the fair price of houses and land to be used as security for a loan. These appraisers use the same criteria as other property appraisers (see chapters 19 and 20), such as the location of the neighborhood, the size of the property, the physical soundness of the structures, the desirability of the architectural design, and the sale prices of similar property in the area. However, they base their evaluation on the probable market value of the property during the entire life of the loan rather than on its value at the time you buy it, since a foreclosure may have to be made at any time during the loan repayment schedule. Inflation and depreciation in the value of the structures during this period are also taken into consideration.

Usually within sixty days of filing a loan application, the lending agency will appraise the property, review your financial and credit history, and notify you as to whether it will grant your loan. Although you will rarely be able to see the results of the appraisal, if your application is rejected, the company probably feels the asking price is too high.

THE LETTER OF COMMITMENT

If your application is accepted, the lender will issue you a letter of commitment detailing the terms of the loan and stating that the money will be delivered at a specific time based on certain conditions that you must meet, such as getting title cleared and having a survey completed and approved. Be sure to get this commitment in writing since lenders sometimes refuse to grant the loan at the last minute, making it impossible for the borrower to go ahead with his purchase.

Sometimes a commitment fee of 0.5 to 2 percent of the amount to be borrowed is required, which is usually refunded when you get the loan. Be sure to have a refund clause included in your letter of commitment, providing that your money will be returned in case you do not purchase the land or close the loan.

MISS PEACH - By MELL LAZARUS

336

THE FINANCE CONDITION IN THE CONTRACT OF SALE

The Model Contract of Sale (chapter 28) conditions the closing of escrow on your ability to obtain a loan under the terms you desire. (See Clause 17 (e).) This is an essential contingency where your ability to make the purchase is dependent on obtaining a loan. Without this condition, if you sign the contract and then are unable to get a loan, you will lose your deposit or earnest money. Read the accompanying explanation to Clause 17(e) and use the information in Part V, "Financing Your Purchase," to fill in the blanks in the financing clause.

DISCLOSURE STATEMENT UNDER THE TRUTH IN LENDING LAW

The Truth in Lending Law requires that the lender supply you with a disclosure statement specifying the total amount of interest you will pay on the loan, the average percentage rate (APR), the percentages of each payment going to interest and to principal, the amount of each payment, when payments are to be made, the number of payments to be made, the date of the last payment, the amount of a balloon payment, and all loan fees and other "extra" costs. You are to sign this disclosure statement as proof that you saw it and approved of its contents. The signed document is the lending agency's proof that it did not violate the law should a problem arise at a later date. Study the statement carefully before signing to be sure it contains all the terms you have agreed to.

PRIVATE MORTGAGE INSURANCE

Most lending institutions today will lend the buyer only between 65 and 80 percent of the appraised value of the property. Since you must come up with the rest of the purchase price as well as all of the closing costs, on a land purchase of $80,000 you might have to supply from $16,000 to $52,000 in cash.

A fairly new innovation in the lending business, however, allows lenders to obtain private mortgage insurance, which enables them to lend the borrower up to 95 percent of the purchase price. The mortgage insurance policy insures the lender for a certain portion of the mortgage loan, usually that amount above the normal loan amount. This is called "assuming the top of the risk."

The oldest and largest company offering this insurance is the Mortgage Guarantee Corporation, referred to as MGIC or "Magic." Its insured funds are mostly available through savings and loan associations, savings banks, and mortgage companies. Under the MGIC plan, you can borrow 90 percent of the purchase price up to a maximum of $54,000.

Before MGIC insures the lender, it evaluates your credit and appraises the property, based on the documents you and the lender supply. You must pay the insurance company a fee of $50 to $100 for processing the application.

You must also pay a premium for the insurance policy, part of which is due at the closing of the loan (when you receive the money), with the rest to be paid in installments during the payment period of the loan. If you borrow 90 percent of the purchase price of the property, your annual MGIC premium will probably be 0.5 to 1 percent of the unpaid balance of the loan during the first year, and 0.25 percent of the balance remaining each year thereafter. You can also pay the entire premium at the closing of the loan, in which case it is usually 3 percent of the amount borrowed.

Although the interest rates are slightly higher than on uninsured loans, a MGIC loan might be the only way you can get enough money to make your purchase. You should discuss the possibilities of obtaining mortgage insurance with your prospective lender if you need more money than he is willing to lend.

VARIOUS LENDERS

The "primary loan market" includes institutional and noninstitutional lenders. The four primary institutional lenders of residential loans for privately owned one- to four-family homes are savings and loan associations, commercial banks, mutual savings banks, and life insurance companies.

The noninstitutional lenders include mortgage companies, private individuals, and nonfinancial organizations. These lenders offer *conventional financing* by lending money directly to the borrower on a long-term basis and holding the land for security until the debt is discharged.

If you qualify, you can turn a conventional loan into a Veterans Administration (VA) Guaranteed Loan or a Federal Housing Administration (FHA) Insured Loan (see chapter 26).

The Federal Land Bank System and the Farmers Home Administration (see chapter 26) are unique loan sources for rural property owners.

Savings and Loan Associations

The largest home lenders in the United States are the federal and state savings and loan associations that were established to promote the investing of money and the sound, economical financing of homes. The federally chartered associations are governed by the Federal Home Loan Bank Board, and the state-licensed associations are regulated by the savings and loan commissioner of the state.

Like most economical lenders, savings and loan associations believe that unimproved land is not a good form of security. Loans are not usually given on active farms and are only occasionally given on unimproved land. Unless a house already exists on the land you are planning to buy, it is not likely that a savings and loan association will lend more than 10 percent of the appraised value, if that much.

However, savings and loan associations are generally more amenable than other institutional lenders to financing second homes that are within 100 miles of a lending office, particularly with a VA or FHA loan. Because of the growing demand for second homes, this requirement is likely to be liberalized in the near future.

Loans for owner-occupied single-family dwellings average 70 percent of the appraised value of the house. The maximum loan permitted depends upon the amount borrowed, with a maximum amortization period of thirty years. The opinions of two appraisers are required. Much importance is placed on the geographical location and age of the home.

Although the interest rate varies in different areas and at different times, it is generally higher than the interest rate on loans given by insurance companies and banks. However, savings and loan associations are generally more liberal in their lending policies. They will usually lend a higher percentage of the appraised value of the property than these other institutions, and they will lend to persons having fairly small incomes. In recent years, interest rates have risen from 6½ percent to 18 percent, and then fallen back to 8 percent. Where they will range in the next ten years is pure speculation.

Loan fees of savings and loan associations are higher than those normally charged by other lenders, ranging from 1 to 10 percent or more of the full amount of the loan. In addition, a prepayment penalty of three to six months' interest is usually charged if more than 20 percent of the loan is repaid before maturity.

Commercial Banks

Banks are general purpose lenders, regulated by federal law and organized under federal and state charters. Loans by both federal and state banks are fairly similar. During the Depression in the 1930s, commercial banks were hit hardest because they had invested heavily in real estate, a nonliquid asset that cannot be quickly turned into cash to meet withdrawal demands. This experience left a bad taste in the mouths of bank presidents, and therefore home loans are low on their priority list of investments.

The most common type of bank loan is for the purpose of building a home. Loans for the purpose of buying land are given only for improved land and for unimproved land that is to be improved after the loan is granted. State banks are more amenable to lending for unimproved property than federal banks. Most banks will lend approximately 50 percent of the appraised value of a second home amortized for ten to twenty years. Since commercial banks are the most common financial institution outside of urban areas, they are the major source of loan funds in rural areas.

Although some banks will not make FHA and VA loans, most will do so at a higher ratio of loan to appraised value for a longer maturity period than is given on a conventional loan.

Mutual Savings Banks

Mutual savings banks are located predominantly in the Atlantic and New England states, where they replace the savings and loan associations. Their policies are similar to those of the latter, and they invest most of their assets in mortgages, with a heavy preference for government-underwritten loans.

Life Insurance Companies

Approximately 30 percent of the assets of life insurance companies is invested in home mortgages. Many insurance companies will make only loans that are insured by the FHA or guaranteed by the VA.

The amount and terms of life insurance company loans are regulated by each state. Loans are usually restricted to an amount not more than two and a half times the borrower's annual income with monthly payments lower than 20 to 25 percent of the borrower's monthly take-home pay. The normal loan has a maximum maturity of twenty-five years and a maximum of 75 percent of the appraised value of the house and land. Although financing is fairly liberal on farm property, insurance companies' appraisal policies tend to be conservative. Getting a loan on an old house is difficult unless it is in exceptionally good condition. Life insurance companies' interest rates tend to be lower than those of other financial institutions, but this is highly variable.

Most life insurance companies require the borrower to purchase a life insurance policy insuring full payment of the loan if the borrower dies during the amortization period.

Life insurance companies lend money at lower interest rates if the borrower has a life insurance policy with the company. As you pay insurance premiums you build up cash value in the policy, which can be borrowed in the form of cash from the company. You will still need to be covered by your policy during the period of the loan if you do this. Find out the specifics from your insurance company on how you can use your life insurance policy to borrow money for the purchase of property.

Mortgage Companies, Mortgage Banks, and Mortgage Brokers

Mortgage companies and mortgage banks are considered to be noninstitutional sources of mortgage funds, and together with other noninstitutional lenders, they supply 25 percent of the loans for all property in the United States. Mortgage companies

are regulated by each state, and they are generally much more liberal than other lending institutions.

In reality, mortgage companies are temporary lenders in that they give loans and then sell the notes to insurance companies, commercial banks, savings and loan associations, other institutions, and private individuals. After selling the notes, they continue to serve the note buyer by collecting the payments, paying the taxes, watching over the property, keeping it insured, and foreclosing when necessary. They charge the buyer of the note a fee of 0.5 percent of the outstanding loan balance for their services.

The mortgage companies prefer government-underwritten loans and generally restrict their loans to low-risk single-family dwellings in the low price range.

Mortgage brokers find investments for potential lenders and are paid a finder's fee for this service. They will often lend on types of rural land that nobody else will lend on and charge extremely high interest rates of 15 to 25 percent. They usually find private lenders to make these loans, promising them fantastic returns on their investment. In fact, these loans for the lenders are usually highly speculative and very risky. I have had cases where borrowers refinanced their rural property at high interest rates, borrowed on the basis of over-inflated appraisals, took the loan funds and walked, abandoning the property to the poor lender-investor who has never even seen the property he lent on through the mortgage broker. In general this is an expensive way to borrow money.

Borrowing from Individuals

The most common source of private loans is relatives and close friends. If they trust you to repay the loan, taking a mortgage is one of the best investments they can make, since the interest rate is higher than they can get by placing their money in a bank or savings and loan association. In fact, they can charge up to the maximum allowed by the state's usury laws, which is commonly 10 percent per year. (Banks, savings and loans, and credit card companies are exempt from the state usury laws.) Obtaining a high-interest loan from a relative might be the only way you can purchase a country home. Many states exempt loans for property purchase from the usury laws, so there is no limit on the amount of interest that can be charged.

Your relative-lender can take back a mortgage or deed of trust. If you make this type of arrangement, be certain that all the terms of the agreement are written in a legally binding contract between you. Never agree to anything by a friendly handshake alone. If you deal with your relatives or friends, you should have an attorney do all the paperwork in a proper legal manner so that everyone has the usual protections. The best way to keep relatives and friends happy is to conduct your affairs in a businesslike manner.

Credit Unions

Credit unions have recently begun to take a greater role in lending for housing purposes. In 1986, 10 percent of the country's 18,000 credit unions offered mortgages. You have to become a member of the credit union to borrow money, but because the credit union is a nonprofit organization, it can lend at lower rates, including lower down payments and fewer loan fees. If you have a credit union available through your place of employment, check out the possibilities of refinancing or borrowing.

Other Nonfinancial Institutional Lenders

Title companies, realtors, and brokers lend money under certain circumstances. These noninstitutional lenders are not regulated and can establish any terms they desire unless they take an FHA or VA loan. Usually they do not have as rigid a credit investigation as the institutional lenders, and often they conduct their own appraisal of the property. They are often a good source for second mortgage loans.

Loans from the Federal Land Bank System (Farm Credit System)

Although the federal land banks were originally funded for farmers, as of 1981 nonfarmers may borrow from the land bank for the purpose of buying, building, remodeling, or refinancing a year-round, single-family, moderately priced home in the countryside. A rural resident can have only one loan outstanding, and the loan cannot be made if the owner intends to resell or rent the home.

Farmers, ranchers, nurserymen, timbermen, commercial fishermen, defined as persons engaged in the production of agricultural products on a full- or part-time basis, can borrow funds for the purchase of farms, farmland, and farm improvements.

In 1916, Congress passed the Federal Farm Credit Act, establishing the federal land banks and the National Farm Loan Association to provide long-term credit for farmers. In 1933 the Farm Credit Administration was created as an independent agency of the executive branch of the federal government to supervise the farm credit system, charged with making loans to farmers and prospective farmers through twelve federal land banks within the twelve farm credit districts set up around the country. These federal land banks have nearly five hundred local federal land bank association offices scattered throughout all parts of the United States, which supply 23.5 percent of the loans on farm property.

Each land bank association is owned cooperatively by the borrowers, who must become members in order to obtain a loan. When you become a land bank borrower, 5 to 10 percent of the amount you borrow must be used to purchase shares in the association, the amount depending on the size of your loan. Stock-purchase requirements are necessary to capitalize the associations so as to insure investor confidence in the securities issued to raise loan funds. Sales of this stock and of federal farm loan bonds are the source of the money for land bank loans. Bonds are sold to private and commercial investors just like other securities. Like other banks, income from interest is exempt from state taxes, although subject to federal income taxes. As of 1983, the sales of all securities have been handled by one office, the Farm Credit Corporation of America. Like other investors, you will get dividends on the shares you have purchased when you obtained your loan.

You can borrow money to purchase land or to make improvements on land you already own. Loans are made for up to 85 percent of the appraised value of the real estate security. But 97 percent financing is available if guaranteed by a state or federal agency. (See chapter 26, ''HUD/FHA- and VA-Insured Loans.'')

The loan must be secured by a first lien on the property. The amortization period can extend from five to forty years, and payments can be made annually, semiannually, quarterly, or monthly. There is no prepayment penalty. In fact, the land bank pays interest on money they receive in advance, and early payments can be put into a future payment fund to meet later installments if you run into trouble making payments later.

Interest rates on most federal land bank loans re variable, being adjusted regularly to reflect the cost of funds. In certain regions of the country, fixed rates are available on certain types of loans.

If you are purchasing forestland rather than farmland, you can obtain a federal land bank forestland loan, which is based on the value of the marketable timber on the land. Check into the requirements for *marketable timber* in your area. Usually a tree must be twelve inches or more in diameter. Although you must be engaged in timber growing, you do not have to cut the timber to get the loan. The land bank simply wants to be sure that they can cut the timber to get their money back, should they have to foreclose. Forestland loans are usually not made on raw timberland, so some building, such as a house, must be on the property. This is an excellent way to finance a vacation home in the woods. You can borrow up to 65 percent of the appraised normal value of the timber and land, and the repayment schedules are the same as those on farm loans.

The current economic health of the federal land banks is rather guarded. The Report to Investors for 1985 opened up with these gloomy words:

For agriculture, 1985 was a year of extraordinary declines in farm and ranch land values. For many agricultural producers it was also a year of continued negative cash flows and inability to pay installments due on borrowed capital. Numerous factors, including changing government agricultural policies, reduced agricultural exports resulting from a strong dollar and expanded foreign agricultural capacity, high real interest rates, abnormal weather patterns and low commodity prices led to an extraordinary number of farm and ranch insolvencies.

The Farm Credit System lost $4.6 billion during 1985 and 1986, and the loan portfolio has declined in recent years from $80 billion to $50.9 billion as of June 30, 1987. Because of the rapidly declining value of farmland in 1986, the federal land banks were faced with approximately $6 billion in outstanding loans that were undercollateralized to the extent that the loan amounts exceeded the estimated market value of the real estate collateral.

In August 1987 the House Agriculture Committee passed a bill to bail out the Farm Credit System without specifying how much should be spent and also ordered consolidation. But the approximately 380 owner-borrower associations that run the 37 regional banks want to try to come up with some alternatives to accomplish the same goals. However, it seems to be difficult for such a large group to reach a consensus on anything. Nevertheless, the banks must continue to lend money because that is how they make money. In 1987, they had $80 billion in loans outstanding to more than one million borrowers, so loans are available.

To apply for a loan go to the local federal land bank association serving the area in which the property is located. Fill out an application regarding your financial status and the purposes of the loan. The property is then appraised for its security value, and your creditworthiness is checked. When the loan is approved, a title search is done on the property and, if it is acceptable, the loan is closed.

Don't assume you will not qualify. Currently, 90 percent of all land bank loans are made to individuals, and of that group 98 percent have a net worth of less than $100,000.

To determine if there is a federal land bank association in the area where you want to buy land look in the phone book under Federal Bank Association. For a packet of information on obtaining a land bank loan and the address of the federal land bank near you, see Useful Resources at the end of chapter 27.

THE DISCOUNT RATE OR POINTS CHARGE

Commercial lenders, which includes everyone except private lenders, have developed a tricky thing called a *discount rate,* or *points* charge, in order to confuse the borrower, beat the legal interest-rate ceilings, and make more on their money.

Every state sets a maximum permissible interest rate, or ceiling, that financial institutions must adhere to. When the prevailing mortgage rates in the business world begin to rise and go higher than the state-controlled ceiling rate, loans may be ''discounted'' to permit the lender to make up the difference between the ceiling rate and the prevailing rate. Although the word *discount* usually connotes a savings, here the term means that the amount to be lent will be decreased by an amount of discount or points, and the borrower must pay back on a larger principal than he actually receives in his pocket at the completion of the loan closing.

Each point is generally $1 for every $100, or 1

percent of the principal amount of your mortgage. For example, if you borrow $90,000 and are being charged four points at this rate—that is, 4 percent times $90,000, or $3,600—you will receive only $86,400 in cash from the lender, but you will have to repay on the basis of a $90,000 principal. If you need to receive a certain amount, like $90,000, to pay your seller, you may want to add the value of the points onto your loan rather than receive less than you need. Often a higher interest rate would be preferable to paying points. You will also pay interest on the points if you do not pay them at the time you take out the loan.

You must be aware of the amount of costs you will have to pay to obtain your commercial loan. On many loans, the fees—loan origination and application fees, title insurance, lawyer's and appraiser's fees, and points—could easily cost you as much as 6 percent of the sales price. So on a loan of $100,000 you pay $6,000 just to get the loan.

Of course, you could avoid most of these costs if the seller finances the sale himself, which is usually the case in the sale of rural property.

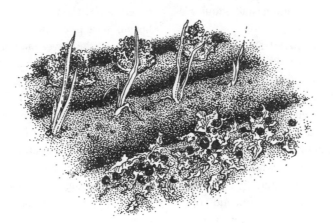

CHAPTER 26

HUD/FHA- and VA-Insured Loans

DEPARTMENT OF HOUSING AND URBAN DEVELOPMENT (HUD)/ FEDERAL HOUSING ADMINISTRATION (FHA)— INSURED LOANS

To enable people to purchase their own homes, the Federal Housing Administration, commonly referred to as the FHA, a subsidiary of the Department of Housing and Urban Development (HUD), has organized a program of mortgage insurance that protects the lender, enabling him to give more liberal financing terms. The HUD/FHA insures the commercial lender against possible loss due to a defaulting borrower by allowing the lender to foreclose and give the property to HUD/FHA in exchange for cash or to assign the defaulted mortgage to HUD/FHA, which proceeds with the foreclosure and reimburses the lender after the foreclosure. Although most of these loans are for urban housing and land, the HUD/FHA programs are available for use in all areas, both rural and urban, as long as a market exists for the property and it meets the objectives of HUD minimum standards. There are also special FHA loans for purchasing property in outlying areas which I will describe later in this chapter.

To obtain a HUD/FHA loan, you first follow the same procedure used in obtaining a commercial loan. When you apply for a loan from a lending institution, it will order an appraisal to be made of the property, check your credit history, employment, and current bank account, and send this information along with its lending terms to the local FHA office. (See Useful Resources in chapter 27 for the addresses of all HUD offices.) If you write or call your local HUD office, it will send you a list of approved lending institutions and additional information on its programs.

Using this information, the HUD examines the applicant's credit history, his motivation for wanting to buy the property, the adequacy of his income to meet future payments, the adequacy of his current assets to meet the down payment and closing costs, and his integrity and motivation to carry through on the repayment of the loan. The incomes of both spouses are considered when it is certain that their employment will continue.

The property, too, must meet certain conditions. General requirements are that the house be soundly built and suitably located. Any defects in the property must be repaired before HUD/FHA will insure a mortgage on it. HUD/FHA makes its own appraisal of the value of the property, to determine the amount it is willing to insure the loan for. However, it does not warrant or guarantee the condition of the property, and HUD recommends that you have the property inspected for hidden defects. If the HUD office finds that the property is acceptable, it issues a *conditional commitment* to the lender.

The office then determines if the loan is reasonable for you. If both you and the property are acceptable, HUD issues a *firm commitment* to the lender which states the estimate of the value of the property and the maximum loan it will insure. The lender then arranges with you to close the loan. The entire process generally takes two months.

The HUD/FHA has approved certain housing counseling agencies in various locations around the country that offer free advice to people regarding the costs and steps involved in buying homes. Check with your local HUD office to get the address of any counseling agency near you.

The maximum interest rate permitted under HUD/FHA-insured loans is usually lower than the current interest rate on conventional loans. Also down payments are usually smaller. Because lenders do not like to accept the lower rates, they are allowed to *discount* the loan or charge *points* (discussed in chapter 25, "Borrowing from Third Party Lenders") to make up the difference between the HUD/FHA interest rate and the current interest rate on the mortgage money market. HUD/FHA prohibits the lender from collecting this discount from the buyer, because to do so would defeat the purpose of the HUD/FHA loan. Therefore, the seller is supposed to pay the points, but often he simply raises his purchase price to cover the amount he will have to pay, so the buyer ends up paying it anyway.

The borrower must pay a small HUD/FHA application fee; a lender's service charge of 1 percent or less of the loan; the charge for a title search and title insurance policy premium; a small fee for an appraisal; a small fee for a credit report; and the fees charged to prepare, record, and notarize the deed, mortgage, and other documents; and other standard closing costs. It is specified in the Model Contract of Sale that the seller is to share the cost of many of these charges with you. (See chapter 28, "The Model Contract of Sale.")

Under a HUD/FHA-insured loan, a special charge, called the mortgage insurance premium, is made on the outstanding balance of the mortgage, which goes into the HUD/FHA fund to pay its expenses and insurance losses on defaults. This premium is paid to the HUD/FHA at the time the loan closes. It may be paid in cash by the home buyer or it may be added to the loan. The amount of the premium at the time of this writing is 3.661 percent of the value of the mortgage if paid in cash or 3.8 percent of the loan if it is added on to the loan and financed.

The borrower is to pay the taxes and special assessments on the property, and he will be charged for the premiums on fire and hazard insurance, taken out to protect the lender's security.

There is no prepayment penalty on an FHA loan, but the buyer must give the lender thirty days' notice if he intends to make more than one month's payment at one time.

You can purchase a home that is already under an FHA-insured mortgage. If you buy *subject to* the mortgage, no FHA approval is needed because the seller's name remains on the mortgage and he bears the responsibility for the mortgage payments if you fail to make them. If you are approved by the FHA, the lender can release the seller from his obligation on the mortgage and substitute you, whereby you *assume* the mortgage.

The FHA has several different insurance programs which you might use. They are described below.

One- to Four-Family Home Mortgage Insurance, Section 203, National Housing Act

The most commonly used program, Mutual Mortgage Insurance, Section 203 (b) of the National Housing Act, provides for the purchase and construction of family homes. Up to four units are eligible under this program. The maximum amount you can borrow varies depending on the area of the country in which the property is located. HUD will insure loans made by private financial institutions for up to 97 percent of the property value and for a term of up to thirty years. The loan-to-value ratio varies depending on the age of the house and whether it was built under HUD/FHA approval. The loan may finance homes in both urban and rural areas except farms. Less rigid construction standards are permitted in rural areas.

The HUD/FHA plan that will probably be applicable to most of you is the Outlying Area Properties Loan, Section 203 (i) of the National Housing Act. Under this plan, HUD/FHA approval is given for mortgages on non-farm housing on five or more acres adjacent to a highway in small communities. Many of the requirements on the standards of construction and the condition of the house are much less rigid than those for mortgage insurance on housing in built-up urban areas. The maximum loan permitted is 97 percent of the appraised value of the property, up to a maximum loan amount permitted by the HUD/FHA. If the purchase price is higher than the HUD/FHA estimate of the value of the property plus closing costs, the buyer must pay the difference in cash. You can choose between ten-, fifteen-, twenty-, twenty-five-, or thirty-year maturity periods.

FHA Cooperative Housing Loan Insurance, Section 213 and Section 221 (d) (3) and (4), National Housing Act

Two unusual loan insurance plans that can be utilized by a group of people purchasing land together are the HUD/FHA Cooperative Housing Loan Insurance, Section 213, and the Multifamily Rental Housing for Low- and Moderate-Income Families, Section 221 (d) (3) and (4). Under these plans HUD/FHA will insure financing for cooperative housing projects that will belong to, and provide housing for, members of a nonprofit cooperative ownership housing corporation. These loans may finance new construction, rehabilitation, acquisition, or improvement or repair of homes already owned. Five or more dwellings must be purchased or constructed by the cooperative. Each purchaser may obtain HUD/FHA insurance. Although the most common use of this program is by large developers building low-cost cooperative housing, there is no reason why a group of people could not get together and form their own nonprofit cooperative and apply for loan insurance to finance construction of their homes. This program does not insure loans for the purchase of land, only for the construction of dwellings. Thus, if your group has the cash only to purchase some inexpensive rural land, it might be able to borrow the money under one of these HUD/FHA plans to build your houses. The first thing to do if you are considering such a project is to discuss your plan with the local HUD/FHA insuring office. For more information on cooperatives, see chapter 32, "Types of Co-ownership."

Experimental Housing Mortgage Insurance, Section 233, National Housing Act

Experimental Housing Mortgage Insurance, Section 233, provides insurance on loans for housing that incorporates new or untried construction concepts aimed at reducing housing costs, raising living standards, and improving neighborhood design. If you can afford to pay for the land itself, you could attempt to get the HUD/FHA to insure a loan to build domes, modular design houses, ferrocement houses, or other experimental buildings. Try to talk the FHA into the idea that your designs are incorporating new and improved construction concepts with the aim of improving conventional construction methods.

Condominium Housing Insurance, Section 234, National Housing Act

Condominium Housing Insurance, Section 234, presents another loan possibility for a group to obtain money for financing the construction of their dwellings on land they have purchased. The program was initiated to help investors develop condominiums, but you can organize a group of "nonprofit investors" seeking insured financing to build four or more dwelling units. After the housing is built, each unit is sold to an individual in the group. His payments go to pay off the insured loan given to construct the dwellings. Each owner has complete title to his dwelling unit and has an undivided interest with the remaining owners in common areas and facilities serving the group. (See chapter 32, "Types of Co-ownership.")

Graduated Payment Mortgage (GPM), Section 245, National Housing Act

A fairly new HUD program can allow you to purchase a house with a reasonable down payment and lower initial monthly payments in the early years of your loan. Your mortgage payments rise gradually for a set period of years, then level off and remain steady for the balance of the mortgage. There are five different GPM plans that vary the rate of monthly payment increases and the number of years over which the payments increase. The greater the rate of increase, or the larger the period of increase, the lower the mortgage payments are in early years. For example, your mortgage payments can start at $350 per month and slowly increase annually until the seventh year, when you might be paying $550 per month, and then stay at that payment level for the duration of the loan.

Adjustable Rate Mortgages (ARM), Section 251, National Housing Act

This HUD-insured mortgage plan allows the lender to vary the interest rate and monthly payments during the life of the loan. The index used for determining the interest rate is the one-year Treasury Constant Maturities. Over the life of the loan, the maximum interest rate change allowed is five percentage points higher and lower than the initial rate of the mortgage, and the interest can change a maximum of one percentage point in any one year. The initial interest rate, the discount points charged, and the margin vary from lender to lender.

Insured Title 1 Manufactured (Mobile) Home Loan Program

If you want to buy a manufactured (also called a mobile) home after purchasing your land, you can get a HUD/FHA-insured loan by a private lending institution through the Insured Title 1 Manufactured Home Loans Program. You can borrow up to $40,500 for a single or multisection manufactured home and $54,000 for a developed lot and manufactured home. The interest rate varies, as does the down payment you must make, and the home must meet HUD standards of construction for a single- or multiple-unit home.

Home Improvement Loan Insurance, Title 1

Once you own your land, you can get HUD-insured loans under Title 1 Property Improvement Loan Insurance to finance major and minor repairs and improvements of existing homes and nonresidential structures and to build new small nonresidential structures, such as agricultural buildings. Improvements can be do-it-yourself or through a contractor.

Solar Energy and Energy Conservation Bank, Title 5, Energy Security Act of 1980

This bank, also called the Solar Bank, operates through the states in providing loan subsidies and matching grants to low- and moderate-income individuals for solar and energy conservation improvements. You must apply through a designated state agency which in turn draws funds from the Solar Bank through the Treasury Financial Communication System (TFCS). Check with your local HUD office if you are interested in this program.

See Useful Resources in chapter 27 for a list of pamphlets about HUD, the FHA, and the various programs listed above.

Veterans Administration (VA)-Guaranteed Loans, GI Loans

Since World War II, the federal government has been guaranteeing loans made by commercial lenders to honorably discharged veterans. Loans may be obtained for purchasing homes and farms, purchasing manufactured homes, certain condominiums, and/or lots, constructing homes, and improving existing dwellings. These loans are called VA- or GI-guaranteed loans.

If you were honorably discharged from active duty, you are eligible for loan guaranty benefits if:

346

—Your active duty service totals 90 days or more, part of which was from September 16, 1940, through July 25, 1947; June 27, 1950, through January 31, 1955; or August 5, 1964, through May 7, 1975; or

—You had 181 days or more of continuous active duty after July 25, 1947, and before June 27, 1950; after January 31, 1955, and before August 5, 1964; or after May 7, 1975, and before September 8, 1980, if enlisted before October 17, 1981, if an officer; or

—You were discharged or released for a service-connected disability.

If you were separated from enlisted service which began on or after September 8, 1980, or if you served as an officer anytime after October 17, 1981, eligibility requirements are (1) completion of 24 months of continuous active duty or the full period (at least 181 days) for which you were called or ordered to active duty, and discharge or release from active duty under conditions other than dishonorable; or (2) completion of at least 181 days of active duty with a hardship discharge or discharge for the convenience of the government, or if you have a compensable service-connected disability; or (3) discharge after a period of less than 181 days for a service-connected disability.

You are also eligible if you have been on active duty more than 180 days and your service continues without breaks. Active duty for training does not count.

A loan guarantee from the VA means that if you default on the loan, the VA will repay the lender for you. You then become liable for payment to the Veterans Administration.

Your entitlement to loan guaranty benefits is available until used. Two or more veterans can put their entitlements together and purchase property as a group if they both reside on the property as their permanent residence. Vacation homes do not qualify. A veteran may also use this entitlement with a nonveteran to purchase a home, but the VA will guarantee only the veteran's half of the loan. Under certain circumstances, you may be eligible to use the benefit more than once. Check with your local VA office.

The first thing a veteran must do is obtain a certificate of eligibility by filling out VA Form 26-1880, Request for Determination of Eligibility and Available Loan Guaranty Entitlement, and submitting it with separation papers (DD214) to the local VA office or financial institution. Usually the VA automatically issues a certificate of eligibility to most newly discharged eligible veterans.

Before the VA will guarantee a loan it appraises the property in the same way the HUD/FHA does. The appraisal report indicates the current fair market value by VA standards at the time the appraisal is made. It does not indicate the physical condition of the residence or whether the purchase is a good one or what the resale value will be at a future date. After completion of the appraisal, the VA sends a Certificate of Reasonable Value to the prospective lender. The maximum maturity allowed is thirty years for a house. The maximum interest allowed under a VA loan varies with market conditions.

First you must find the property you want to buy. Then make a deposit and sign a contract of sale that conditions the sale on your ability to obtain a GI loan. (See Clause 17(e) in the Model Contract of Sale, chapter 28.) A legal description of the property and a survey or sketch of its boundaries must be presented with your certificate of eligibility to the lending institution where you apply for a loan. The lender will run a credit history check and employment report on you, and the VA will conduct its appraisal of the property and run a VA indebtedness check to see if you owe the VA for any other loans. The VA then sends the Certificate of Reasonable Value to the lender. If the lender decides to lend you the money, he gets a guarantee from the regional VA office, then gives you the money.

You will have to pay certain fees on a VA-guaranteed loan. The application fee includes a charge for the appraisal and for the credit report. You must also pay a 1 percent processing fee and a 1 percent finding fee. If the lender charges more points than allowed under the VA loan guaranty, the seller is supposed to pay them rather than the buyer. All the other standard closing costs to be paid by the buyer and the seller are negotiable between you.

In addition to the VA loans, which are federally funded, many states have their own programs that make funds available to veterans through state bond issues. These state programs feature direct loans to veterans, who repay them at a low interest rate. You can obtain information on these loans at the state agencies for veterans affairs listed in the Useful Resources in chapter 27. Also listed are the addresses of all VA regional offices and a list of available pamphlets on GI loans.

LOANS FROM THE FARMERS HOME ADMINISTRATION (FmHA)

Leave it to the federal government to create two separate financial agencies with the initials *FHA*. The Farmers Home Administration is not the same organization as the Federal Housing Administration. The former is operated by the U.S. Department of Agriculture (USDA), the latter by the Department of Housing and Urban Development (HUD). When I speak about the FHA in other parts of this book, unless I specify otherwise, I refer to the Federal Housing Administration that operates under HUD.

The Farmers Home Administration, which is usually referred to as the FmHA to distinguish it from the HUD/FHA, makes housing loans available to low-income farm families and other people in rural areas of ten thousand people or less and in small communities between ten thousand and twenty thousand people. Its intent is to develop the resources of rural areas and upgrade the standard of living of people wishing to live in these places. The FmHA offers both direct loans and/or grants to very low-income people as well as insured loans for up to $200,000 and guaranteed loans for up to $300,000 through private financial institutions. You can use money obtained from an FmHA loan to buy, improve, or repair farm homes and farm service buildings, to drill wells, to develop energy conservation measures, and to refinance debts. Purchasing forestland is permitted if you can show that it will produce income as a commercial or recreational enterprise. After the loan is made, the FmHA will give you technical advice for making profitable use of the land and its resources and help you manage your finances in general.

Insured loans are made directly from an FmHA revolving fund to the borrower. Guaranteed loans are made and serviced by usual commercial sources, such as federal land banks, local banks, insurance companies, and savings and loan associations. FmHA provides the lender with a guarantee against losses on the loan.

FmHA also makes farm ownership loans in participation with other lenders and sellers of farms who supply a part of the needed loan funds. In these cases, FmHA loans may be secured by a junior lien on the property.

Another purpose of the FmHA loan is to assist people who are unable to get reasonable credit elsewhere. Although special provisions are made for low-income families, usually the borrower is expected to have sufficient income to pay the installments, insurance premiums, taxes, and other debts, as well as operating and living expenses. You also must have a satisfactory history of meeting credit obligations and farm experience or training; in addition, you must possess the industry and ability needed to succeed in farming.

Eligibility for a loan is determined by a local committee of the FmHA, consisting of three persons who know local farming and credit conditions and what it takes to succeed. A standard credit and employment check is conducted, and veterans get preferential treatment for any FmHA loan. If your income is not sufficient, a cosigner might be necessary.

Repayment terms and interest rates vary according to the type of loan made. Repayment is scheduled according to the borrower's ability to repay. The interest rate is set periodically, based on the cost of borrowing to the government.

A lower interest rate is available for borrowers with limited resources. Loans to limited-resource borrowers will be reviewed after three years and the interest rate increased if the borrower has sufficient repayment ability. These loans then will be reviewed at least every two years thereafter. However, if at any time the borrower has sufficient income and repayment ability to pay the then-current rate being charged, the borrower's interest rate will be increased to the current rate.

For loans made by other lenders and guaranteed by FmHA, the interest rate and repayment terms will be agreed upon by the borrower and the lender. Interest rates on these loans may not exceed any maximum set by the Secretary of Agriculture.

Each borrower who receives an insured loan is expected to refinance the unpaid balance of the loan when it is financially feasible to rely on commercial credit sources.

Farm ownership borrowers are required to maintain their property, and pay taxes and property insurance premiums when due.

A separate program that might be useful if you are a group of people buying land is the FmHA Self-Help Housing Loan, whereby funds are lent to a group of people to buy building sites and materials. The majority of the construction is then done by the families themselves under an FmHA construction expert. The houses are expected to be modest in size and cost. You are encouraged to submit your own building plans but are advised to keep the house size around 1,100 square feet.

The best way to find out about the FmHA programs available in your area is to write to your local office. See Useful Resources in chapter 27 for the address of the main office and a list of FmHA pamphlets.

CHANGES PLANNED FOR FHA AND VA LOANS

There are some threats to government loan programs. The most serious proposals are to assess user fees on borrowers who participate in Federal Housing Administration and Veterans Administration programs, and to require higher down payments and place limits on income eligibility. There are also plans to increase insurance premiums on loans guaranteed by the FHA and to increase the origination fee for VA mortgages. So get the latest information from the sources listed in chapter 27 to determine current loan information.

CHAPTER 27

Glossary of Financing Terms, Checklist for Evaluating a Loan, and Useful Resources

GLOSSARY OF FINANCING TERMS

Acceleration clause—A clause in the mortgage or trust deed that gives the lender the right to receive the entire principal and interest owed to him by the buyer upon the happening of a certain event such as a missed payment, attempt to sell, or disrepair of the property. They are common but should be avoided by a buyer whenever possible.

Adjustable rate mortgage—See Floating Interest Rate.

Amortization—Paying off a debt by means of installment payments. As each payment toward the principal and interest is made, the loan amount outstanding is reduced, or amortized, by the amount of that payment that applies to the principal.

Annual percentage rate (APR)—A measure of the cost of credit, expressed as a yearly rate. Includes the costs of the loan and interest factors. You can compare the APRs of various loans.

Assignment—A lender sells or gives his rights under a note and mortgage or deed of trust to another party.

Assumption of a loan—The buyer takes title to the property and assumes the liability for payment of a note for which the property has been given as security. The buyer does not become personally liable for payment of the debt if he takes title *subject to* a loan.

Balloon payment—An extra-large installment payment made at the end of the amortization period or at a predetermined time during the amortization period.

Beneficiary—Under a deed of trust the seller or lender is called the beneficiary.

Bond—Another name for a note.

Cap—A limit on how much the interest rate or monthly payment can change. Payment caps don't limit the amount of interest the lender is earning, so this might cause negative amortization.

Closing the loan—Usually done at the same time escrow is closed. It occurs when the money is actually given to the buyer, who gives a mortgage or deed of trust and a note in return.

Commitment—Also called a *letter of commitment*. A pledge or promise by the lender that you will receive the loan you desire.

Conventional loan—Any loan other than a HUD/FHA-insured or VA-guaranteed loan.

Credit check—This is performed by a lender when you apply for a loan. Your credit and employment histories are evaluated, along with your present financial condition, to determine the likelihood that you will repay the loan on time.

Creditor—The person to whom money is owed.

Debtor—The person who owes the money.

Deed of trust (trust deed or trust indenture)—Used in a minority of states in place of a mortgage. The buyer receives title to the property and gives the seller a lien against it as security for the loan. When the debt is paid, the title is reconveyed to the borrower. If the debt is not paid, the trustee can foreclose and sell the property to satisfy the debt to the lender, or beneficiary.

Default—A debtor's failure to make his loan payments. (He is said to default on the loan or mortgage or deed or trust.)

Discount rate (points)—Usually charged by a lender. For example, under an FHA loan, HUD/FHA sets a maximum permissible interest rate that is often lower than the current conventional loan mortgage interest rate. The lender makes the loan but *discounts,* or subtracts, an amount of money from it to make up the difference lost by charging the lower interest rate. Each point is 1 percent, or $1 for every $100 of loan money. The seller is supposed to pay the points under a HUD/FHA

loan. Lenders also charge points to get more money than permitted under current interest ceilings.

Due-on-sale clause—Similar to an acceleration clause. It means that if the borrower desires to sell his property before the loan is repaid, he must pay off the entire amount due on the loan before he can convey title to a purchaser.

Easy money—Means that loans are readily available and interest rates are fairly low or at an average level.

Equity—A buyer's investment in his property, excluding the debt liens against it. When the down payment is made, his equity is the amount of the payment. When the loan is fully paid off, the buyer has 100 percent equity in the property. If the house has a fair market value of $30,000, and the buyer owes $20,000 on an existing mortgage, he has an equity of $10,000.

Escalation clause (escalator clause)—Permits the lender, or seller, to raise the interest rate on the loan during the period of the mortgage or deed of trust. The buyer should always attempt to keep such a clause out of the loan document.

Farmers Home Administration (FmHA–USDA)—A government agency under the U.S. Department of Agriculture (USDA) that makes loans to farmers and rural residents who cannot obtain loans elsewhere.

Federal Housing Administration (FHA)—A government agency under the U.S. Department of Housing and Urban Development (HUD) that insures loans made to borrowers by institutional lenders. The FHA insures that the lender will receive full payment if the buyer defaults. Loans can be for home building, purchase, and improvement. Although they are primarily concerned with ''urban'' areas they do have certain loans that can benefit rural purchasers, such as their ''outlying areas'' loan program.

Federal land bank—An organization owned by the rural residents who borrow from it. It is regulated by the Federal Farm Credit Administration. The land bank lends money, through local land bank associations, to owners and purchasers of farm and timber land. A borrower must purchase shares of stock in the land bank as part of his loan, and he has a vote in selecting the local board of directors who administer the land bank in his area.

Fixed interest loan—Means that the interest rate

on the loan at the time it is borrowed will remain constant throughout the entire amortization period.

Floating or variable interest rate—The opposite of a fixed interest loan. Under a floating interest rate, the interest on the loan goes up or down in relation to the current mortgage interest rate on the money market.

Foreclosure—The procedure used to sell property given as security for a debt when the borrower defaults in payments. The lender attempts to get his money through a foreclosure sale. In some cases, he might keep the property rather than sell it if nobody comes to bid for the property at the foreclosure sale. A foreclosure with a deed of trust is called a *trustee's sale proceeding*.

Homeowner loan or home equity loan—A mortgage or deed of trust on one's primary home given in order to borrow money, for instance to buy a second home. Also called a second-home loan. This loan is based on the amount of equity the owner has in his present home. Interest rates for it are often higher than for a conventional first mortgage or deed of trust.

Installment note—A document that specifies the amount of payment due on specified dates for the repayment of a loan.

Interest rate—A percentage of the principal amount of the loan that the lender charges the borrower for the loan. The borrower should always determine what the interest rate is *per annum*, or per year, for the entire amortization period.

Land contract or installment land contract—A device used to finance the purchase of property. A land contract should never be confused with a contract of sale or other purchase agreement. The seller does not convey title to the land until the buyer has completely paid off the purchase price. This can be a dangerous means of purchasing land and is tempting to the buyer who does not have much cash available for a down payment. It should be used with extreme caution.

Maturity—The end of the length of time for which a loan is made. If a loan is to be repaid in ten years, it has a ten-year maturity.

Mortgage—A document that places a lien on the borrower's property as security for a loan. The borrower keeps title to the property, but the lender has a lien against it until the loan is repaid.

Mortgagee—The seller or lender who receives a mortgage from a mortgagor.

Mortgage insurance premium—The payment made by a borrower under a HUD/FHA loan that helps HUD/FHA defray the cost of its loan insurance program and which provides a reserve fund to use for the protection of lenders if borrowers default in payments. The mortgage insurance premium is made as a one-time payment to HUD/FHA when the loan is closed or added onto the principal and financed.

Mortgagor—The person who borrows the money, or purchases the land, under a mortgage agreement. The mortgagor gives a mortgage to the seller or lender, who is called the *mortgagee*.

Negative amortization—Occurs when the monthly payments do not cover all the interest costs. This unpaid interest is added to the unpaid principal balance. Thus, after several years you would owe more than you did at the beginning of the loan.

Note (promissory note)—Given with a mortgage or deed of trust. It is a signed document wherein the buyer acknowledges the debt and promises to repay it in full. The terms of repayment are specified in the note. See *installment note*.

Partial reconveyance clause (release clause)—In a loan instrument, specifies that the seller or lender is to convey to the buyer a specified portion of the land title free and clear from the overall lien, after a certain amount of the debt is repaid.

Payments—Are made monthly, quarterly, semiannually, or annually under the amortization schedule. A payment will include part of the principal and interest due on the loan.

Points—See *discount rate*.

Prepayment clause—In a mortgage, deed of trust, or land contract permits the buyer to pay off the debt in advance of the maturity date. It also permits the buyer to make a larger installment than what is due and reduce the amount of interest paid on the loan. Normally, the amount of each payment remains the same even if you pay off the loan faster than required.

Prepayment penalty—A clause that specifies the buyer will pay a penalty for paying off any part of the loan at a greater rate than that called for in the loan instrument. The penalty is usually a percentage of the amount due. Sometimes prepayment will be totally prohibited in order for the seller to get all the interest due on the loan.

Principal—The amount of money owed by the purchaser to a lender or seller of land. For example, if the selling price is $45,000 and you pay a $13,000 down payment and give a mortgage for the remainder, the principal of the loan is $32,000. The interest due will be calculated on the basis of this principal amount.

Purchase money mortgage—Any mortgage given for the specific purpose of purchasing a piece of property.

Reconveyance—Of the title to the borrower-trustor is made after the debt is repaid in full under a deed of trust.

Redemption—The right of the borrower to regain his property after a foreclosure has occurred. You always want to have a right of redemption in your loan instrument, if it is not automatic under your state law.

Refinance—Means that the buyer gets a new loan to pay off his original loan. This is commonly done when the interest rates drop and a cheaper loan can be obtained. The borrower gives a new mortgage or deed of trust for the new loan. Owners with large equity in their primary residences often refinance to obtain funds to purchase a second home in the country. If you refinance be sure to figure out if the lower interest rate obtained will be offset by the loan charges, particularly the points.

Release clause—See *partial reconveyance clause*.

Satisfaction—When a debt is paid in full, a satisfaction is signed by the lender, recorded, and given to the borrower as evidence that the lien against his property has been removed.

Second home—A vacation home or part-time residence, usually in the country.

Second-home loan—Same as a homeowner loan.

Second mortgage—A mortgage against the property given for a loan after the buyer has already given a first mortgage to a lender. A holder of a second mortgage can get his money on a foreclosure only after the holder of the first mortgage has received what is due him. There can be third and fourth mortgages. All commercial lenders require a first mortgage when the loan is for the purchase of property.

Subject to a mortgage or deed of trust—When a buyer purchases the land subject to a preexisting lien against the property, he is not personally responsible for the payment of the existing amount that is due. If there is a foreclosure later, he will lose the land. Do not take title subject to a mort-

gage if you can assume it, unless you are prepared to step in and make the payments if your seller does not. See *assumption of a loan*.

Term—Refers to the amortization period or maturity date on a loan.

Tight money—Means that loans are hard to get and interest rates are higher than normal.

Trust deed—Same as deed of trust.

Trustee—The neutral third person who holds the right to foreclose on the buyer during the period a deed of trust is held against the property.

Trust indenture—Same as deed of trust.

Trustor—The person who executes a deed of trust against his property, allowing a trustee to foreclose if payments are in arrears. This person is a purchaser of the property who is paying for it over a period of time or who is repaying a loan.

Unamortized loan—Refers to a loan that must be repaid in one large payment at the end of a specified period of time. It is not usually used for the purchase of land.

Usury rate—The maximum rate of interest allowed under state law.

VA (GI) guaranteed loan—Qualified veterans can obtain a loan that is guaranteed by the Veterans Administration. This makes it easier to obtain a loan with more liberal terms.

Variable interest rate—Same as a floating interest rate.

Wraparound loan—A loan that includes another loan. When a seller conveys the title to the buyer who takes it "subject to" an existing encumbrance, the seller might make the buyer pay a higher interest rate on his mortgage than the seller himself pays on his mortgage to his creditor. Thus, the buyer's mortgage "wraps around" the seller's mortgage. The buyer pays the seller, and the seller pays his lender with the buyer's money.

CHECKLIST FOR EVALUATING A LOAN

—How much will the lender give you? (What is the loan-to-value ratio?)

—How soon can you get the loan?

—Do you need a co-signer or security other than the land you intend to buy?

Interest Rate

—What is the annual interest rate?

—Is the interest rate under a variable interest plan? (See the comparison factors under "Adjustable Rate Mortgages" in chapter 22.)

—What will be the total amount of interest on the loan?

—Is there an escalation clause that permits the lender to increase the interest rate in the future?

Payment Plan

—How long is the amortization period (maturity date)?

—When are the installments to be paid: monthly, quarterly, annually, etc.?

—How much is each installment to be?

—Is there a prepayment clause that allows you to make payments in advance and have them credited in the future if you cannot make a payment?

—Are there any other prepayment privileges?

—Is there a prepayment penalty? Is so, what does it specify? Is prepayment prohibited altogether?

—Is there a provision for a balloon payment? If so, how much is it?

—Does the loan include an acceleration clause that permits the lender to force you to pay the entire amount due if you miss a payment, fail to pay taxes or assessments, attempt to sell the land, or let the property fall into disrepair? Is there a due-on-sale clause?

—Are you supposed to make impound payments for taxes and assessments with your loan payments?

Foreclosure

—What rights does the lender have if you get behind in your payments?

—What procedure does he have to follow to foreclose your loan? Does he have to go to court first in order to foreclose?

—Do you have a period of redemption? If so, how long is it, and what period does it cover?

—Does the loan specify that you are to be reimbursed for all money you have put into the land for improvements if there is a foreclosure?

—Is it stated that you are to receive any surplus money from a foreclosure sale?

—If an insufficient amount of money is received from a foreclosure to meet the debt, can the lender get a deficiency judgment against you?

Assignment Rights

—Is the note negotiable or nonnegotiable?

—Is the lender permitted to assign his interest under the loan?

—Can you sell or assign your interest in the property and have the buyer assume your debt? If so, are there any conditions, such as lender approval?

—Can you place a second mortgage or deed of trust on the property?

—Can you put other liens on the property during the loan period?

—Will you be allowed to borrow on your property and give a second mortgage to the same or another lender?

Extra Fees

—Will you be charged for preliminary costs other than interest—for example, points, extras, origination fees? If so, how much will the charge be for each one?

—When do these fees have to be paid? Can they be included in the loan installments over a period of time?

—How much will you have to pay for having the loan documents drawn up?

—What type of insurance and how much coverage are you bound to carry on the property?

—How do you pay for the insurance?

—How much do you have to pay for a credit and employment report?

—How much do you have to pay for a property appraisal?

—Taking everything into account, how much will it cost you to borrow the money?

USEFUL RESOURCES

Federal Land Bank Loans

The following is a list of federal land banks, sometimes also called Farm Credit Banks, and the states served by each. You can contact your state office to obtain the name of the bank nearest to your property.

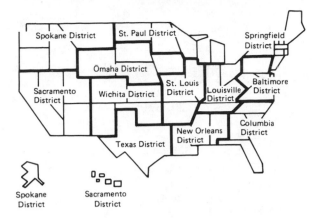

Spokane District · St. Paul District · Springfield District · Omaha District · Sacramento District · Wichita District · St. Louis District · Louisville District · Baltimore District · New Orleans District · Columbia District · Texas District · Spokane District · Sacramento District

92. The Twelve Farm Credit Districts Containing the Federal Reserve Land Banks, and the States Served by Each

Federal Land Bank of Springfield
P.O. Box 141
Springfield, MA 01101

(Covers: Maine, New Hampshire, Vermont, Massachusetts, Rhode Island, Connecticut, New York, and New Jersey)

Federal Land Bank of Baltimore
P.O. Box 1555
Baltimore, MD 21203

(Covers: Pennsylvania, Delaware, Maryland, Virginia, West Virginia, and District of Columbia)

Federal Land Bank of Columbia
P.O. Box 1499
Columbia, SC 29202

(Covers: North Carolina, South Carolina, Georgia, and Florida)

Federal Land Bank of Louisville
P.O. Box 32390
Louisville, KY 40232

(Covers: Ohio, Indiana, Kentucky, and Tennessee)

Federal Land Bank of New Orleans
P.O. Box 50590
New Orleans, LA 70150

(Covers: Alabama, Mississippi, and Louisiana)

Federal Land Bank of St. Louis
Main Post Office, Box 491
St. Louis, MO 63166

(Covers: Illinois, Missouri, and Arkansas)

Federal Land Bank of St. Paul
375 Jackson St.
St. Paul, MN 55101

(Covers: Michigan, Wisconsin, Minnesota, and North Dakota)

Federal Land Bank of Omaha
Farm Credit Bldg.
206 S. 19th St.
Omaha, NB 68102

(Covers: Iowa, Nebraska, South Dakota, and Wyoming)

Federal Land Bank of Wichita
900 Farm Credit Banks Bldg.
151 N. Main
Wichita, KS 67202

(Covers: Oklahoma, Kansas, Colorado, and New Mexico)

Federal Land Bank of Texas
P.O. Box 2649
Houston, TX 77001

(Covers: Texas)

Federal Land Bank of Sacramento
P.O. Box 13106-C
Sacramento, CA 95813

(Covers: California, Nevada, Utah, Arizona, and Hawaii)

Federal Land Bank of Spokane
P.O. Box TAF-C4
Spokane, WA 99220

(Covers: Washington, Oregon, Montana, Idaho, and Alaska)

For free information on obtaining a federal land bank loan and other loans through the Farm Credit Association, write to:
The Farm Credit Council
50 F St., N.W., Ste. 900
Washington, DC 20001

The following are available from the above agency:
Federal Land Banks—How They Operate
Production Credit Associations
Banks for Cooperatives
The Farm Credit System

Federal Housing Administration (FHA)-Insured Loans

The following is a list of area offices of Department of Housing and Urban Development (HUD) and insuring offices of the Federal Housing Administration (FHA). These offices can supply you with information on lending policies in your area. The other source of FHA information is any FHA-approved financial institution. A list of these approved lenders is available from any HUD or FHA office.

HUD Regional and Field Offices

REGION I

Boston Regional Office
Boston Federal Office Bldg.
10 Causeway St.
Boston, MA 02222-1092

FIELD OFFICES

Bangor Office
Professional Bldg., Ground Fl.
263 State St.
Bangor, ME 04401-5435

Burlington Office
110 Main St.
Fairchild Square
Burlington, VT 05401-0989

Hartford Office
330 Main St.
Hartford, CT 06106-1860

Manchester Office
Norris Cotton Federal Bldg.
275 Chestnut St.
Manchester, NH 03101-2487

Providence Office
330 John O. Pastore Federal Bldg. and U.S.
    Post Office
Kennedy Plaza
Providence, RI 02903-1785

REGION II

New York Regional Office
26 Federal Plaza
New York, NY 10278-0068

FIELD OFFICES

Albany Office
Leo W. O'Brien Federal Bldg.
N. Pearl St. and Clinton Ave.
Albany, NY 12207-2395

Buffalo Office
Statler Bldg., Mezzanine
107 Delaware Ave.
Buffalo, NY 14202-2986

Camden Office
Parkade Bldg.
519 Federal St.
Camden, NJ 08103-9998

Newark Office
Military Park Bldg.
60 Park Place
Newark, NJ 07102-5504

REGION III

Philadelphia Regional Office
Liberty Square Bldg.
105 S. 7th St.
Philadelphia, PA 19106-3392

FIELD OFFICES

Baltimore Office
Equitable Bldg., 3rd Fl.
10 N. Calvert St.
Baltimore, MD 21202-1865

Charleston Office
405 Capitol St., Ste. 708
Charleston, WV 25301-1794

Pittsburgh Office
412 Old Post Office Courthouse
7th and Grant Sts.
Pittsburgh, PA 14219-1906

Richmond Office
701 E. Franklin St.
Richmond, VA 23219-2591

Washington, D.C., Office
451-7th St., S.W., 3rd Fl.
Washington, DC 20410-5500

Wilmington Office
800 Delaware Ave., Rm. 101
Wilmington, DE 19801-1387

Atlanta Office
Richard B. Russell Federal Bldg.
75 Spring St., S.W.
Atlanta, GA 30303-3388

FIELD OFFICES

Birmingham Office
Daniel Bldg.
15 S. 20th St.
Birmingham, AL 35233-2096

Columbia Office
Strom Thurmond Federal Bldg.
1835-45 Assembly St.
Columbia, SC 29201-2480

Coral Gables Office
Gables 1 Tower
1320 S. Dixie Hwy.
Coral Gables, FL 33146-2911

Greensboro Office
415 N. Edgeworth St.
Greensboro, NC 27401-2107

Jackson Office
Federal Bldg.
100 W. Capitol St., Ste. 1016
Jackson, MS 39269-1096

Jacksonville Office
325 W. Adams St.
Jacksonville, FL 32202-4303

Knoxville Office
1 Northshore Bldg.
1111 Northshore Dr.
Knoxville, TN 37919-4090

Louisville Office
601 W. Broadway
P.O. Box 1044
Louisville, KY 40201-1044

Memphis Office
100 N. Main St., 28th Fl.
Memphis, TN 38103-5080

Nashville Office
1 Commerce Pl., Ste. 1600
Nashville, TN 37239-1600

Orlando Office
Federal Office Bldg.
80 N. Hughey Ave.
Orlando, FL 32801-2226

Tampa Office
700 Twiggs St.
P.O. Box 2097
Tampa, FL 33601-4017

REGION V

Chicago Regional Office
300 S. Wacker Dr.
Chicago, IL 60606-6765
    and
547 W. Jackson Blvd.
Chicago, IL 60606-5760

FIELD OFFICES

Cincinnati Office
Federal Office Bldg.
550 Main St., Rm. 9002
Cincinnati, OH 45202-3253

Cleveland Office
1 Playhouse Square
1375 Euclid Ave., Rm. 420
Cleveland, OH 44115-1830

Columbus Office
200 N. High St.
Columbus, OH 43215-2499

Detroit Office
Patrick V. McNamara Federal Bldg.
477 Michigan Ave.
Detroit, MI 48226-2592

Flint Office
Genesee Bank Bldg.
352 S. Saginaw St., Rm. 200
Flint, MI 48502-1953

Grand Rapids Office
2922 Fuller Ave., N.E.
Grand Rapids, MI 49505-3409

Indianapolis Office
151 N. Delaware St.
Indianapolis, IN 46204-2526

Milwaukee Office
Henry S. Reuss Federal Plaza
310 W. Wisconsin Ave., Ste. 1380
Milwaukee, WI 53203-2290

Minneapolis–St. Paul Office
220 Second St., S.
Minneapolis, MN 55401-2195

Springfield Office
524 S. Second St., Ste. 672
Springfield, IL 62701-1774

REGION VI

Fort Worth Regional Office
1600 Throcktmorton
P.O. Box 2905
Fort Worth, TX 76113-2905

FIELD OFFICES

Albuquerque Office
625 Truman St., N.E.
Albuquerque, NM 87110-6443

Dallas Office
555 Griffin Square Office Bldg.
525 Griffin St.
Dallas, TX 75202-5007

Houston Office
National Bank of Texas Bldg.
2211 Norfolk, Ste. 300
Houston, TX 77098-4096

Little Rock Office
Savers Bldg.
320 W. Capitol, Ste. 700
Little Rock, AR 72201-3523

Lubbock Office
Federal Office Bldg.
1205 Texas Ave.
Lubbock, TX 79401-4001

New Orleans Office
1661 Canal St.
P.O. Box 70288
New Orleans, LA 70112-0288

Oklahoma City Office
Murrah Federal Bldg.
200 N.W. 5th St.
Oklahoma City, OK 73102-3202

San Antonio Office
Washington Square
800 Dolorosa
P.O. Box 9163
San Antonio, TX 78285-3301

Shreveport Office
6811 New Federal Bldg.
500 Fannin St.
Shreveport, LA 71101-3077

Tulsa Office
Robert S. Kerr Bldg.
440 S. Houston Ave., Rm. 200
Tulsa, OK 74127-8923

REGION VII

Kansas City Regional Office
Professional Bldg.
1103 Grand Ave.
Kansas City, MO 64106-2496

FIELD OFFICES

Des Moines Office
Federal Bldg.
210 Walnut St., Rm. 259
Des Moines, IA 50309-2155

Omaha Office
Braiker/Brandeis Bldg.
210 S. 16th St.
Omaha, NE 68102-1622

St. Louis Office
210 N. Tucker Blvd.
St. Louis, MO 63101-1997

Topeka Office
444 S.E. Quincy St., Rm. 297
Topeka, KS 66683-3588

REGION VIII

Denver Regional Office
Executive Tower Bldg.
1405 Curtis St.
Denver, CO 80202-2349

FIELD OFFICES

Casper Office
4225 Federal Office Bldg.
100 E. B St.
P.O. Box 580
Casper, WY 82602-1918

Fargo Office
Federal Bldg.
653 2nd Ave., N.
P.O. Box 2483
Fargo, ND 58108-2483

Helena Office
Federal Office Bldg.
301 S. Park, Rm. 340
Drawer 10095
Helena, MT 59626-0095

Salt Lake City Office
324 S. State St., Ste. 220
Salt Lake City, UT 84111-2321

Sioux Falls Office
Courthouse Plaza
300 N. Dakota Ave., Ste. 108
Sioux Falls, SD 57102-0311

REGION IX

San Francisco Regional Office
Phillip Burton Federal Bldg. and U.S.
  Courthouse
450 Golden Gate Ave.
P.O. Box 36003
San Francisco, CA 94102-3448

Indian Programs Office, Region IX
1 N. First St., Ste. 400
P.O. Box 13468
Phoenix, AZ 85004-2360

FIELD OFFICES

Fresno Office
1630 E. Shaw Ave., Ste. 138
Fresno, CA 93710-8193

Honolulu Office
300 Ala Moana Blvd., Rm. 3318
P.O. Box 50007
Honolulu, HI 96850-4991

Las Vegas Office
720 S. 7th St., Ste. 221
Las Vegas, NV 89101-6930

Los Angeles Office
1615 W. Olympic Blvd.
Los Angeles, CA 90015-3801

Phoenix Office
1 N. First St., 3rd Fl.
P.O. Box 13468
Phoenix, AZ 85002-3468

Reno Office
1050 Bible Wy.
P.O. Box 4700
Reno, NV 89505-4700

Sacramento Office
777 12th St., Ste. 200
P.O. Box 1978
Sacramento, CA 95809-1978

San Diego Office
Federal Office Bldg., Rm. 553
880 Front St.
San Diego, CA 92188-0100

Santa Ana Office
34 Civic Center Plaza, Box 12850
Santa Ana, CA 92712-2850

Tucson Office
100 N. Stone Ave., 4th Fl.
Tucson, AZ 86701-1467

REGION X

Seattle Regional Office
Arcade Plaza Bldg.
1321 Second Ave.
Seattle, WA 98101-2054

FIELD OFFICES

Anchorage Office
701 C St., Box 64
Anchorage, AK 99513-0001

Boise Office
Federal Bldg. and U.S. Courthouse
550 W. Fort St.
P.O. Box 042
Boise, ID 83724-0420

Portland Office
520 S.W. Sixth Ave.
Portland, OR 97204-1596

Spokane Office
W. 920 Riverside Ave.
Spokane, WA 99201-1075

The following pamphlets are available free from
any HUD or FHA office listed above or from:
U.S. Department of Housing and Urban
  Development
451 Seventh St., S.W., Rm. B-258
Washington, DC 20410

Financing Condominium Housing
  HUD-77-F
*HUD/FHA Non-assisted Program for
  Condominium Housing* HUD-227-F

359

Mobile Home Financing Through HUD
HUD-265-F
Buying and Financing a Mobile Home
HUD-243-F
Wise Home Buying HUD-267-H(1)
Fixing Up Your Home—And How to
Finance It HUD-52-H(9)
Let's Consider Cooperatives HUD-17-F(2)
Home Buying Members of the Armed
Services HUD-121-H(5)
Avoiding Mortgage Default HUD-426-PA(6)
Move In . . . With a Graduated Payment
Mortgage HUD-H-317(4)
Home Mortgage Insurance HUD-43-F
Programs for Home Mortgage Insurance
HUD-97-H
HUD's Home Ownership Subsidy Program
HUD-419-H
Should You Buy or Rent a Home
HUD-328-H
Protecting Your Housing Investment
HUD-346-PA
Home Buyers Vocabulary HUD-383-H
Questions and Answers on FHA Home
Property Appraisals HUD-38-F

Veterans Administration (VA)— Federal Government Guaranteed Loans (GI Loans)

The following is a list of Veterans Administration (VA) Guaranty Service regional offices. You can obtain information and necessary loan forms by sending a note to the director of any of these offices.

Alabama
VA Regional Office
474 S. Court St.
Montgomery, AL 36104

Alaska
VA Regional Office
235 E. 8th Ave.
Anchorage, AK 99501

Arizona
VA Regional Office
3225 N. Central Ave.
Phoenix, AZ 85012

Arkansas
VA Regional Office
1200 W. Third St.
Little Rock, AR 72201

California (Northern)
VA Regional Office
211 Main St.
San Francisco, CA 94105

California (Southern)
VA Regional Office
Federal Bldg.
11000 Wilshire Blvd.
Los Angeles, CA 90024

VA Regional Office
2022 Camino Del Rio, N.
San Diego, CA 92108

Colorado
VA Regional Office
Denver Federal Center, Bldg. 20
Denver, CO 80225

Connecticut
VA Regional Office
450 Main St.
Hartford, CT 06103

Delaware
VA Regional Office
1601 Kirkwood Hwy.
Wilmington, DE 19805

District of Columbia
VA Regional Office
941 N. Capitol St., N.E.
Washington, DC 20421

Florida
VA Regional Office
P.O. Box 1437
144 First Ave., S.
St. Petersburg, FL 33731

Georgia
VA Regional Office
730 Peachtree St., N.E.
Atlanta, GA 30365

Hawaii (including American Samoa, Wake, Midway, and the Trust Territory of the Pacific Islands)

VA Regional Office
PJKK Federal Bldg.
300 Ala Moana Blvd.
P.O. Box 50188
Honolulu, HI 96813

Idaho
VA Regional Office
Federal Bldg. and U.S. Courthouse
550 W. Fot St., Box 044
Boise, ID 83724

Illinois
VA Regional Office
536 S. Clark St.
P.O. Box 8136
Chicago, IL 60605

Indiana
VA Regional Office
575 N. Pennsylvania St.
Indianapolis, IN 46204

Iowa
VA Regional Office
210 Walnut St.
Des Moines, IA 50309

Kansas
VA Regional Office
901 N. Washington Blvd.
Wichita, KS 67211

Kentucky
VA Regional Office
600 Federal Pl.
Louisville, KY 40202

Louisiana
VA Regional Office
701 Loyola Ave.
New Orleans, LA 70113

Maine
VA Regional Office
Togus, ME 04330

Maryland
VA Regional Office
Federal Bldg.
31 Hopkins Plaza
Baltimore, MD 21201

Massachusetts
VA Regional Office
John F. Kennedy Bldg.
Government Center
Boston, MA 02203

Michigan
VA Regional Office
Patrick V. McNamari
  Federal Bldg.
477 Michigan Ave.
Detroit, MI 48226

Minnesota
VA Regional Office
Federal Bldg.
Fort Snelling
St. Paul, MN 55111

Mississippi
VA Regional Office
100 W. Capital St.
Jackson, MS 39269

Missouri
VA Regional Office
Federal Bldg.
1520 Market St.
St. Louis, MO 63103

Montana
VA Regional Office
Fort Harrison, MT 59636

Nebraska
VA Regional Office
Federal Bldg.
100 Centennial Mall, N.
Lincoln, NE 68508

Nevada
VA Regional Office
245 E. Liberty St.
Reno, NV 89520

New Hampshire
VA Regional Office
Norris Cotton Bldg.
275 Chestnut St.
Manchester, NH 03101

New Jersey
VA Regional Office
20 Washington Pl.
Newark, NJ 07102

New Mexico
VA Regional Office
Dennis Chavez Federal Bldg.
U.S. Courthouse
500 Gold Ave., S.W.
Albuquerque, NM 87102

New York (Eastern)
VA Regional Office
252 Seventh Ave.
New York, NY 10001

New York (Western)
VA Regional Office
Federal Bldg.
111 W. Huron St.
Buffalo, NY 14202

North Carolina
VA Regional Office
Federal Bldg.
251 N. Main St.
Winston-Salem, NC 27155

North Dakota
VA Regional Office
655 First Ave., N.
Fargo, ND 58102

Ohio
VA Regional Office
Anthony J. Celebrezze
Federal Bldg.
1240 E. Ninth St.
Cleveland, OH 44199

Oklahoma
VA Regional Office
Federal Bldg.
125 S. Main St.
Muskogee, OK 74401

Oregon
VA Regional Office
Federal Bldg.
1220 S. Third Ave.
Portland, OR 97204

Pennsylvania (Eastern)
VA Regional Office
5000 Wissahickon Ave.
P.O. Box 8079
Philadelphia, PA 19101

Pennsylvania (Western)
VA Regional Office
1000 Liberty Ave.
Pittsburgh, PA 15222

Rhode Island
VA Regional Office
380 Westminster Mall
Providence, RI 02903

South Carolina
VA Regional Office
1801 Assembly St.
Columbia, SC 29201

South Dakota
VA Regional Office
P.O. Box 22nd St.
Sioux Falls, SD 57117

Tennessee
VA Regional Office
110 Ninth Ave., S.
Nashville, TN 37203

Texas (Northern)
VA Regional Office
1400 N. Valley Mills Dr.
Waco, TX 76799

Texas (Southern)
VA Regional Office
2515 Murworth Dr.
Houston, TX 77054

Utah
VA Regional Office
Federal Bldg.
125 S. State St.
Salt Lake City, UT 84147

Vermont
VA Regional Office
White River Junction, VT 05001

Virginia
VA Regional Office
210 Franklin Rd., S.W.
Roanoke, VA 24011

Washington
VA Regional Office
Federal Bldg.
915 Second Ave.
Seattle, WA 98174

West Virginia
VA Regional Office
640 Fourth Ave.
Huntington, WV 25701

Wisconsin
VA Regional Office
VA Center
P.O. Box 6
Milwaukee, WI 53193

Wyoming
VA Regional Office
2360 E. Pershing Blvd.
Cheyenne, WY 82001

The following pamphlets on VA loans are available free from any VA regional office listed above:

A Guide to Veterans Benefits
Pointers for the Veteran Homeowner VA-265
Questions and Answers on Guarantees and Direct Loans for Veterans VA-264
To the Home-Buying Veteran VA-266
A Summary of Veterans Administration Benefits VA-27-82-2

State Agencies for Veteran's Affairs

The following state agencies provide services and information to the state's veterans, their dependents, and survivors. Check with their farm and home purchases division to see if property loans are available to veterans in your state.

Alabama
Department of Veterans Affairs
State Office Bldg.
Montgomery, AL 36130

Alaska
Military and Veterans Affairs Department
3601 C St., Ste. 620
Anchorage, AK 99503-5989

Arizona
Veterans Service Commission
700 W. Campbell, #17
Phoenix, AZ 85013

Arkansas
Department of Veterans Affairs
1200 W. Third St., Rm. 105
Little Rock, AR 72201

California
Department of Veterans Affairs
1227 O St.
Sacramento, CA 95814

Colorado
Division of Veterans Services
Department of Social Services
1575 Sherman St.
Denver, CO 80203

Connecticut
Veterans Home and Hospital Commission
287 West St.
Rocky Hill, CT 06067

Delaware
Veterans Affairs Agency
P.O. Box 185
Milford, DE 19963

District of Columbia
Office of Veterans Affairs
Department of Human Services
941 N. Capitol, N.E., Rm. 1211-F
Washington, DC 20002

Florida
Veterans Affairs
Department of Administration
350 Lesis State Bank Bldg.
Tallahassee, FL 32301

Georgia
Department of Veterans Services
Veterans Memorial Bldg.
Atlanta, GA 30334

Hawaii
Veterans Affairs Unit
Social Services and Housing Department
1060 Bishop St., 5th Fl.
Honolulu, HI 96813

Idaho
Division of Veterans Affairs
Department of Health and Welfare
P.O. Box 7765
Boise, ID 83707

Illinois
Department of Veterans Affairs
208 W. Cook St.
Springfield, IL 62706

Indiana
Department of Veterans Affairs
707 State Office Bldg.
Indianapolis, IN 46204

Iowa
Department of Veterans Affairs
Camp Dodge
Johnston, IA 50131

Kansas
Veterans' Commission
Department of Human Resources
503 Kansas Ave.
Topeka, KS 66603

Kentucky
Center for Veterans Affairs
600 Federal Bldg., Rm. 1365
Louisville, KY 40202

Louisiana
Veterans Affairs Commission
Office of the Governor
Old State Capitol
Baton Rouge, LA 70801

Maine
Bureau of Veterans Services
Defense and Veterans Services Department
State House Station, #33
Augusta, ME 04333

Maryland
Maryland Veterans Commission
Federal Bldg., Rm. 110
31 Hopkins Plaza
Baltimore, MD 21201

Massachusetts
Office of Veterans Services
100 Cambridge St., Rm. 1002
Boston, MA 02202

Michigan
Veterans Trust Fund
Department of Management and Budget
P.O. Box 30026
Lansing, MI 48909

Minnesota
Department of Veterans Affairs
Veterans Bldg.
20 W. 12th St.
St. Paul, MN 55155

Mississippi
Veterans Affairs Board
War Memorial Bldg.
120 N. State St.
Jackson, MS 39201

Missouri
Division of Veterans Affairs
Department of Public Safety
P.O. Drawer 147
Jefferson City, MO 65102

Montana
Veterans Affairs Division
Social and Rehabilitation Services
Department
111 Sanders St.
Helena, MT 59601

Nebraska
Department of Veterans Affairs
301 Centennial Mall, S.
P.O. Box 95083
Lincoln, NE 68509-5083

Nevada
Commission for Veterans Affairs
245 E. Liberty St.
Reno, NV 89504

New Hampshire
State Veterans Council
359 Lincoln St.
Manchester, NH 03103

New Jersey
Veterans Program and Special Services
Department of Human Services
143 E. State St., Rm. 512
Trenton, NJ 08625

New Mexico
Veterans Service Commission
P.O. Box 2324
Santa Fe, NM 87504

New York
Division of Veterans Affairs
194 Washington Ave.
Albany, NY 12210

North Carolina
Division of Veterans Affairs
Department of Administration
227 E. Edenton St.
Raleigh, NC 27611

North Dakota
Veterans Affairs Department
P.O. Box 1287
Fargo, ND 58107-1287

Ohio
Veterans Affairs
Department of Adjutant General
State House Annex, Rm. 11
Columbus, OH 43215

Oklahoma
Veterans Affairs Department
2311 N. Central
Oklahoma City, OK 73105

Oregon
Department of Veterans Affairs
700 Summer St., N.E.
Salem, OR 97310

Pennsylvania
Department of Military Affairs
Fort Indiantown Gap
Annville, PA 17003

Rhode Island
Veterans Home
Department of Social and Rehabilitation
    Services
600 New London Ave.
Cranston, RI 02920

South Carolina
Department of Veterans Affairs
1205 Pendleton St., Rm. 227
Columbia, SC 29201

South Dakota
Veterans Division
Military and Veteran Affairs Department
State Capitol, 1st Fl.
Pierre, SD 57501

Tennessee
Department of Veterans Affairs
215 Eighth Ave., N.
Nashville, TN 37203

Texas
Veterans Affairs Commission
P.O. Box 12277
Capitol Station
Austin, TX 78711

Utah
Division of Finance
Administrative Services Department
2110 State Office Bldg.
Salt Lake City, UT 84114

Vermont
Veterans Affairs
118 State St.
Montpelier, VT 05602

Virginia
Division of War Veterans Claims
P.O. Box 809
Roanoke, VA 24004

Washington
Department of Veterans Affairs
11th and Washington Sts.
Olympia, WA 98504

West Virginia
Veterans Affairs
Atlas Bldg., Rm. 605
Charleston, WV 25305

Wisconsin
Department of Veterans Affairs
77 N. Dickinson, Rm. 263
P.O. Box 7843
Madison, WI 53707

Wyoming
Veterans Affairs Commission
2207 Sheridan
Laramie, WY 82070

Farmers Home Administration (FmHA)

For information on FmHA programs available in your area write to your local FmHA office. To get the address of your local office write to:
The Farmers Home Administration
U.S. Department of Agriculture
Washington, DC 20250

The following pamphlets are available free from any local Farmers Home Administration office or the main office listed above:

Self-Help Housing Loans—Program Aid
    No. 990

Home Improvement Loans and Repair Loans and Grants—Program Aid No. 1184

Home Ownership Loans—Program Aid No. 977

Loans to Limited-Resource Farmers—Program Aid No. 1250

Farm Ownership Loans—Program Aid No. 62

Farm Operating Loans—Program Aid No. 1002

Rental Assistance Program—Program Aid No. 1210

Farm Labor Housing Loans and Grants—Program Aid No. 521

Loans for Resource Conservation and Development—Program Aid No. 799

Water and Waste Disposal Loans and Grants—Program Aid No. 1203

Rural Rental Housing—Program Aid No. 1039

Watershed Loans—Program Aid No. 406

Irrigation and Drainage Association Loans—Program Aid No. 1187

The following is available for $.50 from:
Small Homes Council—Building Research Council
University of Illinois at Urbana-Champaign
One E. Saint Mary's Rd.
Champaign, IL 61820

Financing the Home—A 1.3

The following are available for the specified cost from:
R. Woods
Consumer Information Center
P.O. Box 100
Pueblo, CO 81002

Fair Credit Reporting Act 415P	$ .50
The Mortgage Money Guide	$1.00
Settlement Costs 163P	$1.25
Sales of Federal Real Estate (revised monthly) 581P	free
Are There Any Public Lands for Sale? 128P	$1.00
Consumer Handbook on Adjustable Rate Mortgages 580P	free

The following is available free from:

S. James
Consumer Information Center, Y-6
P.O. Box 100
Pueblo, CO 81002

Consumer Handbook on Adjustable Rate Mortgages

The following is available free from any savings and loan association office:

Your Guide to a Savings and Loan Mortgage

The following are available for the specified cost from:
Superintendent of Documents
Government Printing Office
Washington, DC 20402

Selecting and Financing a Home S/N 001-000-04431-1	$2.25
Condominiums—Their Development and Management HH 1.2:C 75/3 S/N 2300-00202	$1.25
Rent or Buy? S/N 029-001-02309-0	$3.50

The following are free from:
Publications Services
Division of Support Services
Board of Governors of the Federal Reserve System
Washington, DC 20557

Consumer Handbook to Credit Protection Laws
What Truth in Lending Means to You
The Equal Credit Opportunity Act and Credit Rights in Housing

The following is free from:
Public Information Department
Federal Reserve Bank of New York
33 Liberty St.
New York, NY 10045

The Arithmetic of Interest Rates

The following is free from:
California Land Title Association
Box 13968
Sacramento, CA 95853

Understanding Foreclosure

The following is free from:

T.D. Service Financial Corporation
4041 N. Central Ave., Ste. 625
Phoenix, AZ 85012

Your Introduction to a Foreclosure

The following is available for $1.00 from:
ANR Publications
University of California
6701 San Pablo Ave.
Oakland, CA 94608-1239

Shop for Your Loan

For information on the Fair Credit Reporting Act or to register complaints regarding your credit application rights contact any of the offices of the Federal Trade Commission listed below:

FTC HEADQUARTERS

6th and Pennsylvania Ave., N.W.
Washington, DC 20580

FTC REGIONAL OFFICES

1718 Peachtree St., N.W.
Atlanta, GA 30367

150 Causeway St.
Boston, MA 02114

55 E. Monroe St.
Chicago, IL 60603

118 St. Clair Ave.
Cleveland, OH 44114

8303 Elmbrook Dr.
Dallas, TX 75247

1405 Curtis St.
Denver, CO 80202

11000 Wilshire Blvd.
Los Angeles, CA 90024

26 Federal Plaza
New York, NY 10278

450 Golden Gate Ave.
San Francisco, CA 94102

915 Second Ave.
Seattle, WA 98174

General Information

In addition to the lenders and financial agencies mentioned above, you can get financial advice from your local farm advisor and from your local agricultural experiment station. (See addresses in Useful Resources at the end of chapter 5, "The Earth—Soil, Vegetation, Topography.")

VI

THE CONTRACT OF SALE

CHAPTER 28

The Model Contract of Sale

This chapter is the heart of the book. It contains a Model Contract of Sale which I present as a means of evaluating other contracts and which can be used in your land purchase. Some states, such as California, have standard form contracts formulated by reputable organizations that are extremely well done. In my own law practice, I regularly use the form called Real Estate Purchase Contract and Receipt for Deposit, originally drafted by the State Bar of California in conjunction with the California Association of Realtors, which includes every form of protection within it that I include in my Model Contract of Sale in this chapter.

However, most states do not have such standard form contracts available, and even in California it is not mandatory to use the realtor form. Many brokers in California and throughout the country use forms purchased in stationery stores that are usually very inadequate.

Because my book is for use in all parts of the United States and Canada, my Model Contract is rather complex. It attempts to deal with as many conceivable situations as possible. If you use a contract submitted to you by your broker, be sure you read and understand it, and compare its terms to the ones that I tell you are necessary to have in your contract. If you have any questions, I recommend that you consult an attorney who specializes in real property law. It's a lot cheaper to uncover problems before your purchase than afterward.

As stated previously, many times real estate agents

will give documents to buyers to sign without making it clear that they are binding contracts. The *deposit receipt* is the most infamous example of this practice throughout the United States. **Any document that is dated, contains the name of the parties, states what is being sold and for how much and on what terms, and is signed by the parties is a legally binding contract, regardless of what it is called.**

Each section of the Model Contract is accompanied by an explanation of what the terms mean, why they are included, and how you should fill in the blank spaces. Where applicable, you are referred to the other parts of the book that have more information on that section of the Model Contract. First, read the entire contract, then go back over each section while reading the explanation that goes with it. If you have read the rest of this book, you will then have an understanding of how to use this Model Contract in your purchase to protect yourself.

You will not use every clause contained in this contract. Many sections will be deleted for your purposes as explained in the discussion of each section. For example, if there is no house on the land, you will delete each section of the contract that relates to the purchase of a house.

This contract serves three purposes. First, it is a receipt for your deposit money, which you and the broker sign as evidence you have paid it. There is no reason why you should give the real estate agent any money unless you are ready to make an offer to buy the land according to your terms. Thus the contract also serves as an offer to purchase the land. If the seller accepts your offer, the contract becomes the final agreement between the parties. That is its third function. When you fill in the amount of money to be paid for the property, this is really the amount you are offering to pay. If the seller rejects your offer, he will return the contract unsigned. It will not be surprising if this contract passes back and forth between the two of you several times before a final agreement is reached. The seller can cross out or change anything in your offer and sign and return the contract to you. All changes, additions, and deletions in the document must be initialed or signed by both parties. (See chapter 20, ''Bargaining to Get the Seller's Asking Price Down.'')

When a buyer makes an offer and puts a deposit on a piece of property, the real estate agent normally offers him a deposit receipt or contract of sale to fill out and sign. You can tell him that you wish to use your own form or you can write the contingencies you want included onto the agent's form. If you have time, get all the information from him that you need to complete your own contract. Then go through the contract and delete and add whatever is necessary. Type the resulting contract on regular typing paper, fill in the blanks and sign it, and give it to the agent or seller, whichever party you are dealing with. He will probably be shocked. Compared to the simple form that the agent usually gives a buyer, your contract of sale will look like a manifesto. Don't worry about a thing. The purpose of all this is to protect your investment. Should anything go wrong during or after your purchase, forcing you to proceed with legal action against the seller, you will be glad you used this contract. If you decide to include your contingencies on the agent's form, be sure to check through the contract in this book for those contingencies that are important to you. They can be written out on a separate sheet or sheets of paper labeled Exhibit ''A,'' attached to the form, and referred to in the form with the words: close of escrow is contingent upon Buyer's approval prior to the close of escrow of the conditions specified in Exhibit ''A,'' attached hereto and made a part hereof.

If you submit your own contract to the agent, he is bound by law to deliver it to the seller. You may get resistance from the seller about accepting it. However, I mention areas where you can make compromises with the seller without jeopardizing your basic protections. If the seller absolutely refuses to deal with this contract, you can ask him to give you a contract form that is acceptable to him. Take his contract and compare it to the Model Contract. Where his contract has omitted protections you must have, write in the clauses directly from the Model Contract. If his contract has clauses you don't like, cross them out and initial the change. Then you can return the seller's contract to him. Never allow yourself to be buffaloed by the seller or agent. A fair and honest seller will allow you the basic and adequate protections provided for in this Model Contract of Sale. If the agent or seller balks at all the conditions, simply use the one condition that the purchase is subject to the approval of your attorney, and he or she can then tell you what you should have in the deal before it closes.

Don't be surprised if the form is a little difficult to understand the first time through. By the time you have finished reading the book, looked at some land, talked to some real estate agents and public officials, everything will fit into place. Even if you decided to retain the services of an attorney, this chapter will give you a good understanding of what he should be doing for you. It provides you with the information you need to ask him intelligent questions about the transaction. You should com-

pare this Model Contract with the contract your lawyer prepares for you. If you find anything omitted from his contract or if any clauses are in conflict, point this out to him. Lawyers are not infallible.

It is always risky to purchase real estate without consulting an attorney because of the complexity of the laws regarding rural property, so if you feel unsure at any point go to an attorney for a consultation to have it checked over. The minimal expense of doing this is well worth it considering the amount of money you are about to invest.

MODEL CONTRACT OF SALE

City of _____ County of _____

State of _____ Date _____, 19_____

Received from _____ (herein called Buyer), the sum of _____ Dollars ($_____.__) evidenced by __(personal check or cashier's check)__ as deposit on account of purchase price of _____ Dollars ($_____.__) for the purchase of property, situated in City of _____, County of, _____, State of _____, described as follows: _____
_____
(describe real property and personal property, if any)
_____
_____

Said deposit will be held uncashed until acceptance of this offer. Buyer will deposit in escrow with _____ the balance of purchase price as follows:

The sum of _____ Dollars ($_____.__) to be deposited prior to close of escrow, as a down payment, which shall include the above deposit;

The sum of _____ Dollars ($_____.__) to be represented by a __(note and [1] mortgage or [2] deed of trust)__, to be payable _____ Dollars ($_____.__) or more per month with interest on all unpaid principal of _____% per annum, from close of escrow, payable with each monthly payment as part of the same. First payment is due 30 days after close of escrow.

1. Buyer's signature hereon constitutes an offer to Seller to purchase the real estate and personal property described above. Unless acceptance hereof is signed by Seller and the signed copy delivered to Buyer, either in person or by mail to the address shown below within _____ days hereof, this offer shall be deemed revoked and the deposit shall be returned to Buyer within 48 hours.

2. The price of said property is _____ Dollars ($_____.__) per acre. The total number of acres is _____.

3. The total acreage on which the purchase price is computed shall be based on a legal survey completed by a licensed surveyor. The results of the survey are to be approved by Buyer before the close of escrow. The expense of the survey is to be paid by the Seller.

4. Within _____ days of the Seller's acceptance hereof, escrow instructions signed by Buyer and Seller shall be delivered to __(name and address of escrow holder)__.

Escrow instructions signed by both parties shall provide for closing within _____ days from the opening of escrow, subject to written extensions signed by Buyer and Seller.

Close of escrow means the time when the documents transferring title are recorded.

5. Unless otherwise designated in the escrow instructions of Buyer, title shall vest as follows:

_____

6. Seller shall by Warranty Deed or a Grant Deed convey to Buyer a marketable fee simple title as approved by Buyer in the following manner: Title is to be free of liens, encumbrances, easements, covenants, reservations, restrictions, rights and conditions other than current property taxes and those items approved of by Buyer after inspection of a current preliminary title report or abstract of title. Within _____ days of the Seller's acceptance hereof, Seller shall cause to be delivered to Buyer a Preliminary Title Report issued by ___(title company)___ describing the property, and copies of all documents referred to in it. Within _____ days after Buyer's receipt of the Preliminary Title Report and all documents referred to in it, Buyer shall give Seller notice specifying the matters disapproved by Buyer. If these matters are not corrected by the Seller to the satisfaction and approval of the Buyer before the close of escrow, the Buyer may, at his election, terminate this agreement and any deposit shall immediately be returned to him.

7. Seller shall furnish to Buyer a marketable fee simple title as evidenced by a ___(standard or extended)___ Owner's Title Insurance Policy insuring title in Buyer for the amount of the purchase price of said property and issued by ___(title company)___ .

8. The following prorations shall be made in escrow on the basis of a 30-month and shall be prorated as of (1) the date of recordation of the deed:
    (a) Real property taxes;
    (b) Premiums on insurance policies approved by Buyer and to be assumed by Buyer;
    (c) Interest on obligations secured by encumbrances to which the property will remain subject after close of escrow;
    (d) Installments of principal and interest on the following personal property: _____ which are to be included with this transaction.

9. If impounded funds are held by the lender in connection with a mortgage, deed of trust, or other encumbrance remaining of record at close of escrow, Buyer shall be charged and Seller credited with the full amount.

10. If at the close of escrow all or any part of the property is affected by any assessment liens, or bonds, all or part of which are or may become payable, all the unpaid installments of these, including those that are to become due after close of escrow, shall, for purposes of this agreement, be considered due and liens on the property, and except for _____, Seller shall pay and discharge them before close of escrow or, at Buyer's election, allow them as a credit against the ___(cash or note)___ due Seller at close of escrow.

11. Buyer shall pay _____% and Seller shall pay _____% of each of the following: the escrow fee; the escrow holder's customary charges for document-drafting, recording, and miscellaneous charges; the title insurance premium or charge for the Abstract of Title and Certificate of Title; and local transfer taxes.

    In addition, each party will pay reasonable compensation to the escrow holder for extraordinary or unusual services rendered to or for that party, if any, plus costs and expenses incurred in connection with those services.

12. Seller shall deliver possession of the property, all improvements thereon, and all personal property, if any, to Buyer in substantially the same condition, reasonable wear and tear excepted, as on the date of this agreement (strike out inapplicable alternatives below):
    (a) on close of escrow; or

(b) not later than _____ days after close of escrow; or

(c) on _____

(d) If the Seller has not vacated the property by the date Buyer is to take possession, the Seller shall be liable to the Buyer for a daily rental equal to the sum of _____ Dollars ($_____.___) per day for each and every day the Seller remains on the property as a holdover Seller in possession; or the Buyer, at his option, may terminate this agreement and any deposit and other money deposited in escrow shall thereupon be returned to him.

13. If, when neither legal title nor possession of the property has been transferred to the Buyer, any part of the property is destroyed, materially damaged, or taken by eminent domain, the Buyer, at his option, may be relieved of his obligation to complete the purchase, or he may obtain a reduction of the purchase price to the extent of the cost of repairing or replacing the damage from destruction or the diminution in value resulting from eminent domain.

14. Seller recognizes that Buyer will spend time and effort preparing for the acquisition of this property, and Buyer recognizes that Seller's property will be removed from the market during the existence of this agreement. Both parties agree that if either fails to perform under this contract, the other should be entitled to compensation for the detriment described above, but that it is extremely difficult and impractical to ascertain the extent of the detriment. To avoid these problems, the parties agree to liquidate damages as follows:

If Seller fails to perform for any reason, Buyer shall be entitled to recover his deposit and any other money he has deposited into escrow or paid to or for Seller's account and shall also recover from Seller the sum of _____ Dollars ($_____.___) as liquidated damages.

If Buyer fails to perform for any reason, Seller shall be entitled to recover the sum of ___(amount of deposit or less)___ Dollars ($_____.___) as liquidated damages and shall be entitled to obtain the sum out of any deposit made by Buyer to Seller or his agent or into escrow and out of any other money Buyer has deposited into escrow or paid to or for Seller's account.

Both parties agree that these sums stated as liquidated damages shall be in lieu of any other monetary relief to which the parties might otherwise be entitled by virtue of this contract or by operation of law.

15. The Seller, for himself, and his heirs, representatives, and assignees, covenants with the Buyer and his heirs, representatives, and assignees as follows:

(a) That the Seller is lawfully seised of the described property in fee simple, and has the right to convey the same;

(b) That the property is free from all liens and encumbrances, except as aforesaid;

(c) That the Buyer shall quietly enjoy the property;

(d) That the Seller will do any further acts or procure any further necessary assurance of the title for the purpose of perfecting the title to the property;

(e) That the Seller forever warrants and will defend the title of the property against the lawful claims and demands of all persons;

(f) That all of the above covenants shall survive delivery of the deed.

16. The Seller warrants and represents the following:

(a) That the land title conveyed to the Buyer contains legal access rights from the most accessible public road to the building sites on the conveyed land which is the subject of this agreement. These access roads shall include, but not be limited to, the existing access roads to the building sites on the conveyed land if any are in existence at the time of this conveyance.

(b) That as of the close of escrow the property will have a legal survey completed by a licensed surveyor or registered civil engineer with all corners staked on the ground and all boundaries marked and visible on the ground; and will include within its boundaries the following structures and land features: _____.

(c) That as of the close of escrow the property will include a spring, well, creek, or other water supply with a year-round output of at least _____ gallons per _____.

(d) That at this time and as of the close of escrow the property is and will be zoned _____, under the laws of the City of _____, the County of _____, and the State of _____.

(e) That as of the close of escrow the structures will be free of any damage from infestation by wood-destroying pest and organisms, including but not limited to termites, dry rot, and fungi.

(f) That at present and as of the close of escrow no violation exists or will exist with respect to the property or any improvements, of any statute, ordinance, regulation, or administrative or judicial order or holding, whether or not appearing in public records.

(g) That the property is not, and at the close of escrow shall not be, the subject of any proposed liens, assessment liens, or bonds other than those excepted in Clause 10 above, by reason of any work or improvement completed or installed at or before the close of escrow, or to be completed after the close of escrow.

(h) That at present and as of the close of escrow the Seller has no knowledge of any intent to take any part of the property by condemnation or eminent domain.

(i) That at present and as of the close of escrow the Seller owns, in full, those items listed as personal property to be conveyed to the Buyer according to this agreement. The following such items are not owned in full by the Seller: _____.

(j) That no poisonous sprays, insecticides, pesticides, or herbicides have been used in any way on said property or applied to any vegetation growing on said property.

(k) That all of the above warranties and representations shall survive delivery of the deed.

17. Buyer's obligation to perform this agreement is subject to the following terms and conditions:

(a) If Buyer notifies Seller that Buyer disapproves any matter set out in this Clause, or that the condition has not been satisfied, Buyer, at his election, can terminate the agreement without liability on his part, and his deposit shall be immediately returned to him. Buyer shall notify Seller of his disapproval of a condition herein within _____ days of the signing of the agreement. The close of escrow is contingent upon the Buyer approving of all the conditions herein or meeting those conditions prior to the close of escrow.

(b) Buyer's approval, within _____ days after the date of this agreement, of __(survey, soil test, termite and house inspection, appraisal of land and improvements, etc.)__. The cost of this is to be paid __(equally, by Buyer and Seller, by Seller, by Buyer)__. Buyer and his representatives shall have the right from this date to enter on the property to obtain the pertinent information and for any other purposes reasonably related to carrying out the provisions of this agreement.

(c) Buyer's ability to secure the right, under applicable zoning and land use laws, regulations, and ordinances, to __(zoning, or use designation being sought, building permits, etc.)__. Buyer shall file the documents and pay the fees necessary to obtain the change. If Buyer has proceeded with reasonable diligence but has not obtained a final determination by the time scheduled for closing, on Buyer's written election the closing shall be extended until final determination, provided Buyer is diligently pursuing a determination. Seller may terminate this agreement on _____ days' notice if Buyer is not diligent in pursuing a determination. If the final determination is adverse, Buyer alone shall have the election either to terminate his agreement or to waive this condition. Buyer shall make his election within _____ days after final determination.

(d) Buyer's approval, within _____ days after execution of this agreement, of a structural pest control inspection from ___(name of company)___, a licensed structural pest control operator selected by the Buyer, certifying that normally accessible areas of the property are free from infestation by wood-destroying pests and organisms, including but not limited to termites, dry rot, and fungi, and that no corrective work is required, the cost of the report to be borne ___(equally by Buyer and Seller, by Seller, or by Buyer)___.

Buyer shall notify Seller by _____, 19 ___, if the condition is not satisfied, and Buyer may, at his election, terminate this agreement, unless Seller agrees to pay the cost of completing all recommendations made in said report.

(e) Buyer's obtaining from a lender of his choice within _____ days of execution of this agreement a loan of not less than _____ Dollars ($_____.__) secured by ___(first deed of trust, mortgage)___ on the property on terms no less favorable to the Buyer than the following: Interest at _____% per year, principal and interest payable in equal monthly installments of _____ Dollars ($_____.__) for a term of _____ years, privilege of prepayment at any time without penalty, loan fees and costs of not more than _____%, acceleration provisions to be approved by Buyer, and ___(guaranteed by VA or insured by FHA)___.

Buyer shall make diligent application to at least two lending institutions and execute and furnish documents and supply all information reasonably requested by the lending institutions in connection with Buyer's applications

(f) The Seller shall make a diligent effort to locate and develop a year-round adequate water supply for the Buyer's needs on the property. If necessary, the Seller shall drill a well to a maximum depth of _____. The water supply must have a year-round output of at least _____ gallons per minute. If the Seller cannot locate and develop an adequate water supply, then this agreement shall be terminated immediately and all funds deposited and paid by the Buyer shall be returned immediately, and the Buyer shall suffer no further liability under this agreement.

18. The prevailing party in any action or proceeding between the parties shall be entitled to reasonable attorney's fees in addition to all other relief to which he may be entitled.

19. As used in this agreement, the masculine, feminine, or neuter gender, and the singular or plural number shall each be deemed to include the others whenever the context so indicates, and the words Buyer and Seller shall include the respective successors in interest of each, whenever the context so requires.

20. All exhibits to which reference is made are deemed incorporated in the agreement, whether or not actually attached.

21. The waiver by either or both parties of the performance of any covenant, condition, or promise shall not be considered a waiver of any other covenant, condition, or promise. The waiver by either or both parties of the time for performing any act shall not constitute a waiver of the time for performing any other act required to be performed under this agreement.

22. All notices and demands shall be given in writing by registered or certified mail, postage prepaid, and return receipt requested. Notices shall be addressed as appears below for the respective person unless one party notifies the other of a change of address. Notices to any party of any transaction sent after escrow is opened shall also be sent to the escrow holder.

23. This agreement shall apply to and bind the heirs, executors, administrators, successors, and assignees of the respective parties.

24. Any change in or modification of this agreement must be in writing and signed by the parties hereto.

25. Time is of the essence in this agreement.

(Seller's agent's signature)
_____

Name of Seller's Agent

_____
Address

_____
Telephone

The undersigned Buyer offers and agrees to buy the above-described property on the terms and conditions above stated and acknowledges receipt of a copy hereof. Upon acceptance by the Seller and delivery to the Buyer of a copy signed by both Buyer and Seller, this instrument becomes a binding contract between Buyer and Seller.

_____   _____
Dated   Address

_____   _____
Telephone
        (Buyer's signature)   (Signature of Buyer's spouse or partner)

_____   _____
Name of Buyer   Name of Buyer's Spouse or Partner

ACCEPTANCE

The undersigned Seller accepts the foregoing offer and agrees to sell the property described therein on the terms and conditions therein set forth.

The undersigned Seller has employed the Agent above named and for the Agent's services agrees to pay the Agent as a commission the sum of _____ Dollars ($_____.__) payable as follows:

    (a) on recordation of the deed or other evidence of title, or

    (b) upon Seller's default, if completion of sale is prevented by default of Seller, or

    (c) only if and when the Seller collects the damages from Buyer, by suit or otherwise, if completion of sale is prevented by default of Buyer, and then in an amount not to exceed one half that portion of the damages collected after first deducting title and escrow expenses and the expenses of collection, if any.

The undersigned acknowledges receipt of a copy hereof and authorizes the Agent to deliver a signed copy of it to Buyer.

_____   _____
Dated   Address
                                                 (Seller's signature)

_____
Telephone   Name of Seller

                                         _____
                                                 (Signature of Seller's spouse or partner)
                                         Name of Seller's Spouse or Partner

Agent consents to the foregoing:

_____   _____
                                                 (Agent's signature)
Dated   Name of Agent

EXPLANATION OF CLAUSES IN MODEL CONTRACT OF SALE

Where appropriate, an explanation will be followed by an example showing you how the blanks on the contract can be filled in. Reference will be made to other chapters that include more details and information on the subject of each clause.

Place and Date of Signing

Write in the city, county, and state in which this transaction occurs and the date you sign this contract. This date is important because it starts the time period in which the seller must accept your offer, according to Clause 3 below.

Buyer's Name

Your name is inserted here.

Amount and Form of Deposit (Earnest Money)

Next you specify the amount of your deposit. Any time money amounts are given in the contract, they should first be written out and then given numerically, for example, "Two Hundred Dollars; $200.00." This avoids any possibility of confusion due to a typographical error, since the amount written out always takes priority over the numerical figure. Although the deposit can be for any amount, it is generally between $200 and $1,000. The seller will want the amount to be as large as possible, since the seller gets to keep it as a forfeiture penalty if you break the contract and back out of the deal later. Naturally, you as buyer will want to make it a small amount in case of such eventuality. Never deposit more than 1 percent. Generally, on an offer of less than $100,000 I would never deposit more than $1,000. There is a common misconception that a contract is not legally binding without a deposit. This is not true. I have handled transactions in excess of $500,000 without ever making a deposit before the close of escrow. The deposit is basically a means of "hooking" a buyer into a deal. It is standard throughout the country to request a deposit nowadays, but keep it reasonable.

You should pay the deposit in the form of a personal check rather than cash. If the seller won't accept a personal check, use a cashier's check.

Make the check payable to the intended escrow holder. Give it to the real estate agent to hold until the seller accepts your offer and escrow is opened. Since the check is made out to the escrow holder, neither the agent nor the seller can cash and misuse it before the agreement becomes final. When escrow opens, the deposit will go in as part of the purchase price.

If the seller rejects your offer or at any time breaches the contract, the deposit will be returned to you, as indicated in Clause 1 and Clause 14. If the seller accepts your offer but the deal does not close because some condition is not met, you will get the deposit back. Since you did not submit cash or endorse the check to the seller or agent, you should have no problem getting your deposit back. You can instruct your bank at any time to stop payment on the check. If you default on the agreement, the deposit will go to the seller, as indicated in Clause 14. (See chapter 20, "Bargaining to Get the Seller's Asking Price Down.")

Amount of Full Purchase Price (Your Offer to the Seller)

You must also fill in the purchase price here, which is really only an offer until the seller accepts and signs this contract without changing any of its terms. Once he accepts the contract, this figure becomes the final purchase price. (See chapter 20, "Bargaining to Get the Seller's Asking Price Down.")

Location and Description of the Property

Write in the names of the city, county, and state in which the land is located. After "described as follows," you must give the description of the property as it is to appear on the deed. The real estate agent will give you a copy of this description, which you can copy into the contract. The description must identify the land so that it cannot be confused with any other piece of land. If the property has not yet been surveyed, this can be done after you sign the contract and before the close of escrow as a condition of the contract. This is provided for in Clause 3, Clause 16(b), and Clause 17(b). (See chapter 8, "Land Descriptions and Surveys.") If the description is long, it can be attached to the contract as Exhibit A. If that is the case, write in here, "See Exhibit A attached hereto."

This description will sometimes include what will be excluded from the title to the property, such as mineral and timber rights. (See chapter 11, "Mineral, Oil, Gas, Timber, Soil, and other Rights.") Usually, the description will be copied from the seller's deed and will include the easements and reservations. It does not matter if it is incomplete, because your purchase is subject to approval of a title report or abstract and that is where you will get all the details on the title.

Sometimes the broker has only the tax assessor's number for the property and uses that as the legal description. It is preferable, but not mandatory, to attach the entire legal description.

List all personal property to be included in the deal. This is everything except the *real property*, which is the land and the things permanently attached to the land, such as structures and vegetation. *Personal property* can include such things as machinery, tools, furniture, rugs, appliances, and animals. Make this list complete, because if you omit an item that you expect to receive, this could be construed to mean that it is not included in the sale. This list should be an inventory of everything you are buying that could be removed and taken by the seller. If you wish, you can list the property on a separate piece of paper and attach it to the contract as an exhibit. You would refer to it here. See Clause 20.

For example, the following is a property description by reference to the United States Rectangular Survey. Mineral rights are excluded from the title to the land. An easement across the neighbor's land is included, as are several items of personal property:

PARCEL ONE: The South Half of the Northwest Quarter of Section 21, Township 4 South, Range 2 East, New Mexico Meridian.
EXCEPTING therefrom all coal and other mineral rights in said land together with the right to prospect for, mine, and remove the same as reserved by the United States of America in Patent recorded June 8, 1928, in Book 24, Page 214, of Patents in the office of the County Recorder of said County.
PARCEL TWO: A nonexclusive easement in the Southerly portion of the Northeast Quarter of the Northeast Quarter of Section 21, in Township 4 South, Range 2 East, New Mexico Meridian, and extending Easterly to the West line of the County Road, together with the right to convey said easement to others.

PERSONAL PROPERTY included in this purchase shall include:
One (1) Homelite Chain Saw, Model 14, Serial Number A246415.
One (1) Servel Propane Refrigerator.
Fifteen (15) Rhode Island Red Chickens: four (4) roosters, eleven (11) hens.

Deposit Held Uncashed

The deposit check should not be cashed until there is a contract between the parties. As soon as there is a signed contract, the deposit will be placed with the escrow holder.

Name and Location of the Escrow Holder

You should locate a reputable escrow company to manage the escrow proceedings. Every real estate agent has one or two companies that handle his deals, but you do not have to use his company. Often a particular title company regularly acts as the escrow holder for the agent, and if the agent is a good friend of the title officer, you might not get as much help from the title company as you would from another. Title companies rely on escrows to make their money, and they cater to brokers for their business. Although escrow companies are supposed to be neutral, there is no question that some will give you more information and advice than others. In addition, escrow fees vary, and you might be able to find a better deal than the agent's company can offer. It is best for the buyer to pick out the escrow holder. If you are familiar with the local ones, find a properly licensed and reputable escrow or title company or bank and insert its name and location here. Example: "Home Land Title Company of Bronwood, Georgia." (See chapter 30, "Opening and Closing of Escrow and the Role of the Escrow Holder.")

Details of the Purchase Price and Financing

Detail here how you will pay the purchase price. This is actually the amount of your offer and the terms you are offering to pay. State the down payment you are offering to pay the seller. This is usually 10 to 30 percent of the total price. (For example, it could be $25,000 down on a total of $80,000.) It is paid at the close of escrow. The down payment will include the deposit money you are making with this offer. If you are paying all cash, there will be no down payment; if that is the case, omit the down payment and write in the full amount of cash.

If a down payment is made, the rest of the purchase price will be paid under some kind of financing arrangement. Usually, a buyer pays the seller for the land over a period of time. After you fill in the amount of the down payment, state the remaining amount of the mortgage sum and how you will pay it.

For example, "a Note and Purchase Money Mortgage" or "a Note and Deed of Trust."

Then specify the amount of money you want to pay with each installment, and when each installment is to be made (usually monthly). If you want to pay quarterly, semiannually, or annually, then write it in that way.

If you are assuming an existing mortgage, then you will have to write in the approximate balance of the mortgage or mortgages you are assuming and the approximate amount of the mortgage you will be giving back to the seller, if any.

Then give the rate of interest paid on the principal on a yearly, per annum, basis. Interest starts accruing on the unpaid principal on the date escrow closes.

This section gives you the right to prepayment without penalty. It also specifies that each payment will include both principal and interest. The essential words *or more* allow you to prepay any amount you desire and should always be included in your contract.

Example:

The balance of the purchase price is to be paid as follows:

The sum of Twenty-Five Thousand and 00/100 Dollars ($25,000.00) to be deposited prior to the close of escrow as a down payment, which shall include the above deposit;

The sum of Fifty Thousand and 00/100 Dollars ($50,000.00) to be represented by a Note and Mortgage to be payable Five Hundred Thirty-Seven and 31/100 Dollars ($537.31) or more per month, with interest on all unpaid principal of 10% per annum, from close of escrow, payable with each monthly payment as part of

the same. First payment is due 30 days after the close of escrow.

Clause 1—Buyer's Offer and Seller's Procedure for Accepting

This contract is not binding on either party unless the seller signs it without making any changes and returns it within the specified time limit. If you decide to withdraw your offer, you can do so without penalty until you receive the signed contract from the seller. If you want to revoke your offer after you submit it, you must notify the seller in writing that your offer is no longer open and that your deposit should be returned to you.

You will write your address at the end of the contract. You must state the amount of time the seller has to accept or reject your offer. You do not want to give him too much time, because he may stall around waiting for other buyers. Five to ten days is a standard time limit for a response. If you are really anxious to know where you stand, you can make the time limit shorter.

Clause 2—Price per Acre and Number of Acres

Sometimes land is advertised and sold on the basis of a specified amount of money per acre rather than a price for the total piece of land. If this is true of your deal, leave this clause in the contract. Otherwise, omit it. Most sellers are reluctant to state an exact acreage figure because they often don't know how much it is themselves. This is why you will sometimes see a figure like "40+ acres." The advantage of the clause is that if you have the land surveyed during escrow and find that the number of acres actually included in the parcel is less than the amount advertised, you can terminate the deal or get the price reduced accordingly. This relates to Clause 16(b). (See chapter 8, "Land Descriptions and Surveys.")

Clause 3—Requirement of a Survey to be Approved by the Buyer

Here is a protective clause that should not be removed from the contract. It provides that a legal survey must be furnished with the land and that the purchase is contingent on your approval of it. If the survey shows that the land does not include what you thought it did, you will notify the seller in writing that you disapprove of the results, and you can terminate the deal.

This clause states that the seller is to pay for the cost of a survey. In some cases, a survey will already have been done and there will not be a problem. But if the land has not been surveyed, this can be a point of conflict between you and the seller. He will not want to pay the added expense of a survey. This is a point where you can compromise if you wish, by offering to pay half of the cost. In some cases, the real estate agent will pay for it in order to make the sale. If you cannot afford to pay for a survey and the seller refuses to supply one, you can tell him to increase the purchase price by the cost of a survey and that you will pay for it over a period of time, should the deal be finalized. However you work it out, get the land surveyed before you buy. If you buy unsurveyed land, you have no precise idea of what you are buying. (See chapter 8, "Land Descriptions and Surveys.")

Clause 4—Escrow Instructions and Opening and Closing of Escrow

First Paragraph: This provides for delivery of escrow instructions. After the seller accepts this offer to purchase and signs the contract, both of you will submit written escrow instructions to the escrow holder on how to go about closing the deal. A twenty-day time limit for submission of instructions is reasonable. Fill in the name and address of the escrow holder as given in the beginning of this contract. Normally, a copy of the contract is delivered to the escrow holder, who prepares escrow instructions for the buyer and seller based on the terms of the contract.

Second Paragraph: You can set any closing date you desire. You should provide enough time for any condition that must be completed, such as a loan arrangement, pest report, and survey. Usually thirty to sixty days is sufficient time to complete necessary arrangements for the closing of escrow. If you need more time, both parties can mutually agree to an extension.

Third Paragraph: The purchase is final when the deed is recorded and escrow closes. (See chapter 30, "Opening and Closing of Escrow and the Role of the Escrow Holder.")

Clause 5—How Title Shall Vest

Vesting title refers to the form of ownership by which the buyers will take the property; e.g., as husband and wife, joint tenants, tenants in common, a corporation, community property, etc. The method used is important for legal reasons. You should give the buyers' names and the way they will own the property here. If you do not have this information yet, fill in "to be designated prior to close of escrow." (See chapter 32, "Types of Co-ownership.")

If you are buying with partners, you should have your co-owners' agreement drafted and signed during the purchase process.

Example: "Jerry Herbert, a single man, an undivided one-half interest, and Daniel and Louise Varre, husband and wife, as community property, an undivided one-half interest."

Clause 6—Condition of Title, Type of Deed, Preliminary Title Report, and Buyer Approval

Title indicates legal ownership. Many things can interfere with your absolute ownership of a piece of property. There may be liens or encumbrances on the title.

Liens include any taxes, bonds, assessments, mortgages, mechanic's liens, and judgments that have not yet been paid and that could lead to a forced sale of the land in order to obtain money for their payment. (See chapter 17, "Property Taxes and Assessments"; chapter 18, "Insuring Your Property for Yourself and Your Creditors"; chapter 23, "Buying Property That Is Encumbered by a Loan Agreement.")

Encumbrances can include many of the same things as liens but are more general. An encumbrance can be anything that affects or limits your title to the property.

An *easement* is a legal right-of-way belonging to other persons over your land. (See chapter 9, "Easement Rights.")

Covenants are usually included in the deed as *restrictive covenants* that specify what uses will be permitted or prohibited on the land. (See chapter 33, "Deeds and Recording.")

Reservations are rights held by the seller or other persons to do certain things on your land, such as remove minerals or trees from the property. (See chapter 11, "Mineral, Oil, Gas, Timber, Soil, and Other Rights.")

Restrictions, like covenants, include anything that limits what you can do with or on your land.

Rights and conditions is a catchall for anything that can't be included under the other terms.

All of these items, if they are recorded, will be uncovered and indicated by a title search or abstract of title. However, certain possible encumbrances such as *prescriptive easements* are not recorded, but may still be legally binding against the property owner if proven in court. (See chapter 31, "The Title Search, Abstract of Title, and Title Insurance Policy.")

This clause is drafted so that you must approve of any items that affect the title to the property. You will do this after you receive a title report or abstract. You should always ask the title company or abstractor to also give you complete copies of every document referred to in the report so that you can review them for yourself. After reviewing them, you can tell the seller if you disapprove of anything. For example, if the title company indicates that there is a cloud on the title from a prior lawsuit, you tell the seller or broker you disapprove of that and you want it cleared up before the close of escrow.

Example: An easement over the property held by someone else would state that the title is subject to

a nonexclusive easement 60 feet in width for ingress and egress and public utilities over the existing road located in the Northeast Quarter of the Southeast Quarter of said Section 21 as granted to Sheila M. Eisenberg by deed recorded June 19, 1970, in Book 4710 of Official Records, page 122, Elk County Official Records.

The warranty deed gives the buyer good protection. (See chapter 33, "Deeds and Recording.") You must know what your deed will convey before escrow closes. The best way to get this information is by a preliminary title report, which is usually included free as part of the policy of title insurance, and is given to you during the escrow. The report will indicate all recorded items that affect the title to the property. If you want an item removed, you can ask the seller to clear it up before the purchase is finalized and escrow closes. A seller can remove defects, or *clouds on the title,* more easily than the

buyer because he knows the parties involved. You should be able to get a preliminary title report within a couple of weeks of the opening of escrow, but you can fill in the blank with any time period. You should give yourself a week or two to notify the seller of those things you want cleared, and that time limit is stated in the third blank space. The report will also state those items that the title company will not insure. You should find out why they are not being insured. There might be a serious problem for you to know about.

You must state the name of the title company that is to conduct the title search and issue the report and policy. You can choose any title company you desire.

An important part of this clause is the fact that the seller must provide you with copies of each document referred to in the preliminary title report. For example, if the land is subject to an existing mortgage, you must receive a copy of the mortgage so that you can see what its terms are, how much is left to be paid, and who holds the note.

In some areas of the country, title reports are replaced by abstracts of title. In that case, substitute "Abstract of Title" for "Preliminary Title Report" and fill in the name of the abstract company or lawyer who is to prepare the abstract. (See chapter 31, "The Title Search, Abstract of Title, and Title Insurance Policy.")

No matter what contract you use, the following contingency is essential:

The close of escrow is contingent upon Buyer's approval of (1) a preliminary title report or (2) an abstract of title issued in the name of Buyer prior to the close of escrow.

Clause 7—The Title Insurance Policy

Marketable *fee simple* title means that the seller owns the property, and there is no question about his rights of ownership. A policy of title insurance is to be delivered to you by the seller guaranteeing marketable fee simple title. Although a standard policy has limited coverage, it is the most common buyer's policy. For more money you can get extended coverage offering greater protection. This is sometimes required by lending institutions. (See Clause 11.)

The usual amount of coverage of the standard policy is equal to the purchase price of the property.

Thus, if you build a house after escrow closes, and a title problem later develops, the title company is liable to reimburse you only for the price of the land. The value of the house is not included. If you want greater coverage, you will usually have to pay for it later. (See Clause 11.)

State which company is to issue the title insurance policy. It should be the same company named in Clause 6. If you are dealing with an abstract of title and opinions of an attorney, instead of a title search and title policies, amend this paragraph accordingly. (See chapter 31, "The Title Search, Abstract of Title, and Title Insurance Policy.")

Clause 8—Prorations

This clause specifies the proportionate breakdown between the seller and yourself of taxes, insurance premiums, interest on existing loans, and installment payments on personal property. The amount each party pays depends on the respective periods of ownership or possession. Proration occurs at the closing of escrow because that is the date on which the property is transferred to the buyer. In cases where the buyer moves onto the property before escrow closes, the date he takes possession might be used as the proration date. In that case cross out "the date of recordation of the deed" and write in "the date Buyer takes possession."

(a) Since property taxes are calculated on an annual basis, under the proration you should pay taxes for only that part of the year you own the land. (See chapter 17, "Property Taxes and Assessments.")

(b) The proration of insurance premiums occurs only when you take over insurance held by the seller. If he is not transferring his policy to you, omit this section.

If you decide to take over the seller's insurance policy, he must have your name placed on it as the insured. If the seller or a third party lender is taking a mortgage or trust deed, it is usually required that the creditor be named as a coinsured of the policy. Since the property is the creditor's only form of security for the loan, as a beneficiary under the policy he will be protected should the property be destroyed. (See chapter 18, "Insuring Your Property for Yourself and Your Creditors.") During the escrow period, you should speak to the insurance agent and get a binder guaranteeing that you will

be insured the second you take title to, or possession of, the property, whichever occurs first.

(c) If you are taking title subject to a preexisting encumbrance, such as a mortgage or deed of trust, you should prorate the interest to be paid by you and the seller, since you do not want to pay interest on the loan for the period before you take title to the land. If you are taking title to the land free of any existing encumbrance, omit this section. (See chapter 23, "Buying Property That Is Encumbered by a Loan Agreement.")

(d) If the sale includes personal property, such as appliances and machinery, that is not fully paid for, you should prorate the installment payments so that you will begin to take over payments as of the close of escrow. If you are not taking over payments on any personal property as part of the purchase, omit this section.

Any other item that you want to prorate with the seller can be included in Clause 8 by adding a statement identifying what is to be prorated. (See chapter 30, "Opening and Closing of Escrow and the Role of the Escrow Holder.")

Clause 9—Credit for Impounded Funds

When land is bought under a mortgage or deed of trust, the party who holds the land as security, if it is a commercial lender, usually continues to pay the taxes, assessments, and insurance premiums so that it can be certain these obligations get paid. To pay these expenses, the institutional lender takes payments from the buyer called *impounds*. These impounds are prepaid by the borrower in order to be available for upcoming payments. For instance, the buyer might pay the lender for taxes a year in advance.

When escrow closes, some funds that the seller has already paid will be in this account. He will be credited with this amount, and the prorations shown in Clause 8 will determine the breakdown of payments between the buyer and seller. When you see a copy of the existing mortgage or deed of trust, and discuss assuming the loan, you will be given a list of impounded funds.

If you are not assuming or taking title subject to an existing loan, this clause should be deleted from the contract. (See chapter 23, "Buying Property That Is Encumbered by a Loan Agreement.")

Clause 10—Payment of Liens, Assessments, and Bonds

It is indicated here that the seller is to pay all money due on liens, assessments, and bonds before the close of escrow. This clause is used when the county has enacted a special assessment against the property. This is commonly done by local governments to pay for roads, sewer plants, and other major improvements.

It is always best to get the seller to pay these assessments before you take title to the land or to allow you to subtract the amount due from the purchase price. Since this cuts into the seller's profits, he will resist clearing these liens. If he absolutely refuses to pay off the entire amount due, you should prorate these assessments and liens as part of Clause 8. State what assessments exist and the date that is to be used for proration.

Too often these debts are prorated between the parties, with the seller paying for assessments made on work actually started before the date the contract of sale is signed. The buyer then pays for assessments on work begun after that date. I think this is unfair for the buyer and explain why in great detail in chapter 17, "Property Taxes and Assessments."

Clause 11—Apportionment of Escrow Charges and Title Insurance Premium

Usually, the buyer and seller each pay half of the escrow charges, in which case "50" (percent) would be inserted in both spaces here. When you first submit this contract to the seller, you can stipulate that he pay 100 percent of the fee. Later, you can "compromise" and offer to pay half.

The real estate agent may tell you that these charges are apportioned according to local custom, but you can come to any agreement with the seller that you want. For example, you and the seller can split the fees of escrow and title insurance premium equally, or you can pay the recording and drafting fees and the seller can pay the insurance premium. If you use abstracts omit the reference to title insurance, and vice versa. (See chapter 30, "Opening and Closing of Escrow and the Role of the Escrow Holder," and chapter 31, "The Title Search, Abstract of Title, and Title Insurance Policy.")

Clause 12—Delivering Possession of the Property and Penalty for Holdover

Possession is "delivered" when the buyer moves onto the property or when he has the right to do so. The seller can give the buyer the right to possession at any time, even before the buyer takes title to the land. The importance of fixing a date for possession stems from the fact that liability for property damage and personal liability usually follows possession.

The person in possession bears the risk of property destruction because he is the only person in a position to protect the property. Many states have laws, called Risk of Loss Acts, that expressly state this rule. Once title has passed to the buyer, he will always be the one to bear the loss, regardless of who is in possession, unless specified otherwise in the contract.

If you move into a house before title is transferred to you and the house burns down, you are still legally required to go ahead with the purchase. I don't think it is wise to take possession before the close of escrow, but sometimes this can't be avoided when the buyer is desperate for a place to live. Specify here when you are to take possession.

If you are going to take over the seller's property insurance, have him add your name to his policy as an insured person as of the date you take possession and adjust the proration of the premium accordingly in Clause 8. Never permit the seller to insert a clause that states that you are to assume the burden of insuring the land before you take possession of the property. (See chapter 18, "Insuring Your Property for Yourself and Your Creditors.")

The second part of this clause provides that a penalty will be levied on the seller if he does not deliver possession of the property on the specified date. A fine of $50 per day is usually considered a reasonable amount to be paid by a *holdover seller*. If you choose, you can terminate the entire deal and have your money returned. To insure that money will be available for the fine or refund, instruct the escrow holder to keep all money paid into escrow until you have notified him that the seller has vacated. If you are buying land that is already vacant, you can delete this part of this clause.

To avoid a problem, never allow a seller or his tenant to remain in possession after the escrow closes. I have had to legally evict a seller who refused to vacate after he got his money. Although I do have provisions for penalties here, the best policy is always to refuse to close escrow until the seller vacates the property. Of course, he will want all of your money in escrow before he vacates the property, and that is perfectly acceptable. (See chapter 30, "Opening and Closing of Escrow and the Role of the Escrow Holder.")

Clause 13—Buyer's Option if Property Is Destroyed or Taken by Eminent Domain

This section permits you to terminate the deal or have the purchase price reduced if anything happens to the property before you receive possession or title. It is important that you have both of these choices. (See Clause 14; chapter 15, "Eminent Domain and Condemnation"; and chapter 30, "Opening and Closing of Escrow and the Role of the Escrow Holder.")

Clause 14—Default and Liquidated Damages

When the seller accepts the terms of your offer by signing this contract, each of you has specified obligations to perform as stated in the contract. This clause states the damages that will be levied if one party breaks the agreement. Because the amount of damages is specified before any damages actually occur, this is referred to as a *liquidated damages* clause.

If the seller fails to carry through on the contract, you get the deposit and any other money returned in addition to a penalty amount that is to be inserted here. You can make this any figure you wish, but it should approximate what your actual damages will probably be. For example, if you are paying for an appraisal of the property, you would insert the amount you pay here so that you can get your money back if the seller later backs out. If you have no expenses and the return of your deposit is sufficient, you can leave this space blank. But it is preferable to penalize the seller the same amount of money he will penalize you if you back out.

If you default, the seller can keep the amount specified in the blank. You should fill in the amount of your deposit, or less if you put down a large amount. It is standard procedure that if a buyer

defaults he loses his entire deposit, but you should not permit the seller to take any more than that.

Most courts will overlook this clause if the stated amounts do not represent the actual damages that do occur later. The courts can always adjust the amount up or down if a party protests that an inequity exists. Because court costs are so high, however, it is unlikely that either you or the seller will want to go to court, and that is the purpose of this clause. Try to keep the figure as reasonable as possible.

This clause offers only monetary damages for breach of contract. In another type of remedy, called *specific performance,* the court can force a party to go through with the deal, or perform the contract. Thus, if the seller refuses to sell you the land after this agreement has been signed and you have met all the conditions, you do not have to accept money if it is really the land you want. But you will have to get a court order to force the seller to give you the land. Also the seller can force you to complete the purchase if he feels monetary damages are not sufficient. These legal options are available even though they are not specifically mentioned in the contract.

Clause 15—Comprehensive Title Covenant and Warranty

Paragraphs (a) through (e) state that the seller owns the land he is selling, that he has the right to sell it, that no liens or encumbrances exist other than those stated in the contract, that your ownership will not be disturbed by any other person with a valid title to the land, that he will fulfull any other condition you require in order to clear the title to the land, and that he will pay for costs involved if you have to defend your right to the land.

If you get title insurance, the same warranties will be covered and insured by the title company. The title company will defend you if your title is challenged. In states where title insurance is available, this type of clause is often excluded from the contract. But I see no reason why the seller should not warrant these things regardless of whether you are insured. Thus I have included them.

When the seller is vehemently opposed to including this clause, if he intends to give you a warranty deed or grant deed, and if you can obtain title insurance, or certificate of title, then you can remove this clause from the contract and still be adequately protected. The reason for his opposition is that he will be liable to pay for your defense if anybody challenges your ownership.

Paragraph (f), that these covenants will survive delivery of the deed, means that they will still be binding on the seller after you accept the deed for the property. Usually once the deed is accepted, the terms of the contract of sale are superseded by the terms of the deed and are no longer binding. The court assumes that if you accept the deed you cannot complain later that the terms of the contract have been violated. But the warranty negates the assumption that you intend to let the seller "off the hook" by accepting his deed. (See chapter 33, "Deeds and Recording.")

Clause 16—Warranties and Representations by the Seller

In this clause you should insert any elements of the sale for which you want the seller to give a warranty. If you insert a provision that he refuses to warrant, find out why he is reluctant to do so. You might discover something that should discourage you from making the purchase. I have included here a list of the most common warranties used in sales agreements. If the seller accepts the contract and an item that is included as a warranty is later discovered to be untrue, this clause will be extremely useful to you in a court action. If you want the seller to warrant something that is not included here, write out the details of your warranty, using these as a model, and insert it into your contract. If any of the warranties are irrelevant in your case, simply omit them from your contract.

16(a)   This is a warranty that you have a legal right-of-way to your building site from the public road. You may very likely have trouble getting a seller to agree to this because many pieces of land are sold with inadequate access. Do not purchase one of these parcels. If you don't have good access, you cannot use the land. Make sure this warranty stays in the contract. (See chapter 9, "Easement Rights.")

16(b)   The only part of this warranty you might allow the seller to modify is that specifying surveyed boundaries. On a small parcel or on a flat piece of land you will be fairly safe if only the corners of the property are marked by a licensed surveyor because you can often estimate from them where the boundary lines run. However, if you

have any doubt about whether an item, such as a spring, a house, or a creek, is on the property or not, you will definitely want the entire boundary lines marked by a licensed surveyor. You gain additional protection by listing those things that are essential to your purchase, such as structures, waterfalls, springs, creeks, etc. (See chapter 8, "Land Descriptions and Surveys.")

16(c)   This is your guarantee that there is a year-round water supply on the land. Estimate the amount of water you will need for anything you plan to do on the land or use the figures the seller gives you. If he says a well produces 2 gallons a minute every day of the year, then he must be willing to allow this warranty in the contract. This will be a warranty that will be difficult and probably impossible to get the seller to make. But the discussion it generates will give you some idea of the seller's feelings about the water situation. (See chapter 4, "Is There Enough Water on the Land?")

16(d)   If the zoning of the area is changed before the close of escrow, this warranty makes the seller, rather than you, bear the risk that the change might prohibit your intended use of the land. (See chapter 12, "Zoning Laws.")

16(e)   If there is a house or other structure on the land, this warranty should be inserted for your protection, especially where the structure represents a large portion of the purchase price. Because it does not require freedom from pests until the closing of escrow, the seller has time to get the house sprayed or fumigated before you buy it. (See chapter 6, "Evaluating the House, a Manufactured Home, and Other Structures.")

16(f)   This warranty will be important if there are structures or sewage facilities on the land, since it insures that these conform to the local building and health codes and zoning ordinances. Violations that have not yet been cited by the local authorities are also covered. (See chapter 13, "Building and Health Codes.")

16(g)   This warranty insures that there are no liens on the property, including assessments and bonds levied for past and future improvements, or mechanic's liens for work completed and not paid for. A title search or abstract will not cover unrecorded items. But the seller might know of liens, assessments, or bonds that will be levied against the land and are not yet part of the public records, and he is supposed to insert these here. For example, if he had construction work done and owes a material supplier money, doesn't pay the bill, and then sells you the land, the supplier could place a mechanic's lien against the property, even though you did not own it at the time the bill was incurred. This should be needed only if recent construction has been done on the property. (See chapter 17, "Property Taxes and Assessments," and chapter 31, "The Title Search, Abstract of Title, and Title Insurance Policy.")

16(h)   Often if a seller discovers that the government has plans to take all or part of his land by eminent domain, he will try to sell his property quickly at a higher price than he expects to get from the government. The ignorant buyer then suffers the consequences of the condemnation. This warranty is excellent protection should such circumstances arise after you take title. If you have to go to court, you would have the burden of proving the seller knew that condemnation was imminent. But at least you will be able to get to court with this warranty in the contract. (See chapter 15, "Eminent Domain and Condemnation.")

16(i)   This warranty refers to the complete list of personal property included above with the description of the property to be conveyed. The seller is to list those items that will not be fully paid for by the time escrow closes. If personal property is not included in the sale, omit this warranty.

16(j)   For those who are interested in back-to-nature or "organic" living, this warranty will be very important. It is self-explanatory. (See chapter 5, "The Earth—Soil, Vegetation, Topography.")

16(k)   See Clause 15(f) above.

Clause 17—Conditions to the Agreement

This clause, in which you list all conditions or contingencies that you want met before the close of escrow, is one of the most important in the contract. You can specify essential elements for your protection, as well as any aspect of the deal you are unsure of and want to approve before escrow closes.

Some lawyers prefer to list these conditions in a separate document called a *contingency contract*; however, I list these items right in the contract of sale. When the seller signs the contract of sale he agrees to these conditions. If he crosses out anything before he signs the contract, according to the

law of contracts he rejects the entire offer and makes you a counteroffer.

In this Model Contract I include the most common conditions used for the protection of the buyer. You can insert any conditions you like in your contract and hope the seller accepts them. If he won't, you will have to decide whether they are absolutely essential for your protection or whether you should compromise on them. If the conditions he will not accept are necessary for your protection, you had best not buy the land. Irrelevant conditions listed here should be omitted from your contract. If you have a condition you want that is not here, write it up in the same manner as those here and insert it into your contract.

17(a)   If you do not approve of any matters specified in the following conditions, or if the conditions are not satisfied, it is stated here that you are to tell the seller of your objections, and you can terminate the deal and get your money back. Sometimes, when a condition is not satisfied, you and the seller will renegotiate the deal rather than terminate it. For example, if a pest report says that $2,000 worth of work is needed and you refuse to buy the property, the seller and you might agree to split the cost, or to reduce the purchase price of the property by $2,000 to make the deal go, or the broker might agree to pay for the work out of his commission in order to make the sale.

17(b)   State any report you want made on the property, such as a survey, soil test, pest report, termite and structural inspection, potability test, or property appraisal. You can choose who will do these reports and set your own standards for approval. The only rule generally followed in the law is that you cannot disapprove a survey, test, or report unreasonably. If the seller is to have a survey run before closing and it does not include something you want on the property, you can send your disapproval to the seller in writing and you can terminate the deal. You can also put in a condition here that the close of escrow is subject to your attorney's approval.

The time limit you allow should be inserted in the blank in 17(b). The time will depend on what is to be done. A survey usually takes longer than a termite inspection. Give yourself at least thirty days to be on the safe side, but sixty days is more reasonable. As things in the country tend to move at a slower pace. You should also put in here how the survey, tests, or reports will be paid for. If you disapprove of the results of any of these items, you can legally terminate the deal within the terms of the contract and get your deposit back. (See chapter 6, "Evaluating the House, a Manufactured Home, and Other Structures"; chapter 8, "Land Descriptions and Surveys"; and chapter 19, "Evaluating the Price of the Property.")

17(c)   This condition protects you if you need to get the land rezoned or if you need a permit for something you intend to do or build on the property. For example, some areas permit only one dwelling for each 20 acres of land. If you know that you want to build two houses on your 20-acre parcel, you may extend the close of escrow to give you time to seek a variance. If you cannot get the variance and permit you seek, you have the option to terminate the deal or waive the condition. Or if you need a permit to run a commercial venture on the property, you want to be sure you can get the permit before the deal closes. I have stated that you are to pay the costs of getting a permit or whatever you are after. Of course, you should try to get the seller to help with the fees. You must proceed with haste and diligence, or the seller can terminate this contract. Usually, the seller will not agree to allow this process to proceed for very long as it could take months to get a variance from the local government. (See chapter 12, "Zoning Laws," and chapter 13, "Building and Health Codes.")

17(d)   You need this condition if there are buildings on the land. The pest report must be taken after the date the contract is signed so that the seller won't attempt to show you an old report. You can write in the name of the company you want to do the report if you have selected one by the time you sign the contract. Otherwise, put in the words: "a company of Buyer's choice." You should try to get the seller to pay for it. You may also offer to share the cost with him or pay it entirely yourself. I have written in all three options, and you can choose whichever you want. But first submit the contract with the seller specified as having to pay for the test. If he objects you can offer to pay half, or you can try to get the real estate agent to pay for it. (See chapter 6, "Evaluating the House, a Manufactured Home, and Other Structures.")

17(e)   If your purchase is dependent on getting a loan from a party other than the seller, i.e., a commercial lender, you should have this condition in the contract. If the seller is taking back a mortgage or deed of trust, the payment provision at the beginning of the contract will be sufficient, and you do not need this lending clause. The condition states that you must obtain the loan rather than just a commitment for one, since the lender could change his mind before the papers are signed. The date inserted as a time limit for obtaining the loan should allow you enough time to get all the paperwork done. It can easily take sixty days for the loan to be approved.

Specify the terms under which you are willing to take a loan. Keep them low for your initial attempt to obtain financing. You can always raise them later. If you are seeking an FHA-insured or VA-guaranteed loan, you should insert this as part of the condition.

After attempting to get a loan, if it is obvious you cannot get the financing, inform the seller of that fact, so you don't delay his sale of the property unnecessarily.

If you cannot get a loan, you will get your deposit back. Never let the seller omit this clause from the contract if your purchase is dependent on obtaining a loan. You should investigate your loan possibilities before signing the contract so that you don't waste your time. For example, it is almost impossible to get a loan on undeveloped raw land. If your purchase is contingent on your first selling your present home, then you will want to write that in as a condition. (See part V, "Financing Your Purchase.")

17(f)   If the seller does not want to give the warranty specified above in Clause 16(c), this condition must be included in the agreement. One or the other is absolutely essential. Under this clause, he must make a "diligent effort" to search for water, meaning that he must dig a well, if necessary, to a depth not greater than that which you insert here. If you don't obtain the minimum rate of flow you specify, the agreement will be terminated and you should get any money back you have paid the seller. This condition must be met before escrow closes. The problem is that you will not know whether the flow of water will be adequate in the driest time of year until that time. You will have to decide whether you want to go ahead and risk the chance that it will be sufficient. (The well-driller might have a well log that indicates the flow during the dry season.) Since the condition and warranty specify year-round supply, if it develops that it is insufficient, you can always attempt to rescind the contract and get your money back. Of course, the seller will put up a fight. The figures you use here for maximum depth should be at least the average depth for your area, and the output should be the amount you will need.

Often sellers are reluctant to allow this condition in a contract for obvious reasons. Regardless of how beautiful the land is and how good the price is, if no visible means of water supply exists, do not sign a contract without a condition of this type. Even if 90 percent of the landowners in the area located adequate water by drilling a well, you could be in the unlucky 10 percent, in which case the land will be worthless to you. If the seller will not allow this condition in the contract, he is out to cheat you. Your only compromise should be that you will either pay half or all of the costs of water development. I don't think you should pay more than half, but if you are hooked on the land, go ahead and get a well drilled. If no water develops, you can still get out of the contract and you will lose only the cost of drilling, which is better than buying a dry, worthless piece of land. (See chapter 4, "Is There Enough Water on the Land?")

Clause 18—Liability for Attorney's Fees in Case of Lawsuit

If you ever have to sue the seller because of breach of this agreement, you will get your attorney's fees paid as part of the damages. Of course, the same thing applies if the seller sues you and wins. This is a standard clause in a contract of sale.

Clause 19—Explanation of Terms in This Agreement

This is a standard clause in any contract of sale.

Clause 20—Incorporation of Exhibits

Insurance policies, copies of a mortgage or deed of trust, surveys, lists of personal property, and anything else specified in the agreement and included on separate sheets of paper or in other documents are called *exhibits* and, according to this clause, are part of the contract whether or not they are directly attached. Label attached forms as "Exhibit A, B, C," and so on. This is a standard clause in any contract of sale.

Clause 21—Waiver of Performance, Time for Performance, and Remedies

This is a standard clause in any contract of sale.

Clause 22—Requirements of Valid Notice

You must give notice by the means specified here if you want it to be valid. This is a standard clause in any contract of sale.

Clause 23—Other Persons Bound by This Agreement

This is a standard clause in any contract of sale. It protects both you and the seller in the event either of you dies or assigns your rights under the contract after it becomes binding. At that time your successors or assigns will also be bound by the contract.

Clause 24—Requirements for Change or Modification of This Contract

This is a standard clause in any contract of sale. If you submit this contract to the seller and he deletes or adds anything, you must sign your initials or your name next to the change, signifying you agree to the change, before it becomes binding.

Clause 25—Time Is of the Essence

Each time limit specified in this agreement is to be strictly enforced. Any extensions must be agreed to by all parties in writing. If a provision has no time limit indicated, the period allowed is to be a "reasonable" amount of time. It is always preferable to specify exact time limits whenever possible. This is a standard clause in any contract of sale.

Identification of Escrow Holder and Real Estate Agent

Insert the names, addresses, and phone numbers of the escrow holder and the agent. These are needed in case any of the parties must contact them regarding an element of the transaction. If there is no agent, then this is unnecessary.

Buyer Signs the Contract of Sale and States Form of Acceptance by Seller

You, the buyer, sign here. If you are married, both of you should sign the contract. Be sure to keep a copy of this agreement for yourself and give a signed copy to the seller. The seller's acceptance is not valid until you receive the returned contract signed by him.

Before you sign this contract, or any other document, be absolutely certain that everything you want has been expressed in writing, including all conditions of purchase and warranties by the seller. No oral statements made to or by the real estate agent or seller are binding in any way, unless they can be proven, and that is difficult. That is why you want everything in writing.

Acceptance—Details of Real Estate Agent's Commission

Here the seller will fill in the commission he has agreed to pay the real estate agent, if any. The commission will be paid only if the deal closes, if the seller breaks the contract, or if the seller recovers money from you because you default.

Sometimes the broker will not include the details of the commission because it is part of a separate listing agreement between the seller and the broker.

Seller Signs the Contract and Accepts Your Offer

Finally the seller signs his name in acceptance of your offer and the contract of sale. If the seller is married, both husband and wife must sign. Once he signs and delivers a signed copy to you, the contract becomes legally enforceable, and you and the seller are bound by its terms. If all conditions and terms of the agreement are met by both parties, the transaction will close as scheduled on the day escrow closes.

If the seller alters the document in any material way, it is invalid until the changes have been approved and initialed by you. If he makes changes and sends the altered contract back to you, he is making a counteroffer for you to purchase the land on the basis of the contract as he has changed it. Or he might return your offer unsigned and submit his own contract to you for acceptance. You will have to decide whether his new terms are acceptable. The contract of sale may be sent back and forth several times before a final agreement is reached, if one is reached. So many alterations may be made during the course of your bargaining that you might have to type up a new contract three or four times. But usually you will have negotiated enough verbally with the seller before you submit your contract that it will merely put in writing what you have already agreed to verbally. (See chapter 20, "Bargaining to Get the Seller's Asking Price Down.")

If the seller signs the contract, the real estate agent signs below the seller's name as evidence of his consent to the amount of commission stated, and then he returns the contract to you as a representative of the seller. If you are buying directly from the seller, you should omit all reference in this section to a real estate agent and a sales commission.

CHAPTER 29

Option Agreements

OPTION TO PURCHASE

The purpose of an option to purchase is to get the land off the market while you decide if you want to buy it. This option is created when the buyer gives an amount of money, called the *option money* or *consideration,* to the seller who promises, in return, not to sell his property until the end of the specified option period. The amount of consideration can be any amount of money. For instance, suppose you are interested in buying a certain piece of land but cannot decide if you really want it, and you don't want to commit yourself to the extent of

offering the seller a contract of sale. You know that several other prospective buyers are also very interested in the land, so you want the seller to take the land off the market for a while. You offer to pay him $500 if he doesn't sell the land for three months, and he gives you an option to purchase the land. The seller, or *optioner*, gives the option to you, the buyer, or *optionee*, and you sign an *option to purchase contract*. In the option the entire purchase agreement is detailed including price, terms, conditions, cost-sharing arrangements, and warranties.

During the next ninety days, you can exercise that option by offering to buy the land at any time. The seller must not sell his property during that time to anyone but you. If he breaches the option, you can successfully sue him for damages. If you do exercise the option and buy the land within the time period, the contract of sale becomes binding as of the date the option agreement is exercised, and generally the option payment of $500 is credited toward the purchase price. If you do not exercise the option by the time ninety days pass, the seller keeps your consideration of $500 and puts the property back on the market.

Since the option to purchase is a contract, it should contain all essential elements in writing: the names and addresses of the seller and potential buyer; the date the option goes into effect (usually upon signing); the amount of payment, or consideration, given by the potential buyer to the seller for the option; the express statement that an option has been created; the period the option is for and the date of expiration; how the option is to be exercised (usually by written notice to the seller); the full purchase price and terms of the sale; a statement that the option money is lost if the option is not exercised; the right for you to give, or sell, your rights under the option to someone else during the option period; and the signatures of the parties.

The option should be stated in a short contract with all the required details attached to it in the unsigned contract of sale, which is signed if and when the option is exercised. Personally, I do not recommend the use of an option to purchase in the standard land purchase because it is often a waste of money and it destroys much of the flexibility needed for negotiation. An option is almost always taken out on the basis of the seller's asking price.

However, if you would like to have complete freedom to back out of the purchase and you are willing to pay the option price, an option to purchase might give you the flexibility you need.

It is very important to get notice of the option, if you use one, in the public records. If, during your option period, the seller sells the property, the buyer will have a greater right to the land than you unless you have recorded the option to purchase document or a memorandum that an option has been granted with the county recorder's office. (See chapter 33, "Deeds and Recording.")

An option to purchase is a separate transaction from the signing of a contract of sale. Be sure you are not signing a contract of sale under a different name or some other type of sales contract under the pretext that what you are signing is an option. Because of the unique legal aspects of an option to purchase, you should check the whole deal out with your lawyer before signing or promising any-

thing; I am not giving you a Model Option to Purchase agreement here.

THE LEASE WITH AN OPTION TO PURCHASE

The lease with an option to purchase, or lease option, is an excellent way to use an option to buy land for the person who is unsure of whether he really wants to live in the country. This option allows you to move onto the property, live in the dwelling, and pay rent for an agreed-upon time, the lease period. You also have to pay an additional sum of money for the option itself. If you decide to buy the property during that time, you can exercise an option to purchase the property, and all or part of the rent money and/or option money you have paid should be credited toward payment of the total purchase price. Be sure the lease option has that written into it as part of the deal. If you do not exercise the option during the period of your lease, you lose nothing, except the option money. You have had the privilege of living on the property during the lease period.

The purchase price is determined as of the date the lease option is entered into. Since a binding contract occurs when the option is exercised, the original lease option agreement must contain all the essential items of a contract of sale. A contract of sale should be used with the lease agreement. Most options that are handled on a standard pre-printed form by agents are not sufficient, and you would be wise to obtain legal advice if you have any questions about the validity of yours or regarding drafting your own lease option agreement. All terms of the lease option must be in writing, and a memorandum of the agreement must be recorded with the county recorder in order to give the public notice of your rights and to protect you should the seller make a deal with anybody else after signing a lease option with you.

Occasionally a lease option might only give the tenant the *first right of refusal*. A first right of refusal means that if the landlord-owner decides to sell his property during the terms of your lease, you, as holder of the option, will have the first chance to purchase it at the same price and terms that a third party has offered. This is probably not worth paying extra money for. In the normal lease option, the landlord-owner agrees to sell the tenant the land when he signs the lease option, and the final sale is dependent solely on whether the tenant exercises the option, not on whether the seller of-fers to sell the property during the lease period. If it is a regular lease option that you want, be sure you don't get a first right of refusal instead. Read the agreement carefully and seek the advice of a competent real estate attorney.

VII

GOING THROUGH
ESCROW

CHAPTER 30

Opening and Closing of Escrow and the Role of the Escrow Holder

OPENING ESCROW

One of the most important aspects of your land purchase is the function of *escrow*. The *escrow holder* is a disinterested "go-between" for the parties involved in the transaction who safeguards the interest of everyone involved. Although an escrow may be used for many kinds of business transactions, it is primarily used in the sale of real estate.

Through escrow, title to land is transferred from the seller to the buyer according to the written escrow instructions of each party. These escrow instructions constitute the escrow agreement and are submitted to the escrow holder, also called the *escrow agent, escrow officer*, or *escrowee*, who is bound to carry them out before the deed can be transferred to the buyer, the purchase price conveyed to the seller, and the sale consummated. Escrow is *opened* when a file escrow number is given to the parties and then instructions are given to the escrow holder, and escrow is *closed* when the deed is transferred to the buyer.

The most commonly used escrow agents are title insurance and abstract companies, trust companies, banks, savings and loan associations, escrow companies, and attorneys. The function of any escrow agent is the same, although the specific procedures might differ. Lawyers are sometimes used as escrow holders, but the institutional agents can perform the necessary escrow services at a lower fee than an attorney usually can, because they have escrow departments that specialize in these services.

Fees charged by escrow agents vary considerably. You should look for the most reputable and professional escrow holder you can find who charges a reasonable fee.

There Must Be a Valid Contract of Sale before Escrow Can Open

You and the seller must complete your negotiations and sign a valid contract of sale before going into escrow. The contract will state when escrow is to open and when the parties are to submit escrow instructions; when escrow is to close; and who the escrow holder shall be, giving the name and address of the individual or institution involved. These items would be included in Clause 4 of the Model Contract of Sale in chapter 28.

Parties Submit Escrow Instructions, and Buyer Includes His Deposit

Separate instructions to the escrow holder are submitted by both the buyer and the seller, as well as the lender if a third party loan is involved. These instructions must be in writing and signed by each party who submits them. They are legally binding on the parties, as soon as the buyer and seller have signed identical forms of instructions. Escrow opens and remains open until the transaction is terminated according to the terms of the contract of sale and the instructions. Therefore, you must be certain that the instructions contain everything you expect to receive in the purchase. In some areas, both the buyer's and the seller's instructions are included on a single form, but usually both parties submit separate documents.

Escrow holders generally have standard preprinted forms of escrow instructions that the parties are supposed to fill in with the necessary information or that come to the parties already completed, based on the contract of sale. However, the best way to protect your interest is to read carefully any escrow instructions submitted to you for signing. In chapter 28, I gave you a Model Contract of Sale that you can use in your transaction by inserting appropriate information or that you can compare to a contract used by the broker. I am including in this chapter a Model Form for Buyer's Escrow Instructions, which is meant to be used in conjunction with the Model Contract of Sale either for you to fill in and submit, or to use as a sample for comparison with instructions submitted to you.

MODEL FORM FOR BUYER'S ESCROW INSTRUCTIONS
EXHIBIT A:(DESCRIPTION OF REAL PROPERTY AND PERSONAL PROPERTY THAT IS THE SUBJECT OF THE CONTRACT OF SALE)
EXHIBIT B: TERMS AND CONDITIONS OF THE PURCHASE BY BUYER

1. The total acreage on which the purchase price is computed shall be based on a legal survey completed by a licensed surveyor or registered civil engineer. The results of the survey are to be approved by Buyer before the close of escrow. The expense of the survey is to be paid by the Seller. (May be Buyer and Seller equally.)

2. Seller shall by grant or warranty deed convey to Buyer a marketable fee simple title as approved by Buyer in the following manner: Within _____ days of the Seller's acceptance of the Contract of Sale, Seller shall cause to be delivered to Buyer a Preliminary Title Report issued by _____ (name of the title company) _____ of _____ (city and state) _____ describing the property. Within ____ days after Buyer's receipt of the Preliminary Title Report and all documents referred to in it, Buyer shall give Seller notice specifying the matters disapproved by Buyer. If Buyer fails to give notice of approval or disapproval, his silence shall terminate the agreement.

3. (List further conditions which the sale is subject to. See Clauses 17(a) through (f) of the Model Contract of Sale in chapter 28.)

The information you give in these two forms should never be contradictory. As a safety measure, the escrow instructions should specify that an inconsistency is to be interpreted in favor of the contract of sale. (See Clause 9 of the Model Form for Buyer's Escrow Instructions.) Although it is not required, I think you should submit a copy of the contract of sale with your escrow instructions as Exhibit B (see Model Form for Buyer's Escrow Instructions Clause 1(a)) so that the escrow holder will have both documents at his disposal for clarification of the terms of the transaction. Again, if you have any questions, always consult a real estate attorney.

CLOSING OF ESCROW

The Model Escrow Instructions are meant to be a guide to protect you. You may use a preprinted form given to you by the escrow holder if you make changes and additions to it which specify all of the necessary information that is included in the model instructions. It is most important to remember about the instructions to the escrow holder that all the facts of the purchase must be made known to him so that he can carry out the expectations of both parties to their satisfaction.

If you decide to use the escrow holder's preprinted form, beware of clauses that relieve the escrow holder of liability, such as a clause specifying the escrow holder is not bound to inform the parties regarding facts within his knowledge. Also beware of any clauses that might be against your interests, such as a clause specifying the buyer is to "take title subject to all easements, reservations, liens, encumbrances, covenants, conditions, and restrictions of record" without giving you a detailed list of what these are, or without giving you copies of the recorded documents themselves.

The seller's instructions will basically require that before the close of escrow you must deposit the amount of money you and he have agreed upon, either the full purchase price, or else a down payment and mortgage or deed of trust. The contract of sale specified that if you gave the real estate agent any earnest money as a deposit on the land when you signed the contract of sale, he must submit that money into escrow when escrow is opened

or instructions are submitted. This money is to be held until the terms of the contract of sale are met and escrow closes. The seller's instructions should not be in conflict with your instructions or with the terms of the contract of sale. Any conflict must be resolved before escrow can close.

If you are borrowing money from a third party, such as a commercial bank, the lender will submit separate lender's instructions to the escrow holder explaining his role in the transaction and what the escrow holder is to do for the lender.

When you submit your instructions, an escrow number will be issued that will be written at the top of the instructions, and if an institution is to be the escrow holder it will assign an escrow officer who will personally handle your transaction. Ask for this escrow officer and use your escrow number whenever you need to discuss your transaction with the escrow holder.

In some states, the parties submit their instructions in person and meet with the escrow holder to discuss what is to be done before the closing of escrow. It is becoming common, however, for the parties to give their instructions to the real estate agent, who delivers them to the escrow holder. The buyer and seller may never meet the escrow holder. To protect your interests to the fullest extent, I think you should maintain personal contact with your escrow holder throughout the entire escrow process. Illustration 93, page 400, is a simple diagram of how escrow works and what the duties of each party are.

Summary of Things You Must Check Prior to Closing of Escrow

Before escrow closes, you want to be certain that you have examined every aspect of the purchase and that everything meets your approval. Once you accept the deed, it will be difficult to complain later about anything that has not been performed according to the contract of sale, since accepting the document implies you approve of the transaction. Therefore, be sure you have checked each one of the following points before the day escrow is to close. Each of these things is discussed in detail in its respective chapter.

1. Make a complete inspection of the land and structures and give your approval or disapproval of any aspects you find to the seller. If someone is living on the land, determine his status and have

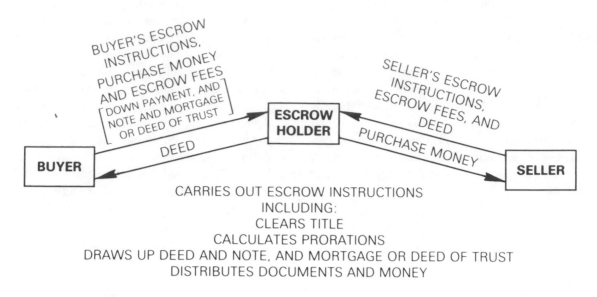

CARRIES OUT ESCROW INSTRUCTIONS
INCLUDING:
CLEARS TITLE
CALCULATES PRORATIONS
DRAWS UP DEED AND NOTE, AND MORTGAGE OR DEED OF TRUST
DISTRIBUTES DOCUMENTS AND MONEY

93. Diagram of How Escrow Works

the seller ask him to leave before escrow closes. Look for and investigate any roads or paths across the land that could be unrecorded easements. Find out if the sale of the land creates an implied easement for the seller or anyone else. Match the description of the easement that will be in your deed with its physical location on the ground to be sure you have access to your building site. If you notice recent repairs or construction when you examine the structures, be sure all costs for the work have been paid by the seller so that future liens cannot be brought against the title. If the closing is contingent upon your approval of an appraisal or report of any kind, be sure the report covers the subject to your satisfaction. Check the water source to determine if it supplies the quantity of water as warranted by the seller.

2. Check any surveys of record to be sure that your land had been surveyed, or check with the local surveyor. Use a legal survey to locate the land's boundaries on the ground, and be sure that all the structures and physical features you expect to get are within them. Also use the survey to check the location of easements.

3. Examine any personal property that goes with the real estate. If you are buying machinery or tools, operate them to see if they are in working condition. Ask the seller to show you records that all personal property is paid for. If any payments are still due, find out how much is owed and whether you are to assume them.

4. Check building, health, and zoning codes to be sure no violations of ordinances or regulations exist regarding the land. Find out whether these permits have all been paid.

5. Examine the title and order the seller to clear any defects you object to. The escrow instructions state that the title must be searched, cleared, and insured before the close of escrow. The seller must furnish you with a preliminary title report, abstract of title, or similar documents showing the results of a title search along with all documents representing encumbrances on the title, such as easements, reservations, mortgages, or other liens. When escrow opens, the first thing the escrow holder will do is order a title search and preliminary title report. He will charge this search to the buyer or seller according to your instructions. The title search will be done by the escrow holder if the escrow holder is a title company.

If you have any objection to the state of the title as shown by the preliminary title report or abstract, you are to inform the escrow holder that the seller is to have the encumbrances removed before escrow closes. For example, if back taxes are due on the land, you want them paid; if money is still owed on a mortgage, you want it satisfied; if a judgment exists against the seller's land, it should be paid off; or if someone has timber rights, you want the reservation removed. The escrow holder will usually obtain the money from the seller to pay and clear these liens. If the seller does not have sufficient funds to remove existing encumbrances but is willing to do so as soon as he obtains the purchase money from you, the escrow holder can take your purchase money on closing day and pay off the liens before closing escrow and delivering the purchase money to the seller. He will then be able to convey a satisfactory insurable title to you with documents that show the encumbrances have been removed. For example, these documents might include a receipt for taxes paid to the tax collector, or a satisfaction of mortgage from the seller's creditor.

Regardless of what encumbrances exist, escrow should never be closed as long as you have objections to the title you are to receive. Provisions for making objections to the title are contained in Clause 6 of the Model Contract of Sale and in Exhibit B, Clause 2, of the Model Escrow Instructions. If all defects in the title that you object to are not cleared within a specified time, you are entitled to have your money returned and the transaction terminated.

When all terms and conditions of escrow have been performed and the title is ready to be transferred, the escrow holder will order the title insurance company to issue a policy of title insurance that insures your title up to the exact minute the deed is recorded. The policy must show your title is free of any defects that you have previously disapproved of. If you cannot get title insurance in your state, you will have to determine from the abstract and certificate of title or similar document that the title is satisfactory. (See chapter 31, "The Title Search, Abstract of Title, and Title Insurance Policy.")

Escrow Holder Transfers the Insurance Policy to the Buyer

If the seller has his property insured and you agree to assume the insurance policy, the seller will give a copy of the policy to the escrow holder. If he obtains permission from the insurance company to assign it to you, he then draws up the document of assignment and gets the insurance policy and assignment form ready to be delivered to you at the close of escrow. Sometimes, the insurance company will draw up a new policy in your name and deliver it to the escrow holder. (See chapter 18, "Insuring Your Property for Yourself and Your Creditors.")

Escrow Holder Makes Prorations and Adjustments

Prorations between you and the seller of property taxes and assessments, insurance premiums, and interest on an existing mortgage are usually made by the escrow holder according to the date escrow closes. The method used in prorating each obligation is explained in the following chapters: chapter 17, "Property Taxes and Assessments"; chapter 18, "Insuring Your Property for Yourself and Your Creditors"; and chapter 23, "Buying Property That Is Encumbered by a Loan Agreement."

Buyer Pays Purchase Price or Down Payment and Submits Loan Agreement and Note

The escrow holder will receive your deposit when escrow opens. You can submit into escrow any other cash you are to pay the seller at any time after escrow opens. However, you should wait until after you receive a preliminary title report or abstract of title and after all other conditions to the contract of sale and the escrow instructions have been met. It is best to submit purchase money on the day escrow is to close.

When the escrow holder receives your funds for the purchase, he will use them to clear up any encumbrances on the title as specified in his instructions, pay the charges owed by the seller, and deliver the rest to the seller after closing.

I caution you against giving the seller any money outside of escrow. The purpose of escrow is to protect you in your dealings with the seller. The seller should not receive your money until you receive what you are paying for. The escrow holder can see that both sides meet their obligations before he disburses the money, deed, and other documents.

If you have arranged a loan from a commercial lender, he will not want to pay you until you have received clear title because he wants to be sure to receive good security for his loan. The seller, on the other hand, does not want to give up his title to the land until, and unless, he is certain of receiving the full purchase price. An escrow holder handles this situation to everybody's satisfaction in the following manner.

Before closing, the escrow holder receives the deed from the seller, a signed mortgage or deed of trust and note from you, and the money from the lender. If all the terms and conditions of the sale have been satisfied, the escrow holder records the deed and delivers it to the buyer. He also records the signed mortgage and note and delivers them to the lender. He then delivers the purchase money to the seller. Thus all parties are protected during the period of escrow and everything is managed by the disinterested escrow holder without the possibility of fraud or violation of any terms of the agreement.

Be sure all financial documents are prepared and ready to be signed before escrow closes. If you are getting a HUD/FHA- or VA-insured loan, finalize all arrangements with the appropriate agency. If the seller is financing the sale, be sure the mortgage or deed of trust and the note or bond are prepared and approved by you before you sign them, before or at closing.

CLOSING COSTS

The closing costs are the expenses in addition to the purchase price that must be paid before you take title. You should be fully aware before escrow closes how much you will be expected to pay and that you will actually receive what you are paying for. Believe it or not, I have met buyers who paid for title insurance and never received a copy of the policy. This should never be allowed to happen.

Your closing costs can be anywhere from $50 to over $1,000. Illustration 94 lists all the items that can be included in closing costs. Your transaction probably won't include all of them. With each item it is stated what party most often pays the charges involved. In many instances, this will be a matter of negotiation between you and the seller, and it is your goal to keep your costs as low as possible. I don't indicate the amount each will

cost because prices are not standard.

In rural areas, closing costs are usually pretty standard within each community. As you get closer to the major metropolitan areas, however, closing costs can vary widely from company to company.

Before hiring anybody, shop around and ask what charges will be levied and particularly how escrow fees are determined. Even after you have an escrow holder, before escrow closes, ask him for an itemized accounting of every single charge that is to be levied against you and make sure you receive a complete preliminary closing statement prior to the close of escrow.

Congress passed the Real Estate Settlement Procedures Act (RESPA) to protect home buyers from unnecessarily high settlement costs. It requires advance estimates of settlement costs, limits the size of escrow accounts, and prohibits referral fees and kickbacks. RESPA requires that all borrowers of federally related mortgage loans receive from the lender a HUD-prepared booklet containing information about real estate transactions, settlement services, cost comparisons, and relevant consumer protection laws when applying for a loan.

One day before the settlement, or closing, the borrower may request information on the settlement costs, and both buyer and seller are entitled to a statement itemizing the costs they paid in the transaction. To find out more about the Real Estate Settlement Procedures Act you may write to: Assistant Secretary for Consumer Affairs and Regulatory Functions, Attention: RESPA Office, US/HUD, 451 7th Street, S.W., Room 9266, Washington, D.C. 20410.

THE CLOSING STATEMENT

The closing statement shows the facts and figures of the closing of escrow for both the buyer and the seller. This document is usually prepared by the escrow holder, although the real estate agent or the seller's attorney might do it in some areas.

A separate closing statement may be used for each party, or both parties may be included on one statement. I recommend using a single closing statement that enumerates the charges for each party on one sheet of paper with the buyer and seller receiving duplicate copies or separate instructions

94. Possible Closing Costs

PAID BY (B = Buyer) (S = Seller)

1. Fees for a title search, title examination, or abstract of title (seller pays to clear existing liens on demand of buyer)	B or S or shared
2. Premium for the policy of title insurance	B or S or shared
3. Escrow fee	Usually shared
4. Fee to draw up and notarize the deed	S
5. Fee to record the deed	B
6. Real property transfer tax	S or shared
7. Termite and structural inspection fee	S or shared
8. Cost of survey	B or S or shared
9. Cost for water drilling and water quality test	B or S or shared
10. Buyer's attorney's fees	B
11. Seller's attorney's fees	S
12. Real estate agent's commission	S
13. Prorations (see 14(h) below)	
14. Possible loan costs	
(a) Fees charged by the escrow holder or the lawyer representing the seller or lending institution to draw up, notarize, and record the mortgage or deed of trust and note or bond	B
(b) Amount of an existing loan to be paid off before closing with possible prepayment penalty fee	S
(c) Credit report fee	B
(d) Appraisal fee	B
(e) "Point" charge	S
(f) Assumption fee charged by the lender, if you are assuming a loan	B
(g) State mortgage tax, in some states, based on the amount of the mortgage (usually 0.5–1 percent of the mortgage amount)	B
(h) Prorations to seller for prepaid taxes, assessments, insurance, and loan impounds	B
(i) First impound installment for taxes, assessments, and insurance to a third party lender	B
(j) FHA insurance premium	B

that enumerate all the charges and the party responsible for paying each of them. All parties should have a complete knowledge of the costs involved, what services are provided, and who is expected to pay each service.

Illustration 95, page 404, is a sample closing statement that includes many of the typical charges and credits for a buyer and seller. Study the sample and read the accompanying explanation so you will be fully prepared to examine your own closing statement for accuracy and understand how the itemization system of *charges* and *credits* functions.

EXPLANATION OF SAMPLE CLOSING STATEMENT

Illustration 94 is an example of a closing statement. The buyer and seller each have a column of charges and credits. Amounts that must be paid into escrow by each party are charged against them. Amounts that have already been paid into, or that are to be paid out of, escrow are credited to each party. The amount charged to each party must equal the amount credited to him. This accounting method is the one

Statement of Escrow No. _____ Office _____

To _____ Date _____

Seller		Item	Buyer	
Charge	Credit		Charge	Credit
	$60,000.00	Purchase Price	$60,000.00	
		Deposit (3/5/88)		$ 500.00
		Deposit (5/1/88)		$14,500.00
$45,000.00		By First Mortgage		$45,000.00
		Prorations as of 5/1/88		
	100.00	Taxes for One-half Year	100.00	
	78.00	Insurance (Premium $468.00)	78.00	
365.00		Policy of Title Insurance		
10.00		Deed		
66.00		Real Property Transfer Tax		
		Recording Deed	7.00	
		Drawing Mortgage	10.00	
		Recording Mortgage	7.00	
		Notary	5.00	
150.00		Escrow Fee (½ Each)	150.00	
4,800.00		Realtor's Commission (8%)		
		Buyer Owes at Closing		357.00
9,787.00		Due Seller at Closing		
$60,178.00	$60,178.00		$60,357.00	$60,357.00

95. Sample Closing Statement

most commonly used. It may not make complete sense to a nonaccountant, but it works.

Purchase Price

In our example, the buyer is paying $60,000 for the property. This amount is charged against the buyer and credited to the seller. The buyer made an initial earnest money deposit of $500, which was submitted into escrow when escrow opened, and he has since submitted into escrow a down payment of $14,500 in escrow. He has arranged to pay the remainder of the purchase price by giving the seller a mortgage and note for $45,000. Although no cash actually changes hands, the seller is "charged" for "lending" the $45,000 to the buyer. In return, the buyer signs the mortgage and note and is credited with having agreed to "pay back" this amount to the seller.

Prorations

Prorations are to be made as of the date of closing, which is May 1, 1988. The property taxes for the year of sale, from July 1, 1987, to June 30, 1988, are $600, to be paid in two equal installments of $300 each. The seller has already paid the first installment, covering the time from July 1, 1987, to December 30, 1987. The second installment was due and paid by the seller before March 10, 1988, so the seller should get credit for the taxes for two months from May 1, 1988, to June 30, 1988, since the closing date is May 1, 1988. Thus the taxes must be prorated. Since the second tax installment is $300, by dividing this amount by 6 (months), we find that the taxes are $50 per month. Thus on the closing statement the seller is credited the $100 worth of taxes he has paid for the two months during which he will not own the land. The buyer is charged this $100.

A similar proration is performed for a fire insurance policy that the buyer is assuming. The policy extends for a one-year period dating from July 1, 1987, to June 30, 1988. The seller has already paid the premium of $468. At the closing date, he will have been covered under the policy for ten months, from July 1, 1987, to May 1, 1988. Since the policy extends for a total of twelve months, the buyer will be covered for two months. The entire premium must be divided into monthly amounts in order to prorate it: $468 divided by 12 equals $39. The buyer owes $39 times 2 (months), or $78, for the period he will own the land under the policy. He is charged this amount on the closing statement, and the seller is credited this amount.

Remaining Fees

The remaining fees are divided between the seller and buyer according to the terms agreed to in the contract of sale and specified in the escrow instructions. The charges shown here are the average fees charged for these services. Separate fees are usually charged for drawing up, notarizing, and recording documents, as done in this statement. The *escrow fee* is usually based either on the amount of money passing through escrow or on the total price of the transaction. In this example, the escrow fee is 0.5 percent of the purchase price and is shared by the buyer and the seller. The state in which this sale occurs has a *real property transfer tax*. This tax requires that for each $500 of the purchase price, $.55 in taxes must be paid to the state. This item will be written on the deed or evidenced by tax stamps on the deed. The $66 transfer tax re-

quired in this purchase is charged to the seller. These taxes vary among the states. Of course, the seller is charged for the real estate agent's commission, given here as 8 percent of the purchase price. The commission usually varies from 6 to 10 percent of the purchase price.

Since the buyer must pay his charges into escrow at closing, all the items from the prorations down to the escrow fees are added to get $357, which he is credited with paying at the close of escrow. The seller must pay all his charges out of money due him that the buyer pays into escrow, in this case the $15,000 down payment, and $78 and $100 from the two prorations. Since the seller's charges equal $5,391, the escrow holder deducts this amount from the money paid in by the buyer ($15,178), leaving $9,787 to be distributed to the seller by the escrow holder after closing.

CHECKING THE STATEMENT

You can personally check the mathematics of the closing statement by using the same system that the escrow holder uses. This check is done by balancing the money he takes in with the money he will pay out. Using our Sample Closing Statement, you see that the escrow holder will receive $15,000 in cash from the buyer as part of the purchase price and $357 for the various fees charged to him. Thus his total receipts from the buyer on closing day equal $15,357.

Now the escrow holder adds up the total amount of disbursements that he will have to make according to the closing statement. I list them in the accompanying table.

Escrow Holder's Balance Sheet

Policy of title insurance	$ 365.00
Drawing up deed	10.00
Real property transfer tax	66.00
Recording deed	7.00
Drawing up mortgage	10.00
Recording the mortgage	7.00
Notary	5.00
Escrow fee	300.00
Realtor's commission	4,800.00
Seller to receive	9,787.00
	$15,357.00

Thus he takes in $15,357 and pays out $15,357, and the figures balance as they should. Never leave the job of calculating your costs and totaling up your money to the escrow holder or anyone else without double-checking all the figures yourself.

PREPARATION OF DOCUMENTS FOR CLOSING

When the title has been cleared to your satisfaction and all other conditions of the sale have been met, the escrow holder will prepare forms necessary to complete your purchase. He, or possibly the seller's attorney or title company, will prepare a new deed in your name. If the contract of sale calls for a warranty deed, he must draw up that type of deed. If the title cannot be cleared as specified in the contract, which prevents the delivery of a proper deed, escrow cannot close. The deed should be signed by the seller and be ready to be recorded before the day of closing arrives. Many states impose a tax on the transfer of all real estate. Evidence of the payment of this tax is shown by having tax stamps placed on the deed or writing the amount paid somewhere on the deed. The escrow holder pays the tax and affixes the stamps, if required. (See chapter 33, "Deeds and Recording.") If the seller is financing your loan, the escrow holder or the seller's attorney prepares the mortgage or deed of trust and note. All forms are sent to the parties for proper signatures and acknowledgments before escrow closes, unless the parties all meet together on closing day.

THE CLOSING DAY (SETTLEMENT DAY)

The *close of escrow* is the last of the "closings" during your land purchase. The first, the *closing of the sale,* occurs when you and the seller sign a legally binding contract of sale. The *financial closing* occurs when you have negotiated a loan and signed all the necessary documents. The close of escrow, or *legal closing,* occurs when all terms and conditions of the sale have been met by both parties

and the title to the land is officially transferred to you by recording the deed with the county recorder. You then own the land, although you may still be obligated to pay off a mortgage or deed of trust for many years to come.

The day of legal closing, also called *settlement day* or paper-signing day, is the day on which the deed and other documents are recorded. This will happen anywhere from a few weeks to a few months after both parties sign the contract of sale. Although the contract will specify a closing date, this date can be and often is postponed or extended, if both parties agree to an extension. (See Clause 4 of Model Contract of Sale in chapter 28.) Occasionally the party granting a requested extension might penalize the other. If the seller has not met all your conditions specified in the contract of sale by the closing date, you have several options. You can grant him an extension or you can terminate the deal if you desire, since the contract of sale specifies that "time is of the essence." If you incur any expenses caused by the seller's delay in closing and transferring possession to you, he should be charged for this.

The closing is generally handled either by mail or in person. If it is to be done by mail, the escrow holder draws up and sends each party the documents to be signed, completes his other duties according to the escrow instructions, such as clearing the title and making the various prorations. Before closing day each party returns the documents and pays the money charged against him. On closing day the escrow holder records the documents with the county recorder, mails copies to each of the parties, and mails to the seller the money due him.

If the closing is to be done in person, all parties including the buyer, the seller, the real estate agent, the escrow holder, any attorneys, and, if a loan is involved, the lender's representative meet to sign the documents. This meeting usually occurs at the escrow holder's office. However, the office of the real estate agent, the buyer's or seller's attorney, or the lender, if the buyer is borrowing the money from a financial institution, may be used.

The person handling the closing will present a closing statement to each person. The buyer submits the money he is obligated to give the seller at closing for the purchase price and other expenses. These payments are usually made by cashier's check or money order, with each check marked as to what it is to cover. If you plan to pay by personal check, send it to reach the escrow company at least 11 days before closing so that the check will have 10 days to clear. The escrow holder will not close escrow until all checks clear. He can then disburse the money as stipulated on the closing statement.

If the seller is financing the purchase, the buyer will sign and give him a mortgage or deed of trust and a promissory note. If a third party lender is involved, he will deliver the loan money at closing, and take back a mortgage or deed of trust and promissory note from the buyer. The lender will want to see the policy of title insurance and get copies of the binders on the fire and insurance before handing over the money. The buyer will pay any money due the lender at this time, such as loan fees and impounds. When all documents have been signed and all money has been submitted into escrow, the documents will be brought to the county recorder to be recorded, after which time all parties will be paid and will receive their documents according to the escrow instructions.

REVIEW THE DOCUMENTS FOR THE CLOSE OF ESCROW

At the closing you must be certain that everything is done exactly right and that the terms are as you have negotiated them. Before closing day you should receive copies of all documents involved in the purchase. Read every word of these documents. Look for clerical errors and double-check all mathematical figuring. Never let yourself be rushed through these procedures. There is a great temptation to just sign the papers, pay your money, and "get the thing over with." Never become casual about any part of your purchase, particularly these final and extremely important details. You are to receive the following items and assure yourself that they are in order:

1. The seller gives you a deed to the property that should be signed by him and notarized. The description of the property and encumbrances in the deed must conform to the contract of sale. Check every word in the deed to see that it is exactly as it should be. A mistake in the property description or a misspelling of any name can cause complications in the future. At closing the deed is recorded with the county recorder, who will make a copy of it and return the original to you by mail usually.

2. You should receive a copy of the final title report or abstract of title and the policy of title insurance. Check the date and time when the policy is to take effect to be sure the title insurance covers you from the exact moment that the deed is recorded. If you are to receive other evidence of title, such as a certificate of title, you will get it at the closing. Your lender will also want a copy of the policy, and he will be named as a co-beneficiary in the policy. You should postpone closing until all liens, or potential liens, on the title have been cleared as specified in the contract of sale.

3. If you are receiving personal property in the sale, get a bill of sale signed by the seller listing everything. Generally, personal property is not included in the deed, so it must be provided for separately. Get all available instructions and warranties for appliances, machinery, and equipment, and get a list of the people who have been servicing them. You should get all keys for locks on the property.

4. You should receive a copy of the survey of the property and copies of any blueprints of the buildings.

5. If you are borrowing money from a third party lender, you will sign a mortgage or deed of trust and a promissory note to the lender, who will give you a check for the loan amount. You will endorse it and deliver it to the seller with your own cash contribution to the purchase price. If the seller is financing the purchase, you will give the escrow holder the down payment, less the amount of earnest money already paid. He should give you a receipt for this payment. You will then sign the mortgage or deed of trust and promissory note to him. These documents will be recorded with the county recorder and remain as a lien against your title until all payments have been completed.

6. If you are to assume an existing mortgage or deed of trust, you must get all pertinent documents, including the seller's receipts for payments he has made already, since you will need these to receive a release deed or reconveyance of title after all payments have been completed. You also want a statement, called a beneficiary's statement, certificate of reduction of mortgage, or estoppel certificate, signed and notarized by the seller's lender, specifying the amount still due on the existing

mortgage or deed of trust, so the lender cannot later claim that more is due him than you expected. This statement should contain all the terms of the loan that you are to accept, and the nature of the lien on the property, such as a first mortgage. Examine the document carefully, checking all the figures to see that they are correct according to your contract of sale. It is also advisable to ask the lender for a written statement that he is aware of the fact that you are to take over payment on the loan and that this arrangement is satisfactory to him if there is a due-on-sale clause in the note and mortgage or deed of trust.

7. If you are borrowing under an FHA or VA plan, you will have to fill out government forms on, or just before, closing day as part of the loan.

8. Get receipts showing the disposition of all liens that you have asked the seller to remove before you take title. For example, you might want the current receipts as evidence that taxes, special assessments, and utilities have been paid for. If you are to pay any bills, you should get a copy of the bill indicating what is due and the final date payment can be made. The bills should be computed to the date of closing in line with the prorations that are to be made by the escrow holder, according to the contract of sale and escrow instructions.

9. Double-check the prorations made on the taxes, insurance premiums, interest on assumed mortgages, utilities, and other items to see that the escrow holder has done his figuring properly.

10. If you are borrowing money from a commercial lender who is going to take impounds, you will have to sign an authorization to the tax collector that instructs the tax collector to have all tax bills on your property sent to the lender for payment. Your lender may have you sign a similar document covering premium payments on your insurance policies.

11. If you are taking over the seller's insurance policy, you will want to get a legal copy of the policy and a binder on closing day. The seller should assign this policy to you in writing, and the insurer should give written recognition that he is aware of this transfer and approves of it. A cover note from the insurance company should state that your property will be protected by the insurance policy from the time of closing until your new policy is prepared and delivered to you. The seller or your lender will

be named as a co-beneficiary. Your lender, if you have one, will also want a copy of this document.

12. If the seller has paid for and received any permits or certificates such as building and sanitation permits, road encroachment permits, or certificates of occupancy, have him give you copies of these documents. If he does not have copies in his possession, it is his responsibility to go to the appropriate agencies and have copies made.

13. If you are purchasing a subdivided parcel, you and the seller may have to complete tax segregation forms at the closing so that you can proceed with the segregation of your land for purposes of proper taxation of the individual subdivided parcels as quickly as possible. If it is possible, the seller should have the segregation completed before the closing and should give you a statement from the tax collector that the segregation has been completed with a breakdown of how it was computed.

THE ROLE OF THE LENDER'S ESCROW DEPARTMENT WHEN MONEY IS BORROWED—LOAN PAYMENTS AND IMPOUNDS

If the seller is financing your purchase, a third party escrow holder will generally not be utilized for the purpose of collecting impounds and land payments. You will make your payments to a bank or the seller, and you or the seller will take care of paying taxes and insurance premiums.

However, if you borrow from a commercial lender, you will make your payments to the lender's special escrow department. These payments will include not only principal and interest on the loan but also the property taxes, assessments, and insurance premiums that will become due during the year. These impounds are usually divided up equally into the number of payments you will make each year and will be added into those payments. The lender's escrow officer pays the taxes, assessments, and insurance bills, thus insuring the protection of the lender's security. The lending institution often acts as the escrow holder throughout the entire purchase and is responsible for preparing all closing documents. (On impounds, see chapter 23, "Buying Property That Is Encumbered by a Loan Agreement.")

LONG-TERM ESCROWS AND LAND CONTRACTS

As explained earlier, in the section on land contracts in chapter 21, "Types of Financing: Land Contract, Mortgage, Deed of Trust," you must be certain to have title held in escrow during the entire payment period if you are buying land under a land contract. Since the seller keeps the title to the land until you complete all of your payments, you must protect yourself against the seller's transferring title to someone else or otherwise encumbering the title before your payments are completed. You should require the seller to make out a deed in your name to give to the escrow holder with instructions to deliver it to you when you make your final payment. If you are to have part of the title conveyed to you after a specified number of payments have been made, this should be written in the escrow instructions. You should also instruct the escrow holder to record the land contract in the county records so that public notice is given that the seller is not free to encumber the title. Nevertheless, because the title to the land does remain with the seller during the payment period, he could have a judgment rendered against the title in a lawsuit, a federal income-tax lien could be placed against the title, or he could go bankrupt, in which case his creditors would be able to attach the title or, at least, create some legal problems for you. For these reasons, among others, it is risky and foolish to buy property under a land contract. Always demand a mortgage or deed of trust.

ESCROW IS NECESSARY

It is absolutely essential that you use an escrow holder in your purchase. Never avoid using an escrow holder to save a little money on escrow fees. A reputable and intelligent escrow holder can be of tremendous assistance to you through all stages of your purchase, and you should maintain close personal contact with your escrow holder at all times.

USEFUL RESOURCES

The following is free from:
  American Land Title Association (ALTA)
  1828 L St., N.W.
  Washington, DC 20036

Closing Costs and Your Purchase of a Home

The following is free from:
  California Land Title Association
  P.O. Box 13968
  Sacramento, CA 95853

Closing Costs—A Primer
  Escrow

The following is available for the specified cost from:
  Superintendent of Documents
  Government Printing Office
  Washington, DC 20402

Settlement Costs (A HUD Guide)
  S/N 023-000-00699-5 $3.50

CHAPTER 31

The Title Search, Abstract of Title, and Title Insurance Policy

When you buy a parcel of land, you are purchasing *title,* or legal ownership, to the land. The deed is the instrument by which title is passed from one person to another.

An owner of land might not have clear title even though he has a deed and a right to legally possess the land. A *defect,* or *cloud,* on his title might exist because someone has a legal right to claim all or part of the property or to make demands on the owner. For example, if the owner has mortgaged the property, he still owns it, but the mortgagee has a lien against the title and can foreclose and take the property to a foreclosure sale if the owner defaults on the mortgage payments; or if a landowner does not pay his property taxes, the county will bring a lien against the land for the collection of back taxes.

The terms *marketable title* and *merchantable title* mean that the seller has the legal right to sell the land. As you will see, any defect that makes the title unmarketable must be removed before you buy the land. To find the defects that exist against a seller's title, and to determine the title's marketability, you must look at its history by researching the public records.

This chapter tells how to do this in order to protect yourself as much as possible when buying title to a piece of land. First, there is a list of the types of defects that can cloud a title. Then there is a description of how a title is searched, going back through the chain of title. The types of documents that you need to determine the state of the title—the abstract of title or title report—are described. Finally the importance of obtaining a policy of title insurance or other title coverage is discussed.

LIENS AND ENCUMBRANCES

Liens and encumbrances are the two most common defects on a land title. They do not make the title unmarketable, because the seller has the legal right to sell the land subject to the liens and encumbrances. Encumbrances include anything that limits or affects the title, such as the following:

—*Mineral, timber, or water rights* held, or *reserved,* by the seller or a third party. These can be in writing or by prescription. (See chapter 10, "Water Rights," and chapter 11, "Mineral, Oil, Gas, Timber, Soil, and Other Rights.") Prescriptive rights will not show up on the public records and are never insured against.

—*Easement rights* permitting others to cross your property. These can be in writing, by implication and necessity, or by prescription. (See chapter 9, "Easement Rights.")

—*Restrictive covenants* in the deed limiting what the property can be used for. (See chapter 33, "Deeds and Recording.")

Liens are also encumbrances, but a lien arises only when the property becomes a security for the payment of a debt or obligation as in the following situations:

—When the owner gives a *mortgage* or *deed of trust* using the land as security. The title will have a lien on it until the debt is paid. If the debt is not paid in the prescribed manner, the creditor can foreclose on the loan. (See chapter 21, "Types of Financing: Land Contract, Mortgage, Deed of Trust.")

—*Federal, state, and local taxes* can become liens against the property when they have not been paid. Real property taxes are automatically liens against the property at all times. Special assessments remain liens against the land until they are paid. The property can be sold for nonpayment of taxes and assessments. (See chapter 17, "Property Taxes and Assessments.")

—A *mechanic's lien* can be held against the property by anybody who furnished labor or material for improvements to the property and was not paid by the owner. This lien could force the sale of the land to satisfy the debts if they remain unpaid.

—A plaintiff initiating a lawsuit against the owner can attach the property, by an *attachment,* to prevent the owner from disposing of the property for the duration of the lawsuit. If the plaintiff wins a *judgment* against the owner, he can force him to sell the property to satisfy the judgment.

—*Lis pendens*: Anybody who brings a lawsuit claiming an interest in the property, such as a suit to establish prescriptive rights or to establish a boundary line or right to water, will file and record a lis pendens which becomes a lien on the property and puts the buyer on notice that there is litigation in progress concerning one aspect of the title to the property.

—*Liens for debts of the decedent* can exist against his property if they remain unpaid. If the creditors cannot get their money from personal property,

REPRODUCED BY PERMISSION

"Unfortunately, when we bought the lot we forgot to inquire about rights of way!"

411

then the real estate can be sold to satisfy their liens.

—*Federal and state inheritance tax liens* can exist against the property of deceased persons. The property can be sold by court order to meet these taxes.

Clause 6 of the Model Contract of Sale (see chapter 28) states that the title conveyed to the buyer is to be free of any defects, including liens, encumbrances, easements, covenants, reservations, restrictions, and rights and conditions of the title except those approved by the buyer prior to the close of escrow. In addition to this protection, you must always search the title and receive an abstract of title or policy of title insurance.

SEARCHING BACK THROUGH THE CHAIN OF TITLE

All land is this country was originally in the possession of the Native Americans. Their various conquerors took their land from them, divided it up, and kept records of who took ownership of each parcel. The transfer of title from owner to owner, eventually to your seller, established a *chain of title* from the present back to the first recorded document of ownership.

The history of New Mexico is a good example of how far back records were kept in this country and how a chain of title develops. In 1539, the area around the present city of Gallup, New Mexico, was claimed by a Franciscan friar from Spain. The fact that American Indians lived on this land already did not deter the "missionaries" from taking it and extending the boundaries of the huge Spanish colony of Mexico. The king of Spain offered large parcels of property to those who would colonize the new land. These gifts were recorded in documents called the Crown Land Grant Records. Spanish immigrants began to move into the area, and the province of New Mexico was established.

Mexico gained its independence from Spain in 1831, and in 1846 the Mexican War began between the United States and Mexico. That war ended in 1848 with the Treaty of Guadalupe Hidalgo, which passed sovereign control of the northern part of Mexico, including the province of New Mexico, to the United States. Spanish and Mexican land

records were transferred with the land. In 1912, the territory of New Mexico became a state. At that time, the federal and state governments traced land ownership back as far as they were recorded to settle all existing claims to title and took control of the rest of the "public lands," which were eventually sold to private owners or retained as government lands. Accurate records of all land transfers have been kept since that time, and make up the chain of title. After you sign the contract of sale you will hire an abstract of title company, a title insurance company, or a lawyer to *search,* or trace back, the land through the chain of title to determine whether the current owner has legal ownership with the right to sell the land, and to discover what, if any, defects exist on the title.

The title does not have to be searched back to the first colonizers. Each state has its own laws (*statutes of limitations*) specifying how far back a title search must extend to be legally sound. This period ranges from twenty-two years in Nebraska to fifty years in Minnesota, to the federal land patents in California.

The primary sources of information that form the links in the chain are the documents recorded with the county recorder or clerk, the tax collector, the various courts, and other government agencies. The person doing the search will trace all of these documents back for the specified number of years to locate anything affecting the title to the land. Since all these records are public, you can do your own title search. However, because of its importance I don't recommend that you rely solely on your own examination. You must obtain a professional title search before the close of escrow, which I discussed in the previous chapter. Nevertheless I will tell you how a title search is performed so that you will understand this vital aspect of your purchase, and perhaps you will do your own search even though you have a professional examination to confirm it. This is one of the most interesting aspects of your investigation because you will learn the history of the land you are preparing to buy.

The deed is the basic instrument for transferring ownership of land, and it includes a description of the title being conveyed. Every state has recording statutes which require that valid deeds be publicly recorded with the county recorder or similar official. When escrow closes on a property transaction, the deed is photocopied by the county recorder, who places it in the deed index, which is arranged chronologically. (See chapter 33, "Deeds and Recording.") Other documents affecting the land are similarly recorded in separate indexes. Each index consists of a set of books or microfilms which together form the official record.

There are two systems of recording and indexing documents affecting real estate. These are the *grantor-grantee index* and the *tract index*.

GRANTOR-GRANTEE INDEX

The most common system used for indexing recorded documents is the *grantor-grantee index*. The grantor index alphabetically lists the name of every seller, or *grantor,* according to the year of the land sale, and the grantee index lists every buyer, or *grantee,* in a similar manner. Leases, mortgages, trust deeds, assignments, wills, liens, lis pendens (i.e., pending legal actions involving the property), and judgments may also be indexed in this general grantor-grantee index. Never hesitate to ask the county recorder to describe the indexing system used in the office.

As an example of how to do a title search using the grantor-grantee index, let's assume that you are buying a parcel of land from a seller by the name of Daniel Lawrence.

Names are listed in the indexes alphabetically for the year the document was recorded. Before you can look up Lawrence's name in the grantee index, you must know the year in which he bought the land. Ask the real estate agent or Lawrence himself for the date. The tax assessor also has this information in the tax rolls, where you can usually find the book and page number of his deed.

In the county recorder's office, locate the grantee index for the year in which your seller bought the land, and look under the section containing last names beginning with *L.* Entries within this section are made according to the date the documents are received for recording during the year and thus are not alphabetical. The first thing you want to locate is the seller's deed. If Lawrence took title on May 9, 1970, the page on which you will find Daniel Lawrence's name as it was recorded when he received his deed might look like this:

The book and page number refer you to the location of Lawrence's deed. This index will also

Grantee	Grantor	Date	Book (Liber)	Page
Leifer, William	Fresquet, Victor	May 2	308	89
Leland, Donald	Inkeles, Gordon	May 4	309	95
Lutz, Dewey	Martin, Arnold	May 4	309	120
Ladrini, Duncan	Herbert, Gerald	May 8	309	142
Lawrence, Daniel	Charles, Edward	May 9	310	3
Lambert, Damon	Howard, Robert	May 12	311	54
Lytle, Drew	Glickman, Raymond	May 20	312	122
Lund, David	Teatro, Susan	May 20	312	132

refer you to the location of other documents in Lawrence's name that have been recorded, such as mortgages. The county recorder can show you where to find the book referred to in the index and how to use it. The book might be a general index of all the county records, or it might contain only copies of deeds.

Look up Lawrence's deed in Book 310 on page 3. Read the deed in its entirety. Does it include a description of the land you are planning to buy from Lawrence? The description might be of a larger parcel that has been subdivided, but it should definitely include the entire parcel you are buying. If it doesn't, then he does not own the land. Note what kind of deed was given, whether it was a quitclaim deed, a warranty deed, or some other kind. (See chapter 33, "Deeds and Recording.") Are there any easements, reservations of mineral, timber, water or other rights, restrictive covenants, or other clouds written into the deed? Write down the names of the sellers who signed the deed to Lawrence.

If there is any indication that the property was conveyed by an administrator or executor after the death of the owner, you must examine the probate court records (ask the county recorder to tell you where they are located) to determine whether the property was properly distributed to the heirs. Keep notes on everything in the deed, including notations referring to the location of other documents.

Next look up all these other documents and copy their contents. For example, there might be a copy of a mortgage Lawrence gave a lender. If so, you want to see a copy of a satisfaction of mortgage or deed of reconveyance to determine if the loan was paid off. After you have examined the deed and all other documents referred to in it, you must search the records to be sure Lawrence hasn't already sold the land to some other party. This part of the title search is very tedious. It involves look-

413

ing in the grantor index to see if Lawrence has ever sold the land he is selling you. Go to the grantor index for the current year and look for Daniel Lawrence's name as a grantor. This index will be arranged in the same manner as the grantee index, except that the grantor and the grantee columns will be reversed. If you find Lawrence's name listed in the grantor column, look up the document referred to and see whether it is a deed selling the same parcel you intend to buy. If it is, you cannot get title since he no longer has title to pass to you. If this is the case, you are being defrauded. However, he may have owned and sold a different parcel of land, so read the description to see if the deed is for another piece of property. If it is, go back to the grantor index and continue looking for Lawrence's name by going backward until you reach the date he received title, which is May 9, 1970.

If you determine that Lawrence has not sold the land to anyone else and that he still owns it, you must then carry your search back another link in the chain of title by repeating the entire process for Lawrence's seller, Edward Charles. If you are lucky, Lawrence's deed in some way referred you to the location of Charles's deed. If not, you must go through the grantee index starting with the year in which Charles sold the land to Lawrence and search backward through each year's list looking for reference to his deed, or you can get the date from the tax assessor. When you find Edward Charles's name in the grantee index, his seller's name will be given, with the date the deed was recorded and the book and page number of its location in the index. Look up his deed and check all those things that you checked in Lawrence's deed. Remember to take notes and to examine all other documents referred to in the deed. Then go backward through the grantor index looking for Charles's name, from the time he sold the land to Lawrence to the time he bought the land, to be sure he did not sell the land to anyone other than Lawrence. Repeat this procedure for each owner of the land back as far as is required by the law of your state.

Usually the grantor-grantee index will include indexing of recorded leases, assignments, mortgages, deeds of trust, attachments, and judgments. The grantor column might include the names of defendants in legal actions involving real property, assignors of loans, mortgagors, and trustors. The grantee index thus includes plaintiffs, assignees, mortgagees, and beneficiaries of deeds of trust.

Instead of a general all-inclusive grantor-grantee index that refers to the location of all the documents, the county recorder might use a *multiple index system,* in which case you must check through each type of index to uncover relevant documents. This makes the general title search much more difficult. For example, there will be a *mortgagor-mortgagee index,* which you must examine to determine whether anyone who ever owned the land gave a mortgage on the property and, if so, whether any mortgage still exists as a lien against the title. Let's assume that Edward Charles gave a mortgage on the property during the period of his ownership. By checking through the mortgagor index, you find that he gave a mortgage to a savings and loan company on July 2, 1984. Note the book and page numbers where a copy of the mortgage can be found, and look it up. If it has been paid off, you will be referred to a book and page number where you will find a copy of the satisfaction of mortgage. Sometimes the satisfaction will be attached to the copy of the mortgage. If you can't find any evidence that the mortgage has been paid off, then it is a lien on the title.

Often these counties have a separate lis pendens index that lists all pending legal actions initiated in the county according to plaintiffs and defendants and refers you to the location of the documents filed in those actions. If such an index exists, check to see whether any previous owner of the land has an action pending against him, such as a foreclosure, mechanic's lien, or civil suit. If a name shows up, check the files to be sure that the property has been cleared of any connection with the legal action. Do not buy land with a lis pendens filed against it, since you must take the property subject to that pending action.

There may also be a separate judgment roll or judgment index that lists creditors and debtors named in judgments resulting from lawsuits. The index will usually name the attorney of the creditor and will indicate whether the debt has been paid off. Look for the name of any previous owner of the property in the column of debtors for the years he owned the property. If a former owner is listed, you must examine the recorded document to determine the status of the debt. You should never purchase land subject to a judgment lien. In some areas, you might have to ask the clerk of the local courts to check for proceedings affecting the property if court records aren't kept in the county recorder's office.

There will also be separate indexes for federal tax liens, lessors-lessees, assignors-assignees, wills, and deeds.

Finally you must examine the county tax rolls located in the tax collector's office to see if any back taxes are due on the land. These tax liens are indexed according to the parcel number, which can be found in the tax books. Ask the tax assessor to show you how to use the books.

The above description of how a title search is conducted probably has you rather confused. Don't worry about it. You will have it done by a professional anyway. But if you go to the county records and start looking through them, you will become familiar with the system of indexing for your area, and everything in this chapter will begin to make sense. The records are always open to the public, and there is no substitute for actually going and investigating yourself. If you are confused, the clerks are public servants and are there to assist you.

TRACT INDEX

A much simpler system used to index recorded documents affecting a piece of land is the tract index. Unfortunately it is found only in a few states: Iowa, Louisiana, Nebraska, North Dakota, Oklahoma, South Dakota, Utah, Wisconsin, and Wyoming. This system has a page for every single parcel or tract of land in the county. Every transaction affecting each particular parcel is indexed on its page with the locations of the recorded documents referred to. For example, if you look up the parcel you are buying, the index page will state the location of every deed used to convey the land since it was first sold by the government. Every mortgage and other recorded instrument affecting the title will also be referred to.

Thus the entire chain of title papers are in one spot, unlike in the grantor-grantee index system where you must trace every transaction yourself. As land is subdivided, the new parcels are added to the tract index.

THE TITLE COMPANY OR ABSTRACTOR'S PLANTS

The title companies maintain their own records at each title office. This is usually done by a computerized system now. Every day the title company orders copies of every document recorded at the recorder's office. Then they see what property is affected by each document. In their private *title plants* they have a file page for each separate parcel of property in the county or parish. Each recorded document is noted on the file page for the parcel it affects with a note of the type of document, and the book and page where it is recorded.

When you order a search for a particular parcel, the title or abstract company simply looks up the parcel in their private files in their plant, and they can turn to the file page and see notes on every recorded document that affects the property. All these are on one page. Thus their job is relatively easy. The escrow fees you pay go for paying their overhead and for maintaining this system.

UNRECORDED ITEMS THAT AFFECT THE TITLE

Some things that affect land title will not be found in the indexes: building and health code regulations, zoning restrictions, renters leasing the land without a recorded lease, persons with a legal right to title by adverse possession, prescriptive easements or prescriptive profits, changes in the boundaries due to erosion or accretion, water rights laws, and work that has been done on the land that could lead to a mechanic's lien being filed after you buy the land.

Therefore, an important aspect of your investigation will be to determine the laws that apply to your land and to personally inspect the property to see what is happening to it. How to do these things is explained in previous chapters.

TYPES OF TITLE PROOF

A professional title search must be conducted be-

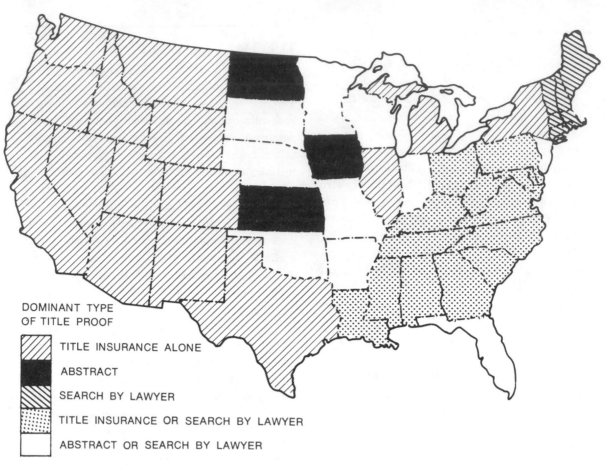

DOMINANT TYPE
OF TITLE PROOF

TITLE INSURANCE ALONE

ABSTRACT

SEARCH BY LAWYER

TITLE INSURANCE OR SEARCH BY LAWYER

ABSTRACT OR SEARCH BY LAWYER

96. Type of Title Proof Used by Each State

fore you can receive proof of good title by an abstract of title, a title insurance policy, or a title certificate by an attorney. Illustration 96 shows which form of title proof is predominant in each state.

THE ABSTRACT OF TITLE

In many parts of the United States, particularly in rural parts of the Midwest, land buyers commonly get an abstract of title after signing a contract of sale. An abstract is a summary of the title history of a parcel of land based on recorded documents for as far back as is required by the state or the buyer. It is prepared by an abstract company using its own records of all transactions in that area. These private files, called *title plants,* are often better organized and more up-to-date than the public records in the county recorder's office. An ab-

stract of title tells the effect on the title of all deeds, mortgages, trust deeds, release deeds, satisfactions, recorded leases, mechanic's liens, foreclosure actions, special assessments, wills, attachments and judgments, tax sales, encumbrances, and other items of record. The contents of each document affecting title are summarized in chronological order in the abstract, and any irregularities in them will be pointed out by the abstractor.

An entry in the abstract will look like this example:

Martin Berman and
Deborah R. Berman,
husband and wife,
        to
Arnold Berschler
Conveys Lot #43 of the Map
    of Happy Acres
Development Company.

Warranty Deed
dated July 23, 1970
ack. July 23, 1970
rec. July 26, 1970
Liber 43, p. 92

When the abstract company delivers the complete abstract, it issues a *certificate of title,* which states that the property title is held by the seller, subject to the encumbrances of record shown in the abstract. This certificate is the abstractor's guarantee that his research and examination of the public records are correct. However, the abstract company is liable for a mistake only to the person who contracts for the abstract. Therefore, if the seller has the abstract done and shows it to you as evidence of his title, you have no protection from the abstract company if you later discover that an error was made in it. If you must use an abstract of title, have it performed in your own name even if the seller pays for it so that the company will be liable to you. Unless you are buying a newly subdivided parcel, an abstract of title probably already exists for the property, completed when an earlier buyer purchased the land. If this is the case, you do not have to get a complete abstract done. Simply have the abstract company bring the existing one up to date. The abstract company will examine the title from the time the last abstract was completed and show any new encumbrances. The company will then give you a certificate called a *reissue* or *recertification* which guarantees that the entire abstract, including the former one and the newly completed section, is correct. This will be much cheaper than getting an entire abstract done, and the recertification makes the company liable to you if it is done in your name. Never accept an old abstract as proof of good title from the seller unless it has been brought up to date and recertified with your name as the insured. Be sure the abstract company is bonded with the state or federal government and is licensed and reputable. Although abstract companies are usually regulated by state agencies, if you must use one, exercise care in choosing.

PRELIMINARY TITLE REPORT AND THE POLICY OF TITLE INSURANCE

An abstract of title only informs you about the contents of documents in public records exactly as they appear there and guarantees you that the search is complete. But the title to the land you are buying is not guaranteed or insured. You are not protected against title defects not shown by the records, nor are you protected against documents that are part of the records but improperly executed. Only the owner's policy of title insurance insures the title you are being sold and protects you if there are defects not shown in the records or if there are forged documents. I strongly recommend that you get title insurance if it is available rather than an abstract of title. Title insurance is increasingly being used throughout the country. Ever since the first title insurance company was founded in Philadelphia on March 28, 1876, real estate purchasers and lenders have been able to obtain protection against land title problems.

Many kinds of defects are so serious that they can render your title unmarketable. Title insurance protects you if any such defect exists. Some of these defects not shown by examining the public record are:

—*Clerical Errors.* A clerk in any of the public offices responsible for recording the documents in the chain of title could have made an error in transcription or filing, or a document could be misstated, incomplete, or misplaced. For example, after you take title if a lien appears that was misfiled by the recorder, the title insurance company will pay your losses up to its coverage if the lien results in your losing title to the land.

—*Forgery.* The deed, or any other document, might be a forged instrument or fraudulent in some other way.

—*Incorrectly Given Marital Status.* A former owner may have been a married person whose spouse was not named in a transaction conveying title to the property during the marriage. The unnamed spouse might later claim an interest in the property under a state law regarding marital rights of spouses. (See chapter 32, "Types of Co-ownership.")

—*Undisclosed Heirs.* If a former owner died while he owned the property and his estate was improperly distributed, the title could be disturbed later by a legal action brought by an undisclosed heir.

—*Post-death Deed Delivery.* A deed might have been signed by the seller but not legally delivered to the buyer before death. The date of delivery on the deed in the records would not indicate a prior death of the seller, and a suit could be brought at a later time by an heir claiming title or by the government claiming estate taxes.

—*Lack of Capacity of a Party to a Transaction.* If a deed or other document affecting title was executed by a person who was a minor, insane, intoxicated or drugged, or acting without the authority of the owner although otherwise a proper agent-employee of his, the deed does not properly convey a valid title to the property.

—*Improper Interpretation of Wills.* Most lands have been conveyed by a will at least once in their history, which may have been improperly interpreted so that title was not conveyed correctly, leaving open the possibility that someone might contest the transaction after you take title to the land.

The possibility of any of the above events occurring might not be very great, but anyone can bring a court action against your title, causing you much grief and expense, even if he does not have a valid and proper claim to make. Title insurance will pay for court costs and legal fees in the event this should happen. Besides insuring you for any possible claim that might arise hostile to your claim of title, the title company insures you against errors made in their title search.

Before issuing insurance, the title company conducts a title search to determine the soundness of the title it will be insuring and the existence of liens and encumbrances. Just as a life insurance company will not insure a man without giving him a thorough physical examination, a title insurance company won't issue a policy without doing a thorough search. Thus, if the title company issues you an insurance policy, you know they are convinced that the seller has valid marketable title to give to you subject to any liens or encumbrances on the title that they list in the policy.

What Do Title Companies Pay under the Policy?

The usual situation where a title company pays money to the insured is when they fail to disclose a recorded lien in their title policy. Although this is a mistake rarely made, it does occur. I have collected thousands of dollars for my clients over the years by filing claims under their policies. For example, one title company failed to disclose a water rights reservation in the policy through negligence of a title searcher who forgot to note it on the policy. I have also had policies that failed to show restrictions on cutting timber, easements through property, reservations of mineral rights, and judgments on record affecting the title.

I have also had title companies pay my attorney fees when my clients have sued over a title matter. Sometimes the title companies use their own attorneys to defend legal actions or to get the title problems cleared up, but it never costs the policy holder any money. That is why you buy title insurance.

Other recent cases of how purchasers have been protected by title insurance policies are quite interesting.

In the East, a buyer purchased real estate from heirs named in the will of its deceased owner. Years later, another will of the same owner was discovered that named different heirs. The second will was probated and found to be valid, leaving the buyers under the other will with no title to the real estate. The title insurance company protected its insured by paying the full amount of the purchase price as provided in its policy of title insurance.

In the Southwest, an affidavit obtained in a title search showed the owner of an undivided one-sixth interest in real estate to be deceased with no heirs. Some time after the transaction was completed, this supposedly deceased person appeared and filed a claim against the buyer for one-sixth of the purchase price. The claim proved to be valid, and the title company insuring the buyer paid the claimant for his interest under its policy of owner's title insurance to settle the matter and avoid loss for the insured.

In the Midwest, a home buyer encountered trouble when the seller paid for two years of taxes on his house with a personal check that later was rejected because of insufficient funds. Since the buyer had obtained owner's title insurance before completing his real estate purchase, the title insurer contacted the seller—who had moved to another state—and collected the full amount of the bad check. When an attempt was made to pay the taxes on the home, it was learned that the amount had been miscalculated in the county office, and as a result additional taxes were owed on the property. The insuring title company paid the initial amount collected from the seller, and paid the additional amount due, to spare the buyer a financial setback.

Preliminary Title Report

Before issuing the insurance policy, the title company will give you, at your request, a preliminary title report showing the status of the seller's title to the land. Often the price for this report is included as part of the final title insurance policy and both are covered by a single fee or premium. All encumbrances and liens on the land will be indicated, and the title company will inform you on what basis they are willing to issue you a final policy. They will indicate which encumbrances are of record and shown as exceptions to the policy of title insurance. The preliminary title report does not insure the title. It simply describes the condition of the title as of the date the report is issued. Never rely solely on this report without getting an insurance policy.

Clause 6 in the Model Contract of Sale (see chapter 28) specifies that the seller is to have a preliminary title report made and delivered to you. If a defect, such as a lien or encumbrance, is shown by the report and you want it removed before the close of escrow, you are to notify the seller of your disapproval. If the seller has not removed the defect by the closing date, you can terminate your purchase and have any money you have paid returned to you.

In those areas where an abstract of title is used rather than a title report and title insurance policy, Clause 7 of the contract of sale should be changed to state when you are to get the abstract for inspection. The abstract of title, as well as the preliminary title report, should cover the title up to the date you receive it. After examining the abstract you should notify the seller of any objections you have, and he should clear the defects before closing. Clause 6 states that at the time you get the abstract or preliminary title report, the seller must include copies of all documents that are listed as encumbrances on the title so that you can examine them in their entirety before the close of escrow, or you can often obtain copies of all documents listed in the preliminary title report from the title company that prepared the report.

The Policy of Title Insurance

Unlike other insurance policies, a policy of title insurance is paid for at one time only and continues as long as you and your legal successors hold title to the property. The premium for a policy is based on the amount of coverage, which is usually the amount paid for the property. Each title company has its own fee schedule. Generally, a $50,000 policy will cost about $325.

Clause 7 of the Model Contract of Sale states that the seller is to furnish and pay for the insurance policy, which is to be issued in your name, with you as beneficiary. Sometimes the seller might object to paying the entire premium, and if you choose you can compromise and split the cost with him. I do not think you should pay the entire amount, since the seller has a duty to provide you with a valid and insured title.

A title insurance policy issued in your name is never assignable or transferable to subsequent purchasers of the property. For instance, the seller cannot transfer his policy to you. Each new buyer of a piece of land must purchase a completely new policy regardless of how recent the seller had a title search conducted. A title company only needs to search back to the date that the seller's policy was issued in order to bring the title up to date for the buyer. Despite the small amount of work sometimes involved in the search, the premiums always remain the same.

A standard coverage title insurance policy usually insures the buyer for the price he pays for the land. This means that if the title company has to defend you in a court action, it will be responsible for bearing costs only up to the amount paid for the property. After you have owned the land for a period of time and have made improvements on it, its value will increase. You can then pay the title company to increase its liability to you based on the increased market value, or you can obtain an inflation endorsement to the policy when you initially purchase it at the close of escrow.

EXAMPLE OF A TITLE INSURANCE POLICY AND AN EXPLANATION OF ITS CONTENTS

The type of title insurance usually taken by a buyer is the standard coverage policy of title insurance. (I discuss extended coverage later in the chapter.) Although each state has its own policy form, the type of coverage granted is basically the same. Illustration 97 is a copy of a standard coverage policy. The policy you will receive will be very similar to this one. The following is an explanation of the terms of the policy.

POLICY OF TITLE INSURANCE

ISSUED BY

Title Insurance Company

TITLE INSURANCE COMPANY, a California corporation, herein called the Company, for a valuable consideration paid for this policy, the number, the effective date, and amount of which are shown in Schedule A, hereby insures the parties named as Insured in Schedule A, the heirs, devisees, personal representatives of such Insured, or if a corporation, its successors by dissolution, merger or consolidation, against loss or damage not exceeding the amount stated in Schedule A, together with costs, attorney's fees and expenses which the Company may become obligated to pay as provided in the Conditions and Stipulations hereof, which the Insured shall sustain by reason of:

1. Any defect in or lien or encumbrance on the title to the estate or interest covered hereby in the land described or referred to in Schedule C, existing at the date hereof, not shown or referred to in Schedule B or excluded from coverage in Schedule B or in the Conditions and Stipulations; or

2. Unmarketability of such title; or

3. Any defect in the execution of any mortgage shown in Schedule B securing an indebtedness, the owner of which is named as Insured in Schedule A, but only insofar as such defect affects the lien or charge of said mortgage upon the estate or interest referred to in this policy; or

4. Priority over said mortgage, at the date hereof, of any lien or encumbrance not shown or referred to in Schedule B, or excluded from coverage in Schedule B or in the Conditions and Stipulations, said mortgage being shown in Schedule B in the order of its priority.

all subject, however, to the Conditions and Stipulations hereto annexed, which Conditions and Stipulations, together with Schedules A, B, and C are hereby made a part of this policy.

In Witness Whereof, Title Insurance Company has caused its corporate name and seal to be hereunto affixed by its duly authorized officers, on the date shown in Schedule A.

Title Insurance Company

BY   PRESIDENT

ATTEST   SECRETARY

97. Example of Policy of Title Insurance

SCHEDULE A

Total Fee for Title Search, Examination

and Title Insurance $

Amount $ Policy No.

Effective Date

Insured

1.   Title to the estate or interest covered by this policy at the date hereof is vested in:

2.   The estate or interest in the land described or referred to in Schedule C covered by this policy is:

SCHEDULE B

This policy does not insure against loss or damage by reason of the matters shown in parts one and two following:
Part One:

1.   Taxes or assessments which are not shown as existing liens by the records of any taxing authority that levies taxes or assessments on real property or by the public records.

2.   Any facts, rights, interests, or claims which are not shown by the public records but which could be ascertained by an inspection of said land or by making inquiry of persons in possession thereof.

3.   Easements, claims of easement or encumbrances which are not shown by the public records.

4.   Discrepancies, conflicts in boundary lines, shortage in area, encroachments, or any other facts which a correct survey would disclose.

5.   Unpatented mining claims; reservations or exceptions in patents or in Acts authorizing the issuance thereof; water rights, claims or title to water.

Part Two:

SCHEDULE C

The land referred to in this policy is situated in the State of   County
of   and is described as follows:

CONDITIONS AND STIPULATIONS

1. Definition of Terms

The following terms when used in this policy mean:

(a) "land": the land described, specifically or by reference, in Schedule A and improvements affixed thereto which by law constitute real property;

(b) "public records": those records which impart constructive notice of matters relating to said land;

(c) "knowledge": actual knowledge, not constructive knowledge or notice which may be imputed to the Insured by reason of any public records;

(d) "date": the effective date;

(e) "mortgage": mortgage, deed of trust, trust deed, or other security instrument; and

(f) "insured": the party or parties named as Insured, and if the owner of the indebtedness secured by a mortgage shown in Schedule B is named as an Insured in Schedule A, the Insured shall include (1) each successor in interest in ownership of such indebtedness, (2) any such owner who acquires the estate or interest referred to in this policy by foreclosure, trustee's sale, or other legal manner in satisfaction of said indebtedness, and (3) any federal agency or instrumentality which is an insurer or guarantor under an insurance contract or guaranty insuring or guaranteeing said indebtedness, or any part thereof, whether named as an insured herein or not, subject otherwise to the provisions hereof.

2. Benefits after Acquisition of Title

If an insured owner of the indebtedness secured by a mortgage described in Schedule B acquires said estate or interest, or any part thereof, by foreclosure, trustee's sale, or other legal manner in satisfaction of said indebtedness, or any part thereof, or if a federal agency or instrumentality acquires said estate or interest, or any part thereof, as a consequence of an insurance contract or guaranty insuring or guaranteeing the indebtedness secured by a mortgage covered by this policy, or any part thereof, this policy shall continue in force in favor of such Insured, agency or instrumentality, subject to all of the conditions and stipulations hereof.

3. Exclusions from the Coverage of this Policy

This policy does not insure against loss or damage by reason of the following:

(a) Any law, ordinance or governmental regulation (including but not limited to building and zoning ordinances) restricting or regulating or prohibiting the occupancy, use or enjoyment of the land, or regulating the character, dimensions, or location of any improvement now or hereafter erected on said land, or prohibiting a separation in ownership or a reduction in the dimensions or area of any lot or parcel of land.

(b) Governmental rights of police power or eminent domain unless notice of the exercise of such rights appears in the public records at the date hereof.

(c) Title to any property beyond the lines of the land expressly described in Schedule A, or title to streets, roads, avenues, lanes, ways or waterways on which such land abuts, or the right to maintain therein vaults, tunnels, ramps or any other structure or improvement; or any rights or easements therein unless this policy specifically provides that such property, rights or easements are insured, except that if the land abuts upon one or more physically open streets or highways this policy insures the ordinary rights of abutting owners for access to one of such streets or highways, unless otherwise excepted or excluded herein.

(d) Defects, liens, encumbrances, adverse claims against the title as insured or other matters (1) created, suffered, assumed or agreed to by the Insured claiming loss or damage; or (2) known to the Insured Claimant either at the date of this policy or at the date such Insured Claimant acquired an estate or interest insured by this policy and not shown by the public records, unless disclosure thereof in writing by the Insured shall have been made to the Company prior to the date of this policy; or (3) resulting in no loss to the Insured Claimant; or (4) attaching or created subsequent to the date hereof.

(e) Loss or damage which would not have been sustained if the Insured were a purchaser or encumbrancer for value without knowledge.

(f) Consumer credit protection, truth in lending or similar law.

4. Defense and Prosecution of Actions—Notice of Claim to be Given by the Insured

(a) The Company, at its own cost and without undue delay shall provide (1) for the defense of the Insured in all litigation consisting of actions or proceedings commenced against the Insured, or defenses, restraining orders, or injunctions interposed against a foreclosure or sale of the mortgage and indebtedness covered by this policy or a sale of the estate or interest in said land; or (2) for such action as may be appropriate to establish the title of the estate or interest or the lien of the mortgage as insured, which litigation or action in any of such events is founded upon an alleged defect, lien or encumbrance insured against by this policy, and may pursue any litigation to final determination in the court of last resort.

(b) In any case any such action or proceeding shall be begun, or defense interposed, or in case knowledge shall come to the Insured of any claim of title or interest which is adverse to the title of the estate or interest or lien of the mortgage as insured, or which might cause loss or damage for which the Company shall or may be liable by virtue of this policy, or if the Insured shall in good faith contract to sell the indebtedness secured by a mortgage covered by this policy, or, if an Insured in good faith leases or contracts to sell, lease or mortgage the same, or if the successful bidder at a foreclosure sale under a mortgage covered by this policy refuses to purchase and in any such event the title to said estate or interest is rejected as unmarketable, the Insured shall notify the Company thereof in writing. If such notice shall not be given to the Company within ten days of the receipt of process or pleadings or if the Insured shall not, in writing, promptly notify the Company of any defect, lien or encumbrance insured against which shall come to the knowledge of the Insured, of if the Insured shall not, in writing, promptly notify the Company of any such rejection by reason of claimed unmarketability of title, then all liability of the Company in regard to the subject matter of such action, proceeding or matter shall cease and terminate, provided, however, that failure to notify shall in no case prejudice the claim of any Insured unless the Company shall be actually prejudiced by such failure and then only to the extent of such prejudice.

(c) The Company shall have the right at its own cost to institute and prosecute any action or proceeding or do any other act which in its opinion may be necessary or desirable to establish the title of the estate or interest or the lien of the mortgage as insured; and the Company may take any appropriate action under the terms of this policy whether or not it shall be liable thereunder and shall not thereby concede liability or waive any provision of this policy.

(d) In all cases where this policy permits or requires the Company to prosecute or provide for the defense of any action or proceeding, the Insured shall secure to it the right to so prosecute or provide defense in such action or proceeding, and all appeals therein, and permit it to use, at its option, the name of the Insured for such purpose. Whenever requested by the Company the Insured shall give the Company all reasonable aid in any such action or proceeding, in effecting settlement, securing evidence, obtaining witnesses, or prosecuting or defending such action or proceeding, and the Company shall reimburse the Insured for any expense so incurred.

5. Notice of Loss—Limitation of Action

In addition to the notices required under paragraph 4(b), a statement in writing of any loss or damage for which it is claimed the Company is liable under this policy shall be furnished to the Company within sixty days after such loss or damage shall have been determined and no right of action shall accrue to the Insured under this policy until thirty days after such statement shall have been furnished, and no recovery shall be had by the Insured under this policy unless action shall be commenced thereon within five years after expiration of said thirty day period. Failure to furnish such statement of loss or damage, or to commence such action within the time hereinbefore specified, shall be a conclusive bar against maintenance by the Insured of any action under this policy.

6. Option to Pay, Settle or Compromise Claims

The Company shall have the option to pay or settle or compromise for or in the name of the Insured any claim insured against or to pay the full amount of this policy, or, in case loss is claimed under this policy by the owner of the indebtedness secured by a mortgage covered by this policy, the Company shall have the option to purchase said indebtedness; such purchase, payment or tender of payment of the full amount of this policy, together with all costs, attorneys' fees and expenses which the Company is obligated hereunder to pay, shall terminate all liability of the Company hereunder. In the event, after notice of claim has been given to the Company by the Insured, the Company offers to purchase said indebtedness, the owner of such indebtedness shall transfer and assign said indebtedness and the mortgage securing the same to the Company upon payment of the purchase price.

7. Payment of Loss

(a) The liability of the Company under this policy shall in no case exceed, in all, the actual loss of the Insured and costs and attorneys' fees which the Company may be obligated hereunder to pay.

(b) The Company will pay, in addition to any loss insured against by this policy, all costs imposed upon the Insured in litigation carried on by the Company for the Insured, and all costs and attorneys' fees in litigation carried on by the Insured with the written authorization of the Company.

(c) No claim for damages shall arise or be maintainable under this policy (1) if the Company, after having received notice of an alleged defect, lien or encumbrance not excepted or excluded herein removes such defect, lien or encumbrance within a reasonable time after receipt of such notice, or (2) for liability voluntarily assumed by the Insured in settling any claim or suit without written consent of the Company, or (3) in the event the title is rejected as unmarketable because of a defect, lien or encumbrance not excepted or excluded in this policy, until there has been a final determination by a court of competent jurisdiction sustaining such rejection.

(d) All payments under this policy, except payments made for costs, attorneys' fees and expenses, shall reduce the amount of the insurance pro tanto and no payment shall be made without producing this policy for endorsement of such payment unless the policy be lost or destroyed, in which case proof of such loss or destruction shall be furnished to the satisfaction of the Company; provided, however, if the owner of an indebtedness secured by a mortgage shown in Schedule B is an Insured herein then such payments shall not reduce pro tanto the amount of the insurance afforded hereunder as to such Insured, except to the extent that such payments reduce the amount of the indebtedness secured by such mortgage. Payment in full by any person or voluntary satisfaction or release by the Insured of a mortgage covered by this policy shall terminate all liability of the Company to the insured owner of the indebtedness secured by such mortgage, except as provided in paragraph 2 hereof.

(e) When liability has been definitely fixed in accordance with the conditions of this policy the loss or damage shall be payable within thirty days thereafter.

8. Liability Noncumulative

It is expressly understood that the amount of this policy is reduced by any amount the Company may pay under any policy insuring the validity or priority of any mortgage shown or referred to in Schedule B hereof or any mortgage hereafter executed by the Insured which is a charge or lien on the estate or interest described or referred to in Schedule A, and the amount so paid shall be deemed a payment to the Insured under this policy. The provisions of this paragraph numbered 8 shall not apply to an Insured owner of an indebtedness secured by a mortgage shown in Schedule B unless such Insured acquires title to said estate or interest in satisfaction of said indebtedness or any part thereof.

9. Subrogation upon Payment or Settlement:

Whenever the Company shall have settled a claim under this policy, all right of subrogation shall vest in the Company unaffected by any act of the Insured, and it shall be subrogated to and be entitled to all rights and remedies which the Insured would have had against any person or property in respect to such claim had this policy not been issued. If the payment does not cover the loss of the Insured, the Company shall be subrogated to such rights and remedies in the proportion which said payment bears to the amount of said loss. If loss should result from any act of the Insured such act shall not void this policy, but the Company, in that event, shall be required to pay only that part of any losses insured against hereunder which shall exceed the amount, if any, lost to the Company by reason of the impairment of the right of subrogation. The Insured, if requested by the Company, shall transfer to the Company all rights and remedies against any person or property necessary in order to perfect such right of subrogation, and shall permit the Company to use the name of the Insured in any transaction or litigation involving such rights or remedies.

If the Insured is the owner of the indebtedness secured by a mortgage covered by this policy, such Insured may release or substitute the personal liability of any debtor or guarantor, or extend or otherwise modify the terms of payment, or release a portion of the estate or interest from the lien of the mortgage, or release any collateral security for the indebtedness, provided such act does not result in any loss of priority of the lien of the mortgage.

10. Policy Entire Contract

Any action or actions or rights of action that the Insured may have or may bring against the Company arising out of the status of the lien of the mortgage covered by this policy or the title of the estate or interest insured herein must be based on the provisions of this policy.

No provision or condition of this policy can be waived or changed except by writing endorsed hereon or attached hereto signed by the President, a Vice President, the Secretary, an Assistant Secretary or other validating officer of the Company.

11. Notices, Where Sent

All notices required to be given the Company and any statement in writing required to be furnished the Company shall be addressed to Home Office of

12. THE PREMIUM SPECIFIED ON THE FIRST PAGE OF THIS POLICY IS THE ENTIRE CHARGE FOR TITLE SEARCH, TITLE EXAMINATION AND TITLE INSURANCE.

The amount of coverage, the cost of the premium, and the names of the buyers taking the title and being insured by the policy are inserted in schedule A, later in the policy.

The policy first states that anyone other than a purchaser who takes title from the parties insured by the policy will have coverage transferred to him. For example, if the insured parties die, their heirs to the property will continue to be insured. The title company agrees to pay all costs of fighting a challenge to the title up to the mount of coverage as provided in conditions and stipulations, Clause 4(a) at the end of the policy.

Liability

The policy then lists the four instances in which the company will be liable for loss or damage to the insured.

1. Protects the insured if the title company makes any mistakes in searching the title. If defects are later found to exist that are not specified in the policy, the damages caused by them are covered. Defects that have been found and thus excluded from coverage are listed in schedule B. Other items not covered are listed in the conditions and stipulations.

2. Protects you against the existence of a defect that would make the title unmarketable, which means the seller did not have a right to sell the land. These are such things as forgeries, undisclosed heirs, and the other defects listed earlier in this chapter. Never accept any policy that does not insure that the title is marketable.

3. Protects the lender, named as an insured, who has a lien on the buyer's title as security for the loan. This could be the seller who has taken back a mortgage from the buyer; both he and the buyer are insured under this policy. The company is liable for a defect in the execution of a mortgage or deed of trust which adversely affects the resulting lien on the property. Before insuring the lender, the company examines the executed mortgage or deed of trust for completeness. If you borrow from a bank or other lending institution, a different type of policy, called a mortgage, lender's, or ALTA (American Land Title Association) policy, is often used. (See below in this chapter.)

4. Insures against the existence of any prior lien or encumbrance, such as a mortgage, not excepted in schedule B, that would adversely affect the mortgage held by the lender or seller who is insured by the policy. For example, if a lender makes a loan to the buyer and he thinks it is the only mortgage on the property, under this policy if another mortgage exists that is superior and not excepted by this policy, any losses suffered by the insured lender will be paid.

Schedule A

First, the cost of the policy, the amount of the coverage, and the policy number are inserted at the top.

Next are spaces that must be filled in with the date and exact time, to the second, that the deed to you is recorded. This is the *effective date* of the policy. You want to be covered for any defects existing at the time you take title. When you get your deed, check the recording time stamped on it with the time and date written into the policy to see if they correspond. If they do not, make an immediate complaint to the title company and have them change the policy to the proper time.

The names of the parties being covered by the policy, the *insured,* are inserted next.

1. Each buyer's name must be inserted and his marital status must be given. The type of ownership by which the buyers are taking title is then given, e.g., tenants in common, joint tenants, husband and wife as community property.

2. Indicates the form of title to be given to the buyers, their names, and type of ownership to be transferred to them. The type of *estate* or *interest* you should get is called a *fee estate* or *fee simple* title, which means you will have complete ownership of the land to sell, give away, or encumber as you wish, subject to the terms of your mortgage or deed of trust.

Schedule B

Part One: Lists the five common exceptions from coverage in standard coverage policies. That is, the policy does not insure against the following:

1. Any taxes or assessments levied against the property before the close of escrow, but not indicated on the public, or tax authority, records, are not insured against by this policy. Thus it is very important to make the seller liable for such liens in the contract of sale, as stated in Clause 10 of the Model Contract of Sale. (See chapter 28.)

2. Encumbrances that can be discovered only by physically inspecting the property and by asking questions of people living on it are not covered by the policy. For example, you could discover an adverse possessor or prescriptive use by inspecting the land, and you will not be insured against a claim for adverse possession or prescriptive use after you purchase the property. (See chapter 16, "Adverse Possession.") Another common unrecorded instrument is a lease held by a renter that is not recorded but that would be binding on the purchaser of the land. Thus you must talk to the people living on the land to ascertain if they have a lease. The policy will not defend you against any legal claims made by such persons in possession after you take title because you had notice they were there by your inspection of the property.

3. The seller of the property may have granted easement rights to an adjoining landowner or other person without recording this grant in the public records, or a person might have gained a prescriptive easement by meeting the requirements for obtaining this right. (See chapter 9, "Easement Rights.") This policy does not insure against easements that could not be discovered by searching the public records. It is your responsibility to determine the status of any right-of-way roads crossing the property or pipelines taking water from the property that are not recorded easements to insure yourself against future claims against the land. The seller is supposed to list all existing easements in Clause 6 of the Model Contract of Sale. (See chapter 28.)

4. This policy does not require the existence of a legal survey and thus insures only that you will receive the seller's title to the property described in this policy and the deed. It does not insure the exact location of that property on the ground. Thus, if you buy land without a survey and later discover that the boundary lines are not where you thought they were, the policy does not protect you. The amount of acreage you will receive is not insured nor are unrecorded "boundary line agreements" made between an owner and an adjoining landowner. Thus you should get a survey as provided in Clauses 16(b) and 17(b) of the Model Contract of Sale.

5. Here the policy excludes from coverage one of the most complicated areas of land ownership, water rights. Since many rights to take water are based on the riparian nature of the property rather than on the recording of any documents, the policy does not take any liability for future water disputes. (See chapter 10, "Water Rights.") Mining claims and mineral rights claims in existence against the property that would not show up in a title search are also excluded from coverage. (See chapter 11, "Mineral, Oil, Gas, Timber, Soil, and Other Rights.")

Part Two: Any encumbrances against the title that the title company found during its title search are listed here, including tax, assessment, and mechanic's liens; mortgages or deeds of trust on the property; easements on the land; covenants, conditions, and restrictions of ownership binding on the owner; attachments and judgments. These are defects in the title, but they do not make the title unmarketable. If an encumbrance did make the title unmarketable, the title company would not issue a policy of title insurance, since it insures the marketability of the title.

Schedule C

A complete description of the property is given. This description should specify any easements, water rights, or other property rights to be included in your purchase so that they will be insured by the policy. If any parts of the property are to be excluded from the conveyance, such as mineral or timber rights, they should also be specified here. Often water rights will be included as part of the description but will not be insured by the title company.

Conditions and Stipulations

These conditions are common to most standard coverage title insurance policies:

1. (a)–(f) The terms used in the policy are defined.

2. The policy covers an insured lender who acquires title to the property to satisfy an obligation owed to him by the insured buyer. For example, if the mortgagee (lender) is one of the insured parties named at the beginning of the policy and he forecloses on the loan at a later date, the mortgagee will be covered by the policy in place of the buyer. But the policy does not continue in favor of another person who purchases the property from the insured party.

3. Further exclusions from the coverage of this policy are listed here. The policy does not insure

the buyer for any losses that he might suffer because of:

(a) Government regulations and laws, such as building codes and zoning regulations, that restrict the use of the property. If the property has been illegally subdivided or the house does not have a legal building permit, any losses you suffer are not covered by this policy. (See chapter 12, "Zoning Laws," and chapter 13, "Building and Health Codes."

(b) Unrecorded police power rights, such as an eminent domain action of condemnation against the property, unless the condemnation has been recorded before the policy goes into effect. (See chapter 15, "Eminent Domain and Condemnation.")

(c) Anything not within the boundaries of the property as described in the policy, except rights-of-way onto adjoining public roads if the property abuts such a public road.

(d) Unrecorded defects known about or agreed to by the buyer but not reported to the title company, or defects that do not result in loss to the insured or that were created after the date the policy was issued. For example, let's say the seller sells the land to someone else before he sells it to you, and the first buyer does not record his deed. If you record your deed before he does and you don't know that the land is already sold, you are the only person with a legal right to the land because you are a *purchaser without knowledge*. If the first buyer sues you, the policy pays for your defense. But if you buy the land knowing it has already been sold, you do not have a legal right to the property because you are a *purchaser with knowledge*. If you are sued, this policy does not cover you, because you knew and assumed the risks when you bought the property.

(e) You are not insured if you are a lender and suffer losses because you violate consumer protection laws, such as the truth in lending law.

4. (a)–(d) This clause establishes the obligation of the title company to protect your title by bringing and defending actions. An interesting part of the defense obligation stipulates that if you make a contract to sell the property and your prospective buyer terminates his purchase because he discovers a defect in your title not excluded from coverage in this policy, the company will cover your damages from the loss of the sale up to the amount of the policy coverage. It is stated that the insured must "promptly notify" the title company of any claim it must fight. The title company also has the right to commence an action to clear on its own initiative. Finally, the policy states that the company shall be allowed to use the insured's name in the prosecution or defense of a case and that the insured shall give the company full cooperation should it have to meet a challenge to the title it is insuring.

5. Additional requirements of notice to the company of its liability are given here. The insured has sixty days after he discovers any loss or damage to notify the company in writing of his claim under the policy.

6. The company has the option to meet its obligations to the insured by either paying his loss up to the amount of coverage or securing his title for him so that he does not suffer a loss.

7. (a)–(e) This section specifies the elements involved in determining and paying for any losses covered by the policy: (a) and (b) deal with the determination of loss—the title company is liable for the actual loss incurred by the insured plus court costs and legal fees up to the amount of coverage; (c) states the limitation of liability—the company has the right to obtain the removal of a defect, if possible, to prevent the insured from suffering a loss. The insured cannot initiate any type of action relating to any matter covered in the policy without the consent of the company. The company is not bound to pay for a loss covered by the policy until all legal proceedings have terminated and resulted in a judgment against the insured; (d) deals with the reduction of the company's liability—if the company makes any payment to the insured for a partial loss due to a defect in the title, the amount of liability under the policy decreases by that amount; (e) specifies the time for payment of loss—the company must render payment within thirty days after liability has definitely been determined.

8. If you have given a mortgage on the land and a judgment later renders your title unmarketable or it is discovered that a lien or encumbrance exists that is covered by the policy, the company must first pay any money to the lender-mortgagee before it can pay you, the insured. If the defect results in

a partial loss only, the amount paid, whether to the lender or to you, will reduce the future liability of the company by that amount in order to prevent the accumulation of liabilities beyond the amount of the policy.

9. To *subrogate* means to substitute. For example, assume that the seller did not reveal in the contract of sale an unrecorded defect in the title when he sold the land to the insured buyer, and the insured buyer suffers a loss because of the defect. After the title company pays the insured for his loss, if it is covered by the policy, the company then has the right to subrogate, or substitute, itself in the place of the insured and sue the seller for his breach of contract of sale. The company can sue in its own name and in the name of the insured, and if any damages are awarded, the title company keeps the money.

The second paragraph of this section applies only to a lender who is insured under the policy and will not affect you.

10. All the terms of the insurance agreement between the company and the insured persons are expressed only in the policy. Any changes made in the policy must be approved in writing by a valid representative of the title company.

11. The address given here should be used if you have to make a claim or notify the company for any reason.

WHY YOU NEED TITLE INSURANCE IN ADDITION TO THE CONTRACT OF SALE

The Model Contract of Sale includes every protection that you receive in the policy of title insurance. Under the contract the seller is liable to you for your damages, while under the policy of title insurance, the title company assumes liability. Therefore, it might appear that getting a policy of title insurance is an unnecessary expense. However, if you are not insured and you have to proceed against the seller for any defect in title and breach of the contract of sale, you will have to pay the legal expenses prior to a judgment, you might not be able to locate the seller to collect a judgment from him, and he might not have any money to

pay a judgment. A title insurance policy pays your legal costs, insures you coverage for any losses included in the policy, and pays for your defense if you are sued over any title problems after your purchase. At this time, it is the best insurance you can have when buying land. It should be an essential part of your purchase, and must always include a preliminary title report issued to you during the escrow so that you will know what liens exist in the title to the land well before you pay your money and take title. Then you will be able to demand the removal of those liens that you don't accept, and if they cannot be removed you can cancel the transaction and get your deposit returned to you.

THE LENDER'S POLICY OF TITLE INSURANCE

If the seller takes back a purchase money mortgage or deed of trust and note when he sells you the land, usually he is included as an insured party in your standard coverage owner's policy of title insurance. But if a commercial lender extends a loan to you for the purchase and takes back a mortgage or deed of trust with the land as security, you will be charged the expense of obtaining a more inclusive form of title insurance called a loan policy or lender's policy, which was established by the American Land Title Association (ALTA) for the protection of lenders.

All those items excluded from coverage in the owner's policy are included in the loan policy, which includes a legal survey and physical inspection by the insurer before a policy will be issued. The cost of this type of coverage is much greater than that of a standard coverage policy, but since a lender usually wants as much protection for his security as possible, he will demand an ALTA policy.

Usually the buyer pays for the lender's policy as part of the loan. This policy insures only the lender-mortgagee and does not protect the buyer. Thus you must also get your own policy of title insurance. The amount of coverage is for the amount of the debt owed to the lender, since that would be the extent of his loss should there be a defect in the title to the land. As the amount of the debt is paid off by the buyer, the amount of coverage decreases by an equal amount. When the debt is totally paid, the lender's policy terminates since there is no longer anything to insure the lender for.

If you order a lender's policy at the same time you order an owner's policy, a discount is usually given by the title company. A few states combine the owner's policy and the lender's policy in a joint protection policy, issued in the amount of the purchase price. As the buyer pays off his loan, the company's liability to the lender decreases and its liability to the buyer increases. When the loan is completely paid, the buyer remains as the only party insured by the policy.

THE EXTENDED COVERAGE OWNER'S POLICY OF TITLE INSURANCE

The greater protection given to a lender by the loan policy can be obtained by a buyer if he extends the standard owner's policy to cover these possible defects. The extended coverage owner's policy generally gives buyers what the ALTA policy gives lenders, except that insured access rights are usually not included. The main advantage of extended coverage is that it insures a survey and everything that can be found by a physical inspection of the property. But the survey taken by the title company is usually more expensive than any survey you can have done elsewhere. Therefore, because it is easy to inspect the property for unrecorded easements and to determine the status of persons in possession of the land, if you get your own legal survey done, you will get adequate coverage with a standard owner's policy of title insurance. Of course, if the seller is willing to pay for it, get the extended coverage policy.

If you desire you can specify in Clause 7 of the Model Contract of Sale that the seller is to pay the entire amount of an extended policy. It is very easy to change the clause in the contract of sale if you want to provide for this. (See chapter 28, "The Model Contract of Sale.")

If you want any information about title insurance in your state, write to your state insurance com-

missioner or the land title association in the Useful Resources at the end of this chapter.

ATTORNEY'S CERTIFICATE OF TITLE

In a few states in the East (see illustration 95 earlier in this chapter), abstracts of title by abstract companies and title insurance policies are not commonly used. Instead, an attorney is hired to examine all of the recorded documents relating to the title, and he makes up the abstract of title. He issues the results of his title search in a certificate of title that details what records were examined and what encumbrances exist against the title, if any. This certificate is basically the same as an abstract of title certificate. It is not insurance of marketable title and does not insure against undisclosed defects, such as forgery and the others listed earlier. Thus, like an abstract of title, it is not an adequate form of protection for the buyer.

If the attorney makes a negligent mistake in his title search, you will have to sue him for any losses you suffer due to his negligence. In contrast, under a title insurance policy, you will be compensated if the company is negligent and for unknown defects in the title subject to any exception in the policy.

Always insist on a policy of title insurance if it is available in your area. If the real estate agent or seller tells you that they are not issued in your area, do some investigating on your own to determine the location of the nearest title company. Title insurance is becoming more widespread every year. Look in the yellow pages under Title Companies. If you can't locate a title company, send an inquiry to: The American Land Title Association (ATLA), 1828 L Street, N.W., Washington, D.C. 20036.

THE TORRENS TITLE SYSTEM AND TORRENS CERTIFICATE

Less than 1 percent of the country uses a completely different method of guaranteeing title to land, called the Torrens Title System. In this system, the county recorder maintains a record of all encumbrances that exist on the title to each piece of property in the county. Before a parcel of land can be sold or mortgaged, the buyer and seller must go to court for a hearing. The county recorder sends a notice of the hearing to anybody who he determines could have a claim against the title according to the county records. Anybody with a claim must sue to have his claim settled before title is passed to the buyer. The court dismisses or settles all the claims, orders the title to be registered in the buyer's name, and issues the new owner a Torrens certificate, which lists any liens and encumbrances against the title. If a Torrens certificate is issued, the title is declared marketable and no undisclosed defects can be used later to cause a loss of title.

USEFUL RESOURCES

The following are available free from:
American Land Title Association (ALTA)
1828 L St., N.W.
Washington, DC 20036

The Importance of the Abstract in Your Community
Buying a House of Cards?
Protecting Your Interest in Real Estate
Land Title Insurance—Consumer Protection Since 1876
Blueprint for Home Buying

In 1976, ALTA produced its first volume of *White Papers*. The topics featured in that volume were:

1. The Nature of and Need for Title Insurance Services
2. The Importance of Title Insurance in the Availability of Mortgage Funds and in the Development of the Secondary Mortgage Market
3. The Benefits of Title Insurance
4. Popular Misconceptions of the Title Industry
5. The Torrens System

It is available for $2.50 from the ALTA address above, and a *Torrens Summary Booklet* is available for $1.50.

The following are available free from:
California Land Title Association
P.O. Box 13968
Sacramento, CA 95853

Why Do You Need Title Insurance?
Solar Access—A Potential Title Problem
Closing Costs—A Primer
Title Insurance—Where Does Your Dollar Go?
Understanding Foreclosure
The Function of an Escrow
Mechanic's Liens
Forgery—A Cause for Alarm
Creative Financing—Carrying Back a Second? You Need a Lender's Title Policy
The Title Consumer—Understanding Supplemental Property Taxes
Pinning Down Your Property
Understanding Closing and Title Costs

The following are available free from:
Safeco Title Insurance Home Office
P.O. Box 2233
Los Angeles, CA 90051

Title Insurance—Why and How
Title Insurance Facts
Owner's Title Insurance
Your Safeco Title Policy Issuing Agent

CHAPTER 32

Types of Co-ownership

In this chapter, I describe the advantages and disadvantages of the various types of co-ownership by which a married or unmarried couple or a group can take title to a parcel of land. Today more and more people are joining together with others willing and able to share the costs of owning country land and are buying as a group. Generally, the larger the parcel of land, the cheaper it is per acre. As a group the individuals can pool their funds to buy a larger parcel. Even if you do not want to share ownership of your land with anyone else, you might agree to buy a large parcel of land with some other people and then subdivide the property among yourselves with each of you taking separate

title to your individual parcel. However, you must check the local zoning regulations first to be sure that you will be allowed to subdivide, or partition, your land after purchasing it. Some areas have minimum acreage laws for parcel splits and limits to the number of residences per parcel. (See chapter 12, ''Zoning Laws.'')

Whenever two or more people plan to buy land together, before signing the contract of sale all the buyers should understand what each person's goals and desires are regarding the land. It is often useful to draw up an owners' agreement specifying the group's goals and desires on paper. I have included a Model Owners' Agreement at the end of this chapter which your group can use as a basis for drawing up your own contract. Then the group should decide on the form of co-ownership best suited to it.

The two most common forms of land co-ownership are tenancy in common and joint tenancy. People can also join together in a corporation, non-profit association, or cooperative. Since all the legal aspects of these legal entities could fill another book of this size, I will merely summarize their advantages and disadvantages to give you a basic idea of the possibilities available to your group.

I also include some information pertaining to property ownership by a husband and wife, specifically tenancy by the entireties, dower and curtesy, and community property rights.

OWNING LAND AS TENANTS IN COMMON

When buying land as tenants in common, each purchaser shares an undivided interest in the total parcel of land. This means that one party cannot claim any specific portion of the land as his alone unless it is specified in a contract among all the owners. Each cotenant does not necessarily have to own an equal share. For instance, one person might have a quarter interest, another a half interest, and two others might each have a one-eighth interest in the land. Usually each person is financially responsible only to the extent of his ownership.

A cotenancy in a deed might read as follows: "Gordon Iris, a single man, an undivided ⅓ interest, and Wendi Campbell, a single woman, an undivided ⅔ interest, as tenants in common."

The only way one tenant can destroy the tenancy in common, or cotenancy, without the other owners' approval is by going to court and filing an action to *partition* the land among the owners. There is no way to stop such an action unless all parties have waived these rights by a legal agreement between themselves. The judge will appoint a commissioner, or referee, who will equitably divide the land into separate parcels according to the amount of interest held by each tenant. Each person then becomes the sole owner of his respective portion. If, for geographical or legal reasons, the land cannot be split up in this manner, the court will order that the entire piece of land be sold and the proceeds split up among the owners according to their respective interest. If all the owners are willing, of course, they can partition the land themselves as local law permits or sell it and divide the proceeds without initiating a court action, although getting everyone to agree on a fair division of the land is usually difficult. The owners can also mutually agree in writing to replace the cotenancy with another form of co-ownership.

Each individual cotenant can sell or mortgage his interest in the land, but he acts only for his own share and cannot bind anyone else's interest. Thus, if a person's mortgage on his share were to be foreclosed, his lender would take his share as a tenant in common with the other owners. Because the lender would then have to either sell his interest in the land or file for a partition in order to sell the land and get the money owed him, a commercial lender will not likely grant a loan to just one cotenant in a tenancy in common.

To avoid possible problems with lenders or a purchaser of a cotenant's interest, the owners can specify in a contract among themselves that no tenant may sell or mortgage his share, or that the remaining owners have the *right of first refusal* if one tenant wants to sell his interest. The right of first refusal means that the cotenant who wants to sell his interest must first offer to sell it to the other owners before he can offer it to anyone else. The Model Owners' Agreement at the conclusion of this chapter illustrates how such an agreement can be written.

If a cotenant fails to make his payments on the land and other expenses, the other co-owners can sue him, get a judgment, and foreclose on his interest in the property. If a cotenant dies, his interest in the property goes to his heirs, who take his place as tenants in common with the other owners. This inheritance rule is the most important legal aspect of a tenancy in common differentiating it from other forms of co-ownership. Under a joint tenancy (see next section), if an owner dies, his interest in the property goes to the surviving owners. Because most people want their property to go to their heirs, unrelated land buyers usually buy as tenants in common rather than joint tenants. Most states assume that, unless stated otherwise, title to property will be under a tenancy in common. Nevertheless, you should specify in your contract of sale, in your escrow instructions, and in your deed that you are to take the property as tenants in common if that is your choice.

OWNING LAND AS JOINT TENANTS

Whereas tenants in common may hold undivided unequal interest in the land, joint tenants always share an undivided equal interest in the land. The major legal difference between these two types of co-ownership is that under a joint tenancy the co-owners have the *right of survivorship*, which means that if one of the parties dies, his interest automatically passes to the surviving owners. A joint tenant cannot will his interest to his heirs or anyone else, and his interest does not become part of his estate on his death. The surviving joint tenants inherit the deceased's interest free from personal debts and liens. Since no will is involved, an expensive and lengthy probate proceeding is unnecessary. Depending on the state where the property is located, an inheritance tax may be levied, based on the value of the deceased person's interest in the land.

Since each person owns an equal interest in the land, all expenses, including land payments, taxes, repairs, insurance, and other items, must be shared equally. If one party fails to contribute his share, the other joint tenants can sue him for contribution or breach of contract, obtain a judgment against him, place a lien against his interest in the property, and eventually obtain a writ of possession against his share of the property.

Once a joint tenancy has been created, no joint tenant can get out of it without destroying that form of ownership. If a party sells his interest, his buyer comes in as a tenant in common rather than a joint tenant to the others. For example, if X, Y, and Z hold a piece of land as joint tenants and Z sells his interest to A, A buys in as a tenant in common. If A dies, his share goes to his heirs, rather than to X and Y. X and Y remain joint tenants, and each has a right of survivorship to the other's interest. Upon death, their interests never go to A. If X and Y choose, they can change their arrangement to become tenants in common with A. If only two people are joint tenants, and one sells his interest, the joint tenancy is automatically terminated and transformed into a tenancy in common when the new owner takes title. (See illustration 98.) If a joint tenant chooses to sell his interest, he can do so without the consent of the other owners, unless the owners specify otherwise in a contract among themselves.

If a joint tenant, like a tenant in common, wants to borrow money for a private loan, he can mortgage his interest in the property. However, if his loan is foreclosed, his lender will take his interest as a tenant in common, and the remaining tenants then automatically become tenants in common. A joint tenant, like a tenant in common, would probably have a hard time finding a lender willing to lend him money solely on the security of his joint tenancy interest.

If a money judgment is rendered against one tenant for personal debts, his interest can be split off from the others and used to pay his obligations.

Any owner, or creditor, can go to court to file an action for partition of the individual interests just as in a tenancy in common, or the owners can mutually agree in writing to change the arrangement.

If you choose to take ownership under a joint tenancy, you must specify in your contract of sale, escrow instructions, and deed that you are to take title as *joint tenant* or as *joint tenant with the right of survivorship*. A few states, Florida, Georgia, Kentucky, North Carolina, Ohio, Oregon, Pennsylvania, South Carolina, Tennessee, Texas, Virginia, Washington, and West Virginia, have abolished the right of survivorship in joint tenancy, and title passes to the heirs on the death of a joint tenant as if he were a tenant in common.

A typical joint tenancy would read as follows: "John Rael, a single man, an undivided ½ interest, and Mary Smith, a single woman, an undivided ½ interest, as joint tenants."

OWNING LAND AS TENANTS BY THE ENTIRETIES

This type of ownership applies only to a husband and wife. In some states—Arkansas, Delaware, Florida, Indiana, Kentucky, Maryland, Massachusetts, Michigan, Missouri, New Jersey, New York, North Carolina, Oklahoma, Oregon, Pennsylvania, Rhode Island, Tennessee, Vermont, Virginia, West Virginia, Wisconsin, and Wyoming—a sale to a married couple can create a tenancy by the entireties between the spouses. In some states it is automatic unless specified otherwise, and in other states it must be specifically stated in the deed.

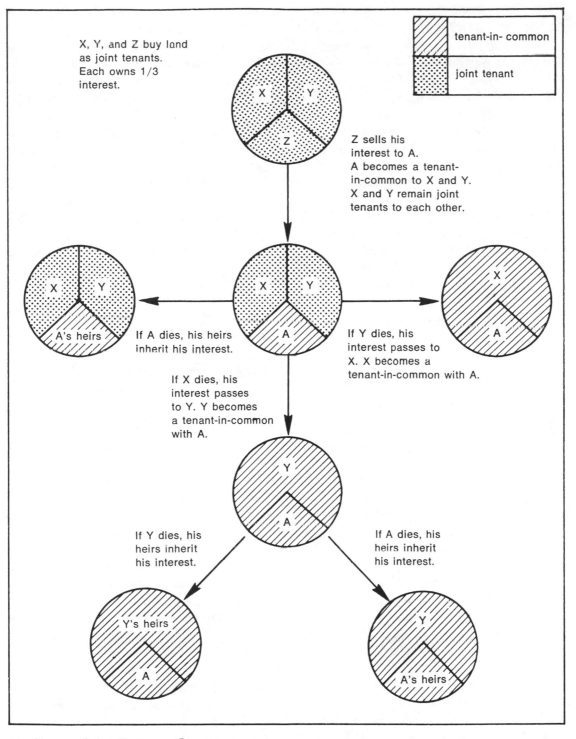

X, Y, and Z buy land as joint tenants. Each owns 1/3 interest.

Z sells his interest to A. A becomes a tenant-in-common to X and Y. X and Y remain joint tenants to each other.

tenant-in- common

joint tenant

If A dies, his heirs inherit his interest.

If Y dies, his interest passes to X. X becomes a tenant-in-common with A.

If X dies, his interest passes to Y. Y becomes a tenant-in-common with A.

If Y dies, his heirs inherit his interest.

If A dies, his heirs inherit his interest.

98. How a Joint Tenancy Operates

Under a tenancy by the entireties, title is held by both persons as if they were one owner. Each has complete ownership of the property, and when one dies the other keeps full ownership rights. Thus, like joint tenants, they have the right of survivor-ship. If the deceased spouse had individual debts, his creditors cannot get a lien against the property. However, if the debtor spouse is the one who sur-vives or if the husband and wife had common debts, the creditors can attach the property.

433

If a married couple buys land with a single person, another couple, or a group of people, each married couple may be considered as tenants by the entireties within a group of joint tenants. For instance, if X and Y, a husband and wife, buy land with Z a single person, X and Y can be considered one person under the law of tenancy by the entireties and own an undivided half interest in the property as a joint tenant with Z, who also owns an undivided half interest in the land. Compare this with a strict joint tenancy under which X, Y, and Z would each own an undivided one-third interest in the land. If a divorce occurs, X and Y split their half interest and become tenants in common with Z, and the right of survivorship terminates.

No action for partition can be forced by only one of the spouses in a tenancy by the entireties, and no sale of the property can be made by one spouse without the written consent of the other.

DOWER AND CURTESY RIGHTS AND COMMUNITY PROPERTY

Several states recognize either dower and curtesy rights or community property rights of a husband and wife, which, like a tenancy by the entireties, require both spouses' consent to a purchase or sale of their mutual property. Although these rights are not a type of ownership, strictly speaking, they will affect your title if you are a married couple, and they could affect the title of the land you are buying if the sellers include a married couple.

Dower and Curtesy Rights

Where recognized, dower rights give a widow one-third of her husband's real estate upon his death. Some states have increased this to a half interest. On the other hand, curtesy is the husband's right to one-third of his wife's real estate upon her death, but he obtains the right only if a child was born during the marriage.

Dower and curtesy rights cannot be cut off by one spouse's selling the land without the permission of the other. Both parties must consent to the sale in writing and must sign the deed. For instance, in a dower and curtesy state, if you buy land from a husband and the wife does not sign the deed, you run the risk that if her husband dies before she does, she can collect her share of her husband's estate from you, since she never signed away her dower interest in the land. To be sure both parties will agree to sign the deed, you should get both the husband and wife to sign the contract of sale. If both parties do not sign the contract of sale, either party can refuse to sign the deed without legal liability.

The states that still recognize dower and curtesy rights are Alaska, Arkansas, Delaware, Georgia, Hawaii, Kentucky, Maryland, Massachusetts, Ohio, Oregon, Rhode Island, Tennessee, Virginia, West Virginia, and Wisconsin. New Jersey abolished dower and curtesy rights as of May 28, 1980.

Community Property

Eight states—Arizona, California, Idaho, Louisiana, Nevada, New Mexico, Texas, and Washington—regard any property purchased during a marriage as community property. Both husband and wife have an equal right to own and possess the property purchased during marriage, and upon the death of either spouse the survivor automatically receives half of the community property and the other half passes to the lawful heirs, or in some states, the surviving spouse automatically receives the entire amount of community property. Check with a lawyer to determine what the law is in your state if you are in a community property state. Of course, the deceased spouse may will the other half to the surviving spouse regardless of the state law. In a divorce, the community property is always split in half between the spouses. Community property laws, like dower and curtesy laws and tenancy by the entireties, were enacted to prevent a surviving spouse from being totally deprived of property under the will of the deceased.

It is now common for a married couple to take title to property in community property states as follows: "Victor Marci, husband, and Mary Marci, wife, as community property."

You must be sure that both the husband and the wife sign the contract of sale and the deed when conveying any community property to you. Regardless of the state law, you must always have both spouses sign a contract of sale and deed if you are purchasing land from a married couple.

FORMING A CORPORATION TO BUY LAND

If you have a fairly large group that wants to purchase land together, you might consider corporate ownership. Its unique feature is that a corporation has all of the legal aspects of a single person. When a corporation is formed, each person puts in a sum of money in return for shares of stock and becomes a shareholder in the corporation. This money goes to make the down payment for the land. The shares are issued as in any other type of corporation, and the shareholders' agreement can entitle the shareholder to live on the land and obligate him to pay assessments to the corporation to cover its cost of owning the property.

The shareholders must draw up articles of incorporation, bylaws, and a shareholders' agreement. Each state has its own requirements regarding the proper legal form of these documents, but every state requires, at least, the filing of the articles of incorporation with the secretary of state (of the state) for approval. A filing fee is required, and in most states an annual corporation tax, or franchise tax, is due.

The corporation is managed according to the bylaws, and by a board of directors. Each shareholder can be a member of the board and thus take part in all the decision making. The voting power of each member will depend on the number of shares of stock he owns. For simplicity, it is preferable in a large group to keep things equal. The group will specify in the bylaws the number of votes required to approve an action taken by the board. For instance, the group might decide that 75 percent of the shareholders must agree on any decision. The shareholders pass resolutions authorizing the corporation's officers, including a president, vice president, secretary, and treasurer, to handle particular problems involving the land, such as paying taxes and insurance premiums, hiring someone to do roadwork, and paying off the mortgage. Each board member can take turns being an officer.

The shareholders' agreement specifies any terms the group wants binding on the shareholders. It must be in writing, but it does not have to be filed with the secretary of state. The agreement is a contract signed by all the shareholders and states their rights and obligations. For example, the agreement can specify that no share can be sold or transferred by a shareholder without the approval of the board or that the use or occupancy of the land by any person other than a shareholder is prohibited unless approval is granted.

To form a corporation, it is not necessary to have an income-producing business. I have had articles of incorporation approved which state that "the specific business in which the corporation is primarily to engage is to own and occupy certain real property." This type of corporation will have no income and, therefore, will be charged no federal income tax. Of course, a profit will be made when the land is sold, and a tax will be levied at that time. Although the corporation has no regular income, it will have regular expenses, such as mortgage payments, property taxes, and maintenance costs, which the individual shareholders must pay according to the terms in the shareholders' agreement. Thus the corporation operates at a loss each year.

Some states permit each shareholder to deduct from his annual personal income tax return the amount of the corporation's net loss in proportion to the number of shares of stock he owns; for example, a subchapter S corporation in California allows this. Thus the shareholder receives an annual tax benefit because the corporation "loses" money. If the shareholder lives on the land, an amount equal to the appraised rental value of the land must be subtracted from the above-allowed deduction unless he can show that he is living on the land to perform duties for the corporation, such as maintenance and care of the property.

If a shareholder fails to pay his obligations as specified in the shareholders' agreement, the board of directors can vote to sell his shares to recoup the money owed to the corporation. When a buyer is found and approved, the transfer of ownership merely necessitates changing the name of the shareholder in the corporate books instead of the usual foreclosure procedure. A reserve "slush" fund is always maintained by the corporation to use if a shareholder falls behind in his payments in order to prevent a default on the mortgage payments.

If the shareholders vote to sell the entire corporate land, the profits will be divided according to the amount of stock each shareholder owns.

An advantage of a corporation is that the shareholders do not have personal liability for the acts of the corporation, and conversely the corporation does not have liability for the acts of the individual shareholders. Thus land owned by a corporation cannot be attached for personal debts or judgments rendered against any of its shareholders. A creditor can attach only the person's shares in the corporation. He then becomes a shareholder and must abide by the rules of the corporation. In this way, the other landowners are protected from having their ownership disrupted by an unwelcome stranger. If the board of directors must approve the sale of any stock, the creditor might find it difficult to collect his money.

On the other hand, if the corporation cannot pay its debts, none of the shareholders can individually be forced to pay a creditor, although the corporation's assets, such as its land, can be reached and sold to make up a debt. If the land is worth less than the amount of debts, the creditors cannot get a deficiency judgment against the shareholders.

The major disadvantage of a corporation is the cost involved in incorporating, since you will probably need an attorney to draw up the documents, and you will have to pay state filing fees and state corporation taxes. But the corporate form of ownership has many advantages for a group that wants to own a large undivided parcel of land.

Cooperative Corporation

If your group plans to buy land primarily for the purpose of living on it rather than for the purpose of investment, you might see whether your state recognizes a specific corporation called the *cooperative corporation*. Under a cooperative corporation, the corporate organization is seen as a "landlord" and the individual shareholding members are viewed as "tenants." Because this arrangement is more a type of property ownership than a true corporation, some states have placed the cooperative corporation under the supervision of the real estate commissioner rather than the secretary of state, who normally oversees corporations. Instead of issuing shares of stock, the cooperative corporation issues a certificate entitling the holders to a vote in the corporation's management and the right to live on the land. Everything else in this type of corporation is arranged in basically the same way as the profit-type corporation. Each state has its own laws on cooperatives, particularly with regard to their tax status.

The Nonprofit Corporation

Another type of corporation you might investigate if you are not planning to make money on the land is the nonprofit corporation. Your group must fit into one of the special nonprofit and nonpolitical categories, such as religious, educational, scientific, or charitable. If you qualify, the nonprofit corporation may not have to pay income taxes, and, in many states, will also be exempt from paying property taxes. However, you will have to maintain thorough financial records and file detailed tax returns covering the nature of your nonprofit operation.

Instead of issuing stock, the nonprofit corporation may sell or give "memberships" to individuals, who elect a board of directors and vote on the operation of the corporation. Like a profit-oriented corporation, articles of incorporation and by-laws are required, and an additional application for nonprofit status must be made to the Internal Revenue Service and to the appropriate state agency, which determine whether the corporation is truly nonprofit and therefore eligible for tax exemptions.

Once formed, the nonprofit corporation remains in existence until it is dissolved. This dissolution process could present problems to the individual owners of the corporation because the secretary of state or state corporations official will likely determine that the corporation's assets were held in trust for the nonprofit purpose which the corporation claims to represent. This causes delays and legal problems when you try to sell the property and divide the profits among yourselves because the secretary will attempt to prevent the profits from going to private individuals. If your group is now, or wants to become, a church or other nonprofit organization and buy land, you will need a lawyer to get you through the legal paperwork involved in setting up the corporation in the best manner possible to meet your needs.

FORMING AN UNINCORPORATED NONPROFIT ASSOCIATION

A religious, social, educational, or other nonprofit group can also form an unincorporated nonprofit association to buy land. Although the group must appoint one of its members as a trustee who takes the title to the land in his name, the organization, rather than the trustee or other members of the group, retains liability for its own debts. The trustee only acts according to the charter and bylaws of the organization.

In a nonprofit association, no single person owns any part of the land. The members of the group usually agree to pay rent to the association for living on the land, which can be used by the association to pay its mortgage and other expenses without making a profit. This type of purchase appeals primarily to communes, ecological groups interested in preserving open space, and people interested in forming some type of community in the country without actually being personal landowners.

Arrangements must be made in writing at the time the association is formed as to how the funds from a future sale of the property will be disbursed. Each state has its own rules regarding the formation of an unincorporated nonprofit association, and you can get all the necessary information from your secretary of state or commissioner of corporations. Forming such an association is usually easy, but you will require the services of an attorney. Associations are easier to form because the regulations for corporations are avoided. You must be sure the zoning will allow the construction of multiple dwellings on a single parcel of property.

A MODEL OWNERS' AGREEMENT

If you are going to buy land with other people, you should get together to discuss and write out in detail the terms of the co-ownership before making your purchase. The entire group should understand as completely as possible the intentions and desires of each person. The best of friends one year can become bitter enemies the following year over conflicts involving such things as mate switching, being a vegetarian versus being a meat eater, whether to hunt or not, nudity versus modesty, religious fervor versus atheism, or other basic personality clashes. Or the issues can be more ordinary, like failure or inability to pay the mortgage, tax, or insurance payments; or disagreement over where the houses are to be built. The best-intentioned people cannot possibly predict what will happen to them when they become co-owners of land, with all the responsibilities that that entails, particularly if they are living in the country for the first time.

Often people who have never lived together in the city think they will automatically be able to commune together in the country. Actually, life in the country is more difficult because you must rely to a much greater extent on yourselves, not only for the basic necessities of survival, such as providing water, heat, shelter, but also for more subtle psychological reinforcements. The distractions of the city, which help relieve the pressures of living and working together with the same people day after day, are gone, and individual levels of awareness and personal conflicts are therefore emphasized. Although you cannot prevent problems from arising, you can eliminate basic misunderstandings and decide how to deal with potential future problems in an owners' agreement. If you are a married couple and you want to define your respective interests in your property differently than is specified by the laws governing marital property rights, you will need to make a postnuptial agreement. See chapter 39, "Preserving Your Separate Property: Prenuptial and Postnuptial Agreements."

Each buyer signs the agreement, which should state in writing all the details of the purchase, including such items as each person's rights and obligations regarding the property and its use; the construction of improvements; future resale of the property; financing; decision making; the sale of one person's interest; individual personal liability; and what happens in the event of a death, divorce, separation, or insolvency.

All financial aspects of the purchase should be specified. Some people might want to live on the land year-round while others might want to use the property only as a vacation home. Are you all going to want to pay an equal share? Each person should understand what his financial obligations will entail, including mortgage payments and maintenance costs, and must be willing and able to meet them.

The group must decide how the members want to live on the land. For instance, is the group going to build one communal house and share the rest of the land without dividing it up? Are the members of the group going to build houses on separate building sites and share a portion of the land communally? Or is the group going to divide up the entire land into proportionate sections for each person with none of the land shared by the group? Regardless of how it is done, be sure that adequate building sites exist for everyone who wants to construct his own house. Every site is not equally inviting, so decide who gets what before you take title to the property.

The Model Owners' Agreement I am including at the end of this chapter covers the two basic areas required in any co-owner's agreement. First, it details each buyer's ownership rights and obligations, and second, it states the rules to be observed in relating to the land. This model agreement assumes that there are three partners, each having an equal third interest in the land, and that agreements will be made on the basis of a simple majority. You can use any figure you want for approval of co-owner decisions. If there are married couples, or partners sharing an interest, you may want to give the couple only a single vote between them.

You should have no problem understanding the agreement. Each owner is responsible for building his or her own house, and the respective values of each house will be paid to each owner upon the sale of the total property. It provides for the possibility that one owner might want to sell his interest and get out of the agreement, in which case the remaining owners have the "right of first refusal."

I include three alternative methods of setting up the first right of refusal. Select the one you and your partners wish to use, and remove the other two from the agreement. You can also change my interest rate of 8 percent to any figure you desire.

The contract specifies the terms under which the remaining owners can buy the seller's interest; if they decide not to buy it, they have the right to approve a new buyer.

To preserve the natural environment as much as possible, it specifies in great detail what can and cannot be done on the land.

You can use this agreement as a guide to your specific group needs, whether there are two or twenty of you. You can insert and omit specific clauses depending on your situation. Whatever agreement you make, it must be in writing, dated, and signed by all the owners. It is always advisable to notarize all the signatures. This is a simple and inexpensive process. You should also prepare a *memorandum of agreement* for recording, so it will be of record that there is an agreement affecting the rights of the owners of the property. I include here a sample memorandum of agreement. The agreement should be drawn up and signed before you buy the land, so that you can iron out basic problems in advance. Some group members might come to realize that they do not see eye to eye with the other members on major issues and will decide to drop out of the deal before it's too late. I have seen this happen many times. Our agreement is very formal and legal sounding, but yours can be expressed in any manner you choose. Informality or choice of language is irrelevant, as long as you express clearly and thoroughly what each individual's rights, obligations, and expectations will be after the group takes title to the property.

If necessary, consult an attorney as a group to work out your own specific agreement.

MODEL OWNERS' AGREEMENT

This Owners' Agreement is made this _____ day of _____, 19____, by and between _____, _____, _____, whereby it is agreed as follows:

1. The purpose of this Owners' Agreement is to specify the rights and obligations of the undersigned Owners with regard to that certain real property situated in the County of _____, State of _____, described as _____.

2. The purpose of this Owners' Agreement is also to specify the rules and regulations regarding the use and enjoyment of said property.

3. Each Owner shall have one vote in any decision regarding said property or any condition specified in this Agreement.

4. Each Owner shall pay an equal amount of the principal and interest on the existing mortgage; and each Owner shall pay an equal amount of the property taxes, assessments, insurance, and maintenance costs, including road repair.

5. If any owner is in default in any obligation under the terms of this Agreement, any Owner may bring an action in court for breach of contract or other appropriate causes of action. If a judgment is obtained against a defaulting owner, it shall be recorded as a lien against his interest in the property, and legal recourse may be had to seek to execute against the interest of the defaulting owner, and cause his interest to be sold in order to satisfy the judgment for the breach.

Right of First Refusal—Alternative #1

6. In the event any Owner should desire to sell his or her interest in said property, the first right of refusal shall be accorded to the remaining Owners. The option vested in the remaining Owners shall entitle them, individually or as a group, to purchase all rights and liabilities of the selling Owner at a price equivalent to the total investment to date made by the selling Owner in said property, plus interest on that investment. The interest shall be computed at a rate of 8 percent per annum from the date of investment. The term "investment" shall include all money paid in the form of mortgage payments, including that portion of the payment which is accorded to principal and that portion of the payment which is accorded to interest.

The selling Owner shall also be entitled to reimbursement for his or her portion of the investment in any improvements made on said property. The term "improvement" shall include structures, orchards, gardens, development of water systems, sewage systems, and drainage systems, and any other construction or development on said property that increases its value for sale. For this Agreement, the term "improvements" shall also include any items that will remain on said property, such as machinery, tools, and animals. The term "investment," with regard to improvements, shall include all money paid for the improvement. The value of an Owner's labor shall not be included in the computation of said Owner's investment.

The selling Owner shall be entitled to have all monies due him paid in a period not to exceed four years at a rate of one-fifth (⅕) of the principal amount due, or more, per year, plus 8 percent interest per annum on the unpaid principal, with a cash down payment of one-fifth (⅕) of the selling price.

Right of First Refusal—Alternative #2

In the event any Owner should decide to sell his or her interest in said property, the first right of refusal shall be accorded to the remaining owners. The option vested in the remaining Owners shall entitle them, individually or as a group, to purchase all rights and liabilities of the selling Owner at the same price and the same terms as those offered to the selling Owner by any third person.

Should the selling Owner receive an offer to purchase his or her interest, the Owner must immediately notify the remaining Owners of the terms of the offer, and allow the Owners 15 days to exercise their first right of refusal to purchase the interest of the selling Owner. If the Owners elect not to purchase the interest, then the selling Owner must sell to the third party on the same terms previously offered, subject to paragraph 7 below. If the terms are changed, then the selling Owner must again offer his or her interest to the remaining Owners, who have 15 days to exercise their first right of refusal.

If one or more Owners elect to purchase the selling Owner's interest, they shall have thirty days to close escrow on the sale. If they fail to close escrow in a timely manner, they shall be held to be in breach, and the selling Owner shall be free to sell his or her interest to any third party on any terms the selling Owner desires, subject to paragraph 7 below.

Right of First Refusal—Alternative #3

In the event any Owner should desire to sell his or her interest in said property, the first right of refusal shall be accorded to the remaining Owners. The option vested in the remaining Owners shall entitle them, individually or as a group, to purchase all rights and liabilities of the selling Owner on the following terms:

The selling Owner and the Owner or Owners who desire to purchase the seller's interest shall mutually agree on a real estate appraiser to appraise the selling Owner's interest in the said property, including his share of the value of the land and the value of his improvements on the land, such as a house. Once the written appraisal has been submitted by the appraiser, the purchasing Owner has 15 days to exercise his first right of refusal to purchase the seller's interest.

If an Owner elects to purchase the seller's interest, the Owner shall close escrow in 30 days and shall pay the seller's price over a period not to exceed four years at a rate of one-fifth ($\frac{1}{5}$) of the principal amount due, or more, per year, plus 8 percent interest remaining on the unpaid principal, with a cash down payment of one-fifth ($\frac{1}{5}$) of the selling price.

If no Owner elects to exercise his or her right of first refusal, the selling Owner is free to sell his interest on any terms he desires to any third person, subject to paragraph 7 below.

7. Any Owner desiring to sell his or her interest in said property shall so advise the other Owners in writing, and subject to the rights granted in paragraph 6 above, all Owners shall use their best efforts to locate a buyer for the interest. No interest shall be sold to any person without the written consent and approval of the majority of all the Owners, which consent shall not be unreasonably withheld.

8. No Owner shall encumber or permit the encumbrance of his or her interest in said property by any person or legal entity without the written consent of a majority of Owners, which consent shall not be unreasonably withheld.

9. No Owner may make a gift or donation of his or her interest in said property without the written approval and consent of a majority of all the Owners.

10. No Owner shall split or divide his or her interest in said property with any other persons for any reason except for a spouse. Should an Owner attempt to do so, such action will be interpreted as a desire to sell his or her interest in said property, and the rules of this Agreement regarding the sale of an interest shall apply.

11. In the event of the death of an Owner, the heir or devisee to his or her interest shall be bound by the terms of this Agreement and the remaining Owners shall have the right to purchase the decedent's interest in the property from his estate on the same terms as those for the Right of First Refusal.

12. This Agreement secures for each Owner the right, should he or she choose, to construct a habitation on said property. A majority approval is required with regard to the exercise of said right to the extent that the Owners may consider aesthetic, environmental, and other considerations relevant to the location and construction of said habitation.

13. Any physical alteration of said property must be approved by a majority of the Owners. "Physical alterations" shall include, among other things, the construction of any structures, such as houses, barns, garages, and greenhouses; roads, dams, wells, water tanks, and other forms of land development. The term "physical alterations" shall also include the cutting of any trees and vegetation and the clearing of any part of said property.

14. There must be approval by a majority of the Owners before any gas, water, or sewage pipes or electrical lines can be installed on said property from outside sources.

15. There shall be no use of pesticides, herbicides, or other poisons at any time or any place on said property without the approval of all the Owners.

16. The hunting and killing of wildlife shall be absolutely and strictly prohibited on said property at all times and during all seasons, except that killing of wildlife will be permitted for the protection of dwellings. The wildlife in the category of animals that threaten dwellings shall include mice, rats, and skunks. Under no circumstances shall bears, wildcats, deer, or birds be killed. The taking of any fish from the creeks on said property shall be in accordance with state and local regulations.

17.   The keeping of all domestic and farm animals shall be subject to approval by a majority of the Owners.

18.   There shall be no unnecessary discharge of firearms at any time or any place on said property. The term "unnecessary discharge" shall include the use of firearms for target or practice shooting.

19.   If, at any time, none of the Owners is willing or able to live on said property, then the Owners will allow one or more persons to act as caretakers of said property. The caretakers must be approved by a majority of said Owners. If any caretakers operate to the dissatisfaction of the majority of Owners, they shall be asked to leave. Under no circumstances may an Owner permit a nonowner to live on said property without the prior approval of all Owners living on said property.

20.   The entire property may be sold if approval for such sale is given by a majority of the Owners in writing. In the event the entire parcel of said property is sold, a majority of the owners shall agree on a selling price. The Owners may hire a licensed appraiser to determine the fair market value of said property and improvements. The fees and cost of said appraisal, and the fees and cost of any other expenses involved in the selling of said property, shall be borne by each Owner in proportion to his ownership interest in the property.

21.   In the event the entire parcel of said property is sold, the proceeds shall be divided equally among the Owners, with regard to the portion of the selling price attributed to the value placed on the land. In addition, each Owner shall be entitled to receive a separate share of the proceeds based on the value of each Owner's respective improvements, as determined by agreement between the Owners or by an appraisal of the respective improvements.

22.   In exercising the majority approval and vote rule of this Agreement, the Owners shall make all reasonable efforts to contact and consult with an absentee Owner and accord to him or her the right to exercise a vote whenever any matter subject to approval should arise. "Reasonable efforts" shall include express mail and telegrams, if necessary. Should the absentee Owner be unavailable after the expenditure of a reasonable amount of time and effort to locate him or her, then the remaining Owners shall proceed with the granting or denying of approval.

23.   Any Owners shall have the right to initiate legal action against any Owner who violates the terms of this Agreement.

24.   If any legal action arises due to a violation of the terms of this Agreement, the prevailing party shall be entitled to reasonable court costs and attorney fees.

25.   Any amendments or additions to this Agreement must be approved in writing by a majority of the Owners of said property.

26.   This Agreement is written and approved in the spirit of fairness to all the Owners in the hope that no Owner shall derive any benefit at the unfair expense of any other Owner.

27.   This Agreement is binding on the heirs and successors-in-interest of the parties hereto.

28.   A memorandum of this agreement stating that there is an agreement between the owners relating to their rights to sell or encumber their interest in the property shall be recorded in the county records.

_____
(Owner's signature)

_____
(Owner's signature)

_____
(Owner's signature)

MODEL MEMORANDUM OF AGREEMENT

When Recorded, Return To:

[name]
[street]
[city & state]

Memorandum of Agreement

_____ and _____

and _____, Owners of that real property, in the County of _____, State of _____, described in Exhibit A, (legal description of the property) attached hereto and made a part hereof, have executed an agreement among themselves which gives certain rights of first refusal and which contains other terms and conditions regarding the subject real property. A copy of the Owners' Agreement, dated _____ should be inspected to determine all the matters regarding the subject real property.

Dated:

_____

(signature)   Owner

_____   (NOTARY SEAL)

(signature)   Owner

_____

(signature)   Owner

CHAPTER 33

Deeds and Recording

The development of the deed as a method of transferring title is perhaps the most important element to evolve during the history of private land ownership. Not until 1676, when the Statute of Frauds was enacted in England, were written documents required and widely used as evidence of land ownership. Prior to that time, the transfer of land titles was mainly done orally and symbolically. A seller would simply hand the buyer a stick, an acorn, a rock, or a handful of dirt from his land and pronounce that he was passing title to the land. Many problems arose under this system, the most common of which was the lack of evidence of the conveyance. Nothing prevented the seller from re-

turning to his land and claiming he never sold it. Buyers, demanding greater protection, began to call on neighbors to witness land transactions. The seller, standing on his land, would make a public statement to the buyer and the witnesses, who stood a short distance off the land. After stating that he was selling his land to the buyer, the seller would walk off the land and the buyer would walk onto it. Thus many witnesses heard and saw the seller convey his land to the buyer. But witnesses eventually died or moved away, and a better system had to be found.

The first written documents showing land transfers eventually evolved into what we now call deeds. A deed is not the title to the land being conveyed. *Title* represents ownership. A *deed* is the instrument used to transfer the title or ownership of property from one person to another. A person holding a deed to a parcel of land holds the title as represented by the writing in the deed, which states that title was transferred by the former owner to the party now holding the deed.

A deed is not a contract between the buyer and seller and should never be used as one. The terms and conditions of the sale are stated in the formal contract of sale. (See chapter 28, "The Model Contract of Sale.") Do not confuse a deed, which transfers title, with a *deed of trust,* which is a means of financing a land purchase in some states. (See chapter 21, "Types of Financing: Land Contract, Mortgage, Deed of Trust.")

BASIC PROVISIONS OF ANY LEGAL DEED

Although various types of deeds are used to convey property, any deed must contain basic elements to be legally valid.

1. A deed must be in writing, and all of its terms must be contained within it. The seller, who must be legally and mentally competent, is responsible for having the deed drawn up and delivered to the buyer.

2. The date of the conveyance must be stated.

3. The name of each person who owns the land, including both spouses, must be given in full.

4. The names of all the buyers must be given in full and their marital status specified. Also the deed must state how title is to be taken, e.g., joint tenants, tenants in common, etc. (See chapter 32, "Types of Co-ownership.") If the buyers are dividing their interests in the property into unequal portions, the division should be specified; e.g., "to A, a single man, an undivided one-half (½) interest; to B, a single man, an undivided two-sixths (²⁄₆) interest; and to C, a single man, an undivided one-sixth (⅙) interest."

5. All owners, including both spouses, must sign the deed, as sellers, using the same names by which they took title to the property. If a seller was single at the time he bought the property but is now married, both spouses must sign the deed. Some states require witnesses to sign the deed also. The buyer does not usually sign the deed.

6. Words of conveyance must be used in a *granting clause* which states that the seller is conveying, or transferring, his title to the buyer. For example,

the seller does hereby "bargain and sell," "grant and convey," or "quit claim and release" his title.

7. Although most states do not require that the purchase price be given, the deed must state that something of value was given. The phrase "good and valuable consideration" or "for value received," is often used in place of an actual monetary figure.

8. The property being conveyed must be described in full, preferably including easements, water rights, and other property rights that the buyer is getting. The description should also include reservations, exceptions, and restrictive covenants in the title. For example, if mineral rights will not be included in the conveyance, the deed might state that they are excepted from the title and identify the person in whose name the rights are reserved. Since these are not always mentioned in the deed, it is essential to get a title report or abstract of title to determine the nature of the grants and reservations.

9. Depending on the type of deed, various warrants and covenants of title must be included, either specifically in the document or implied by law. These are described later in this chapter.

10. If the title is being conveyed "subject to" an existing encumbrance, such as a mortgage, deed of trust, tax, or other lien, the encumbrance might be stated and fully described in a "subject to" clause. This is not a legal requirement for a valid deed.

11. The deed must be authenticated by an "acknowledgment," whereby the seller declares before a public official, usually a notary public, that he is in fact the person who signs the deed, i.e., that it is not a forgery. The notary signs the deed and stamps it with his official notarization.

12. Real property transfer tax stamps must be placed on the deed or the amount of taxes must be written on the deed in states that levy such a tax. (See chapter 19, "Evaluating the Price of the Property.")

13. Before the transfer of title is valid, the deed must be delivered to the buyer. Acceptance of the delivery is considered complete when the deed is recorded in the county records, whereby notice is given to the world that the seller has transferred his title to the buyer.

14. Some states require the buyer to state his address on the deed to facilitate communication

with him for purposes of sending him property tax bills.

RESTRICTIVE COVENANTS IN A DEED

Restrictions are often placed in a deed to a piece of land that are binding on anybody who purchases the land thereafter. A restrictive covenant limits what you can do on the property. For example, a covenant might specify that the land can be used only for residential purposes, or only during certain times of the year. Only private dwellings or only one building per parcel might be permitted. A line might be established, called a building line restriction, beyond which no buildings can be constructed. These are not government restrictions, like zoning, building, and health codes. Restrictive covenants are established and enforced by private parties to a transaction, usually a subdivider or seller.

If any restrictions exist, they should be listed in the Model Contract of Sale in Clause 4. (See chapter 28.) The real estate agent should show you what restrictions exist, and you can also look them up in the seller's deed in the county records. Chapter 31, "The Title Search, Abstract of Title, and Title Insurance Policy," tells how to look up deeds.

Restrictive covenants might be written in a declaration of covenants, conditions, and restrictions, which is a form used when land is being subdivided and all the parcels are to be bound by the same restrictions. The declaration of restriction is filed with the subdivision public report and plat (see chapter 14, "Subdivisions and Condominiums") and may not appear in your deed. Instead the deed will refer to the location of the recorded restrictive covenants. For example, the deed might state "title is conveyed subject to the restrictions listed in the Declaration of Covenants, Conditions, and Restrictions recorded in the Office of the County Recorder, Case 5, Drawer 12, Page 68." You should locate and examine this document thoroughly to see what restrictions exist. It will also be referred to in your title report or abstract of title.

How will existing restrictions affect your intended use of the land? If a subdivision was formed with the same restriction included in each buyer's deed, any landowner in the subdivision can bring a legal action against any other owner who is violating the restrictions.

If the restriction will hinder your use, before you purchase the land ask the seller to either release the restriction himself or get it released by whoever initially placed it on the land. If that can't be done and you will be prevented from using the land as you wish, you had better look elsewhere.

A restriction might not be to your disadvantage. Particularly in a subdivision, you may want restrictions prohibiting commercial development or placing a minimum size on subdivided parcels. If another landowner in the subdivision violates a restriction, you can take legal action against him if the restriction has been established for the entire subdivision as shown in the plat and report. If the restriction is made only in each individual purchaser's deed or contract of sale, the seller alone can take action for violations.

WARRANTY DEED

In Clause 6 of the Model Contract of Sale (chapter 28) I specify that the seller shall convey title by a grant deed or warranty deed because these deeds offer the best protection to the buyer in the states that use this kind of deed. A variety of deeds are used throughout the United States. You might be told by the real estate agent or title company that local custom or law favors the use of a different kind of deed. If you find out that a deed other than a warranty or grant deed is customarily used in your state, ask what protections are included in your deed and fill out your contract of sale accordingly. Deeds are fairly uniform within each state. For example, California uses a grant deed, Wisconsin uses a warranty deed, and New Jersey uses a bargain and sale deed.

The advantage of the warranty deed (also called full covenant and warranty deed or general warranty deed) is that when the seller gives the title to the land, he includes five specific warranties, called covenants of title. These warranties must be written into the deed as: covenant of seisin, covenant against encumbrances, covenant of quiet enjoyment, covenant of further assurance, and covenant of warranty of title.

1. The *covenant of seisin* guarantees that the seller is *seised* of the full title to the land, which means he has possession of a *fee simple estate*. In this covenant the seller also warrants that he has a legal right to sell the land and that he has not previously sold it to any other person.

2. The *covenant against encumbrances* assures the buyer that the only encumbrances existing against the title are listed in the deed. Encumbrances include mortgages, deeds of trust, tax and assessment liens, judgment liens, restrictions, easements, rights of spouses, and all other liens. If you should find out later that a lien does exist against the property which is not included in the deed, the covenant is breached, and you can take legal action against the seller.

3. The *covenant of quiet enjoyment* assures the buyer that neither the seller nor any other person will have a better title to the land than the buyer himself and that his "quiet enjoyment" of the land will not be disturbed by the actions of anyone after he receives the deed to the property. If the buyer is forced to leave the property because of a court order, he can take legal action against the seller for breach of this covenant. Furthermore, if the buyer sells the property, his buyer will also be covered by this covenant.

4. The *covenant of further assurance* guarantees that the seller will do anything necessary to give the buyer the title promised in the deed. For example, if the seller is to pay off an existing mortgage before the deed is delivered and later it is discovered that a mistake was made and the mortgage was not legally paid, the seller must clear the defect on the title. Or if there is a mistake in the deed, the seller must rewrite the deed to correct the error. Regardless of when the mistake is discovered in the title, the seller must do whatever is necessary to put the title to the land in the condition in which he promised to deliver it to you.

5. The *covenant of warranty of title* guarantees the buyer good title and possession of the land forever. If a third party presents a rightful claim to the title of the land, the seller must defend the buyer's title. If the buyer loses his title, the seller must pay him damages for the loss.

These five warranties give basically the same protection as a standard owner's policy of title insurance. But title insurance places liability for a defective title on the title company, whereas a warranty deed makes the seller responsible to you. Thus you get double protection if you have both, and it is always desirable to get as much protection as possible. In an area where the title insurance is not available, a warranty deed is essential.

You will notice that Clause 15 in the Model Contract of Sale also includes the five covenants of title. A sixth provision states that the covenants survive delivery of the deed, thus protecting the buyer after he receives title to the land. (See chapter 28.) If the seller wants to delete the warranties from the contract, there might be some question in his mind regarding the state of the title, and if you detect this in his actions, you must proceed with extreme caution and determine the cause of his reluctance.

GRANT DEED

A few state legislatures have established a special warranty deed called a grant deed. The law states that a grant deed automatically includes certain warranties that do not have to be written into the document. You should find out from the title company or escrow holder what warranties are included in the deed by state law. Usually a grant deed includes only a few of the five warranties I have discussed above. For example, in California the grant deed signifies that the seller has not previously sold the property to anyone else and that a fee simple title is being conveyed, unless specified otherwise. Illustration 99 shows a typical form of grant deed.

BARGAIN AND SALE DEED

Most bargain and sale deeds make two warranties. First, the seller warrants that he owns the land he is conveying. The second guarantee is "that the seller has not done or suffered anything whereby the said premises have been encumbered in any way." Under the warranty, called a covenant against grantor's acts, the seller is liable only if he has caused a defect to be placed on the title, whereas

RECORDING REQUESTED BY

LES SCHER, ESQ.

AND WHEN RECORDED MAIL TO

NAME

ADDRESS

CITY &
STATE

Title Order No._____Escrow No._____

MAIL TAX STATEMENTS TO

NAME

ADDRESS BUYER'S NAME & ADDRESS

CITY &
STATE

SPACE ABOVE THIS LINE FOR RECORDER'S USE

Documentary transfer tax $........................
☒ Computed on full value of property conveyed, or
☐ Computed on full value less liens and encumbrances
remaining thereon at time of sale.

....
Signature of declarant or agent determining tax — firm name

Individual Grant Deed

FOR VALUE RECEIVED,   [SELLERS]

GRANT_S_to   [BUYERS]

all that real property situate in the

County of   State of California, described as follows:

[Legal description of property being sold.]

_____   _____
                                     [SELLER'S SIGNATURE]
_____

STATE OF CALIFORNIA

_____ County of _____ } ss.

On _____, 19___, before me, the undersigned, a Notary Public
in and for said State, personally appeared _____

_____, personally known to me or proved to me
on the basis of satisfactory evidence to be the person_ whose name ____ _____
subscribed to the within instrument, and acknowledged to me that _ he _ executed it.

_____
            NOTARY PUBLIC

FOR NOTARY SEAL OR STAMP

MAIL TAX STATEMENTS AS DIRECTED ABOVE

in a warranty deed the seller is also liable if any other person, including his seller, has placed an encumbrance on the title to the land.

For example, if your seller intends to use a bargain and sale deed and he has given a mortgage on the property, he must pay off that mortgage before conveying title to you. However, if your seller's seller had mortgaged the property during his ownership, your seller would not be liable under a bargain and sale deed for giving you the title subject to the mortgage, whereas under a warranty deed he would. This type of deed is also called a bargain and sale deed with covenant against grantor's acts; a grant, bargain, and sale deed with covenant against grantor's acts; or, because the protection is less than a warranty deed, a special warranty deed or limited warranty deed.

There can also be a bargain and sale deed without covenant against grantor's acts. The only warranty in this deed is that the seller owns the land he is conveying. No guarantees are made against liens and encumbrances on the title.

THE QUITCLAIM DEED

In the quitclaim deed, the seller makes no warranties or guarantees about anything. Whenever you see the word *quitclaim* in a deed, such as "the seller does hereby quitclaim and release," or "remise, release, and forever quitclaim," that deed transfers to the buyer only whatever interest the seller has in the land. If he has full title, the buyer will get full title. If the seller has nothing, the buyer will get nothing. When you are buying land never, under any circumstances, accept a quitclaim deed. Somebody could legally sell you the Grand Canyon with such a deed. Regardless of what the title search shows and despite the fact that the seller is willing to give you a policy of title insurance, don't buy land under a quitclaim deed. Quitclaim deeds are usually used for transfers between spouses or partners.

PATENTS

When the federal or a state government transfers or sells land it owns, a patent rather than a deed is used. A patent serves the same function as a deed and also gives notice that the land was formerly owned by the government. Almost every parcel of land in the United States has a patent in its chain of title since most land was originally owned by the government. If you buy land that has oil, mineral, timber, or other rights reserved by the government, your deed will generally state that those rights are reserved in a patent recorded in the county recorder's office. Ask the county recorder how to look up this patent so you can read it.

RECORDING YOUR DEED AND OTHER DOCUMENTS

The deed to your land must be recorded as soon as you receive title to the property. Only recording it protects you against the possibility that the seller will convey the title to another person after selling it to you. For instance, suppose escrow closes and you receive a warranty deed to the land on May 1, and you do not record it. On May 2 the seller sells the same land to another person and gives him a warranty deed. The second buyer knows nothing about the sale to you the day before, and since you are not living on the property, he cannot tell by inspecting it that the land has already been sold to you. On the same day, May 2, he records his deed with the county recorder. On May 3, you record your deed. Under every law regarding title to land, you will not have legal title to the property because you did not have your deed recorded first. If you and the second buyer were to go to court, the judge would undoubtedly declare that the other purchaser holds the only legal title to the land. The first person to record a deed to a parcel of land is the owner. Once a deed is recorded, the law declares that everybody in the world has full knowledge, or has *constructive knowledge,* of the deed. Thus, if you have recorded your deed first, the second buyer could not claim that he did not know the land had already been sold, since the deed would be part of the public record. The recording system was established to show the chronological sequence of the land transfers and other actions affecting the title to the land.

If your name is not on a recorded deed and the

seller dies, or is sued and has a judgment against him, this will impair your ability to get clear title to the property.

When you are receiving a deed to property, all the owners must sign it, including both husband and wife.

A deed is recorded in the recorder's office of the county where the land is located. The county recorder will either photograph, photocopy, microfilm, or microfiche the deed, and the original will be returned to you. The copy is filed with the other documents and indexed in the grantor-grantee index or the tract index. (These indexes are discussed in detail in chapter 31, "The Title Search, Abstract of Title, and Title Insurance Policy.") A recording fee, which is usually $10 or less, will always be charged, usually to the buyer.

The escrow holder usually records the deed as a routine part of escrow. Be sure your escrow holder is to do this and that your policy of title insurance goes into effect at exactly the same time. The burden of making sure the deed is recorded is on the buyer. If, for any reason, the deed is returned to you before it is recorded, you must take it to the county recorder and have it recorded immediately. Generally, the title insurance company will also be watching to be sure the deed is recorded since the policy of title insurance insures the title up until the moment the deed is recorded. They usually walk the deed over to the recorder's office and personally record it.

Most deeds contain a space in which the buyer is to write an address where all the tax statements and other official notices are to be sent. Be sure to give a current address where you are certain to receive your mail, and keep the county informed of any changes. Nonreceipt of mail is not a good defense for failure to pay property taxes.

Any other document affecting title to land is also recorded and open to public inspection in the county recorder's office. Some of these documents include mortgages; deeds of trust; release deeds; satisfactions of mortgages or deeds of trust; deeds of reconveyance; assignments of mortgages or deeds of trust; easement grants; and covenants, conditions, and restrictions.

A FINAL NOTE AND WARNING

I have included a copy of one type of deed in this chapter. You can see copies of the types of deeds used in your state by looking through any of the record books in your local county recorder's office. I cannot encourage you strongly enough to become familiar with these records. Look up the seller's deed to the land you are planning to buy. (I tell you how to do this in chapter 31, "The Title Search, Abstract of Title, and Title Insurance Policy.") What kind of deed did he receive, and what is included in it?

You must specify in your contract of sale the type of deed you want the seller to give you. Your escrow instructions should also specify the same type of deed. I recommend that you state you want a warranty deed, or grant deed, or bargain and sale deed, depending on the laws in your state. You can find out what is customary in your state from a real estate attorney, title or escrow company, or bank or other financial institution. If the seller tells you he cannot give you such a deed, find out why. What is he afraid of? Does he doubt that he has full and clear title to the land, or does he have good title but simply wants to avoid liability by giving you a policy of title insurance that places liability on the title company? If you do not specify what type of deed you are to receive, the seller might deliver you a quitclaim deed. Maybe he'll sell you part of the Grand Canyon while he's at it.

VIII

ALASKA, HAWAII, AND CANADA

CHAPTER 34

Alaska

FEDERAL LANDS

Alaska was the last state that allowed homesteading of federal lands. Unfortunately, on October 21, 1986, the settlement laws were repealed, bringing an end to homesteading on federal lands in Alaska. However, there is a program still operating that allows hardy settlers to obtain five-acre homesites on federal lands in very remote areas of the state. Details can be obtained from any BLM office below:

Bureau of Land Management
Department of Interior
Washington, DC 20240

Manager, Land Office
344 6th Ave.
Anchorage, AK 99501

Anchorage Land Office
555 Cordova St.
Anchorage, AK 99051

Manager, Land Office
2nd Ave.
Fairbanks, AK 99701

Manager, Land Office
Box 1481
Juneau, AK 99801

STATE LANDS

The Alaska Department of Natural Resources offers state land for private ownership at least once a year through some or all of the following programs:

1. *Subdivision and agricultural parcels.* Surveyed parcels awarded by lottery and purchased at fair market appraised value.
2. *Homesite parcels.* Surveyed subdivision lots awarded by lottery. Title is acquired either by proving-up or paying fair market appraised value.
3. *Homesteads.* Large, remote parcels, usually unsurveyed. Homesteaders have the option of proving-up or paying fair market value.
4. *Agricultural development projects* award agricultural interests only, and are based on fair market value.
5. *Over-the-counter parcels.* Subdivision lots, agricultural parcels, homesites, and homesteads that were not taken in a lottery or auction. They are available on a first-come, first-served basis under the same terms and conditions as the original program at each of the department's regional offices.
6. *Auctions.* May be held several times a year. Contact any of the regional offices of the Alaska Department of Natural Resources listed below for information about upcoming auctions.

On July 1, 1985, Alaska repealed the old remote parcel program and created a new homesteading program. Homesites of 5 acres or less may be acquired by building a permanent dwelling within 5 years and living on the land for 35 months. Homesteads of up to 40 acres of nonagricultural land or up to 160 acres of agricultural land may be acquired by building a permanent dwelling within 3 years and living on the site for 25 months within 5 years.

The annual sale brochure, *Land for Alaskans,* gives information on program requirements, procedures, conditions, parcel locations, access, and prices. Copies can be picked up at no charge at region and area offices listed below and at numerous other distribution points throughout the state during the application period. The brochure is usually available by June of each year.

You may receive a copy by mail if you send a request and $3.00 for postage and handling to *Land for Alaskans,* at any regional office listed below.

Auctions and lotteries not held on a regular basis will be advertised in newspapers throughout the state.

Additional information is available at regional offices' information counters. You can also write to any regional office listed below for the free brochure:

Fact Sheet, State Land Offerings

The offices of the Alaska Department of Natural Resources are:

Office of the Commissioner
Alaska Department of Natural Resources
P.O. Box 7005
Anchorage, AK 99510

Southcentral Regional Office
Frontier Bldg., 10th Fl.
3601 C St.
P.O. Box 7005
Anchorage, AK 99510-7005

Mat-Su Area Office
Century Plaza, Ste. 202
Mile 5, Knik Rd.
P.O. Box 874008
Wasilla, AK 99687

Northern Regional Office
4420 Airport Wy.
Fairbanks, AK 99701

Southeastern Regional Office
400 Willoughby St., Ste. 400
Juneau, AK 99801

For information on climate, farming conditions, and markets for produce, and many other available publications, write to:

Publications
Agricultural Experiment Station
University of Alaska
309 O'Neal Resources Bldg.
905 Koyukuk Ave., N.
Fairbanks, AK 99701

State of Alaska
Department of Natural Resources
P.O. Box 949
Palmer, AK 99645-0949

Agricultural and Forestry Experiment
  Station
University of Alaska, Fairbanks
Fairbanks, AK 99775-0080

U.S. Department of Agriculture
P.O. Box AE
Palmer, AK 99645

For maps, write to:
  Alaska Distribution Section
  U.S. Geological Survey
  New Federal Bldg., Box 12
  101 Twelfth Ave.
  Fairbanks, AK 99701

CHAPTER 35

Hawaii

I recommend retaining an attorney to help you purchase any Hawaiian real estate. Because of the unique nature of real property in the Hawaiian Islands, the rules of investment and property purchase are unique. For some reason, many mainlanders seem willing to buy Hawaiian property sight unseen. This is a tremendous risk. I recently had to help a couple attempt to get their money back on a parcel they bought sight unseen that was on a lava bed, totally unbuildable and within a dangerous area of volcanic activity. It seems Hawaii still has a way to go in enforcing laws for the protection of the real estate consumer.

On the other hand, many mainlanders have purchased parcels and been very happy. A major dis-

appointment for those returnees with whom I have spoken is not their land, but a general dissatisfaction with life on an island, regardless of the weather, beauty, and relaxed life-style.

Naturally, you should spend a couple of vacations there before deciding to invest your money. But Hawaii may not remain as exotic as it presently seems to be. Between 1980 and 1985, there was a net immigration (excepting military personnel and their dependents) of 39,000, accounting for 44 percent of the total civilian population growth during that time. The resident population is expected to reach 1,138,400 in 1990; 1,211,500 in 1995; 1,267,800 in the year 2000; and 1,310,000 in 2005. The population is young—the median age in 1980 was 28.3 years. Native Hawaiians are slowly becoming a minority. In 1983 the Caucasians were 24.5 percent, while Hawaiians and part-Hawaiians were only 20.0 percent.

It is becoming increasingly more expensive to

live in Hawaii. In 1981, an intermediate budget for a four-person family living on Oahu was $31,893, 26 percent higher than the corresponding U.S. average. The consumer index tripled from 1967 to 1985.

Nevertheless, growth continues as owner-occupied homes increased from 116,000 in 1975 to 150,000 in 1985. The average selling price of single family homes on Oahu during 1984 was $187,000, while the more rural areas on Kauai had homes with an average price of $89,700, and homes on the island of Hawaii went for an average of $71,200.

Homes in Hawaii are generally smaller than mainland homes and designed for a different style of living. The homes usually have outdoor lanais (patios) and smaller bedrooms. There is frequently no heating or cooling because it is unnecessary. Home lots are often very small, even in the rural areas, because of the high value of property.

Condominiums and time-share units are very popular in Hawaii because of the high cost of home construction. I always prefer a private home to a condo, but for the person who only wants a place to stay a short time out of the year, a condo may be desired. Each owner owns his apartment individually and has a share of common facilities. All apartment owners have a vote on the board of directors regarding maintenance standards and fees to be collected for operation of the condominium.

Time-share or interval ownership is one step away from full condominium ownership. Time-share divides usage of a condominium unit into equal portions of time, usually several weeks each year. The owners who share the unit divide the cost of time usage and upkeep equally according to the amount of time they use the unit. For example, twelve families might each "own" one month of time in a condo unit and pay one-twelfth of the maintenance costs.

At this time, I cannot recommend purchase of time plans. It seems as though they would be very difficult to manage, expensive to maintain, and not worth the hassle in the end. Those persons who purchase a condominium and have a manager rent it out to tenants when the owners are not using it appear to make a better investment. They maintain total control over their unit and have a salable commodity, at least in Hawaii. Just be careful when investing there.

When you visit Hawaii you will be bombarded with real estate advertisements, especially in the newspapers. Even if you don't buy a place there, it's a great place for a vacation. I should know, I was born there.

Take your time, do your research, and don't drink any mai tais before signing a contract.

For more free information on the various islands, write to the following:

Department of Planning and Economic
  Development
State of Hawaii
P.O. Box 2359
Honolulu, HI 96804

*Facts and Figures on Hawaii County (The
  Island of Hawaii)*
*Maui County (The Islands of Maui,
  Molokai, Lanai, and Kahoolawe)*
*Kauai County (The Islands of Kauai and
  Niihau)*
*City and County of Honolulu (Island of
  Oahu)*
The State of Hawaii.

Small Business Information Service
Starting a Business in Hawaii
Have Some Energy on the House—Solar
The Population of Hawaii, 1970–1984
  SR173
Hawaii's Immigrants, 1984 SR174
County Trends in Hawaii, 1975–1985
  SR181
Statistics by Islands, 1984 SR183
*Estimated Population of Hawaii by District,
  1984 CTC64*
*Department of Planning and Economic
  Development Newsletter (General
  Information and Annual Report)*

The above agency also publishes a detailed statistical report annually called *The State of Hawaii Data Book.* It is available for $5.00 in the islands or $15.00 elsewhere. It contains more than 680 statistical tables on Hawaii's population, economy, environment, etc.

Specific information on the individual islands can be obtained as follows:

HAWAII COUNTY (Covers: island of Hawaii)

Department of Research and Development
County of Hawaii
34 Rainbow Dr.
Hilo, HI 96720

MAUI COUNTY (Covers: islands of Maui, Molokai, Lanai, Kahoolawe)

Department of Economic Development
County of Maui
County Bldg.
Wailuku, HI 96793

KAUAI COUNTY (Covers: islands of Kauai and Nihau)

Department of Economic Development
County of Kauai
4191 Hardy St.
Lihue, Kauai, HI 96766

HONOLULU COUNTY (Covers: island of Oahu)

Department of Planning and Economic
Development
P.O. Box 2359
Honolulu, HI 96804

CHAPTER 36

Canada

There has often been, on the part of Canadians, a desire to own a piece of land. . . . Land, air and space were perceived as free or public goods. Today, increased land costs are a major component of high house prices, but the desire for land and space, engendered generations ago, is still with Canadians.

—Canada's Special Resource Lands

Canada has the third largest land mass of any country in the world, with an area of over 4 million square miles. The population is now over 26 million with over 80 percent inhabiting areas within a hundred miles of its three-thousand-mile border with the United States. This is mainly because of the Canadian climate, but also because of trade and transportation access. Only about 10 percent of the land is viable farmland, with the balance being forest and tundra with rich mineral deposits. The country is divided into ten provinces and two territories, each with its own legislative body that can enact laws on landownership. Because of the complexities of land purchase, it is essential to retain an attorney to help you in any land purchase in Canada.

GENERAL INFORMATION

Canada is commonly seen as being divided into six geographical regions, as shown in illustration 100, page 460.

1. The Atlantic Provinces
The maritime provinces and the island of New-

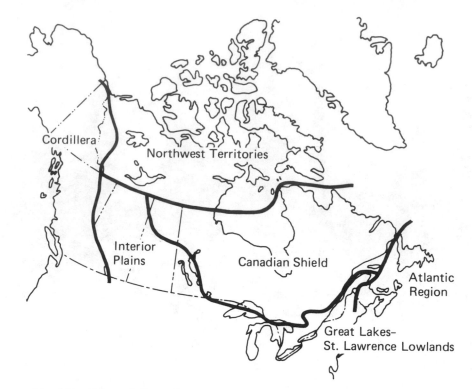

Cordillera

Northwest Territories

Interior
Plains

Canadian Shield

Atlantic
Region

Great Lakes–
St. Lawrence Lowlands

100. Geographical Regions of Canada

foundland. These provinces are known to have lower income and a less expanding economy. This is a very rural area with few places with high concentrations of people, characterized by low hills and mountains, and rugged, indented coasts.

2. The Great Lakes–St. Lawrence Lowlands
A high intensity agricultural and urban area, with the highest density of industry, commerce, and population in Canada. The lowlands area here holds more than half of Canada's population. This includes an area of French-speaking Canadians with a rural landscape of long, narrow farms and rural villages.

3. The Canadian Shield
Occupies half of the mainland of Canada and contains few people. It is a region of forests, lakes, and rocks where people come mostly for recreation or holidays.

4. The Interior Plains
The largest area of nearly level land in Canada and filled with large grain farms. A main characteristic is the geometric spacing of its villages, towns, and

cities, which service the needs of the surrounding farms. This means that every six miles along the main road and railway line is a depot for grain storage, etc., providing equal access for all farms. Larger depots have a number of grain pool bins.

5. The Cordillera
The mountainous region, with most of the population concentrated into the southwestern corner of British Columbia. Many variations can be found here in its topography. The east side of British Columbia has the Rocky Mountains, which are solid rock, not treed, and have many glaciers. The coastal mountains in the West are well treed with the famous British Columbia spruce and fir. The central Okanagan area is desertlike and famous for its fruit and wine grape growing areas. Summer temperatures here reach up to 110° F.

6. The Northwest Territories
Characterized by their diversity of natural environment, lack of developed resources, scanty population, and different government. This is the wild, unspoiled area of Canada where hunting is still practiced as a means of earning a livelihood.

460

POPULATION AND IMMIGRATION

For many years the country's center of population has been moving slowly westward; central Canada, especially Ontario, is growing faster than the eastern part of the country but less vigorously than the western region. British Columbia and Alberta in particular have experienced rapid population growth in the past two decades. Most of this expansion has been due to interprovincial migration; all provinces east of Alberta suffered net migration losses between 1971 and 1981, with Ontario being the only exception between 1961 and 1971. British Columbia continues to draw from other provinces, while Quebec loses in population exchanges.

The population of Canada has more than doubled since World War II. Its rate of growth has not been steady, however, gradually subsiding from the high levels of the late 1940s and the 1950s to a very low ebb in recent years.

Historically, immigration has been a key factor in the growth of Canada's population. In the 1981 census, one of every six people reported having been born outside Canada. As a result of the economic slump that recently affected the entire western world, the Canadian government cut immigration levels to less than 100,000 in 1983 and 1984.

Traditionally, the majority of immigrants came from Europe, especially England. In the past ten years, however, there has been much greater diversity in the countries of origin of those who come to settle in Canada. In particular, there has been a sharp increase in the number of Asian immigrants.

Of course, Canada continues to be a popular place for Americans to live, either permanently or seasonally. Many Americans maintain vacation homes in Canada, and that is becoming an increasingly popular idea because land prices are so much lower in Canada than in the United States.

Canada is primarily an urban country, with over 75 percent of the population in urban areas. The most urbanized provinces are Ontario, Quebec, British Columbia, and Alberta. At the other end, Prince Edward Island has a majority of its population in rural areas.

According to Canadian real estate investors, the most popular areas for Americans buying Canadian rural property are in British Columbia, Ontario, and the maritime provinces of Nova Scotia and New Brunswick.

Year	Urban population	Percentage of total population		Rural population
1976	17,366,965	75.5	24.5	5,625,635
1971	16,410,785	76.1	23.9	5,157,525
1966	14,726,759	73.6	26.4	5,288,121
1961	12,700,390	69.6	30.4	5,537,857
1956	10,714,855	66.6	33.4	5,365,936
1951	8,628,253	61.6	38.4	5,381,176
1941	6,252,416	54.3	45.7	5,254,239
1931	5,572,058	53.7	46.3	4,804,728
1921	4,352,122	49.5	50.5	4,435,827
1911	3,272,947	45.5	54.5	3,933,696
1901	2,014,222	37.6	62.4	3,357,093
1891	1,537,098	31.8	68.2	3,296,141
1881	1,109,507	25.7	74.3	3,215,303
1871	722,343	19.6	80.4	2,966,914

Sources: Dominion Bureau of Statistics, 1963b. Population: Rural and Urban Distribution. Catalogue 92-536.
Urquhart and Buckley, 1965. Historical Statistics of Canada.

101. Canada's Urban and Rural Population, 1871–1976

Province	Population 1966	Population 1971	Population 1976	Population growth 1966 to 1971	Population growth 1971 to 19
				(per cent)	
Newfoundland	493,396	522,104	557,725	5.81	6.82
Prince Edward Island	108,535	111,641	118,229	2.86	5.90
Nova Scotia	756,039	788,960	828,571	4.35	5.02
New Brunswick	616,788	634,557	677,250	2.88	6.73
Québec	5,780,845	6,027,764	6,234,445	4.27	3.43
Ontario	6,960,870	7,703,106	8,264,465	10.66	7.29
Manitoba	963,066	988,247	1,021,506	2.61	3.37
Saskatchewan	955,344	926,242	921,323	− 3.05	− 0.53
Alberta	1,463,203	1,627,874	1,838,037	11.25	12.91
British Columbia	1,873,674	2,184,621	2,466,608	16.60	12.90
Yukon and Northwest Territories	43,120	53,195	64,445	23.37	21.15
CANADA	20,014,880	21,568,311	22,992,604	7.76	6.60

Sources: Statistics Canada, 1972. Advance Bulletin: Population of Census Divisions.
Catalogue 92-753.
_____, 1977a. Population: Geographic Distributions: Federal Electoral
Districts. Catalogue 92-801.

102. Population Growth, by Province, 1966–1971 and 1971–1976

The population distribution of Canada, 1951-85

Province or territory	1951 %	1966 %	1981 %	Estimated population on June 1, 1985 '000
Newfoundland	2.6	2.5	2.3	580.4
Prince Edward Island	0.7	0.5	0.5	127.1
Nova Scotia	4.6	3.8	3.5	880.7
New Brunswick	3.7	3.1	2.9	719.2
Quebec	28.9	28.9	26.4	6,580.7
Ontario	32.8	34.8	35.4	9,066.2
Manitoba	5.5	4.8	4.2	1,069.6
Saskatchewan	5.9	4.8	4.0	1,019.5
Alberta	6.7	7.3	9.2	2,348.8
British Columbia	8.3	9.4	11.3	2,892.5
Yukon	0.1	0.1	0.1	22.8
Northwest Territories	0.1	0.1	0.2	50.9
Canada	100.0	100.0	100.0	25,358.5

103. Population Distribution of Canada, 1951–1985

Province or territory	Number employed	Average weekly earnings
	'000	$
Newfoundland	124.4	389.24
Prince Edward Island	29.6	324.55
Nova Scotia	249.2	360.22
New Brunswick	185.2	374.12
Quebec	2,149.6	397.48
Ontario	3,541.6	404.57
Manitoba	347.0	378.79
Saskatchewan	267.7	387.68
Alberta	813.1	439.27
British Columbia	920.2	429.41
Yukon	8.3	483.38
Northwest Territories	17.6	564.14
Canada	8,653.6	405.13

104. Employment and Average Weekly Earnings, 1984

TAX SALES

There are some municipal tax sales held in towns and cities across the country, but in general the famous rural tax sales have been discontinued. This is because of a number of factors, but mainly the realization of governments that they have to acquire large tracts of land for their own use as provincial parks, game refuges, and open space. Other reasons include the many legal challenges to tax sales because of incorrect data and imperfect titles. There were also cases of manipulation by local officials as well as sales of properties that did not exist or, in some cases, were under water!

One notable exception is the province of Ontario which, under 1984 legislation, requires tax authorities to offer for sale by tender all properties taken for nonpayment of taxes that are not required for official use. These properties are listed throughout the year in the *Ontario Government's Gazette*, obtainable from the Queen's Printer, Parliament Buildings, Toronto, Ontario, Canada. The gazettes are published weekly, and listings are sporadic and located all over this large province, so that an annual subscription is really required if one is interested in a specific area.

CANADIAN PROPERTY TAX FEATURES

It is a common misconception that if one is paying taxes on a property in Canada, the land belongs to him. These people will base their stand on the fact that they receive a bill which has their name on it each year from the local tax office.

What they do not understand is that the Registry of Deeds Office has nothing to do with the tax office. The tax office will gladly deal with anyone who is willing to pay the taxes, since their main objective is to collect as much tax as they can for the municipality, and they do not concern themselves with ownership. Many persons pay taxes on a parcel of land without going through the formalities of deed registration and never become the legal owners.

In most provinces, you will receive one tax bill a year covering all charges on the property, but there are exceptions. In some northern Ontario areas, there are three taxing authorities, and therefore three bills each year. These are for land tax, which is collected by the Ontario Provincial Government; Statute Labour Tax, which is usually collected by the local Roads Board of the township where the land is located (this is really a road maintenance tax); and school board tax, which is collected by the local district school board.

There may be other taxes imposed by these authorities, such as a wolf bounty tax (to keep the local wolf population under control, mainly for the sheep farmers) and a fence tax (to keep the neighboring farmer's cattle on his property). Also, if title to the property includes mining rights as a separate parcel, there will also be a tax bill for these.

If any of these taxes are outstanding for the pre-

105. Percentage of Households Owning Vacation Homes

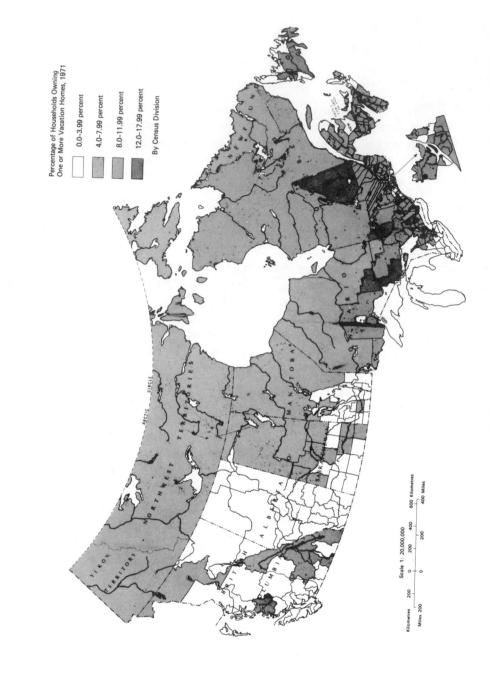

Percentage of Households Owning
One or More Vacation Homes, 1971

0.0–3.99 percent

4.0–7.99 percent

8.0–11.99 percent

12.0–17.99 percent

By Census Division

Scale 1: 20,000,000

scribed legal period, the taxing authority can take over the property and sell it to the highest bidder if it is not required for their own use.

In the province of Nova Scotia, they recently enacted a change-of-use tax. This was based on the classification (forest, resources, farming, etc.) into which the county assessors had categorized each and every property. When a property changes hands, they may deem a ''change of use'' has occurred and impose a one-time tax of 20 percent of the assessed value. Therefore, one has to be careful what the category of the property is before buying, since the purchaser is responsible for the additional cost.

RULES REGARDING LAND PURCHASED BY NONRESIDENT

The following are the main restrictions imposed by provincial authorities on land transfers to nonresidents and non-Canadians. Non-Canadians means non-Canadian citizens. Nonresidents means persons who do not legally reside in the providence, whether or not they are Canadian citizens.

Alberta	Nonresidents cannot purchase more than twenty acres of land without provincial approval.
British Columbia	None, but province records citizenship data.
Manitoba	Nonresidents cannot purchase more than four acres of land without provincial approval.
New Brunswick	None at present, but ownership statistics are recorded.
Newfoundland	None at present.
Nova Scotia	None at present, but ownership statistics are recorded.
Ontario	Non-Canadians must pay a provincial one-time tax of 20 percent of the value of the property at the time of deed registration, which occurs after the property is fully paid for.
Prince Edward Island	Non-islanders cannot purchase more than ten acres or three hundred and thirty feet of water frontage without the approval of the Legislative Assembly of Prince Edward Island.
Quebec	Non-Canadians are subject to a provincial one-time tax of 33 percent of the value of the property at the time of deed registration.
Saskatchewan	Nonresidents cannot purchase more than ten acres of land without provincial approval.

WITHOUT QUESTION EVERY BUYER OF CANADIAN LAND MUST USE A LAWYER

Because of the complex manner in which Canada has developed, systems of real estate practice differ widely from province to province. In Quebec, local buyers don't ever use a lawyer; they use a notary. A *notary* is similar to a lawyer, but is used especially for real estate deals. It is not similar to what is known as a notary in the United States.

In Canada, the lawyers prepare the abstract of title or the lawyer's opinion regarding the condition of title to a piece of property. This is the equivalent of the American title search or abstract of title. Illustration 106, pages 466–67, is a sample portion of an abstract of title typical for lands in Nova Scotia and other provinces using abstracts. Illustration 107, pages 467–68, is a sample of a lawyer's opinion letter regarding the condition of title of an Ontario parcel of land.

Usually a deed is transferred from the seller to the buyer, and then a certificate of indefeasible title is issued by the land title office or land registry. Illustration 108, pages 469–70, is a sample deed called a *transfer of an estate in fee simple*, illustration 109, pages 470–71, is a sample of a *certificate of indefeasible title*, and illustration 110, page 472, is a sample of a *warranty deed*.

Different recording systems are used in some provinces. For example, in Ontario the rural northern tracts are under the Land Titles Act and the

ABSTRACT OF TITLE TO LANDS OF EDWARD
BENOIT'S ISLAND, TRACADIE,
ANTIGONISH COUNTY, NOVA SCOTIA

Searched For: Purchaser
Searched By: Attorney

Searched:
File:

1. DEED   Francis L. Jones & wife,
    58/16   Jennifer
    June 2, 1900   - to -
    July 4, 1900   Sarah J. Landon
    $375.00

Conveys, inter alia, lands under search. Refers to Book 27, Page 192.

2. WILL   Will of Sarah Jean Wilcox
    81/728
    Sept. 2, 1929
    Jan. 7, 1930

Leaves everything to her husband, Samuel Wilcox.
NOTE: It would appear that Sarah J. Landon became Sarah J. Wilcox.

3. DEED   Samuel Wilcox & wife, Georgina
    91/25   - to -
    April 19, 1948   Edward Johnson and Weldon Berman
    May 17, 1948
    $1.00

2nd lot describes lands under search. Refers to Book 58, Page 16 and Will in 81/728.

4. QUIT CLAIM DEED   Weldon Berman & wife, Myrtle
    95/31   - to -
    July 8, 1953   Edward Johnson
    July 22, 1953
    $1.00

Second lot appears to describe lands under search.

5. PETITION FOR ADMINISTRATION   Est. of Edward Johnson
    100/300   - to -
    July 12, 1962   Mildred Johnson
    July 16, 1962

106. Sample of a Partial Abstract of Title

Recites that Edward Johnson died intestate on June 26, 1962, leaving his widow, Mildred Johnson, and three children: William, Claire, and Richard, surviving.

6. DEED 104/219 May 16, 1968 June 6, 1986 $1.00	William Johnson, one of the heirs of Edward Johnson - to - Mildred Johnson

Lot #2 describes lands under search.

7. ORDER OF SALE 104/220 June 5, 1968 June 6, 1968	In the matter of the interest of Claire Johnson and Richard Johnson, infants

Authorizes the sale of the interests of Claire and Richard Johnson in lands, including lands under search to Mildred Johnson, for the sum of $8,371.50. Appoints Mildred Johnson as next friend of infants. Lot 2 describes lands under search.

BARRISTER, SOLICITOR

Re: H. M. _____ purchase from
The Royal Bank of Canada - Lot 1,
Township of Harvey, County of Peterborough

I would advise that the above transaction was completed in accordance with the provisions of the Agreement of Purchase and Sale, the Statement of Adjustments, and your instructions on October 22, 1986, at which time a conveyance under Power of Sale by The Royal Bank of Canada pursuant to the provisions of its First Mortgage on the subject lands, as Transferor in favour of H. M. _____ as Transferee with respect to Lot 1, _____ for the Township of Harvey, was registered as Instrument Number _____ for the Registry Division of Peterborough on the 22nd day of October, 1986.

In my opinion, you have a good and marketable title in fee simple to the lands set out therein without encumbrance and without execution and subject only to the reservations as set out in the original conveyance from the Subdivider, Sumcot Development Corporation Limited, as contained in its conveyance being Instrument Number _____, a copy of which is enclosed herewith and which was discussed with you by telephone and in particular the reservation of mines and minerals as a Vendor's Lien for unpaid purchase money in favour of Sumcot Development Corporation Limited. This conveyance was in favour of _____ and _____ at which time a Mortgage back from Messrs. _____ and _____ was given in favour of Sumcot Development Corporation Limited as Instrument Number _____ and which was later Discharged by Instrument Number _____.

I am enclosing herewith a copy of that portion of the Plan pertaining to the subject lands together with the duplicate registered conveyance.

107. Sample of a Lawyer's Opinion Letter

The Power of Sale documents were deposited on title at the time of closing as Instrument Number _____, and I am enclosing the duplicate copy herewith, for your records.

A search of executions initially carried out at the time of the completion of the search of title on _____ indicated no executions outstanding against the previous owners as evidenced by the enclosed Certificate of the Sheriff of the County of _____ being Certificate Number _____ which was updated at the time of closing with a search of executions against the Transferor, _____, on the _____ day of _____ which indicated no executions outstanding as evidenced by the enclosed Certificate of the Sheriff of the County of _____ being Certificate Number _____.

I would advise that we carried out a search of work orders and zoning and find no outstanding work orders issued against the property and that the property is zoned Recreational Residential as evidenced by the enclosed Report of the Clerk of the Municipality dated _____.

Pursuant to the provisions of the Agreement of Purchase, we have determined the arrears of taxes for the years _____, _____, and _____ totalling _____ and have paid same from the proceeds received on closing and I am enclosing a copy of my letter to the Municipality paying the aforementioned tax arrears and further advising them of the change of ownership. I would advise that the final installment of _____ taxes is due _____ in the sum of _____, which said installment has been paid to the Municipality together with the arrears of taxes as reflected in my letter to the Municipality dated the _____ day of _____.

I would like to take this opportunity to thank you for permitting me to act on your behalf in this matter and I hope that everything has been handled to your satisfaction.

Yours very truly,

[Sample Letter]

LAND TITLE ACT
(Section 307)

STATE OF TITLE CERTIFICATE

Land Title Office, Nelson   , British Columbia

This is to certify that, at 10 a.m./3 p.m. on ...., 19............, the state of the title to the land described on the copy certificate of title commencing overleaf, is as on the copy stated, and is subject to the NOTATIONS appearing below. The copy certificate of title comprises __1__ pages including the page overleaf.

.... *Ce M Marion*
Registrar DS

NOTATIONS

Pending applications received:

No. ...., see copy annexed hereto.

This certificate is to be read subject to the provisions of section 23 (1) of the *LAND TITLE ACT* as amended and may be affected by the *LAND ACT* sections 52–55 (*see* R.S.B.C. 1979, chapter 214).

108. Sample Deed

ABBREVIATIONS

AR	= assignment of rents
CBL	= claim of builder's lien
CML	= claim of mechanic's lien
CVT	= caveat
E	= easement
J	= judgment
L	= lease
LE	= life estate
LP	= lis pendens
M	= mortgage
OP	= option to purchase

PA	= priority or postponement agreement
RC	= restrictive covenant
RFR	= right of first refusal
RP	= right to purchase
RW	= right-of-way
SC	= statutory charge
SBS	= statutory building scheme
SRW	= statutory right-of-way
TA	= timber agreement
TSN	= tax sale notice
U	= undersurface rights

To:

Duplicate certificate of title
issued   Yes/No

Your File No.

DK-16   W-60   R1 R2

LAND TITLE ACT
(FORM 21, Section 173(1))

CERTIFICATE OF INDEFEASIBLE TITLE

Land Title Office, ... Kamloops ....
...., British Columbia

Title No. ....

From Title No. ....

The undermentioned owner in fee simple is indefeasibly entitled to an estate in fee simple, subject to such charges, liens, a
interests as are notified by endorsement on this certificate and subject to the conditions, exceptions, and reservations set out
the back hereof, to the land in British Columbia described below.

Registered owner in fee simple: (Application for registration received on ....

Description of land:

109. Sample Certificate of Indefeasible Title

470

Minerals only F to C R5496 17.3.82

CHARGES, LIENS, AND INTERESTS*

Nature of Charge; Number; Date and Time of Application	Registered Owner of Charge	Remarks

Signed and sealed by me, this .... day of ...., 19 ....

....

DUPLICATE CERTIFICATE OF TITLE

Date Issued	Name and Address of Person to Whom Delivered	Filing Reference of Request for Duplicate Certificate of Title	Date of Cancellation of Duplicate Certificate of Title

Title Cancelled and Interests Disposed of as Follows	Date	Signature of Registrar

450.161

*Each endorsement affects all the land described, unless otherwise indicated in "Remarks." See back hereof for abbreviations.

471

THIS WARRANTY DEED   made this   day of

BETWEEN:

being the Owner of the lands described in Schedule "A" herein
(hereinafter called the "GRANTOR")

                                                  - and -

(hereinafter called the "GRANTEE")

                                                  - and -

being the spouse (of the Grantor) who holds no title to the said lands
(hereinafter called the "RELEASOR")

WITNESSETH THAT in consideration of One Dollar and other good and valuable consideration;

THE GRANTOR hereby conveys to the GRANTEE the lands described in Schedule "A" to this Warranty Deed and hereby consents to this disposition, pursuant to the Matrimonial Property Act of Nova Scotia.

THE GRANTOR covenants with the GRANTEE that the GRANTEE shall have quiet enjoyment of the lands, that the GRANTOR has good title in fee simple to the lands and the right to convey them as hereby conveyed, that the lands are free from encumbrances, and that the GRANTOR will procure such further assurances as may be reasonably required.

THE RELEASOR hereby consents to the within conveyance and releases any claim that the RELEASOR had, has, or may have pursuant to the Matrimonial Property Act of Nova Scotia and hereby conveys any land and all right, title, and interest which the RELEASOR may have with respect to the lands described in Schedule "A."

IN THIS WARRANTY DEED the singular includes the plural and the masculine includes the feminine, with the intent that this WARRANTY DEED shall be read with all appropriate changes of number and gender.

IN WITNESS WHEREOF, the Grantor and Releasor have properly executed this deed on the date first shown above.

SIGNED, SEALED, AND DELIVERED   )
)
   in the presence of   )
)
)
) _____

_____
A Notary Public in and for
the State of _____   _____

SAMPLE WARRANTY DEED

110. Sample Warranty Deed

urban areas in the south are under the Registry System. The method of deed and document recording is very different than the system utilized in the United States.

The method of surveying in Canada is not based on the U.S. Rectangular Survey method. Instead, Canadian surveyors use the Coordinate Method with three dimensional coordinates used as property identifiers. Boundary lines are described in metes and bounds, bearings and distances. All land should be positively defined on the ground by a licensed surveyor prior to the purchase of any parcel of property.

Illustration 111, page 474, is a sample of a real estate purchase agreement as used in British Columbia. However, it is important to use an attorney in Canadian land purchases. If you do not know of one, the Canadian Bar Association will help you in obtaining appropriate legal services in Canada. Write to them at:

Canadian Bar Association
130 Albert St., Ste. 1700
Ottawa, Ontario KIP 5G4

This is the national lawyer's association of Canada. While they do not deal directly with the public, if they receive a real estate inquiry, they will direct it to the provincial bar association, which will supply the inquirer with the names of lawyers in the specific area of interest.

Specific information for each province can be obtained from the following sources, which will direct you to a lawyer specializing in real estate:

Alberta
Alberta Law Society
344 12th Ave., S.W.
Calgary, AB T2R 0H2

British Columbia
The Law Society of British Columbia
300 1148 Hornby St.
Vancouver, BC V6V 2C4

British Columbia Lawyer Referral Service
504 1148 Hornby St.
Vancouver, BC V6V 2C3

(They will refer you to a lawyer who will give you an interview of up to 30 minutes for $10.00)

Manitoba
The Law Society of Manitoba
201 219 Kennedy St.
Winnipeg, MB R3C 1S8

New Brunswick
The Barristers Society of New Brunswick
305 Justice Bldg.
P.O. Box 1063
Fredericton, NB E3B 5C2

Newfoundland
The Law Society of Newfoundland
Court House
Duckworth St.
P.O. Box 1028
St. John's, NF A1C 5M3

Northwest Territories
Northwest Territories Law Foundation
P.O. Box 2594
Yellowknife, NWT X1A 2P9

Nova Scotia
Nova Scotia Barristers' Society
Lawyer's Referral Service, Kerth Hall
1475 Hollis St.
Halifax, NS B3J 3M4

Ontario
The Law Society of Upper Canada
Lawyer's Referral Service
130 Queen St., W.
Toronto, ON M5H 2N6

(They will refer you to a lawyer for an initial 30-minute consultation for $20.00)

Prince Edward Island
The Law Society of Prince Edward Island
Law Courts Bldg.
42 Water St.
Charlottetown, PEI C1A 1AY

Quebec
La Maison du Barreau
445 Blvd. St.-Laurent
Montreal, PQ H2Y 3T8

Chambre des Notaires de la Province de Quebec
1700 630 Dorchester
Montreal, PQ H3B 1T6

Saskatchewan
The Law Society of Saskatchewan
201 Woodbine Plaza
2212 Scarth St.
Regina, SK S4P 2J6

PLEASE PRESS HARD FOR COPIES

MULTIPLE LISTING BUREAU
INTERIM AGREEMENT

LIST No _____

Salesman _____

OFFER TO PURCHASE

I (WE) the undersigned, _____ Occupation _____

_____ Occupation _____

Address _____ Phone No. _____

(herein called "Purchaser(s)"), having inspected the real estate property listed by _____ Agent for the Vendor,

and owned by _____ Occupation _____

_____ Phone No. _____

(herein called "Vendor(s)"), hereby offer and agree to purchase the property at _____ (Place)

and known as _____
(Street Address)

and described as (Legal Description) _____

_____

free and clear of other encumbrances except restrictive covenants, existing tenancies, reservations and exceptions in the original grant from crown, easements and/or rights of way in favour of utilities and public

authorities and except as set above. _____

and save existing tenancies at the price of _____ $ _____
payable as follows:

Cash Deposit paid herewith _____ $ _____

Balance of Cash Payment on or before _____ $ _____

All cash funds to be held in trust until completion of registration on _____

of the necessary documents and the balance if any as follows

_____ $ _____

_____ $ _____

_____ $ _____

_____ $ _____   Total Purchase Price $ _____

_____

AND adjustment of taxes, tolls, local improvement rates, irrigation taxes and tolls, insurance premiums and water rates, sewer and garbage rates as hereinafter provided, such price to include all existing blinds, awnings, screen doors and windows, fixed floor coverings, electric, plumbing and heating fixtures and attachments as owned by the vendor.

_____

_____

_____ as shown to me by your agent on or about _____
(Date)

Possession (subject to existing tenancies) shall be given to me on, and taxes, local improvement rates, rentals, insurance premiums and water rates shall be adjusted as

of _____
(Date)

THE PROPERTY SHALL BE AT MY RISK FROM _____ Registerable documents shall be prepared at my expense
(Date)
and shall contain the terms herein set out and shall contain, in addition thereto such covenants, terms and conditions not inconsistent therewith as may be agreed upon between us or, failing such agreement, as may be specfied by the solicitor for the time being of the Multiple Listing Bureau of the Kootenay Real Estate Board. Time shall be of the essence

I/WE HAVE READ AND CLEARLY UNDERSTAND THE ABOVE OFFER TO PURCHASE, ACKNOWLEDGE THAT IT ACCURATELY SETS OUT ALL THE TERMS OF MY/OUR OFFER, THAT I WAS/WE WERE NOT INDUCED TO MAKE IT BY ANY REPRESENTATIONS, WARRANTIES, GUARANTEES OR PROMISES NOT CONTAINED THEREIN, AND ACKNOWLEDGE HAVING RECEIVED A COPY OF THE SAID OFFER ON THIS DATE.

This offer shall be open for acceptance by you until 11:59 p.m. on _____ 19 ____

DATED at _____ on _____ , 19 ____
WITNESS:

_____   _____
                              Purchaser

_____   _____
                              Purchaser

RECEIPT FOR DEPOSIT

To(Purchaser) _____

I/We (Agent) _____
                              (Selling Broker)

acknowledge receipt of the sum of _____ ($)
being the deposit referred to in the above Offer to Purchase.

Dated at _____ on _____

                              _____
                              (Selling Broker)

ACCEPTANCE   Per _____

To (Purchaser) _____

And to (Listing Broker) _____

I/We Vendor _____
hereby accept the above offer and its terms and covenants and agree to pay to my/our said agent a commission as heretofore agreed upon.

_____

Dated at _____ on _____ , 19 ____
WITNESS:

_____   _____
                              Owner

_____   _____
                              Owner

1 White—Selling Broker 2 Green—Purchaser 3 Blue—Vendor 4 Red—Bureau 5 White—Purchaser

111. Sample Real Estate Purchase Agreement

Yukon
The Law Society of the Yukon
3081 Third Ave.
Whitehorse, YT Y1A 1B5

USEFUL RESOURCES

Much of the resource information throughout this book is useful for Canadian land purchases, particularly the five chapters in Part II, "Checking Out the Land." See that part for many publications printed in Canada as well as the following information, which is specifically applicable to Canada.

The following pamphlets and general information on climate in Canada are available from:

The Director
Meteorological Branch
Department of Public Transport
315 Bloor St., W.
Toronto 5, ON MS5 155

Precipitation Normals for (the province you want)	$ .10
Temperature Normals of (the province you want)	$ .10

For additional information about publications, climatic data, and climate-related activities of national scope, contact:

Canadian Climate Centre
Atmospheric Environment Service
4905 Dufferin St.
Downsview, ON M3H 5T4

Information about regional climatic programs and services is available from these regional offices of AES (Atmospheric Environment Service):

Pacific Region
1200 W. 73rd Ave., Ste. 700
Vancouver, BC V6P 6H9

Western Region
Argyll Centre
6325 103 St.
Edmonton, AB T6H 5H6

Central Region
266 Graham Ave., Rm. 1000
Winnipeg, MB R3C 3V4

Ontario Region
25 St.-Clair Ave., E.
Toronto, ON M4T 1M2

Quebec Region
100 Alexis Nihon Blvd., 3rd Fl.
Ville St.-Laurent, PQ H4M 2N6

Atlantic Region
1496 Bedford Highway
Bedford, NS B4A 1E5

and in Quebec,
Service de la Meteorologie
Ministère de l'Environment du Quebec
194 St.-Sacrement
Quebec, PQ E1N 4S5

A list of maps and aerial photographs for every region in Canada can be obtained free from:

National Geodetic Survey and Mining
Office
601 Booth St.
Ottawa, ON K1A 0E8

An index and list of topographic maps showing the agricultural value of the land and the grade of the terrain in every region in Canada is available from:

Map Distribution Office
Department of Mining and Technical
Surveys
615 Booth St.
Ottawa, ON K1A 0E9

Information on soil, water, agriculture, and other land-related matters can be obtained from:

Agricultural Economics Research Council of
Canada
55 Parkdale Ave.
Ottawa, ON K1Y 1E5

Queen's Printer
Daly Bldg.
Ottawa, ON K1N 9E1

Canada Handbook, published annually to record social, cultural, and economic developments in Canada, is available for the specified costs from:

Statistics in Canada
Publication Sales and Services
Ottawa, ON K1A 0T6

Canada, $15.00
Other countries, $16.50

Information on evaluating homes and building sites can be obtained from:

Canadian Mortgage and Housing
   Corporation (CHMC)
Box 9975
Ottawa, ON K1G 3H7

On all orders below include $1.00 handling charge.

CMHC Publications Catalogue   (Free publication list available)

A Home Selection Guide NHA 5179	$ 3.00
Details of House Construction NHA 5011	$11.00
CMHC Septic Tank Standards NHA 5213	$ 3.00
Choosing an Energy-Efficient House—	
A Buyer's Guide NHA 5662	$ 3.00

Problem Lands. Each pamphlet identifies the building problems described:

Conditions to Avoid NHA 5698	$ 1.00
Building on Clay NHA 5699	$ 1.00
Building on Peat NHA 5700	$ 1.00
Building in a Flood Risk Area NHA 5701	$ 1.00

The Research Centers Directory lists all agencies in Canada involved in land-related research. (See Useful Resources at the end of chapter 5, "The Earth—Soil, Vegetation, Topography.")

Real Estate Agents and Catalogues

Information on buying land in Canada and a listing of licensed real estate agents and realtors in all regions of Canada can be obtained from:

The Canadian Real Estate Association
Place DeVille, Tower A
320 Queen St., Ste. 2100
Ottawa, ON K1R 5A3

Ask for a list of agents in the area where you are interested in purchasing property. A letter to the agents will get you their current property listings.

Canadian Institute of Realtors
20 Eglinton Ave., E.
Toronto, ON M4P 1A9

(See also the listing of real estate agents within each province section in this chapter.)

H. M. Dignam Corporation Ltd.
Cedar Pointe Business Park, Unit 807
370 Dunlop St., W. (Hwys. 400 and 90)
Barrie, ON L4N 5R7

This unique company is probably the premier national rural property seller in Canada. They have been offering Canadian recreation properties since 1916, and from all accounts are a trustworthy outfit to deal with. They are not brokers. They own and sell their own land. The average property is around $6,000 Canadian. They put out a regular catalogue of their offerings, with complete details for each parcel. They will also send you aerial photographs, road maps, and a sectional map for any parcel you are interested in from the catalogue.

This company specializes in buying land at tax sales in order to resell at a profit. You can buy on all-cash or on time, and a deed conveying clear title is guaranteed by them after you have made all of your payments. They have a unique exchange program where you can exchange your parcel for another of equal or greater value within two years of purchase. Below is a sample ad from one of their recent land catalogues.

NEW BRUNSWICK
Property 654-NB
Portions of Lot D and F, Adamsville, East Settlement, Harcourt Parish, Kent County, New Brunswick, *193 acres* or *78.2 hectares*. Well located on the south side of a year-round road which runs between secondary highways 126 and 465, this would definitely be a good location for permanent residence. The property is mainly high and dry being about two hundred and fifty feet above sea level but there is a low area in the center which drains off to a small branch of the Coal Branch River as it crosses the southern end of the acreage. There is an old road along the west side of the parcel which will allow access to almost any portion along its forty-five-hundred-foot depth. The frontage totals about one thousand and five hundred feet on the paved road, and hydro and telephone are available at the lot line. Moncton, the "Hub City of the Maritimes," is just over thirty miles south and the Atlantic Ocean about the same distance east. Highway 126, running north and south, is about

two miles west and connects Moncton with the Newcastle, Chatham, Miramichi area. The local residents are very likeable, hardworking people, mainly engaged in forestry and fishing and justly proud of their heritage. *Price $18,690.00* payable *$2,690.00* cash with order and fifty monthly payments of *$320.00* each, and interest; or *$15,886.50* (being 15% off) if paid *$2,690.00* cash with order and *$13,196.50* within thirty days thereafter.

Remember, as much care should be used in purchasing land from H. M. Dignam as in any other purchase of real estate. The burden is always on you to check out your land purchases.

The current prices of the H. M. Dignam sale lists are as follows. They can be obtained from the addresses given above:

Twelve issues (including monthly newsletter)	$15.00
Maps for any parcel in catalogue	$ 4.00

The staff at Dignam is extremely helpful and will answer any questions you have about purchasing land in Canada. You can write to the address above or telephone (705) 721-1515. Ask for Tom Willcock if he is available.

For information on immigration to Canada, write to:

> The Department of Citizenship and
> Immigration
> Ottawa, ON K1A 0J9

Alberta

Maps showing available public lands and geographic features of the area are available from the address below. Information on climate, soil, water, and land conditions is also available on request. The following pamphlets are also available free from:

> Director of Lands
> Department of Lands and Forests
> Natural Resources Bldg.
> 109th St. and 99th Ave.
> Edmonton, AB

> *General Information concerning Acquisition of Recreational Land and the Sale or Leasing of Land in Alberta* Department of Lands and Forests Leaflet
> *Information regarding Homestead Sales in the Government of the Province of Alberta* LH 48

A list of real estate agents who can send you their land listings is available free with other general information on purchasing land in Alberta from:

> Secretary-Treasurer
> Alberta Real Estate Association
> 503 7th St., S.W.
> Calgary, AB T2P 1Y9

> Canadian Real Estate Association
> 1410 Fint St., S.W.
> Calgary, AB T2R 0V8

> Brooks Real Estate Board Co-operative Ltd.
> Box 97
> Brooks, AB T0J 0J0

> Calgary Real Estate Board Co-op Ltd.
> 503 7th St., S.W.
> Calgary, AB T2P 1Y9

> Cold Lake and District Real Estate Board
>   Co-op Ltd.
> Box 1678
> Grand Centre, AB T0A 1T0

> Drumheller and District Real Estate Board
> Box 2936
> Drumheller, AB T0J 0Y0

> Edmonton Real Estate Board
> Box 25000, 14220 112 Ave.
> Edmonton, AB T5J 2R4

> The Fort McMurray Real Estate Board
> 108 10012-A Franklin Ave.
> Fort McMurray, AB T9H 2K6

> Grande Prairie Real Estate Board
> 10012 97-A St.
> Grande Prairie, AB T8V 2C1

> Hinton-Edson Real Estate Board
> Box 2386
> Hinton, AB T9E 1C0

> Lloydminster Real Estate Board
> Box 1607
> Lloydminster, AB S9V 1K5

> Medicine Hat Real Estate Board Co-op Ltd.
> 403 4th St., S.E.
> Medicine Hat, AB T1A 0K5

Red Deer and District Real Estate Board
Co-op Ltd.
4824 51st St.
Red Deer, AB T4N 2A5

British Columbia
A list of available maps of British Columbia is available free from:
Director, Surveys and Mapping Branch
Geographic Division
Department of Lands, Forests, and Water
Resources
Victoria, BC

Maps and nautical charts of British Columbia are also available from:
Dominion Map Limited
626 Howe St.
Vancouver 1, BC V6C 3B8

Geographic Bulletins 1 through 10 on geographic materials for British Columbia are available from:
Province of British Columbia Lands Service
Department of Lands, Forests, and Water
Resources
Victoria, BC

Information on climate, soil, water, land use, and agriculture is available from both of the following agencies:
Canadian Agriculture Research Station
University of British Columbia
6660 Northwest Marine Dr.
Vancouver, BC V6T 1X2

Department of Agriculture
Government of British Columbia
Victoria, BC

For information on the availability and requirements to buy Crown lands, write to:
British Columbia Lands Branch
Victoria, BC

The following pamphlet is free from:
Government Printing Bureau
Victoria, BC

The Acquisition of Crown Lands in British Columbia Land Series Bulletin No. 11

For homestead and general land information, write to:
Director, Surveys and Mapping Branch
Geographic Division
Department of Lands, Forests, and Water
Resources
Victoria, BC

The following pamphlets are available free, as well as any other necessary information on homesteading and purchasing land next to, or on, the Queen Charlotte Islands. Write to:
Director of Lands
British Columbia Lands Service
Parliament Bldg.
Victoria, BC

Status Map 103F of Available Land Land Bulletin No. 8

For information on leasing or buying land in British Columbia, write to any of the following:
Land Commissioner
Burns Lake, BC

Land Commissioner
1600 Third St.
Prince George, BC

Land Inspector
British Columbia Lands Service
Department of Lands, Forest, and Water
Resources
Victoria, BC

Director of Lands
British Columbia Lands Service
Department of Lands, Forest, and Water
Resources
Victoria, BC

For information on buying land and for listings of land for sale, write to any of the following:
Cariboo Real Estate Board
Box 2386, 4166 15th Ave.
Prince George, BC V2M 1V8

Chilliwack and District Real Estate Board
Box 339, 46177 Yale Rd., E., Ste. 2
Chilliwack, BC V2P 6J4

Fraser Valley Real Estate Board
Box 99, 15483 104th Ave.
Surrey, BC V3T 4W4

Kamloops Real Estate Board
101 418 St. Paul St.
Kamloops, BC V2C 2J6

Kootenay Real Estate Board
Box 590
Nelson, BC V1L 5R4

Northern Lights Real Estate Board
1101 103 Ave.
Dawson Creek, BC V1G 2G8

Northwest Real Estate Board
117 4546 Park Ave.
Terrace, BC V8G 1V4

Okanagan-Mainline Real Estate Board
1889 Spall Rd.
Kelawna, BC V1Y 4R2

Powell River Sunshine Coast Real Estate
    Board
Box 206
Powell River, BC V8A 4Z6

South Okanagan Real Estate Board
212 Main St., Ste. 3
Penticton, BC V2A 5B2

Real Estate Board of Greater Vancouver
1101 W. Broadway
Vancouver, BC V6H 1G2

Vancouver Island Real Estate Board
Box 719, 6374 Metral Dr.
Nanaimo, BC V9R 5M4

The Victoria Real Estate Board
3035 Nanaimo St.
Victoria, BC V8T 4W2

British Columbia Association of Real Estate
    Boards
475 Howe St., Rm. 502
Vancouver, BC V6C 2Z3

Real Estate Institute of British Columbia
608 626 W. Pender St.
Vancouver 2, BC V6B 1V9

Canadian Real Estate Association
205 1847 W. Broadway
Vancouver, BC V6J 1Y6

Manitoba
Information on Crown land for sale and the free

pamphlet *Available Crown Land in Manitoba* can
be obtained from:
    Lands Branch
    Department of Mines and Natural Resources
    810 Norquay Bldg.
    Winnipeg 1, MB

Information on maps and available homestead
land can be obtained from the director of surveys
at the same address.

Information on soil, water, agriculture, and other
land-related matters can be obtained from:
    Canada Agriculture Research Station
    University of Manitoba
    25 Dafoe Rd.
    Winnipeg 19, MB R3T 2N1

Information on buying land and land for sale in
Manitoba can be obtained from:
    Brandon Real Estate Board
    930B Lorne Ave.
    Brandon, MB R7A 6K7

    The Portage La Prairie Real Estate Board
    160 Saskatchewan Ave., W.
    Portage La Prairie, MB R1N 0M1

    Thompson Real Estate Board
    The Place, 50 Selkirk Ave.
    Thompson, MB R8N 0M7

    The Winnipeg Real Estate Board
    1240 Portage Ave.
    Winnipeg, MB R3G 0T6

    Canadian Real Estate Association
    1240 Portage Ave.
    Winnipeg, MB R3G 0T6

New Brunswick
Information on Crown lands and other lands for
sale in New Brunswick can be obtained from:
    Director of Lands Branch
    Department of Natural Resources
    Fredericton, NB

Information on buying land and land for sale in
New Brunswick can be obtained from:
    Real Estate Board of the Fredericton Area,
        Inc.
    Box 1295, 516 Queen St.
    Fredericton, NB E3B 5C8

Moncton Real Estate Board, Inc.
107 Cameron St.
Moncton, NB E1C 5Y7

Northern New Brunswick Real Estate Board
Box 185
Bathurst, NB E2A 3Z2

Greater Saint John Real Estate Board
560 Main St., Bldg. A
St. John, NB E2K 1J5

Valley Real Estate Board, Inc.
14 Court St.
Edmundston, NB E3V 3K9

Newfoundland and Labrador
Information on Crown lands and other lands for sale can be obtained from:
    Director, Crown Lands and Surveys
    Department of Mines, Agriculture, and
        Resources
    Confederation Building
    St. Johns, NF (Newfoundland)

Information on buying land and land for sale can be obtained from:
    Central Newfoundland Real Estate Board
    Box 733
    Grand Falls, NF A2A 2K2

    Humber Valley Real Estate Board
    Box 532
    Corner Brook, NF A2H 6E6

    St. John's Real Estate Board
    77 Portugal Cove Rd.
    St. John's, NF A1B 2M4

Northwest Territory
Information on Crown lands and other lands for sale can be obtained from:
    Water, Forest, and Lands Division
    Development Branch of the Department of
        Indian Affairs and Northern Development
    Ottawa, ON

    Igloo Real Estate Ltd.
    Box 2698
    Yellowknife, NWT X0E 1H0

    Government of NWT
    Box 1320
    Yellowknife, NWT X1A 2L5

Department of Public Works NWT
Box 1320
Yellowknife, NWT X0E 0T0

Nova Scotia
Information on Crown lands and other lands for sale can be obtained from:
    Director of Immigration and Land
        Settlement
    Truro, NS

Information on buying land and land for sale can be obtained from:
    Anapolis Valley Real Estate Board
    376 Main St.
    Kentville, NS B4N 1K8

    Cape Breton Real Estate Board
    Box 945, 188 Charlotte St.
    Sydney, NS B1P 6J4

    Halifax-Dartmouth Real Estate Board
    6132 Quinpool Rd.
    Halifax, NS B3L 1A3

    Highlight Real Estate Board
    Box 727
    Port Hawkesbury, NS B0E 2V0

    Northern Nova Scotia Real Estate Board
    183 Provost St.
    New Glasgow, NS B2H 2P8

    South Shore Real Estate Board
    6 King St.
    Lunenburg, NS B0J 2C0

Ontario
Information on agriculture and land use including maps and charts can be obtained from:
    Ontario Ministry of Agriculture and Food
    Legislature Bldg.
    Queens Park
    Toronto, ON M7A 1B6

Information on Crown lands and other lands for sale can be obtained from:
    Director, Lands and Surveys Branch
    Department of Lands and Forests
    Parliament Bldgs.
    Toronto 5, ON

Information on buying land for sale for nonpayment of taxes can be obtained from the following:

Publications Centre
880 Bay St., 5th Fl.
Toronto, ON N7A 1N8

Ask for: *The Ontario Gazette*, published weekly
by the government, can be ordered from:
Tax Sale Lands
Queen's Printer
Parliament Bldgs.
Toronto, ON

Director
Tourist Industry Development
Department of Tourism
Parliament Bldgs.
Toronto, ON

Information on buying land and land for sale can
be obtained from:
Bancroft District Real Estate Board
Box 1522
Bancroft, ON K0L 1C0

Barrie and District Real Estate Board, Inc.
Box 412, 105 Dunlop St., E., Ste. 202
Barrie, ON L4M 4T5

Brampton Real Estate Board
119 West Dr.
Brampton, ON L6T 2J6

Brantford Regional Real Estate Association, Inc.
Box 1013, 9 Queen St.
Brantford, ON N3T 5S7

Real Estate Board of Cambridge, Inc.
Box 693, 75 Ainslie St., N
Cambridge, ON N1R 5W6

Central St. Lawrence Real Estate Board
Box 1465, 51 King St., E., Ste. 2
Brockville, ON K6V 5Y6

Chatham-Kent Real Estate Board
Box 384, 303 Merritt Ave.
Chatham, ON N7M 5K5

Cobourg-Port Hope District Real Estate Board
Box 160, 1011 William St., 2nd Fl.
Cobourg, ON K9A 4K5

Collingwood and District Real Estate Board
168 Hurontario St.
Collingwood, ON L9Y 2M2

Cornwall and District Real Estate Board
135 Augustus St.
Cornwall, ON K6J 3V9

Grey Bruce Real Estate Board
504 10th St.
Hanover, ON N4N 1R1

Guelph and District Real Estate Board
400 Woolwich St.
Guelph, ON N1H 3X1

Haliburton District Real Estate Board
Box 760
Minden, ON K0M 2K0

Metropolitan Hamilton Real Estate Board
194 James St.
Hamilton, ON L8P 3A7

Huron Real Estate Board
Box 244, 151 Wellington St.
Goderich, ON N7A 3Z2

Kingston and Area Real Estate Association
155 Brock St.
Kingston, ON K7L 1S2

Kitchener-Waterloo Real Estate Board, Inc.
530 Queen St.
Kitchener, ON N2G 1X1

Lindsay and District Real Estate Board
22 Pearl St.
Lindsay, ON K9V 3L8

London and St. Thomas Real Estate Board
311 Oxford St., E.
London, ON N6A 1V3

Midland-Penetang District Real Estate Board
Box 805, 188 Woodland Dr.
Midland, ON L4R 4E3

Mississauga Real Estate Board
249 Lakeshore Rd., E.
Mississauga, ON L5G 1G8

Muskoka Real Estate Board
Box 2219, 49 Manitoba St.
Bracebridge, ON P0B 1C0

Niagara Falls–Fort Erie Real Estate Association
Box 456, 4411 Portage Rd.
Niagara Falls, ON L2E 6V2

North Bay Real Estate Board
Box 774, 387 Fraser St., Ste. 206
North Bay, ON P1B 8J8

The Oakville Milton and District Real Estate
  Board
152 Trafalgar Rd.
Oakville, ON L6J 3G6

The Orangeville and District Real Estate Board
228 Broadway Ave.
Orangeville, ON L9W 1K5

Orillia and District Real Estate Board
Box 551, 100 Coldwater St., E.
Orillia, ON L3V 1W7

Oshawa and District Real Estate Board
Box 190, Unit 14, 50 Richmond St., E.
Oshawa, ON L1H 7L1

Real Estate Board of Ottawa-Carleton
1745 Woodward Dr.
Ottawa, ON K2C 0P9

Owen Sound and District Real Estate Board
124 Tenth St., W.
Owen Sound, ON N4K 3P9

Parry Sound Real Estate Board
Box 29
Parry Sound, ON P2A 2X2

Peterborough Real Estate Board, Inc.
Box 1330, 273 Charlotte St.
Peterborough, ON K9J 7H5

Quinte and District Real Estate Board
Box 1086, 268 Dundas St., E.
Belleville, ON K8N 5E8

Renfrew County
377 Isabelle St.
Pembroke, ON K8A 5T4

Sarnia-Lambton Real Estate Board
555 Exmouth St.
Sarnia, ON N7T 5P6

Sault Ste. Marie Real Estate Board
498 Queen St., E., Ste. 1
Sault Ste.-Marie, ON P6A 1Z8

Simcoe and District Real Estate Board
44 Young St.
Simcoe, ON N3Y 1Y5

Ste.-Catharines District Real Estate Board
116 Niagara St.
Ste.-Catharines, ON L2R 4L4

Stratford District Real Estate Board
42 Albert St., Upper Fl.
Stratford, ON N5A 3K3

Sudbury Real Estate Board
Box 1091, 280 Larch St.
Sudbury, ON P3B 1M1

Thunder Bay Real Estate Board
1135 Barton St.
Thunder Bay, ON P7B 5N3

Tillsonburg District Real Estate Board
Box 35, 1 Library Ln.
Tillsonburg, ON N4G 4H3

Timmins Real Estate Board
47 Pine St., S., Ste. 204
Timmins, ON P4N 2J9

Toronto Real Estate Board
183 Yonge St.
Toronto, ON M4S 1Y7

Welland District Real Estate Board
Box 486
Welland, ON L3B 5R2

The Windsor-Essex County Real Estate Board
815 Riverside Dr., W.
Windsor, ON N9A 5K7

Woodstock-Ingersoll and District Real Estate
  Board
Box 185, 491 Upper Dundas St.
Woodstock, ON N4S 7W8

York Region Real Estate Board
Box 400
Aurora, ON L4G 3L5

Prince Edward Island
Information on Crown lands and other lands for
sale can be obtained from:
    Commissioner of Public Lands
    Department of the Attorney General
    Province House
    Charlottetown, PEI

Information on buying land and land for sale can
be obtained from:

Secretary
Prince Edward Island Real Estate Brokers
  Association
92 Kent St.
Charlottetown, PEI C1A 1M9

Prince Edward Island Real Estate
  Association
202 Queen St.
Charlottetown, PEI C1A 4B6

Quebec
Information on Crown lands for sale and the free
pamphlet *Canada Land* can be obtained from:
  Deputy Minister
  Department of Lands and Forests
  Parliament Bldgs.
  200 Ste.-Foi St.
  Quebec City, PQ

Information on agriculture can be obtained from:
  Deputy Minister
  Department of Agriculture and Colonization
  Parliament Bldgs.
  200 Ste.-Foi St.
  Quebec City, PQ G1R 4X6

Information on soil, water, and other land-re-
lated matters can be obtained from:
  Geographical Branch
  Department of Mines and Technical Surveys
  Parliament Bldgs.
  200 Ste.-Foi St.
  Quebec City, PQ

Information on buying land and land for sale can
be obtained from:
  Executive Secretary
  Corporation of Real Estate Brokers of
    Quebec
  1080 Beaver Hall Hill, Rm. 802
  Montreal 128, PQ

La Chambre d'immeuble du Bas St.-
  Laurent, Inc.
14, est rue St.-Germain
Rimouski, PQ G5L 1A2

Chambre d'immeuble Centre du Quebec,
  Inc.
660, rue de Boucherville
Drummondville, PQ J2C 5C8

Chambre d'immeuble de l'Estrie, Inc.
Bureau 103, 2654 ouest rue King
Sherbrooke, PQ J1J 2H1

La Chambre d'immeuble de Lanaudiere,
  Inc.
70, sud place Bourget, Local 301
Joliette, PQ J6E 5E8

Chambre d'immeuble des Laurentides
CP 1615 155, boul. Ste.-Adèle
Ste.-Adèle, PQ J0R 1L0

La Chambre d'immeuble de La Mauricie,
  Inc.
Bureau 102, 1640 6e rue
Trois-Rivières, PQ G8Y 5B8

Chambre d'immeuble de Montreal
Bureau M-102, 180 côte du Beaver Hall
Montreal, PQ H2Z 1T3

La Chambre d'immeuble de l'Outaouais,
  Inc.
197, boul. St.-Joseph
Hull, PQ J8Y 3X2

Chambre d'immeuble de Quebec
Bureaux 101 et 102, 2480 chemin Ste.-Foy
Ste.-Foy, PQ G1V 1T6

La Chambre d'immeuble de Saguenay-Lac
  St.-Jean, Inc.
980, est boul. Université
Chicoutimi, PQ G7H 6H1

Saskatchewan
Information on Crown lands and other lands for
sale and the pamphlet *Available Crown Land in
Saskatchewan* can be obtained from:
  Controller of Surveys
  Department of Natural Resources
  Administration Building
  Regina, SK

Information on soil, water, agriculture, and other
land-related matters can be obtained from:
  Canada Agriculture Research Station
  University of Saskatchewan
  University Campus
  Saskatoon, SK

Information on buying land and on land for sale
can be obtained from:

Canadian Real Estate Association
2602 8th St., S.
Saskatoon, SK S7H 0Y7

General Manager
Saskatchewan Real Estate Association
100 Ross Block
116 Third Ave., S
Saskatoon, SK S7K 1L3

Battlefords Real Estate Board
Box 611
North Battleford, SK S9A 2Y7

Melfort Real Estate Board
Box 3157
Melfort, SK S0E 1A0

Moose Jaw Real Estate Board
35C Ominica St., W.
Moose Jaw, SK S6H 1W8

Prince Albert Real Estate Board
160 17th St., W.
Prince Albert, SK S6V 3X5

Regina Real Estate Association
1854 McIntyre St.
Regina, SK S4P 2P9

Saskatoon Real Estate Board
1149 Eighth St., E.
Saskatoon, SK S7H 0S3

Swift Current Real Estate Board
211 12 Cheadle St., W.
Swift Current, SK S9H 0A9

Weyburn Real Estate Board
140 First St., N.E.
Weyburn, SK S4H 0T2

Yorkton Real Estate Association, Inc.
103 5th Ave., N.
Yorkton, SK S3N 0Z3

Yukon Territory
Maps and other information on buying land can be obtained from:
> Map Distribution Office
> Department of Mines and Technical Surveys
> Ottawa, ON

Information on Crown lands and other lands for sale can be obtained from:
> Supervisor of Lands
> P.O. Box 1767
> Whitehorse, YT Y1A 4N1

> Yukon Real Estate Association
> Box 5292
> Whitehorse, YT Y1A 4Z2

IX

USING A LAWYER

CHAPTER 37

Do You Need a Lawyer?

In a profession where unbounded trust is necessarily reposed, there is nothing surprising that fools should neglect it in their idleness, and tricksters abuse it in their knavery, but it is the more to the honor of those, and I will vouch for many, who unite integrity with skill and attention, and walk honorably upright where there are so many pitfalls and stumbling blocks for those of a different character.

—Sir Walter Scott, *The Antiquary*

In this book I have tried to anticipate the major legal questions and problems you might encounter when purchasing land. Every transaction is unique,

however, and you might have an unusual problem involving complicated legal questions I do not cover. If there is any matter you do not fully understand, do not sign anything at any stage until you see a lawyer.

Because laws and practices vary throughout the country and are constantly being revised, you will have to investigate which laws apply to your area. Some of you will not have the time or inclination to do a thorough job of investigation and negotiation yourselves and will want a lawyer to do some of this for you. Although a lawyer cannot tell you if the property is satisfactory with reference to location, water, soil, climate, amenities, and condition of the structures, or if the price is reasonable, he can help you write the contract of sale, negotiate with the seller, or decide whether you have the necessary easements, water rights, and other legal rights.

If you retain a lawyer to handle your real estate

487

deal, he will be working exclusively on your behalf, doing everything he can to see that you receive what you expect to get. All other parties, such as the title company, mortgagee, lending institution, local and state government officials, the seller, and the real estate agent, will have interests different from your own. As explained in chapter 2, "Real Estate Agents, Realtors, and Salespeople," the real estate agent works for the seller. He cannot give you legal advice and may, in fact, give you false advice due to ignorance or intent. Beware of the agent who discourages you from obtaining an attorney or who asks you to rely on his advice. A broker's interest is in making a quick and easy sale so that he can collect his commission. A lawyer's interest is in protecting the client who employs him.

WHAT A LAWYER CAN DO FOR YOU

You can retain a lawyer to do anything from drafting or double-checking your contract of sale to handling all the legal aspects of the purchase from start to finish.

By the time you start negotiating to get the price down, you might be too friendly with the agent to become a hard bargainer. Sometimes it is to your advantage to have an attorney negotiate on your behalf with the real estate agent and seller. When the agent tells you that your demands are unreasonable, you can blame your lawyer for insisting on them. A lawyer also might have connections with a bank or finance company and be able to help you obtain a loan.

Drawing up contracts and examining forms you are asked to sign are important functions of a lawyer. In many states, a real estate agent is permitted to write contracts, but these contracts will not give you sufficient protection. The Model Contract of Sale in this book is drafted to protect the interests of the buyer, but its details must be carefully studied and adjusted to fit your situation. If you have doubts about any document involved in the transaction, a lawyer can determine its legality and explain its contents.

You can have an attorney investigate the zoning and other ordinances that affect your property and tell you whether your intended use will be permissible. An attorney can do a title search or obtain one for you. Most importantly, he can read all the legal documents pertaining to your property, such as easements, reservations, and restrictions and explain them to you. He or she can ensure that you have adequate water rights and easements. He can personally examine the land for any constructive defects of title that would not be recorded in the county records such as prescriptive easements or adverse possession claims. (See chapter 9, "Easement Rights," and chapter 16, "Adverse Possession.") Then he can help you get the seller to clear any defects of title before you buy, such as an unwanted easement or tax lien.

The means by which you take title and the financial terms of the purchase have tax consequences that can be to your benefit or detriment, and you might want to ask an attorney's advice on these matters if you have an unusual situation. The retention of a lawyer is mandatory if you are a group planning to incorporate or form a nonprofit organization such as a church or foundation. Certain state regulations must be satisfied, and the legal problems involved can be complex.

CHOOSING YOUR LAWYER

You must decide whether to use a city or a country lawyer. Then you must choose between a general practitioner or a real estate specialist.

If you already have a lawyer in the city who has handled other matters for you, you may want him to handle your land deal. This is usually not advisable. Most attorneys are reluctant to oversee a real estate transaction more than 100 miles away because it is difficult to inspect the land and speak with parties involved. Your regular attorney will probably recommend that you retain local counsel, and that is my advice also. A local lawyer not only knows the land, or can easily reach it, he knows everybody in town and has established a working relationship with surveyors, well-diggers, appraisers, inspectors, government officials, title company officials, bankers and other lending institution officials, escrow holders, sellers, and real estate agents. Your city lawyer may be able to refer you to a local attorney he knows personally or by reputation. If you still want your regular attorney's aid, you can make an arrangement whereby he will double-check the local country lawyer's work and advice, but that is really not necessary if you find a competent attorney in the area where the land is located.

You must be careful that the lawyer's association with the local residents does not interfere with his work on your behalf. If your lawyer is trying to talk you out of necessary protections such as surveys, appraisals, and contingencies in the contract, or if you read anything in this book that your lawyer does not mention to you, question him on the matter and try to determine if he has any ties with the real estate agent, seller, or other party that might be a conflict of interest. It is illegal for a lawyer to take a case in which he has a conflict of interest.

Many lawyers in the country specialize in real estate law because the majority of their cases involve land problems. Often such a specialist will charge more than a general practitioner, but it is worth the extra expense because he is the most knowledgeable. He is more familiar with the problems and laws involved and will have to do less research and spend less time on the case than the lawyer who handles such deals only occasionally. You should compare the estimated fee of the local specialist with that of the local practitioner. Beware of an attorney who tells you he has to research the law on some point that you feel he should know. This is not a specialist, and he should be avoided.

In most rural areas, your choice of attorneys will be limited because of the scarcity of lawyers practicing in the country. Usually several lawyers practice in the county seat, and the farther you go from that base, the fewer lawyers you will encounter. If a local, state, or federal legal assistance office is located in the area, ask for recommendations and information on who are the most trustworthy and reasonable lawyers in the area. Call the county bar association and ask for a list of real estate specialists. If you know a lawyer in the city, ask if he can recommend a good lawyer in the area in which you intend to purchase land. Talk to local people and try to get an idea of the reputation of local attorneys. You may find that one lawyer will be consistently referred to as being the most honest and knowledgeable lawyer in town.

Whatever you do, never pick a lawyer solely by his or her ad in the yellow pages of the telephone book. Any lawyer can take out an ad, but the best lawyers continue to operate on the basis of reputation.

Sometimes a large real estate agency will have an attorney who works for the office drawing up papers and overseeing the legalities of sales. Do not rely on him to represent you. If he draws up any documents, you should examine them yourself very carefully, and if you hire an attorney, he must also inspect them.

HOW TO RELATE TO YOUR LAWYER

Good feelings between you and your lawyer are essential. If you don't feel comfortable with him after you retain him, you should fire him and go to someone else. Since your lawyer needs to be able to contact you, keep him informed of your whereabouts at all times. Keep him up to date regarding all conversations you have with the real estate agent or seller, give him copies of every document you receive, and inform him of any other matters relating to your purchase. When giving information, don't tell him only what you think is relevant. Tell him everything. He should also keep you informed about everything he is doing for you.

Sometimes a lawyer will put you off when you try to contact him or will seem to be very slow in getting his job done for you. This is probably because he has many clients, but if you do not think he is giving your case enough attention, do not hesitate to stay on his back and prod him along at a reasonable pace.

HOW TO KNOW WHETHER YOUR LAWYER IS DOING A GOOD JOB

Check everything the lawyer does against the information contained in this book. If his advice or information conflicts with what I say, bring it to his attention and resolve the problem. He does not necessarily have to agree with everything I say, but he should give you an adequate explanation of why he disagrees. New laws may have been passed, or practices may be different in your area.

If your lawyer uses standard forms, which are preprinted forms containing blank spaces for inserting the necessary information, be certain that they protect you adequately. Forms drawn up specifically for your individual situation are much better, since preprinted forms often do not satisfactorily deal with your individual circumstances. Nevertheless, most lawyers will use them to save time. In some states, the bar association and/or realtors have established preprinted forms that are very adequate. In California I use the printed contracts supplied by the California Association of Realtors daily without hesitation. Check the forms used by your attorney against those that I include in this book for completeness. After any forms are drawn up, carefully review them with your attorney to be sure they include everything you expect to get out of the deal, particularly regarding conditions of the sale and financing. Show my Model Contract of Sale to your attorney so he can use it, making the appropriate changes. (Of course, the purpose of including it is to enable you to draw up your own contract, but you might want to have it double-checked by an attorney if you are uncertain about something.)

HOW MUCH WILL A LAWYER COST?

A lawyer's fee is based on several factors, including the time and labor that he estimates will be required, the difficulty of the problems involved, the amount of skill involved and the level of his expertise, the standard fees of lawyers in his community, the amount of money and benefits that you will receive from his services, and whether you are an established or a new client.

When you see a lawyer, after explaining what you want him to do, ask him what his fee is. Depending on the situation, he will either quote you a single fee as a package price or an hourly fee with an estimated time involved. The method he chooses will largely depend on what you hire him to do. If you want him to handle the whole purchase, including all the negotiations, execution, and examination of documents, he will probably give you a package rate. If you simply want to come to him whenever a problem arises that you think you cannot deal with, he will charge by the hour, and he will probably keep track of every letter he writes, every phone call he makes, and every minute he spends talking to you, in person or on the phone. If you run into any time-consuming problems in the middle of the transaction, the amount of the fee could easily be as much as, or more than, it would be if the lawyer handled the entire purchase for a package price. In a legally complicated land deal you might find that it is cheaper to pay a set fee and let the lawyer handle it entirely.

If a lawyer charges a single fee, he usually bases it on the purchase price of the property since that is the value of the item he is making "safe" for you. The common fee is 1 to 3 percent of the purchase price, with a minimum of $100. Thus, on an $80,000 purchase price, the lawyer's fee would probably be between $800 and $2,400, but it could go higher. All fees are negotiable, and you can offer goods or services as part or all of the fee. Hourly fees usually start at a minimum of $65 to $90 and can go as high as $150 per hour.

If you draw up your own contract of sale based on the Model Contract in this book, or have a broker draft a contract, you can take it to an attorney for an "examination and opinion." The charge for that and/or checking out all aspects of the title to the property would probably run $200 to $1,000.

If you are buying as a group and want to form a corporation or nonprofit entity, you will have to retain an attorney to draw up and file the proper documents. This service could cost several hundred dollars, although if it is combined with other aspects of the purchase, such as examining and executing other documents, you can get a deal on the total price.

Whatever your decision is regarding the use of a lawyer, one thing is certain: It will cost you more time and money to go to court after the transaction is completed than to pay a lawyer to oversee your purchase from the beginning or to double-check your own legal work. Buying property is the largest investment you will make in your life, and paying a few hundred dollars to insure that you are proceeding properly is a small price to pay for security.

By considering your responses to the following questions you will be able to better determine whether or not you need to retain an attorney: What is your business experience in general and your prior experience in land and real estate transactions? How large is your purchase, and what could you lose if something goes wrong? Is a good lawyer available? What are his fees? What do you want a lawyer to do for you? After reading this book, do you feel confident that you can handle the entire deal on your own? If you do retain an attorney, this book can be used to help you understand what is involved in the purchase and to enable you to oversee his work.

"My lawyers will handle the fine print."

X

PROTECTING YOUR PROPERTY AFTER YOUR PURCHASE

CHAPTER 38

How to Be a Nice Neighbor without Paying for It in the End

Good fences make good neighbors.

—Robert Frost

We know that a person's home is his or her castle. In the past a physical moat was constructed around the castle for protection. Today, we need to have a figurative moat of legal protection for our homes. This chapter will cover some important areas that you should be aware of to allow you to defend yourself against potential litigation with your neighbors, your spouse, your creditors, and the future threat of the federal government taking minerals from your land.

In my legal career I have had numerous cases involving lawsuits between neighbors. One neighbor will allow another to take water from his land or cross his land with a vehicle for a number of years. Then they get into a fight, the neighbor is asked to stop taking water and crossing the land, and a lawsuit follows. In many cases, the courts will issue an injunction preventing the owner from cutting off his neighbor. Those kinds of actions rarely occur in the urban environment but are frequent in the country.

For example, your neighbor comes to you and says he would like to start developing his property and asks your permission to take water from your land. You assent to this and allow him to plug his pipe into your spring and take water. He then takes his raw land, puts in an orchard and garden, and builds a nice home for his family. Ten years later you want to develop your property some more, and you ask him to please remove his pipes from your spring. He knows he has inadequate water for his needs on his own parcel, so he hires a lawyer to sue you for permanent water rights to your property. He may very likely win his case even though you let him take water by permission and as a friendly gesture.

Many states enforce an old doctrine known as an *irrevocable oral license*. This law states that if you give your neighbor verbal permission to take something from your land and if in reliance on the continuation of that permission, your neighbor expends money improving his property, you cannot come along after the property is improved and cut off your neighbor's permission.

Therefore, the only way you can be a good neighbor anymore without paying a price in the end is to get your arrangement in writing. I include herein a sample form I have developed called a revocable license which spells out what the extent of the permission is between you and your neighbors. This sample is for a road easement, but it can be modified for the taking of water, gravel, or other things. The basic import of this document is that it establishes in writing the fact that your neighbor should not spend any money developing property relying on the continuation of your permission, because you are telling him in the beginning that you can revoke it at any time in the future.

There are other means of protecting your property against prescriptive users that are different in every state. For example, in California, a property owner can send a registered letter to each person using his property stating that "the use is by permission and subject to the control of owner, Section 1008, Civil Code." Signs stating the same message should be posted at appropriate points along the property.

Because of the importance of legally protecting yourself against future litigation over prescriptive rights, or court-ordered irrevocable licenses, you should always seek the advice of an attorney before allowing your neighbor to do anything on your property. Because it is for the benefit of your neighbor, he should pay the legal fees in drafting the appropriate documents.

If a neighbor already has deeded rights to use your property, then the above information does not apply. However, you should be aware that an easement can be overburdened. This problem frequently arises when a parcel being served by an easement is subdivided, increasing the traffic across your land. If one parcel and one residence are being served by an easement over your land, the traffic will be increased if that parcel is split up and more houses are built. This could overburden your easement, and you might be able to stop the overuse by going to court.

Sometimes, the easement reservation will state that it is "for the benefit of the parcel, and any divisions thereof." In that case, you will be helpless to stop the development. Be aware of the encumbrances on your land and the neighbor's use of recorded or unrecorded rights to use your property.

REVOCABLE LICENSE FOR INGRESS AND
EGRESS AND RELEASE AND INDEMNIFICATION FORM

_____, hereinafter referred to as "Licensor," and _____,
hereinafter referred to as "Licensee," hereby agree as follows:

Licensor agrees to give a revocable non-exclusive license to Licensee for the purpose of

112. Sample Revocable License for Ingress and Egress

496

ingress and egress, to be used in common with others, over and across the existing road across Licensor's property, located _____.

Licensor's property is described in Exhibit "A," attached hereto and made a part hereof.

This license is only for non-commercial use and is only for Licensee's use in obtaining ingress to and egress from Licensee's property, which property is described in Exhibit "B," attached hereto and made a part hereof.

This license will be terminable at the will of the Licensor and Licensor agrees to give Licensee ten (10) days' notice prior to the termination of this license.

Licensee agrees that any use of this license for ingress and egress has been, and will continue to be, solely by the permission of Licensor or his predecessors in interest. Licensee agrees that he has no rights to use the roads on Licensor's property, either by deed, prescription, or any other means, except as herein provided.

Licensee understands that he is not to expend any monies in the development of his property or to improve his property in reliance on the continuance of the license herein, as this license is revocable at any time at the option of the Licensor.

Licensor shall not be liable for personal injury or property damage sustained by Licensee or others caused by conditions or activities during the period of this license agreement.

Licensee hereby waives, releases, and discharges any and all claims for damages for death, personal injury, or property damage which he may have, or which may hereafter accrue to him, as a result of his exercise of the license rights herein. This release is intended to discharge in advance the Licensor, his agents, and employees from and against any and all liability arising out of or connected in any way with Licensee's use of Licensor's property, even though that liability may arise out of negligence or carelessness of the Licensor, his agents, or employees. It is further understood and agreed that this waiver, release, and assumption of risk is to be binding on my heirs and assigns.

Licensee agrees to indemnify, defend, and hold harmless Licensor, his agents, and employees against and in respect of any and all claims and demands, losses, costs, expenses, obligations, liabilities, damages, and attorney's fees that Licensor shall incur or suffer, which arise, result from, or relate to any matters arising out of the use of this license by Licensee, his heirs, agents, or employees.

If Licensor should incur any legal expenses or other costs enforcing the terms of this license, then Licensee agrees to reimburse Licensor for all expenses, including attorney's fees and court costs.

Licensee agrees that this agreement and license is not transferable and is non-assignable by him or any other parties or persons.

As used in this agreement, the masculine, feminine, or neuter gender, and the singular or plural number shall each be deemed to include the others whenever the context so indicates.

Dated:

_____
Licensor

_____
Licensee

CHAPTER 39

Preserving Your Separate Property: Prenuptial and Postnuptial Agreements

Every state has rules about the status of property when it is owned by a married couple. A problem often arises when one spouse has substantial assets prior to marriage and then property is purchased after marriage. Most states have laws which hold a presumption that property purchased after marriage is community property or owned equally by the spouses.

But if the money being spent on the property is yours and you want to conserve the property as being yours alone in the event of a divorce, then you must take precise legal steps to ensure this result. Usually a couple will sign a contract between themselves before they get married, called a prenuptial or ante-nuptial agreement. Both future spouses consult separate attorneys who advise them accordingly.

The agreement will spell out their intentions after marriage. For example, both future spouses will keep individual bank accounts in their own names wherein they will keep their separate holdings. They will open up one joint account after marriage, and they will contribute funds to that account as they desire. That is the account they will use for their mutual benefit, for living expenses, or a home purchase. Any real estate purchases made from separate funds will remain the separate property of the spouse paying for it, according to the agreement.

A common legal problem that occurs in a divorce is when two persons marry and one of them brings substantial assets into the marriage and the other has few assets. The couple buys a home, both names go on the title to the home, and shortly thereafter a divorce is filed. In most cases, if the husband's and wife's names are both on the deed, they will each be entitled to one-half of the value of the house, regardless of the source of the funds.

If you marry and then inherit funds and want to buy a house, you will need a postnuptial agreement setting forth your rights. For example, you might agree that you will put the money in for a down payment, but all mortgage payments will be made from joint income. If a divorce occurs later, you will be reimbursed for the down payment before the rest of the sales proceeds are equally divided.

If you find yourself in an unequal financial position with your spouse at the time of marriage, you certainly will want to seek the advice of an attorney. Because of the extremely high rate of divorce in this country, it is more likely than not that you will remarry with assets saved during a prior marriage. You will want to be sure you protect those assets, particularly in the event of purchase of real estate. You can be married and still take title to property in your name alone as your sole and separate property. If you wish to continue to keep the separate nature of your property, then all mortgage payments should be made from your separate bank account.

CHAPTER 40

Getting Your Minerals Back from the Federal Government

The federal government holds the mineral rights on thousands of privately owned parcels of land throughout the United States. The main reason for this is that when the government granted patents for homesteading, they automatically reserved the mineral rights in every grant. (See chapter 11, "Mineral, Oil, Gas, Timber, Soil, and Other Rights.") These rights were reserved without regard to whether there actually existed any minerals of value on the conveyed land.

As a result, clouds hang over the title to these parcels, as abstracts or title searches show that the government holds the right to enter the property and conduct mineral examinations forever.

In 1979, new legislation was passed providing for the conveying back of mineral rights to the landowner under certain circumstances. Write to any Bureau of Land Management office for a copy of Circular No. 2439:

Title 43—Public Lands: Interior

CHAPTER II—BUREAU OF LAND MANAGEMENT, DEPARTMENT OF THE INTERIOR

[Circular No. 2439]

SUBCHAPTER B—LAND RESOURCES MANAGEMENT

[Group 2700—Disposition; Sales]

PART 2720—CONVEYANCE OF FEDERALLY-OWNED MINERAL INTERESTS

You can file for reconveyance with your local BLM office. You will pay a $50 nonrefundable fee. You must be able to show either that (1) you have reason to believe that there are no known minerals of value in the land, or (2) the reservation of ownership of the mineral interests in the United States interferes with or precludes appropriate non-mineral development of the land and such development would be a more beneficial use of the land than its mineral development.

The interference with your land is obvious. You cannot get a commercial loan, and depending on the size of the parcel, mineral extraction could cause serious interference with a homestead. The government's current political approach is to release unnecessary ownerships to the private sector, so the time to apply to have your minerals back is now.

The BLM does have to send out geologists to study your land and take soil samples, which are analyzed in a laboratory. That process could cost $1,000. After that, more exploratory work might be done, depending on the initial findings. This work costs additional money and is done to determine the value of the minerals, if any are found. You might then have to pay to buy back these mineral rights. Although this might cost some money before you are through, I think it is well worth it to remove such an encumbrance on the title to your property. I pursued this for my own land and am very glad I did.

It also helps if you enlist the aid of your local congressperson to aid you in dealing with the BLM, should you encounter any problems. You probably will not need a lawyer in pursuing this project.

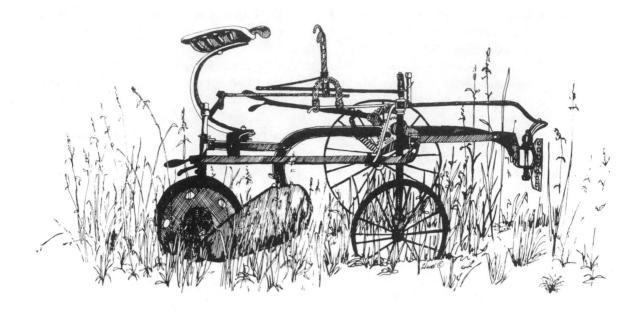

CHAPTER 41

The Homestead Exemption

In some states, homestead exemption laws protect your family's home against possible attachment by creditors up to a certain amount of the value or equity of the home. The amount of protection varies among the states that have enacted such laws. If no homestead protection exists in your state and you are unable to pay a debt, such as a personal loan or judgment lien resulting from a lawsuit, your home can be attached along with your personal property. After attachment an order of execution or writ of possession can be obtained, and your home may be forcibly sold to raise enough money to pay your debts.

If a homestead exemption exists, however, your home will be protected up to the amount of the exemption. Suppose your state has a $45,000 homestead exemption for a married couple, and you and your wife have a joint debt of $40,000 that you cannot pay. Your creditor cannot attach your family home and sell it to make up your debts if it is worth $45,000 or less because the first $45,000 of home value is exempt under the law. If your house is worth more than $45,000 but your equity (value of home less mortgages against it) is less than $45,000, you are similarly protected. If your home is worth more than $45,000 and you own it free and clear, your creditor can get a court order to sell it. Say it sells for $80,000. You will keep $45,000, and your creditor will get $35,000. Even though you still owe him $5,000, most states will not allow the creditor to collect any more of the money you received from the home sale. However, you must use the funds to purchase a new home within a specified period of time, usually six months to a year. If you have not bought a home in that time, your creditor can go after the rest of the money you owe him.

In most states, the homestead exemption law applies only to married couples and their families who occupy the land as their permanent home. A few states also have a *single person exemption* or *head of household exemption* for two or more people living together as a family unit with one person supporting the other members of the "family." The head of the family must own the property or have an interest in it. Thus, in these states, a partnership or other group together can take advantage of the homestead exemption as individuals within the group.

If the person or family sells the homestead property, the exemption rights terminate. If one spouse dies, the survivor and any children can live on the property under an exemption until the survivor dies and the youngest child reaches age twenty-one.

Exemptions are not automatic in every state that grants them. Sometimes you must file a declaration of homestead document that must be recorded in the county records as notice to possible creditors of your limited liability. The single person, husband or wife, or the head of household, depending on the state's law, files the declaration and in it states that he or she is single or married or is the head of household, describes the land, and estimates the land's value. The document is signed, notarized, and given to the county recorder. To see what a form looks like, go to the recorder's office. If a homestead exemption exists, the public files will be full of them.

Some types of debts are superior to the homestead exemption. Unpaid property taxes and special assessments can be collected from exempt property. If you don't pay a person whom you hired to make an improvement on your land, that person can place a mechanic's lien on your property and have it sold to collect his money, despite a homestead exemption, because you had the work done on your own initiative for the purpose of increasing the value of your property. If you give a mortgage or deed of trust using the property as security, you cannot then hide behind a homestead exemption to avoid paying the debt. Land under a homestead exemption law often cannot be given as security for a loan unless both spouses consent in writing to give up the exemption. The mortgage or deed of trust also will usually have a clause that both parties must sign waiving all homestead rights. Thus the exemption is usually good only against *unsecured debts,* those created without using the property as security in any way. Such things as unsecured loans, credit on the purchase of consumer goods, medical bills, and gambling debts fall within most exemption regulations.

The amount of exemption permitted and the requirements to qualify vary greatly among the states that offer a homestead exemption. You should find out the exact information for your state in order to be fully protected. An attorney can tell you what, if any, exemptions exist and can prepare the papers for you at a cost of somewhere between $50 and $150. The states that offer some kind of homestead exemption are: Alabama, Arizona, Arkansas, California, Florida, Georgia, Idaho, Illinois, Kansas, Louisiana, Michigan, Minnesota, Mississippi, Missouri, Montana, North Carolina, North Dakota, Ohio, Oklahoma, Oregon, South Dakota, Texas, Vermont, Washington, West Virginia, Wisconsin, and Wyoming. The value of the protection varies among states; e.g., Wisconsin, $25,000; Arkansas, $2,500, except that 80 acres may be exempt regardless of value; Illinois, $7,500; and Mississippi, $30,000 for a dwelling, or 160 acres of raw land regardless of value.

Your exemption can cover a mobile home as well as a regular dwelling.

There is also a federal exemption in the event of bankruptcy, in the amount of $7,500 equity. These figures are subject to change, so check with an attorney if you plan to apply for an exemption.

CHAPTER 42

What to Do if You Are Having Trouble Making Payments

If you find after you buy your land that you are unable to keep up with the agreed-upon payment schedule, immediately inform your creditor of this fact. Never let payments pass in the hope that your money will not be missed. Payment plans can often be reorganized by mutual agreement to more reasonably meet your capabilities, but you will have to convince the creditor that you will be able to meet the new obligation if he agrees to rework the payment plan. Call and explain your predicament before he calls you demanding to know why you aren't making your payments. If he sends you notices or letters, answer them rather than ignore them.

If you have a commercial lender, call them or write them immediately if you think you cannot make the payments or you are already late. Explain why you cannot make the payments, and ask to speak to a loan representative. Explain the facts of your financial situation and your expected future income.

Then call a housing counseling agency if there is one near you. The U.S. Department of Housing and Urban Development (HUD) has approved over six hundred such agencies and provides funds to counsel homeowners who can't keep up with HUD–insured payments. The housing counselors are skilled in assisting persons faced with the possibility of losing their homes through foreclosure. HUD has a temporary mortgage-relief assistance program (TMAP). Information on housing counseling agencies and HUD aid programs can be obtained from any local HUD offices. (See Useful Resources in chapter 27 for addresses of local HUD offices.)

If you bought your home with a Veterans Administration (VA) guaranteed loan and are having trouble making payments, call the VA office nearest you for assistance. (See Useful Resources in chapter 27 for addresses of local VA offices. Also, read the material on foreclosure in chapter 27 and see the Useful Resources section of that chapter for literature on foreclosure.)

Believe it or not, the fact is that most creditors, like their debtors, do not want to be subjected to the legal and monetary problems of a foreclosure, since they may lose money if deficiency judgments are not allowed. They usually must hire an attorney to carry through the foreclosure in the courts, which is also costly. A creditor would rather get his payments and interest without these hassles. Therefore, never try to avoid your creditor if you feel he may be amenable to changing your payments in order to facilitate your repaying your obligations.

If you know that you cannot keep up with the payments, even if the creditor agrees to lower them, always try to sell the land before the creditor forecloses on your loan. If you can keep up your payments long enough to find a buyer to assume your payments or to pay cash so that you can pay off your creditor and transfer full title to your buyer, you stand a chance of realizing a profit and need not suffer the consequences of a foreclosure, loss of your property, and possible deficiency judgment. Try to stay on good terms with your creditor to make stalling easier if you have to resort to

selling your land in order to avoid a foreclosure.

If you find that you cannot get the lender to give you some slack in your payments and you are desperate, put the property up for sale. If the lender starts to foreclose, go see a bankruptcy attorney, because it is easy to stall off the loss of your property for many months to allow you time to sell it.

The attorney will prepare bankruptcy papers, usually a Chapter 13 wage-earner debt reorganization plan. This bankruptcy immediately stops all foreclosure proceedings the minute it is filed. A plan is then submitted to the bankruptcy court wherein your unsecured debts are cut by 50 to 70 percent, or sometimes wiped out totally. You are then permitted to make up overdue land payments over a period of time so long as you keep the post-bankruptcy payments current. If you find a buyer for your property during the bankruptcy *stay* or *hold* on the foreclosure proceedings, you can prepare to sell it, seek to get the bankruptcy dismissed, and proceed with the sale. Or you can get court approval to sell the property within a certain period of time during the bankruptcy.

This is a very effective tool for saving your property. Never just walk away from your property. At all costs, avoid the ostrich mentality—refusing to deal with the problem. I have seen people in foreclosure who were offered money for their property, refused to sell the property because they wanted more money, and ended up losing everything. It is better to walk away with something in your pocket than nothing, so be realistic.

And above all, do not wait until the last minute to see an attorney. Plan your strategy with the attorney well in advance of the day before you are going to lose your property.

CHAPTER 43

Appealing the Tax Assessor's Valuation of Your Property

Each tax assessor is responsible for appraising hundreds of parcels in a given area, and he rarely gets more than a surface glimpse of any one piece of land and its improvements. Often, significant depreciation factors in a home are overlooked. In addition, appraisals are sometimes determined on the basis of who the property owner happens to be. Political, economic, and personal friendships often play a large part in rural tax appraisals. If you feel your taxes are unfair in any way, either because your property is appraised too high on its own

standards or in relation to the surrounding land, you should not hesitate to protest and present your case for reappraisal.

Every county has a procedure for appealing the results of the tax assessor's valuations before a body that hears appeals, called the board of review, tax review commission, or assessment appeals board.

GRIEVANCE PERIOD

If the appraised valuation of a parcel is increased by the assessor, he sends the landowner a card before taxes become due indicating the new appraisal for that year. This notification should include instructions on protesting the new valuation. If it doesn't, call the tax assessor's office and ask for instructions on appealing. A form, usually called a notice of protest, will be sent that you must fill out and present to the appeals board during an allotted grievance period, which might be only a single day. You might be required to speak to the assessor first to see if you can come to some kind of an agreement. If you do not get satisfaction, you will be allowed to present your case in person before the board, either alone or with a lawyer. The aid of a lawyer probably won't be necessary.*

PREPARING YOUR CASE

Your case will be very strong if you can demonstrate that an inequity exists between the valuation of your property and that of other property in the area. Go to the tax assessor's office and look at the parcel maps of your area, noting the parcel numbers and acreage of surrounding pieces of property. If you know that some property in your area has been held by the same person for many years, make a special effort to locate those parcels.

Look up the properties in the tax files the same way that I told you to look up your own tax records earlier in this chapter. Note what the appraised fair market value (full cash value) is on each of the parcels you are using for comparison. Look only at the land value. If differences exist, try to figure out if there is any justification for them. For instance, land fronting a public road might be appraised higher than other land. If you can find no justification, you probably have a good cause for a protest of unequal treatment.

If you know what structures exist on the neighboring lands, you can compare their appraised values to the values given for the improvements on your land. Compare the size, age, and other factors that are used in evaluating the worth of a house. You might discover inequities in the improvement valuation as well as the land valuation. This is usually where the assessor makes his mistakes, intentional or not.

*You only want to attempt to lower your taxes if there is an extreme inequity. This is because you will be trying to convince the appraiser or assessor that your property is worth less than he says it is. To do this you have to attempt to "downgrade" your property, and this kind of information in the public files could hurt you if you go to sell the property at a higher price.

Next make a list of all the factors contributing to the depreciation and "unmarketability" of your improvements, such as termite infestation, wood rot, a sagging foundation, the small size of the rooms, the lack of electricity or running water, the peculiar design, and anything else you can think of.

Then list those things about the land itself that decrease the resale value or its potential for development, such as a lack of building sites, poor roads, insufficient water to support further development or subdivision, the great distance from shopping areas, schools, or other facilities. If you have some extra money, get a professional appraisal made of the property to use as evidence on your behalf. The taxes you might save could pay for the cost of the appraisal.

MAKING YOUR APPEARANCE

Carefully prepare your case in writing before the appeals board hearing. Make a detailed list of those things you think lower the value of your land and improvements. Make a chart comparing your land to similar neighboring lands, and compare the valuations made on the land and improvements to show the inequity. Refute any questionable statements the tax assessor made to you on how he arrived at his evaluation of your land. For instance, state that the amount of time he told you he spent examining the property was too short for a thorough evaluation of its deficiencies. If he based his figures on current asking prices given to him by local real estate agents, refute them by stating that they are inflated prices. Then state a figure that you think represents a reasonable value of the land.

Take several copies of your written statement with you when you appear so that you can give one to each member of the board and retain one for yourself. If you have had a professional appraisal made, also have copies of those results ready for distribution—assuming, of course, they are in your favor. Quote the opinions of several local real estate agents, if they are in your favor.

Your oral presentation will be a review of the information contained in your statement. If you hire a lawyer, he may charge you a percentage of the taxes he saves you if the amount is considerable, or he may charge you a flat fee. However, because the tax appeal board resembles a small-claims court and the members of the board are used to hearing cases presented personally by protesting taxpayers, I don't think you will gain much by hiring an attorney.

After you present your case, the tax assessor may present his. When the board arrives at some de- cision of what your valuation should be, the results will be publicly posted on the final assessment rolls in the tax assessor's office.

Since relatively few taxpayers ever complain, you will have an advantage simply because you are willing to take the time and trouble to appear in person to protest. It doesn't hurt to protest your taxes.

CHAPTER 44

The 1986 Income Tax Reform Act and Tax Exemptions Affecting Your Property

GOOD NEWS FOR SECOND-HOME OWNERS

Recently, the federal government passed the 1986 Tax Reform Act, a new "simplified" tax code. Although significant changes were made regarding how real estate is taxed, the tax laws regarding first and second homes were left virtually unchanged. Primary and secondary homeowners are still al-

lowed to write off their mortgage interest and real property taxes on their income taxes. Thus the tax benefits of owning a second, or vacation, home are still with us.

The changes in the tax law were directed toward those real estate investors who previously could write off their losses if they made a bad investment. Now the tax laws encourage people to invest in real property that makes economic sense.

Basically, the new tax law reclassifies real estate investments other than first and second homes as *passive investments*. Losses from passive investments can be written off only from other passive income, which means income from similar sources, such as other real estate. It can no longer be written off *active income,* such as wages and salaries, or portfolio income, such as dividends and interest. The exceptions to this rule are primary and secondary residences and actively managed real property. If you "materially participate" in the management of your real property, you can deduct up to $25,000 from your active or portfolio income if your adjusted gross income is under $100,000. Between $100,000 and $150,000, the deductible amount is phased out. Also, you are not allowed to deduct mortgage interest and property taxes from your income tax except on your first home, your second home, and in some cases on your actively managed real property.

The new tax laws do affect second-home owners, however. Previously, if you owned a vacation retreat you were advised, for tax purposes, to limit your visits to two weeks a year. Now you are advised to convert it to a second-home status, which means you must use it more than 14 days a year or more than 10 percent of the number of days the property is rented out, to avoid the passive loss limitations. This is certainly good news for those who enjoy spending time in their vacation homes. In addition, if you rent it out fewer than 15 days a year, you don't have to report any rental income.

However, the lower tax rates mean there will be a reduction in the value of these tax benefits. For instance, a person in the 35 percent income tax bracket paying a total of $9,500 in mortgage interest and property taxes saved $3,325 in taxes in 1986. Under the new tax law, which limits the rate to 28 percent in 1988, the tax saving would be only $2,660. Thus it will cost this person an additional $665 a year ($55 a month) to be a homeowner. The cost will be even higher for a person who was in a higher tax bracket before.

Keep Track of Home Improvements to Save Taxes When You Sell

When you sell your country home you will have to pay taxes on your profit. The way to save taxes is to cut your taxable profit, i.e., keep your *cost basis* as high as you can. One means of doing this is by adding the cost of improvements on to the original purchase price of your home.

Therefore, you arrive at a new cost basis on which to determine profit. Any improvements are considered in this factor, such as building on a new bedroom, bathroom, dining room, game room, or laundry room, or installing a new roof. These are items that the IRS has determined materially add to the value of your home.

Regular home maintenance costs do not help you in calculating the basis. These would be things such as painting, fixing foundation cracks, and graveling

the driveway. Only your initial investment plus money put into improvements and selling expenses make up the cost basis of your home.

Therefore, it is very important to maintain good records of receipts for all monies spent improving your property. Obviously, you should keep these for some period of time after you sell your home, in case of a tax audit.

Also, if you are selling your city home to buy a place in the country, all funds spent on fixing up your home for sale are deductible from the selling price of your home. The fixing-up expenses must have been incurred by you within 90 days prior to the sale and paid no later than 30 days after the sale. These deductible items can include rug cleaning, painting, chimney sweeping, and selling expenses such as broker's commission, newspaper ads, legal expenses, and title company and abstract fees.

The After-Tax Benefits of Home Ownership

You can defer capital gains on the sale of your city home entirely by reinvesting the proceeds within two years on a country home costing at least as much. If you buy a country home for less money than you receive on the sale of your city home, you will pay some capital gains tax, but it will be far less than if you did not reinvest at all.

Also, if you are 55 or older, you have a once-in-a-lifetime $125,000 exclusion from taxation on gain from a sale of a home.

Finally, if you refinance your primary residence and use the funds to purchase a second home, you may continue to write off all the interest charged for the refinancing loan.

Therefore, the advantages of second-home ownership are still with us even after the passage of the most sweeping tax reform act in decades. This is certainly good news for those of us who seek the enjoyments of a place in the country.

TAX EXEMPTIONS

Homeowners

Several states offer a homestead or homeowner's exemption that allows some tax relief for the homeowner. This permits a specified amount to be deducted from the assessed value of your house. For example, assume your state has a $2,500 homestead exemption. If the assessed value (assessment ratio) is 50 percent of the appraised fair market value and your house is appraised at $75,000, the assessed value will be $37,500. You can then subtract the $2,500 exemption from that amount, which reduces the assessed value for tax purposes to $35,000.

To qualify, your property must be your principal place of residence, and the claimant must be an owner, co-owner, or a purchaser under an installment land contract of sale. The dwelling can be a structure, a condominium, a trailer, or a mobile home.

Since each state's laws are different, ask the tax assessor if such an exemption is offered in your area, and if so, how much it is for. The taxpayer usually must file for an exemption each year during a specified filing period. The following states are some that have homeowner's exemptions: Alabama, Arkansas, California, Florida, Georgia, Iowa, Louisiana, Minnesota, Mississippi, Missouri, Oklahoma, South Dakota, Texas, West Virginia, and Wyoming.

Veterans

Veterans' exemptions offer a discount on the assessed value of homes owned by veterans who were residents of the state when they were inducted. The amount of exemption may depend on the value of the home and the marital status of the veteran. For example, one state allows a married veteran to deduct $1,000 from the assessed value of his home if its appraised value is less than $10,000. See your tax assessor or local Veterans Administration regional office. (See addresses in chapter 27.) They will have all the information on available veterans' exemptions in your state.

Timber

When the value of the standing timber is assessed on your land, your state might allow you to claim an exemption for all immature timber or other timber that will decrease your tax liability. Since the definition of mature timber varies, so does that of immature or exempt timber.

For example, in California, forest trees are exempt if they are on lands from which 70 percent

of all trees over 16 inches in diameter have been removed. The remaining trees are exempt from taxation even though some or all of them are merchantable timber.

As with other types of tax exemptions, the taxpayer must file an application to gain the benefits of an exemption. Once you file the forms, the assessor will place an initial value on the total property you own. He will then allocate separate values to the land and the timber, and finally he will apply the timber exemption to the resulting total.

The permissible exemptions in your area for timber, young fruit trees, other crops, and other forms of real property can be investigated at the office of your local tax assessor or farm advisor.

Preferential Tax Assessment for Rural Land

Some states assess certain rural land on a preferential basis to help small farmers and ranches stay in business and preserve large areas of open land. Lands with favored tax status include vineyards, orchards, pasturelands, dairies, ranch lands, timberlands, and other large rural land holdings.

Three ways of applying preferential assessments are now in use in various parts of the country. The first method, called the *plain preferential assessment system,* provides that land that qualifies is to be assessed on the basis of the present productivity of the land rather than on its potential value. The law often cuts the taxes in half on rural lands that qualify.

If you own raw land in a rapidly developing area, ordinarily your taxes will increase because the area's development makes your land more valuable for commercial use. But under preferential assessment, land is taxed as if there were no excessive growth in the area's development.

The second method, called the *tax deferral system,* allows part of the property taxes each year to be deferred by the landowner until the land is either sold or put into nonagricultural use. This method really only postpones your taxes until you can sell your land at a presumably healthy profit.

The third method, called the *planning and zoning system,* allows those lands that are zoned for agriculture or open space to be treated like lands under the plain preferential assessment system. Farms and other open lands that are located in areas with other types of zoning, for example residential or industrial zoning, are now allowed.

511

In order to receive preferential treatment, some states require that the landowner have a minimum number of acres and sign a contract with the state promising not to develop or subdivide his land for a specified length of time. Since the laws in each state are different and new laws are being introduced each year, you should check with your local planning commission and tax assessor to see if some kind of preferential tax assessment is available for your land. The last federal study found preferential tax benefits for rural land in the following states: California, Connecticut, Florida, Hawaii, Indiana, Iowa, Maryland, Massachusetts, Michigan, Minnesota, Nebraska, Nevada, New Jersey, New York, Ohio, Oregon, Pennsylvania, Rhode Island, Texas, Virginia, Washington, and Wisconsin.

XI

PROPERTY EVALUATION CHECKLIST

CHAPTER 45

The Property Buyer's Complete Checklist

The following pages contain a complete summary of all essential points to consider when evaluating any piece of property, whether improved or un-improved.

Nothing should be overlooked. Room has been left for you to write in the necessary information. A space has been placed next to each number for you to check off the information as you proceed with your research. If a particular point does not apply to your parcel, write in N/A (not applicable).

You should remove this list from the book so you can carry it with you on a clipboard. You might even show it to the real estate agent so he knows what information you will want to evaluate for your prospective purchase.

Check blank when question is answered.

A. GENERAL INFORMATION

____   I. Location:

____   II. Property owner; if being sold by seller:

____   A. Address:

____   B. Phone:

____   III. Acreage and/or size of property:

____   IV. Legal description:

____   V. Tax assessor's parcel number:

____   VI. Improvements:

____   VII. Special qualities:

____   VIII. Income produced by land:

     IX. Lay of land:
Steep ____
Tillable ____
Flat ____
Open ____
Hilly ____
Forested ____

____   X. Availability and cost of power, telephone, cable TV, sewer, and water

B. REAL ESTATE AGENT

____   I. Name of broker or salesman and real estate agency:

____   II. Address of agency:

____   III. Phone:

____   IV. Type of listing, if known:
Multiple listing ____
Exclusive ____
Open listing ____

C. FACTS FOR PRICE NEGOTIATION AND FINANCING

____   I. Total asking price:
Per acre:

____   II. Terms:

____   A. All cash or cash down payment plus mortgage or deed of trust?

____   B. How much money down?

____   C. Assume existing mortgage or deed of trust?

____   D. How much will note to seller be?

____   III. When did the seller buy the property, and how much did he pay, if you can determine this? See tax stamps on deed and seller's existing mortgage on the property.

____   A. Why is seller selling the property?

____   IV. Does the seller or broker have a written appraisal of the property? Get a copy. What does tax assessor have the land and buildings appraised at for tax purposes?

____   V. How firm is seller on price?

____   VI. Can you afford this property?

____   VII. Existing mortgage to be assumed by you:

—   **1st:**
—   A.   Amount to be assumed:
—   B.   Interest rate:
—   C.   When each payment is
         due and amount of
         payment:
—   1.   Balloon payments?
—   2.   Acceleration clause
              or prepayment
              penalty?
—   3.   Who is trustee or
              title company?
—   4.   Any other liens to
              be assumed?

—   **2nd:**
—   A.   Amount to be assumed:
—   B.   Interest rate:
—   C.   When each payment is
         due and amount of
         payment:
—   1.   Balloon payments?
—   2.   Acceleration clause
              or prepayment
              penalty?
—   3.   Who is trustee or
              title company?
—   4.   Any other liens to
              be assumed?

—   *New Note and Mortgage or
       Deed of Trust given back to
       Seller:*
—   A.   Amount:
—   B.   Interest rate:
—   C.   When each payment is
         due and amount of
         payment:
—   D.   Balloon payments?
—   E.   Acceleration clause or
         prepayment penalty?
—   F.   Can it be subordinated
         to construction loan?
—   G.   FHA/VA

       Third Party Lenders
—   A.   Name:
—   B.   Branch:
—   C.   Address:

—   D.   Attention:
—   E.   Loan number:
—   F.   Verbal commitment
         received:
—   From:
—   Date:
—   G.   Written commitment
         dated:
—   H.   Terms:
—   Amount:
—   Points:
—   Fees:
—   Points and fees paid
            by:
               Seller _____
               Buyer _____
—   I.   Interest rate:
—   J.   Monthly payments:
—   K.   FHA/VA:

D. WATER

—   I.   Above-ground source:
         Creek _____
         Springs _____
         Pond _____
         Lake _____
         River _____
         Other _____

         Flood hazards?
         Property in flood zone?

—   A.   Amount (during dry
         season). Ask:
—   1.   Neighbors
—   2.   Farm advisor
—   3.   Well-driller
—   B.   Potability—health
         department
—   C.   Location:
—   1.   Within boundaries
—   2.   In relationship to
              sewage disposal
              system—health
              department
—   D.   Others' rights to use
         water. See seller's
         deed, title report,

abstract of title. Do you get water from someone else's land? Do others get water from your land? What are terms? Enough water for everyone at *all* times of the year? Do you really want to share water?

_____ E. Prescriptive rights. Water being taken by surrounding landowners?

_____ F. Provided by irrigation district or water company? Talk to supplier about costs and amounts available.

_____ II. Underground source (existing well)
_____ A. Observe system in use
_____ B. Check well-driller's log
_____ C. Health department and building department—permits
_____ D. Others' rights to use water. See seller's deed, title report, abstract of title. Do you get water from someone else's land? Do others get water from your land? What are terms? Enough water for everyone at *all* times of the year? Do you really want to share water?

_____ III. Underground source (no existing well)
_____ A. Check with local well-drillers. Compare with other wells in the area.
_____ 1. Depth
_____ 2. Estimated cost (drilling, casing, pump, holding tank, etc.)
_____ 3. Probability of getting water

_____ B. Health department and building department
_____ 1. What permits required
_____ 2. Percolation test
_____ 3. Potability
C. Condition in contract that water be obtained prior to close of escrow
_____ D. Others' rights to use water. See seller's deed, title report, abstract of title. Do you get water from someone else's land? Do others get water from your land? What are terms? Enough water for everyone at *all* times of the year? Do you really want to share water?

_____ IV. Contamination potential
_____ A. Waste disposal sites in area
_____ B. Pesticide, insecticide, or chemical fertilizers used?
_____ C. What is upstream—livestock, homes, industry, farms, etc.?
_____ D. Test water before escrow closes. What is result?

E. SOIL

_____ I. Type of soil:
Sandy _____
Clay _____
Rocky _____
Acid _____
Hardpan _____
How much topsoil? _____
Tillable? _____

_____ II. Soil test reports available?
_____ A. By whom?
_____ B. Summary of tests
_____ C. Additional testing needed?

_____   D.   Any foreseeable problems caused by soil conditions; e.g., special site engineering creating extra building costs; drainage problems for septic system?

_____   III.   Vegetation growth:
Heavy _____
Moderate _____
Light _____
What kind?_____

_____   IV.   Timber:
Marketable _____
Anyone else have timber rights? _____
Kind of trees _____
Firewood supply _____

_____   V.   Is USGS topo map available? _____
Aerial photos _____
Timber and soil maps _____

_____   VI.   Drainage, irrigation, and agricultural potential. Talk to neighbors and surrounding farmers; see USGS data, farm advisor, etc.

F.   BOUNDARIES AND SURVEY
(not covered by title insurance; only by a survey by a licensed surveyor or registered civil engineer)

_____   I.   Existing survey
_____   A.   Copy of recorded survey—county recorder's office and/or local surveyor
_____   B.   Find markers on ground; use aerial photographs and topographical maps with survey
_____   C.   If in doubt that something is within boundaries, put a condition in contract
_____   1.   Line(s) to be surveyed—flagged and approved by

buyer prior to close of escrow
_____   2.   Specify that improvements, water supply, etc., are within boundary lines of property

_____   II.   No existing survey
_____   A.   Estimated cost of survey from licensed surveyor
_____   B.   Condition in contract that survey be completed and approved, and paid for by sellers

_____   III.   Talk to neighbors to see if any boundary conflicts exist

G.   MINERAL AND TIMBER RIGHTS

_____   I.   Check deeds, preliminary title report, abstract of title

_____   II.   Evaluate reserved/excluded rights carefully to determine if they are so undesirable you do not want the land

H.   EASEMENTS AND ROAD ACCESS

_____   I.   Your easement
_____   A.   Existing easement
_____   1.   Check deed, preliminary title report, or abstract of title
_____   2.   Check deed description against available maps
_____   3.   Maintenance
_____   a.   Check with neighbors
           b.   Examine road condition (culverts, gravel, ditching, etc.)
_____   c.   Accessible year-round?

____

____   B.   Easement needed

          1.   Condition in contract requiring recorded easement in deed. Never buy land without deeded access rights. If none, cancel purchase now.

____   2.   Road construction company

____   a.   Possibility of construction

____   b.   Estimated cost of construction and annual maintenance

____   c.   Seller should pay for road construction as part of sale

____   II.   Others' easements over the land

____   A.   Check deeds, preliminary title report, or abstract of title

____   B.   Decide whether they will interfere with your enjoyment of land

____   C.   Prescriptive easements (not ocvered by title insurance). Examine land for evidence of access usage by adjoining owners. Talk to them regarding their rights and future intentions.

I.   SEWAGE DISPOSAL SYSTEM

____   I.   Public or private? If public available—cost of running pipes, hookup fees, monthly charges.

____   II.   Existing septic tank on property

____   A.   Observe location of tank and leach field,

open lids, concrete, wood, or metal

____   B.   Pumping information

____   1.   Who installed system?

____   2.   Who does pumping?

____   3.   How often is system pumped?

____   4.   When last pumped?

____   C.   Health department and building department

____   1.   Permits and percolation test results

____   2.   Relationship to water source

____   3.   Size of tank for needs, size of lot; flush toilets, run shower and faucets.

____   4.   Is system legal?

____   III.   No existing septic tank

____   A.   Health department and building department

____   1.   Percolation test rules

____   2.   Permits required

____   3.   Estimated cost

____   B.   Condition in contract requiring approval of percolation test and permits before close of escrow. Never buy land without prior approval of percolation test—or you might not be able to build.

J.   HOUSE

____   I.   Condition in contract

____   A.   Pest and structural report

____   B.   Appraisal

____   C.   Cost to do improvements on house (if needed). Subordination clause needed in mortgage?

_____ D. Personal property included: Check conditions of equipment and appliances. List everything in contract.

_____ II. Bargaining over conditions of property. Get price lowered if repairs are needed, or get repairs done before deal closes.

K. HOUSE INSPECTION CHECKLIST:
Number each blank
1–10
1—Excellent condition
10—Rebuild

I. STRUCTURAL INTEGRITY

Foundation:

_____ Concrete perimeter
_____ Pole frame
_____ Sinking
_____ Cracked concrete
_____ Termites
_____ Is all wood in the house above the level of the soil?
_____ Was the soil under house treated with insecticide during construction?
_____ Afterward?
_____ Any termite shelter tubes visible on foundation?
_____ On pipes?
_____ If house is in zone of high termite hazard, is there a structural pest control contract on it?
_____ Include guarantee?

_____ Concrete slab
_____ Chemically treated
_____ Floor joist sag
_____ Irregularities
_____ Wood rot
_____ Does the crawl space have adequate clearance and ventilation?
_____ Is the soil covered with a moisture barrier?
_____ Has soil under any addition been treated?
_____ Does crawl space contain stumps or wood debris?
_____ Are there any small holes in any unfinished wood with powder in them indicating infestation?

Comments:

Basement:

_____ Cement
_____ Wood
_____ Flood evidence
_____ Sump pump
_____ Drains

_____ Dirt
_____ Rock
_____ Mud
_____ Water stains

Comments:

Roof:

_____ Wood
_____ Shingle
_____ Tar paper
_____ Gravel
_____ Plywood
_____ Flashing
_____ Is roof decking completely covered, especially at roof edge?

_____ Fireproof
_____ Gutters and downspouts intact?
_____ Leader condition
_____ Leaks
_____ Roof extension over walls sufficient?
_____ Roof sag (rafter decay)?
_____ Water stains on ceilings under roof indicating leaks?

Comments:

Exterior Walls:

_____ Sagging
_____ Square
_____ Pest damage
_____ Wood rot
_____ Caulking around windows, doors, and joints?

_____ Paint peeling or blistering due to condensation?
_____ Siding material
_____ Interior walls buckling?
_____ Are decorative and other items attached to house likely to admit or trap moisture?

Comments:

521

Drainage:

_____ Grading slope away from house

_____ Leaders drain proper distance away

_____ Drainage ditches

_____ Pest and fungus inspection

Comments:

Attic:

_____ Insulation under roof

_____ Insulation on floor

_____ Louver ventilation in attic

_____ Leaks

_____ Water stains

_____ Beam ceiling insulated

Comments:

Porches:

_____ Are earth-filled porches separated from house?

Comments:

II.   EFFICIENT INSULATION

Insulating Material:

_____ Foil

_____ Fill

_____ Slab

_____ Board

_____ Other

_____ Snow on roof

_____ In ceiling

_____ Condition

_____ Thickness

_____ Clammy

_____ Mice damage

_____ Drafts

_____ Under floors

_____ In walls

Comments:

III.   INTERIOR

Doors, Windows, and Floors:

_____ Do doors or windows sag or stick?

_____ Are frames decayed?

_____ Are floors level?

_____ Any spongy spots in floors, particularly in bathroom or kitchen?

Comments:

Electrical:

_____ Fuse box

_____ Circuit breaker

_____ Frayed or loose wires

_____ Capacity (120 and 240 volt)

_____ Load system can carry—number of amps?

Comments:

_____ Meet code standards?

_____ Number of outlets in kitchen?

_____ Other rooms?

_____ Rewiring necessary?

_____ Estimated cost?

Plumbing:

_____ Water pressure Turn several faucets on at once and flush toilet

_____ Toilets flush well?

_____ Do floors feel spongy when walked on in bathroom or kitchen?

_____ Faucets drip?

_____ Rusty water?

_____ Rusty pipes?

_____ Water stains on walls?

_____ Main shutoff valve location good?

_____ Ask about all appliances, i.e., dishwasher, washing machine

_____ Caulking around tubs, sinks, and showers intact?

_____ Leaks anywhere, including drains?

_____ Standing water indicating poor drainage?

_____ Water stains on ceiling?

_____ Separate shutoff valves for individual rooms?

_____ Frozen pipes or valves?

Comments:

IV. CHIMNEY

_____ Code freestanding wood stove?

_____ Code fireplace?

_____ Good draft?

_____ Smoke or burn marks?

_____ Loose or missing bricks?

_____ Good location?

L. COMMERCIAL FARMING CAPABILITIES

_____ I. Kinds of crops/livestock or animals

_____   A. Annual income (for last 5 years)

_____   1. Net profit

_____   2. Overhead breakdown

_____   B. Equipment for crops/livestock or animals

_____   1. List items and examine condition, age, and repair history

_____   C. Who gets existing crops and animals?

_____   D. Who has been buying the crops?

        1. Talk to them

_____ II. Get complete profit and loss statements and seller's tax returns for past 5 years, reflecting farming income and expenses

_____ III. Talk to neighbors, farm and agriculture officials, and read as much as possible about the current economic situation in the area for your intended business

M. CONTRACT, TITLE EXAMINATION, RESTRICTIONS ON DEVELOPMENT

_____ I. Current preliminary title report or abstract of title available?

_____   A. GET COPY AND READ IT

_____ II. Put ALL conditions of sale in contract to purchase

_____   A. Sale is subject to:

_____   1. Buyer's approval of a preliminary title report or abstract of title

_____   2. Guarantee of water availability. (Get reports by soil and water engineers, hydrologists, well-drillers.)

_____   3. Guarantee that property is buildable (percolation and engineering study)

_____   4. Pest, termite, and structural report and approval

_____   5. Review by buyer's attorney

_____   6. Buyer's approval of a survey of the property

_____   7. Buyer obtaining a building permit for the property

_____   8. Buyer's obtaining financing or selling his home in the city to obtain purchase money

_____ III. If deal is made, order preliminary title report or abstract of title in your name

_____ IV. Get copies from title company of all documents contained in preliminary title report or abstract of title necessary to evaluate condition of title. Read every document. If you don't understand something, see an attorney.

_____ V. Anything detrimental in report that cannot be cleared BEFORE escrow closes; e.g., property subject to easements, reservation of water rights, timber rights, mineral rights. If detrimental and can't be cleared, stop the deal and don't buy the property.

_____ VI. Anything detrimental that can be found only by physical inspection of property that cannot be cleared BEFORE escrow closes; i.e., prescriptive easements, prescriptive water rights, boundary line in dispute, present or prospective dispute with a neighbor, etc.
  _____ A. Physically examine property carefully and talk to neighbors
  _____ B. If problem cannot be taken care of by seller now, stop the deal and don't buy the property

_____ VII. Any back taxes due, judgment liens, mechanic's liens, or other monetary liens on property should be paid by seller prior to close of escrow

_____ VIII. Restrictions on development of property by property owner's association or government agency
  _____ A. Building or architectural and design restrictions
  _____ B. Lot size restrictions
  _____ C. Zoning (commercial or industrial) restrictions
  _____ D. Have existing buildings been condemned for violation of health codes? Do they have any valid building permits?

_____ IX. Taxes/assessments
  _____ A. Sewage or water assessments
  _____ B. Property taxes
  _____ C. Proposed easements?

_____ X. Obtain and read public report if one has been isused

_____ XI. If part of homeowners association, obtain and read all documents pertaining to the operation, rights, and powers of the association

N. YOUR OFFER

_____ I. Date you made offer

_____ II. How much offered

_____ III. What terms offered

_____ IV. Seller's response to your offer:
  _____ A. Silence
  _____ B. Rejection
  _____ C. Counteroffer
    _____ 1. Are you willing to respond to Seller's counteroffer?
      _____ a. How much?
      _____ b. What terms?
      _____ c. Date you respond to counteroffer

IF NO DEAL IS MADE, DON'T WORRY. THERE IS PLENTY OF GOOD LAND AVAILABLE. KEEP LOOKING. DON'T GET BUYER'S FEVER.

AGENCIES WITH INFORMATION

1. County recorder's office
   A. Deeds
   B. Surveys
   C. Liens
   D. Any other recorded documents

2. Tax assessor
   A. Delinquent taxes
   B. Value of land and improvements by tax assessor
   C. Amount of yearly taxes

3. Planning department
   A. Zoning
   B. Use permits
   C. Mobile homes
   D. Violations

4. Building department
   A. Permits already granted
      a. Well
      b. Septic tank
      c. House
      d. Other buildings
   B. Permits needed
   C. Violations

5. Health department
   A. Permits already granted
      a. Well
      b. Septic tank
      c. Percolation tests
   B. Permits needed
   C. Violations

6. BLM (Bureau of Land Management)
   If land is near federally owned lands, find out BLM's future plans for the area; have mineral information.

7. Farm advisor, soil conservation agent, Forest Service, U.S. Geological Service, Department of Water Resources.

CHAPTER 46

Some Final Words

I hope that the information in this book has not only made you more aware of the complexities involved in finding and buying your place in the country, but has also given you the confidence to handle many aspects of your purchase yourself. By referring to this book, you should be able to find the answers to any questions and the solutions to any problems that might arise. If you encounter a unique problem or an example of a fraudulent real estate practice I have not discussed, I will be interested to read about it. Your information might be useful to include in future revisions. You can write or call me at my office:

Les Scher
Attorney at Law
P.O. Box 780
Garberville, CA 95440
(707) 923-2128

Even after you buy your land, you will find that much of the information herein will continue to be useful. When you decide to sell your property, you can take this book from the shelf and refresh your memory on many aspects of buying and selling real property. You will find that by having been a wise land buyer, you will also be a successful land seller.

APPENDIX

APPENDIX

APPENDIX A

Real Estate Catalogues and Useful Magazines for the Country Property Owner

Land Catalogues are available free from:
United National Real Estate
4700 Belleview
Kansas City, MO 64112

Horizons, Preferred Property Listings in the U.S.
Realtors Land Institute
430 N. Michigan Ave.
Chicago, IL 60611

Many real estate agencies put out catalogues of their properties for sale. Check through the classified ads in magazines specializing in country land, and you will see free and low-priced catalogues offered.

MAGAZINES OF SPECIAL INTEREST FOR FOLKS IN THE COUNTRY

Mother Earth News
P.O. Box 3122
Harlan, IA 51593-2188
    or
Mother Earth News
P.O. Box 70
Hendersonville, NC 28793-9989
    6 issues for $14.97

529

Farmstead Magazine
P.O. Box 111
Freedom, ME 04941

Rodale's Organic Gardening
Emmaus, PA 18099-003
  12 issues for $12.97

Country Living
P.O. Box 10124
Des Moines, IA 50347-0124
  10 issues/year for $9.97

The New Farm
Department 61122
Emmaus, PA 18049
  7 issues/year for $15.00

Harrowsmith
The Creamery
Charlotte, VT 05445
  1 year for $18.00

Whole Earth Review
P.O. Box 15187
Santa Ana, CA 92705
  4 issues/year for $18.00

Country Home
Locust at 17th
P.O. Box 10635
Des Moines, IA 50380
  6 issues/year for $16.00

Practical Homeowner (formerly *New Shelter*)
Rodale's Practical Homeowner
33 E. Minor St.
Emmaus, PA 18099-0017
  9 issues/year for $10.97

Country Accents (decorating the country home, etc.)
GCR Publishing Group, Inc.
Circulation Department
888 Seventh Ave.
New York, NY 10106

Country Almanac (country kitchens and country decorating ideas)
Harris Publications, Inc.
115 Broadway
New York, NY 10010

Log Home Guide
1 Pacific, Ste.-Anne de Bellevue
Quebec, PQ, Canada H9X 1C5
  or
Log Home Guide
Box 1150
Plattsburgh, NY 12901

Better Homes & Gardens Country Home
Locust at 17th
Box 10245
Des Moines, IA 50380-0245

Small Farmer's Journal
Box 2805
Eugene, OR 97402

The New Settler Interview
P.O. Box 730
Willits, CA 95490
  12 issues/year for $10.00

American Country (by editors of *Mother Earth News*)
P.O. Box 3132
Harlan, IA 51593-2198
  6 issues/year for $11.97

Solar Earthbuilders International
P.O. Box 16119
Las Cruces, NM 88004-6119

Fine Homebuilding
The Taunton Press
63 S. Main St.
Box 355
Newtown, CT 06470
  7 issues/year for $22.00

The Old-House Journal (restoration and maintenance techniques)
69-A Seventh Ave.
Brooklyn, NY 11217
  10 issues/year for $18.00

Progressive Builder (formerly *Solar Age*)
P.O. Box 470
Peterborough, NH 03458-0470
  12 issues/year for $28.00

The Owner Builder
Owner Builder Center
1516 5th St.
Berkeley, CA 94710
  4 issues/year for $4.00

Storey's Books for Country Living (a
catalogue of hundreds of books on
country arts, crafts, and skills)
Department 7022
Schoolhouse Rd.
Pownal, VT 05261

APPENDIX B

The Bureau of Land Management (BLM) State and District Offices

The following offices are state and district branches
of the BLM. They will have the information you
need about present and future uses of federal land
adjoining or near the land you wish to buy. Look
at their maps and studies of projected multiple uses.
They also have lots of useful information that is
referred to throughout this book.

Main Office
U.S. Department of the Interior
Bureau of Land Management
Eighteenth and C Sts., N.W.
Washington, DC 20240-0001

Alaska
Alaska State Office
701 C St.
P.O. Box 13
Anchorage, AK 99513

DISTRICT OFFICES
Anchorage, AK 99507
Fairbanks, AK 99707

Arizona
Arizona State Office
2400 Valley Bank Center
Phoenix, AZ 85073

DISTRICT OFFICES
St. George, UT 84770
Phoenix, AZ 85017
Stafford, AZ 85546
Yuma, AZ 85364

California
California State Office
Federal Office Bldg.
2800 Cottage Wy., Rm. E-2841
Sacramento, CA 95025

DISTRICT OFFICES
Bakersfield, CA 93301
Folsom, CA 95630
Redding, CA 96001
Riverside, CA 92507
Susanville, CA 96130
Ukiah, CA 95482

Colorado, Kansas
Colorado State Office
1037 20th St.
Denver, CO 80202

DISTRICT OFFICES
Canon City, CO 81212
Craig, CO 81625
Grand Junction, CO 81502
Montrose, CO 81401

Idaho
Idaho State Office
3380 Americana Terr.
Boise, ID 83706

DISTRICT OFFICES
Boise, ID 83702
Burley, ID 83318
Coeur D'Alene, ID 83814
Idaho Falls, ID 83401
Salmon, ID 83467
Shoshone, ID 83352

Montana, North Dakota, South Dakota
Mountain States Office
222 N. 32nd St.
P.O. Box 30157
Billings, MT 59701

DISTRICT OFFICES
Butte, MT 59701
Dickinson, ND 58601
Lewistown, MT 59457
Miles City, MT 59301

Nevada
Nevada State Office
300 Booth St.
P.O. Box 12000
Reno, NV 89520

Battle Mountain, NV 89820
Carson City, NV 89701
Elko, NV 89801
Ely, NV 89301
Las Vegas, NV 89102
Winnamucca, NV 89445

New Mexico, Oklahoma, Texas
New Mexico State Office
South Federal Place
Federal Bldg. and U.S. Post Office
P.O. Box 1449
Santa Fe, NM 87501

DISTRICT OFFICES
Albuquerque, NM 87107
Las Cruces, NM 88001
Roswell, NM 88201
Socorro, NM 87801

Oregon, Washington
Oregon State Office
825 N.E. Multnomah St.
P.O. Box 2965
Portland, OR 97208

DISTRICT OFFICES
Baker, OR 97814
Burns, OR 97720
Coos Bay, OR 97420
Eugene, OR 97440
Lakeview, OR 97630
Medford, OR 97501
Prineville, OR 97754
Roseburg, OR 97470
Salem, OR 97302
Spokane, WA 99201
Vale, OR 97910

Utah
Utah State Office
University Club Bldg.
136 E. South Temple
Salt Lake City, UT 84111

DISTRICT OFFICES
Cedar City, UT 84720
Moab, UT 84532
Richfield, UT 84701
Salt Lake City, UT 84119
Vernal, UT 84078

Wyoming, Nebraska, Kansas
Wyoming State Office
2515 Warren Ave.
P.O. Box 1828
Cheyenne, WY 82001

DISTRICT OFFICES
Casper, WY 82601
Rawlins, WY 82301
Rock Springs, WY 82901
Worland, WY 82401

States east of the Mississippi River, plus
Arkansas, Iowa, Louisiana, Minnesota,
Missouri
Eastern States Office
350 S. Pickett St.
Alexandria, VA 22304

APPENDIX C

Federal Lands for Sale

Business and householders do not retain items they do
not need; neither should the Government.
—Official federal government policy statement

The federal government regularly disposes of excess public land. This is done by the Bureau of
Land Management (BLM). Almost all of the lands
are in the western states of Alaska, Arizona, California, Colorado, Idaho, Montana, Nevada, New
Mexico, Oregon, Utah, and Wyoming.

There are also small amounts of such land in
Alabama, Arkansas, Florida, Illinois, Kansas,
Louisiana, Michigan, Minnesota, Missouri, Mis-
sissippi, Nebraska, North Dakota, South Dakota,
Oklahoma, Ohio, Washington, and Wisconsin.

There are no public lands managed by BLM in
Connecticut, Delaware, Georgia, Hawaii, Indiana,
Iowa, Kentucky, Maine, Maryland, Massachu-
setts, New Hampshire, New Jersey, New York,
North Carolina, Pennsylvania, Rhode Island, South
Carolina, Tennessee, Texas, Vermont, Virginia,
and West Virginia.

The excess lands have been identified as un-
needed by the federal government or as better utilized in private ownership. By law, these lands are

made available for sale at no less than fair market value.

The law states that BLM can select lands for sale if, through land-use planning, they are found to meet one of three criteria: (1) they are scattered, isolated tracts, difficult or uneconomic to manage; (2) they were acquired for a specific purpose and are no longer needed for that purpose; (3) disposal of the land will serve important public objectives, such as community expansion and economic development.

Land types vary widely. Some may be desert; some, higher elevations. Some are close to towns; some are rural. Some are small parcels of just a few acres; some, several hundred acres in size. Any lands with agricultural potential will be clearly identified in the sale notice. However, most public lands have little or no agricultural potential.

The source of information for these sales is the local BLM office (see appendix B, "The Bureau of Land Management (BLM) State and District Offices") or the General Services Administration (addresses at the end of this appendix).

The sales are held near where the land is located. Details of any sale are specified in the sale notice available from BLM. By writing to any BLM office, you can find out what sales are currently scheduled. They will send you a description of the property, method of sale, bidding procedure, a general map, special conditions of sale, and other facts. More detailed information, such as land reports, and environmental assessments are available upon request for a small copy fee.

In the late 1980s and the early 1990s, there will be a major sale of public lands by the Bureau of Land Management. For example, in California, the federal government has announced that it will sell 2 percent of the public lands, or approximately 330,500 acres.

The following types of land will be sold:

(a) Land in or near population centers that can be used for community expansion;
(b) Isolated or scattered land tracts that are expensive and difficult for BLM to manage;
(c) Land whose appropriate use is agricultural, commercial, or industrial development by nonfederal entities;
(d) Other types of land identified for disposal in existing or future land-use plans.

The fair market value of these lands will be advertised in advance. They will then be sold by scaled bids. You can obtain all information regarding these sales free from the Bureau of Land Management. You do not have to pay any commercial service to obtain this information. There will be no free land. Never believe any source that tells you otherwise. Except in Alaska, there has been no "free" land since the Homestead Act was repealed in 1976 by the passage of the new Federal Land Policy and Management Act. Homesteading of federal lands in Alaska ended in 1986, though there is still homesteading of state lands in Alaska.

Just as much care should be utilized in buying these federal sale properties as for any land purchase, including obtaining a title report; examination of easements and reservations, such as timber, water, and minerals; and examination of suitability for residential construction.

NATIONAL FOREST LANDS

The U.S. Forest Service has very limited authority for the sale of national forest system land. New legislative authority will be necessary to allow the sale of national forest system lands. In the unlikely event that any forest lands will be offered for sale, you can find out about it through the local U.S. Forest Service office or the National Forest Service, P.O. Box 2417, Washington, D.C. 20013. (See Useful Resources, chapter 5, for addresses.) There are areas of private lands intermingled with national forestlands in most areas. Local realtors are generally a good source of information regarding such land. Check with those realtors operating in the area nearest the forestlands you are interested in. If Congress authorizes the sale of forest system lands, details can be obtained from the Forest Service, P.O. Box 2417, Washington, D.C. 20013.

Occupancy or residence on public lands is now allowed only in conjunction with specific types of public land uses. Ongoing mining activities allow a miner, through an approved plan of operation, to have a residence on a valid mining claim (see appendix E, "Mining Claims.") The Bureau of Land Management may also issue leases and permits for occupancy in conjunction with other uses such as grazing and servicing of rights of way. These permits allow temporary residences. Information can be obtained from the local Bureau of Land Management office.

The following is available for the specified price from:

Superintendent of Documents
Government Printing Office
Washington, DC 20402

Are There Any Public Lands for Sale? $1.00

The following are available free from:

California State Office
Bureau of Land Management
2800 Cottage Wy., Rm. E-2841
Sacramento, CA 95825

*Questions and Answers on the Public Land
Sales Program in California*
California Desert: Occupying Public Lands

The following is available for $1.00 from:

R. Woods
Consumer Information Center, A
P.O. Box 100
Pueblo, CO 81002

Are There Any Public Lands for Sale?
Important information about the federal program to sell excess undeveloped public land. Explains why there are no more lands available for homesteading.

Inquiries regarding sale information of public lands managed by the Bureau of Land Management may be obtained by writing any of the BLM offices listed in appendix B.

The Government Services Administration does not maintain a mailing list for each property sale. You must request a list each time, as indicated in their brochures. Each list tells you when, where, and how surplus properties will be sold, and where to go for more information on specific pieces of property. To get the latest free issue of *U.S. Real Property Sales List*, write to:

Properties
Consumer Information Center
Pueblo, CO 81009

In addition to the sales listings in the above material, the Government Services Administration also provides information on specific upcoming sales through the *GSA Real Property Mailing List*. This list affords prospective buyers the opportunity to receive notices of government sales of property in which they are listed.

To obtain a free copy of the *Real Property Mailing List Application Card*, write to:

General Services Administration
Centralized Mailing List Service, 8-BRC
Denver Federal Center, Bldg. 41
Denver, CO 80225

Information on available federal real property can also be obtained from the following General Services Administration (GSA) regional offices:

Connecticut, Maine, Massachusetts, New Hampshire, New Jersey, New York, Rhode Island, and Vermont:

McCormack Post Office and Courthouse
Boston, MA 02109

Alabama, Delaware, District of Columbia, Florida, Georgia, Kentucky, Maryland, Mississippi, North Carolina, Pennsylvania, Puerto Rico, South Carolina, Tennessee, Virginia, and West Virginia:

Russell Federal Bldg.
75 Spring St., S.W.
Atlanta, GA 30303

Illinois, Indiana, Michigan, Minnesota, Ohio, and Wisconsin:

230 S. Dearborn St.
Chicago, IL 60604

Arkansas, Iowa, Kansas, Louisiana, Missouri, Nebraska, New Mexico, Oklahoma, and Texas:

819 Taylor St.
Fort Worth, TX 76102

Arizona, California, Hawaii, and Nevada:

525 Market St.
San Francisco, CA 94105

Alaska, Colorado, Idaho, Montana, North Dakota, Oregon, South Dakota, Utah, Washington, and Wyoming:

GSA Center
Auburn, WA 98001

APPENDIX D

Homesteading

There is no longer land available free through homesteading. The Federal Homestead Act was repealed in 1976, when Congress passed the Federal Land Policy and Management Act which applied to all public lands in the United States. However, Congress did allow the Homestead Act to continue in Alaska until 1986, at which time federal homesteading was ended. But it is still possible to homestead Alaska state lands. (See chapter 34, ''*Alaska*.'')

Do not let anybody tell you homesteading is still available, and do not waste any money buying books or advertising brochures on homesteading. It is gone, probably forever.

APPENDIX E

Mining Claims

The federal and state laws regarding mining claims are very complex. Many people have staked claims and constructed cabins for occupying while engaged in their mining operations. There are still many adventurous types chasing the mineral rainbow. The best way to start is to order all the pamphlets described below. Good luck.

The following are available for free from any Bureau of Land Management office listed in appendix B.

Patenting a Mining Claim on Federal Lands
Questions and Answers about Mining the
    Public Lands

*Mining Claims under the General Mining
    Laws of 1872*
*Requirements for Recordation of Unpatented
    Mining Claims*
*Laws and Regulations Governing Mining in
    California*
*How to Research a Mining Claim Using
    BLM Records*
Exploration and Mining in Wilderness Areas
Mining in National Forests
Annual Assessment Work (Proof of Labor)

The following is available for $1.25 from any BLM Branch Office:

Staking a Mining Claim on Federal Lands

The following is free from:
    R. Woods
    Consumer Information Center, Y6
    P.O. Box 100
    Pueblo, CO 81002

The Federal Oil and Gas Lottery

The following are available for the specified prices from any U.S. Geological Survey public inquiry office listed in chapter 5, "The Earth—Soil, Vegetation, Topography":

Prospecting for Gold in the United States
    S/N 024-001-02036-0   free
*Availability of Federal Land for Mineral
    Exploration and Development in Western
    States: Colorado, 1984*
    S/N 024-004-02157-8 $7.00
*Availability of Land for Mineral Exploration
    and Development in Southeastern Alaska*
    S/N 024-004-02158-6 $5.25
Suggestions for Prospecting   free
*Replenishing Non-Renewable Mineral
    Resources*   free

The following is free from:
    Branch of Publications Distribution
    Bureau of Mines
    4800 Forbes Ave.
    Pittsburgh, PA 15213

*Assaying Ores, Concentrates, and Bullion: Bureau of
Mines Information. Circular 8714r*

APPENDIX F

Special Uses of the National Forests, Including Habitation for Summer Homes and Sale to the Public

Long-term exclusive private use of national forest system lands involving erection of a building for residential or second-home use is no longer authorized by the Forest Service. Some years ago, a limited number of summer-home lots were made available in national forests to persons interested in building a recreation residence for seasonal use. All of these lots have now been developed. While the special-use permits authorizing summer homes on those lots continue, no new lots are being established, and there are no plans to establish additional lots in the future. Annual rental fees for the existing lots are based on fair market value and range from a few hundred dollars to over $2,000 a year. The improvements on these lots are frequently offered for sale by the owners. When this happens, a special-use permit may be reissued to the new owners.

At this time there are approximately 6,500 recreational residences (summer homes) in the national forests in California alone. Most recreational residences are in tracts established long ago when public recreation in national forests was just beginning. The current owners are using their property under a permit, and own only their improvements on the land, not the land itself. The special-use permits for this use are issued for a maximum term of 20 years.

If you are interested in buying the improvements from a permitee, prior to completion of the sale, you should meet with the seller and a local Forest Service representative to discuss conditions and requirements for preparing a new special-use permit.

Be very careful, because there is no guarantee that a new special-use permit will be issued or renewed at the end of the stated term. If it is not, you will be required to remove all improvements from the lot and restore it to the original condition at your sole expense. Remember, special-use permits for recreation residences are for recreational use only. They may not be used for a primary residence. A permitee must have a primary residence elsewhere.

For current information on these kinds of permits, the following are free from:

Forest Service
U.S. Department of Agriculture
Washington, DC 20250

or any Forest Service office.

Field Offices of the Forest Service FS-13
National Forest Lands
Recreational Residence in National Forests

The Forest Service doesn't handle the sale of recreation residences, nor keep track of them. This information will be obtained from a local realtor, or from For Sale signs posted on recreation residence sites. There is a national organization of thousands of persons who own recreation resident permits on national Forest Service lands. They have banded together to protect their rights as permitees. If you are interested in this program, or want information on permits that might be for sale, contact the following and ask for a copy of the N.F.R.A. newsletter:

National Forest Recreation Association
Route 3, Box 210
Highway 89, N.
Flagstaff, AZ 86004

For information on leasing summer homes in national forests in each state, write to the U.S. Forest Service regional field office for your state. All addresses are given in the Useful Resources at the end of chapter 5.

APPENDIX G

State Lands for Sale

The following agencies manage state-owned lands.

Alabama
Division of Lands
Conservation and Natural
Resources Department
64 N. Union St., Rm. 702
Montgomery, AL 36130-1901

Alaska
Department of Natural Resources
Pouch M
Juneau, AK 99811

Arizona
Land Department
1624 W. Adams St., 4th Fl.
Phoenix, AZ 85007

Arkansas
State Land Commissioner
109 State Capitol
Little Rock, AR 72201

California
State Lands Commission
1807 13th St.
Sacramento, CA 95814

Colorado
Board of Land Commissioners
Department of Natural Resources
1313 Sherman St.
Denver, CO 80203

Connecticut
Land Acquisition and Management
Environmental Protection Department
165 Capitol Ave., Rm. 102
Hartfort, CT 06106

District of Columbia
Department of Administrative Services
613 G St., N.W., Rm. 1104
Washington, DC 20001
    or
Redevelopment Land Agency
1350 Pennsylvania Ave., N.W., Rm. 401
Washington, DC 20004

Florida
Division of State Lands
Department of Natural Resources
3900 Commonwealth Blvd.
Tallahassee, FL 32303

Georgia
  State Properties Commission
  1 Martin Luther King Jr. Dr.
  Atlanta, GA 30334

Hawaii
  Board of Land and Natural Resources
  1151 Punchbowl St.
  Honolulu, HI 96813

Idaho
  Department of Lands
  Statehouse
  Boise, ID 83720

Illinois
  Department of Conservation
  Lincoln Towers Plaza
  524 S. Second St.
  Springfield, IL 62706

Indiana
  Department of Administration
  507 State Office Bldg.
  Indianapolis, IN 46204

Kansas
  Secretary of State
  State Capitol, 2nd Fl.
  Topeka, KS 66612

Kentucky
  Facilities Management Department
  Finance and Administration Cabinet
  Capitol Annex Bldg.
  Frankfort, KY 40601

Louisiana
  Division of State Lands
  Department of Natural Resources
  P.O. Box 44124
  Baton Rouge, LA 70804

Maine
  Bureau of Public Lands
  Department of Conservation
  State House Station, #22
  Augusta, ME 04333

Maryland
Office of Real Estate
Department of General Services
301 W. Preston St., Rm. 1309
Baltimore, MD 21201

Massachusetts
Deputy Commissioner
Division of Capital Planning
1 Ashburton Pl., Rm. 1501
Boston, MA 02108

Minnesota
Real Estate Management Division
Department of Administration
50 Sherburne Ave., Rm. G-22
St. Paul, MN 55155

Mississippi
Public Lands Department
Office of Secretary of State
401 Mississippi St.
Jackson, MS 39201

Missouri
Division of Parks and Historic Preservation
Department of Natural Resources
P.O. Box 176
Jefferson City, MO 65102
    or
Divisions of Fisheries, Forestry and Wildlife
Department of Conservation
P.O. Box 180
Jefferson City, MO 65102

Montana
Department of State Lands
1625 11th Ave.
Helena, MT 59601

Nebraska
Educational Lands and Funds Board
301 Centennial Mall, S.
P.O. Box 94986
Lincoln, NE 68509-4986
    or
Game and Parks Commission
2200 N. 33rd St.
P.O. Box 30370
Lincoln, NE 68503-0370

Nevada
Soil Conservation Districts
Conservation and Natural Resources
    Department
201 S. Fall St.
Carson City, NV 89710

New Hampshire
Forest and Lands Division
Resources and Economic Development
    Department
6 Loudon Rd.
Concord, NH 03301

New Jersey
Green Acres and Recreation Program
Environmental Protection Department,
    CN-404
Trenton, NJ 08625

New Mexico
State Land Office
310 Old Santa Fe Trail
Santa Fe, NM 87501

New York
Department of Environmental Conservation
50 Wolf Rd.
Albany, NY 12233

North Carolina
Office of State Property
Department of Administration
300 N. Salisbury St.
Raleigh, NC 27611

North Dakota
Land Department
State Capitol, 6th Fl.
Bismarck, ND 58505

Ohio
Office of Real Estate
Department of Natural Resources
Fountain Square
Columbus, OH 43224

Oklahoma
Land Office Commission
Jim Thorpe Bldg.
Oklahoma City, OK 73105

Oregon
Division of State Lands
1445 State St.
Salem, OR 97310

Pennsylvania
  Department of General Services
  515 N. Office Bldg.
  Harrisburg, PA 17120

Rhode Island
  Department of Environmental Management
  83 Park St.
  Providence, RI 02903

South Carolina
  Director of Property Management
  Division of General Services
  Budget and Control Board
  1203 Gervais St.
  Columbia, SC 29201

South Dakota
  School and Public Lands
  State Capitol, 2nd Fl.
  Pierre, SD 57501

Tennessee
  Department of Conservation
  701 Broadway
  Nashville, TN 37219-5237

Texas
  General Land Office
  837 Stephen F. Austin Bldg.
  1700 N. Congress
  Austin, TX 78701

Utah
  State Lands and Forestry Division
  Department of Natural Resources and
    Energy
  3100 State Office Bldg.
  Salt Lake City, UT 84114

Vermont
  Agency of Environmental Conservation
  79 River St.
  Montpelier, VT 05602

Virginia
  Department of General Services
  Ninth Street Office Bldg.
  Richmond, VA 23219

Washington
  Commissioner of Public Lands
  Department of Natural Resources
  Public Lands Bldg.
  Olympia, WA 98504

West Virginia
  Public Land Corporation
  Department of Natural Resources
  1800 Washington St., E.
  Bldg. 3, Rm. 713
  Charleston, WV 25305

Wisconsin
  Board of Commissioners of Public Lands
  P.O. Box 7857
  Madison, WI 53707

Wyoming
  Public Lands
  Herschler Bldg.
  Cheyenne, WY 82002

APPENDIX H

U.S. Government Printing Office Bookstores

In addition to the mail-order service provided by the office of the Superintendent of Documents, Government Printing Office, there are also twenty-one retail bookstores outside of Washington, D.C. They stock the most popular of the 16,000 titles in the GPO inventory, and they will special order any publication currently offered for sale.

The locations of these stores are:

Alabama
  Birmingham GPO Bookstore
  9220 B Parkway, E.
  Birmingham, AL 35206

California
  Los Angeles GPO Bookstore
  ARCO Plaza
  505 S. Flower St., C Level
  Los Angeles, CA 90071

  San Francisco GPO Bookstore
  Federal Office Bldg.
  450 Golden Gate Ave., Rm. 1023
  San Francisco, CA 94102

113. Locations of U.S. Government Printing Office Bookstores

Colorado
  Denver GPO Bookstore
  Federal Office Bldg.
  1961 Stout St., Rm. 117
  Denver, CO 80294

  Pueblo GPO Bookstore
  World Savings Bldg.
  720 N. Main St.
  Pueblo, CO 81003

District of Columbia
  Commerce Department
  GPO Bookstore
  14th and Pennsylvania Sts., N.W.
  Washington, DC 20230

  Main GPO Bookstore
  710 N. Capitol St., N.W.
  Washington, DC 20402

Florida
  Jacksonville GPO Bookstore
  Federal Office Bldg.
  400 W. Bay St., Rm. 158
  Jacksonville, FL 32202

Georgia
  Atlanta GPO Bookstore
  Federal Office Bldg.
  275 Peachtree St., N.E., Rm. 100
  Atlanta, GA 30303

Illinois
  Chicago GPO Bookstore
  Everett McKinley Dirksen Bldg.
  219 S. Dearborn St., Rm. 1365
  Chicago, IL 60604

Maryland
  Retail Sales Branch
  8660 Cherry Ln.
  Laurel, MD 20707

Massachusetts
  Boston GPO Bookstore
  Kennedy Federal Bldg.
  Sudbury St., Rm. G-25
  Boston, MA 02203

Michigan
  Detroit GPO Bookstore
  McNamara Federal Bldg.
  477 Michigan Ave., Ste. 160
  Detroit, MI 48226

Missouri
    Kansas City GPO Bookstore
    120 Bannister Mall
    5600 E. Bannister Rd.
    Kansas City, MO 64137

New York
    New York GPO Bookstore
    26 Federal Plaza, Rm. 110
    New York, NY 10278

Ohio
    Cleveland GPO Bookstore
    Federal Office Bldg.
    1240 E. Ninth St., 1st Fl.
    Cleveland, OH 44199

    Columbus GPO Bookstore
    Federal Office Bldg.
    200 N. High St., Rm. 207
    Columbus, OH 43215

Pennsylvania
    Philadelphia GPO Bookstore
    Federal Office Bldg.
    600 Arch St., Rm. 1214
    Philadelphia, PA 19106

    Pittsburgh GPO Bookstore
    Federal Office Bldg.
    1000 Liberty Ave., Rm. 118
    Pittsburgh, PA 15222

Texas
    Dallas GPO Bookstore
    Federal Bldg.
    1100 Commerce St., Rm. 1-C-50
    Dallas, TX 75242

    Houston GPO Bookstore
    9319 Gulf Fwy.
    Houston, TX 77017

Washington
    Seattle GPO Bookstore
    Federal Bldg.
    915 Second Ave., Rm. 194
    Seattle, WA 98174

Wisconsin
    Milwaukee GPO Bookstore
    Federal Bldg.
    517 E. Wisconsin Ave., Rm. 190
    Milwaukee, WI 53202

APPENDIX I

Federal Information Centers

If you have questions about any service or agency in the federal government, you may want to call the Federal Information Center (FIC) nearest you for a free call or minimum long-distance charge. FICs are prepared to help consumers find needed information or locate the right agency for help with problems.

Alabama
    Birmingham (205) 322-8591
    Mobile (205) 438-1421

Alaska
    Anchorage (907) 271-3650

Arizona
    Phoenix (602) 261-3313

Arkansas
    Little Rock (501) 378-6177

California
    Los Angeles (213) 894-3800
    Sacramento (916) 551-2380
    San Diego (619) 293-6030
    San Francisco (415) 556-6600
    Santa Ana (714) 836-2386

Colorado
    Colorado Springs (303) 471-9491
    Denver (303) 236-7181
    Pueblo (303) 544-9523

Connecticut
    Hartford (203) 527-2617
    New Haven (203) 624-4720

Florida
    Ft. Lauderdale (305) 522-8531
    Jacksonville (904) 354-4756
    Miami (305) 350-4155
    Orlando (305) 422-1800
    St. Petersburg (813) 893-3495
    Tampa (813) 229-7911
    West Palm Beach (305) 833-7566

Georgia
    Atlanta (404) 221-6891

Hawaii
Honolulu (808) 546-8620

Illinois
Chicago (312) 353-4242

Indiana
Gary (219) 883-4110
Indianapolis (317) 269-7373

Iowa
From all points in Iowa
(800) 532-1556 (toll free)

Kansas
From all points in Kansas
(800) 432-2934 (toll free)

Kentucky
Louisville (502) 582-6261

Louisiana
New Orleans (504) 589-6696

Maryland
Baltimore (301) 962-4980

Massachusetts
Boston (617) 223-7121

Michigan
Detroit (313) 226-7016
Grand Rapids (616) 451-2628

Minnesota
Minneapolis (612) 349-5333

Missouri
St. Louis (314) 425-4106
From elsewhere in Missouri
(800) 392-7711 (toll free)

Nebraska
Omaha (402) 221-3353
From elsewhere in Nebraska
(800) 642-8383 (toll free)

New Jersey
Newark (201) 645-3600
Trenton (609) 396-4400

New Mexico
Albuquerque (505) 766-3091

New York
Albany (518) 463-4421
Buffalo (716) 846-4010
New York (212) 264-4464

Rochester (716) 546-5075
Syracuse (315) 476-8545

North Carolina
Charlotte (704) 376-3600

Ohio
Akron (216) 375-5638
Cincinnati (513) 684-2801
Cleveland (216) 522-4040
Columbus (614) 221-1014
Dayton (513) 223-7377
Toledo (419) 241-3223

Oklahoma
Oklahoma City (405) 231-4868
Tulsa (918) 584-4193

Oregon
Portland (503) 221-2222

Pennsylvania
Philadelphia (215) 597-7042
Pittsburgh (412) 644-3456

Rhode Island
Providence (401) 331-5565

Tennessee
Chattanooga (615) 265-8231
Memphis (901) 521-3285
Nashville (615) 242-5056

Texas
Austin (512) 472-5494
Dallas (214) 767-8585
Fort Worth (817) 334-3624
Houston (713) 229-2552
San Antonio (512) 224-4471

Utah
Salt Lake City (801) 524-5353

Virginia
Norfolk (804) 441-3101
Richmond (804) 643-4928
Roanoke (703) 982-8591

Washington
Seattle (206) 442-0570
Tacoma (206) 383-5230

Wisconsin
Milwaukee (414) 271-2273

APPENDIX J

Alternative Energy Resources

If you have any interest in developing alternative energy on your property—either water, wind, or solar—you must take this into account when evaluating a piece of property. In order to properly assess the layout of the land, some basic knowledge of energy systems is essential.

The resources in this appendix provide a good source of basic information to help you gain the knowledge necessary to purchase a parcel that is appropriate for alternative energy production. Start by checking with your local library, as numerous books and periodicals have been written on this subject in the last ten years.

The following is available for the specified cost from:

> Progressive Builder
> P.O. Box 470
> Peterborough, NH 03458

Homeowners Energy Handbook $4.95

For a list of some interesting publications put out by the Energy Performance of Buildings Group in the Applied Science Division at Laurence Berkeley Laboratory, write to:

> Energy Performance of Buildings Group
> Laurence Berkeley Laboratory
> University of California
> Bldg. 90, Rm. 3074
> Berkeley, CA 94720

Write to the following agencies and groups for a list of their publications:

> National Appropriate Technology Assistance
>   Service (NATAS)
> U.S. Department of Energy
> Box 2525
> Butte, MT 59702

This government agency supplies technical advice on energy matters in any area. If you call their 800 numbers, you will be connected with a group or individual with the answers to your energy questions. Below are the numbers and available calling times:

> (800) 428-1718 (in Montana)
> (800) 428-2528 (everywhere else)
> Call from 9:00 A.M. to 6:00 P.M. Central
>   Time on weekdays only.

Also write to the addresses above for their brochures on the services they have available for you.

> National Center for Appropriate Technology
>   (NCAT)
> Box 3838
> Butte, MT 59702

Write to the above agency for a list of their publications, which are written for the layperson, on all areas of alternative energy, building construction ideas, and energy-saving in all aspects of your life.

> National Solar Heating and Cooling
>   Information Center
> P.O. Box 1607
> Rockville, MD 20885
> Toll-free numbers:
> (800) 523-2929
> (800) 462-4983 (in Pennsylvania)
> (800) 523-4700 (in Alaska and Hawaii)

> National Technical Information Service
>   (NTIS)
> 5285 Port Royal Rd.
> Springfield, VA 22161

> Solar Energy Research Institute
> 1617 Cole Blvd.
> Golden, CO 80401

REGIONAL SOLAR ENERGY CENTERS:

> Western Solar Utilization Network (WSUN)
> Pioneer Park Bldg.
> 715 S.W. Morrison, Ste. 800
> Portland, OR 97205

> Mid-American Solar Energy Complex
>   (MASEC)
> 8140 26th Ave., S.
> Minneapolis, MN 55420

> Southern Solar Energy Center (SSEC)
> 61 Perimeter Park
> Atlanta, GA 30341

Northeast Solar Energy Center (NESEC)
470 Atlantic Ave.
Boston, MA 02110

American Section of the International Solar
Energy Society (AS of ISES)
American Technological University
P.O. Box 1416
Killeen, TX 76541

Passive Solar Industries Association
c/o Potomac Energy Group
401 Wythe St.
Alexandria, VA 22314

Passive Solar Products Association
350 Endicott Bldg.
St. Paul, MN 55101

Solar Energy Industries Association
1001 Connecticut Ave., N.W.
Washington, DC 20036

If you are interested in having an alternative energy system designed and engineered specifically for your site, write to the company whose motto is: "We solve power problems."

Photron, Inc.
77 W. Commercial St.
Willits, CA 95490

The following are available from:
Superintendent of Documents
U.S. Government Printing Office (GPO)
Washington, DC 20402

Biomass: Solar Energy from Farms and Forests S/N 061-000-00333-9	$2.00
Direct Normal Solar Radiation Data Manual S/N 061-000-00593-5	$4.75
Drying Wood with the Sun: How to Build a Solar-Heated Firewood Dryer S/N 061-000-00613-3	$3.50
Inexpensive Economical Solar Heating System for Homes S/N 033-000-00632-2	$4.75
Insolation Data Manual: Long-term Monthly Averages of Solar Radiation, Temperature, Degree-Days and Global Kit for 248 National Weather Service Stations S/N 061-000-00489-1	$8.50
Passive Design: It's a Natural S/N 061-000-00401-7	$4.50
Installation Guidelines for Solar DHW Systems in One- and Two-Family Dwellings S/N 023-000-00520-4	$5.50

Progress of Solar Technology and Potential Farm Uses S/N 001-000-04290-4	$5.00
Solar Dwelling Design Concepts S/N 023-000-00334-1	$2.30
A Survey of Passive Solar Buildups S/N 023-000-00473-2	$3.50
Site Planning for Solar Access: A Guidebook for Residential Developers and Site Planners S/N 023-000-00545-0	$6.50
Solar Greenhouses and Sunspaces: Lessons Learned S/N 061-000-00622-2	$2.25
Energy Potential from Livestock and Poultry Wastes in the South S/N 001-019-00359-6	$2.25
Turning Great Plains Crop Residues and Other Products into Energy S/N 001-019-00354-5	$2.25
Energy and United States Agriculture: Irrigation Pumping, 1974–80 S/N 001-019-00329-4	$4.50
Home Heating: Systems, Fuels, Controls S/N 001-000-03823-1	$1.75
Regional Guidelines for Building Passive Energy Conserving Homes S/N 023-000-00481-0	$8.50
Solar Heating and Cooling Demonstrative Program S/N 023-000-00338-4	$1.15
Solar Dwelling Design Concepts S/N 023-000-00334-1	$2.30
Solar Design Package—Design drawings, climate maps, solar building, cost estimates. Order "Solar Package."	$8.00
Earth Sheltered Passive Solar House Model Order "Earth Pamphlet."	$1.00
Energy-efficient Features Inherent in Older Homes S/N 024-005-00838-1	$4.75
Energy Efficiency in Light-Frame Wood Construction S/N 001-001-00465-1	$4.75
Energy Management Checklist for the Home S/N 001-000-03440-5	$1.00
Building Hobby Greenhouses S/N 001-000-03692-1	$2.75
Energy-wise Homebuyer S/N 023-000-00518-2	$5.50
Bio Gas: Energy from Animal Waste S/N 061-000-00451-3	$5.00

CONSERVATION AND RENEWABLE ENERGY INQUIRY AND REFERRAL SERVICE (CAREIRS)

This service provides information on the full spectrum of renewable energy technologies—solar, wind, hydroelectric, photovoltaics, geothermal— and on energy conservation. In addition, the service maintains contact with a nationwide network of public and private organizations that specialize in highly technical or regionally specific problems, and can provide referrals for someone who may need detailed assistance on technical problems.

CAREIRS does not send out lists of their publications, due to their frequent changes in inventory. But if you are interested in a specific topic, they will send you a list of what they have available.

Here is a partial list of publications that CAREIRS offers. There are many others available upon request:

> *Efficient Air-Conditioning*
> *Solar Water-Heating Bibliography*
> *Passive and Active Solar Domestic Hot Water Systems*
> *Sunspaces and Solar Greenhouses*
> *Caulking and Weatherstripping*
> *Learning about Renewable Energy*
> *Low-Cost Passive and Hybrid Solar Retrofits*
> *Is the Wind a Practical Source of Energy for You?*
> *Sources of Solar and Energy-efficient House Plans*

For information on services offered by CAREIRS, write to:
Renewable Energy Information
Box 8900
Silver Spring, MD 20907

or call toll free:
(800) 523-2929 United States
(800) 462-4983 Pennsylvania
(800) 233-3071 Alaska and Hawaii

The following are available for the specified cost from:
National Association of Home Builders
15th and M Sts., N.W.
Washington, DC 20005

Designing, Building and Selling Energy Conserving Homes	$12.50
Fuel Savings—A Kit of Solar Ideas for Existing Homes	$ 3.25

The following are free from:
Thermal Insulation Manufacturers
Association
7 Kirby Plaza
Mt. Kisco, NY 10549

Energy Saving Booklet T-302
Wall Chart T-303
Thermal Insulation/Energy Conservation T-306
Cutting Back on Fuel Cost T-310
Roof Insulation Folder T-324

The following are available for the specified cost from:
Brick House Publishing Co.
3 Main St.
Andover, MA 01810

The New Solar Home Book: Bruce Anderson and Michael Riordan	$18.95 (postpaid)
Common Sense Wind Energy	$10.95 (postpaid)

The following is available for the specified cost from:
National Fenestration Council
White Lakes Professional Bldg.
3310 Harrison
Topeka, KS 66611-2279

Builders Guide to Passive Solar Home Design and Land Development	$12.00

The National Association of Home Builders puts out a catalogue of books on various subjects. For a copy of their free catalogue write to:
NAHB Bookstore
15th and M Sts., N.W.
Washington, DC 20005

The following pamphlets can be ordered for the specified cost from:
The National Association of Brick
Distributors
1000 Duke St.
Alexandria, VA 22314

Energy Efficient Fireplaces	$ .85
Brick for Passive Solar Heating	$ .85
Build with the Sun	$ .50
Save Energy, Build with Brick	$ 1.25

Brick, the Greatest Building Material under
    the Sun $ .90

Catalogues and Magazines

    Alternative Sources of Energy (ASE)
    107 S. Central Ave.
    Milaca, MN 56353
       10 issues/$48.00 per year

    Progressive Builder Magazine (formerly
      Solar Age)
    Energy Efficiency and Quality Home
      Construction
    Subscription Services
    P.O. Box 985
    Farmingdale, NY 11737-9685
      12 issues/$28.00 per year

    Solar Earthbuilder International
    P.O. Box 16119
    La Cruces, NM 88004-6119

You can obtain a very informative 80-page catalogue and design guide for solar, wind, and water energy systems put out by Alternative Energy Engineering, Inc. Send $3.00 to:

    Alternative Energy Engineering, Inc.
    P.O. Box 339
    Redway, CA 95560

Wind-Driven Electrical Systems

A very complete source of scientific and product data on wind energy is the Wind Energy Research Center. Write for their catalogue, manufacturers' list, bibliography, and brochure entitled *Is the Wind a Practical Source of Energy for You?* All are available from:

    Solar Energy Research Institute
    1617 Cole Blvd.
    Golden, CO 80401

Another group that publishes books on wind energy is:

    American Wind Energy Association
    1017A King St.
    Alexandria, VA 22314

Wind Energy: How to Use it $16.95
The New Alchemy Water-Pumping
    Windmill Book $10.00

The Wind Power Book $14.95
Windy Land Owner's Guide $15.00

Ask for their publications list for other titles.

    Regular periodicals publishing information on wind energy are:
    Wind Technology Journal
    Wind Energy Weekly (published 8 times per
      year)
    American Wind Energy Association
    1516 King St.
    Alexandria, VA 22314

    National Technical Information Service
    U.S. Department of Commerce
    5285 Port Royal Rd.
    Springfield, VA 22161

Solar Wind-Powered Irrigation Systems
    PB 82-177486 $ 4.50

Pumping and Raising Water and Hydro Power

Catalogues and information about pumping and raising water with various alternative energy sources such as windmills and hydraulic rams can be obtained from:

    Dempster Industries
    Box 848
    Beatrice, NE 68310
      Free catalogue

    Baher Manufacturing
    Evansville, WI 53536
      Free catalogue

    Rife Hydraulic Engines
    Box 790
    Norristown, PA 19404
      Catalogue $2.00

    High Lifter Water Systems
    P.O. Box 397
    Willits, CA 95490
      Information free

    Heller-Aller Co.
    Corner of Perry and Oakwood
    Napoleon, OH 43545
      Information $1.50

The most current comprehensive book on hydro-electric power for residential purposes is:

The Residential Hyro Power Book, Keith
  Ritter, available for $10.00 from:
Homestead Engineering
32801 Hwy. 36
Bridgeville, CA 95526

The definitive resource catalogue is still *The Essential Whole Earth Catalogue* (1986), available in bookstores, or send $18.00 (postpaid) to:
  Whole Earth Access
  2990 Seventh St.
  Berkeley, CA 94710

State Agencies' Energy Programs

The following state agencies develop and administer programs relating to energy conservation, alternative energy research and development, and energy information.

Alabama
  Energy Division
  Economic and Community Affairs
    Department
  P.O. Box 2939
  Montgomery, AL 36105

Alaska
  Office of Energy
  Commerce and Economic Development
    Department
  3601 C St., Ste. 722
  Anchorage, AK 99503

Arizona
  Energy Division
  Department of Commerce
  1700 W. Washington, 5th Fl.
  Phoenix, AZ 85007

Arkansas
  Energy Office
  1 Capitol Mall, Rm. 2-C-105
  Little Rock, AR 72201

California
  Energy Resources Conservation and
    Development Commission
  1516 Ninth St.
  Sacramento, CA 95814

Colorado
  Office of Energy Conservation
  Department of Regulatory Agencies
  112 E. 14th Ave.
  Denver, CO 80203

Connecticut
  Energy Division
  Office of Policy and Management
  80 Washington St.
  Hartford, CT 06106

Delaware
  Facilities Management Division
  Administrative Services Department
  O'Neill Bldg.
  Dover, DE 19901

District of Columbia
  District of Columbia Energy Office
  420 Seventh St., N.W., Rm. 500
  Washington, DC 20004

Florida
  Governor's Energy Office
  Office of the Governor
  301 Bryant Bldg.
  Tallahassee, FL 32301

Georgia
  Governor's Office of Energy Resources
  270 Washington St., S.W.
  Atlanta, GA 30334

Hawaii
  State Energy Division
  Planning and Economic Development
    Department
  335 Merchant St.
  Honolulu, HI 96813

Idaho
  Office of Energy
  Department of Water Resources
  450 W. State St.
  Boise, ID 83720

Illinois
  Department of Energy and Natural
    Resources
  325 W. Adams St.
  Springfield, IL 62704

Indiana
  Division of Energy Policy
  Department of Commerce
  1 N. Capitol, Ste. 700
  Indianapolis, IN 46204

Iowa
  Energy Policy Council
  Lucas State Office Bldg.
  Capitol Complex
  Des Moines, IA 50319

Kansas
  Research and Energy Analysis Division
  Corporation Commission
  State Office Bldg., 4th Fl.
  Topeka, KS 66612

Kentucky
  Energy Cabinet
  Iron Works Pike
  P.O. Box 11888
  Lexington, KY 40578

Louisiana
  Office of Conservation
  Department of Natural Resources
  P.O. Box 94275
  Baton Rouge, LA 70804-9275

Maine
  Office of Energy Resources
  Executive Department
  State House Station, #53
  Augusta, ME 04333

Maryland
  Energy Administration
  Department of Natural Resources
  Tawes State Office Bldg., B-3
  Annapolis, MD 21401

Massachusetts
  Executive Office of Energy
  100 Cambridge St., Rm. 1500
  Boston, MA 02202

Michigan
  Energy Administration
  Department of Commerce
  P.O. Box 30228
  Lansing, MI 48909

Minnesota
  Energy Division
  Department of Energy and Economic
    Development
  150 E. Kellogg Blvd., 9th Fl.
  St. Paul, MN 55101

Mississippi
  Department of Energy and Transportation
  510 George St.
  Jackson, MS 39202

Missouri
  Division of Energy
  Department of Natural Resources
  P.O. Box 176
  Jefferson City, MO 65102

Montana
  Energy Division
  Natural Resources and Conservation
    Department
  25 S. Ewing
  Helena, MT 59601

Nebraska
  Energy Office
  State Capitol, 9th Fl.
  P.O. Box 95085
  Lincoln, NE 68509-5085

New Hampshire
  Governor's Energy Office
  2½ Beacon St.
  Concord, NH 03301

New Jersey
  Department of Energy
  1100 Raymond Blvd.
  Newark, NJ 07102

New Mexico
  Energy and Minerals Department
  525 Camino de los Marquez
  Santa Fe, NM 87501

New York
  Energy Office
  Empire State Plaza, Bldg. #2
  Albany, NY 12223

North Carolina
Division of Energy
Department of Commerce
430 N. Salisbury St.
Raleigh, NC 27611

North Dakota
Office of Intergovernmental Assistance
Office of Management and Budget
State Capitol, 14th Fl.
Bismarck, ND 58505

Ohio
Division of Energy
Department of Development
30 E. Broad St., 34th Fl.
Columbus, OH 43215

Oklahoma
Division of Conservation Services
Corporation Commission
302 Jim Thorpe Bldg.
Oklahoma City, OK 73105

Oregon
Department of Energy
111 Labor and Industries Bldg.
Salem, OR 97310

Pennsylvania
Governor's Energy Council
1625 N. Front St.
Harrisburg, PA 17105

Rhode Island
Public Utilities Commission
100 Orange St.
Providence, RI 02903

South Carolina
Division of Energy Policy
Office of the Governor
1205 Pendleton St.
Columbia, SC 29201

South Dakota
Office of Energy Policy
Commerce and Regulations Department
Trucano Bldg.
Pierre, SD 57501

Tennessee
Energy Division
Economic and Community Development
Department
320 Sixth Ave., N.
Nashville, TN 37219

Texas
Public Utilities Commission
7800 Shoal Creek Blvd.
Austin, TX 78757

Utah
State Energy Office
Department of Natural Resources and
Energy
355 W.N. Temple, 3 Triad Center
Salt Lake City, UT 84180-1204

Vermont
Department of Public Service
120 State St.
Montpelier, VT 05602

Virginia
Energy Division
Mines, Minerals and Energy Department
2201 W. Broad St.
Richmond, VA 23220

Washington
Washington State Energy Office
Mail Stop ER-11
Olympia, WA 98509

West Virginia
Department of Energy
State Capitol Complex
Charleston, WV 25305

Wisconsin
Division of State Energy and Coastal
Management
Administration Department
P.O. Box 7868
Madison, WI 53707

Wyoming
Office of Energy Conservation
Barrett Bldg.
Cheyenne, WY 82002

INDEX